10/6/2001

# NIMITZ

E. B. POTTER

# NIMITZ

NAVAL INSTITUTE PRESS
ANNAPOLIS, MARYLAND

Library of Congress Catalogue Card No. 76-1056
ISBN 0-87021-492-6

Printed in the United States of America on acid-free paper ∞

The author is grateful for permission to quote from the following publications: George Allen & Unwin, Ltd., for *Nice to Have You Aboard* by Captain Harold Hopkins, RN; Harold Ober Associates Incorporated for *Admiral Halsey's Story* (published by McGraw-Hill Book Company, Inc.) by William F. Halsey and J. Bryan III, copyright © 1947 by William F. Halsey, copyright © 1947 by the Curtis Publishing Company; Random House, Inc., for *The Rising Sun: The Decline and Fall of the Japanese Empire, 1936–1945*, by John Toland, copyright © 1970 by John Toland; Hawthorne Books for *General Kenney Reports: A Personal History of the Pacific War* by George C. Kenney, copyright © 1949 by George C. Kenney; Little, Brown and Company for *The Quiet Warrior* by Thomas B. Buell, copyright © 1974 by Thomas B. Buell; *U.S. Naval Institute Proceedings*, July 1966; W. W. Norton and Company, Inc., for *Fleet Admiral King: A Naval Record* by Ernest J. King and Walter Muir Whitehill, copyright © 1952 by Ernest J. King; *Once a Marine: The Memoirs of General A. A. Vandegrift, United States Marine Corps*, by A. A. Vandegrift and Robert B. Asprey, copyright © 1964 by A. A. Vandegrift and R. B. Asprey; *Present at the Creation: My Years in the State Department* by Dean Acheson, copyright © 1969 by Dean Acheson.

The author also thanks Samuel Eliot Morison for permission to use material from *The Rising Sun in the Pacific* (published by Little, Brown and Company, copyright © 1948 by Samuel Eliot Morison) in the preparation of the map on page 38 in this book.

Unless otherwise indicated, all photographs are official U.S. Navy.

15  14  13

*To Grace, Katherine, and Lorraine*

# CONTENTS

# MAPS

# PREFACE

FLEET ADMIRAL NIMITZ's almost obsessive discretion may have had its roots in the notorious Sampson-Schley controversy, which was going on while Nimitz was a student at the Naval Academy. The controversy embarrassed friends of the Navy and permanently injured the reputations of both Rear Admiral William T. Sampson and Commodore Winfield S. Schley. Young Nimitz, shocked by the undignified bickering, vowed to himself that there would be no more such washing of the Navy's dirty linen in public if ever he was in a position to prevent it. During the rest of his life, he avoided and, insofar as possible, forestalled public controversy—particularly where it involved personalities. He made every effort to protect the feelings and reputations of his subordinates, even when they failed to measure up.

Admiral Nimitz deplored the "rushing into print" of many World War II officers, particularly when their revelations tended to dim the prestige of other officers or to stimulate public wrangling. For his own part, he would not write his biography or permit it to be written during his lifetime, and even in his personal letters he carefully withheld censure and all facts on which censure might conceivably be based. There was one exception. In his daily wartime letters to his wife he freely let off steam, expressing his exasperation at the conduct or shortcomings of some of his associates. She understood that these comments were for her eyes alone. "It was just sort of a safety valve for him to do this," she said. To ensure that the contents of the letters should never be made public, she burned all except a few of the blandest.

To his friend Andrew Hamilton, Admiral Nimitz said, "People ask me why I haven't written my memoirs. My answer has always been that history is best written by the professional historians. A wartime military commander is likely to be too emotionally involved to present an objective picture of himself or his associates—and his prejudices might hurt the people he served with."

For the use of his future biographer, Nimitz carefully collected his papers and saw that they were deposited in the Operational Archives of the Naval History Division in Washington, D.C., under the care of Rear Admiral Ernest M. Eller, then Director of Naval History. In January 1965, he submitted to two long interviews by John T. Mason, Jr., representing the Columbia University oral history project, but he would not permit his replies to be recorded on tape. Mason made copious notes and then rushed to his hotel and reproduced the interviews as completely as possible on his tape recorder.

Not long after Admiral Nimitz's death in 1966, Admiral Eller interested the eminent historian Allan Nevins in writing the Nimitz biography. Nevins had begun his research and engaged C. M. Nelson as his research assistant when he was stricken with an illness from which he did not recover.

In 1969, the U.S. Naval Institute established its own oral history program with John Mason at its head. Mason took as his first project the collecting of more materials for Nimitz's biographer, whoever he might be. He began by interviewing Chester Nimitz, Jr., and his wife Joan at their home in Connecticut. Chester, Jr., expressed the opinion that the time was ripe for a biography of his father but told Mason that his mother, Mrs. Chester Nimitz, Sr., was the one to give the green light for such a work.

Mrs. Nimitz, Sr., then living in San Francisco, readily granted Mason a series of interviews. She told him that she wanted the biography written and that she would like Professor Potter to write it. "He knew the admiral," she said. "Professor Potter worked with him and he has been a guest in our home. I think that's important."

The rest of the family agreed with Mrs. Nimitz. All granted extensive interviews, which were recorded on tape, transcribed, and submitted to the interviewees for correction. Mason and his assistant, Etta-Belle Kitchen, then traveled to various parts of the United States and even abroad to interview former associates of Admiral Nimitz. Unfortunately, by 1969 some of the senior officers who had been most closely associated with Nimitz in World War II were dead, and others were too ill to be interviewed.

I learned of these proceedings shortly after Mason's visit with Mrs. Nimitz. Commander R. T. E. Bowler, Jr., Secretary-Treasurer and Publisher, U.S. Naval Institute, invited me to his office and offered me a contract to write a biography of Admiral Nimitz. I promptly accepted the offer, and signed the contract early in 1970.

I caught my first glimpse of Admiral Nimitz in 1943 when I was on duty as a naval reserve officer at Pearl Harbor. He was riding by in the back seat of a big, black car. Later the same year, I heard him address the personnel of the 14th Naval District. I was at that time working in the vaultlike basement of the district administration building. This was the basement described at the beginning of Chapter 5 of this book, though by 1943 it was being used for distributing codes rather than breaking them.

After the war I was surprised and delighted to receive a letter from Admiral Nimitz congratulating me on a recently published book of which I was editor and chief author. I first spoke to him in 1955, when he attended the 50th anniversary homecoming of his Naval Academy class. I made my first visit to his home, Longview, in Berkeley, California, early in 1957 to discuss with him the writing of *Sea Power: A Naval History*, for which he had agreed to act as adviser and associate editor. During the next two years, the admiral and I corresponded regularly concerning the book, and we conferred during his visits to the East Coast. In the summer of 1959, as the book was nearing completion, Admiral and Mrs. Nimitz invited my wife and me to stay with them during the final discussions.

As we were leaving Longview, I told Admiral Nimitz that if ever he wanted somebody to write his biography I hoped he would think of me. He smiled and said, "You know where my papers are." In March 1963, Commander Bowler wrote to the admiral and asked if I might begin writing his life's story for publication by the Naval Institute. Nimitz declined, indicating that he thought the time was not ripe. He was then considering having his children write the book after his death. Nevertheless, from time to time he sent me papers and articles that would be useful to a biographer, and I filed them away. When Admiral Nimitz died in 1966, I used these materials to write a 10,000-word sketch of his life for publication in the *U.S. Naval Institute Proceedings*.

After I had signed the contract for the Nimitz biography and had absorbed and catalogued the scores of interviews that Mason and his assistant had recorded, I flew with my wife to Texas where I did some interviewing of my own among Nimitz's friends and relatives in Fredericksburg and Kerrville, where the admiral was born and reared. We then went on to the West Coast for more interviews, including two final tape recordings with Mrs. Nimitz.

In the course of writing this book, while also teaching history at the Naval Academy, I have been encouraged and assisted by the Navy Department and by the Nimitz family. Whenever I needed a detail that I could not find for myself, I wrote to whichever Nimitz was most likely to know the answer and always received a prompt reply. I did not, however, submit this book before publication either to the Navy Department or to the Nimitz family. It is proper that I alone be responsible for what appears on these pages. The Nimitzes and my naval friends understand and approve of this view.

*History Department*                                                      E. B. Potter
*United States Naval Academy*
August 1975

# NIMITZ

*Passed Midshipman Chester W. Nimitz and his "wonderful white-bearded grandfather," Charles Henry Nimitz, Texas, February 1905.*

*Lieutenant Chester and Catherine Freeman Nimitz in April 1913, two weeks after their marriage. Courtesy of Mrs. Chester W. Nimitz, Sr.*

*Rear Admiral Russell Willson relieving Rear
Admiral Nimitz as Commander, Battleship Division One,
on board the USS* Arizona *at San Pedro, California, May 1939.*

*Admiral Nimitz assuming command of the Pacific Fleet on
board the submarine* Grayling *at Pearl Harbor, December 31, 1941.*

22 March 42.

I am glad you went to Mrs Knox's luncheon. I have not seen anything K. recently so believe he is lying low. I'm afraid he is not so keen for me now as he was when I left - but that is only natural. Even so many people were enthusiastic for me at the start but when things do not move fast enough - they own on me. I will be lucky to last six months. The public may demand action and results faster than I can produce.


24 Nov. 43

If all goes well I should be back in my headquarters by 9. a.m. Tomorrow after a most interesting trip. With me are Gen. Richardson and Col. Powell of the Army and from my staff - R Adm. Sherman, Capt Redman, Vice Adm. Newton, Lt Col Jones. U.S.M. C and Lamar. We have been on Tarawa where our Second Marine Div. under Maj. Gen. Julian Price covered itself with glory. Our losses were very heavy and will be announced in due time but the morale of the Troops was very high after the battle and inspite of their heavy losses. I have never seen such a desolated spot as Tarawa. Gen. Richardson who saw the battlefields in France last war says it reminded him of the Ypres field over which the battle raged back and forth for weeks. Not a cocoanut tree of thousands, was left whole. The Japs had prepared a magnificent defense and fought to the last man, except that a few wounded or dazed Japs were taken. The stench was terrific from bodies yet unburied even though our troops were working hard to bury the dead. I was relieved when we left the place for a neighboring island in the atoll - to eat our supper and to sleep - Even there we could get occasional whiffs when the wind shifted. But enough of that. We are all working hard to consolidate our gains and to prepare for the attacks which we know are inevitable

With the Lords help we will not only hold on to what we have got but will use the new places to attack the Japs when we get the fields ready for planes.

*Admiral Nimitz wrote to his wife, Catherine, every day during World War II. His letters took the form of a diary, with daily entries, which he mailed, usually, once a week. In the first of the above entries, he expresses his dejection at having achieved so little by the spring of 1942. In the second, he describes his visit to Tarawa.*

*Admiral Nimitz and Admiral William F. Halsey, ComSoPac,*
*aboard the USS* Curtiss *at Espiritu Santo, New Hebrides, January 1943.*

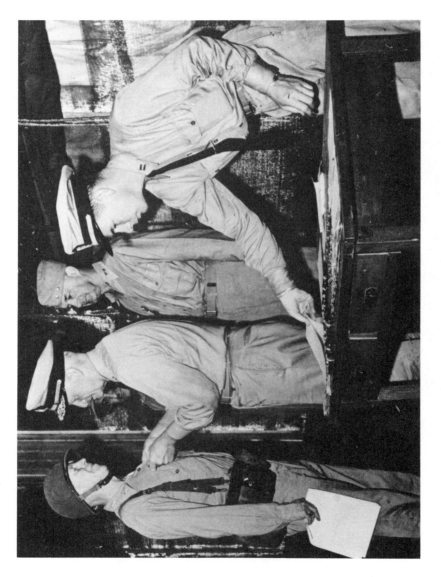

*Admiral Nimitz presenting the Navy Cross to Colonel M. A. Edson, USMC, at Guadalcanal, while Major General A. A. Vandegrift looks on. The "indispensable" Lieutenant H. A. Lamar, aide to the admiral, is bending over the table.*

*Admiral Nimitz gives a dinner party at Makalapa for Mrs. Franklin D. Roosevelt on September 22, 1943 following her visit to the South Pacific. Left to right: Rear Admiral William R. Furlong, Rear Admiral William L. Calhoun, Rear Admiral Charles A. Lockwood, Mrs. Roosevelt, Admiral Nimitz, Vice Admiral Raymond A. Spruance, Captain Thomas C. Anderson, and Vice Admiral John H. Towers.*

*Lieutenant General Robert C. Richardson talking with
Admiral Raymond A. Spruance in July 1944 aboard the latter's
flagship, the heavy cruiser* Indianapolis. *He complained to Spruance
about the dressing-down he had received at the hands of Admiral Kelly Turner.*

*Admiral Nimitz walking with Admiral Raymond A. Spruance on
the deck of the* Indianapolis *as she rode at anchor off Saipan in July 1944.*

*General MacArthur, President Roosevelt, and Admiral
Nimitz on board the USS* Baltimore *at Pearl Harbor, July 26, 1944.*

*Fleet Admiral Nimitz with, left, Vice Admiral C. H.
McMorris, his chief of staff, and Rear Admiral Forrest P. Sherman,
his war plans officer, at CinCPac-CinCPOA headquarters, Guam, 1945.*

*Vice Admiral Kelly Turner (center) with Lieutenant
General Holland M. Smith (left) and Rear Admiral Harry W. Hill.*

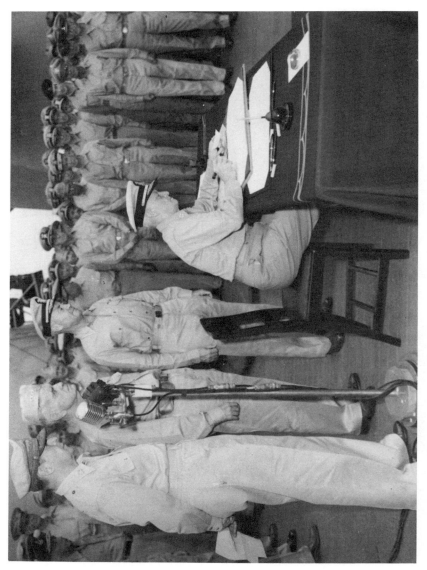

*With General MacArthur and Admirals Halsey and Forrest Sherman standing directly behind him, Fleet Admiral Nimitz signs the Japanese surrender document on board the USS Missouri in Tokyo Bay, September 2, 1945. Official U.S. Army photograph.*

*Fleet Admiral Nimitz returns in triumph to Washington, D.C., at the end of World War II, October 1945. At Nimitz's right is Admiral Forrest P. Sherman; on his left, Commander H.A. Lamar.*

*Fleet Admiral Nimitz being sworn in as Chief of Naval
Operations, as his predecessor, Fleet Admiral Ernest J. King, looks
on. The oath was administered by Rear Admiral Oswald S. Colclough, Judge
Advocate General, in a ceremony at the Navy Department, December 15, 1945.*

*On board the USS* Franklin D. Roosevelt, *of the Eighth Fleet, during maneuvers off the Virginia Capes, April 1946, left to right: Fleet Admiral Nimitz, Fleet Admiral William D. Leahy, President Harry S. Truman, and Admiral Marc A. Mitscher.*

*Fleet Admiral and Mrs. Nimitz in the garden of*
*Longview, their home in Berkeley, California, early in the 1960s.*

*Nimitz Day, October 17, 1964, at Berkeley, California.*
*Fleet Admiral Nimitz acknowledges the cheers of football fans at*
*the game between the University of California and the Naval Academy.*
*To the admiral's left are Clark Kerr, Chancellor of the University of California,*
*and Rear Admiral Charles S. Minter, Superintendent of the Naval Academy.*
*To his right is Edmund Brown, Governor of California.*

# CHAPTER 1

# THE APPOINTMENT

I**N** W**ORLD** W**AR** II, Fleet Admiral Chester W. Nimitz commanded thousands of ships and aircraft and millions of men, amounting to more military power than had been wielded by all the commanders in all previous wars. The operations he directed and, to a large extent, devised involved projecting across the Pacific Ocean forces that blasted Japan and defeated an enormously expanded Japanese empire.

Admiral Nimitz was link and buffer between imperious, often caustic Admiral Ernest J. King, Commander in Chief of the U.S. Fleet, and his own subordinates, men of stubborn convictions, usually expressed in emphatic language. The press aptly nicknamed three of them "Bull" Halsey, "Terrible" Turner, and "Howling Mad" Smith. Nimitz molded these strong-willed men, and others like them, into one of the most effective fighting teams in history.

His success derived in part from a remarkable knack for anticipating events. This ability is illustrated in a forecast he made in the mid-1930s in a conversation with his son, then a midshipman at the U.S. Naval Academy. Chester Junior put the question: "Pop, where do you expect to get in the Navy, and how do you expect to get there?" His father replied that he would like some day to be Chief of Naval Operations, the Navy's topmost professional command. As to how he hoped to get there, he intended to do his best, as he had in the past, and was convinced that in the Navy one got what one deserved. Of course, chance and timing played their part.

"Let me say one thing," continued the elder Nimitz. "I do believe that we are going to have a major war, with Japan and Germany, and that the war is going to start by a very serious surprise attack and defeat of U.S. armed forces, and that there is going to be a major revulsion on the part of the political power in Washington against all those in command at sea, and they're all going to be thrown out, though it won't be their fault necessarily. And I wish to be in a position of sufficient prominence so that I will then be considered as one to be sent to sea, because that appears to be the route."

Some three years later, Nimitz, then a rear admiral, attained his "position of sufficient prominence." Following a tour of sea duty, he reported in August 1939 to the Navy Department to serve as Chief of the Bureau of Navigation— as the Bureau of Naval Personnel was called at that time. He was 54 years old, trim and vigorous, with a pink complexion, and light blond hair just turning white. The position, though high-level indeed, was a desk job and, as such, did not entirely please him. He would have preferred to remain in command of forces at sea. Moreover, he disliked living and working in Washington, D.C.

1

The post, however, concerned as it was with the "procurement, training, promotion, assignment, and discipline of officers and enlisted personnel in the Navy," made good use of Nimitz's skills and interests. The training function, of particular concern to him, gave him general jurisdiction over the Naval Academy, over the Naval Reserve Officer Training Corps, of which he was a founder, over the officer candidate schools, and over all the boot camps and other training facilities in the Navy.

In retrospect Chester Junior considered that the post had been ideal for his father. Said he, "Dad was a people man entirely—Bureau of Navigation. Dad never heard of the Bureau of Ordnance. He really wasn't interested in the guns and technology of the Navy." In fact, of course, as a young officer, Nimitz had been much involved with naval technology and tactics. He was a recognized authority on submarines and marine diesel engines. Later he was instrumental in introducing into the Navy such technological improvements as underway replenishment and the circular formation.

Chester Junior regarded those achievements as far less important to his father's career than his tours as Assistant Chief and Chief of the Bureau of Navigation and his earlier duty as Assistant Chief of Staff to the Commander in Chief, U.S. Fleet. He said, "The rest of the jobs, his submarine duties and so forth, were simply, so far as I'm concerned, familiarization with the mechanics of the seagoing Navy, but didn't tend to fit you for higher command. You didn't see much of the broad picture, as you do in the CinC staff and in the Bureau of Navigation trying to man the Navy. So far as those in which he learned most, and in which the evaluation of his superiors was probably most critical to his subsequent success, I'd say those were the jobs."

Admiral Nimitz took over as chief of the bureau with little fanfare, but his presence was soon felt. At first there was nothing specific—only a kind of invigorating appreciation of a big task ahead that had to be performed superbly well. Later, more specific things began to happen: lines of communication became more direct, archaic processes were abandoned or simplified.

Reorganization was of course necessary to meet new demands. A congressional act of 1934 had authorized building the fleet up to treaty strength; a second act in 1938 appropriated a billion dollars for a two-ocean navy. Obviously commanding, manning, and servicing all these new warships and their supporting bases was far beyond the capacity of the regular Navy. Great numbers of men and, later, of women would have to be brought into the Navy from the civilian population and trained as reservists to take over most of the assignments. The outbreak of war in Europe in 1939, with the possibility that the United States might be drawn in, made the rapid expansion of all naval training programs the more urgent. This expansion was the responsibility mainly of the Bureau of Navigation.

The Bureau's training program soon ran afoul of plans drawn up by the Bureau of Aeronautics, which believed that it should control the training of the Navy's aviators and make important command assignments in naval aviation.

All training and assignment had of course been the responsibility of the Bureau of Navigation long before the Bureau of Aeronautics came into existence. Inevitably the friction between the bureaus led to a confrontation between Rear Admiral Nimitz and Rear Admiral John H. Towers, Chief of BuAer. Each respected the other's abilities, but Towers regarded Nimitz, no aviator, as a battleship admiral—the best, perhaps, of the old school that had been made obsolescent by the aircraft carrier and by aviation in general. Being reasonable men, they reached a workable compromise. Towers seems to have been surprised by Nimitz's flexibility and understanding of the aviator's point of view. Each remained somewhat wary of the other, however, and each continued a gentlemanly campaign against the other's plans and ideas.

As the Navy began to expand, Admiral Nimitz made the wise decision that the reservists should wear uniforms identical with those of the regulars. That decision was not popular among some of the professionals, but Nimitz stuck to it—despite the example of Britain's Royal Navy, in which reserve officers wore undulating gold stripes, from which they got the nickname Wavy Navy. Nimitz saw in such differentiation a real handicap. It marked the reservists as different from and somehow inferior to the regulars, whereas regulars and reservists would for the most part have the same authority and the same responsibilities. Difference in uniform implied a lack of unity that did not, or should not, exist.

The Bureau of Navigation was rapidly outgrowing its assigned space in "Main Navy," a building on Constitution Avenue constructed to house the Navy Department in World War I. A "temporary" building, it continued in use through World War II and long beyond. To find room for its growing secretariat, the Bureau began moving to a Navy Department annex in Arlington, a building it was to share with Marine Corps headquarters. The move imposed a hardship on Nimitz, who had to keep in close touch with the Secretary of the Navy and the Chief of Naval Operations while supervising his own bureau, part of which was housed on the far side of the Potomac River.

Nimitz was also regularly in touch with the White House. President Franklin D. Roosevelt personally selected his top naval commanders and he relied on advice from Nimitz, who was acquainted with every senior officer in the Navy and knew the special qualifications of each. Between the two men there developed a curious bond. Nimitz deeply respected Roosevelt as President and recognized his political genius. At the same time he was somewhat repelled by the feeling that Roosevelt was less than natural, that he was always playing a role. Roosevelt, on the other hand, seems unqualifiedly to have admired Nimitz.

Early in 1941 the presidential favor brought Nimitz an extraordinary offer, nothing less than the post of Commander in Chief, U.S. Fleet (CinCUS). For so relatively junior an admiral to be offered the command second only to Chief of Naval Operations (CNO) was such a signal honor that it perhaps invites some background explanation.

At the time of the offer, the war that Nimitz had predicted had already broken out in Europe. The Germans had annexed Austria and most of Czechoslovakia and had overrun Poland, Denmark, Norway, Holland, Belgium, and France. In the Orient the Japanese, in an undeclared war, had invaded China and occupied northern Indochina.

The United States was expanding its Patrol Force in preparation to assist beleaguered Britain by escorting convoys as far as Iceland. Americans were forbidden to sell aircraft, aviation gasoline, iron, or steel to Japan. In 1939, on President Roosevelt's orders, Admiral Claude C. Bloch, then CinCUS, began shifting his lighter vessels from their West Coast ports to Pearl Harbor. In April 1940, Bloch's successor, Admiral James O. Richardson, completed the transfer of the U.S. Fleet to Hawaii. Shortly afterward the CNO, Admiral Harold R. Stark, notified Richardson that the fleet would be based on Pearl Harbor indefinitely.

"Why are we here?" asked Richardson in some dismay.

"You are there," replied Stark, "because of the deterrent effect which it is thought your presence may have on the Japs going into the East Indies."

To Richardson such reasoning was nonsense. He considered Japanese expansion in Asia and the Indies to be of slight concern to the United States. Anyway, he believed that a fleet kept in readiness in mainland ports was a more credible deterrent than one half-starved at the then-primitive Hawaiian base. He rushed the construction of facilities and housing at Pearl Harbor but continued to complain; twice he visited Washington to urge the President, the State Department, and the Navy Department to bring the fleet back home. Roosevelt finally lost patience and early in 1941 ordered Richardson relieved.

Nimitz, despite his lack of seniority, had some qualifications that made him a suitable relief for Richardson. He had shown himself a gifted administrator and was noted for making do with next to nothing. It was he who had built the submarine base at Pearl Harbor, using materials that he scrounged from East Coast naval shipyards. Evidently, if Nimitz found the fleet base at Pearl Harbor inadequate, he was the man to make it adequate, and to do so at minimum expense.

Nimitz asked to be excused. He explained that he considered himself too junior to be CinCUS. Were he, in time of peace, to be jumped over the heads of half a hundred more senior officers, he said, it would reap him a harvest of ill will that might impair his usefulness. He had no scruples about declining the command, since he knew that the alternate choice was his friend, the able Rear Admiral Husband E. Kimmel.

Nimitz's rejection of the fleet command may have been, for him, the most fortunate decision of his career. Kimmel, in accepting the duty, took the temporary rank of full admiral, jumping up 31 numbers and doubtless earning the ill will that Nimitz had avoided. Moreover, he took command of a naval force that, as events were to prove, was both inadequately protected and exposed to enemy attack. There is not, however, any indication that Admiral Nimitz in declining the command of the United States Fleet had any motive beyond the one he professed, lack of seniority.

On the day that Admiral Kimmel assumed his new duty, February 1, 1941, the expanding Patrol Force became the United States Atlantic Fleet, and Kimmel's force based at Pearl Harbor became the United States Pacific Fleet. Kimmel thus became Commander in Chief, Pacific Fleet (CinCPac), but he also retained Richardson's old title of Commander in Chief, U.S. Fleet (CinCUS). This CinCUS title was henceforth to be rotated among the three fleet commanders but the title was to be exercised only when two or more of the fleets operated together or to prescribe uniform procedures or training standards for all United States forces afloat.

Because Nimitz, as a bureau chief, was not directly concerned with diplomacy or military operations, he was not informed concerning high-level negotiations between the United States and Japan. He was not aware that American cryptanalysts had broken Japan's diplomatic code and were reading messages between the government in Tokyo and Japanese embassies and consulates in Washington and elsewhere. Yet, as a voracious reader of books, magazines, and newspapers and a keen analyst of events, he was able to keep himself almost as well informed concerning Japanese moves as were the nation's topmost military and political leaders.

In the summer of 1941, while Nimitz and his bureau were working overtime to meet the manpower needs of an explosively growing Navy, the situation in the Pacific was deteriorating rapidly. When the United States began restricting sales to the Japanese of the oil they urgently needed to carry on their war, Japan completed its occupation of Indochina, thus acquiring bases that menaced Borneo, the Philippines, and Singapore. In retaliation, the governments of the United States, Britain, and the Dutch East Indies froze Japanese assets, thereby threatening to cut off Japan's oil purchases entirely.

The Japanese then had a choice of three courses of action: (1) induce the United States to unfreeze their assets and provide them with oil; (2) terminate their aggressions and pull back their forces to the homeland; and (3) assure themselves of a supply of oil by seizing the petroleum-rich East Indies. Because neither the United States nor Japan was willing to change its policies, informed observers expected Japan to execute the third option.

As Stark had pointed out to Richardson in 1940, the U.S. Fleet had been moved from the West Coast to Pearl Harbor precisely to deter the Japanese from such a move. By autumn 1941, however, it had become apparent that they were not going to be deterred—even at the risk of war with the United States and the British Commonwealth. Indeed, it appeared that, in order to protect the flanks of their southern advance, the Japanese might occupy the Philippines, Singapore, Hong Kong, and possibly Guam.

Britain's deep concern at the growing crisis was demonstrated by the arrival at Singapore of the battleship *Prince of Wales*, the battle cruiser *Repulse*, and other vessels—evidently as a further deterrent. Japan showed its anxiety by rushing to Washington a special negotiator, Saburo Kurusu, to assist the Japanese ambassador and his staff in dealing with the U.S. State Department. President Roosevelt appealed directly to Emperor Hirohito to withdraw Japanese military forces from southern Indochina.

In early December American newspapers reported an assemblage of many Japanese ships in Camranh Bay, on the southeast coast of Indochina. On December 6 they summarized reports from British aviators of a huge Japanese attack force rounding the southern tip of Indochina and entering the Gulf of Siam. Like many thoughtful Americans, Admiral Nimitz doubtless studied the map and concluded that this fleet was headed for the Malay Peninsula to launch an attack toward Singapore. On the other hand, he did not suspect that Japan's only carrier force was simultaneously heading eastward for a raid on Pearl Harbor. Nor did any other American suspect anything of the sort, not the President or the Secretary of the Navy or the Chief of Naval Operations— and certainly not Admiral Kimmel, whose Pacific Fleet was the main target of the oncoming enemy carriers.

Admiral Nimitz was spending Sunday, December 7, 1941, at his apartment at 2222 Q Street, Washington, D.C. With him, besides Mrs. Nimitz, were his youngest daughter Mary, aged 10, his daughter-in-law Joan, and her daughter Frances. The two older Nimitz daughters, Catherine, then aged 27, and Nancy, 22, lived in a separate apartment across the hall in the same building. Chester Junior was in a submarine operating out of the Philippines.

After a late midday dinner, Admiral and Mrs. Nimitz, as was their custom, settled down to read and to listen to music. At 3:00 p.m. the admiral turned on the radio to hear a CBS broadcast of Artur Rodzinski conducting the New York Philharmonic Orchestra. Almost immediately the broadcast was interrupted by a flash announcement that the Japanese had bombed Pearl Harbor.

Admiral Nimitz leapt from his chair. Hardly had he got his overcoat on when the telephone rang. It was his assistant, Captain John F. Shafroth, saying that he was driving to the Navy Department and would pick Nimitz up. The admiral asked Mrs. Nimitz to call his flag secretary, Lieutenant (j.g.) H. Arthur Lamar, and tell him to get down to the Department. Said Nimitz as he went out the door, "I won't be back till God knows when."

At the Navy Department Admiral Nimitz conferred with members of his staff in his own office and then hurried off for further conferences in Secretary Frank Knox's and Admiral Stark's offices. Knox had been talking by telephone to Admiral Bloch, Commandant of the 14th Naval District, whose headquarters were at Pearl Harbor. Bloch had described the damage he could see from his office window: the *Oklahoma* and the *Arizona* had been badly hit, he said, and the *Pennsylvania* and the *Tennessee* superficially damaged; the *California* was down on the shallow bottom but could be raised. Luckily the navy yard and oil reserves had not been touched. Admiral Stark, with the President's consent, had radioed the U.S. Navy's first combat directive to all commanders in Panama and the Pacific area: "Execute unrestricted air and submarine warfare against Japan."

That Sunday Nimitz felt as never before the awkwardness of a physically divided bureau, with its head on Constitution Avenue and its body in Arlington. In the late afternoon he arrived for consultation at the Arlington Annex. By then news reaching the Navy Department from Pearl Harbor revealed that there was a great deal that Admiral Bloch had not seen from his window. The *Nevada* and *West Virginia* and a number of smaller vessels, 18 ships in all, had been damaged, some beyond repair. Hangars and other buildings had been set afire. Nearly 200 planes had been destroyed, most of them on the ground. Americans killed and injured, chiefly U.S. Navy personnel, numbered in the thousands. To his old friend Captain F. E. M. ("Red") Whiting, the Bureau of Navigation's director of recruiting, Nimitz expressed his despair. "Red," he said, "we have suffered a terrible defeat. I don't know whether we can ever recover from it."

Back at home, Nimitz's daughter Catherine had taken over her father's accustomed chore of walking Freckles, the family cocker spaniel. She used no leash, which she considered unnecessary in view of Freckles' sterling record for good behavior. Mistress and dog turned into Massachusetts Avenue and there beheld an astonishing sight. On the side lawn of the Japanese embassy a fire was blazing, and employees were lugging out boxes of official papers to dump on the flames. Crowds looked on under the watchful eyes of District of Columbia police. The press was well represented, and photographers were everywhere, even in the trees.

Mustering her dignity, Catherine proceeded to march past the embassy with her dog at heel. Suddenly, to her horror, the usually well-behaved Freckles dashed onto the front lawn of the embassy and there, in full view of public, police, and reporters, incontinently committed a nuisance. Catherine, red-faced, chased the dog off the lawn and headed for home. She said to her mother, "There's all the press up there, and if they only knew they could write a headline: ADMIRAL'S DOG HURLS DEFIANCE AT NIPPON."

Mrs. Nimitz soon set forth with warm food, a thermos of hot coffee, and a thermos of hot soup. This was only the first of several trips she made to the Navy Department in the next few days in an effort to keep her husband and his associates properly fed. It was long after midnight when Admiral Nimitz arrived home. He caught three or four hours' sleep, took a quick bath, shaved, and was off to the Department again.

The newspapers that morning, quoting a naval communiqué, mentioned only the *Oklahoma* as having been damaged. The Navy Department had decided not to inform the Japanese, via the American press, how successful their attack had been and how badly the U.S. Navy had been hurt. Some officers speculated that if the attacker knew the whole truth he might be encouraged to come back and invade Hawaii.

Also, the Department, via newspapers and public radio broadcasts, had

ordered all officers in the Washington area to present an appearance of prepar-
edness by reporting for duty Monday morning in uniform—an order that very
nearly backfired. Admiral Nimitz and Lieutenant Lamar had no problem, for
their duties required them to have uniforms ready to wear at certain funerals in
Arlington Cemetery. Other officers, however, had not worn a uniform in three
years of shore duty, and some of them had gained weight or permitted their
uniforms to lapse into disrepair. Lamar had spent Sunday afternoon and evening telephoning naval tailors, urging them to open store and repair shop as a
means of meeting the crisis. Despite mighty strivings, not every officer was
prepared to look his best by Monday morning. Some arrived at the Navy
Department in jackets that would not button or that had buttons missing or
tarnished braid. One flag officer showed up sporting a very loud Scottish tweed
overcoat topped by his admiral's cap.

The President that day requested, and Congress voted, a declaration of
war against Japan. Germany and Italy, in fulfillment of treaty commitments to
Japan, soon declared war on the United States. It was up to the Bureau of
Navigation to man a wartime Navy, an undertaking that would have been far
more difficult had not Admiral Nimitz forehandedly prepared for just this
contingency—sometimes in defiance of restrictive regulations.

At the same time the Bureau of Navigation was swamped with emergency
duties resulting from the Pearl Harbor raid. Conflicting information had to be
sorted out, families of the killed notified, bodies brought home, and, in many
cases, arrangements made for burial. Thousands of officers and men who were
left stranded and stripped of everything by the sinking of their ships had to be
provided for. Calls poured into the bureau demanding information. Excited
congressmen telephoned, wanting to enlist in the Navy. For these Nimitz, bone
weary and almost sleepless, had a set answer: "Go back and vote us appropriations, for we're going to need them."

On December 9 Secretary Knox left by air to make a quick inspection of
Pearl Harbor and to confer with officers on the scene. The next day Admiral
King, the hard-nosed Commander in Chief of the Atlantic Fleet, arrived in
Washington to confer with the Navy chiefs, including Admiral Nimitz. It
would be difficult to find personalities more sharply contrasting than those of
the rough, tough King and the calm, courteous Nimitz, but the two men got
along well together. There had earlier developed between them a friendship
based on respect for each other's ability, integrity, and devotion to duty.

On Monday, December 15, Knox, back in Washington, met representatives of the press. He told them that the *Arizona* had been sunk, as had a target
ship, a minelayer, and three destroyers, and that the *Oklahoma* had capsized
but could be righted. Though that, of course, was not the whole story, the fact
that the Secretary had told so much appalled some officers. But Knox, who in
private life was publisher of the Chicago *Daily News*, knew his business. He
had revealed only what could plainly be seen from the heights flanking Pearl
Harbor and must already be known to the enemy. The Secretary blamed the

disaster in part on the defense forces at Hawaii, whom he accused of not being on the alert.

Knox's bad news was only another phase of the story of mounting catastrophe for the Americans and their British friends, now allies. The Japanese attack force that had been sighted entering the Gulf of Siam had landed troops in Malaya, and these were driving on Singapore. The *Prince of Wales* and the *Repulse*, advancing to interrupt this invasion, had been promptly sunk by Japanese planes. The Japanese had captured Guam, invaded the Philippines and the British Gilbert Islands, bombed Singapore and Hong Kong, and bombarded Midway Atoll and Johnston Island. U.S. marines had hurled back an enemy drive to occupy Wake Island, but the atoll was under air attack from the Marshalls, evidently preliminary to a renewed invasion attempt.

That evening Knox conferred with President Roosevelt, to whom he made three recommendations: (1) that a board of inquiry be set up to investigate the reasons for the failure of the Pearl Harbor defenses and to determine who, if anybody, was to blame; (2) that Admiral Kimmel, his name now inescapably associated with catastrophe and defeat, should be immediately relieved as CinCUS-CinCPac; and (3) that CinCUS be separated from the area fleet commands and given the operational control of the entire Navy. Roosevelt concurred with all three recommendations, and he and Knox agreed that Admiral King should be appointed to the new, independent post of Commander in Chief, U.S. Fleet. Apparently President and Secretary decided to sleep on the question of who should relieve Kimmel, for the next morning, Tuesday, December 16, Knox was back at the White House. They then quickly agreed on Nimitz for CinCPac. "Tell Nimitz," said Roosevelt, "to get the hell out to Pearl and stay there till the war is won."

Knox hastened to the Navy Department and at once sent for Nimitz. The latter, completely unaware of the decisions reached at the White House, trudged wearily down to the Secretary's office. Knox, seated at his desk and obviously excited, did not ask the admiral to sit down. He blurted out, "How soon can you be ready to travel?"

Nimitz, his nerves on edge from fatigue, answered a little crossly, "It depends on where I'm going and how long I'll be away."

"You're going to take command of the Pacific Fleet, and I think you will be gone for a long time."

Nimitz was startled. The year before he had begged off from the command for lack of seniority. That reason still applied, and now he would have the additional embarrassment of relieving an old friend. But in time of war one does not question an order. He thought of his immediate responsibilities.

"I'll have to get someone to relieve me."

"Whom do you want?"

"Randall Jacobs." Captain Jacobs, until recently Assistant Chief of the Bureau of Navigation, knew the bureau's problems almost as thoroughly as Nimitz did.

"You can't have him," replied Knox. "FDR doesn't like him."

"God damn it," Nimitz exploded, "he's the only man who can do the job!"

"Where is he?"

Nimitz replied that Jacobs was somewhere in the Atlantic and that he would find him. Leaving the Secretary's office, he set out down the corridor, his thoughts awhirl. Suddenly he was brought to a startled standstill at the sight of a pudgy figure coming toward him. It was Captain Jacobs. Jacobs explained that he was steaming into Norfolk when he heard the news of the attack on Pearl Harbor. As soon as he could get away, he had come to Washington to find out what was going on.

Said Nimitz, "Come up with me."

The admiral led Jacobs to his own office and sat him down at the desk. "From now on," said he, "you are chief of the bureau. Get your orders drawn up."

Leaving behind a slightly bewildered new chief of bureau, Nimitz spent several hours preparing instructions, getting off correspondence, conferring with Shafroth and others—all necessary to get the new chief off to a clear start. Late in the afternoon he was summoned to the White House with Knox and King for a brief interview with the President. Then he walked home to Q Street, as usual.

He found Mrs. Nimitz in bed trying to throw off a head cold. The admiral came into the bedroom and sat down beside her. After a long pause, he asked, "Have you got a fever?"

She could see that something was on his mind. "No, sweetheart," she replied. "What is it? What's happened?"

With a distraught expression he replied, "I'm to be the new Commander in Chief in the Pacific."

"You always wanted to command the Pacific Fleet. You always thought that would be the height of glory."

"Darling, the fleet's at the bottom of the sea. Nobody must know that here, but I've got to tell you."

After dinner, Mrs. Nimitz got out a couple of suitcases, and she and the admiral began to pack his things. When she noticed that he was distractedly packing his tuxedo, she made him sit down while she took over the job, putting in several sets of whites and khakis. Having lived in Hawaii, she knew that he would not need blues there. She could send his blues later to enable him to take any necessary trips to cooler climes.

The Nimitzes, it turned out, had packed a little prematurely. The admiral was obliged to attend a whole series of day and night discussions and planning sessions, climaxed by a conference at the White House on Thursday morning. A major topic of discussion was what should be done with the weakened U.S. forces in the Pacific. The main striking power of the Pacific Fleet now consisted of three task forces built around the carriers *Saratoga*, *Enterprise*, and

*Lexington*. Admiral Kimmel, with the approval of the Navy Department, on December 16 had committed all three forces to the relief of Wake. The *Lexington* force was to make a diversionary raid on the Marshalls, while the *Saratoga*, with a marine corps fighter squadron aboard, headed directly for Wake, backed by the *Enterprise*, which was also to cover Pearl Harbor.

After the relief of Wake, what next? Despite a secret prewar commitment to the British for a policy of "beat Hitler first," U.S. naval leaders expected to use the Pacific Fleet aggressively. At the outbreak of war they planned to capture the Marshalls and the Carolines, in order both to divert the Japanese from the East Indies area and to open the way for the relief of the Philippines. The raid on Pearl Harbor automatically canceled that ambitious plan. Apparently all that could be expected of the remnant of the Pacific Fleet was that it would protect U.S. positions and shipping—with emphasis on Midway and communications with Australia, which appeared most threatened by the enemy advance.

Thursday morning's newspapers announced the President's decisions in reaction to the Pearl Harbor attack. A five-man board headed by Supreme Court Justice Owen J. Roberts would investigate the failure of U.S. defenses. Admiral Kimmel was to be relieved by Admiral Nimitz. Pending the latter's arrival in Hawaii, the command of the Pacific Fleet was assigned to Vice Admiral William S. Pye, commander of the Battle Fleet. Lieutenant General Delos C. Emmons would replace Lieutenant General Walter C. Short as head of the Hawaiian Department. Brigadier General Clarence L. Tinker was to relieve Major General Frederick L. Martin in command of the Hawaiian Air Forces. Until a new commander in chief of the Atlantic Fleet had been selected, no announcement was to be made of the appointment of Admiral King as Commander in Chief, U.S. Fleet. And of course no hint was published of the Wake relief expedition.

Secretary Knox notified Nimitz that a plane was waiting to convey him to Pearl Harbor. "Look," replied the admiral, "I am just simply too tired to make that quick trip by air." He preferred, he said, to go to the West Coast by rail in order to catch up on his sleep, regain his strength, and read some reports.

Accordingly, it was arranged that Nimitz should leave Washington the following afternoon, Friday, December 19, on the B. & O.'s Capitol Limited. He seems to have worked late Thursday evening as usual, but on Friday morning he relaxed to the extent of accompanying Mrs. Nimitz to Jackson School, where daughter Mary was to perform in a Christmas pageant that they had promised to attend.

Back home, as the family was finishing a late lunch, Flag Secretary Lamar arrived with a car and driver. Captain Shafroth had ordered Lamar to accompany Nimitz on the train, and the Navy Surgeon had instructed him to consider himself the admiral's head keeper and nurse for the next few days. Lamar was to see that Nimitz ate and slept properly, and he was to try, at least for the first day or so, to keep his boss's mind off his coming responsibilities.

The lieutenant was also advised to pick up a couple of bottles of whiskey and make sure the admiral got two good slugs as a relaxer each evening before dinner.

On instructions from the White House, both the lieutenant and the admiral were to travel incognito in civilian clothes. Nimitz decided to call himself "Mr. Freeman," using his wife's maiden name. Lamar chose to be "Mr. Wainwright," after Rear Admiral John Drayton Wainwright, whom he admired.

After conversing with the family for a while, Lamar tactfully withdrew, saying, "I'm going down and wait in the car."

So as to entrain as inconspicuously as possible, Admiral Nimitz said goodbye to his family then and there in the apartment. Though Mrs. Nimitz and the girls had no idea when they would see the admiral again—certainly not for many months, perhaps years—there were no tears. They were a Navy family, in which separations were to be expected—and accepted.

Mrs. Nimitz said later: "At no time did I break down. I was brought up by my mother to take what's coming, and you don't weep over it. You have to go through things. It was very sweet because when he left, it was just as if he was going off for the day."

Nimitz left home early enough to drop by the Navy Department. Stark wrung his hand and offered to accompany him to the station, then thought better of it, for his uniform would attract attention. Knox, just back from speaking at the graduation ceremony of the Naval Academy's accelerated class, was exhausted and so emotionally worn that his voice trembled as he said goodbye. Meanwhile, Stark had summoned Lamar to his office and handed him a heavy canvas bag. "Don't let this out of your possession," he said, "and don't open it until you are well along the way outside Chicago, and then show Admiral Nimitz what's inside."

During the ride to the station, Nimitz was silent and preoccupied. Lamar knew better than to intrude upon his chief's thoughts. Their association, necessarily close, had never been intimate, for Nimitz, though kindly and accessible, usually kept his subordinates psychologically at arm's length. Luckily, at Union Station they encountered not a soul they knew. They were allowed to board the Capitol Limited at once and were given adjoining rooms with a door between.

Hardly had the train pulled out of the station when Nimitz showed a side of himself that was new to his aide. He shucked his cares, told funny stories, and tossed off atrocious puns. He tried to teach Lamar cribbage, but the lieutenant was too excited to keep his mind on the game. He was beginning to wonder who was looking after whom. At length the admiral gave up on his aide and began playing his own highly mathematical version of solitaire.

The admiral's newfound gaiety was somewhat deflated at dinner that evening when a fellow diner looked fixedly at him and then, on leaving the car, addressed him by name and rank. It was a college professor whom Nimitz had met recently while addressing a convention of the Association of American

Universities. Nimitz could only hope that his identity would not spread through the train and reach the press.

In Chicago, between trains, Nimitz took a taxi to the Navy Pier for a much-needed haircut and made a quick visit to a Naval Reserve midshipmen's school. He was gratified to learn that Wake was still holding out despite repeated air raids.

In the early afternoon the Santa Fe's Superchief pulled out of Chicago with the admiral and his aide aboard. After lunch Lamar opened the canvas bag that Stark had entrusted to him and handed Nimitz the contents—the complete report on the material and human casualties at Pearl Harbor, together with grim photographs of the sunk and damaged ships. Nimitz instantly became serious and began scrutinizing the report carefully. He found it shocking, but it tended to confirm his growing conviction that Knox was wrong in blaming Kimmel and the other commanders in Hawaii. "It could have happened to anyone," he said sympathetically.

Most distressing to Nimitz was a photograph of the battleship *Arizona* wreathed in smoke, her foremast leaning crazily askew. A Japanese bomb had exploded in one of her forward magazines. More than a thousand of her company had lost their lives. Three years before, when Nimitz was Commander, Battleship Division One, the *Arizona* was his flagship. Her commanding officer then was Nimitz's old friend Captain Isaac Kidd. At the time of the Pearl Harbor attack, Kidd, promoted to rear admiral, had succeeded to command of Battleship Division One, and his flagship was the *Arizona*. He was on board when the attack came, and he was among the missing.

Nimitz at length took time out from his studies to dash off a letter to Mrs. Nimitz, the first of hundreds written during World War II. These took the form of a journal, with daily entries, some long, some very brief, which he mailed once a week. "Here we are westbound thru western Illinois," he began, "through lovely rolling country, nice farms and wide vistas and far off horizons."

To relieve the monotony of the long ride across the plains, Nimitz and Lamar got off the train during its infrequent stops and strolled about the station platform. On one such occasion, as he headed to leave the train, the admiral stepped into a men's room. Along came the porters routinely locking the toilets before the engine came to a stop. The one who locked the facility Nimitz occupied failed to check whether the room was in use. Hence when "Mr. Freeman" was ready to emerge, he found he could do nothing of the sort. Worse, when the train pulled out of the station, the porter forgot to unlock the door.

The admiral banged on the door to no avail. Equally unavailing were his efforts to unfasten the lock from the inside. He had designed and installed naval machinery and had been a national authority on diesel engines, but that little lock defeated him. Somehow the irony of the prospective commander in chief of the Pacific Fleet being trapped inside a two-by-four jakes failed to commend itself to his sense of humor. For fifteen minutes the sweating admiral alternately tinkered with the lock and pounded on the door.

At long last the porter, passing along the narrow passage, heard the banging. Taking out his key, he unlocked the door, to be instantly confronted by a wrathful "Mr. Freeman." The porter turned a scornful look upon what he took to be a bungling middle-aged civilian.

"Now, look," he said pityingly, "if you're inside, you can always get out by just moving this latch."

"Oh, you think so?" said Nimitz. "Well, good. Try it. Give me the key and get in there."

Nimitz shut the door and turned the key, leaving the porter as helpless to get out as he himself had been. Back in his compartment the admiral concentrated a quarter of an hour on the report. He then arose and, swinging the borrowed key, marched back down the aisle and released the impounded porter, now exhausted with fruitless banging and yelling. Nimitz returned to his compartment in a merry mood. In retrospect he began to find the whole caper, including his own discomfiture, vastly amusing. Here was another anecdote to add to the store of humorous stories that he delighted in telling.

On Sunday afternoon, while rolling through New Mexico, the admiral wrote Mrs. Nimitz again:

> Had a fine sleep and awoke much refreshed—but after spending most of to-day reading reports and estimates I find it difficult to keep on cheerful side. Perhaps when I actually arrive and get over the first shock things will be better.
>
> Last night's paper announced King as C in C U.S. and he is apparently displacing Stark insofar as concerns operations. Ingersoll is C. in C. Atlantic. What a grand overall shakeup! At any rate I am convinced that there will be more action in the Pacific than elsewhere for many a day to come.
>
> Lamar has continued to be a great comfort.
>
> Hope the weather is favorable to prompt flying departure.

At Los Angeles, Nimitz and Lamar parted company. While the lieutenant headed back to Washington, the admiral went on to San Diego, arriving in the late afternoon of December 22. There he was met by Captain E. Robert Anderson, who was in a state of some agitation. Finding no "Mr. Freeman" on the first and second sections of the incoming train, Anderson checked with the stationmaster and had been assured that all the cars from Los Angeles had arrived. He was about to conclude that the admiral had met with some mishap, perhaps even foul play, when, contrary to the stationmaster's information, a final section of the train came rolling in, bearing the missing "Mr. Freeman." Anderson, a journalist serving in the Naval Reserve, conducted Nimitz by navy car to the home of his San Diego host, Rear Admiral Ernest Gunther, at the Air Station, 11th Naval District.

A Catalina flying boat was standing by to take Admiral Nimitz to Pearl Harbor, but a southeast gale delayed its departure. It made an abortive start on

December 23, but a gust caught the wing of the plane, plunging its engines under water, and the flight had to be abandoned. The next morning it appeared that the winds were abating and that the flight would be possible that day.

The morning newspapers announced that enemy forces had landed on Wake, but that the marine and naval defenders continued to resist. Admiral Nimitz wondered what was holding up the relief expedition, which should have reached the atoll by that time.

Before taking off that afternoon, Nimitz managed to write a few lines to Mrs. Nimitz, concluding: "I only hope I can live up to the high expectations of you and the President and the Department. I will faithfully promise to do my best. I am sorry I could not get out to P.H. before the [Roberts] inspecting board got there."

Nimitz's Catalina was airborne at 4:00 p.m. The admiral apologized to the crew for taking them away from their families on Christmas Eve.

# CHAPTER 2

# CINCPAC FROM TEXAS

FOR SECURITY REASONS, Admiral Nimitz's plane did not head directly for the island of Oahu in the Hawaiian chain. Instead, at dawn on Christmas morning, it dropped down out of low clouds over Molokai, the next island to the east, where it was met by several fighter aircraft and escorted to Pearl Harbor.

The admiral, chilled and half-deafened by the roar of the motors, had scarcely slept. As his plane circled for a water landing, he looked down through pelting rain at a disheartening spectacle. East Loch, the main anchorage, was covered with black fuel oil; the battleship *Oklahoma* and the target vessel *Utah* were bottoms up, and a minelayer was lying on her side. In the distance the battleship *Nevada*, heavily damaged, was aground in the shallows. The battleships *California*, *West Virginia*, and *Arizona* were sunk in deeper water, only their topsides visible, with blackened and twisted masts.

At 7:00 a.m., exactly on time, the admiral's plane touched down and came to a stop. When the door was thrown open, his nostrils were assailed by a miasma of black oil, charred wood, blistered paint, and burned and rotting bodies. Alongside came a whaleboat, foul inside and out with oil. With some distaste Nimitz, still in civilian clothes, stepped down into the filthy craft and shook hands with the reception committee—Rear Admiral Patrick Bellinger, commanding the naval air arm in Hawaii, and Captains William W. Smith and Harold C. Train, chiefs of staff to Admirals Kimmel and Pye, respectively.

Nimitz at once asked the question that was uppermost in his mind: "What news of the relief of Wake?" Told that the relief expedition had been recalled and that Wake had surrendered, he remained silent for some time.

The trip to shore was miserable. The surface was choppy. The rain continued to fall. All four men with considerable difficulty remained standing to avoid soiling their clothing. In reply to another Nimitz question, Captain Smith explained that the boats moving about the harbor were fishing out the bodies of sailors which, grotesquely bloated, were still rising to the surface. Another long silence.

"When you get back to your office," said Nimitz at last to Smith, "call Washington and report my arrival." Then, gazing back over East Loch, he murmured, "This is a terrible sight, seeing all these ships down."

At the submarine-base wharf, which the whaleboat presently came alongside, Captain Train escorted Nimitz to the official car beside which Admiral Pye was waiting to conduct him to his quarters at Makalapa, a long-extinct volcano rising from behind the submarine base. Carrying Pye and Nimitz, the car moved up the hill and presently stopped before a comfortable-looking dwelling.

"Whose quarters are these?" asked Nimitz.

"They are yours. Nobody else is there."

Nimitz asked Pye if he had eaten breakfast. Pye replied that he had.

"Well," said Nimitz, "you'll have another one, for I won't eat alone— after what I've seen."

When Nimitz had completed his first and Pye his second breakfast, Admiral Kimmel joined them. He was wearing two stars instead of the four he had worn as CinCPac. A portly man of imperious presence, he now appeared a little stooped, somehow deflated. On that terrible morning, more than a fortnight earlier, as Kimmel with horrified fascination watched his fleet being smashed, a spent .50-caliber bullet broke through the window and struck his breast. "Too bad it didn't kill me," Kimmel had said quietly.

Nimitz, shocked at his old friend's appearance, warmly pressed his hand. "You have my sympathy," he said. "The same thing could have happened to anybody."

Kimmel, an inveterate workhorse, had left his wife at home in the United States so that he would not be in any way diverted from his job as CinCPac. Until recently he had lived in the quarters prepared for Nimitz. Now he, Admiral and Mrs. Pye, and a navy captain were housed together across the street, a result of the crowding at Pearl Harbor caused by the loss of so many quarters afloat.

Nimitz offered to share his four-bedroom house, but Pye and Kimmel pointed out that their crowded condition was temporary, for Kimmel soon would be leaving. So would Mrs. Pye, since all dependents had been ordered back to the States. The new CinCPac, they said, would need his spacious quarters to house some of his staff and to lodge visiting dignitaries. Nimitz insisted that they at least mess with him and they agreed to do so for the time being. Thus, Admirals Nimitz, Kimmel, and Pye, and Mrs. Pye had Christmas dinner together.

Admiral Nimitz promptly plunged into the task of learning his new job. In this he was loyally assisted by Pye and other admirals who were much senior to him and would remain so until he assumed his four stars as CinCPac. In preparation for that occasion, he received from the officers and men of the submarine base, which he had built twenty years earlier, the gift of a pair of four-star shoulder marks. Admiral Kimmel made himself available to Nimitz whenever possible, but Kimmel had to spend several hours a day before the Roberts Commission, which usually met in a suite of a hotel in Honolulu.

Between briefings and conferences, Admiral Nimitz made a series of inspections, carefully studying machine shops, offices, communication facilities, and everything else of importance, including damaged ships and salvage operations. From his studies and inspections he drew two major conclusions. One was the disappointing realization that Commander in Chief, Pacific Fleet, could no longer be a seagoing command. Its responsibilities were too far-flung, its contacts too numerous, for the incumbent in time of action to leave the complex communication center at Pearl Harbor and move with the fleet. It appeared that Nimitz, who had gone through the First World War without hearing a shot fired in anger, was unlikely to see battle in the Second. His other conclusion was more cheering. It had become clear to him that the "Pearl Harbor disaster" was not nearly so disastrous as it might have been. The damage could, in his words, "very easily have been devastatingly greater."

Had Admiral Kimmel received timely warning of the enemy's approach, he would "by all the rules" have had the fleet at sea to intercept the attacking force. With luck he might have joined Vice Admiral William F. Halsey's *Enterprise* force, which was approaching Oahu after delivering a marine fighter squadron to Wake. But the Japanese striking force included six carriers and it had at least a 2-knot speed advantage. Hence, had Kimmel put to sea and met the enemy, his whole fleet would almost certainly have been sunk—in deep water beyond salvage, with a loss of 20,000 men. As it was, all but two of the eight battleships damaged at Pearl Harbor could eventually be returned to the fleet. The *Maryland*, the *Pennsylvania*, and the *Tennessee*, with temporary repairs, were already limping back to the West Coast for rehabilitation.

To many Americans the raid on the fleet at Pearl Harbor seemed a catastrophe beyond measure, and indeed the loss of 2,000 men was a tragedy for their friends and families and a serious loss to the armed forces. But what few people, even naval officers, realized in 1941 was that the old battleships at Pearl Harbor were, to a great extent, superfluous. They were too vulnerable to operate without air cover and too slow to operate with the carriers. In modern carrier warfare only planes could reach the enemy fleet; ship guns could not. In 1944, however, having been raised, repaired, and renovated, they were invaluable for shore bombardment under cover of planes from the new escort carriers. In the meantime, their damaged state made many thousands of trained men, then in short supply, available for service in the carrier and amphibious forces that proved decisive against Japan.

The Japanese missed the U.S. carriers because none were at Pearl Harbor. They failed to hit the tank farm with its 4,500,000 barrels of fuel oil. Had this immense reservoir been destroyed, the fleet would have been forced back to the West Coast. They did not hit the vital repair facilities of Pearl Harbor, or the submarine base, from which the first American attack was launched. Most important, the raid on Pearl Harbor galvanized a dangerously divided nation into one implacably determined to fight the war through to final victory. On balance, then, the raid truly strengthened rather than weakened the United States. Admiral Isoroku Yamamoto, who planned and launched the attack despite the vigorous opposition of the Japanese Naval General Staff, had committed a first-class blunder.

Admiral Nimitz, while carrying out his interminable tasks, sometimes glanced longingly at the green heights and sparkling beaches of Oahu, which provided fine hiking and swimming, but for him there was now no time for such pleasures. It was probably lack of the physical activity to which he was accustomed, as much as his baffling problems, that kept him awake through part of each night. Despite sleeplessness, he arose every morning at 6:30, did a few setting-up exercises, breakfasted alone at 7:15, and then proceeded to Pacific Fleet headquarters at the nearby submarine base. He lunched at the BOQ with one or more officers, then went back to his office or made inspections until 6:00 p.m., when he returned to his blacked-out house.

After dinner with Kimmel and the Pyes, Nimitz enjoyed his only relaxation of the day by playing a game or so of cribbage with them. For many men, this association could have been more trying than relaxing, for over them all there hung like a shadow the embarrassing matters of Kimmel's relief and of the failure to rescue Wake. Kimmel had launched the Wake relief expedition, which, had it succeeded, might have restored his damaged reputation. Pye, after assuming command, had recalled it. But nothing that had happened in any way marred the friendship of the three admirals, then or later.

One of Admiral Nimitz's most important and perplexing problems at this time was selecting a staff to serve with him. He had an embarrassment of riches, because in addition to force commanders who had lost their commands, he had the staffs of Admirals Kimmel and Pye and of Rear Admiral Milo F. Draemel, Commander, Destroyers, Battle Force. After the raid, of course, Pye's and Draemel's staffs had nowhere to go but ashore.

Nimitz concluded from discussions and from general sensitivity to the atmosphere around him that morale at Pearl Harbor was sinking rapidly. The angry defiance with which the garrison and the ships' companies had reacted to the initial attack had become eroded by inaction, by continuing bad news, and, above all, by the failure to relieve Wake. At year's end, Nimitz decided that he could wait no longer to assume command.

At ten o'clock on the morning of December 31, 1941, on the deck of the submarine *Grayling* moored alongside the submarine-base wharf, Admiral Nimitz took command of the Pacific Fleet, and his brand-new, four-star flag was hoisted at the *Grayling*'s mast. He liked to say that he assumed command aboard a submarine because the Japanese attack had left no other sort of deck available at Pearl Harbor. He may have been influenced by the fact that he wore the submariners' dolphins himself.

After the ceremony Admiral Nimitz stepped ashore and addressed a small group of officers, including General Emmons and Admirals Kimmel, Pye, and Draemel. The speech, a short fight talk, was intended partly for the benefit of a group of newsmen standing by. "We have taken a tremendous wallop," Nimitz concluded, "but I have no doubt as to the ultimate outcome."

One of the newsmen asked, "What are you going to do now?"

Nimitz thought a moment and then replied with a Hawaiian expression which, as he explained, meant, "Bide your time, keep your powder dry, and take advantage of the opportunity when it's offered."

Grumbled Robert Casey of the Chicago *Daily News*, "He was reasonably frank about saying nothing."

Later that day Admiral Nimitz called a conference of Kimmel's, Pye's,

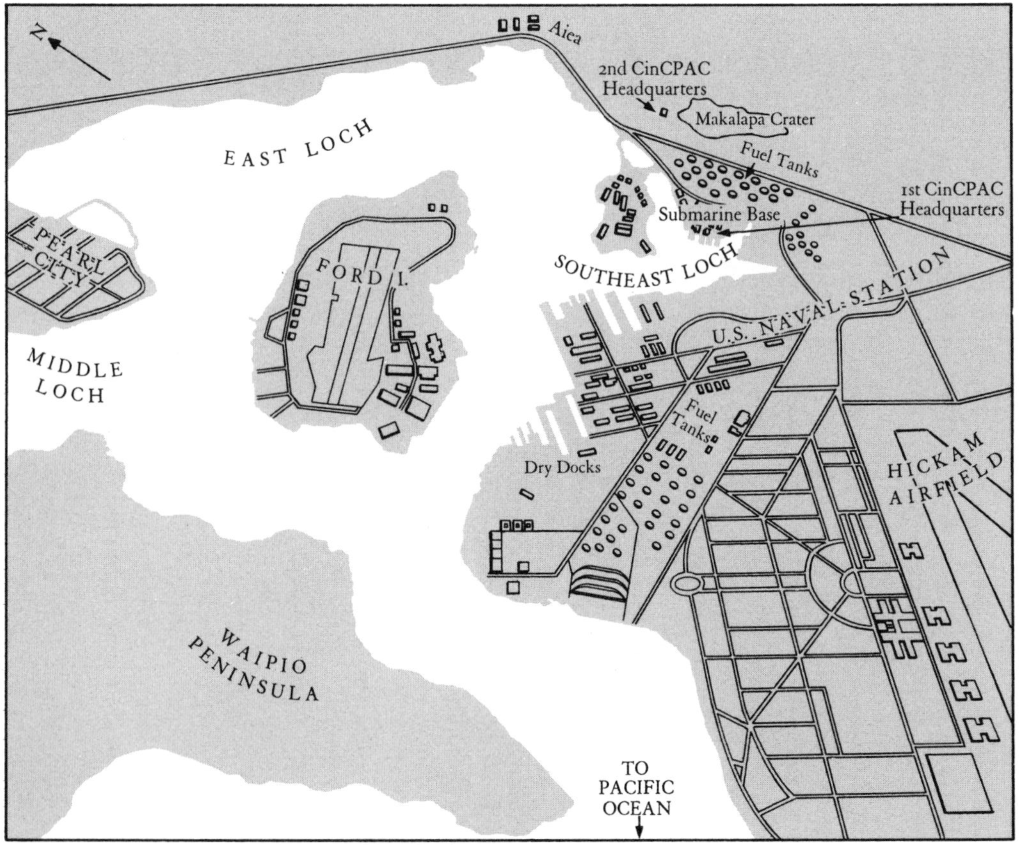
N
Aiea
2nd CinCPAC
Headquarters
Makalapa Crater
Fuel Tanks
1st CinCPAC
Headquarters
Submarine Base
EAST LOCH
SOUTHEAST LOCH
U.S. NAVAL STATION
PEARL CITY
FORD I.
MIDDLE LOCH
Fuel Tanks
Dry Docks
HICKAM AIRFIELD
WAIPIO PENINSULA
TO PACIFIC OCEAN

*Pearl Harbor, 1942*

and Draemel's staff officers. It was a gloomy assemblage. They were prepared to hear the worst, for they all felt more or less tainted by the Pearl Harbor defeat, and some members of Pye's staff felt personally disgraced by the failure to relieve Wake. This meeting, they supposed, was the new chief's farewell party before sending them away to far-off, inhospitable billets. If Admiral Kimmel was being called to account for the Pearl Harbor disaster, it seemed hardly likely that his underlings would escape penalty.

Nimitz promptly dropped a bombshell, but not the sort the assembled officers were expecting. He said that he had complete and unlimited confidence in every one of them and that he did not blame them for what had happened at Pearl Harbor. Moreover, he continued, as former Chief of the Bureau of Navigation, he knew that it was because of their competence that they had been sent to the Pacific Fleet. Now he wanted them to stay on with him to provide continuity through their familiarity with their duties. If there were any who wanted to leave he would listen to them individually, discuss their futures, and do what he could to get them the assignments they wanted. "But," he concluded, "certain key members of the staff I insist I want to keep." Somehow, in that simple, short speech, Admiral Nimitz lifted an incubus off the spirits at Pearl Harbor.

Most of the officers who expressed a desire to leave Pearl Harbor did so because they were due for sea duty, which was necessary to the advancement of their careers. Among these was Kimmel's chief of staff, Captain Smith, who was up for promotion to rear admiral. As soon as his new commission arrived, Nimitz gave him command of a heavy cruiser division. For his own chief of staff, Nimitz selected Admiral Draemel. He retained Captain Charles H. McMorris as war plans officer, the post McMorris had held under Kimmel. It is worth noting that Draemel and McMorris had taken diametrically opposed positions regarding the recall of the Wake expedition, the former recommending recall and the latter opposing it.

Of all the officers at the meeting, probably none less expected to be retained than Kimmel's intelligence officer, Lieutenant Commander Edwin T. Layton, who reproached himself for having failed to foresee and to warn his chief of the impending attack. But Nimitz did retain him. Layton was in fact the only officer besides Nimitz himself who remained attached to CinCPac headquarters throughout the war.

Nimitz was well aware that such advice and guidance as he could get from Kimmel were temporary, for it was not in the books that that unhappy officer would remain at Pearl Harbor after he had finished testifying before the Roberts Commission. Nimitz did, however, secure permission for Pye to remain for a while as his unofficial adviser.

In a sense Nimitz had spent his whole life preparing for the post of CinCPac. He was, probably as much as any commander in history, a self-created officer. Evidence suggests that, observing the qualities of commanders under whom he served, he conceived the image of an ideal officer and consciously molded himself to conform to that image. Yet the raw material with which he began was never obliterated. Always discernible in his character and personality was his inheritance from the mercurial Nimitzes and from his mother's family, the solid, hard-working Henkes.

The ancestors of the Nimitzes were among the Saxon Germans who in the thirteenth century, spearheaded by the Knights of the Sword, invaded and overran Livonia, on the eastern shore of the Baltic Sea, in the names of Christianity and quick profits. Indeed the Nimitz family crest implies that the Nimitzes were among the knightly conquerors, later absorbed into the Knights of the Teutonic Order, and that the head of the family bore the title *freiherr*, an aristocratic rank somewhere between baron and count.

In 1621 the Swedish king, Gustavus Adolphus, seized northern Livonia. As a result, Nimitz men served in the Swedish army. They accompanied Gustavus Adolphus when he invaded Pomerania in 1630, thus returning to their ancestral Germany. In 1644 Major Ernst von Nimitz was serving as adjutant to Swedish General Gustav Wrangel. With the signing of the Peace of Westphalia in 1648, ending the Thirty Years' War, Major Nimitz settled in northwest Germany, not far from Hanover.

Later Nimitzes, through disaffection from the government and inability to keep up with the social demands that their title entailed, simply dropped the title and discontinued using the *von* before their family name. Going into business as dealers in cloth, they gradually restored the family fortunes.

In Admiral Nimitz's ancestral line, this growing prosperity came to an abrupt halt with the admiral's great-grandfather, Karl Heinrich Nimitz. Karl Heinrich, it appears, was something of a playboy, hunting by day, partying by night, and grossly neglecting business. His estate squandered, his business bankrupt, he took work as a supercargo on a merchant vessel. His youngest son, also Karl Heinrich, the admiral's grandfather, at 14 years of age followed his father in seeking employment in the merchant marine. Three of the older children emigrated to the United States, settling in 1840 in Charleston, South Carolina. Here they were joined by their parents in 1843 and by young Karl Heinrich in 1844.

After his venturesome life at sea, Karl Heinrich, Jr., was by no means satisfied by the quiet city of Charleston. Attracted by tales of the western frontier, he went by sea to Texas and there joined a group of German immigrants led by Baron Ottfried Hans von Meusebach. The Germans, mostly clerks, teachers, lawyers, and other professional people, were poorly prepared for the hardships they faced—insufficient food, lack of shelter from the almost incessant rains. En route to land purchased for them by a society of aristocrats in Germany, many died either of cholera or of sheer exhaustion.

At last, in May 1846, the survivors reached the purchased land, considerably to westward of territory settled by the Anglo-Americans. There, they founded their town, which they named Fredericksburg in honor of their most aristocratic patron, Prince Friedrich of Prussia. Many of the settlers anglicized their Christian names. Their leader became plain John O. Meusebach. Karl Heinrich thenceforth called himself Charles Henry Nimitz.

The Germans set about constructing log huts for shelter. They laid out very wide streets, almost as if they foresaw the advent of the automobile, but actually to permit wagons to make U-turns easily. Meusebach through a friendly approach, deft diplomacy, and judicious distribution of gifts obtained from the local Comanche Indians a treaty permitting the Germans to share their country, a treaty that was never violated by either side.

The settlers brought with them their love and knowledge of music—the works of Bach, Haydn, and Beethoven, and also of less classical composers. They formed bands and orchestras and held regular saengerfests and other musical events. To these they soon added schuetzenfests, to demonstrate and compete in their new marksmanship skills.

Charles Henry Nimitz worked for a while as bookkeeper for a cypress lumber company on the nearby Pedernales River. In April 1848, he married Sophie Dorothea Muller, daughter of a fellow settler, and the next year she presented him with the first of twelve children. In 1851 Charles Henry joined and served briefly in the Texas Rangers. In 1852 he found his true vocation when, at the eastern end of Fredericksburg, on the broad Main Street, he built a tiny hotel of sun-dried brick. The enterprise prospered, being frequented by ranchers, soldiers, and westward-bound pioneers. Until El Paso came of age, there was no inn between the Nimitz Hotel and San Diego.

Charles Henry soon enlarged his hostelry. Reflecting his love of the sea, he added a kind of marquee shaped like the bow of a ship. Above this he eventually added rooms, balconies, and a mast so that the inn looked more and more like a ship and was often called the Steamboat Hotel.

Mrs. Nimitz, despite almost continuous pregnancy, did much of the cooking and superintended the cleaning and straightening of the rooms and the fueling of the stoves and fireplaces. Charles Henry supervised the building program, which in time included the addition of a saloon, a combination ballroom and theater, and, in the rear, a smokehouse, a brewery, and a bathhouse, all surrounded by a wall of sun-baked bricks topped with broken glass to keep out thieving Indians.

Nimitz, blond of beard and hair, was, above all, the affable host. Interested in people, he had the knack of making each guest feel especially welcome. Officers passing between San Antonio and the frontier forts paused frequently to partake of the Nimitz hospitality. Colonel Robert E. Lee was a favorite at the hotel. Nimitz, when possible, assigned him the same room, which after the Civil War was exhibited as "General Lee's room." Other notable guests were Phil Sheridan, James Longstreet, Kirby Smith, Adolphus W. Greeley, and O. Henry, who used the Nimitz inn as his model for the Quarrymen's Hotel in his story "A Chaparral Prince."

When the Civil War broke out and the army contingents were removed from the nearby frontier forts, Nimitz organized and was named captain of the

Gillespie Rifles, composed of young men from the surrounding Gillespie County, who took over the soldiers' task of controlling the Indians. Not long afterward the Confederate States government appointed Nimitz enrolling officer for his district—a position that temporarily alienated him from his German neighbors, most of whom were Union sympathizers.

Following the Civil War, the Nimitz Hotel achieved new prosperity as a regular stop for stage coaches. Captain Nimitz presided over operations with a zest and heartiness that sometimes verged on rowdyism. A favorite stunt of his was to secrete hotel silver in the baggage of a departing guest and then organize a posse to overtake the "thief" and bring him back for a mock trial. Such treatment of a guest would scarcely commend itself to a modern innkeeper, but Nimitz's pranks were all in the spirit of the time in what was aptly called the Wild West.

Nimitz too was master of the "tall tale," a Texas specialty. Finding a possibly squeamish guest enjoying the hotel's famous smoked sausage, Captain Nimitz would draw up a chair and launch into a story he reserved especially for guests with queasy stomachs. A local shooting last summer, he would explain, had produced an unidentified corpse. Examination of the dead man's effects revealed that the defunct had a wife in New York. To her Nimitz sent a telegram asking what disposition to make of the body. The woman wired back, so the story went, that she would come herself to identify the remains.

It was August and he had no means of preserving the corpse by refrigeration. So, said Nimitz, he did the best he could. He hung the body in the smokehouse along with the sausages. The trains from New York being slow and the connections poor, it took the wife quite a while to reach Fredericksburg. By that time, of course, her husband was well smoked. Shown the body, she protested that this could not be her husband; her husband was a white man. Captain Nimitz then explained to her that unless she recognized her husband, she couldn't collect any insurance money. Whereupon, she recognized him and took him home.

In fact, Nimitz rarely reached his punch line. His squeamish diner usually left the room, pale and in some haste, before the end of the tale.

Charles Henry's brief employment at sea as a mere boy grew in the telling until it was generally believed that he had once been a master mariner and a captain of merchant vessels. To his growing circle of wide-eyed grandchildren he spun yarns of such outlandish fascination that they begged for more. He explained that he could never make another ocean voyage. "I turned my back on the sea," he said, "and when you do that you can never make an ocean trip. The sea will swallow you up as punishment."

Later, having forgotten this particular piece of fabricated sea lore, Captain Nimitz sailed for New York, leaving his small fry anxious lest "Opa" Nimitz be swallowed up. On his safe return, "Opa" thought it expedient to set their minds at rest, explaining, "I begged forgiveness and promised to give the sea one of my grandsons—as an admiral."

From his New York trip, Captain Nimitz brought back another tall tale for the edification of his guests and neighbors. During his visit, he related, he had attended the theater, where he witnessed a startlingly realistic fire scene. Returning to his hotel and climbing several flights of stairs to his room, he couldn't get that scene out of his mind. "Gee," he said to himself, "I'm way up above the ground level. Suppose this hotel caught on fire!"

He went to bed but he couldn't sleep for thinking about what he had witnessed at the theater and the possibility of fire in the hotel. At last he rose, so the story went, and turned up the gas light. Then he noticed for the first time under his window a coil of rope beneath a sign saying FIRE ESCAPE. That was quite a relief, but he thought he'd feel safer if he gave the thing a trial run. So he opened the window and threw out the free end of the rope. Then he started down, not bothering to change from his nightshirt, for he was sure that nobody would be able to see him in the darkness.

He lowered himself to the courtyard easily enough, but climbing back up was something else again. He tired quickly. It was several flights up and he could not quite make it. He got as far as the story below his room and, in a state of exhaustion, entered an open window—only to be greeted by the screams of the female occupant. He backed out in a hurry and lowered himself to the courtyard again.

By then the woman's shrieks had alerted everybody in the hotel. Lights went on, windows were raised, faces peered down into the court, where Nimitz was illuminated by light streaming from opening doors. Out from the hotel saloon poured late revelers to see this former Texas Ranger, exposed in his nightshirt. They hauled him into the bar as Exhibit A and made him buy a round of drinks for everybody.

This tale duly impressed the captain's Fredericksburg hearers, but Nimitz could never satisfactorily explain where in his nightshirt he found the money to pay for the drinks.

Nimitz, despite his high jinks and tall tales, enjoyed the respect and affection of his neighbors, who made him a school trustee and a member of the examination board for Gillespie County schoolteachers. In 1891, when the years had somewhat toned down his boisterous spirit, and his tow-colored hair and beard had turned a dignified white, he was elected to the Texas state legislature.

The most improbable of the gregarious Captain Nimitz's four sons who lived to maturity was quiet, reserved Chester Bernard. With blue eyes and flaxen hair, he had the ethereal look one expects in poets, and he was so unassuming as to be often overlooked at gatherings. He was always frail, for he had weak lungs and a rheumatic heart. In pursuit of health, he became a cowboy and helped to drive cattle from Texas to Nebraska.

Doctors advised Chester never to marry, but he fell in love with Anna Henke, daughter of Henry Henke, the butcher. Anna, despite her fragile beauty, had inherited the Henkes' strength of will and character. The eldest of twelve children, she had necessarily learned to assume responsibilities. She was popular and had many suitors, but she accepted the marriage proposal of bashful young Chester. Perhaps his frailty appealed to her strong maternal instinct. They were married in March 1884, when Chester Bernard was 29 years old and Anna was in her early twenties. Five months later Anna was a widow, and pregnant.

At least during the last stages of her pregnancy, Anna lodged at her parents' small limestone cottage across the street from the Nimitz Hotel, occupying the tiny back bedroom on the ground floor. Here, attended by midwife Lisette Mueller, she gave birth on February 24, 1885, to a boy with hair as blond as his father's had been. She named him Chester William. He was the future fleet admiral.

Captain Nimitz was so excited about the approaching birth of a grandchild that he forgot to lower the flag raised on the mast of the hotel on the 22nd, to honor the memory of George Washington. The proximity of President Washington's and Admiral Nimitz's birthdays has often been remarked, but Anna Nimitz had another date in mind. To her, little Chester was "my Valentine boy."

Captain Nimitz, tenderly fond of Anna and touched by the orphaned state of her son, moved both into his hotel and devoted a good deal of time to the boy. For the captain their presence was a welcome diversion because, recently widowered and semiretired, he was at loose ends. His second son, Charles Henry Junior, now did much of the managing of the hotel. Most of the rest of his children had married and moved away. His youngest son, William, was in Massachusetts, attending Worcester Polytechnic Institute. He was the only one of the Nimitz sons that the captain had been able to send to college.

While still a baby, Chester was christened in the Lutheran Church. Like all children of his generation in Fredericksburg, he grew up bilingual in an atmosphere that was at least as German as it was American. At Christmastime a cedar tree was set up in the hotel parlor, its branches festooned with chains of popcorn and colored paper and hung with fruits, gilded nuts, and cookies. Available at the hotel and also in "Oma" Henke's stone cookie jar in her kitchen across the street were Zimmet Sterne and Pfeffernuesse, cookies flavored respectively with cinnamon and, oddly enough, pepper. At children's Christmas Eve parties a very American Santa Claus was likely to appear and be greeted with the recited prayer: "Ich bin klein; mein Herz ist rein; soll niemand drin wohnen also Jesus allein."

The two great attachments of Chester's early childhood were his mother and his paternal grandfather. Of the latter, the fleet admiral long afterward wrote: "I didn't know my father, because he died before I was born. But I had a wonderful white-bearded grandfather. He was Charles H. Nimitz, who settled in Fredericksburg, Tex., and built a steamboat-shaped hotel. Between chores and homework I listened wide-eyed to stories about his youth in the German merchant marine. 'The sea—like life itself—is a stern taskmaster,' he would say. 'The best way to get along with either is to learn all you can, then do your best and don't worry—especially about things over which you have no control.'"

So impressed was Chester with his grandfather's wisdom that he did not venture to protest when the old gentleman handed him a small derby hat to wear on his first day at school, though he was barefooted and wearing only a pair of jeans and a shirt. Thus incongruously clad and hatted, off went the boy, somewhat timidly, for until then he had not had much contact with other children. Hardly had he entered the schoolyard when another boy knocked the hat off his head. Chester made a dive for it and slammed it back on, only to have it knocked off again. Before he got into the school, Chester's eyes were black, his clothes torn, and the derby was a shambles. But he fought all day for that hat and brought the fragments home.

Chester could never figure out why his beloved "Opa" Nimitz should do such a thing. Said the admiral a few months before his death, "Why, why, do you suppose Grandfather ever gave me that hat to wear to school?" One would like to speculate that the old gentleman was trying to instill in the boy a determination to be himself, however different from those around him. The chances are, however, that the old boy simply could not resist an opportunity for a practical joke, even when little Chester was the butt.

By this time William Nimitz, Chester's Uncle Willie, had returned from Massachusetts the proud possessor of a degree in engineering. He was thus probably the best-educated man in Fredericksburg. His family and friends expected great things of him. He seemed at the threshold of a brilliant career. But nothing much happened. His engineering skills were apparently in no demand in the Fredericksburg area. Uncle Willie did, however, cause general rejoicing by winning the hand of the widowed Anna, still a beauty. They were married on Christmas Day, 1890. Chester thus acquired a new father without any change of name.

Willie was rescued from the ranks of the unemployed by an elder sister, who engaged him to manage at Kerrville, Texas, the St. Charles Hotel, that she had evidently acquired through marriage. So Willie moved his family the 24 miles from picturesque Fredericksburg to Kerrville, on the Guadalupe River, and installed them in the hotel. The St. Charles was in fact nothing more than an overgrown boardinghouse, a rambling two-story, white-clapboard building with porches and balconies and much gingerbread about the eaves. Most of the guests were ranchers, traveling salesmen, and consumptives seeking a cure in the healthful Texas hill country.

Anna, like her late mother-in-law, supervised the kitchen, did most of the cooking, and directed the one or two maids who cleaned and straightened the rooms. As it turned out, she also did most of the managing of the hotel. Willie sat on the front porch chatting with the guests or went for strolls. He became a familiar sight about Kerrville, with his billy-goat beard and growing paunch. He tried each day to observe all construction work in town and generally was accounted the city's most persistent sidewalk superintendent. Anna, perhaps not uncharacteristically, had married another weakling. He was conscious of his own inadequacies. "If I had an unlimited supply of silver dollars," he used to say sadly, "I couldn't show a profit selling them at 50 cents apiece."

Anna bore her load cheerfully and without reproaches. She presented Willie with two children, Dora, born in 1895, and Otto, born two years later. Hard work never robbed her of her looks, for she remained slim, and lines and shadows merely added character to a basically lovely face. Her friends and neighbors admired and respected her, and her children revered her. In 1924 when she lay dying, Chester rushed by ship and plane from maneuvers in the Pacific to his mother's bedside in time to hear her last conscious words, "I knew my Valentine boy would come to see me."

Chester had a normal small-town boyhood. Friendly as a puppy, nick-named Cottonhead, he made many friends among the boys in Kerrville—and also in Fredericksburg, where he visited frequently during holidays. With other boys he swam, fished, and hunted, seeking rabbits and doves along the Guada-lupe River at Kerrville, or along Town Creek in Fredericksburg. The great highlights of his vacations were the week-long camping trips he took with Grandfather Nimitz. The captain would tell Chester to invite a friend. Then he would roll out the big, horse-drawn prairie schooner, and away they would go, sometimes as far away as the Llano River to the north. Grandfather would do the cooking and camp-tending while the boys hunted, fished, or just roamed the woods.

Chester also cherished his visits to the ranch where Grandfather Henry Henke raised cattle for his meat business. There he would spend the day on the range with the cowboys, then return for one of Grandmother Dorathea Henke's wonderful German meals, consumed with much lively conversation, always in German. Equally memorable for Chester were visits to Uncle Otto's ranch on Owl Creek, between Fredericksburg and Kerrville. An exciting sport there was to push a mowing machine through the oatfield to flush out rattle-snakes, which the boys killed. They then strung the rattles together to create super-rattles, which were the wonder and envy of the boys in town.

Though Chester was probably poorer than any of his companions, some of whom were the sons of well-to-do ranchers, he seems never to have devel-oped feelings of inferiority or insecurity—or if he did, he conquered them early in life. The chief inconvenience resulting from his poverty was that he felt obliged to go to work at the age of eight to help out his family. For a dollar a week he worked as delivery boy at a Kerrville meat market owned and oper-ated by his mother's brother.

Anna, fearful that Chester might have inherited some of his father's phys-ical frailties, must have impressed upon her son the need to take care of his health. At any rate, he ran regularly, swam often, and rarely rode when he could walk—even the fourteen miles out to Uncle Otto's. Chester's Cousin Guenther Henke, in recalling their boyhood together, said, "Nothing stands out more than his utter determination to remain physically fit." In fact, Chester became a notably swift runner and developed a robust constitution, though he was somewhat prone to pneumonia, with which he had several bouts, and which finally carried him away.

Friendly though he was, Chester was subject to violent outbursts of temper. Although these led to a good many fights, he rarely held grudges. In one notable scrap, he took on two brothers simultaneously and came away victorious but bloody. "Those boys fight like girls," said he disgustedly; "they scratch." Somewhere in the process of growing up, he learned to curb his outbursts. Probably he discovered that brain power achieved more effective solutions than did fist power. At any rate, from an early period he evidently operated on the conviction that there are better ways to manipulate people than by use of force and violence.

At the age of fifteen Chester began working at the St. Charles. From 9:00 a.m. to 4:00 p.m. he attended Tivy High School, where he made top grades. Returning to the hotel, he raked and otherwise cared for the lawns surrounding the building. He split kindling, filled woodboxes, and tended the dozen or more stoves and fireplaces in the hotel. After supper he took his turn as clerk at the desk, until 10:00 p.m., studying as best he could between interruptions. In exchange for these services his aunt, the proprietor, gave him $15 a month and board and lodging.

Chester was thus exposed to the less glamorous aspects of the Henke family's meat business and the Nimitz family's hotel-keeping. Attracted to neither and with no prospect of an education beyond high school, he made vague plans to apprentice himself to a surveyor. But he longed for a broader stage on which to exercise his talents.

In the summer of 1900, Chester for the first time caught a glimpse of an opportunity to broaden his experiences. From Fort Sam Houston, outside San Antonio, came Battery K, Third Field Artillery, for training and gunnery practice in the hills across the Guadalupe from Kerrville. On their way to join Battery K, Second Lieutenants William M. Cruikshank and William I. Westervelt, both brand-new West Point graduates, stopped at the St. Charles Hotel. Chester was much impressed by their military bearing, their well-fitting new uniforms, and above all their air of worldly sophistication.

To Chester of course army officers were no novelty. From earliest infancy he had been bounced on their knees at his grandfather's hotel. What fascinated him about Lieutenants Cruikshank and Westervelt was that, with all their fine bearing and polish and their impending responsibilities in the Army, they were only a little older than himself. They had been plucked but recently from humdrum situations like his own and had been educated and launched on a career of travel and high adventure, all at no cost to their families, all for the asking—plus, of course, hard study and stiff competition.

Young Nimitz had no fear of hard study or competition. For him, at last, a door seemed to be opening. All afire with hope and anticipation, he applied to Congressman James Slaydon to take the West Point examination. Slaydon shut the door. He said that all his appointments for the Military Academy were filled. Nor were there likely to be any for Nimitz in the future, he implied, for with numerous forts in his district, army families were waiting in line to get their sons into West Point. Then Congressman Slaydon reopened the door a little. "But," he said, "I have an opening for the U.S. Naval Academy. Are you interested?"

Chester had never so much as heard of the Naval Academy, but he swallowed his disappointment and said yes, determined to seize any opportunity to get an education. To prepare for the entrance examinations, he advanced his rising time to 3:00 a.m. and studied until 5:30. At that hour began his first daily stint as the hotel's janitor and general handyman—lighting fires, attending stoves, and calling early risers. After a quick breakfast, off he went to school.

Uncle Willie, constitutionally pessimistic, was certain that Chester could never pass the examinations. For one thing, he would have to miss his final year at high school, along with plane geometry and other subjects on which he would be examined. Nevertheless Uncle Willie worked long and hard to help his stepson to fill this gap in his education. To his credit it must be said that Willie never made any distinction between Chester and his own children. He labored as diligently to assist the former as he later did to aid his son Otto to follow Chester's footsteps toward a naval career.

As young Nimitz's hopes and expectations became known in Kerrville, helping him to achieve them became something of a community project. A devoted teacher, Susan Moore, tutored Chester in algebra, geometry, history, geography, and grammar. John Graves Toland, principal of Tivy High School, found time to coach him in mathematics.

With such help, plus his native intelligence, Chester won out over all competitors in the local Naval Academy examination held in April 1901. The following July, he made the rounds of his friends and relatives in Kerrville and Fredericksburg to say goodbye. Then, accompanied by Congressman Slaydon, he went by train to Annapolis. There, he entered the Werntz Preparatory School for two months of further preparation for the late-August national examinations, which he passed easily.

On September 7, 1901, Chester W. Nimitz was sworn in at the Naval Academy as a naval cadet. He had broken out of the narrow confines that had circumscribed his childhood. He renewed his allegiance to the United States of America, that fantastic country which had plucked him out of the Texas hills to be educated at public expense and launched on an honorable career with chances for high distinction.

# CHAPTER 3

# HOLDING THE LINE

On December 30, 1941, the day before Admiral Nimitz became CinCPac, Admiral Ernest Joseph King assumed the duties of Commander in Chief, U.S. Fleet, and thus became Nimitz's immediate superior.

King had earned a reputation for brilliance and toughness, not to say harshness. He was generally reputed to be cold, aloof, and humorless. Ladislas Farago, who served under King, in his book *The Tenth Fleet* describes the new commander in chief: "Tall, gaunt and taut, with a high dome, piercing eyes, aquiline nose, and a firm jaw, he looked somewhat like Hogarth's etching of Don Quixote but he had none of the old knight's fancy dreams. He was a supreme realist with the arrogance of genius.... He was a grim taskmaster, as hard on himself as others. He rarely cracked a smile and had neither time nor disposition for ephemeral pleasantries. He inspired respect but not love, and King wanted it that way."

The description is, of course, a stereotype, as Farago readily admitted. King could turn a reasonably benevolent eye upon a subordinate who produced to suit him, and in return elicit a degree of wry affection. On the other hand, he was utterly intolerant of stupidity, inefficiency, and laziness. He hated dishonesty and pretension, despised yes-men, and had no patience with indecisive Hamlet types. He could be completely ruthless. On one occasion he sent a commander to relieve a rear admiral who, in King's opinion, had failed to measure up—with orders that the admiral be out of the Navy Department building by five o'clock that afternoon.

King rejected the short title CinCUS used by his predecessors because after Pearl Harbor it sounded like a bad joke. For it he substituted the acronym CominCh. In fact, the CominCh command, concocted by President Roosevelt and Secretary Knox in the opening days of the war, encompassed very different responsibilities from those of the CinCUS command that the fleet commanders had rotated among themselves in peacetime. King, as Commander in Chief, U.S. Fleet, was to run the Navy and report directly to the President.

Because Admiral King did not hesitate to exercise the full authority vested in him, it soon appeared that Admiral Stark, the Chief of Naval Operations, was left with little or nothing to do. President Roosevelt's solution to this quandary was simple and drastic. He made King CNO as well as CominCh. Stark he sent to London as Commander in Chief, U.S. Naval Forces, Europe.

King, in addition to heading the Navy, served as a member of the U.S. Joint Chiefs of Staff, which also included General George C. Marshall, Army

Chief of Staff, General Henry H. ("Hap") Arnold, Commanding General, Army Air Forces, and, later, Admiral William D. Leahy, Chief of Staff to the President. The U.S. Joint Chiefs of Staff and the British Imperial Chiefs of Staff, when meeting together, comprised the Combined Chiefs of Staff, the senior executive body controlling Allied military operations. The CCS delegated most of the control of Pacific theater operations to the JCS, who for this function relied heavily on the advice of Admiral King.

In actual practice much of the strategy of the war in the Pacific was devised by Admirals King and Nimitz. They were thus thrown into the closest cooperation, though most of the time they were far apart geographically. They maintained a constant dialogue in the form of radio dispatches, often several a day, letters, exchanges of representatives, and periodic meetings, usually in the Federal Building, San Francisco, King flying there from Washington and Nimitz from his headquarters in the Pacific. Though Admiral King's tone in communicating with Nimitz was occasionally acerbic, as was his nature, it is clear that the two commanders greatly respected each other. At the end of the war, King recommended Nimitz to be his successor as Chief of Naval Operations.

Although their styles were in sharp contrast, King and Nimitz were more alike than different. Simplicity and directness were the keynotes of their characters. They were both dedicated to their country and to the Navy, though King's interests were more narrowly naval. Both were men of integrity and keen intelligence, and both were born strategists and organizers, with a genius for clarifying and simplifying and a jaundiced eye for useless complications and waste motion. Their chief difference lay in their attitudes toward their fellow human beings. King had little of Nimitz's understanding of, and empathy for, people. Said one of King's wartime associates, "Every great man has his blind spot, and his was personnel." King went to great lengths to draw into his command the sort of men he wanted and to eliminate those he did not. The results were not always fortunate. Several cases of his placing the wrong man in the wrong spot for the wrong reason could be cited.

King's immediate and gravest concern as CominCh was the deteriorating military situation in the Pacific theater. By early January 1942, the small U.S. Asiatic Fleet had retreated southward from the Philippines into the Java Sea, and the Japanese had occupied Hong Kong and Manila and were advancing on Java and Singapore. In the Central Pacific, they had advanced from the Marshall Islands into the British Gilberts. Their planes had struck at Ocean and Nauru islands west of the Gilberts, and their submarines had shelled Johnston and Palmyra islands between the Gilberts and Pearl Harbor. To the American war planners the Japanese moves in the Central Pacific appeared to be preparation for a drive to the southeast via the Ellice Islands to Samoa. From Samoa Japanese aircraft, submarines, and carrier forces would be able to intercept shipping between the United States and Australia, thus eliminating the latter as a potential base for Allied offensives. The shelling of Midway by submarines seemed to imply Japanese intentions to operate again against the Hawaii area.

King's first act as CominCh was to remind Nimitz by radio dispatch that the latter's primary tasks were to guard the Hawaiian Islands including Midway and to protect shipping between Hawaii and the United States and between the United States and Australia as far southwest as Samoa. To guard Samoa some 5,000 marines had been alerted and the first of these would soon depart San Diego for the island base, escorted by the carrier *Yorktown*, then en route from the Atlantic. Understandably, the Australian government was pleading for protection of shipping all the way to Australia, but the United States could not immediately fortify the islands southwest of Samoa—the Fijis, the New Hebrides, and New Caledonia.

King recommended to Nimitz that he stage raids against the Gilberts and the mandates, that is, the enemy-held islands in the Central Pacific.* For such limited offensives the Pacific Fleet had three carrier task forces: the *Saratoga* force (Task Force 14), commanded by Vice Admiral Fairfax Leary; the *Lexington* force (Task Force 11), commanded by Vice Admiral Wilson Brown; and the *Enterprise* force (Task Force 8), commanded by Vice Admiral William F. Halsey, Jr. To these soon would be added the *Yorktown* force (Task Force 17), commanded by Rear Admiral Frank Jack Fletcher. Carrier attacks on the mandates might divert Japanese drives on Java and Singapore or at least upset their plans for advances east and southeast. With any success at all, such attacks could go far toward restoring morale in the services and at home.

At Pearl Harbor, King's directive and recommendation had been anticipated. All available light forces, including ships drawn from the carrier screens, were being used to escort shipping in convoy from the United States to Hawaii. Palmyra and Johnston islands were being developed into air bases to provide additional protection for convoys heading south from Hawaii. At the same time, U.S. submarines were out reconnoitering the Marshalls and Wake. Nimitz, even before officially taking command, had asked the CinCPac war plans staff to prepare for offensive operations.

The staff on January 2, 1942, submitted to Nimitz a plan for carrier strikes against the Gilberts and Marshalls. On January 8, Admiral Pye offered a modified plan. Pye began with the assumption that the Japanese "by means of agents communicating via Mexico" knew of the Samoa reinforcement expedition and might try to forestall the marines' landing. He therefore recommended dispatching an additional carrier force from Pearl Harbor to beef up the *Yorktown* force in covering the debarkation. Both carrier groups would then head for the Marshalls and Gilberts in order to meet any approaching enemy force. If no enemy were encountered, the two U.S. task forces should attack points in the Gilberts and Marshalls, while a third U.S. carrier force attacked the airfields at Wake, partly to prevent planes flying from there to support the Marshalls. The fourth carrier force would remain near Hawaii to cover Pearl Harbor.

* The Marshalls, the Carolines, and the northern Marianas, former German island groups, occupied in 1914 by Japan, which following World War I administered them as League of Nations mandates. Since 1947 they have been U.S. trust territories under the United Nations.

Admiral Nimitz favored raiding enemy bases, but not without thorough preliminary study and discussion. As was his custom in formulating war plans, he invited any interested senior officers in the area to attend his general conferences. A good listener, he heard their opinions and advice before making his decisions. Among those attending the discussions was Rear Admiral Raymond A. Spruance, who strongly approved the innovations in command and methods that Nimitz had introduced, saying the change of atmosphere was "like being in a stuffy room and having someone open a window and let in a breath of fresh air."

Others would have said that the discussions were more like windstorms, for opinions were sharply divided and loudly defended. Loudest in supporting the proposed raids was war plans officer Captain McMorris. Aggressive, not to say pugnacious, his homely face and loose-hung frame had earned him among his juniors at Pearl Harbor the nickname Phantom of the Opera,* but the nickname for him that stuck was "Soc," conferred on him at the Naval Academy for his Socratic wisdom.

Most of the officers were opposed to sending carrier forces against land bases. Such attacks had succeeded at Taranto, Italy, in 1940, and of course recently at Pearl Harbor, but those bases had been caught by surprise. There was little chance of surprising the Japanese. Their own success at Pearl Harbor would have alerted them to the threat of carrier attack. They were bound to realize that if the U.S. Pacific Fleet intended to counterattack it had to do so with carriers. The obvious targets would be the Japanese bases nearest Pearl Harbor—the Gilberts, the Marshalls, and Wake.

The officer most vocal in opposing the raids was Rear Admiral Claude Bloch, commandant of the 14th Naval District, which included Pearl Harbor. Two years earlier Bloch had worn four stars at Pearl as CinCUS. He was much senior to Admiral Nimitz until the latter put on his own temporary four stars as CinCPac. Bloch had seen another junior admiral, Kimmel, raised over senior heads to CinCPac and then lose the Pacific Fleet battleships. He was damned if he was going to sit back now and see Nimitz lose the Pacific Fleet carriers. They were the nation's last mobile line of defense. With them gone, the Japanese would be able to go where they pleased in the Pacific and take what they wanted.

Bloch pressed his views on Nimitz, both in conference and in private. In effect, he put an avuncular arm around Nimitz's shoulders and proceeded to tell him how to run the war. Nimitz considered himself fully competent to do the job without such tutelage, but he was at a disadvantage because most of the air officers agreed with Bloch, and Nimitz was not an aviator and had never commanded carriers.

On Wednesday, January 7, the *Enterprise* force returned to Pearl from

---

* The title of a movie character conceived and played by the actor and makeup artist Lon Chaney. The Phantom, usually masked to conceal his skull-like face, haunted the sewers under the Paris opera house.

patrol, and its commander, crusty warrior Vice Admiral Halsey, came ashore. Halsey's ferocious scowl, which announced to all that he hated the enemy like sin, could not conceal the twinkle in his eye that bespoke his affection for his fellow sailors, particularly those who served under him.

We lack eyewitness records of what happened next, but we know that Halsey barged into the CinCPac conference that day or the next and cleared the air by sounding off loudly, and no doubt profanely, against the defeatism he found. He then and there permanently endeared himself to his commander in chief by backing him and the raiding plan to the hilt. Because he was a vice admiral and Commander, Aircraft, Battle Force, and was liked and respected by all, his words carried decisive weight. Long afterward, when Halsey came under criticism, Nimitz recalled this difficult period and refused to participate in the general censure. "Bill Halsey came to my support and offered to lead the attack," he said. "I'll not be party to any enterprise that can hurt the reputation of a man like that."

On the 10th, in response to a summons, Halsey reported to CinCPac headquarters. He and Nimitz, both notable story-tellers, usually began their conversations by swapping a yarn or two. Not this time. Nimitz was in deadly earnest. He told Halsey that he was to implement Pye's plan by taking his *Enterprise* force to join the *Yorktown* force at Samoa, where they would cover the landing of the marines. The two carrier forces, under Halsey's overall command, were then to head for an attack on the Gilberts and Marshalls.

"How does that sound?" he concluded. "It's a rare opportunity."

Halsey agreed, but now that the die was cast, he had some sober thoughts. He was fully aware of the risk that was being taken and of the consequences to his country if he failed. The following day he dropped by headquarters for last instructions and "to say what I hoped was au revoir." Nimitz walked with him down to the wharf. "All sorts of luck to you, Bill!" he called as Halsey stepped into his barge.

Early the next day, Sunday, January 11, the *Enterprise*, with Halsey aboard and escorted by three heavy cruisers, six destroyers, and one oiler, departed Pearl Harbor. Officers in the know, ashore and afloat, had cause for apprehension. Left guarding the Hawaiian Islands were only the *Saratoga* and *Lexington* forces, with the latter scheduled to attack Wake. Radio intelligence indicated that the same six-carrier Japanese striking force that raided Pearl Harbor had departed Japan on January 6. It could be heading for Midway, Pearl Harbor, the Marshalls, or Samoa.

Late on the 11th came the shocking news that the *Saratoga*, patrolling 450 miles southwest of Oahu, had been struck by a submarine torpedo. On the 13th she came limping into Pearl Harbor, where an examination in dry dock revealed that she would have to retire to the West Coast for major repairs and rebuilding that would keep her out of the war for several months.

One wonders if Admiral Nimitz was tempted to recall the *Enterprise*. Certainly there must have been those around him who urged such a move.

Now he felt the loneliness of high command, for nobody in the Pacific theater could share his appalling responsibility. "I lie awake long hours," he wrote to Mrs. Nimitz but could not tell her what was troubling him.

In the midst of this period of anxiety, Admiral Nimitz was startled to learn that all work had been stopped on the Palmyra and Johnston island air bases. The stoppage, it appeared, was by order of Admiral Bloch, who was convinced that these outlying islands could not be held and saw no point in building facilities for use by a conquering enemy. For the same reason, Bloch had failed to spur on or cooperate with the army teams assigned to fortify Christmas and Canton islands. Nimitz called a conference to settle these matters and to look into the slack handling of supplies by the 14th Naval District. He neither shouted nor thumped the table, but he made clear what he expected and intended to have done. Bloch got the message. Though sometimes bull-headed and mischievous, he was a loyal and disciplined officer. He accepted his instructions from the younger but now senior Nimitz with a respectful "Aye, aye, sir."

During the debate about whether to raid or not to raid, rumblings reached Nimitz from discontented newsmen assigned to the Pacific Fleet. One reporter, frustrated by censorship, tried to smuggle out forbidden copy. The Chicago *Daily News's* Robert Casey wrote a complaining letter to his publisher, who, of course, was the Secretary of the Navy. To make sure that the letter would be brought to Knox's personal attention, Casey included a cock-and-bull story about being shadowed by "security guards." A censor showed the letter to Nimitz, who let it pass, trusting in the Secretary's good sense to discredit such poppycock.

Knox apparently assessed the security-guard story for what it was, but he was sufficiently impressed to fire off a radio dispatch to Admiral Nimitz: "Bob Casey, Chicago *Daily News*, now in Honolulu, will call on you. Please listen to him on Navy censorship question. You can rely on whatever he tells you. Hope you can correct present conditions that are complained of. Regards, Knox."

Nimitz evidently found this patronizing message not a little irritating. He declined to invite Casey to tell him how to run his command; he was already getting enough of that sort of thing from Bloch. Instead, he summoned all the visiting journalists to a meeting. "All right, men," he said, once they were assembled, "let's hear your gripes."

Quite simply, what the newsmen wanted most of all was news. At home the public was asking, "Where is the Navy? What is the Navy doing?" and editors were demanding that their reporters on the scene provide some answers.

Nimitz pointed out that thus far the Navy had no news but bad news. It would be poor policy, he said, to inform the Japanese via the American press of the extent of their success. The press would, however, be promptly supplied with all news that was safe to print.

The newsmen's other complaint concerned censorship. Their stories, it appeared, had to run the gauntlet of both the CinCPac and the 14th Naval District censors, who refused to tell the correspondents what had been changed in or deleted from their copy. Whole news stories had been thrown out, the reporters not being informed of the fact until the home office sent out a blast.

Admiral Nimitz immediately relieved the 14th Naval District of all news censorship duty and ordered the CinCPac censor to provide "each correspondent a copy of all censored material." The more ardent newsmen, including Casey, he shipped off with Halsey to the Gilberts and Marshalls to gather their own news stories. He thus silenced the grumbling, at least for the time being.

Right on schedule, January 20, Halsey arrived off Samoa, then cruised around while waiting for Fletcher's *Yorktown* force, which had been delayed beyond expectation by refueling en route. On the 24th it at last arrived with the marines, who began disembarking.

On January 15, King, impatient, had ordered the Gilberts-Marshalls raid speeded up, to be followed by an attack on Wake by the *Lexington* force two or three days later, "at which time enemy endeavors to oppose Halsey can be expected to have reduced coverage of Wake." Though Nimitz was reluctant thus to tie up all his carriers at once, on the 22nd he radioed Vice Admiral Brown, then cruising with the *Lexington* some 500 miles southwest of Pearl, to advance and take Wake under attack. He had sent out the *Neches*, his only available oiler, to refuel Brown's vessels, but on the 23rd the *Neches* was sunk by a submarine, so Nimitz canceled the Wake raid and ordered the *Lexington* to return to Pearl Harbor.

On January 25, the marines having been landed on Samoa, the *Enterprise* and *Yorktown* forces began their run to the Gilberts and Marshalls. Until their attack on the islands had revealed their presence to the enemy, they were of course to maintain radio silence. But Nimitz could and did keep in radio communication with them. He informed Halsey and Fletcher that their prospects were better than first estimated. The reconnoitering submarines had found that the Marshalls were not nearly so well developed and fortified as had been feared. More important, the Japanese carriers were not coming their way. They were busy down south supporting a Japanese landing in New Britain to capture the port of Rabaul.

In the circumstances, Nimitz recommended to Halsey that he raid not only the assigned atolls in the northeastern Marshalls but that he penetrate to the heart of the archipelago and strike at Kwajalein, the world's largest atoll and presumably the local Japanese headquarters. "It is essential that the attacks be driven home," said Nimitz in a later message. "Exploit this situation by expanding operations, utilizing both task forces in such repeated air attacks and ship bombardments as developments and logistics make feasible. If practicable, extend offensive action beyond one day."

It is perhaps fortunate that Halsey was operating under radio silence, or else he might have replied in more or less official language with a resounding

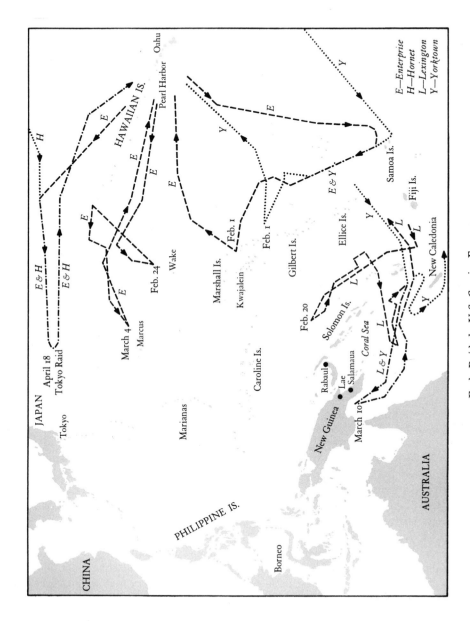

*Early Raids by U.S. Carrier Forces*

"Shut up!" for the messages from CinCPac seem to have exasperated him. Having commanded carriers since 1935, he felt he could handle his assignment without any coaching from non-aviator Nimitz.

The *Enterprise* and *Yorktown* forces began their raids at dawn on January 31 (February 1 in the Gilberts and Marshalls, which lay beyond the International Date Line). At Pearl Harbor the first information arrived that afternoon in the form of radio exchanges between Halsey and Fletcher, with CinCPac cut in as an information addressee. Halsey's preliminary report to CinCPac reached Pearl in the early evening.

Basing his estimate chiefly on aviators' reports, Halsey claimed two submarines, one light cruiser, one small carrier, and four auxiliaries sunk, many ships damaged, and widespread destruction ashore. The heavy cruisers *Northampton* and *Salt Lake City*, under Rear Admiral Spruance, had bombarded Wotje Island, believed to be the most strongly fortified of the Marshalls. The price paid by the Americans was not excessive: thirteen planes lost, the heavy cruiser *Chester* hit by an aerial bomb, the *Enterprise* slightly damaged by near misses.

The American aviators, not experienced in recognizing ship types and assessing damage, had grossly overestimated their achievements. Halsey's true score amounted to one transport and two smaller vessels sunk, eight other ships damaged, various shore installations set afire, and a few enemy planes destroyed. Fletcher, because of bad weather in his sector and perhaps because of excessive caution, had achieved very little.

The newsmen at Pearl Harbor, however, so long starved for good news, not only accepted the exaggerated claims of the raiders but shamelessly puffed them up. Stateside editors added their bit, so that many American newspapers ran such nonsensical headlines as PEARL HARBOR AVENGED! But, although the attack was only a minor inconvenience to the enemy, it more than attained its goal of restoring the morale of American civilians, sailors, and soldiers. The national frustration was replaced by a feeling of "At last, we're on our way!"

When the *Enterprise* force came steaming back into Pearl on February 5, the carrier had her largest colors flying triumphantly. Every ship in the harbor blew its siren. Crews yelled. Soldiers, sailors, and civilian shipyard workers lined the shores and cheered. As the carrier came alongside the wharf, Admiral Nimitz, not waiting for the gangway to be lowered, went over the side in a bos'n's chair. "Nice going!" he shouted, grabbing Halsey's hand. Rear Admiral Robert A. Theobald, Commander, Destroyers, Pacific, who had been one of the chief opponents of the carrier raids, came aboard right behind Nimitz and shook his finger in Halsey's face. "Damn you, Bill," he said, "you've got no business getting home from that one! No business at all!"

Nimitz soon turned the beaming Halsey over to the press and retired into the background. Halsey, a charming, genial, approachable fellow, was smiling from ear to ear but glad to turn on his famous scowl to oblige photographers. He was equally ready to accommodate the reporters with quotable statements about what he intended to do to the enemy, all couched in the salty language that quickly became his trademark. He was a swashbuckler of the old tradition and, like most swashbucklers, part little boy who never grew up. For the newsmen Halsey seemed made to order—a likable fellow who could be built up into a national hero. The press lost no time at all in enshrining him as the nemesis of the Japanese, a half-fictitious character whom they named "Bull Halsey."

Pearl Harbor seems to have exhausted itself cheering the *Enterprise* force. When the *Yorktown* and her escorts arrived in port the following day, they attracted only moderate attention. The newsmen, with the colorful Halsey to write about, could spare few words for Frank Jack Fletcher or for the even quieter Raymond Spruance.

The Gilberts-Marshalls raid had no discernible effect on enemy operations elsewhere. In the Philippines the Japanese continued to push the American and Filipino troops into the tip of Bataan Peninsula and nearby Corregidor Island. Their drives on Rangoon and Singapore and into the Netherlands East Indies showed no signs of slowing.

The American, British, Dutch, and Australian defenders in the East Indies combined their efforts in an ABDA command. The ABDA Striking Force, eight cruisers (two American) and twenty-two destroyers, could not, however, delay the comparatively light fleets Japan was sending southward along the coasts of Borneo because the latter were always supported by superior air power from fields that the Japanese built as they advanced. Three days after Halsey's raid on the Marshalls, bombers from a field in southern Celebes damaged one of the U.S. ABDA cruisers and put the other out of action.

In response to the Japanese occupation of Rabaul, the Allied high command promptly established, adjoining and to the southeast of the ABDA Area, a new special defense zone, the ANZAC Area, enclosing Australia, New Zealand, British New Guinea, New Caledonia, and the Loyalties, New Hebrides, Fijis, and Solomons. Rabaul was obviously being developed by the enemy into a major base, from which bombers would be able to strike at Port Moresby, the Australian base on the south coast of New Guinea. From Rabaul also, military intelligence warned, the Japanese planned to advance via the Solomons and the New Hebrides to seize New Caledonia, which lay athwart the United States-Australia communication line.

Neither Australia nor New Zealand could defend the threatened islands because any of their forces that were not needed for home defense were guarding the Middle East or Singapore. The Joint Chiefs of Staff therefore rushed 20,000 U.S. troops to the Pacific, the great majority of them to garrison New Caledonia. They ordered Nimitz to send to the ANZAC Area the *Lexington* force, all the navy patrol planes and army bombers he could spare, and a heavy cruiser and two destroyers to join Australian cruisers and corvettes in an ANZAC Striking Force.

As the Allied situation worsened, King called on Nimitz for still greater support for the southwest areas, either in the form of reinforcements or of aggressive diversionary operations against the mandates, using all available forces including the half-dozen battleships then based on the West Coast. This order, dated February 5, was followed on the 6th by two messages warning of an imminent stepped-up Japanese offensive in the southwest, accompanied probably by strong raids elsewhere, and calling for "prompt action to check enemy advance."

After conferring at length with his staff and other advisers, Nimitz on February 7 replied to King:

> Pacific Fleet markedly inferior in all types to enemy. Cannot conduct aggressive action Pacific except raids of hit-and-run character which are unlikely to relieve pressure Southwest Pacific. Logistic problems far surpass peacetime conception and always precarious due to fueling at sea and dependence upon weather. . . . Offensive employment battleships does not fit in with hit-and-run operations, and their independent or supporting use precluded by lack air coverage and antisubmarine protection. Such employment considered inadvisable at present. Continued operation of one or more Pacific Fleet task forces in ANZAC Area will involve dependence upon logistic support from Australia and New Zealand, which support appears limited. . . . Unless this fleet is strengthened by strong additions, particularly in aircraft, light forces, carriers, and fast fleet tankers, its effectiveness for offensive action is limited. . . .

He concluded by reporting that, in compliance with King's initial directive to guard Hawaii and the shipping line as far as Samoa, he planned to send one of his remaining carrier forces southward toward Samoa and keep the other in reserve at Pearl.

To the CinCPac staff King's directive that the battleships be used for raiding seemed particularly quixotic. The newest had been commissioned in 1923, and none could make better than 21 knots, much too slow to operate with the 34-knot carriers. There were not enough cruisers and destroyers in the Pacific Fleet to screen carriers and also battleships. As between carrier forces and battleship forces, the former were more effective because they had both planes and guns for offense and defense.

In the afternoon of February 9, there arrived from CominCh a reply to CinCPac's message that rocked Nimitz and his staff back on their heels:

> Pacific Fleet not, repeat *not*, markedly inferior in all types to forces enemy can bring to bear within operating radius of Hawaii while he is committed to extensive operations in Southwest Pacific. Your forces will however be markedly inferior from Australia to Alaska when the enemy has gained objectives in Southwest Pacific unless every effort is continuously made to damage his ships and bases. Action by you towards and in the mandates will of itself cover and protect Midway-Hawaii line while affording badly needed relief of pressure in Southwest Pacific. . . . Review situation in above premises and consider active operations against mandates and Wake from northward and eastward or otherwise vary pattern of operations.

At a hastily called conference the CinCPac staff could not think of any objective within reach of the Pacific Fleet, even if its range were extended by fueling at sea, that could be attacked with any reasonable expectation of affecting Japanese activities in other areas. At length they decided to adjourn overnight to cool off and meet again the next day when Admiral Halsey would be present.

Meanwhile, Admiral Nimitz put Admiral Pye on a Pan American clipper and headed him for Washington to explain the situation in the Central Pacific to CominCh. As an emissary to King, Pye was an inspired choice. He was a highly respected strategist and an experienced commander of large forces. Somewhat cautious by nature, he could be counted on to council prudence. Since until lately he had been Commander, Battle Force, Pacific, his advice against attempting to use the old battleships would carry weight. By no means least important, he was a Naval Academy classmate of King and one of his few intimate friends.

In addition to information and council on strategy, Nimitz sent to King, via Pye, a small personal request. It appears that Admiral Bloch still could not refrain from advising Nimitz how to run the war. The latter was anxious not to injure Bloch's service reputation, but he would be most grateful to have King remove him to a command where his advice was needed.

At the next day's conference, with Halsey and other senior officers present, the suggestion was made that Halsey with the *Enterprise* force be sent to join Brown's *Lexington* force in a raid on Rabaul while Fletcher's *Yorktown* force attacked Wake. The double blow might be enough to shock the enemy into shifting a few ships. A more daring proposal was for a raid on Tokyo. The Japanese would have to react to the resulting loss of face. But the latter idea was shelved, at least temporarily, because of the difficulty of refueling in northerly latitudes in winter weather.

Nimitz finally decided to combine the *Enterprise* and *Yorktown* forces and send them against Wake and Eniwetok or Marcus. Such raids, if nothing more, would give the men experience and raise American morale, and he hoped they would satisfy King. As for the battleships, he refused to send them out on offensive missions with the inadequate screens he could provide them and have them sunk by enemy aircraft.

Halsey raised no objections when he was assigned to lead the new raid, but he blew up when he learned that his carrier force had been designated Task Force 13 and that it was scheduled to sail for Wake on Friday, February 13. Off he sent his chief of staff, hot-tempered Captain Miles Browning, to raise hell at CinCPac headquarters over the outrage. Striding into the war plans office, Browning demanded of Captain McMorris, "What goes on here? Have you got it in for us, or what?"

The Phantom of the Opera was not a superstitious man, but he agreed that too many hoodoos were being hung on Halsey's risky enterprise. He changed the command designation to Task Force 16 and assured Browning that an overdue oiler would hold up Halsey's sortie until the 14th.

On the 14th, then, Halsey with the *Enterprise* and screen got under way. Fletcher's *Yorktown* force was to follow the next day. On Sunday the 15th came a conciliatory dispatch from CominCh, apparently reflecting the good offices of Pye. King would be satisfied, it now appeared, with occasional raids by Pacific Fleet forces on the Japanese island bases in the Central Pacific. Ships should be held in reserve, he continued, to meet possible surprise thrusts by the enemy, and he suggested that one carrier be retained in a central position in the area of Canton Island.

To Canton therefore, CinCPac sent Task Force 17, the *Yorktown* force. Task Force 16 continued westward, maintaining radio silence. Rather to Nimitz's annoyance Halsey remained silent, even though Japanese radio traffic on February 24 plainly indicated that Wake was being raided and on March 4 that Marcus Island was under attack. It is not known whether Halsey, while at Pearl, complained to Nimitz about being coached from headquarters during the Marshalls operation. At any rate, his subsequent refusal to make radio contact with CinCPac appears to have been his counterpart to the Civil War general's cutting of the telegraph lines to forestall interference from Washington. On March 5 at last came a brief message from Commander, Task Force 16, a request for an oiler with the added laconic report: "This force not, repeat not, damaged."

Nimitz got the point. Thenceforth he made it his firm practice, once a commander had departed on a mission with an approved operation plan, not to send out any directive or advice as to how the mission should be carried out.

Mixed news had arrived at Pearl from the ANZAC Area. Admiral Brown had attempted a raid on that troublesome base at Rabaul, but Japanese patrol planes had detected his approaching force 350 miles short of the target. Most of the bombers that flew out from Rabaul to attack were shot down by the *Lexington*'s fighters, at the cost of only two planes and no damage at all to the ships. Nevertheless, Brown felt that with surprise lost he had no choice but to withdraw. He insisted that if he had an additional carrier he could go back and finish the job. Nimitz therefore ordered Fletcher to take the *Yorktown* force down and join Brown.

On March 10 Halsey's Task Force 16 came steaming into Pearl Harbor. The force had indeed raided Wake and Marcus, but even the optimistic Halsey could not claim much success—a few buildings and possibly a fuel-storage tank set afire, one small patrol craft sunk, at the cost of two American bombers. In the opinion of one officer who had participated in the raids, "The Japs didn't mind them any more than a dog minds a flea."

The Japanese advance in the ABDA Area had not been slowed down in the slightest. Singapore had surrendered on February 15. In the Battle of the Java Sea, February 27–28, the remnant of the ABDA Striking Force had been shattered. Four U.S. destroyers escaped, but the other vessels, including the heavy cruiser *Houston*, were sunk while trying to escape from the Java Sea. Rangoon fell on March 8; Java, the following day.

On February 19, bombers from the Japanese carrier force raided Darwin,

Australia's chief northern port. The carriers then cruised south of Java, supporting the Japanese invasion there and picking off Allied vessels escaping from the southern ports. After the fall of Java, the carrier force headed into the Indian Ocean to take a few cracks at the British Eastern Fleet and at the bases on Ceylon.

Meanwhile, the combined *Yorktown* and *Lexington* forces under Wilson Brown were cruising in the Coral Sea. Instead of returning to attack Rabaul, Brown ducked under the New Guinea bird tail and on March 10 sent 104 planes over the Owen Stanley Range to attack shipping at two tiny Japanese footholds, Lae and Salamaua, on the north coast of New Guinea. Then, leaving the *Yorktown* force behind in the Coral Sea, Brown with the *Lexington* force headed for Pearl Harbor, where he arrived on March 26. After 54 days at sea, he had only one raid to his credit.

Nimitz accepted Brown's explanation that raiding powerfully fortified enemy bases across badly charted seas was too risky for carriers. But King insisted that Brown was not aggressive enough to lead combat forces, so Nimitz detached him from the *Lexington* force and appointed him to command the new Amphibious Force, with headquarters at San Diego. Brown's relief was Rear Admiral Aubrey W. ("Jakey") Fitch, who was younger than Brown but the most experienced carrier flag officer in the Navy.

For Brown the transfer was no demotion; his new responsibility was the vital one of training forces to capture bases in support of an eventual advance on Japan. Here was an example of Nimitz's custom, when kicking had to be done, of kicking a man upstairs, if at all possible. Whatever King or anybody else might think about Brown's aggressiveness, there was no question that he was an expert organizer, and he had demonstrated his skill as a trainer and educator at the U.S. Naval Academy, where he had recently served as superintendent.

Brown's new command had been created by a reorganization of the Pacific Fleet. King and Nimitz, reasoning that scouting at sea would henceforth be performed by submarines and aircraft, abolished the Scouting Force. Convinced that there would be no more Jutland-type battles between lines of dreadnoughts, they also abolished the Battle Force. To replace the defunct commands, they established the Amphibious Force and the Covering Force. The latter command, comprising the old battleships and their accompanying light forces, was assigned the task of protecting and supporting the former. A few days after CinCPac appointed Admiral Brown to command the Amphibious Force, he made Admiral Pye commander of the Covering Force, a command with an uncertain future since nobody had yet figured out how to use 21-knot dreadnoughts in support of 34-knot carriers, or vice versa.

Meanwhile, President Roosevelt, anxious not to lose his senior and most experienced officer, had ordered General Douglas MacArthur out of the Philippines. MacArthur, reluctant to abandon his besieged and starving troops, stalled until March 11, when he slipped away from Corregidor by night in a PT boat. From Mindanao he flew by B-17 bomber to Australia, where he announced: "The President of the United States ordered me to break through the Japanese lines and proceed from Corregidor to Australia for the purpose, as I understand it, of organizing the American offensive against Japan, a primary object of which is the relief of the Philippines. I came through and I shall return."

The general was mistaken if he believed that he was to be the sole organizer of the Allied offensive in the Pacific theater. In anticipation of his arrival in Australia, Allied representatives had worked out a new division of the theater of operations and a new assignment of commands. These were set forth in directives dated March 30 to Admiral Nimitz and General MacArthur.

General MacArthur was designated Supreme Commander, Allied Forces in the Southwest Pacific Area, which included Australia, the Solomons, the Bismarcks, New Guinea, and the Philippines. Admiral Nimitz was appointed commander in chief of the Pacific Ocean Area (POA), which comprised all the rest of the Pacific except for a shipping zone off South and Central America. As CinCPOA, he commanded all U.S. and allied forces in his area—land, sea, and air. Since CinCPac was subordinate to CinCPOA and Nimitz retained both titles, he was in a sense his own commanding officer.

The Combined Chiefs of Staff directed that the Pacific Fleet should remain under Nimitz's control, even if strategic considerations required it to enter MacArthur's Southwest Pacific Area. To free MacArthur from too much dependence on the Pacific Fleet, however, most of the ANZAC Striking Force was assigned to the general as the nucleus of a fleet of his own.

Because of its size, the Pacific Ocean Area was divided into the North Pacific Area, north of latitude 42° N; the Central Pacific Area, from 42° N to the equator; and the South Pacific Area, south of the equator.* Since both the Japanese and the Americans were planning offensive moves in the south, an overall commander, subordinate to CinCPOA, was required in the South Pacific Area. For this command Nimitz nominated Admiral Pye.

As a battleship commander in prewar days, Pye had regarded the carrier as an auxiliary type. He was moreover tarred with the failure of the Wake Island relief expedition. But he had a quick, flexible intellect; he could see where he had been mistaken and adjust his thinking accordingly. He had grown steadily in Nimitz's esteem. CinCPac had given him the Covering Force in order to permit him to exercise his command skills, but he came to consider him qualified for a position of even higher responsibility in the new kind of warfare that was unfolding in the Pacific.

Admiral King evidently thought otherwise. His tendency was to pigeonhole a man once and for all. He left Pye, the experienced battleship officer, in command of the battleships. For Commander, South Pacific Area, he selected Vice Admiral Robert L. Ghormley. This proved to be one of King's least

* Hence the inclusive designation came to be expressed in the plural, as Pacific Ocean Areas.

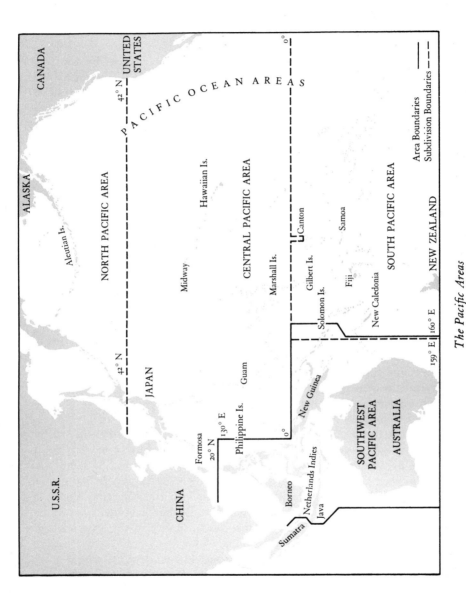

*The Pacific Areas*

BROKEN VERTICAL LINE IS SOUTH-SOUTHWEST PACIFIC BOUNDARY AS REVISED AUGUST 1, 1942

fortunate choices. Ghormley, widely experienced and outstandingly intelligent, proved unequal to heading off military crises or dealing with them when they came.

In his inherited staff Nimitz found a few officers who failed to measure up. In due course he transferred them out, but until he did so he was unable to attain his objective of so delegating authority that he, as commander in chief, would have to do only what nobody else could do. By spring 1942, however, he had cleared his desk well enough to find time for an occasional game of tennis, and, adjacent to his quarters, he had a space prepared where he could toss horseshoes to work off tension. With the help of such limited exercise he gradually overcame the uncharacteristic insomnia that had vexed him since his arrival at Pearl.

Sharing quarters with Nimitz at that time were his chief of staff, Admiral Draemel, and the fleet surgeon, Captain Elphege Alfred M. Gendreau. Most evenings they had guests for dinner, but such socializing was not for Nimitz just a matter of relaxation. His twofold purpose was to meet his subordinates in an informal atmosphere and to bring together and get to know other commanders in the area. "Am trying my best," he wrote Mrs. Nimitz, "to get the heads of the services here together."

Admiral Nimitz played the genial host, but in his private moments he could not throw off the depression that had burdened him since his arrival. He was frustrated that he could do so little to turn the tide of war, and he suspected that he had disappointed his sponsors. Because Secretary Knox had not communicated with him since sending that snippy little message about censorship, he was surprised to learn from Mrs. Nimitz that she had been entertained by Mrs. Knox.

"I am glad you went to Mrs. Knox's luncheon," he wrote in reply. "I have not seen anything [from] K. recently so believe he is lying low. Am afraid he is not so keen for me now as he was when I left but that is natural. Ever so many people were enthusiastic for me at the start but when things do not move fast enough they sour on me. I will be lucky to last six months. The public may demand action and results faster than I can produce."

# CHAPTER 4

# BACKGROUND OF
# A STRATEGIST

In his lectures at the Naval War College, Alfred Thayer Mahan frequently stressed the proposition that "communications dominate war."* This dictum was especially applicable to highly mechanized World War II. Certainly it was one on which Admirals King and Nimitz and the Japanese leaders were in agreement. We have noted the relentless Japanese drive to cut communications between the United States and Australia and American exertions to protect them. Japan, by blocking supplies flowing along this direct route, could prevent the Allies from using Australia as a base for offensive operations. By such means, however, she could do no more than postpone her own defeat, not ensure her own victory.

On the other hand, Japan faced inevitable defeat if her communications with the East Indies were interdicted. For her there was no other possible source of oil, and without oil her war machine would quickly grate to a halt. Up from the south via the South China and East China seas, fleets of tankers transported oil from the East Indies to Japan. King and Nimitz agreed that the primary objectives of the Allied armed forces were to safeguard their own supply lines and then drive westward in order to capture bases from which Japan's indispensable "oil line" might be blocked.

From the beginning, Nimitz had sent Pacific Fleet submarines to attack ships plying this and other Japanese lines of communication. It was conceivable that insular Japan might be defeated by submarines alone, as submarines twice nearly defeated insular Britain. With Japan the task should have been simpler, for not only oil but most of her other war-making raw materials flowed to her along a single line from her newly conquered southern area, and most of the finished materials and refined fuel had to be shipped over long, vulnerable routes to distant fighting fronts.

Veteran submariner Nimitz was disappointed when his submarines failed to achieve the results he had anticipated. Had he known how scanty the sinkings in fact were, he would have been even more distressed. He had about 50 submarines and, by the end of April 1942, they had sunk one 1,900-ton destroyer, three submarines, and some twenty cargo vessels, only four of which exceeded 6,000 tons. Since the beginning of the year, an average of fewer than 50 U-boats operating daily in the Atlantic and Arctic oceans had sunk 271

---

* As used here, the word *communications* means a "system of routes and transport." *Communications* also means "transfer of information," by radio, flag hoist, and so forth.

ships amounting to nearly 1,600,000 gross tons. In Washington the tendency was to blame the disparity on the inexperience or ineptitude of the American submariners, but the latter were beginning to suspect, correctly, that the fault lay elsewhere.

To King and Nimitz the Pacific Ocean was no *aqua incognita*. When King was a student at the Naval Academy, and shortly before Nimitz's arrival there, the United States, and the U.S. Navy in particular, had their attention powerfully drawn to the Pacific by Commodore George Dewey's victory over the Spanish fleet in the Battle of Manila Bay and by the subsequent U.S. annexation of Hawaii, the Philippines, Guam, Wake, and part of Samoa. A series of war scares then focused the Navy's attention on the problem of protecting the Philippines from an expanding Japan. Hence, at the Naval Academy, at the Naval War College, and elsewhere in the Navy, Japan was studied as a potential enemy, and the Pacific Ocean came under intense scrutiny as a possible theater of war. The Navy's war games and fleet exercises were generally geared to the probability of a war with Japan. To King, Nimitz, and other U.S. naval officers of the early twentieth century, therefore, Tongatabu, Fiji, Funafuti, and Efate were not just exotic names; they were potential bases that they encountered repeatedly in their studies and problem-solving.

When Chester Nimitz entered the Naval Academy in 1901, the U.S. Navy was undergoing a glorious renaissance. Having neglected the Navy for nearly two decades, Congress in the 1880s began authorizing the new fleet of steam and steel that in 1898 earned the enthusiastic appreciation of the American nation by winning crushing victories in Philippine and Cuban waters. Around the turn of the century Mahan's books on the influence of sea power and their imperialist, pro-navy message became known to the American public through the pronouncements of President Theodore Roosevelt, long-time friend and disciple of Mahan. From 1898 to 1916 Congress authorized the building of at least one battleship per year—the sole exception being 1901, and that only because of congestion in the shipyards. By congressional authority also, the Naval Academy's decaying brick buildings, most of them dating back to before the Civil War, were to be replaced by sparkling new buildings of granite and gray brick in French Renaissance style. The cadet quarters built by Admiral David Dixon Porter, superintendent in the late 1860s, would be replaced by palatial Bancroft Hall, the largest dormitory in the world.

It was in this heady atmosphere that Chester Nimitz began his career in the Navy. His class, consisting of 131 cadets, was much the largest that had entered the Naval Academy since its founding in 1845. The increase was to offset the shortage of naval officers revealed by the Spanish-American War and to provide leadership for Theodore Roosevelt's expanding navy. Pending the building of Bancroft Hall there were not enough rooms to house such an influx of plebes. As a result, Chester and a good many of his classmates had to be berthed in a temporary wooden annex, which was hard to keep clean, lacked adequate bathing facilities, and was hot in the summer and cold in the winter.

To offset his uncompleted high-school education, Chester continued his old routine; he rose at 4:30 a.m. and studied till reveille. His roommate, Albert Church, of Idaho, adopted the same routine, and their zeal resulted in top grades. Midway through the first semester, however, Chester suffered a serious setback. One afternoon, sweaty from a workout in the field, he became chilled while standing in line in the drafty annex to get into the bathroom. As a result, his chief physical weakness asserted itself: he came down with pneumonia and had to spend a month in the hospital, thereby missing the Army-Navy football game and falling far behind in his studies.

Making up for the lost time required a mighty effort. He had missed part of the basic foundation in French. His mathematics course assumed a prior knowledge of geometry and logarithms, to both of which he was a complete stranger. French continued for some time to give Chester trouble, but he had the logical type of mind that readily absorbs mathematics. Sent to the board one day to work an algebra problem, he astonished the instructor by finding the right answer, not as prescribed in the book but through a method of his own devising.

By the end of 1901 Nimitz had caught up with Church and was again near the academic forefront of his class. Some of their classmates, possibly on the advice of the faculty, then came forward with the request that Nimitz and Church separate and take as roommates cadets who were "less academically efficient." Somewhat reluctantly they agreed, Chester selecting John Sumpter, of Kentucky. Nimitz and Church goaded their new "roomies" into adopting their own early-morning study habits and thus succeeded in pulling them over the passing line for the rest of the academic year.

The Naval Academy that Nimitz attended was in some respects intentionally made grim, for one of its functions—regarded by some officers as its most important—was the relentless weeding-out of the unfit. Plebes were subjected to "running" by the upper classes. This, when kept within bounds, was a mild form of hazing involving no physical contact but plenty of harsh words and onerous regulations, all calculated to discourage the faint-hearted. Chester Nimitz, whom the cadets had nicknamed Natchew or Natty, took the whole program in stride.* He accepted the running so good-naturedly that the upper classmen lost interest in trying to give him a hard time.

The method of instruction at the Academy threw the students on their own resources. They were tested almost daily on material that had been assigned to them without explanation or clarification. As soon as a section (class) had been formally presented to the instructor by the cadet section leader, the

---

* Strange and wonderful are the origins of some naval officers' nicknames, nicknames that often stick with them throughout their careers. "Natty" derived from "Natchew," the nickname conferred on Chester by other cadets who teasingly professed to note a facial resemblance between him and Mathew ("Matchew") Strohm, Naval Academy instructor in gymnastics and, of all things, ballroom dancing, a man with cauliflower ears, flattened nose, and ferocious mien. Nimitz's nicknames seem not to have survived his Academy days.

instructor was likely to say, "Gentlemen, draw slips and man the boards." The slips of paper contained material from the assignments which the students were to answer, solve, or translate on the blackboards. Only afterward, as the instructor moved around the room correcting, grading, and commenting on the answers, did he give any explanation.

Chester's months of boning up for the Naval Academy entrance examinations had made him sufficiently self-reliant to require no help in interpreting textbooks. Not all of his classmates were so lucky. Cadet George V. Stewart, of Virginia, complained to Nimitz that the instructors never taught him anything.

"I could do a lot better, Natty," he said, "if they would only explain and show me."

"Of course they don't," replied Natty, who endorsed the Academy's methods of weeding-out and of forcing the cadets to teach themselves. "You are here to learn, to do things for yourself."

Nobody took a livelier interest in Chester's progress at the Naval Academy than did his Grandfather Nimitz. Writing from Fredericksburg on February 19, 1902, the old innkeeper began a letter as follows:

> My dear grandson Chester,
>
> Next Monday you will reach your 17th birthday, and I hope these lines will find you in the best of health and in good spirits at the progress of your new studies in trigonometry and Spanish, and I hope that you will not find it unusually difficult to master these as well as you have so far succeeded in other studies. Your grade cards have come to me, and I as well as your Papa and Uncle Charlie rejoice at your classification. If we understand the numbers right, your marks place you between good and very good. A better standing could not be expected by anybody. Even Professor Toland is delighted.
>
> We hope the most severe part of the winter is over for you, and that you can take outdoor exercises. That will be appreciated by all. We have seen in the paper that the German training ship *Moltke*, having a lot of German cadets on board, was to pay your academy a visit. I hope it has come to pass, and you have some fun, as no doubt you will also have from the visit of Prince Heinrich on the last of this month. You will probably have to dress for a grand parade. I know of nothing acceptable to send you for a birthday present, so I will overhaul a lot of old letters and give you some family history.

There followed many pages of the annals of the Nimitz family, reaching all the way back to the thirteenth century. It was obviously a labor of love on the old man's part, and Chester cherished it as much as he would have appreciated a costly birthday gift. He kept the letter among his papers as long as he lived.

Each Saturday morning Chester and other cadets were drilled in seamanship by sailing the steel square-rigger *Chesapeake*. Her captain, also head of the Department of Seamanship, was Commander William Frederick Halsey, father of the future Admiral Bill Halsey. Bill was a cadet too, in the class of 1904. He was thus a year ahead of Chester, and he was fullback on two of the most inept varsity football teams in the history of the Naval Academy. Bill always claimed to have been the worst fullback on the Academy's two saddest teams.

Chester made the varsity crew and became a stroke but was never a standout. He participated in various sports for pleasure, however, and always did well, particularly in tennis. He never neglected exercise—walking, running, and swimming—when not engaged in competitive sports.

It is worth noting that most of the naval leaders of World War II attended the Naval Academy with Nimitz. Ernest King and William Pye graduated the June before Chester's arrival, but among his fellow cadets, besides Halsey, were Harold Stark, Husband Kimmel, Royal E. Ingersoll, Robert Ghormley, Frank Jack Fletcher, Raymond A. Spruance, John Towers, Milo Draemel, John S. McCain, Aubrey Fitch, Thomas C. Kinkaid, Wilson Brown, H. Kent Hewitt, and R. Kelly Turner. Though the period of Nimitz's cadetship was one of rapid growth for the Academy, there were never more than 700 cadets present. Everyone knew everyone else and many close friendships were formed. Thus the officers who commanded U.S. naval forces in World War II were far from being strangers to one another.

Chester's first summer cruise was in the *Chesapeake*, which sailed down the Chesapeake Bay, passed through the Capes of Virginia into the Atlantic, and conveyed her crew of cadets up to Bar Harbor, Maine. There the student-sailors were entertained at parties given by the wealthy owners of summer homes. Chester was beginning to encounter the great world of achievement and sophistication that he had left Texas to explore.

Cadet Nimitz subsequently cruised in the battleships *Massachusetts* and *Indiana*, veterans of the Spanish-American War, and in a destroyer. While in the destroyer he developed an abscess in his ear. Since there was no doctor aboard, the captain sent to the engine room for an oil syringe with which to squirt boric acid into the affected ear. Nimitz's lifelong slight deafness may have been the result of the abscess, though he himself tended to blame it on the fact that the syringe was probably not sterile. He learned to offset his hearing difficulty by inconspicuously watching the lips of speakers.

During Nimitz's plebe year the third volume of Edgar S. Maclay's *History of the United States Navy* was published and used as a textbook at the Naval Academy. The new volume, dealing with the Spanish-American War, put the severest interpretation on Commodore Winfield Scott Schley's actions in the Caribbean Sea campaign, finding him disobedient of orders, lacking in aggressiveness, dilatory in blockading the enemy, and, in the Battle of Santiago, downright cowardly.

The battle came about when the U.S. fleet commander, Rear Admiral William T. Sampson, left Schley in command of the blockade while he himself went in his flagship to confer with the U.S. general ashore. The Spanish fleet, seizing the opportunity, burst out of the harbor, firing as it went, broke through the blockaders, and sped off westward along the Cuban coast.

All the American ships except Schley's cruiser *Brooklyn* turned west to give chase. The *Brooklyn*, on Schley's orders, turned east. She nearly rammed the *Texas* and steamed a complete circle before joining the chase, which ended with the destruction of the Spanish fleet. In telling the story, Maclay deplored what he called "the shameful spectacle of an American war ship, supported by a force superior to the enemy's ... deliberately turning tail and running away."

When Maclay's charge was published, newspapers all over the country let out a roar. The American public was deeply shocked, for they had enshrined Dewey, Sampson, and Schley as heroes, the three U.S. naval victors over Spain. To brand one of them incompetent, hesitant, and craven was a blow to national pride. Schley wrathfully demanded that Maclay's third volume be thrown out of the Naval Academy, and so it was. The publisher recalled all unsold copies and had the author revise the offending passages.

But the damage had been done; the original passages had already been quoted in the press. Schley demanded a court of inquiry as a means of retrieving his military reputation. The court, with Admiral Dewey as president, sat for forty days and accumulated 2,000 pages of testimony and findings. Unfortunately the proceedings degenerated into the notorious Sampson-Schley controversy, in which adherents of the two officers squabbled in and out of court over whether Sampson or Schley was the true victor in the Battle of Santiago. The public was at first amused and then bored by the undignified spectacle. Drawings of the court proceedings published in *The Washington Post* verged on being cartoons. When a split finding of the court intensified rather than settled the dispute, President Theodore Roosevelt in effect ordered all parties to desist from further argument, because there was "no excuse whatever from either side for any further agitation on this unhappy controversy."

Thus the Navy, which in contrast to the bumbling Army, had come out of the war in a blaze of glory, was made faintly ridiculous by the subsequent behavior of its leaders. Navy men and friends of the Navy were deeply embarrassed. Most of the students at the Naval Academy, however, were able to shrug off any vexation they felt, and some no doubt were delighted at the discomfiture of their elders.

To Cadet Nimitz, dedicated as he was to the Navy, the effect seems to have been nothing less than traumatic. He made a vow then and there that, if ever he was in a position to prevent it, there would be no washing of the Navy's dirty linen in public. The shock of the Sampson-Schley controversy may indeed have been at the root of Nimitz's later almost obsessive discretion.

It must not be supposed that Chester Nimitz was all study and duty. He was still the sunny-natured, gregarious fellow of his Texas boyhood. Nothing delighted him more than a party with plenty of talk and nonsense. No doubt he offered some of his Texas tall tales for the general amusement. Unless Academy students have greatly changed since the turn of the century, such corny fare must have brought forth a certain amount of headshaking and groaning. At any rate, Nimitz soon shifted to a more sophisticated sort of story, usually just a shade risqué and with a surprise punch line. Continuing after Academy days to tell such stories, he became an accomplished raconteur. During World War II, Nimitz stories were widely repeated throughout the Navy.

At cadet parties, non-alcoholic punches prepared by Chester were consumed in large quantities and widely appreciated. Sometimes, by his own admission, he and his friends defied regulations and risked expulsion by quaffing beverages stronger than punch. Chester and his classmates also defied regulations and the wrath of Congress by going beyond "running" plebes and actually hazing them, an old if not particularly intelligent Academy custom. Once Chester's entire class was suspended for hazing.

When Chester's class returned from leave in September 1904, they found the first wing of Bancroft Hall completed. They, as first classmen (seniors), occupied it. Nimitz, then a three-striper and commander of the 8th Company, was assigned commodious quarters on the northeast corner of the third floor. He had a bedroom of his own and shared a large adjoining study with his old friend Midshipman (new title replacing "cadet") George Stewart.

Nimitz's class of 1905 learned that because of the pressing need for junior officers in Roosevelt's expanding fleet, they were to graduate at the end of January 1905 instead of in the following June, as scheduled. Hence among the new first classmen there was a rush and an increased pressure of duties. Some of their less important subjects and some drills were canceled. In other subjects their assignments were lengthened. They were granted a "free gate" to Annapolis during non-study hours so that they might visit their tailors and expedite completion of the uniforms they would require on graduation. "You may be sure," said Nimitz, "we made good use of this extraordinary privilege."

Midshipmen Nimitz and Stewart soon had the happiness of discovering that from their quarters they could reach the roof of the new dormitory, which was still under construction. Here, completely concealed from below by the roof overhang, they could and did hold beer parties with their friends. As a midshipman drained off a bottle, over the side it went, smashing into the piles of granite blocks awaiting placement in the uncompleted building. The racket quickly drew blue-uniformed civilian guards, known as Jimmy-Legs, who to the satisfaction of the culprits on the roof, dashed about in bewilderment trying to discover the source of the descending bottles.

One Saturday afternoon Chester and a number of his classmates decided to seek relaxation from their frenetic pace by having a roof party. They drew lots to determine who should go into Annapolis and get the beer. Chester "won." Out through the Main Gate carrying an empty suitcase bravely he went, wearing three stripes on his sleeve and gold stars on his collar. The Jimmy-Legs and marine guards gave him only a cursory glance, recognizing him as a first classman with town privileges.

In the back room of a tailor's shop on Maryland Avenue, a couple of blocks away, Nimitz had his suitcase loaded with a dozen bottles of cold beer. With the proprietor, who had procured the beer as a friendly service, was a handsome, dark-haired gentleman whom he did not introduce to Chester. With his loaded suitcase, Nimitz returned to the Academy and passed again, somewhat tremulously this time, through the Main Gate. He was not challenged. The rooftop beer-and-sandwich party that night was a resounding success.

The following Monday morning when Chester marched his section into navigation class, he was horrified to see in the instructor's chair the handsome, dark-haired gentleman of the tailor's shop, now in uniform. He was Lieutenant Commander Levi Calvin Bertolette, USN, class of 1887, who had only recently reported for duty at the Naval Academy. With dreadful anticipation, Nimitz foresaw a summons at the end of the hour and an early conclusion to his naval career. But Bertolette gave no indication that he had ever beheld Chester before.

The chances are that Commander Bertolette simply did not recognize the beer purchaser of the preceding Saturday. But Nimitz, judging him on the basis of his own memory for names and faces, always believed otherwise. He said later: "This escapade taught me a lesson on how to behave for the remainder of my stay at the Academy. It also taught me to look with lenient and tolerant eye on first offenders when in later years they appeared before me as a Commanding Officer holding Mast."

Nimitz hoped some day to meet Bertolette in the Service and thank him for what he took to be "understanding forbearance," but their paths never crossed. Bertolette died in 1912.

One experience during Chester's first-class semester gave him an early foretaste of a type of operation that was to play an important part in his later career. The Navy's first commissioned submarine, the *Holland*, was based at Annapolis, and Nimitz and his classmates took turns going aboard for training runs in the mouth of the Severn River. His submergence in this slow, 54-foot-long device does not seem to have inspired Nimitz at this time with any burning desire to specialize in submersibles.

The truncated first-class year came rapidly to an end. The midshipman who wrote up Nimitz for the *Lucky Bag*, the Naval Academy yearbook, showed remarkable perceptiveness in selecting a line from Wordsworth to characterize him: "A man he seems of cheerful yesterdays and confident tomorrows." The writer added: "Possesses that calm and steady-going Dutch way that gets to the bottom of things."

On January 30, 1905, Nimitz and his classmates were graduated and became passed midshipmen. As such, they were "appointed officers," not commissioned officers. They were eligible to be commissioned ensigns only after serving the Navy satisfactorily for two years. Meanwhile, records of their service were kept at the Naval Academy and periodically reviewed by the Academic Board.

In his class of 114 graduates, Midshipman Nimitz stood seventh in overall achievement. His best subjects were modern languages (French and Spanish), ordnance, mathematics, and navigation, and he earned very high marks on practice cruise. Standing fourth in the class was Royal E. Ingersoll, who became Commander in Chief, Atlantic Fleet, one day after Chester Nimitz took over as Commander in Chief, Pacific Fleet. Standing fifth was Fairfax Leary, who in World War II commanded successively the *Saratoga* force, the ANZAC Striking Force, the Allied Naval Forces, Southwest Pacific, and the Eastern Sea Frontier. Sixteen members of the class of 1905 made rear admiral or better.

Passed Midshipman Nimitz went home to Texas for a short leave, at the close of which he took a train at San Antonio for the West Coast. On the same train, by prior arrangement, was his friend and classmate Passed Midshipman Bruce Canaga, who had orders identical to his own. Together they proceeded to San Francisco and reported for duty aboard the battleship *Ohio*. This was not the last time Chester's and Bruce's duties brought them together. They remained lifelong friends.

The *Ohio*, one of four battleships authorized by Congress in 1898, had just finished her acceptance trials. She displaced 12,000 tons, was armed with four 12-inch and sixteen 6-inch guns and could make 17 knots. Her skipper was Captain Leavitt C. Logan, of the class of 1867.

Soon after Midshipman Nimitz came aboard, the *Ohio* headed for the Orient to serve as flagship of the U.S. Asiatic Fleet. Captain Logan, in his first quarterly report to the Naval Academy's Academic Board, wrote: "During the short time Midshipman Nimitz has been on board the Ohio his services have been satisfactory." By the end of the next quarter, when Chester had come to the captain's attention as boat officer and assistant officer of the deck, Logan wrote: "Midshipman C. W. Nimitz is an Excellent Officer and I cheerfully commend him to the very favorable consideration of the Academic Board."

When the *Ohio* reached Far Eastern waters, Japan and Russia were at war. Hostilities at sea reached a climax in May 1905 with the Battle of Tsushima, in which a Japanese fleet under Admiral Heihachiro Togo defeated and virtually destroyed the Russian Baltic Squadron. Since Togo had previously destroyed most of the Russian Far Eastern Squadron, and the Japanese army had captured Port Arthur, the Czar acknowledged Russia's defeat by accepting the proffered mediation of President Theodore Roosevelt.

To mark the restoration of peace, the Japanese emperor gave a garden party to honor his victorious army and navy commanders, with Admiral Togo as chief guest. Invitations were sent to the officers of the *Ohio*, then in Tokyo Bay, but since the more senior officers had no interest in attending the affair, six midshipmen, including Nimitz, were detailed to represent the ship. Scattered about the imperial palace grounds were two or three hundred tables, each with several bottles of Russian champagne captured at Port Arthur. Because of transportation difficulties, the midshipmen arrived late and were seated at the table nearest the exit.

Toward the end of the party, the Americans saw Admiral Togo coming down the path to take his departure. Somewhat flushed with wine, they decided to intercept him, and it was Midshipman Nimitz whom they selected to step forward and invite the admiral to their table. Togo smilingly accepted the invitation and came over. He shook hands all around, took a sip of champagne, and chatted briefly in English, a language he spoke fluently, for he had spent seven years in England, first as a student and later as overseer of the building of a light cruiser. The admiral made a deep impression upon Nimitz, who never again saw him alive but was repeatedly involved over the years in honoring the old sea dog's memory.

The long-standing cordial relationship between the United States and Japan was severely strained by the latter's stunning victory over the most populous of the Western powers. For Americans, the need to protect their newly acquired Philippine Islands from a possibly expansionist Japan took on a new urgency. President Roosevelt's mediation did nothing to preserve the old cordiality. It brought the war to a close with the Treaty of Portsmouth (New Hampshire), but infuriated the Japanese, who were denied an indemnity to shore up their war-wrecked economy.

In the circumstances, Roosevelt deemed it expedient to call home his capital ships. When the *Ohio* headed for the United States in mid-September 1906, Midshipmen Nimitz and Canaga were among the Americans left behind, both transferring to the venerable cruiser *Baltimore*, which had fought with Dewey in the Battle of Manila Bay. Nimitz and Canaga believed, probably correctly, that it was the more capable of the American officers and men who had been selected to remain in the Orient.

In a letter written to Grandfather Nimitz from Cavite, Philippine Islands, on December 12, 1906, Chester reported that he and the other passed midshipmen had taken their examinations for ensign and would probably learn the results about the end of January. He was not worried over the chances of passing. He had other good news.

> I told you about trying to get one of the gunboats down here. Well, the powers that be have assured me that I will have command of the U.S. gunboat *Panay* just as soon as she is ready to go into commission. She will be ready in about two weeks from now, and she will cruise in the southern islands of the Philippine group. Just look at a large map of this section and you will see what a large area it covers. These little boats get roving commissions—that is, they can visit any ports they choose. There will be another officer on board besides myself, McCain* of the class below mine will go along. The crew will consist of about 30 all told, and I have been allowed to take my pick of this ship's company, and the whole ship's company is practically a picked crew, so you see I shall get a bunch of good men.

---

* Passed Midshipman John S. McCain. As vice admiral with the U.S. Pacific Fleet in World War II, he relieved Vice Admiral Marc Mitscher in command of the Fast Carrier Task Force.

Though his ex-Spanish gunboat was only 92 feet, 8 inches long, Nimitz was delighted to get this small command because, as he said, "I can practice piloting and navigation and so forth as well as on a small ship, and besides it should teach me a certain amount of self-reliance and confidence."

Chester and Bruce were commissioned ensigns on January 31, 1907. Not long afterward, Nimitz departed Cavite in the *Panay* and Canaga set out in command of a similar gunboat, the *Paragua*. They planned to cruise together and, insofar as practical, they did. Their job was to "show the flag" to the recently subdued Filipinos and Moros in the Sulu Archipelago, to assist the natives when possible, and to settle troubles where necessary. As it turned out, the two young ensigns encountered no serious problems. For them the roving duty was a period of high adventure.

In addition to his gunboat, Nimitz commanded a tiny naval station at Polloc, Mindanao, where 22 marines were stationed. "I had one foot ashore and one at sea, so to speak," said Nimitz, "but I lived aboard the *Panay*. Those were great days. We had no radio, no mail, and no fresh food. We did a lot of hunting. One of the seamen said one day he 'couldn't look a duck in the beak again.' "

Events elsewhere brought this idyll to a sudden end. At the conclusion of the Russo-Japanese War, Japanese veterans, seeking new homes, flocked to California, where the low wages they accepted upset the West Coast labor market. San Francisco retaliated by segregating Japanese schoolchildren, an implication of racial inferiority that outraged the people of Japan. Under pressure from President Roosevelt San Francisco agreed to end the practice. In return he secured from Japan an agreement to limit the immigration. Then, as a restraint on Japanese warmongers, Roosevelt announced on July 9, 1907, that he was transferring the U.S. battleship fleet from Atlantic waters to San Francisco.

A war scare shook the U.S. Asiatic Fleet into frantic activity that reached all the way to Polloc. After all, the Japanese had not hesitated in 1904 to attack the Russian fleet, which had fifteen modern battleships to their six. Togo and his admirals had first defeated Russia's divided Far Eastern Squadron piecemeal and then awaited the arrival of Russia's Baltic Squadron from the Atlantic and destroyed that also. If Japan intended to use that strategy against the U.S. Navy, the obvious place for her to begin was in the Philippines, and the time was now, before the U.S. Atlantic fleet could reach the Pacific.

Nimitz, with the *Panay*, was summoned to the big naval base at Cavite. "There was so much talk of war with Japan," he said, "that when we approached Manila Bay, I almost sent a landing party ahead to see if we still held the place."

Mooring his gunboat, Nimitz donned white uniform and sword and went ashore to report to the base commander, Rear Admiral Uriah Rose Harris, whom his subordinates nicknamed "Uriah Heep." He was a frozen-faced martinet who believed in never cracking a smile while on duty. Harris brusquely informed Nimitz that he was to take command of a destroyer, the *Decatur*, which had been for some time out of commission, and get her into dry dock without delay. The admiral might have permitted himself at least a small paternal smile at this extraordinary announcement. Twenty-two-year-old ensigns are not now and were not then normally given command of destroyers, even in times of grave emergency. Among Nimitz's contemporaries destined for the highest ranks, Spruance had his first destroyer command at the age of 26; Halsey, at the age of 30; King, at 36.

Permitting Nimitz no time to return to the *Panay* for his gear, Admiral Harris sent him at once in his own launch to the *Decatur*, which was swinging at a buoy. He was to have the destroyer in dry dock at Olongapo, 60 miles away, in 48 hours. "Your clothes will catch up to you," said Harris.

Ensign Nimitz arrived aboard his new command still in whites and with sword, to be greeted by a couple of Filipino watchmen. The ship appeared little more than a hulk. Vital equipment was missing. There were no provisions aboard and no water or fuel. Before Chester could grasp the enormity of his problem, officers and crew began arriving.

Recalling his helpless and hopeless feeling at that moment, Nimitz afterward remembered the *Decatur* at their first meeting as a "beat-up old destroyer." In fact, she was a fine, comparatively new vessel, a product of the 1898 congressional appropriation, which also provided for the *Ohio* and two other battleships. The sixteen destroyers authorized, the first in the U.S. Navy, were four-stack, 420-ton, coal-burners capable of 28 knots. The *Decatur* and her sisters served through World War I and were stricken in 1920.

Nimitz returned to shore in the launch that had brought the first contingent of his crew. The trip gave him a little time to think. As he gazed at the blue waters of Manila Bay and at the distant jungled hills, he grew calmer. He was determined, despite his inexperience, to show himself worthy of his seniors' confidence in him.

Now, as so often in his career, Nimitz profited by his habit and gift of making friends, without regard to rank or status. He turned to some warrant officers at Cavite with whom he had played poker when the *Panay* was being readied for service. They promised to do what they could. Soon bargeloads of equipment, coal, and water began to arrive at the *Decatur*. By laboring night and day, Nimitz and his scratch crew finally got steam in one boiler but they did not have time to test the engines.

Nimitz planned to back away from the buoy, but when he rang up quarter speed astern, the destroyer moved forward. When he ordered full speed astern, she darted ahead. The engine telegraphs had been hooked up in reverse. Despite this contretemps, a storm, and inadequate charts, Nimitz and his crew got the *Decatur* to Olongapo on time. In two weeks she was out of dry dock and ready for war with Japan.

The war scare began to subside when the Japanese government indicated its peaceful intentions by formally inviting the Pacific-bound American battleships to visit Tokyo Bay. This was exactly what Roosevelt wanted. He then created an international sensation by announcing that his "Great White Fleet" of sixteen battleships would cruise not only to the U.S. West Coast and to Japan but all the way around the world on a good-will tour, which incidentally would demonstrate to all countries the U.S. Navy's strength and skill.

In advance, Roosevelt dispatched his Secretary of War, William Howard Taft, to tour the world as his ambassador of peace and good will. It is open to question whether the 300-pound Taft with his neatly curled white mustachios and imposing paunch was any less impressive as a good-will envoy than one of Roosevelt's battleships. After visiting Japan, he proceeded to the Philippines, where he had been the successful and popular civil governor from 1901 to 1904. Arriving at Manila in the fall of 1907, Taft officiated at and spoke at the opening of the general assembly. Then, accompanied by Mrs. Taft and their ten-year-old son Charles, he made a brief tour of several Philippine cities.

Ensign Nimitz became involved in the tour when he was assigned the duty of conveying the Taft party from Olongapo back to Manila. Seeking a means of making the portly envoy comfortable on the deck of the *Decatur*, Nimitz obtained two wicker chairs and had his carpenter lash them together and saw off the two inside arms. He thus provided a lounge chair that proved snug but ample for the ambassador and strong enough to sustain his weight. Taft and party soon departed Manila by sea for Vladivostok, whence they proceeded overland to Moscow, St. Petersburg, Berlin, and Paris.

Nimitz, having been nearly three years in the Orient, hoped to be sent home before long. Instead, he was ordered south in the *Decatur* to his old cruising grounds off Mindanao and the Sulu Archipelago. Again Chester found time to hunt—wild pig, deer, duck. For a while the *Decatur* served as a sort of flagship for the American governor of the archipelago, a Colonel Rogers. On arriving off a Sulu village, the destroyer would expend a few rounds from its rapid-fire guns to impress the natives. Then the Moro chieftains would come aboard and present Colonel Rogers with their problems and differences as a court of last appeal.

While the colonel was making decisions and dispensing justice, Ensign Nimitz was making friends. He became particularly attached to a Moro chief named Datu Piang. After World War II, the latter's son, Major Datu Gumbay Piang, of the Philippine Constabulary, sent Admiral Nimitz a kris, the Moro short knife, that had belonged to his father. It was the major's way of thanking the admiral for his part in liberating the Philippines.

One break from routine that Nimitz particularly enjoyed was a voyage across the South China Sea in the spring of 1908 to Saigon, river port and capital of French Indochina, then known as "the Paris of the East." Wrote Chester to Grandfather Nimitz:

> The French there made a good deal of us, and we enjoyed ourselves immensely. They were interested a great deal in the *Decatur* and admired her very much on account of her size. Their largest torpedo boat destroyers are about half the

size of the *Decatur*. Also, coming back from Saigon I encountered my first,
and I hope it may be my last, real live typhoon, and although my ship
behaved remarkably well, for one of its size, we spent three very uncomfortable
days. The ship rolled 50 degrees continually, and when the sea was ahead or
astern I thought she would surely break in the middle, as a former destroyer,
British, once did in a heavy sea. However, we arrived safely in Manila only a
few hours after our scheduled time.

Nimitz was beginning to long for a visit to Texas and his family, whom he
had not seen in three and a half years. There was a chance that he might be
sent back in the *Maine* or the *Alabama*, but he hoped not. These battleships, in
bad shape, had been detached from the Great White Fleet at San Francisco
and were returning at slow speed to the U.S. East Coast the long way around,
rather than risk the dangerous passage back through the Strait of Magellan.
The White Fleet itself, after visiting New Zealand, Australia, Japan, and China,
was to leave Manila early in December. Had Nimitz joined it, as he suspected
he might be ordered to do, he would have encountered many of his Annapolis
friends, including Ensign Bill Halsey. But the White Fleet was not due back in
the United States until February 22, 1909.

Speculation about such matters was brought to an abrupt end by an
unforeseen mishap. In the evening of July 7, 1908, Ensign Nimitz in the
*Decatur* became a little careless. Entering Batangas Harbor, south of Manila
Bay, he estimated his position instead of taking bearings. He also failed to
check on whether the tide was running in or out. Suddenly the leadsman
shouted, "We're not moving, sir!"

At first Nimitz was puzzled. Then came the sickening realization that his
destroyer had run aground on a mudbank. Attempts to back her down were
fruitless. Here was a situation that could easily wreck a young officer's career.
"On that black night somewhere in the Philippines," Nimitz later recalled, "the
advice of my grandfather returned to me: 'Don't worry about things over
which you have no control.' So I set up a cot on deck and went to sleep."

Not long after daybreak a small steamer appeared, heaved a line to the
*Decatur*, and pulled her off. Ensign Nimitz dutifully reported his accident.
Navy regulations required that the grounding be investigated and the guilty
party, if any, be punished. Nimitz was therefore transferred to the cruiser
*Denver* to stand court-martial for "culpable inefficiency in the performance of
duty."

The court, taking into account the flawless record of the accused and the
poor state of the charts for the Batangas area, reduced the charge. It found
Nimitz guilty, but only of "neglect of duty," and sentenced him "to be publicly
reprimanded by the Commander-in-Chief, U.S. Naval Forces in Philippine
waters." Rear Admiral J. N. Hemphill, the commander in chief, wrote at the
end of the proceedings: "The promulgation of these findings and sentence will
be regarded as constituting in itself a public reprimand, as required by the
sentence of the court."

Except for inconvenience and embarrassment, the court-martial brought

Nimitz only good luck, and did no harm at all to his career. He had of course been relieved of command of the *Decatur* and, instead of waiting for the White Fleet to reach Philippine waters, he was on his way home two weeks after sentencing. Eighteen months later, he was promoted from ensign to lieutenant, having skipped the rank of lieutenant, junior grade.

For Ensign Nimitz the voyage home was a lark. He sailed in the gunboat *Ranger*, a venerable craft that had been sent out for use as a training ship by the Philippine Nautical School. The Filipinos had found her too expensive to maintain, and now Ensigns Nimitz, Glenn Owen Carter, John H. Newton, and Alexander Wadsworth, all of the Naval Academy class of 1905, were assigned as watch officers to take her back to the United States. There she was to be turned over to the Massachusetts State Nautical School.

Happily for the four ensigns, there were no guns on board the *Ranger*, so no battle drills could be held. Under steam the old gunboat puffed along at 9 knots, but whenever the wind was favorable, they made sail, which increased their speed to 10 or 10½ knots. Recalled "Go" Carter several years later:

> Nimitz, Newton, Wadsworth and I had a really glorious trip, except for the fact that we made the trip in half the time we would like to have taken. Three months and a week from Manila to Boston was good time for that relic, but still left a little time for us to spend ashore at Singapore, Colombo, Perim, Port Said, Naples, Villefranche (which we will never forget), Gibraltar, Madeira, and Bermuda.

The *Ranger* reached Boston in early December. Nimitz visited his family, and on January 25, 1909, reported for duty under instruction in the First Submarine Flotilla. At that time the Great White Fleet, following nearly the same route as the *Ranger* had taken, was still in the Mediterranean.

Chester was disappointed to be assigned to submarines, which at that time were considered hardship duty without extra pay. "In those days," said Nimitz, "they were a cross between a Jules Verne fantasy and a humpbacked whale." What Chester had requested was more duty on battleships, then the glamour vessels of the fleet, under the impression that this was what he needed to further his career. In fact, of course, in a capital ship senior officers got all the interesting and responsible jobs, and ensigns had to settle for routine duties. Moreover, although contemporary naval leaders did not even suspect it, the heyday of the battleship was approaching an end, whereas submarines were yet to reveal their extraordinary capacity as offensive weapons.

Nimitz swallowed his disappointment and threw himself wholeheartedly into his new assignment, thereby learning the important lesson that most projects, however unprepossessing, repay devotion and hard work with interesting and instructive experiences. Having commanded successively the submarines *Plunger, Snapper,* and *Narwhal,* he began to campaign for the removal of gasoline engines from submarines because of their noxious fumes and tendency to explode. He advocated their replacement with the new diesel engine and made himself a recognized authority on diesels.

# CHAPTER 5

# CONFRONTATION IN THE CORAL SEA

ADMIRAL NIMITZ shortly after his arrival at Pearl Harbor inspected the 14th Naval District's Combat Intelligence Unit. He was conducted down some cellar steps and through a vaultlike steel door into a long, narrow, windowless basement under the district administration building. Here he was shown around by the officer in charge, Lieutenant Commander Joseph J. Rochefort. There was not much to see except rows of desks and filing cabinets, at which sailors and officers were working, and a line of clattering International Business Machine Corporation tabulators, walled off behind a partition because of the noise they made.

Nimitz learned that this local unit, called Station Hypo, was a branch of Op-20-G, the Communication Security Section of the Office of Naval Communications in Washington. There was another branch, Station Cast,* on Corregidor Island in Manila Bay, and the British maintained a cooperating station at Singapore. Op-20-G and its branches, Nimitz was told, were mainly concerned with enemy radio communications—analyzing traffic, locating and tracking transmitters, and decoding the messages through cryptanalysis.

Theoretically, the traffic analysts, by studying the volume and destination of Japanese radio messages, were able to forecast the direction and weight of impending enemy thrusts. Japanese transmitters, ashore and afloat, attempted to conceal their identity by frequently changing their number-letter call signs, but the analysts soon identified them again by location, direction of movement or, most often, by the radio operator's touch on the key, his "fist," which to an expert was as distinctive and recognizable as a human voice.

In the Pacific area the system included subsidiary receiving stations with high-frequency direction-finders. These stations were situated in a great arc from Dutch Harbor in the Aleutians, through Hawaii, to the Philippines. They listened continuously to enemy transmissions, pinpointed the transmitters, and reported directly to Station Hypo.

Station Hypo's specialty in the field of cryptanalysis was the Japanese Navy's operational code, which the Americans called JN25.† The clattering IBM tabulators were even then tackling the day's transmissions. In Washing-

---

* "Hypo" and "Cast" were at that time the English phonetic words for H (here meaning Hawaii) and C (for Corregidor).

† Not to be confused with the widely publicized "Purple Code," the Japanese diplomatic cipher, which the U.S. Army's Signal Intelligence Service had broken in September 1940, or with "Ultra," the cipher based on the German Enigma machine, which the British reproduced.

ton, on Corregidor, and at Singapore, other such machines were unraveling the same messages, and all four stations continually pooled their findings.

Admiral Nimitz showed polite interest, asked a few questions, and departed. He was not impressed. If the radio intelligence units could do what they were set up to do and do it efficiently, why had they not warned of the impending attack on Pearl Harbor?

Code JN25 consisted of roughly 45,000 five-digit groups (such as 53875, 45089, 37158), most of which represented words or phrases. As a means of frustrating cryptanalysis, a book of 50,000 random five-digit groups was issued to Japanese communicators. The sender added a series of these random groups to the code groups of his message. A special five-digit group included in the message told the receiver page, column, and line in the random-group book where the sender had selected his first group to begin adding. To find the meaning, the receiver located the same numbers in his own random-group book, subtracted them, and looked up the resulting groups in the decode book. To further foil cryptanalysis, the Japanese from time to time issued new random-group books. Less frequently they scrambled their code groups—just as one might redistribute the telephone numbers in a telephone book.

Such measures were supposed to render the JN code invulnerable. They did nothing of the sort, partly because of the heavy traffic in the code—up to 1,000 messages a day—and especially because Op-20-G, and Station Hypo in particular, enjoyed the services of some of the world's most skilled cryptanalysts. In such heavy traffic, the same random and code groups were bound to come together time and time again. When this happened often enough, it became possible by a mathematical process to "strip the additives" and disclose the basic code groups, which were then dealt with by standard cryptographic methods. Shortly before the Pearl Harbor attack, the Japanese had issued a new random-group book. Before the American cryptanalysts could again come to grips with the basic JN code, the additive groups had to be cleared away, a process carried out for the most part by the IBM tabulators.

Only a fraction of the 45,000 meanings that the JN code groups represented was ever brought to light by cryptanalysis. The code-breakers, after weeks of attacking a new version of the code, were lucky to recover 15 per cent of any message text. This much, however, when combined with the results of traffic analysis and related to previously recorded message fragments, was usually enough to yield useful information. The IBM tabulators, which stored on cards quantities of data from the radio dispatches, did most of the work of connecting new messages with old ones. Equally important in this process was the fantastic memory of Commander Rochefort, who could recall details of enemy messages filed weeks earlier.

The partially recovered messages were forwarded to the Chief of Naval Operations and to Pacific Fleet headquarters, and also of course to Op-20-G and to the remaining units, which, to escape the advancing Japanese, shifted from Corregidor to Melbourne, Australia, and from Singapore to Colombo,

Ceylon. At CinCPac headquarters the receiving agent was Commander Layton, the fleet intelligence officer held over from Admiral Kimmel's staff. Layton brought the more important decrypted messages promptly to Admiral Nimitz or to his chief of staff, Admiral Draemel. The rest he made use of in preparing his intelligence briefings, which opened Nimitz's daily morning conferences. In addition to this passage of messages, Layton and Rochefort communicated with each other several times a day by scrambler telephone. They had been friends since 1929 when the Navy sent them both to Japan to study the language and Japanese customs, and their paths had crossed many times since.

Layton had early impressed Nimitz with his detailed knowledge of the location and movements of Japanese naval forces. He had also demonstrated a remarkable understanding of Japanese psychology—about which Nimitz himself was knowledgeable as a result of his tours of duty in the Far East. The admiral told Layton, when the latter joined his staff, that he expected him henceforth to assume the role of Admiral Osami Nagano, Chief of Japan's Naval General Staff, or "whoever else is calling the shots." In that capacity Layton was, insofar as possible, to think like a Japanese, and, as such, keep Nimitz informed of the Japanese Navy's strategic concepts, plans, and operations.

When Layton had gained the admiral's confidence still more by accurately predicting enemy moves, he undertook to explain to him why Station Hypo had not been able to give advance warning of the Pearl Harbor raid. The failure, it appeared, was a result less of American inefficiency than of Japanese caution. No mention of the plan was passed by radio in any code that the Americans were then breaking. Several weeks preceding the attack, the Japanese carrier force had simply disappeared from the radio traffic pattern, all its ships maintaining the most rigid radio silence.

Layton's intelligence briefing of April 9, 1942, contained little but bad news. Corregidor remained in American hands, but Bataan had just fallen to the enemy. The Japanese carrier force was still operating in the Indian Ocean. After raiding the base at Colombo, Ceylon, it had sunk two British cruisers at sea. Signs pointed to a Japanese offensive against eastern New Guinea in the latter part of April.

That last item Admiral Nimitz found particularly disturbing. He knew it had been obtained through radio intelligence, which he had by then come to trust. Task Force 16, under the command of Admiral Halsey in the *Enterprise*, was off on a dangerous mission—nothing less than a raid on Tokyo. Even if the *Enterprise* survived the raid, she would not be able to get to the New Guinea area by the end of the month.

The scheme for raiding Tokyo, which CinCPac had shelved the preceding February, had been picked up by the Army Air Forces, and the airmen believed they had worked out a nearly foolproof plan. On March 19, an emissary from the Joint Chiefs of Staff, Captain Donald B. Duncan, had arrived at Pearl Harbor to lay the plan before Nimitz.

One of the main objections to raiding Tokyo was that carrier bombers had a relatively short range. To launch such an attack, the carriers would have to approach suicidally close to Japan's numerous airfields. The Army proposed substituting B-25s, long-range medium bombers. Lieutenant Colonel James H. Doolittle had trained 16 crews to take off from an airstrip the length of a carrier deck. The army bombers, to be sure, could not *land* on so short a runway. The plan was to transport them across the Pacific by carrier. At a point 500 miles east of Japan, they would take off, drop their bombs on Tokyo and other Japanese cities, and go on to friendly airfields in China. The new carrier *Hornet*, then en route from the Atlantic, would take on the B-25s at Alameda Air Station near San Francisco. Since the *Hornet*, with the army bombers lashed to her flight deck, would not be able to use her own planes for search and air patrol, another carrier force was needed to escort her to Japanese waters. Would CinCPac provide one?

Nimitz turned to Halsey. "Do you think it would work, Bill?"

"They'll need a lot of luck."

"Are you willing to take them out there?"

"Yes, I am."

"Good!" said Nimitz. "It's all yours."

Halsey's Task Force 16 departed Pearl Harbor on April 8 in order to rendezvous at sea with the *Hornet* and her surface escorts as they passed en route to Japan.

The warning about the impending new Japanese offensive must have disturbed Admiral King too, for he took the unprecedented step of communicating directly with Commander Rochefort at Station Hypo. The Japanese carrier force had raided Trincomalee, another base in Ceylon, and had sunk a British carrier, the *Hermes*. What, King wanted to know, did radio intercepts indicate about Japan's immediate and long-range plans?

Rochefort, after reviewing his sources of information and consulting with his staff, replied with a four-part estimate, which he sent to both CominCh and CinCPac: (1) The Japanese had concluded operations in the Indian Ocean, and their fleet was withdrawing to home bases; (2) they had no plans to attack Australia; (3) they would soon launch an operation to seize the eastern end of New Guinea; (4) they would follow this move with a much bigger operation in the Pacific, an operation involving most of the Combined Fleet.

Admiral Nimitz and his staff tentatively accepted the Rochefort estimate and based their own assumptions upon it. To control eastern New Guinea, they reasoned, the Japanese would have to seize the Australian base at Port Moresby on the Coral Sea, because bombers from there could reach not only all of the New Guinea bird tail but also the Japanese base at Rabaul.

As for the coming Pacific Ocean operations, Nimitz and his planners estimated that the enemy would attack the Aleutians, Pearl Harbor, or Midway. Whatever their ultimate objective, it seemed unlikely the Japanese would bypass Midway, the westernmost fortified U.S. outpost in the Central Pacific.

Nimitz recognized as a cardinal rule that he must not risk such losses in defending New Guinea that he would be helpless to counter the later Pacific Ocean offensive.

By mid-April the radio intelligence unit in Australia, Station Cast, was able to predict that a group of Japanese transports would soon enter the Coral Sea escorted by the light carrier *Shoho** and supported by a striking force that included two big carriers, veterans of the Pearl Harbor raid, probably the *Shokaku* and the *Zuikaku*. When the Japanese began to refer to their coming attack as Operation MO, Admiral Nimitz was strengthened in his assumption that their main objective was Port Moresby. He soon had reason to believe also that they would first seize Tulagi, an islet north of Guadalcanal, for use as an early-warning seaplane base, and that their operations would begin May 3.

Admiral Nimitz and General MacArthur were deeply alarmed at the threat to Port Moresby. MacArthur was planning to develop it into a major base, both as a place from which to block a Japanese advance on Australia and as a jumping-off point for his promised return to the Philippines. The admiral and the general were agreed that the enemy must be stopped.

The means were slim. MacArthur had a couple of hundred army planes, but the pilots were not trained for over-water operations or for ship recognition. If the Japanese were to be thrust back, it would have to be by means of carrier planes. Recognizing this, Nimitz ordered Fletcher's *Yorktown* force, Task Force 17, then operating in the Coral Sea, to retire to Tongatabu for hurried upkeep and replenishment and to return to the Coral Sea ready for action before the end of April. He ordered Fitch's *Lexington* force, which was at Pearl Harbor, to head south and report to Fletcher on May 1. MacArthur's little fleet, the former ANZAC force, sent Fletcher a support group of one U.S. and two Australian cruisers and a pair of destroyers, commanded by Rear Admiral J. G. Crace, of the Royal Navy. All these additions were to be integrated into Task Force 17.

The Allied vessels were equipped with radar and with aircraft homing devices and those of the Japanese were not, but the *Shokaku* and the *Zuikaku* had the priceless advantage of having operated together for six months against a variety of targets, including the ill-fated carrier *Hermes*. On balance, the chances for an Allied victory did not seem favorable. The scribe of the CinCPac Command Summary probably reflected Admiral Nimitz's opinion when he wrote on April 18: "CinCPac will probably be unable to send enough force to be *sure* of stopping the Jap offensive."

Nimitz, who had from the first been dubious about the plan to raid Tokyo, was now seriously regretting the operation. In the face of the impending crisis, the Tokyo attack, a mere military gesture, had deprived CinCPac of his most skilled and aggressive commander and of two of his four available

---

\* Her name was at first mistakenly transliterated *Ryukaku* and was so spelled in all early Allied records and narratives. The correct transliteration was later provided by a Japanese prisoner of war.

carriers. There was, moreover, the distinct possibility that, in approaching close to Japan, Halsey, carriers, and all might be lost. Radio intercepts on April 17 (April 18 in Japan) indicated that Tokyo and other Japanese cities were being bombed. Since no mention was made of the origin of the bombers, it could be assumed that the *Enterprise* and the *Hornet* had not been discovered or attacked. Halsey was maintaining strict radio silence.

In the afternoon of April 24, in response to an earlier summons, Admiral Nimitz and members of his staff left Pearl Harbor by flying boat for San Francisco to confer with Admiral King. Their plane landed in San Francisco Bay early on the 25th. King and Nimitz and their parties were housed at the St. Francis Hotel in a lavish oak- and mahogany-paneled apartment occupying the top floor of the northeast wing. It was leased to Mrs. George A. Pope, who had turned it over to the Navy for the duration of the war. The meetings were held several blocks away in the main conference room of the 12th Naval District headquarters, which occupied the San Francisco Federal Building.

The first item taken up at the opening meeting concerned radio intelligence. Nimitz expressed the opinion that the Japanese were efficient at traffic analysis and direction-finding but that only the Americans were reading the enemy's secret radio messages. CinCPac and ComInCh agreed that every effort should be made to ensure that there be no leaks concerning this source of information, which was providing American forces with a priceless advantage over the Japanese.

Next taken up was personnel. Both King and Nimitz were concerned about Frank Jack Fletcher's possible lack of aggressiveness. Unless Halsey got to the Coral Sea in time, which was extremely unlikely, Fletcher would be the senior admiral present and the responsibility for throwing back the assault on Port Moresby would be his. Nothing could be done at the moment, they concluded, to improve the outlook. But Fletcher's conduct of operations should be watched critically.

King explained and supported Secretary Knox's desire to bring youth into positions of command. Junior flag officers, he said, should be fed into the lower echelons of command at sea with opportunities to rise through demonstrated merit. Flag officers about to retire should not be employed.

Nimitz agreed in general with ComInCh and the Secretary, but he expressed a desire that the Bureau of Navigation make the assignments of officers to positions of high command. As former chief of the bureau, he knew that more dependable data on personnel was available in Washington than at Pearl Harbor. Perhaps also he realized that his own tendency to give a man another chance might not always be in the best interests of the nation. At any rate, having the reliefs and assignments made in Washington would save him much, sometimes painful, deliberation, not to say embarrassment.

CinCPac outlined his views concerning the employment of carrier forces, which he believed were destined to be the principal means of carrying the war to the Japanese. King, Nimitz, and the other officers present discussed the subject at length, with special attention to details of composition and problems of command. For the time being, with the *Wasp* in European waters and the *Saratoga* still undergoing repairs, the Japanese had a clear advantage in carrier strength. The immediate and critical problem was how to thwart the enemy's thrusts into the Coral Sea and then into the Pacific. By the middle of 1943, however, America's building program would begin to give the U.S. Navy a decided edge in carriers. When that time came, the Navy must be prepared to make the best possible use of its favorable margin.

On April 25, while the CominCh-CinCPac conference was getting under way, Halsey with the *Enterprise-Hornet* force steamed jubilantly into Pearl Harbor, his mission accomplished, his ships intact. Instead of the period of rest and relaxation he and his men had anticipated, he was allowed just five days' upkeep for his force, after which he was to hasten with it to the Coral Sea. It was unlikely that he could complete the 3,500-mile voyage in time to participate in the coming battle, but there was a chance the enemy might be behind schedule. In that event, Halsey was to join Fletcher and assume overall tactical command.

When Admiral Nimitz returned to Pearl Harbor on the 28th, he conferred with Halsey and confirmed decisions made in his absence. He ordered Admiral Pye, who on Nimitz's orders had brought his battleships out to Pearl Harbor, to take them back to the West Coast, where they would be out of the way and would not deplete the carriers' limited fuel supply. As soon as the situation in the Coral Sea area had been stabilized, all the American carriers and their escorts were to return to Pearl Harbor to meet the expected Japanese thrust in that sector. The naval forces were reminded of their standing orders to break silence as soon as their location was known to the enemy and report by radio to CinCPac so that General MacArthur's aircraft and Captain Ralph Christie's Brisbane-based submarines could be advised how best to lend support.

On April 30, Admiral Halsey departed Pearl Harbor with his two carriers, escorted by five cruisers and seven destroyers and accompanied by two oilers. On the same date, the *Yorktown* and *Lexington* forces, under radio silence, presumably made rendezvous in the Coral Sea, where it was already May 1, east longitude date. Radio-traffic analysis revealed that Japanese naval forces were on the move in the Southwest Pacific and that at least one enemy group was advancing into the Solomons. Apprised of the enemy's approach, the small Australian garrison at Tulagi began hastily to clear out.

Admiral Nimitz at his morning conference on the 30th discussed new evidence of the coming enemy operation in the Pacific and grimly remarked that it might be a good thing if the Japanese staged a small raid on Oahu. Then, perhaps, Washington might find a way to strengthen the meager force of sixteen B-17s available to protect Pearl Harbor. Nimitz was inclined to believe, however, that the Japanese objective in the forthcoming Pacific Ocean operation would not be Pearl Harbor but Midway. On May 1, despite the impending battle in the Coral Sea area, he flew the 1,135 miles out to lonely Midway Atoll for a personal inspection of its defenses. He was back at Pearl on the 3rd.

During his absence, word had come from MacArthur's headquarters at Brisbane that one of his Australia-based search planes had sighted transports debarking troops at Tulagi, with several Japanese warships nearby. The next morning sensitive Allied radio receivers picked up a call for help from the newly installed Japanese base commander at Tulagi. He was under air attack.

Nimitz assumed that the attacking planes had come from one or both of Fletcher's carriers. This assumption was confirmed toward noon the following day by Fletcher himself. Having by his raid revealed his presence and approximate location to the enemy, he broke radio silence to report to CinCPac. Leaving the *Lexington* force behind to refuel, he had steamed north at high speed in the *Yorktown* and sent his planes winging across the mountains of Guadalcanal for a day-long series of attacks on Tulagi in the sound beyond. He then hastened back south to rejoin the *Lexington*.

"Fitch delayed by fueling," Fletcher signaled. "All joined up now." He listed "positive enemy losses: sunk 2 destroyers, 4 tugs or gunboats, 1 cargo ship. Beached and sunk: 1 light cruiser. Very badly damaged, possibly sunk: 1 9,000-ton seaplane tender, 1 large tender. Badly damaged: 1 large cruiser, 1 transport. Shot down: 5 seaplanes." He concluded: "Some fun!"

The Americans thus had opened the battle with a first blow, and apparently a hard one. From Pearl Harbor, Admiral Nimitz jubilantly radioed Fletcher: "Congratulations and well done to you and your force. Hope you can exploit your success with augmented force."

Subsequent air reconnaissance and radio intelligence revealed that Fletcher's claims were grossly exaggerated, reflecting the extreme difficulty aviators had in correctly assessing their results in the heat of battle. In fact, only a few minor naval craft had been sunk, though one Japanese destroyer, damaged and beached, later slid off into deep water and went down. Admiral Nimitz, in his final endorsement of Fletcher's action, called the Tulagi operation "certainly disappointing in terms of ammunition expended to results obtained" and emphasized "the necessity for target practice at every opportunity."

In Operations Plot at CinCPac headquarters, staff officers entered Fletcher's position and course on their plotting board. They then sat back and awaited further intelligence, adapting themselves to the east longitude date and the zone-minus-11 time of the Coral Sea area. The CinCPac plotting board at that time consisted of a chart of the Solomons-Coral Sea-Bismarcks area fastened on a piece of plywood laid across a pair of sawhorses. Over the chart was placed a large sheet of tracing paper, and on this the plotting officers sketched in blue pencil the positions and movements of U.S. ships and forces. Japanese ships, forces, movements, reported sightings, and estimated positions they marked in orange. Remarks, notes, guide lines, and such were in ordinary pencil. Fresh tracing-paper overlays were laid out on the chart each midnight, Pearl Harbor time. Admiral Nimitz, though kept fully posted in his office, came occasionally to Operations Plot in order better to visualize the situation.

On May 5 MacArthur's headquarters began transmitting confusing information. His search planes were reporting enemy ships of every type south of the Solomons. At least some of these sightings were evidently phantoms, resulting from the inexperience of the aviators and an overcast that shrouded part of the Coral Sea. Nevertheless Brisbane relayed the reports to Fletcher, on the chance that they might give his own planes something to look for. In the late afternoon CinCPac passed to Task Force 17 the day's findings from radio intelligence. In response to Fletcher's raid on Tulagi, the Japanese striking force, including the carriers *Shokaku* and *Zuikaku* and two heavy cruisers, had left the Rabaul area, passed northeast of Bougainville, and had evidently swung southward around the eastern end of the Solomons and entered the Coral Sea. These ships were obviously hunting for Task Force 17. The force that first located the other might well get the jump on its opponent.

Night fell on the 5th without any clear contacts. At 10:30 the next morning B-17s from Australia, staging through Port Moresby, found the covering group that was advancing to escort the Japanese invasion convoy. The covering group, coming down on a southwesterly course from the Solomons, included the 12,000-ton carrier *Shoho*, which the B-17s attacked without making any hits. Their bombs fell so wide of the mark, in fact, that the *Shoho* was able to launch agile Zero fighters, which chased the bombers away. At 1:00 p.m. some of MacArthur's planes sighted the Port Moresby invasion convoy off New Britain. It was apparent that the covering and invasion groups were heading to round the tip of New Guinea via Jomard Passage, an opening in the Louisiade Archipelago.

From the Allied point of view, the most alarming sighting of May 6 was made by a Japanese search plane out of Rabaul, which at 11:00 a.m. located Task Force 17 refueling some 350 miles south of the central Solomons. Several Allied radio stations picked up the report as it was broadcast by the Rabaul transmitter. An early attack on Task Force 17 could now be expected from the *Shokaku* and the *Zuikaku*, which Allied planes had not yet located. At CinCPac headquarters, tension mounted by the hour, but no indication reached Pearl Harbor that Fletcher had come under attack. What Nimitz and his staff did not know was that the big Japanese carriers had failed to pick up the contact report, either directly from the search plane or as it was relayed from Rabaul. The Japanese thus missed an exceptional opportunity to beat the Americans to the punch.

The watch at Pearl Harbor greeted the coming of night with considerable relief, although for them, as for all their fellow Americans and for the people of the Philippines, May 6 had been a day of mourning. Lieutenant General Jonathan M. Wainwright, whom General MacArthur had left in command on Corregidor, had been obliged at last to surrender his beleaguered, half-starved army, thereby relinquishing the whole Philippine archipelago to the Japanese. The naval radio station on Oahu intercepted Wainwright's farewell message to President Roosevelt: "...With profound regret and with continued pride in my gallant troops, I go to meet the Japanese commander. Good-bye, Mr. President."

Early on May 7 a Japanese search plane over the Coral Sea made a new

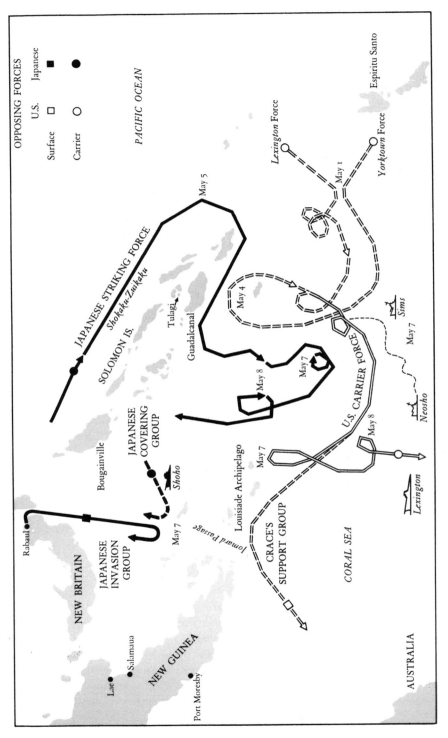

*The Battle of the Coral Sea, May 4–8, 1942*
TRACKS APPROXIMATE

contact, which it reported by voice radio. The report was expressed in pre-scribed Japanese military form: "TE-TE-TE (for *teki*, meaning 'enemy'); BO-BO-BO (*bogan*, 'carrier'); JUN-JUN-JUN (*junyokan*, 'cruiser')," followed by the bearing and distance of the ships from Rabaul. As the result of a curious skip-distance phenomenon, this supposedly short-range transmission was picked up by some of the 14th Naval District combat intelligence unit intercept stations. Rochefort relayed the report via the secure "hot line" to Layton, who promptly informed Admirals Nimitz and Draemel, Captain McMorris, the war plans officer, and the Operations Plot watch officer, who began to enter the contact on the plot.

CinCPac headquarters was aquiver with excitement and apprehension. If the Japanese had again sighted Fletcher's ships, it was unlikely that the latter would once more escape being attacked. The location reported by the Japanese worked out to be latitude 16° S, longitude 158° E—an unlikely position for Task Force 17, which U.S. estimates placed at least 250 miles to the north-west.

Somebody noticed that the reported position coincided with Point Rye, a fueling rendezvous through which the oiler *Neosho*, accompanied by the de-stroyer *Sims*, was scheduled to pass that morning at sunrise. The *Neosho*, having fueled the American force, was following a set cruising pattern in order to be available for more fueling, as needed. It dawned on the CinCPac officers that the "carrier" and the "cruiser" reported by the Japanese pilot were in fact the oiler and her escort. This surmise was confirmed a little after 9:00 a.m. when the *Neosho* and the *Sims* flashed distress signals. Three successive at-tacks by high-level bombers scored no hits on either ship, but a strike at noon by 36 dive-bombers, attacking simultaneously, sank the *Sims* and left the *Neosho* a barely floating hulk.

At Pearl Harbor concern for the oiler and the destroyer and their crews was mingled with elation. The attacking planes, so far from any enemy base, could have come only from carriers, evidently the *Shokaku* and the *Zuikaku*. The *Neosho* and the *Sims* had unwittingly and unwillingly drawn off a strike that was obviously intended for the American carrier force.

On the plot at CinCPac headquarters, it became clear that, from the Allied point of view, a dream setup was in the making. MacArthur's head-quarters reported that one of its planes had sighted Japanese forces approach-ing Jomard Passage from the north. These were of course the covering and invasion groups, including the light carrier *Shoho*. Japanese planes out of Rabaul reported the American carriers coming up from the south, steadily closing the range. The *Shokaku* and the *Zuikaku*, whose mission it was to support their invasion forces by attacking Fletcher's carriers, were off to the east, busily bombing the *Neosho* and the *Sims*. Thus Fletcher, unmolested, was free to attack the enemy invasion forces.

At CinCPac headquarters hours passed without any more information. In the early afternoon Admiral Nimitz betrayed his nervousness in a radio dispatch to Admiral King: "From reports of enemy forces in the Louisiade area, believe Fletcher and Fitch should have been able to strike excellent objectives today but have not heard from them."

In fact, Fletcher had that morning located the enemy force to the north and launched an attack against it. Before noon he knew that his planes had sunk a carrier, for Lieutenant Commander Robert Dixon, one of his squadron leaders, had radioed back from the scene of action: "Scratch one flattop! Dixon to carrier. Scratch one flattop!"

Dixon's voice transmission was not picked up by any Allied intercept stations. CinCPac had to wait until the planes of Task Force 17 had returned to their carriers, the aviators had been debriefed, and their reports had been evaluated before Fletcher made his report. This was correct and prudent procedure, but for Nimitz and his staff it meant a long, nerve-racking wait.

Fletcher reported the *Shoho* sunk and an enemy light cruiser sent down, but the cruiser-sinking report turned out to be incorrect—another example of pilot error. The elimination of the light carrier was good news, indeed, but it scarcely relieved the tension at CinCPac. The big carriers *Shokaku* and *Zuikaku* were still somewhere in the Coral Sea, and the commander of the Japanese striking force would surely try to retrieve his blunder of the morning by attacking Task Force 17.

Meanwhile, Allied interceptor stations were picking up reports from Japanese aircraft that they had sunk a battleship and a cruiser and had torpedoed another cruiser. Since there were no battleships in the Coral Sea, and Fletcher's force was intact at the time of his report, these interceptions were received by CinCPac with puzzlement. The explanation became clear at Pearl Harbor several days later. Early on the 7th Fletcher had detached Admiral Crace's support group and sent it forward so that it would be ready to block Jomard Passage, should the American carriers be sunk or disabled. These ships, three cruisers and three destroyers, were attacked from the air four times on May 7, once by U.S. B-17s whose crews mistook them for enemy. It was this group of vessels that Japanese pilots reported having hit, mistaking cruisers for battleships and destroyers for cruisers. In fact, Crace's ships, by expert use of maneuver and antiaircraft fire, escaped, ultimately to Australia, having suffered only minor damage, caused by strafing.

Radio intercepts at the end of the day on the 7th seemed to indicate that Japanese search planes had again located Task Force 17, but there was no evidence that the carriers on either side had come under attack. During the night, U.S. radio intelligence made an all-out effort to help Fletcher by locating the enemy. The Japanese were transmitting a great deal, but their carriers were apparently in an area of squally weather and such heavy static that no dependable radio-direction-finder fixes could be established. Evidently Fletcher would have to find them himself by sending out a dawn search.

Task Force 17 having been sighted by Japanese land-based aircraft and also, it appeared, by carrier planes, it was unlikely that another day could go by without a battle between the opposing carrier forces. The early daylight hours of May 8 passed, however, without any news from the Coral Sea reaching Pearl Harbor. At last, a little after 10:00 a.m., CinCPac received an intercepted message from Fletcher to General MacArthur giving the location of both Task Force 17 and the enemy striking force. From this communication CinCPac staff drew the following inferences: (1) that Task Force 17 search planes had sighted and reported the enemy force; (2) that enemy search planes had sighted Task Force 17 and Fletcher knew they had done so; otherwise he would probably not have broken radio silence; (3) that since the forces were only 175 miles apart, each must have launched aircraft against the other, and history's first battle between carrier forces was imminent; and (4) that Fletcher, by his message, was suggesting that MacArthur send out land-based planes to join in the attack on the Japanese striking force. This last was a forlorn hope; the army bombers were making another fruitless attack on the Port Moresby invasion force, which was retreating toward Rabaul.

CinCPac staff sweated out two more hours. Then just before noon came Fletcher's preliminary report: "First enemy attack completed. No vital damage our force." So far so good. What about the enemy? Half an hour later Nimitz was handed another intercepted message from Fletcher to MacArthur: "Task Force 17 damaged one enemy carrier: two 1,000-pound bomb hits, two torpedo hits. Recommend your bombers attack."

"What is position damaged target?" asked Commander in Chief, Southwest Pacific. Fletcher replied with longitude and latitude, but still got no help from army air. The army bombers were busy keeping the Japanese invasion force in full retreat, and incidentally demonstrating that high-level bombing rarely hits moving targets.

In a series of radio messages sent to CinCPac in the early afternoon, Commander, Task Force 17, reported that the *Yorktown* had been hit by one bomb, which had penetrated several decks, and the *Lexington* had been struck by two torpedoes and by a couple of bombs, which had done minor damage. In a separate dispatch he noted: "At least four and probably more hits made on enemy carrier. At least three 1,000-pound bomb hits. Burning badly." A little later he reported: "*Yorktown* can now make 30 knots. I propose retire tonight to fill *Yorktown* complement planes as far as possible from *Lexington* and send that ship to Pearl."

The CinCPac staff officers were smiling with relief. The news from the Coral Sea could have been better, but it could have been much worse. The damaged Japanese carrier, identified as the *Shokaku*, was reported by U.S. aviators as "settling fast." Nimitz radioed to Fletcher, with information copy to King: "Congratulations on your glorious accomplishment of the last two days. Your aggressive actions have the admiration of the entire Pacific Fleet. Well done to you, your officers, and men. You have filled our hearts with pride and have maintained the highest traditions of the Navy." The CinCPac Command Summary opened the evening's entry on a cautiously cheerful note:

This is a red-letter day for our forces operating in the Coral Sea area. As a result of the exchanges between carriers in the past 36 hours we have sunk the RYUKAKU [i.e., the *Shoho*] and badly damaged the SHOKAKU, while they have badly damaged the LEXINGTON and slightly damaged the YORKTOWN. . . . At the end of the daylight period the YORKTOWN and the LEXINGTON were retiring to the south. . . .

Early in the evening the euphoria at Pearl Harbor was dampened by another intercepted message from Fletcher to MacArthur: "*Lexington* condition much worse. Request all possible air coverage." This was followed by location, course, and speed of Task Force 17, which was making 20 knots "but may have to slow." This was surprising news. CinCPac staff had concluded correctly that the *Lexington* had been made safe, brought to an even keel, and enabled to resume flight operations. That she was "much worse" implied some oversight or failure in damage control. In mid-evening (still afternoon in the Coral Sea), Admiral Nimitz and his staff were appalled to learn that the carrier had been abandoned and scuttled. As they learned later, gasoline vapor from ruptured fuel lines had exploded deep within the *Lexington*'s hull, setting off unquenchable fires and a series of explosions of increasing violence. When she had been abandoned, Fletcher ordered a destroyer to send her down with torpedoes.

At CinCPac headquarters the good cheer of the afternoon was replaced by gloom. Admiral Nimitz was shocked and subdued. "The *Lexington* could have been saved," he murmured. Then, noting the long faces around him, he continued: "Remember this, we don't know anything about the enemy—how badly he's hurt. You can bet your boots he's hurt, too. His situation is no bed of roses either."

It turned out that the Japanese were not hurting as badly as reports and estimates had implied. Station Hypo, in its May 9 morning summary of Japanese communications, revealed that the *Shokaku* had not sunk, after all. She had in fact received no torpedo hits, had been only moderately damaged by three bombs, was proceeding under her own power, and was transferring planes to the *Zuikaku*. The Japanese, also overestimating their successes, claimed to have sunk both the *Yorktown* and the *Lexington*.

It was becoming clear that the Japanese had won a tactical victory. Their loss of the converted 12,000-ton *Shoho* and a few small vessels sunk off Tulagi was a small price to pay for the sinking of the *Neosho*, the *Sims*, and the 33,000-ton *Lexington*. For the United States, however, the Battle of the Coral Sea was definitely a strategic victory: the main Japanese objective, the capture of Port Moresby, had been thwarted. For the first time in World War II, a Japanese advance had been turned back.

Admiral Nimitz considered ordering Fletcher not to retire but to remain in the Coral Sea. Halsey, who was fast approaching the area, could add the *Yorktown* and her escorts to his two-carrier Task Force 16 and seek out the enemy. He reconsidered, however, and decided not to do so because of the vulnerability of the damaged *Yorktown*. With an all-out enemy attack impending in the Central Pacific, he could not afford to risk a carrier. The enemy, in his coming operation, might even be able to employ his striking force intact, for Japanese radio reported the *Shokaku* making 16 knots and expected in Japan on May 17. Nimitz ordered his submarines to attempt a shot at the crippled carrier. He also radioed the Puget Sound Navy Yard to expedite repairs on the *Saratoga*, concluding, "Services urgently required."

On May 10 the Japanese, in a face-saving gesture, sent a force out from Truk to occupy the phosphate islands of Ocean and Nauru. When he heard this, CinCPac ordered Halsey to steam within 500 miles of the Eastern Solomons so that Japanese search planes out of Tulagi would be sure to see and report the presence of the *Hornet* and the *Enterprise*. The Japanese, as Nimitz expected, on discovering that there were two newly arrived American carriers in the South Pacific, hastily recalled the Ocean-Nauru occupation force. Nimitz had another reason for having Halsey display his task force to the enemy: the Japanese would suppose that all of CinCPac's available carriers were in the South. Acting on this assumption, the enemy might be expected to retain forces in that area and also to be less wary in his forthcoming attack in the Pacific.

Admiral Nimitz, his earlier doubts erased, expressed the opinion that Rear Admiral Fletcher had "utilized with consummate skill the information supplied him, and by these engagements in the Coral Sea between the 4th and 8th of May won a victory with decisive and far-reaching consequences for the Allied cause." To Admiral King he recommended that Fletcher be promoted to the rank of vice admiral and awarded the Distinguished Service Medal.

King, less favorably impressed than Nimitz with Fletcher's performance, radioed back: "I must express my feeling that destroyers might have been used in night attacks on the enemy." Nimitz pointed out that Fletcher had had barely enough destroyers for screening duty, that, lacking radar, they had little chance of finding fast carriers in the darkness, that the difficulty of fueling at night did not permit high-speed night operations, and that, had the destroyers done distant night cruising, they would not have been able to get back to their own force by dawn. King nevertheless refused either to promote Fletcher or to award him the medal, at least until the battle had been more thoroughly studied.

Nimitz, in his effort to keep the enemy guessing, released news of the Coral Sea battle in only the most general terms. He provided few details and concealed the loss of the *Lexington* until after the Battle of Midway. The Allied peoples, however, sensed that the battle, by thwarting an aggressive Japanese move, had vastly improved their military position in the Pacific. The action in the Coral Sea to a large degree offset the crushing news of the surrender of Corregidor.

# CHAPTER 6

# PREPARING TO
# DEFEND MIDWAY

ADMIRAL NIMITZ'S VISIT to Midway Atoll in early May 1942 was the result of a hunch based on a study of the map. If the Japanese were about to launch an offensive in the Pacific Ocean, as Commander Rochefort was predicting, they were going to have either to seize or bypass the armed U.S. outpost of Midway, which stood squarely in their way. And, thus far, the Japanese juggernaut had shown no tendency to bypass strong points. Busy as he was, the commander in chief decided that he had better fly out and have a look at the atoll's defenses.

Nimitz and members of his staff spent May 2 inspecting thoroughly the fortifications of the atoll's two islets, Eastern and Sand. The admiral crawled into gun pits, let himself down into underground command posts, examined the hangars, questioned the marine defenders, and observed the operations of the communication facilities, especially the priceless cable connection with Honolulu. By means of this cable, a segment of the old transpacific cable system, Midway and Pearl Harbor could communicate in plain English without having to worry about static or enemy interception and traffic analysis.

Nimitz liked what he saw, and was particularly pleased with the obviously close liaison between Commander Cyril T. Simard, the atoll commander, and Lieutenant Colonel Harold Shannon, USMC, commander of the ground forces. At the end of the day he asked them what they would need if they had to defend Midway against a powerful attack from the sea. Shannon, who had already given the problem much thought, reeled off a list.

"If I get you all these things you say you need, then can you hold Midway against a major amphibious assault?"

"Yes, sir," replied Shannon.

Nimitz smiled and appeared to relax. He asked Shannon to put his list in writing and to add to it any other supplies and reinforcements that he or Simard thought would ensure the defense of the atoll. The next morning he and his staff boarded his PBY-5A and flew back to Pearl Harbor. In his usual quiet way he had thoroughly alerted the defenders of the atoll and at the same time instilled confidence in them.

During the next few days, Admiral Nimitz was deeply immersed in the progress of the Battle of the Coral Sea and in advising Admiral Ghormley and his staff on plans for setting up the new South Pacific command. By the second week of May, radio traffic analysis revealed that Japanese ships were assembling in great numbers in home waters and in the Marianas. Rochefort and his assistants concluded that the Japanese objective was, indeed, the capture of Midway.

This estimate Nimitz tentatively accepted, but he could not disregard conclusions reached elsewhere. The Army Air Force, for example, was expecting a raid on San Francisco and for that reason would not release to Admiral Nimitz all the bombers he felt he needed. General MacArthur was of the opinion that the Japanese would resume their drive on the New Guinea-Solomons area. British army planners were arguing, contrary to all evidence, that Japan's next move would again be into the Indian Ocean.

When the Japanese began calling their forthcoming attack Operation MI, everyone recalled that they had used the designator Operation MO for their aborted descent on Port Moresby. For Commander Rochefort the clincher was repeated references to AF, which he knew to be the Japanese code-designator for Midway. Station Hypo had long since noticed that the Japanese identified American positions in the mid-Pacific by code groups of two or three letters beginning with A. They had identified the place they raided on December 7, 1941, as AH. Early in 1942, flying boats from the Marshalls, en route to drop more bombs on Pearl Harbor, had refueled from submarines at French Frigate Shoals, identified as AG. These bombers had been warned to evade air searches from AF, which could only have been nearby Midway.

When this evidence failed to convince all parties, Commanders Layton and Rochefort dreamed up a scheme to draw out the Japanese still further. Layton suggested to Admiral Nimitz that he order Midway to send out a fake radio message stating that their distillation plant had broken down, a serious matter since the atoll had no other source of fresh water. Nimitz agreed, and directions went out by way of the cable. Midway made the report in the clear; two days later Hypo decrypted a Japanese intercept reporting that AF had a shortage of fresh water.

By mid-May Admiral Nimitz, drawing most of his evidence from Hypo, had assumed for purposes of planning that the Japanese would attack Midway, and that this blow would be preceded by a secondary attack on the Aleutians. To tighten his control over available American forces, he first notified General Emmons of what he was about to do, then ordered a condition of "fleet-opposed invasion," whereby all forces in the Hawaiian area, except army ground forces, were brought directly under the control of CinCPac. Though the defense of Hawaii itself remained the general's responsibility, Nimitz removed the Seventh Air Force bombers from his control and sent most of them to Midway.

Emmons, deeply disturbed, forwarded to Nimitz, with an approving endorsement, a critique prepared by army intelligence. CinCPac's planning, the critique pointed out, was based on an estimate of the enemy's probable intentions, but it was more prudent to plan on the basis of everything the enemy was capable of doing, and the Japanese were definitely capable of attacking Oahu. At this elementary lesson in intelligence procedures, some of the CinCPac staff exploded with indignation, but Nimitz took the prod good humoredly. It was, he said, a well-meant and useful warning and he proposed to do something about it. What he did was assign to Captain James M. Steele, of his staff, the task of reassessing the findings of fleet intelligence. Specifically, Steele was to challenge every bit of information put forward by Layton and Rochefort and their assistants.

What Nimitz did not do, and had no intention of doing, was to diffuse his efforts and scatter his limited forces in an attempt to meet every sort of attack of which the Japanese were capable. His situation was desperate and he knew it. The enemy had ten carriers while the Americans could be sure of having only two, the *Enterprise* and the *Hornet*. Admiral Fitch had estimated that it would take 90 days to make the *Yorktown* battleworthy. The *Saratoga* had been repaired and was en route to San Diego to form a task force, but it was unlikely she could do this and reach mid-Pacific in time. The *Wasp*, Pacific-bound, was still on the far side of the Atlantic. Much nearer were three British carriers operating in the Indian Ocean. Nimitz requested the loan of one of these, but the Admiralty, still bemused with the notion that the next Japanese drive would be into those waters, replied that none could be spared. As for other major types, the Japanese had twenty-three cruisers, Nimitz had eight; they had eleven fast battleships, including the new *Yamato*, reputed to be the world's largest warship, Nimitz had six, none fast enough to operate with the carriers.

Admiral Nimitz lost no time in assembling and deploying such forces as he could collect. He ordered Admiral Halsey's Task Force 16 and Admiral Fletcher's Task Force 17 to return from the South Pacific to Pearl Harbor on the double. He detached Admiral Fitch from Task Force 17 and sent him to San Diego to expedite the assembling of the *Saratoga*'s task force and to take command of it. Nimitz briefly considered ordering out the battleships from San Francisco but discarded the notion as impractical. Rear Admiral Robert H. English, Commander, Submarines, Pacific Fleet, wanted to scatter his boats in search-and-attack missions, but Nimitz believed there was not time for such needle-in-haystack operations. He assigned search-and-attack missions to aircraft, which had wider-ranging eyes, and ordered the submarines, as they came in from patrol, to stations on the approaches to Midway, close enough to interfere seriously with any attempt at invasion.

Because Nimitz assessed the coming blow against the Aleutians as a diversionary raid, he was tempted to concentrate everything he had in the defense of Midway and leave the Aleutians to defend themselves. There was evidence, however, that the Japanese intended making landings on some of the western islands in the Aleutian chain. It would be hard to find positions of less strategic value, but the fact remained that they were U.S. territory. Should Nimitz let them go by default, he would face public condemnation out of all proportion to the worth of what had been lost. Concluding that he had no choice but to allot at least a token force to Aleutians defense, he formed a North Pacific Force, composed of cruisers and destroyers, and declared a state of fleet-opposed invasion in the Alaska sector, thereby placing all defense forces in the area under the naval commander, Admiral Theobald. Lacking carriers, Theobald could scarcely hope to hurl back an enemy carrier attack, but by placing his force in the right place at the right time, he had a reasonable chance of derailing any attempt the Japanese might make actually to invade the northern islands.

To Midway, Admiral Nimitz sent Catalina patrol planes newly arrived at Pearl Harbor from the United States. Thither also he dispatched the converted railroad ferry *Kittyhawk* loaded with eighteen dive-bombers, seven Wildcat fighter planes, five light tanks, a quantity of antiaircraft guns, and men to fly, drive, and fire them. To Simard and Shannon, in anticipation of, and as a spur to, heroic efforts on their part, he sent promotions to captain and colonel, together with new silver eagles for their collars.

Meanwhile, Op-20-G and Stations Cast and Hypo were ferreting out details of forthcoming enemy operations. Cast decrypted and translated a long message which revealed that the Japanese had canceled the plan to take Port Moresby by amphibious assault. Instead, they would drive overland, advancing by the trail from Buna, on the north coast of New Guinea, across the Owen Stanley mountain range, to Port Moresby. Japanese engineers were to widen the trail into a road that would be usable by trucks as well as by troops.

This information alarmed General MacArthur, who considered sending his own soldiers over the range to seize Buna before the Japanese could land there. To Admiral Nimitz it meant that practically every Japanese warship, including all the carriers, would be available for the attack on Midway.

During mid-May the Japanese sent an astonishing amount of top-secret information by long-range radio. From numerous intercepts Rochefort and Layton were able to piece together a remarkably complete intelligence estimate of the Japanese plan for the attack on Midway and the Aleutians, as ordered by Admiral Yamamoto, Commander in Chief of the Combined Fleet.

According to the estimate, the Combined Fleet was to be divided into (1) a Northern Force, (2) a First Carrier Striking Force, and (3) a Midway Invasion Force. The Northern Force included a Second Carrier Striking Force, which was to open the attack with a diversionary air raid on the American base at Dutch Harbor in the Aleutians. Transports of the Northern Force would then land troops on the western Aleutian islands of Attu, Kiska, and Adak. The First Carrier Striking Force, coming down from the northwest, would launch the main attack with an air raid on Midway. Meanwhile, the Midway Invasion Force, from Guam and Saipan, would be approaching Midway from the southwest. It would be met at sea and escorted the last 650 miles by the Japanese Second Fleet, including part of Battleship Division 3.*

* Battleship Divisions 1 and 2, comprising the First Fleet, would also be at sea, backing up the whole operation. Admiral Yamamoto was to be with this fleet in the superbattleship *Yamato*. Because Yamamoto had been for some time with the First Fleet in the Inland Sea, it had not been necessary for him to transmit orders to these divisions by means of long-range radio, which the Americans could intercept. Hence the Americans did not know about Yamamoto's and the First Fleet's active participation in the battle until several months later.

The Second Carrier Striking Force included the light carrier *Ryujo* and a new fleet carrier, whose name was indecipherable. The First Carrier Striking Force, coming against Midway, was the original Japanese carrier force, commanded by Vice Admiral Chuichi Nagumo, that had attacked Pearl Harbor and then raided as far as Ceylon. Rochefort was convinced that it would include only the veteran carriers *Akagi*, *Kaga*, *Hiryu*, and *Soryu*, with a screen of two battleships, three cruisers, and eleven destroyers. He believed, correctly as it turned out, that the *Shokaku* and the *Zuikaku*, newest and largest carriers assigned to this force, would not be able to take part in the forthcoming battle. Intercepts indicated that the *Shokaku* was still undergoing repair from the damages she had received in the Battle of the Coral Sea, and that the *Zuikaku* had not been able to replace the trained aviators she had lost in that battle. Rochefort estimated that the Midway-Aleutian attack would come early in June, but he could give no precise times, for these were concealed in a special date-time cipher.

Nimitz authorized Layton to send an outline of the Yamamoto plan, without revealing the source of the information, to certain interested radio addressees in a cipher specially reserved for flag officers. Among the recipients was Admiral Fitch, who was en route to San Diego in the cruiser *Chester* to take command of the *Saratoga* force. Aboard the *Chester* also were Fitch's staff and other survivors of the *Lexington*, including the lost carrier's skipper, Captain Frederick C. ("Ted") Sherman, Sherman's executive officer, Commander Morton Seligman, and Stanley Johnston, a war correspondent for the *Chicago Tribune*. Seligman violated security regulations by showing the CinCPac dispatch, with the Yamamoto plan, to Johnston, with whom he had become friendly.

On May 24, Admiral Nimitz, deciding that it was time he and his planners had a personal interview with Rochefort, set up an appointment with him at CinCPac headquarters for the next day. At the appointed hour the admiral and members of his staff were assembled, but Commander Rochefort failed to make his appearance. Those present exchanged glances. One did not ordinarily fail to keep appointments with the commander in chief.

At last, half an hour late, Rochefort, looking a bit rumpled and distraught, was admitted. The admiral eyed him icily. Rochefort apologized, explaining that he and his assistants had been up all night trying to break the date-time cipher. One of his assistants, Lieutenant Commander Wesley Wright, had succeeded to the extent that he could predict that enemy operations would begin against the Aleutians on June 3 and against Midway on June 4. There was little chance of more information becoming available through cryptanalysis before the attack, said Rochefort, because the Japanese had changed their operational code, as they did routinely, or at least issued a new set of additives. Weeks would pass before traffic in the new code built up to the point where the repetitions on which cryptanalysts relied for code-breaking occurred.

The exposure of Admiral Yamamoto's purported plan, instead of convincing the doubters at CinCPac headquarters, merely deepened their suspicions. Why, they asked, should practically the whole Combined Fleet be assigned to the capture of one tiny Central Pacific atoll and a couple of useless islands in the Aleutians? Might not the messages be fakes, deliberately planted to mislead the Americans? Such top-secret information is not usually transmitted by radio, even in the securest codes, for all the world to record, scrutinize, and perhaps cryptanalyze. Nimitz pointed out that the Japanese could be operating in strength in order to meet any American opposition. Their main objective might even be to draw out the inferior U.S. Pacific Fleet so that it could be destroyed. The transmission of the plans by radio could mean that Yamamoto was operating on so tight a schedule that he could get them distributed in time by no other means.

Admiral Nimitz, for want of anything better, decided to base his plans on the assumption that the intelligence estimates were correct. He ordered his plotting officers, drawing their colored lines in Operations Plot, regularly to check the supposed Yamamoto plan against all other sources of military intelligence. He gave the same order to Layton. He told the latter to make a careful review of all the data he had from radio intelligence and other sources of information and to derive as precise a forecast of the coming attack as possible.

A decoded message from the Japanese carrier command setting up a program of weather reports contained the words "we plan to make attacks from a generally northwest direction." For want of more precise information, Layton estimated that the carriers would move toward Midway on bearing 315 degrees, that is, from due northwest. He assumed that they would approach under cover of darkness, just as they had approached Pearl Harbor six months earlier. He believed that they would launch their bombers at first light and then race toward Midway to shorten their return flight. At first light also Midway would launch its search planes. Apprised now of the date of the attack, he looked up in the appropriate tables the hour and minute of sunrise on June 4, 1942. Knowing approximately the course and speed of the four-carrier striking force and the speed of the American search planes, he was able to forecast with fair accuracy when and where they would make contact. In his final report to Admiral Nimitz, Layton estimated that the Japanese would come in on bearing 315 degrees and that they would be sighted 175 miles from Midway at about 0600.

This was a good deal more precision than Nimitz had counted on, but he knew that Layton would not have gone into such detail unless he had very good support for each fact and figure that he reported. The admiral thanked him and ordered the information promptly passed on to Midway and also to the officers in Operations Plot.

To Nimitz is was clear that in Yamamoto's disposition of force, the crucial elements were Nagumo's four veteran carriers. Only they could provide the punch needed to knock out Midway's ground and air defenses, and only they could provide a concentration of air power great enough to cover the other components of his fleet. They along were essential to the attack. Therefore Nimitz and his staff laid plans to eliminate the Nagumo carriers.

At dawn on May 26 the tops of Halsey's task force appeared on the southwest horizon, and soon his twenty-one ships were filing into Pearl Harbor. That afternoon Admiral Halsey's barge came alongside the submarine-base wharf and the admiral entered CinCPac headquarters. When he appeared before Nimitz, the latter was shocked. Halsey forced a grin but that did not conceal his haggard appearance, for he had lost twenty pounds. He was suffering from dermatitis, a torturing skin eruption that had become increasingly severe and had deprived him of sleep by night and of peace of mind by day. The cause of the disease was undoubtedly nervous strain. Except for brief stays in port, Halsey had been on the bridge, pioneering carrier warfare, for six months' straight. He had hoped against hope to command the forthcoming operation, whatever it was, and Nimitz had expected him to do so, but the doctor had ordered him to the hospital. Halsey later called this forced relinquishment of command "the most grievous disappointment of my career."

He had dropped by, Halsey said, to pay his respects and to make an urgent recommendation—that the fleet command be turned over to his cruiser commander, Rear Admiral Raymond Spruance. That Nimitz could not promise, but he did agree to give Spruance temporary command of Halsey's Task Force 16, the *Enterprise-Hornet* force. Halsey then departed for the hospital.

For Nimitz, loss of his most aggressive and most combat-experienced carrier admiral on the eve of a crisis was a severe blow. Yet he must have suspected that the substitution of Spruance for Halsey as task force commander was not altogether for the worse. With stakes so high and available U.S. strength so limited, Halsey's impulsive boldness might have invited disaster. In the impending battle, what was needed was not so much bellicosity as the ability to calculate coolly under stress. Admiral Nimitz believed that the intellectual Spruance had just that ability. He had long since appraised him as a first-rate organizer and strategist and had already requested orders for him to join CinCPac as chief of staff.

Spruance, informally notified of the change of command, promptly reported to CinCPac headquarters. There Admiral Nimitz confirmed the news: Spruance was indeed to take Task Force 16 to sea, using Halsey's experienced staff. Nimitz further informed Spruance that this seagoing command was temporary. After the battle he would be ordered ashore to relieve Admiral Draemel. Spruance received the latter announcement with mixed feelings. He said afterward: "Having had two previous tours of staff duty during my career, I was not too happy about going ashore in the early stages of a big naval war."

For the time being, however, Spruance swallowed his disappointment and gave his full attention to the briefing that followed. He saw at once the advantage of placing his force on Nagumo's flank and the possibility of attacking the Japanese carriers while their planes were raiding Midway. Spruance also made the prudent observation that the U.S. carrier forces should not proceed west of Midway in search of the enemy before the enemy carriers were substantially disabled. The Japanese might alter their plans and head for Pearl Harbor, in which event the American forces might find themselves bypassed and unable to intervene.

For Admiral Nimitz, the next day, May 27, was especially exhausting. His workday began with a full-dress conference. Admiral Spruance and General Emmons were there. A newcomer present was Lieutenant General Robert C. Richardson, informally representing General Marshall. After the conference, Nimitz visited the *Enterprise* and decorated three of her pilots. As he pinned the Distinguished Flying Cross on Lieutenant Roger Mehle, he remarked, "I think you'll have a chance to win yourself another medal in the next few days."

Early that afternoon, Admiral Fletcher's Task Force 17 arrived off Oahu, the *Yorktown* trailing an oil slick ten miles long. As the damaged carrier threaded her way through the narrow entrance to Pearl Harbor, she was greeted with cheers, sirens, and steam whistles. She was ordered straight into dry dock, where blocks, shaped and emplaced the previous night, were waiting to receive her. Before the dock had been completely drained, Admiral Nimitz arrived, pulled on long boots, and led an inspection party in a sloshing examination of the *Yorktown*'s hull. This was Nimitz the marine engineer, no new role for him.

Nimitz had already concluded from reports radioed ahead of the *Yorktown*'s arrival that Fitch's estimate of the time needed to repair her was unrealistic. In 90 days the Pearl Harbor yard could make her as good as new. That was out of the question now—and unnecessary. It would take much less time to make her battleworthy. She had propulsion, her elevators were working, and her wooden flight deck had already been repaired. Her bomb-damaged compartments could be temporarily braced with timbers. It was necessary to patch her hull, perforated by near misses, only well enough to keep fish out for a few days more.

Speaking quietly but emphatically, Nimitz told the men in his inspection party, "We must have this ship back in three days." The men glanced at one another. Then, after a pause, Lieutenant Commander Herbert J. Pfingstad, the hull-repair expert, answered for all, "Yes, sir." Within an hour welding equipment, steel plates, and other materials were being assembled at the dock and the repairs were begun which would continue around the clock until the job was done.

Scarcely had Nimitz returned to his office when Fletcher arrived to report, accompanied by his cruiser commander, Rear Admiral William Ward Smith. Fletcher's usual ramrod posture and jaunty stance had somehow gone a little limp. To Nimitz's inquiry how he felt, he replied, "Pretty tired." Nimitz nodded and said that normally, after so long a spell of sea duty with combat, he would have sent him home for leave, but unfortunately he needed Task Force 17 in another important mission.

Then Nimitz, assisted by Admiral Draemel, proceeded to fill Fletcher in on the Japanese plan to capture Midway. "Do you know," said Nimitz a little crossly, "they've even named the officer who is to take over the naval station there on August 1?" Fletcher, who had known Nimitz since their days together at the Naval Academy, sensed that the latter was both exhausted and deeply disturbed.

Nimitz was indeed disturbed, and not only because of the uncertainties of the approaching battle. The fact is he had a job to do that for a man of his nature was particularly distasteful. With Halsey out of the picture, Fletcher was entitled by virtue of seniority to the overall seagoing command in the impending operation. Nimitz must now, without delay, either convince a doubting Admiral King that Fletcher was the man for the job or convince himself that Fletcher fell short. That meant nothing less than questioning Fletcher's competence and even his courage. Nimitz kept putting off the grilling.

At last, after discussing a number of other subjects, Admiral Nimitz reluctantly began his review of Fletcher's wartime record. As the reason for this probing gradually dawned on Fletcher, both he and his interrogator became increasingly embarrassed. Frank Jack, never fluent of speech, found himself virtually tongue-tied. He muttered something about wanting to consult his records, and Nimitz agreed that that was a reasonable request. The little group of admirals was relieved when Spruance unexpectedly joined them. Spruance had now learned something of the damage to the *Yorktown* and questioned whether she could be readied in time for action. "She'll be joining you," said Nimitz.

The next morning Fletcher made his verbal report to Nimitz, who asked him to submit it in writing. What Fletcher produced was no mere apologia but a full and manly account of his stewardship of Task Force 17. By the time Nimitz had finished reading it, he knew that Frank Jack Fletcher would command the U.S. carrier forces at Midway.

Admiral Nimitz promptly forwarded the statement to CominCh with a covering letter. "Dear King," it said, "I have finally had an opportunity to discuss with Fletcher, during a three day stay in port, his operations in the Coral Sea area, and to clear up what appeared to be a lack of aggressive tactics of his force. . . . I hope, and believe that after reading the enclosed letter, you will agree with me that Fletcher did a fine job and exercised superior judgment in his recent cruise in the Coral Sea. He is an excellent, seagoing, fighting naval officer and I wish to retain him as a task force commander in the future."

Nimitz concluded with a general survey of the situation at Pearl Harbor. It was an optimistic report, in which he emphasized his advantages and made light of his difficulties.

In the evening of May 27, the CinCPac and task force staffs held a joint conference under the direction of Admiral Draemel to hammer out battle plans. Present, among others, were Admirals Fletcher and Spruance, Commander Layton, and the operations officers: Captain McMorris from CinCPac, Commander William H. Buracker from Task Force 16, and Commander Walter G. Schindler from Task Force 17. The guiding principles were that the

Americans, with inferior forces but presumably better information concerning the opposition, must achieve surprise, must get the jump on the enemy, and must catch the enemy carriers in a vulnerable state. It was assumed that the Japanese Striking Force would begin launching at dawn—attack planes southward toward Midway, search planes north, east, and south. At that hour the American task forces, on course southwest through the night, should be 200 miles north of Midway, ready to launch on receiving the first report from U.S. search planes of the location, course, and speed of the enemy. With good timing and good luck they would catch the Japanese carriers with half their planes away attacking Midway. With better timing and better luck they might catch the enemy carriers while they were recovering the Midway attack group. That the Americans might catch the Japanese carriers in the highly vulnerable state of rearming and refueling the recovered planes was almost too much to hope for.

On the morning of May 28, Task Force 16, with Admiral Spruance in command, steamed, single file, out of Pearl Harbor, assumed circular formation, took on planes, and headed northwest. Spruance and his squadron and division commanders had been issued CinCPac Operation Plan No. 29-42. Officers qualified to read the bulky plan found it a fascinating and chilling document. Without revealing its sources of information, it stated in astonishing detail what enemy forces would attack Midway and when. Commander Richard Ruble, navigator of the *Enterprise*, evidently a reader of spy thrillers, could only mutter in wonder, "That man of ours in Tokyo is worth every cent we pay him."

The CinCPac operation plan directed Fletcher and Spruance to "inflict maximum damage on the enemy by employing strong attrition tactics," which meant by air attacks on the enemy ships. In a separate letter of instruction to both Fletcher and Spruance, Nimitz added: "In carrying out the task assigned in Op Plan 29-42, you will be governed by the principle of calculated risk, which you will interpret to mean the avoidance of exposure of your force to attack by superior enemy forces without prospect of inflicting, as a result of such exposure, greater damage to the enemy."

In the morning of May 29, Dry Dock No. 1 began to flood, and a little after 11:00 a.m. the *Yorktown* was towed out into the harbor, electricians and mechanics still working on her. The workmen continued their operations throughout the day and the following night. The next morning, a bosun's whistle announced the arrival of Admiral Nimitz. He had come to the *Yorktown* to thank the repairmen for winning their battle against time and to wish officers and crew "good luck and good hunting." He was sorry, he told the commanding officer, Captain Elliott Buckmaster, that the men could not go stateside after their long, arduous tour of duty. But he assured Buckmaster that, when they had finished the upcoming job, he would certainly send the *Yorktown* home for liberty and overhaul.

Shortly after the admiral left, the carrier's engines started, and an intercom announcement "all ashore that's going ashore" brought the last of the repairmen topside and into a waiting launch. The ships of Task Force 17, the *Yorktown*, two heavy cruisers, and five destroyers, filed out of the harbor, formed up, and headed for their rendezvous with Task Force 16 at a position 350 miles northeast of Midway—a position optimistically designated Point Luck.

Also on May 30 two heavy cruisers left Pearl Harbor for the Alaskan Sector to beef up Admiral Theobald's North Pacific Force. Nimitz had notified Theobald that Attu, Adak, and Kiska were the Aleutian islands that the enemy intended to invade. Theobald refused to believe that anybody would bother to occupy such worthless bits of land. He decided that the information was a ruse, planted by the Japanese to draw him westward so that they could get behind him for a landing at Dutch Harbor or perhaps in Alaska. So Theobald stationed his force 400 miles south of Kodiak, where it proved about as useful as if it had been in the South Atlantic.

Admiral Fitch with the *Saratoga* and an improvised screen of cruisers and destroyers at last sortied from San Diego on June 1. This force could not possibly reach Midway in time to participate in the battle, however, unless the Japanese attack was behind schedule, or Layton's predicted dates were not the right ones.

Down in the Coral Sea a U.S. cruiser, on orders from Admiral Nimitz, began broadcasting on frequencies normally assigned to carrier air groups. Nimitz was sure that Japanese listening stations would pick up these signals. He hoped the enemy would thus be deceived into believing that the U.S. carriers were still operating off the Solomons and would thus be lulled into overconfidence as he approached Midway.

In the last week of May, U.S. traffic analysis indicated that all segments of the Combined Fleet were under way. In CinCPac Operations Plot, staff officers were estimating speeds and drawing on the plotting board with colored pencils the courses of the various elements of the opposing fleets as they moved toward their objectives. Radio intercepts indicated that Japanese seaplanes and submarines were en route to scout Pearl Harbor. The seaplanes never arrived because they could not complete the long flight from the Marshall Islands and back without refueling from tanker-submarines that were supposed to meet them in the lagoon of French Frigate Shoals, and Admiral Nimitz had fore-handedly stationed a vessel in the lagoon. The submarines did arrive off Pearl Harbor and formed picket lines, but there was nothing for them to report. Task Forces 16 and 17 had already departed.

On the morning of the 30th, twenty-two Catalinas took off from Midway to begin the first of daily searches out to 700 miles westward. It soon appeared that Japanese bombers were patrolling northeastward from Wake. Two of the lumbering Catalinas encountered the enemy bombers and were badly shot up. This unprecedented contact warned both sides that the other was on special alert. Nimitz hoped that the warning would not make the Japanese alter their plans.

With possible defeat staring him in the face in the Central Pacific, Admiral Nimitz daringly recommended going on the offensive in the quiescent South Pacific. What he suggested was a spoiling raid on Tulagi and adjacent positions. Such a raid would presumably delay any Japanese preparations to build an airfield in the area and thus simplify the coming advance via the Solomons, which Admiral King had proposed. It seemed the ideal time for such an operation, while practically the whole Japanese Navy was deployed to the north.

Admiral King heartily approved of the project, and Admiral Nimitz offered to provide it with the 1st Marine Raider Battalion, then at Samoa, and also with transports to convey the marines to the New Hebrides. But because General MacArthur, who would have to provide the cruisers, destroyers, and aircraft to support the raid, concluded that the forces available were too small for the task, the idea was dropped.

Meanwhile Simard and Shannon, with the equipment sent by Nimitz and the aid of their marines, were earning their spot promotions by converting Sand and Eastern islands into the most strongly fortified two square miles in the Pacific. By the end of May the 3,000 defenders on Midway, protected by ground mines, underground shelters, guns in concealed emplacements, and a wilderness of barbed wire, were prepared to hurl back any force that was likely to try a landing.

Nimitz was still dubious about what Midway's planes could do against enemy carriers. Tiny Eastern Island, where the airfield was, could handle only so many planes, and those available were ill adapted for attacking ships. The slow, vulnerable Catalinas were not much good for anything other than patrolling. The Midway combat air force consisted of 16 obsolete Vindicator dive-bombers, which the marines called "wind indicators," and 21 equally outdated Buffalo fighters, known locally as "flying coffins." To these Nimitz was able to add only 18 Dauntless dive-bombers, 7 TBF torpedo planes, and 7 Wildcat fighters, all carrier castoffs, and 19 army bombers. Four of the army bombers were B-26 Marauders rigged with torpedoes and flown by pilots who had never fired a torpedo. The rest were high-level B-17 Flying Fortresses, whose bombs could easily be eluded by moving ships. Not a flyer on Midway had had any combat experience. About the best that could be expected of them was that, by breaking up the formation of the enemy fleet and drawing off its fighters, they would set it up for the better-trained carrier aviators.

CinCPac and his staff had shot their bolt. They had deployed available forces to the best of their ability to meet impossible odds. There was little more they could do until the enemy appeared. Then they would have their hands full again, particularly since Admiral Nimitz, acting as coordinator, was retaining overall tactical command—land, sea, and air.

In the evening of May 31, the admiral prepared to retire earlier than he had for several weeks. In his daily letter to Mrs. Nimitz, he said: "I expect the next few days to be *full* and *long* so will bank up some rest." He could not violate security by telling her what he would be doing, but he added: "Some day the story of our activities will be written and it will be interesting—but not for now."

Staff officers continued to brood over the CinCPac plotting board and its steadily advancing colored lines. Their growing tension spread into the lower echelons where junior officers and enlisted men could only guess what was impending. To them, the appearance of the commander in chief, moving about, head erect, apparently calm and collected, was a source of reassurance. A young naval reservist and public relations officer on the CinCPac staff, Lieutenant (j.g.) James Bassett, long afterward recalled the comforting presence of what for him, as for others, had become a father figure. "This," he remarked, "was a very unflappable man."

On June 2, the orange lines on the plotting board drew close to their objectives, and Task Forces 16 and 17, under radio silence, were assumed to have made rendezvous at Point Luck. If the lines on the chart were correct, contact between the Catalinas patrolling westward from Midway and the oncoming Midway Invasion Force was imminent. The invasion force was scheduled to arrive at the atoll on the morning of June 5, following an all-day attack on Sand and Eastern islands by Nagumo's carriers.

When night fell on the 2nd, no reports had come in. For the officers who had staked the safety of America's Pacific bases on the accuracy of their intelligence, this was a bewildering and distressing situation. But, that evening, Admiral Nimitz wrote to Mrs. Nimitz: "Another busy day and one of anxious waiting for something to develop—and for which we are better prepared than ever before."

# CHAPTER 7

# THE BATTLE OF MIDWAY

AT DAWN ON June 3, key members of the CinCPac staff were at their stations. A little after 4:00,* U.S. radio-intercept stations began to pick up bits of radio traffic suggesting unusual, possibly enemy, air activity in the eastern Aleutians. Dutch Harbor had in fact been raided from the air, but a report from that base seems to have got no farther than Admiral Theobald, who was at sea under radio silence. Analysis of the intercepts, however, at length convinced CinCPac staff that there had indeed been enemy planes over Dutch Harbor.

Admiral Nimitz conservatively assessed the overflights as enemy reconnaissance, possibly by cruiser planes, rather than as part of the Japanese operation plan, unfolding right on schedule. Even if he could be sure that the planes were from the Japanese Second Carrier Striking Force, he would still not be certain that Midway was the enemy's main target or that Nagumo's First Carrier Striking Force was speeding down from the northwest in the fog to attack Midway. The best evidence of that would be a sighting of the slower Invasion Force from Saipan heading for the atoll.

Several hours passed without any further word from the north and none at all from the west. At last, a little after 11:00 a.m. (12:30 p.m. at Pearl Harbor), the cable from Midway came to life. It was relaying a report, sent in segments from a Catalina patrolling 700 miles to westward: "Main Body . . . bearing 262, distance 700 . . . eleven ships, course 090, speed 19." Nine B-17s, held in readiness at Midway for just such a contact, had promptly taken off and headed west to attack the oncoming enemy force with bombs. At Pearl Harbor, Commander Maurice E. Curts, the CinCPac communication officer, rushed the contact report to Nimitz's office, where the admiral was consulting with Commander Layton. Nimitz glanced at the dispatch, then sat suddenly erect.

"Layton," he said excitedly, "have you seen this?"

"What is it, sir?"

"The sighting of the Japanese forces!"

Nimitz was smiling. That in itself was nothing unusual, for he smiled often. His expression now, however, was nothing less than radiant, what Layton called "that brilliant white smile."

---

* Commands and combatants involved in the Midway-Aleutians operations used different dates and a variety of times. Following the practice of most published accounts in English of the Battle of Midway, this narrative uses West Longitude date and Zone-plus-12 (Midway) time.

"It just lights up," said Layton, as though "somebody let in the sun by raising a window shade. His smile and his blue eyes would go right through you." Nimitz had successfully concealed his anxiety, but now he made not the slightest attempt to hide his relief. He handed the dispatch to Layton.

"This ought to make your heart warm," he said, chuckling. "This will clear up all the doubters now. They just have to see this to know that what I told them is correct."

Though the U.S. task forces would almost certainly have picked up the radioed contact report directly from the Catalina, CinCPac communications took the elementary precaution of relaying the report to Admiral Fletcher. In view of the report's misleading phrase "Main Body," Nimitz warned: "That is not, repeat not, the enemy striking force." Thus far, only the Invasion Force had been sighted, he added, and he reminded Fletcher that the Japanese carriers were due to strike from the northwest the following morning. The chances of sighting them on June 3 were slight because, from the foggy area almost all the way to Midway, dense clouds obscured the ocean.

Before sunset on the 3rd, Admiral Nimitz knew that Dutch Harbor had been bombed that morning and that four Japanese carrier planes had been shot down over the Aleutians. From Midway he learned that the B-17s sent against the Invasion Force found and attacked it 570 miles out. They reported having hit two battleships or heavy cruisers and two transports—news that the CinCPac staff received with a certain amount of skepticism. In the early evening, four Catalina amphibians took off from Midway for a moonlight torpedo attack on the Invasion Force. CinCPac relayed all this information to the appropriate commands. Then to Midway and to his task force commanders Nimitz sent a special message: "The situation is developing as expected. Carriers, our most important objective, should soon be located. Tomorrow may be the day you can give them the works." The concluding words of the entry in the CinCPac Command Summary for June 3 were prophetic: "The whole course of the war in the Pacific may hinge on the developments of the next two or three days."

Though few persons on Oahu knew exactly what was going on or what to expect, all felt the tension that spread throughout the area like a tangible presence. At nightfall CinCPac headquarters, not aware that the scheduled Japanese seaplane reconnaissance had been canceled, passed an air-raid warning to 14th Naval District, which sounded an all-out "red" alert. Pearl Harbor Navy Yard was promptly blacked out. Machinery in the repair shops was shut down. Workmen and marines manned machine guns. Trucks blocked the gates. On the ships in the harbor, gun crews hurried to their stations. At Schofield Army Barracks, many patients were discharged from the hospital to make way for anticipated casualties. In Honolulu civilian defense workers were summoned to duty.

Few CinCPac staff officers slept that night. One of them recalled that Admiral Nimitz dozed on a cot in his office—storing up rest against the coming forty-eight or more hectic hours, yet ready for any eventuality. Around 2:00 a.m., the staff communication office, which operated twenty-four hours a day, received and passed on to Nimitz a report, relayed via Midway, from the Catalina amphibians. It stated that they had torpedoed two of the oncoming Invasion Force's ships.

At dawn, June 4, all the CinCPac staff were at their stations. They knew that when first light came to Midway, where the sun rose 1½ hours later than it did at Pearl, Catalinas would be out to the northwest, patrolling at the edge of the overcast. They were aware also that the report they were awaiting might well be the pivotal communication of the war. Shortly after 6:00 a.m. it came, an urgent message in plain language, sent via the cable from Midway: "Plane reports two carriers and Main Body ships bearing 320, course 135, speed 25, distance 180."

Though the Catalina pilot had reported seeing only two carriers, Nimitz was sure that there were four, perhaps five. He glanced at the date-time group on the dispatch. He then went into Operations Plot and pinpointed the enemy's position. Afterward he remarked to Layton, "Well, you were only five miles, five degrees, and five minutes off." At least half the credit for the remarkable accuracy of Layton's prediction is due to Admiral Nagumo's navigator, who, through three days of fog and overcast had guided his force unerringly toward its objective.

Here at last was the target the Americans had been waiting for—Nagumo's First Carrier Striking Force, the force that had opened the war six months before with its raid on Pearl Harbor, the force that now had to be defeated. The brief contact report made clear to Nimitz and his staff that Nagumo had already launched an air attack on Midway. He must have launched his planes much farther out than a mere 180 miles, and he would have done so while his ships were still hidden by the overcast. He had remained on course 135°, toward Midway, so that his returning aircraft could find their carrier decks and in order to shorten their return flight. Nagumo could not have known at the time of launching that the American carriers were on his flank, or he would have launched his planes and shaped course in their direction.

CinCPac staff took for granted that, on receiving the contact report, Midway had launched all its planes so that none could be caught on the ground. The Midway-based bombers and torpedo planes would be heading to attack Nagumo's carriers, the 28 marine fighters to tackle his oncoming planes. Off to the northeast, Fletcher had undoubtedly heard the contact report and was acting upon it. Nevertheless, CinCPac communications faithfully relayed the report to him—just in case.

The CinCPac staff was sure that, despite resistance from the 28 fighter planes, some, perhaps most, of the Japanese bombers would get through to Midway. An attack on the atoll was inevitable, and imminent. At 6:25 the expected message came in via the cable, a three-word dispatch: "Air raid Midway."

Two hours of trying uncertainty ensued, with no messages at all reaching

Pearl from U.S. forces at the battle front. Fletcher and Spruance would of course maintain radio silence until they had been located by the enemy. Then, at 8:30 there came in from Midway a sad little message: "Only 3 undamaged fighting planes remain. No contact our dive-bombing planes."

Meanwhile Rochefort and Layton were in excited conversation on the scrambler telephone. Rochefort's Radio Intelligence Unit had picked up a Japanese voice contact report, evidently from one of Nagumo's search planes. The report was expressed in the usual triplicate, abbreviated form: "TE-TE-TE, etc." As interpreted by Rochefort, it read: "Sighted 10 surface ships, apparently enemy, bearing 10°, 240 miles from Midway, course 150°, speed over 20 knots."

Layton took the sighting report immediately to Admiral Nimitz, who glanced at it.

"Are you sure the report didn't include our carriers being sighted?"

"Yes, sir."

Nimitz, report in hand, strode into Operations Plot and handed it to the watch officer, who entered it on the plot. If the reported ships were one of the American carrier groups—and they could hardly be anything else—then the opposing forces were about 150 miles apart, that is, just within effective attack radius, and the Japanese carrier force was about 150 miles from Midway.

The Midway-based aircraft must have been attacking Nagumo at about the same time that Nagumo's search plane was informing him of nearby U.S. forces afloat. Intense static in the area through which Nagumo was steaming had, however, blotted out all radio reports from the American aircraft. Only as they returned to Midway were the aircraft able to forward reports to CinCPac, thanks to the cable connection. Their reports were not particularly encouraging. The dive-bombers had apparently hit one enemy carrier, which they said was left smoking. The B-17s reported making three hits on two carriers. On the other hand, the American planes had encountered heavy opposition from Zero fighters and suffered severe losses.

Nagumo's myopic search pilot, transmitting outside the zone of intense static, continued to send in reports that were heard at Pearl. At 8:09 he identified the "10 surface ships, apparently enemy" as "five cruisers and five destroyers." Eleven minutes later, having taken another look, he reported, "the enemy is accompanied by what appears to be a carrier bringing up the rear."

This report brought the CinCPac staff crowding around the plot. They were sure that Nagumo now had information on which he was bound to act. He had to do something, and do it quickly, about that American carrier. CinCPac staff agreed that the Japanese admiral had two choices. He could launch an attack at once with his reserve aircraft. If he did that, the planes returning from Midway would have to remain in the air until the launching had been completed. There was a strong possibility that many of them, low in fuel after their long flight, would crash into the sea. Or Nagumo might first recover, refuel, and rearm the Midway planes before launching. He would thus be able to send out a much more powerful attack, but the attack would be delayed at least an hour. Meanwhile American planes would certainly be en route to strike Nagumo's force. Should they succeed in bombing the Japanese carriers while the latter were refueling and rearming aircraft, the carriers would explode like giant firecrackers.

Although Midway-based Catalinas were out patrolling, no new information about the position or course of the Japanese carriers came over the cable. Nimitz was equally uninformed about the operations of the American forces. Fletcher continued to maintain radio silence, even though the Japanese now knew where he was.

Thus, just as the crucial battle of the war was reaching a climax, CinCPac suffered an information blackout. Nimitz managed to look unruffled, but officers who knew him well could see that he was deeply worried. One officer said, "Admiral Nimitz was frantic; I mean, as frantic as I've ever seen him." The admiral sent for Commander Curts. "Why aren't we getting messages?" he demanded. "Why aren't we hearing something?" Curts replied somewhat lamely that he didn't know, but that he didn't want to send a message out there saying, "I'm having no reports. Report something." Nimitz agreed that that would not do at all.

The Japanese were not so reticent. Before 10:00 a.m. two fairly long radio messages emanated from their carrier force. The Americans could not read the encoded messages, but Rochefort's men reported that they came from the carrier *Akagi*, Nagumo's flagship. One of them had recognized the touch on the key as that of one of the *Akagi's* chief warrant officers, an operator whose fist was so bad that someone had remarked that he "hits the key like he's kicking it with his foot." If Station Hypo could not read the messages, it at least now had Nagumo's current call sign for future reference.

Nimitz's sole source of information concerning the U.S. carrier forces continued to be the Japanese search pilot. A little before nine o'clock, the pilot had radioed to the Japanese force: "Ten enemy torpedo planes heading toward you." The planes could only be from the American carriers. CinCPac and his staff concluded that Nagumo was now either just completing the launching of his reserve aircraft or, as seemed more probable, he was recovering his planes from Midway, in which case he would not be able to launch until after 10:00.

At 9:26 the cable relayed to Pearl a Catalina report placing the oncoming Invasion Force 320 miles from Midway. Next over the cable came reports from Midway-based bombers and torpedo planes newly returned to the atoll. Apparently the Midway aircraft were continuing to take heavy losses while inflicting little or no damage on the enemy. Finally at 10:08 the *Enterprise* broke silence in an unexpected manner. In CinCPac's communications center a voice on the carrier's audio frequency was heard to shout, "Attack immediately!" Someone identified the voice as that of Captain Miles Browning, the chief of staff whom Spruance had inherited from Halsey. Browning's cry must have been in response to a report from American aviators that they had found the enemy.

After another long period of silence, Nimitz sent out inquiries, and Lay-

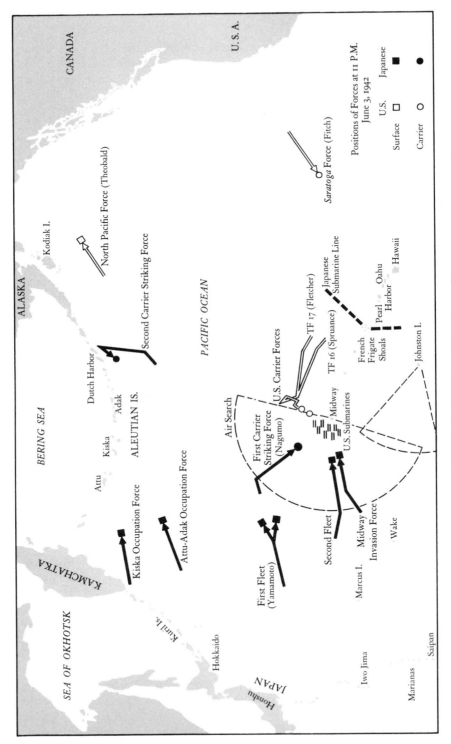

The Battle of Midway: The Approach

ton asked Rochefort via the hot-line telephone whether the U.S. carriers had attacked Nagumo's force and, if so, what the Japanese reaction was. "Don't we have anything on this?" Layton inquired.

"Not a thing."

"Have we tried the other frequencies?"

"We've tried every frequency we know they've got."

Admiral Nimitz and his staff concluded that in this instance no news might be good news. If the enemy carriers were not transmitting, it could be because they were no longer able to do so. At eleven o'clock Rochefort's Radio Intelligence Unit intercepted a transmission, or a fragment of a transmission, in plain-language Japanese: "Inform us position enemy carriers." This message, which obviously had been sent from the Nagumo force to one of its search planes, implied that at least one Japanese carrier was able and ready to counterattack. Fifty minutes later Nagumo himself radioed a long message in code to an unidentified addressee. The call sign was his, but the operator was not the heavy-handed warrant officer of the *Akagi*. One of Rochefort's people had made a study of identifying operators and recognized the fist as that of the chief radioman in the cruiser *Nagara*. Evidently the *Akagi* had been damaged too heavily to serve as flagship, and Nagumo had shifted to the cruiser.

Admiral Fletcher, informed of these intercepts, at last broke radio silence, but only to report that *Yorktown* planes had attacked two enemy carriers. He added: "Have no indication of location of additional carriers which have sighted this force." Shortly afterward, the Pearl Harbor Radio Intelligence Unit intercepted the report of an airborne Japanese flight leader, "We are attacking the enemy carrier." The flight leader was then heard ordering the aircraft under his command, "Attack! Attack! Attack!"

Then into CinCPac communications center came a message in plain English: "Am being attacked by large number of enemy bombers." It was sent by ship's radio to CinCPac, but no originator was shown, and attempts to authenticate it were fruitless. The explanation came twenty minutes later, when Fletcher sent a correctly identified coded message, "Have been attacked by air 150 miles north of Midway."

CinCPac was kept informed, if somewhat belatedly, of what was happening to the *Yorktown*. Three bomb-hits having left her dead in the water, Admiral Fletcher and his staff had transferred to the cruiser *Astoria*. Shortly after 3:00 p.m., when the damaged carrier was again under way, she was the target of a second attack, this time by torpedo planes, which hit her at least twice. Because the *Yorktown* began to list badly and was apparently about to capsize, Captain Buckmaster gave the order to abandon ship. Hours later, after the last of her crew had been fished out of the water, the carrier was still afloat and had undergone no appreciable change in trim. Fletcher therefore requested CinCPac to send tugs and told him that, unless otherwise directed, he and his Task Force 17 would protect and attempt to salvage the *Yorktown*, while

Spruance's Task Force 16 continued to engage the enemy. Admiral Nimitz raised no objections; he wanted no effort spared to save the carrier, and in his opinion Spruance was entirely capable of taking over the tactical command.

The bad news about the *Yorktown* was somewhat offset by a dispatch from Spruance. He reported that between 9:30 and 11:00 that morning "air groups from Task Forces 16 and 17 attacked carriers of enemy force consisting of probably 4 carriers, 2 battleships, 4 heavy cruisers, and 6 destroyers. All 4 carriers believed badly damaged." He concluded his report: "Our plane losses heavy."

Aircraft from Midway and from the *Yorktown*, the latter launched before she was damaged, were frantically searching the ocean for the source of the attacking planes. A shore-based Catalina found three burning ships 170 miles northwest of Midway. Some 45 miles farther out on the same bearing, the *Yorktown* planes found an undamaged enemy carrier, identified as the *Hiryu*. She was accompanied by two battleships, three cruisers, and four destroyers. Against this target the *Enterprise* and the *Hornet* launched forty dive-bombers, while Midway sent a dozen B-17s, six of which were just approaching Eastern Island, having been ordered from Hawaii to Midway.

By the early evening of June 4, Admiral Nimitz and his staff were reviewing the events of the day with guarded optimism. If the information thus far received was to be taken literally, the Americans had defeated the Nagumo force. But most of the favorable reports were based on observations by army aviators, and they were not trained in assessing battle damage at sea. Even the careful Spruance had reported "all 4" enemy carriers badly damaged that morning. Yet in the early afternoon planes from one of those carriers had knocked out the *Yorktown*.

Results of the attack launched against the *Hiryu* from Midway and by Task Force 16 were not transmitted to CinCPac until the bombers had returned from their mission, the crews had been debriefed, and repetitions had been removed from their reports. Midway's dispatch arrived at Pearl Harbor a little after 10:00 p.m.; Task Force 16's, some twenty minutes later.

Said Midway: "Fortresses en route from Pearl made 2 hits on smoking carrier bearing 320, distance 170. Reported 2 other ships in area burning and 2 additional on fire about 125 miles on same bearing."

Spruance reported: "At 1700 to 1800 air groups of Task Force 16 attacked enemy force consisting of 1 carrier, 2 battleships, 2 or more heavy cruisers, several destroyers. Carrier hit several times with 500- and 1000-pound bombs and when last seen burning fiercely. At least 4 hits on battleship, which was burning. One heavy cruiser also hit and burning. At 1750 enemy force in position lat. 30-41 north, long. 177-41 west, course west, speed 15 knots, with destroyers joining from southeast. Three ships believed carriers previously attacked were observed to southeastward still burning...."

When Nimitz had read that far, he looked up. His countenance was glowing with "that brilliant white smile." If the *Hiryu* was burning fiercely and the *Akagi, Kaga,* and *Soryu,* hit that morning, were still burning, all four carriers were almost certainly beyond salvage. An American victory seemed assured unless Spruance were to blunder badly, and Nimitz believed Spruance was no blunderer. Nimitz immediately had Admiral Draemel release a prepared message to all his forces, with Admiral King and General Emmons as information addressees: "You who participated in the Battle of Midway today have written a glorious page in our history. I am proud to be associated with you. I estimate that another day of all-out effort on your part will complete the defeat of the enemy." The CinCPac Command Summary, probably echoing Nimitz, called the day's operations "the start of what may be the greatest sea battle since Jutland. Its outcome, if as unfavorable to the Japs as seems indicated, will virtually end their expansion. We lost a high percentage of highly trained pilots who will be difficult to replace."

Some of the CinCPac staff, reading to the end of Spruance's report, had plotted his anticipated position for 4:00 a.m., June 5: lat. 30° 31' N. long. 175° 20' W. That was a puzzler, for it was considerably to the east of Task Force 16's last-known afternoon position. Spruance had reported the enemy on course west. Why was Spruance not on the same course in hot pursuit?

When this anomaly was pointed out to Admiral Nimitz, he refused to intervene—or even to take the matter seriously. "I'm sure Spruance has a better sense of what's going on out there than we have here," he said. "I'm sure he has a very good reason for this. We'll learn all about it in the course of time. From here we are not in a position to kibitz a commander in the field of action."

Some of the officers continued to grumble then and later that Spruance had thrown away a golden opportunity. Others took a second look at the chart and decided that what Spruance was doing made sense. If Task Force 16 continued through the night at sustained speed, it would at 4:00 a.m. be far to eastward of its 10:00 p.m. position, and it dared not slow down lest it be overtaken and attacked by enemy submarines. The only possible conclusion was that Spruance was heading east only temporarily and that he planned to turn back west at some time during the night.

What was he backing off from? Had the battleships and cruisers of the Japanese Second Fleet detached themselves from the Invasion Force at noon, they could have picked up Nagumo's westbound remnant at nightfall and all then headed east. Spruance, had he headed west, might have collided with this force and probably would have been overwhelmed in a night battle. He must therefore have drawn back temporarily out of reach, argued some of the CinCPac staff, so that he should encounter no enemy before dawn, when he could use his carriers.

Not all the CinCPac staff accepted this line of reasoning, but Admiral Fletcher, a thousand miles closer to the enemy than they were, obviously did. He detailed the destroyer *Hughes* to stand by the *Yorktown* through the night and sink her if she appeared in danger of capture. Then, with the rest of Task Force 17, he hauled off eastward in Spruance's wake.

There was little sleep in CinCPac headquarters that night, for it was believed that Yamamoto, whose determination and resourcefulness were well known, would make every effort to retrieve the battle. The first alert was at 1:30 a.m., when the cable transmitted a report that Midway was being bombarded. Said Nimitz, "I guess the Japs still intend to land," and turning to Layton, his stand-in for Yamamoto, he asked, "Do you think so?"

"Yes," replied Layton, "I think so."

"Despite the damage?"

"Well, they're a pretty stubborn outfit. If they have plans, they always try to carry them out until it's obvious they can't."

Minutes later cable dispatches identified the bombarding vessel as a submarine, which Midway's shore batteries had soon chased away.

At 3:00 a.m. the U.S. submarine *Tambor* reported "many unidentified ships" about 90 miles west of Midway. An hour later, as dawn began to break in the Midway area, the *Tambor* identified the ships as Japanese. When it grew lighter, she saw that two of them were *Mogami*-class heavy cruisers. Apparently, the Japanese were going through with their invasion. Admiral English, after conferring with Admiral Nimitz, radioed all submarines of the Midway patrol to "proceed at best speed to position five miles west of Midway." If the enemy really was coming in, his force would have to run an ominous gauntlet.

Reports from Midway-based search planes, however, soon changed the picture. The aircraft had found all Japanese forces to westward of Midway and all heading west. Their observations supported Station Hypo's earlier report that radio direction-finding revealed the Second Fleet on course northwest. Evidently the enemy, instead of advancing, was everywhere withdrawing. The planes also reported that the two *Mogami*-class cruisers directly west of Midway were trailing oil, evidently from damages. A little after 8:00 a.m. dive-bombers and B-17s from Midway attacked the cruisers and reported that they had scored at least two hits.

Spruance at last broke radio silence to warn the U.S. submarines off Midway that he was coming through in pursuit of Japanese units. Task Force 16 was on course west but was only 50 miles north of the atoll, having been drawn southward during the night by the enemy activities in the Midway area. That afternoon Task Force 16 launched an air strike against a group of enemy ships reported to the northwest. The strike did not reach the enemy ships, giving Spruance's critics at CinCPac headquarters occasion to further deplore his eastward withdrawal during the preceding night.

The general feeling at CinCPac, however, was relief that the enemy evidently had been repulsed and pride that it had been achieved against overwhelming odds. After their sleepless night, the staff officers sat around smoking and relaxing. Admiral Nimitz, though he shared the general relief, had no intention of letting down his guard. The Japanese still had ample strength to ambush Spruance at night. Or they might refuel and regroup their forces and come back, spearheading a renewed attack with the two carriers that had raided Dutch Harbor and the one or two light carriers believed to be with their forces at sea. Nimitz warned his commanders by radio: "There are strong indications the Japanese will attempt assault and occupation Midway regardless past losses."

Admiral Spruance, concluding that he had little chance of overtaking the ships to the northwest, went in pursuit of the two damaged *Mogami*-class cruisers, and on June 6 launched three strikes against them. Analysis of reports, pictures taken from the *Enterprise*'s photographic planes, and interrogation of survivors revealed that one of the cruisers, the *Mikuma*, had been sunk, while her sister, the *Mogami*, severely battered and barely afloat, had escaped, accompanied by two destroyers.

That morning Admiral King sent Admiral Nimitz a radio message of congratulation. It was broadcast in plain English so that all ships and stations, including the enemy's, could intercept and read it: "The Navy, Marine Corps, and Coast Guard join in admiration of the American naval, marine, and army forces who have so gallantly and effectively repelled the enemy advance on Midway and are confident that their comrades in arms will continue to make the enemy realize that war is hell."

That was enough for General Emmons. If hard-nosed Admiral King was ready to concede that victory had been achieved, Emmons was prepared to acknowledge handsomely that he had been wrong in questioning Admiral Nimitz's strategy. The general presently appeared at CinCPac headquarters bearing a jeroboam of cold champagne decorated with Navy blue and gold ribbons. Following him an aide carried a container holding two dozen champagne glasses. With a little speech of congratulation, Emmons presented the wine to Nimitz, who ordered it opened and served.

In the midst of the celebration, someone, probably Layton, suggested that Joe Rochefort deserved to be in on the festivities. Nimitz agreed, whereupon a staff officer telephoned the summons to Station Hypo and sent a car to fetch the master cryptanalyst from his basement office. Rochefort was late again. Hard at work, in need of a shave, wearing a rumpled smoking jacket and carpet slippers when the call came, he took so long to get cleaned up that when he arrived at CinCPac headquarters the party was over and a high-level conference was in progress. Nimitz nevertheless welcomed him, introduced him to officers he had not met, and said, "This officer deserves a major share of the credit for the victory at Midway."

Rochefort, embarrassed, muttered something about merely doing what he was paid to do, and added that credit was owing not just to him but to everybody in Station Hypo. He then settled back and listened to the continuation of the discussion that had been under way when he entered. Thereby he was treated to a sample of Nimitz's sometimes pixieish sense of humor.

It seemed that as fears for an attack on the West Coast diminished, the Army Air Force* had begun releasing bombers in increasing numbers from the United States. As fast as they arrived at Pearl, these bombers had been hurried

---

* Shortly after the United States entered World War II, the American army command was divided into Army Ground Forces and Army Air Forces. The latter were often informally called Army Air Force.

out to Midway. The latest arrivals, B-17s, were being held on Oahu. A CinCPac staff officer suggested that, since the Japanese might return to the attack, these too should be sent to Midway. Admiral Nimitz concurred.

An Army Air Force general objected, pointing out that they were the only planes the Army had on Oahu and that the Navy had none. Take the B-17s away, he said, and Oahu would be defenseless. The general went on at some length, arguing the necessity of keeping the bombers where they were. Nimitz listened patiently; then he offered to make a deal. The *Saratoga*, he said, was due at Pearl Harbor within an hour, and she was bringing in a load of planes as well as her own air groups. Nimitz said that if the general would send all his B-17s out to Midway, operational control of the *Saratoga* planes would be turned over to the Air Force for the entire period of their stay at Pearl Harbor.

At that, the general brightened and agreed to send out his B-17s. Admiral Nimitz asked him to use the telephone to put the order through at once, and the general did so. Pat Bellinger looked a little bewildered, as did some of the other naval officers, but they said nothing, and the discussion went on, covering a number of subjects.

Some forty-five minutes later, when the B-17s were airborne and on their way, a thought occurred to the general. "By the way, Admiral," he said, "you say that the *Saratoga* is due today at Pearl?"

"Yes, it should be in at any moment now."

"How long may we expect the *Saratoga* to be here?"

Replied Nimitz with a straight face, "Long enough to fuel, and then she will proceed to sea and load up the planes again."

There was a general burst of laughter, in which the Air Force general joined, a little wryly, one may suppose. Actually, as everyone knew, Oahu was in no immediate danger. The Combined Fleet was not likely to hazard an attack on Hawaii unless it had first sunk or disabled the *Enterprise*, the *Hornet*, and the *Saratoga* and captured Midway. What probably disturbed the general was the prospect of having nothing to command.

Far out at sea that evening, 400 miles west of Midway, Task Force 16 abandoned the chase and turned back east. Included among the reasons Spruance gave for taking this action were the need to refuel destroyers and general fatigue, but to the officers around the CinCPac plotting board a more compelling reason was obvious. Spruance, had he continued westward, would soon have come within bombing range of Wake Island, and both he and the CinCPac staff knew that Japanese bombers were stacked up at Wake anticipating an early transfer to Midway. With the support of these planes, Yamamoto could be expected to set an ambush for Task Force 16. That he was attempting something of the sort became apparent when U.S. radio listening stations picked up and relayed to Pearl plain-language distress messages, such as might be sent by a sinking ship, emanating from a position west of Task Force 16. CinCPac warned Spruance to pay no attention to what was evidently Yamamoto's final, desperate effort to lure the Americans into his clutches. "Sometimes," said Admiral Nimitz, "they can be quite transparent, can't they?"

The good news of June 6 was offset to a large degree by very bad news indeed. The *Yorktown*, under tow toward Pearl Harbor, with a salvage team aboard and escorted by a half-dozen destroyers, had been torpedoed by a submarine. The destroyer *Hammann*, secured alongside the carrier to provide power for the salvage work, had also been torpedoed and had gone down. Said Admiral Nimitz disgustedly, "If a Japanese submarine can come in there and torpedo the *Yorktown* when we've got five or six destroyers out there to keep that submarine away, there is something wrong with our submarine tactics." Hope lingered that, since the carrier had survived one torpedo attack, she might survive this one. At breakfast time the next morning, however, CinCPac's hopes were dashed. Captain Buckmaster radioed: "As result yesterday's attack *Yorktown* sank 0500."

On the morning of June 8, the CinCPac staff and Station Hypo were thrown into a tailspin by a dispatch from CominCh stating that someone had apparently leaked to the press the intercepted Japanese operation plan for the Midway campaign. Their fears were confirmed when a copy of the June 7 *Chicago Tribune* reached Pearl Harbor. On the front page was a column-long story headlined Navy Had Word of Jap Plan to Strike at Sea. Datelined "Washington, D.C., June 7," it began: "The strength of the Japanese forces with which the American navy is battling somewhere west of Midway Island in what is believed to be the greatest battle of the war, was well known in American naval circles several days before the battle began, reliable sources in the naval intelligence disclosed here tonight."

The story went on to summarize the Japanese deployment and, citing the names of major warships, to describe the Invasion Force and the First and Second Carrier Striking Forces. Though the article did not mention the broken code, Japanese intelligence agents who read it would be certain to suspect some such leak and to tighten their cryptographic security. The United States thus stood to lose the priceless fountainhead of information that had made the American victory at Midway possible.

An investigation revealed that the story was, in fact, filed in Chicago by *Chicago Tribune* correspondent Stanley Johnston, whose source was of course the copy of Yamamoto's plan that Morton Seligman had shown him. Luckily no Japanese—or German or Italian—spy read that issue of the *Chicago Tribune*, and so the Japanese kept on using their JN25 code, with occasional changes of additives. Since a grand jury found that Johnston had broken no law, he was not brought to public trial—which was just as well, for that would inevitably have drawn the attention of the Japanese to the leak they had missed. Seligman's promising naval career was ruined. He was passed over for promotion to captain, and he retired from the Navy in 1944.

For his Midway victory, Admiral Nimitz received congratulations from all over the world, except the Axis countries. Army and navy officers and other students of warfare recognized the Battle of Midway as decisive in that it erased Japan's military advantage in the Pacific, bringing the antagonists to something approaching equality. Those who best knew the facts recognized that Japan's severest loss was not in carriers or planes but in trained aviators. Military analysts predicted that the United States would soon shift to the offensive.

Admiral Nimitz did his best to share the praise and give credit to those who deserved it. He was not always successful. For example, Admiral King rejected his recommendation that Joseph Rochefort be awarded the Distinguished Service Medal. CominCh recognized the vital part that cryptanalysis had played in recent American successes, but he considered it the work of too many people, in Washington, at Pearl Harbor, and at Melbourne, for any one man to be singled out. With that example, Nimitz must have been thankful that he had secured promotions for Colonel Shannon and Captain Simard in advance. When Simard, on his way from Midway to a new duty post, called on Nimitz, the admiral praised him for his gallant fight and, pointing to his new silver eagles, remarked, in dubious metaphor, "I sent you the flowers before the funeral."

From Midway the army bombers, the few B-26s and the many B-17s, came back in small groups. Admiral Nimitz could not meet them all, but he saw to it that he was at least represented and that each squadron leader received his personal thanks to pass down to the individual aviators. On June 13 Admiral Fletcher with part of Task Force 17 entered Pearl Harbor, followed a few hours later by Admiral Spruance with Task Force 16. Ships in the harbor dipped their flags in salute. Admiral Nimitz and members of his staff, standing on the wharf, awaited each task force. They went aboard the flagships and shook hands with the commanders and as many of the officers and enlisted men as possible, thanking all, in the name of the nation, for a splendid performance.

Distributing proper credit now became something of a problem. The army flyers were the first to return to Pearl and had given representatives of the press their version of the Battle of Midway. The aviators knew that they had dropped bombs and that enemy ships had been damaged and sunk, but the B-17s had bombed from such a height that it was impossible for their crews to recognize ship types or to tell a hit from a near miss. Quite honestly they took the credit. None of them recognized that the "cruiser" they had reported sinking in fifteen seconds on June 6 was, in fact, the U.S. submarine *Grayling* indignantly crash diving. None of these flyers was more than dimly aware that the Navy had been involved in the battle. On June 12, the day before Task Forces 16 and 17 returned to Pearl Harbor, *The New York Times* ran an article with the interesting headline: ARMY FLIERS BLASTED TWO FLEETS OFF MIDWAY.

Admiral Nimitz, recognizing that the aviators made up in gallantry what they lacked in aim and damage-assessment, declined to contradict the Army's extravagant pretensions. His spokesman merely claimed for the Navy a share in the victory. Later, when the battle had been carefully analyzed, Nimitz issued a statement that went a little further: "The performance of officers and men was of the highest order, not only at Midway and afloat, but equally so among those at Oahu not privileged to be in the front line of battle. I am proud to report that the cooperative devotion to duty of all those involved was so marked that, despite the necessarily decisive part played by our three carriers, this defeat of the Japanese arms and ambitions was truly a victory of the United States' armed forces and not of the Navy alone."

Nevertheless the myth that the B-17s had won the Battle of Midway persisted until some time after the end of World War II, when extensive questioning of Japanese officers made it clear that all the army bombs fell in the water. Not one of the 322 bombs dropped by the B-17s scored a hit.

Postwar research in U.S. and Japanese sources brought out the following details concerning the Battle of Midway.

The Midway-based Catalina amphibians that attacked the Japanese Invasion Force on the night of June 3 succeeded in torpedoing an oiler, temporarily slowing her down.

The following morning, June 4, the Nagumo force launched 108 aircraft against Midway, retaining an equal number in reserve. The Japanese planes inflicted widespread damage on the atoll and shot down most of the defending marine fighters.

Midway counterattacked with more than 60 bombers and torpedo planes, which struck the enemy, not together, but in five separate waves. The attackers took severe losses, mainly from the agile Zero fighters, but made not a single hit. Next came three separate attacks by torpedo planes from the *Hornet*, the *Enterprise*, and the *Yorktown*. Nearly all these were shot down without inflicting any damage whatever.

The Nagumo force had come unscathed through eight successive attacks. But the strikes by the American planes were not entirely fruitless. Their disastrous showing caused Nagumo to relax caution, and the low-flying torpedo planes drew the airborne Zeros, and Japanese attention, down to low altitude.

At 8:30 a.m. on June 4 Rear Admiral Tamon Yamaguchi, commanding Carrier Division 2 in the *Hiryu*, upon learning of the American carrier force to the northeast, advised Nagumo to launch an immediate attack on it with his reserve planes. Nagumo disregarded this advice and made the fateful decision to delay until he was prepared for a massive, coordinated strike with all his planes. He began replacing the instant-contact bombs, with which his reserve planes were armed in anticipation of a second strike on Midway, with armor-piercing bombs and torpedoes. He recovered his combat air patrol of Zeros and also his planes returning from the initial raid on Midway. Most of these operations were carried out while under attack; they cost Nagumo two hours.

No student of warfare, fully apprised of the situation in the Midway area at 10:00 a.m., June 4, 1942, would have predicted that the Americans had the slightest chance for victory. The four Japanese carriers had on their flight decks a strike force armed, fueled, and ready to take off, and a second strike force being readied below. Few of the American Midway-based aircraft, except the B-17s, were fit for further service, and the B-17s could not hit moving ships. Task Forces 16 and 17 were losing their torpedo planes, and their bombers were all flying in wrong directions.

Then the American potential improved. The *Hornet* bombers continued southeast, away from the enemy, but the *Yorktown* bombers turned to follow their own torpedo planes, and the *Enterprise* bombers adopted the course of a straggling destroyer. Approaching from different directions, the *Yorktown* and *Enterprise* groups arrived over the enemy force at the same time, unobserved by the Japanese and unaware of each other's presence. No amount of planning or rehearsal could have attained such precision.

The last of the American torpedo-plane strikes had been snuffed out, Nagumo had finally ordered his counterattack, and his carriers were just turning into the wind to launch. They had armed and fueled planes spotted on their flight decks about to take off, and other planes on their hangar decks arming and fueling. Discarded instant-contact bombs were still lying on the hangar decks awaiting return to the magazines. The force was thus in the ultimate state of vulnerability.

In five minutes the Japanese strike would be on its way. Before it could be launched, however, bombers from the *Yorktown* and *Enterprise* dove from 15,000 feet and, in seconds, changed the whole course of the war. They released bombs that hit the *Soryu*, the *Kaga*, and Nagumo's flagship *Akagi*, setting off lethal fires and explosions in all three.

The carrier *Hiryu*, escaping unscathed to the north with some of the Japanese surface vessels, first launched bombers, then torpedo planes that found and disabled the *Yorktown*. At 5:00 p.m. dive-bombers from the *Enterprise* located the *Hiryu* just as she was about to launch an attack on the other American carriers. They scored four direct hits on the Japanese carrier, setting off explosions and uncontrollable fires. A dozen B-17s from Midway participated in the attack on the *Hiryu*: none of the bombs they dropped hit the target, but one of the army bombers succeeded in strafing the burning vessel.

On orders from Yamamoto, the Japanese Second Fleet had separated from the Invasion Force. Four of its heavy cruisers, screened by two destroyers, advanced to shell Midway, while the majority of its remaining vessels, including two battleships and four heavy cruisers, sped to the support of Nagumo's carriers. Arriving too late, the Second Fleet picked up Nagumo's two battleships and most of his other surface ships, and headed east in the darkness, seeking the Americans—an encounter which Spruance avoided by his temporary eastward withdrawal. At 2:55 a.m. Admiral Yamamoto, concluding that his eastbound ships were less likely to be victors of a night battle than victims of a dawn air attack, canceled the Midway operation and ordered a general retreat.

The Second Fleet's four-cruiser bombardment group, then nearing Midway, reversed course and presently sighted the U.S. submarine *Tambor*. In maneuvering to avoid torpedoes they mistakenly supposed the *Tambor* had fired, the *Mogami* and *Mikuma* collided. The other two cruisers sped away, leaving the damaged vessels with the two escorting destroyers to make what speed they could.

By 9:00 a.m., June 5, all four of Nagumo's carriers had gone down. That morning B-17s and Marine Corps bombers from Midway attacked the *Mogami* and *Mikuma*. All their bombs missed, but Marine Captain Richard Fleming crashed his flaming plane into the *Mikuma*'s after turret, starting fires which caused numerous casualties and widespread damage. On June 6, as we have seen, Task Force 16 attacked the battered cruisers with dive-bombers, sinking the *Mikuma* and damaging the *Mogami* so badly that it took almost a year to repair her.

On June 7 the Japanese began landing without opposition on the Aleutian islands of Attu and Kiska, having canceled their plan to take Adak when it was discovered that there was a secret American base nearby. During the landings, Admiral Theobald's North Pacific Force was cruising uselessly a thousand miles away, south of Alaska.

Directly following the battle of June 4 and for several days thereafter, U.S. air and surface craft searched the seas north and west of Midway, picking up downed airmen and other survivors, Japanese and American.

For the Americans the victory was not cheap: one carrier and one destroyer sunk, 307 men killed, 147 aircraft lost, extensive damage to installations at Midway, moderate damage to installations at Dutch Harbor, and Attu and Kiska lost. Japanese losses were not as severe as U.S. wartime estimates indicated, but they were severe enough to reverse the course of the Pacific war: four carriers and one heavy cruiser sunk, another heavy cruiser wrecked, one battleship, one oiler, and three destroyers damaged, 322 aircraft lost, and 2,500 men killed, including many experienced pilots.

In the first euphoria of victory, before the cost in lives had been totted up, Admiral Nimitz could not resist making a pun in his famous communiqué of June 6: "Pearl Harbor has now been partially avenged. Vengeance will not be complete until Japanese sea power is reduced to impotence. We have made substantial progress in that direction. Perhaps we will be forgiven if we claim that we are about midway to that objective."

# CHAPTER 8

# CHESTER AND CATHERINE

CATHERINE NIMITZ soon tired of the frenetic pace of wartime Washington, with its rumormongering and its intrusions upon her privacy. In June 1942, when her daughter Mary's school closed for the summer, she gave up her apartment, loaded the family Chrysler, and with eleven-year-old Mary set out across country to Berkeley, California, where she and Chester had spent some of the happiest years of their married life. Daughter Nancy, then just twice Mary's age, took leave from her library job to go along and help her mother with the driving.

Admiral King asked Catherine to provide him with her itinerary and to let him know if for some reason she could not stick to it. On his instructions, she checked in by telephone to various naval offices across the country. She was not greatly surprised when the tollman at a Mississippi River bridge greeted her with "Good evening, Mrs. Nimitz, you're earlier than we expected," but she was a bit startled on arriving in Burlington, Iowa, at the far end of the bridge, to find a police escort waiting to conduct her to her hotel.

While Mrs. Nimitz and Nancy took turns driving, Mary shared the back seat with her family of paper dolls and a menagerie consisting of Freckles, the cocker spaniel; Tamagno, a canary, named after the famous Italian opera singer and carried in a small cage; and John, Jack, Helen, and Helena, little green turtles, who nearly came to grief when the car sped too fast over a dip in the road and sloshed them and the water out of their bowl.

Mary understandably became restless long before the journey was over. She began, moreover, to fret over the prospect of spending the summer in Berkeley where she might not have any playmates. Accordingly, when they reached Lake Tahoe and were entranced with the beauty of the country, Mrs. Nimitz began to look about for a camp for girls. At State Line, Nevada, she found Camp Chonokis and enrolled Mary for the summer weeks. Then with Nancy she went on to Berkeley and took temporary residence at the Hotel Durant. Shortly afterward Nancy returned by train to Washington.

A major reason for Catherine's moving to the West Coast was to be on hand when Chester flew to San Francisco for his periodic conferences with Admiral King. In a recent letter, Nimitz had intimated that another such conference would be forthcoming that summer. For security reasons, however, he had not informed her in so many words. To pass on secret information in letters that might be intercepted, they had developed a kind of private language, a matter of nuances and references that would not mean anything to outsiders.

Admiral Nimitz retained his inherited staff members until the stigma of their having been surprised by the attack on Pearl Harbor had been expunged. By the spring of 1942, he had begun rotating them out. His stated reason, perfectly true, was that he believed in regularly reinvigorating his staff by bringing in officers fresh from combat experience and in sending those ashore out to the war zone before they grew stale from desk work. Officers' careers, he pointed out, profited from variety of experience. To Mrs. Nimitz he confided a third reason. "My staff," he wrote, "will gradually change from those I found to those I choose." Then he added a bit of information he knew would interest her: "Mercer will be my flag secretary before many weeks."

Commander Preston V. Mercer had earlier been a most efficient flag secretary to Admiral Nimitz, and he and his wife, also named Catherine, had become close friends of the Nimitzes. Not long after receiving news of this impending appointment, Catherine Nimitz was not at all surprised to learn that Catherine Mercer had taken up residence in nearby Piedmont. The latter's husband had done no more than point out in a letter that flag secretaries normally accompany their admirals to important conferences. This hint was enough to attract his wife to the West Coast.

Catherine Nimitz had routinely notified 12th Naval District headquarters in San Francisco of her presence in the area. Toward the end of June, Vice Admiral John W. Greenslade, the district commandant, called her by telephone and asked if she would like to go to the air station at nearby Alameda on the morning of the 30th. Instantly grasping his concealed meaning, she replied that she would indeed. Afterward she conveyed the good news to Catherine Mercer in equally discreet language.

Thus it was that the two Catherines met at the air station on the morning of June 30. Present also was a small group of officers headed by Admiral Greenslade. Mrs. Nimitz and Mrs. Mercer were conducted to a waiting room near the pier to which Admiral Nimitz's plane was scheduled to taxi after landing. Here they were made comfortable and offered hot coffee.

Presently there hurried into the room an agitated-looking officer who explained that Admiral Nimitz's plane had just touched down and that there had been a "slight accident." The admiral and his staff members, he assured them, however, had only been shaken up a little. Would the ladies let him drive them over to the dispensary near where boats from the plane were landing? The two Catherines assured him they would. Admiral Greenslade and other officers followed in another car.

It was a short but alarming ride. En route two ambulances and a fire engine, sirens wailing, passed the two cars. As the cars arrived at the dispensary, out came a pair of hospital corpsmen bearing a stretcher on which lay a man with a bleeding head. Mrs. Nimitz, recognizing the patient as Captain Lynde D. McCormick of her husband's staff, was seized with panic. Had all the men in the "slight accident" been "shaken up" as badly as that—or worse? Almost immediately afterward she and Mrs. Mercer were relieved to see their husbands walking toward them—both in wet blue uniforms, the admiral capless, the commander clutching a briefcase. There were damp embraces.

The plane, a four-motor Sikorsky amphibian, had been, in a sense, the victim of tail winds, which had brought it over San Francisco Bay ahead of schedule, before the boats sent out from the Alameda station to clear the landing area of floating objects had completed their patrols. When the plane began to descend, none of the passengers bothered to fasten seat belts. Admiral Nimitz and Captain McCormick were playing cribbage. Commander Mercer, seated by a window, was guarding a briefcase that contained the CinCPac action report of the Battle of Midway. In the cabin also were crew members, including a couple of relief pilots, and an officer who had hitchhiked a ride to a new stateside billet.

Just before the plane touched down, they heard Mercer exclaim, "Oh-oh!" He had just seen a box in the water. Almost immediately afterward the plane struck a floating pile as big as a telegraph pole. Up flew its bow and it flipped completely over, its bottom ripped out. In the cabin bodies hurtled through the air, smashing open doors and dogged-down hatches. McCormick, besides head wounds, suffered two cracked vertebrae. Nimitz and Mercer were saved from serious injury by being seated with their backs toward the direction of the plane's motion. But the admiral had his share of bumps and contusions, and a man landed on Mercer's chest with such force that the commander had trouble breathing for several days afterward.

When the inverted cabin began to fill with water, everyone inside, disregarding broken bones, made for an open freight hatch. As they clambered out onto what had been the underside of a wing, Mercer anxiously asked Nimitz if he was hurt. "I'm all right," replied the admiral, "but for God's sake save that briefcase."

Already the debris-collecting boats were heading for the topsy-turvy plane, which was slowly settling. Everybody in the cabin was able to get out, but rescuing the pilots and crew members from the cockpit and adjacent spaces took some doing. Admiral Nimitz refused to go ashore while men were still trapped inside the plane. He and his fellow passengers, soaking wet and shivering, were still standing on the wing when a crash boat arrived with crew, two medical officers, and several corpsmen.

The medics climbed onto the wing, and while the doctors examined the more seriously injured men, corpsmen and boat crews guided or lifted passengers and plane crewmen into the boats. Everything had to be done in haste before the plane went down. Each time a corpsman with an armful of blankets draped one around Nimitz's shoulders, the admiral took it off and wrapped it around an injured man.

At last everybody was out of the plane. All except Nimitz and Mercer had suffered at least broken bones. One of the pilots had been killed. Corpsmen tried politely to lead Nimitz into one of the boats, but in his deep concern he would not let himself be conducted from the wing while there were still injured men there. Inadvertently he was making a nuisance of himself. At last an 18-year-old boat crewman from Texas, a seaman second class with vague notions about insignia and rank, turned to the admiral and shouted, "Commander, if you would only get the hell out of the way, maybe we could get something done around here." Without replying, Nimitz meekly stepped into the crash boat.

As the boat pulled away from the plane, Nimitz, at last wrapped in a blanket, stood in the stern watching the rescue proceedings.

"Sit down, you!" yelled the coxswain.

When Nimitz obeyed, the sailor caught sight of his uniform sleeve with more gold stripes than he had ever seen before. He reddened and tried to apologize.

"Stick to your guns, sailor," said Nimitz gently. "You were quite right."

After meeting their wives, Nimitz and Mercer were examined and had their bruises treated at the dispensary. The doctors there advised them to spend the night under observation in the naval hospital at Mare Island, where the more seriously injured men were being sent. Both men declined. The ladies' cars had now been brought to the dispensary. Before departing, the admiral checked on all the injured men still at the dispensary. Then Admiral Greenslade helped him and Mrs. Nimitz into her car and sent his personal aide, Lieutenant Marshall Smith, along to drive and to be of assistance.

When they arrived at the Durant, Mrs. Nimitz was horrified at the prospect of conducting the admiral through the hotel lobby in the disreputable condition to which he had been reduced. "Let's take the elevator from the basement up," she said, "because I don't want to take my husband looking like a drowned rat, soaking, dripping wet, up to the main floor."

So up they went, not letting the elevator operator stop until they reached Mrs. Nimitz's floor. She rushed the admiral, who was beginning to sniffle, into a hot bath and, while he was soaking, sent Lieutenant Smith out to buy him some dry underwear. She dried the admiral's uniform on the radiators and touched it up with a hot iron.

Presently there came a worried telephone call from 12th Naval District headquarters. Proper security, it seemed, could not be afforded the Commander in Chief, Pacific Fleet and Pacific Ocean Areas, at the Hotel Durant. The Pope suite was awaiting them at San Francisco's St. Francis Hotel. Would Admiral and Mrs. Nimitz come over and occupy it? A car would be sent for them.

Mrs. Nimitz consulted the admiral, who said yes, it was the right thing to do: there was no use worrying people who were responsible for his safety. He was quite well enough for another ride. While he dressed, Mrs. Nimitz packed suitcases, not neglecting to include the civilian clothes she had brought to the West Coast for him.

At the St. Francis, Admiral and Mrs. Nimitz were whisked by special elevator to their apartment. There an unexpected bit of good news awaited them: Admiral King's arrival would have to be delayed until he had completed a series of emergency conferences with General Marshall, which would take two or three days. Thus Chester was vouchsafed time not only to get over his hurts but also for a little vacation with Catherine.

Admiral Nimitz had more than an inkling of what the emergency conferences were about, for he himself had been much involved in the preliminaries. Directly after the Battle of Midway, General MacArthur, who had rejected Nimitz's suggestion for a raid on Tulagi as too risky, came forward with a far more daring plan. Give him, he said, the amphibiously trained 1st Marine Division and two carriers with adequate screen. With them and the three army divisions he already had, he would at once assault New Britain and seize control of Rabaul and the Bismarck Archipelago, thus forcing the Japanese back to their island base of Truk, 700 miles to the north.

Admiral King was appalled at the mere notion of sending precious carriers and the Pacific theater's only amphibious troops across the reef-strewn, poorly charted Solomon Sea into the teeth of a complex of enemy air bases. He insisted that Rabaul had to be approached via the Solomon Islands in a series of steps, so that airfields could be established to support each successive invasion with land-based bombers and fighters. Moreover, King asserted, since the invasion forces—the marines, the carriers, the transports, and most of the supporting vessels—would have to come from the Pacific Fleet and Pacific Ocean Areas, Admiral Nimitz should command all operations in the Solomons, with Admiral Ghormley as his deputy. The Army's contribution, he said, would be to provide garrisons for the islands that the Navy and the Marine Corps captured.

It was now General MacArthur's turn to protest, for the Solomons lay entirely within his Southwest Pacific Area. MacArthur insisted that it was he who should command all forces operating in his area. On this point General Marshall backed him up. King replied that if it made sense for the Army to have the top command in Europe, where most of the forces were ground troops, as Marshall had recommended, then it made equally good sense for the Navy to have the top command in the forthcoming Solomons campaign, where all the operational forces would be naval and marine.

King was, he said, prepared to launch the assault using naval and Marine Corps forces, "even if no support of Army forces in the Southwest Pacific is made available." At this, MacArthur fired off a radiogram to Marshall expressing his opinion that the Navy was trying to reduce the Army in the Pacific to a subsidiary role which would consist "largely of placing its forces at the disposal of and under the command of Navy or Marine officers."

Marshall waited a couple of days to let himself, and the general situation, cool off a bit. Then, on June 29, he replied to King with a conciliatory memorandum, suggesting that they get together and work out a compromise.

This was the basis of the emergency conferences that delayed King's departure for the West Coast.

Not long after the Nimitzes had settled themselves at the St. Francis, Captain E. U. Reed, the District Medical Officer, arrived at the hotel. After identifying himself to the suspicious marine who guarded the door of the special elevator, he was allowed to proceed to the Pope apartment. He gave Admiral Nimitz another physical examination and confirmed that his injuries, though extensive, were not really serious. He suggested, however, that his bruises might become increasingly painful for a while, in which case he should have himself brought to the District Medical Office for a diathermy treatment. For the time being, he was to remain in bed.

Chester and Catherine, closer and with more interests in common than most married couples, had a great deal to tell each other after six months' separation. During their day-long conversation, the admiral seems to have forgotten, or at least succeeded in making light of, his aches. In the silence of the ensuing night, however, his bruises kept him so uncomfortably awake that early the next morning he followed Captain Reed's advice and visited the medical office for a diathermy treatment. He then returned to the St. Francis and, on doctor's orders, went back to bed.

That afternoon, July 1, Admiral Nimitz, who had become increasingly restless, suddenly sat up. "I'm not going to stay in bed any longer," he announced. He asked Catherine to bring him his civilian clothes. "Let's go down," he said, "and let's take a walk in the streets and do some window shopping."

So the admiral donned his civvies. Then, with Catherine on his arm, he left the apartment, told the startled marine guard to step aside, descended in the special elevator, and joined the crowds in the street. Unrecognized, limping slightly, he did his window-shopping with Catherine at his side. When they reached the foot of California Street, they decided to take the cable car to the top of the hill and go to call on some old friends, a recently retired admiral and his wife.

As the cable car stopped near the summit and the Nimitzes were about to get off, they encountered more old friends about to get on. These were Commander Atherton McCondray and his mother. McCondray, "a most charming bachelor," in Mrs. Nimitz's words, had been a student of the admiral when the latter had taught reserve officers at the University of California in the 1920s.

The admiral seized the commander's hand, and there was a burst of chatter, with Mrs. Nimitz, never at a loss for words, eagerly entering the conversation. Meanwhile, the cable-car conductor, irked at the delay caused by this middle-of-the-street chitchat, was loudly thumping his bell for the Nimitzes to get off his car and the McCondrays to get on.

Finally the admiral took his hand off the car, the McCondrays climbed aboard, and the vehicle got under way with as much speed as a San Francisco cable car going uphill could muster. The conductor was indignant, particularly at the older gentleman, who appeared to have been the principal cause of the delay. He growled in a loud voice to the whole car, "Who does that man think he is, holding up the car like this?" Commander McCondray, suppressing his laughter, could hardly resist saying, "You'd be surprised."

During the next two days, Chester and Catherine whirled about the San Francisco area happily calling on friends. Chester forgot his bruises, discovering anew that for him people and conversation were the best medicine. Even a visit to the Mare Island hospital failed to subdue his and Catherine's spirits, for they found the victims of the airplane accident getting along famously.

The impromptu Nimitz vacation came to a close at the end of July 3. That afternoon Admiral King and his retinue arrived from Washington. The following morning the formal conference would convene and, at the close of this, Nimitz would fly back to Pearl Harbor and resume his onerous duties.

A solomonic compromise had at last allowed King to leave Washington. The Joint Chiefs of Staff, to get around the problem of the Navy having the senior command within General MacArthur's assigned area, had straightened out the north-south line of demarcation so that it ran only along the 159th east meridian northward to the equator. Thus, the Eastern Solomons, including Tulagi and Guadalcanal, were inside the South Pacific Area. Within this enlarged area, Pacific Fleet forces under the overall command of Nimitz would seize and occupy Tulagi, the Santa Cruz Islands, and adjacent positions. This operation was designated Task I, and its target date was August 1.

Task II, which would follow, required the seizure and occupation of the rest of the Solomons and of the northeast coast of New Guinea, including Lae and Salamaua. In this phase, General MacArthur was to be in overall command. Task III called for the seizure and occupation of Rabaul and adjacent positions, again with MacArthur in overall command.

The King-Nimitz conference opened on the morning of July 4 in the Federal Building. Commander Mercer showed up in a racy blue-and-white-check suit, which so obviously irked Admiral King that, with Mrs. Mercer's help, the commander patched up his torn uniform sufficiently to make it wearable at the second session. Rear Admirals Pye and Jacobs were present and, at the beginning, so was Rear Admiral Richmond Kelly Turner, lately chief of War Plans in the CNO's office, but newly appointed Commander, South Pacific Amphibious Force. In the latter capacity he would be in direct command of the seizure of Tulagi.

Admiral King opened the meeting by outlining and commenting upon the compromise command solution for the forthcoming Solomons campaign. There was no need to go into plans for the Tulagi operation, for these in broad outline had been worked out and agreed upon by King and Nimitz via radio dispatch. Admiral Turner submitted a more detailed project, which was quickly approved. When it was apparent that nothing more was to be said about Tulagi, Turner left the meeting and headed by plane for Pearl Harbor and the South Pacific to make final plans and assemble his forces.

Like most of the King-Nimitz conferences, this one dealt largely with details left over from the major decisions already agreed upon by radio. King did, however, excite the imagination of all present with another of his long looks ahead. Following the completion of Tasks I, II, and III, and the conquest of Rabaul, he announced, the next advance toward Japan would be via Truk, Guam, and Saipan.

In the late afternoon of July 5, before the conference adjourned, word came from Pearl Harbor that Station Hypo had broken a radio dispatch indicating that a Japanese naval party had landed on Guadalcanal. From the fact that the party included Pioneer Forces, fleet intelligence deduced that the enemy was about to construct an airfield on that island.* This startling information altered the objectives of the new operation and gave it a heightened urgency. A tentative plan to occupy the Santa Cruz Islands was dropped and Guadalcanal substituted. The latter would have to be seized before the airfield could be completed and made operational by the enemy.

When the meeting broke up, Admiral Nimitz returned to the St. Francis, where he had a final visit with Catherine. Then with Commander Mercer he headed back by plane to Pearl Harbor. Captain McCormick had to remain in the hospital a little longer.

In the admiral's absence, Mrs. Nimitz made herself useful. She helped to establish and supervise a new naval family hospital in Oakland. Officially designated U.S. Naval Hospital, Oakland, it was soon familiarly known as Oak Knoll. Catherine joined the project at the request of the hospital's commanding officer, who needed help because most of his physicians and surgeons were reserve officers, unaccustomed to navy ways.

In the evenings she spoke frequently over the radio on behalf of war-bond sales, the Red Cross, and other causes. She wrote her own speeches, which the program directors soon learned needed no checking or editing. One Christmas she broadcast special messages to Burma, the Philippines, and Australia. On a nationwide hookup, when she was one of several speakers in different cities, an urgent request reached San Francisco from New York: "Ask Mrs. Nimitz if she will please help us out. Somebody's made a mistake, and we've got to have somebody talk for a minute more than was scheduled. Will she do it?" She would, and she calmly ad-libbed for 60 seconds on behalf of the Navy Relief Society.

Catherine was quite as well informed as her husband and the many eminent people with whom his rank and offices brought him into association. She respected ability and high office, but was never awed by them. Like the admiral, she was natural and at ease with the mighty, and equally so with the lowly. She handled the family's finances, not because she particularly liked managing money but because the admiral was too busy to do so. Neither he nor she ever felt straitened by navy pay because their tastes did not run to luxuries or to display and neither had any ambition to amass wealth.

Chester and Catherine, despite the periodic separations consequent upon

---

* To conceal the source of this information, a cover story was later released stating that a Southwest Pacific search plane had observed the field under construction.

his career, had grown so close together through the years that they had developed the same interests and tastes and had come even to think alike. People who knew the Nimitzes well and appreciated the admiral's mind often remarked that in her own way Catherine was every bit her husband's intellectual equal.

They first became acquainted in November 1911 over a game of bridge. Chester, then 26, had been at sea in command of the submarine *Narwhal* with additional duty as Commander, Third Submarine Division. He had been ordered, via the Boston Navy Yard, to the Fore River Shipbuilding Company at Quincy, Massachusetts, to oversee the installation of diesel engines in the submarine *Skipjack*, which he was next to command. Almost at once he ran into Lieutenant Prentice Bassett, his friend since their days at the Naval Academy together. Bassett, delighted at the encounter, insisted that Nimitz come to have supper with him and his mother, with whom he lived in nearby Wollaston. Before supper he took Nimitz down the street to meet the Freeman family. The father of the family, Mr. Richard Freeman, a ship broker, invited them to come back later for an evening of bridge. This was the evening that changed Chester's life.

The elder Freeman daughter, Elizabeth, in her mid-twenties, was the belle of the household. Most of her callers of late had been naval officers, among whom it was understood that courtesy required them to be available for a game or so of bridge, known to be Mr. Freeman's favorite pastime. The younger Freeman daughter, Catherine, was then all of 19, but in her family she was still the kid sister, and was particularly so considered by Elizabeth. Catherine for her part, rather resented the naval officers because her sister's admirers cluttered up the house when Catherine would have liked to have her own friends there more often.

In the ordinary course of events, both Prentice Bassett and Chester Nimitz would have been considered callers on the very eligible Miss Elizabeth Freeman, and she would have made the fourth at bridge that evening. But as fate would have it, Elizabeth was not at home, and so Catherine was drafted to take her place both at tea and afterward at bridge.

Right away Catherine decided that as naval officers went, Lieutenant Nimitz was something special. "As we sat there in the afternoon having a cup of tea," she afterward recalled, "I looked over at this young gentleman that Prentice had brought, and I thought he was the handsomest person I had ever seen in my life. He had curly, blond hair, which definitely was a little bit too long because he had just come in from weeks at sea and had not had a chance to have it cut. I kept thinking what a really lovely person this was—those beautiful blue eyes and a lovely smile with which he greeted my mother and looked at her."

That evening Catherine was particularly impressed with young Nimitz's good nature. Prentice was in high spirits, she remembered. "He carried on a sort of wild conversation and teased Lieutenant Nimitz terrifically, but it seemed to roll off Chester's back. He didn't seem to mind it in the slightest."

Another of Chester's old Naval Academy acquaintances, Lieutenant Clarence Hinkamp, was at Quincy overseeing the fitting-out of the submarine *Sturgeon*, which was to be his next command. Hinkamp, nicknamed Heinie, and Chester took rooms in the grubby, run-down Greenleaf Hotel, Quincy's only hostelry, and ate in equally unattractive restaurants. In the circumstances, Chester was delighted to get an invitation from the Freemans to dine at their home and even more pleased when he sampled Mrs. Freeman's cooking. The next time he was asked to a meal at the Freemans', out of sheer mercy he finagled an invitation for Heinie to accompany him.

Chester and Heinie proved such merry company and were so obviously appreciative of good food served in a comfortable home that Mrs. Freeman invited them frequently, at first only to dine, eventually to spend whole weekends in the Freeman home. For the two Freeman girls those weekends in the winter of 1911–12 were memorable. Chester, Heinie, Elizabeth, and Catherine took long walks together, went bowling, and from time to time journeyed to Boston to attend shows at Keith's Vaudeville. Everybody thought it was awfully decent of Elizabeth to let her kid sister Catherine tag along—apparently as a sort of combination mascot and junior chaperon. Elizabeth, for her part, played the role of surrogate mother to the hilt and with apparent relish, telling Catherine at every opportunity precisely what she should and should not do. It was nearly spring before it dawned on Elizabeth that Chester had ceased to regard Catherine as a mere tagalong, if he ever did, and was acting as the younger sister's escort.

By this time the *Skipjack* and the *Sturgeon* had been launched and, commanded by Lieutenants Nimitz and Hinkamp, began making trial runs as far south as Chesapeake Bay. Chester, now seriously interested in Catherine, wrote to her every day they were apart, though sometimes his duties permitted him time to dash off only a brief note. The briefest of all came one day in March: "I had to go swimming yesterday, and it was awfully, awfully cold." A letter soon arrived from Heinie with an explanation. In Hampton Roads a sailor had lost his footing on the *Skipjack* and slipped overboard into a strong current. Lieutenant Nimitz, perceiving from the man's struggles that he was no swimmer, instantly jumped into the frigid water after him. Chester had to fight the man as well as the water, and hence had no strength left to fight the current that was carrying them both out to sea. Luckily, the struggling men were sighted from the battleship *North Dakota*, which sent out a boat to pick them up. Heinie assured the Freemans that the icy immersion had done Chester no harm. He was in perfect health. For this rescue the Treasury Department awarded Lieutenant Nimitz the Silver Lifesaving Medal, a medal he was always proud to wear.

In the spring of 1912, Nimitz was invited to address the Naval War College on the subject of submarines—an extraordinary honor for a 27-year-old lieutenant. He worked hard on his text and at length journeyed to Newport, Rhode Island. On June 20, 1912, he delivered his lecture, "Defensive and Offensive Tactics of Submarines." The lecture was classified confidential, but an unclassified, somewhat expanded version was published the following December in the *U.S. Naval Institute Proceedings*. Thus young Nimitz was launched on a fruitful secondary career as a lecturer and writer.

It would be pleasant to report that Nimitz foresaw the submarine as the unparalleled commerce-destroyer it turned out to be. He anticipated nothing of the sort and would no doubt have been astonished, and possibly horrified, to learn that the submersibles would find their most effective wartime use against unarmed freighters. Like most naval officers of the time, he saw the submarine as a defender of harbors and coasts and as an auxiliary to the fleet. Amusingly, Nimitz suggested "a ruse which might assist in forcing the enemy to keep away from certain areas and thus increase the chances of making the enemy cross the submarine danger zone": fast scouts of the fleet would "drop numerous poles, properly weighted to float upright in the water, and painted to look like a submarine's periscope."

In the summer of 1912, the submarines were based at Provincetown Harbor, at the end of Cape Cod. As luck would have it, Prentice Bassett, who had recently been married, was assigned to a ship operating in the same area. He and his wife had a cottage on the cape and invited the Freeman sisters to come out and spend a week with them. They gladly accepted, of course, and the three couples—Chester and Catherine, Heinie and Elizabeth, and Prentice and his wife—had some wonderful times together. By now, however, Catherine, beginning to feel grown up, chafed under her sister's constant, "Catherine, don't do this. Catherine, don't do that."

All such dictates came to a rather sudden end one day when the couples were having lunch aboard Bassett's ship. Chester and Catherine were seated at a table with friends, Elizabeth with several people at another, when wine was served. Elizabeth rose from her place, rushed over to the table where Catherine was seated, and said in a voice that all could hear, "Don't take that wine. You mustn't drink any wine."

While Catherine, embarrassed, turned away, Chester rose and looked big sister in the eye. "Elizabeth," he said evenly, "I'm looking after your sister, and I have no intention of letting her drink too much wine, but she's going to have a glass of wine." At that moment something snapped in the relationship between Catherine and her sister and jelled between Catherine and Chester. Catherine knew that thenceforward she would look not to father, mother, or sister for advice and support but to this young man who had declared himself her protector.

Shortly after this episode, on August 28, 1912, Chester Nimitz wrote from Provincetown to Mrs. Anna Nimitz at Kerrville, Texas:

> My dear Mother,
>
> If you love me at all, I want you to congratulate me on becoming engaged to Catherine B. Freeman of Wollaston, Massachusetts, to be married sometime in April or May of 1913, just after I leave the submarines and just before I start my tour of shore duty. I have written to you of the Freemans

several times and you have their pictures. I spent the last winter, December and January, living with them. I will be home on leave to see you in December, near Christmas, I hope, and then you can tell me whether I'm right or wrong. You may accuse me of not knowing my mind because two years ago I wanted to marry someone else. Well, two years is a long time and I am no longer the vague-minded person I was then. I need tell you no more of the Freemans, because I have written you from time to time about them. Ask Otto. He has met them. Now, if you want me to be happy, please write this young lady a nice letter, for my sake. I'm not going into this unprepared. In April of next year I will have saved $1,500 which will give me enough to start on. I look for no outside assistance at all. Whatever my Grandfather left for me belongs to you absolutely and without conditions. I don't know anything about my shore duty or where it will be, but I don't care very much where it is. Will write you more details from time to time. Please let me know that you approve of my plans, because you must remember that I am no longer such a young man. Your son is getting older and bolder every year.

> Very best love to the family.
> Hoping to hear from you soon,
> your son, Chester.

Not long afterward Lieutenant Nimitz, with the imposing title of Commander, Atlantic Submarine Flotilla, headed south in the *Skipjack* accompanied by several other submarines, including the *Sturgeon*, Lieutenant Hinkamp commanding. The flotilla spent the winter in Cuban waters. As always, and through life when they were separated, Chester and Catherine exchanged letters daily. By mail they agreed on arrangements for their wedding, which was to take place immediately on his return. Chester got back to Wollaston on April 8, 1913, and they were married the next day.

The Freemans had the wedding at home. The house was decorated with daffodils, and for the ceremony they enlisted the services of a bearded Unitarian minister who lived across the street. Elizabeth was maid of honor, and Lieutenant George Stewart, Chester's roommate at the Naval Academy, was best man. All but one of the ushers were submarine officers. The exception was Catherine's brother, six years her senior, who had come from Michigan, where he was studying mining engineering. Because of the short notice, none of Chester's family could be present.

Following the ceremony the newlyweds left by train for New York, a journey which in itself was a major adventure for Catherine, who had only once before traveled outside Massachusetts. In the big city they took a room on an upper floor of the then-new Hotel McAlpin on Seventh Avenue. That evening they were convulsed to discover atop a building opposite their window an electric sign advertising Wrigley's Spearmint Gum and featuring a gigantic girl who winked at them all night. "We thought this was absolutely lovely," Catherine recalled.

The Nimitzes attended a couple of shows, but for the most part they simply walked about, window-shopping and seeing the sights. The fact was that the couple had to observe strict economy because Chester's pay at that time was only $215 a month and out of this sum he regularly sent his mother $25. Moreover, they planned next to make the long journey to Texas so that Chester could introduce his bride to his family.

The Texas visit very nearly proved disastrous. Grandfather Nimitz would doubtless have welcomed Catherine, but he had died two years before. Chester's mother greeted her daughter-in-law warmly and then, in her self-effacing way, remained in the background. In the forefront were Henke and Nimitz aunts and uncles, whose reception for the girl from Massachusetts was something less than cordial. They evidently had expected Chester to return home and follow the family custom of marrying into the clan, descendants of the Fredericksburg settlers. They did considerable muttering among themselves in German and made it clear that they were not prepared gladly to accept this Yankee into the family.

To Chester his relatives' attitude was both intensely irritating and completely unforeseen. In the twelve years since he had left Kerrville, he ceased to think of himself as a German-American or a Texan or a Southerner and considered himself simply a citizen of the United States. This change became apparent to all one evening when, at a family gathering, one of his aunts asked, "Chester, if there was another war between the North and the South, which would you fight for?" As she spoke, Auntie gave the bride a look that said, "Now you'll see exactly where you stand."

Catherine was startled. From childhood she had been brought up with the view that the Civil War was over, that the old antipathy between North and South was something one never mentioned. Chester, for his part, scarcely dreamed that it would occur to anyone to ask such a question. "Why," he said, "I'd stay by the Union, of course." Auntie, thus put in her place, gave Catherine a look that was nothing less than poisonous.

The Nimitzes and the Henkes were provincial and prejudiced, to be sure, but there was not a fool among them. They could see that Catherine, Yankee or not, was a fine, intelligent girl and that she and Chester adored each other. Before the brief visit of the newlyweds was over, they had dropped their bias and accepted the young lady from Massachusetts into the family.

Of all the Texas clan, Catherine was most attracted to her mother-in-law, Anna, and to Anna's mother. The latter came over from Fredericksburg to call on Catherine and Chester in the tiny house in Kerrville where Anna and her husband were then living. Grandmother Henke proved to be a very stout, black-eyed little lady with a merry twinkle in her eye. Catherine was eager to meet her, in part because Mrs. Henke had been the subject of some discussion, not to say bewilderment, in the Freeman family. Before his marriage to Catherine, Chester in describing his mother's relatives to Mrs. Freeman had said, "My grandmother Henke is 96 years old and she's very wonderful." Then he added, "You know, I have an uncle younger than I am. Yes, Grandmother Henke's youngest son is 26."

To Catherine, Mrs. Henke did not appear to be 96 or anywhere near that old. She was dying to ask her how old she really was, but she was hesitant, lest the question embarrass the old lady and also because Mrs. Henke spoke little English and Catherine spoke no German. Finally she got Mrs. Henke aside and, screwing up her courage, asked "Grandmother, how old are you?" Without the least hesitation Mrs. Henke replied, "I'm 69."

Catherine, chuckling over Chester's mistake, managed to convey to Mrs. Henke the substance of her grandson's remarks to Mrs. Freeman, whereupon the old lady burst into gales of laughter. From time to time that afternoon, grandma would look at Chester, then at Catherine, and go into shrieks of laughter while the rest of the family, who had not heard the story, wondered what on earth ailed her.

At length, as Chester's leave drew to an end, Lieutenant and Mrs. Nimitz headed for Washington and a return to duty. The honeymoon was over, or so it seemed. In a sense, however, it was just beginning, for in Washington Chester was surprised and delighted to receive orders to proceed to Europe.

The Navy, impressed by the performance of diesel engines in submarines, had decided experimentally to power a few large ships with diesels, but the technology for constructing and installing big enough engines was lacking in the United States. These matters could be learned only abroad, mainly in Germany. Two civilians from the New York Navy Yard, Albert Kloppenberg, a draftsman, and Ernest Delbose, an engineer, were being sent to study the techniques. The Navy also sent Lieutenant Nimitz, who had a reputation as the foremost diesel expert in a U.S. naval uniform.

The Nimitzes went first to the submarine works at New London, where Chester was given a quick survey of the latest developments in the smaller diesels. In May 1913 he and Catherine sailed for Europe in the liner *Kaiserin Augusta*.

# CHAPTER 9

# RISING STAR

IN EARLY JUNE 1913, all Germany began to celebrate the silver jubilee of Emperor William II. The festivities were to reach a climax on the 15th, the anniversary of his accession to the imperial throne. The city of Hamburg had an additional reason for celebration, for there on the ways at the Blohm and Voss shipbuilding yard stood a huge warship scheduled to be launched on Saturday the 14th as part of the national observance. Intended for service with the High Seas Fleet, she was temporarily designated "Cruiser K," and was in fact a battle cruiser, as big and as heavily armed as a battleship. Political, military, and naval dignitaries from all over Germany were expected in Hamburg for her launching.

Among the 10,000 workmen and supervisors at the Blohm and Voss works were three Americans, Lieutenant Chester Nimitz, Ernest Delbose, and Albert Kloppenberg. Their mission, assigned by the U.S. Navy through arrangement with the German government, was to study diesel engines, particularly the working drawings of diesels prepared at this yard. Nimitz found the Blohm and Voss executives and other personnel cooperative enough, but he early learned to avoid German officers in and out of the yard. They were an arrogant lot, and most of them treated him with lofty contempt, at least until they learned that he was an officer out of uniform.

When the day of the launching arrived, Nimitz and his men, though not invited to be present, were permitted to stand in back, behind the guests, and watch. Chester had never beheld such an array of military finery—colorful uniforms, plumes, spiked helmets, and miles of gold braid. Presiding over the ceremonies was General August von Mackensen, Commanding General of the 17th Army Corps. Striding up to the platform erected at the bow of the giant cruiser, Mackensen clicked his heels and launched into a eulogy of the hero from whom the new ship was to take her name. This was Baron Georg von Derfflinger, "the Great Elector's boldest and most successful cavalry general." Mackensen expressed a devout hope that the crews of this ship and her commanders might emulate the great Field Marshal's determination and concentration of purpose. Then, turning toward the cruiser, he solemnly named her Derfflinger, smashed a bottle of wine on her bow, and concluded with the words, "I commit thee, proud fabric of men's hands, to thy element."

The guard of honor presented arms, the band struck up *Deutschland über Alles,* and the hundreds of officers present leapt to their feet and smartly saluted. It was a dramatic moment. As the last notes of the national anthem died out, workmen down below were heard knocking the blocks out from under the cruiser. They next applied hydraulic pressure, whereupon with a deep rumbling sound the *Derfflinger* moved eight or ten inches. There followed a loud thumping and more hydraulic pressure, but the cruiser stubbornly refused to continue down the ways. General Mackensen and the other officers lowered their saluting arms and at length took seats. Except for thumping, banging, and hissing below, a long, embarrassed silence followed. Finally a red-faced Blohm and Voss official announced that, because the tide was ebbing, the launch would have to be abandoned for that day.

Nimitz, Delbose, and Kloppenberg were out of the shipyard in a flash—well ahead of the invited dignitaries. With war clouds looming on the horizon, the Germans were jittery. No telling what they might do to a trio of foreign witnesses to their discomfiture.

A few days later Lieutenant and Mrs. Nimitz made a quick trip to Nürnberg so that Chester could arrange to have himself and his men attached for an extended period to the local diesel engineering works. The Nimitzes stopped at the Sign of the Red Rooster, which had been recommended by one of Chester's German aunts. The hostelry proved to be a picturesque old place with customs a little too quaint for American tastes. When the Nimitzes asked to be shown to the bathrooms, they were told to get into their bathrobes and, when they had done so, they were conducted down two flights of stairs and past all the guests in the lobby. "Well," said Chester, "this may be a very nice hotel, but we're not staying here any longer than we can help." That day they shifted to the more cosmopolitan Grand Hotel, where they were able to get a little room under the eaves with a bath attached.

Before the end of June, Chester and Catherine were back in Hamburg. At the Blohm and Voss yard the *Derfflinger* still sat forlornly on the ways despite two more attempts to get her moving. On the 30th, Chester wrote to his mother in Texas:

Dear Mother,

We're back in Hamburg again, after staying in Nürnberg some four days. We will be in Hamburg for about a month more, and then we will go to Nürnberg again, and stay longer than we first stopped in that place. We are now living at the Aussenalster, a wonderful place right in the center of Hamburg, and we have two fine rooms with a lovely balcony looking out over a beautiful garden. We spend our time out on the lake in rowboats and of course sailboats.

Hamburg is a wonderful city, and I believe it is more beautiful than any I have ever seen. Certainly none of our cities can equal it. There are more gardens, parks, and such places, and believe me there are lots of beer kellers. That's what the Bavarian beer halls and places are called. I never saw so much beer consumed in my life. Even the small girls sit down to a half litre glass at breakfast.

Catherine and I are certainly enjoying it, and we have managed to pick up a little German now and then. I can easily understand everything, and she's beginning to pick it up too. I couldn't begin to tell you about all the things here, but I will send you a book of views of lovely places we visit, so that you can see for yourself how things are. . . .

I will close now with very best love to you from us both.

Your son, Chester

From this one might suppose that Lieutenant and Mrs. Nimitz were on a carefree holiday but, in fact, Chester had little time for boating or any other amusements. Each morning around 7:30 he left the apartment for Blohm and Voss, and he rarely returned before 7:00 in the evening. On July 1 the shipyard workmen finally got the *Derfflinger* launched, but Nimitz was not present. Evidently the Blohm and Voss authorities, in sheer embarrassment, had decreed the launching site off limits to all but essential personnel.

Before returning to Nürnberg, the Nimitzes stopped at Augsburg, where Chester visited the plant in which sixteen years before Rudolf Diesel had completed his first commercially successful engine. In Augsburg they stayed at a famous old hotel and were given an enormous room, the one Napoleon had occupied while passing through the area a century earlier. From the look of things, nothing had been changed since Napoleon's visit, with the exception of one notable and questionable improvement: a corner of the huge chamber had been converted into a bathroom and toilet. Since this was separated from the rest of the room only by a four-foot-high wall, it provided the user with a view but little privacy.

Toward the end of a summer of hard work, Lieutenant Nimitz concluded his investigations with visits to Bruges and Kiel. At a trade fair in Bruges, he spent three days minutely studying and taking notes on a large, late-model diesel engine that was performing on blocks. After visiting the diesel works at Kiel, he wound up his stay in Europe by going with Catherine on a brief pleasure trip to Denmark and southern Sweden. The Nimitzes then took ship back to the United States. For Catherine the return voyage was a time of both joyous anticipation and misery. She was pregnant, and happy to be so, but she was also seasick and spent most of her time resting in her cabin.

Back in the States, Lieutenant Nimitz was given a desk in a small office, which he shared with another officer, in the Machinery Division of the New York Navy Yard in Brooklyn. His task here was to supervise the construction and installation of two 2,600-horsepower diesel engines in the new oiler *Maumee*, the hull of which had been built on the West Coast and towed around to New York.

He and Catherine found an apartment nearby at 415 Washington Avenue —living room, dining room, kitchen, three bedrooms, and bath for $50 a month—and began to furnish it. Here they had numerous visitors, for at any given time several submarines were likely to be at New York, and on Sundays all the young submarine officers whom the Nimitzes had known before their marriage came to lunch with Chester and Catherine.

The Nimitzes loved having them come, but feeding so many hungry young men on a lieutenant's salary took some figuring. They hit upon a simple plan. At the market they would buy a whole shoulder of lamb, boned and rolled, for 90 cents. They would season and simmer it, then put it in a baking pan, spread currant jelly over it, and bake it until it was brown.

The men usually came early and the Nimitzes had them take off their jackets and get to work, peeling potatoes, setting table, and generally helping out. One Sunday, when Chester was taking the lamb shoulder out of the kettle where it had been simmering, he dropped it on the floor. Catherine was horrified because all the guests were watching. But Chester just stabbed the shoulder with a fork, held it under a faucet to wash it off, saying, "Just a lamb gambol," and put it in the pan to bake. At lunch it was eaten, every bit.

Completing a 14,500-ton oiler and building and installing her engines was no overnight task. Chester was still at the job when the Nimitzes' first child, Catherine Vance, was born on February 22, 1914. He was still at it when Chester Junior arrived on February 17, 1915.

Chester and Catherine left Washington Avenue and moved out to Flatbush. On Sunday mornings, Chester, together with other daddies, would take the babies to the park while mamma cooked dinner. Surrounding them in the park were busts of great musicians, Handel, Haydn, Mozart, which pleased Chester and also doubtless other Flatbush fathers, most of whom were Germans and Jews who, like Nimitz, were devoted to music. Chester pushed Chester Junior in a carriage ahead of him and pulled Catherine Vance in a little wagon behind. Chester Junior got a bottle and Catherine a cracker and some lessons in walking. Then, after a bit of sunning and watching the sights, the babies were rolled home to mamma's waiting Sunday dinner.

By this time diesel engines were beginning to be much in demand in the United States, and American diesel builders and dealers were becoming aware that Lieutenant Nimitz was probably the U.S. Navy's most skilled diesel expert. The Busch-Sulzer Brothers Diesel Engine Company of St. Louis, the country's first diesel manufacturer and distributor, in an effort to obtain Nimitz's services and know-how for itself, sent a hotshot recruiter to Brooklyn to try to lure him away from the Navy. It is pertinent to note that at this time Nimitz's navy pay was $240 a month, plus $48 as commutation of quarters. Lieutenant Walter S. Anderson, who occupied the desk next to Nimitz's, tells the story:

> One day in 1915 a man came into our office and introduced himself as representing a company in St. Louis which was trying to manufacture diesel engines. As the conversation developed, I inferred that they were having some problems in this work. Finally it became plain that they wanted to employ Nimitz. This would of course have meant his resignation from the Navy. The man made Nimitz a definite offer of $25,000 a year and a five-year contract. This was when a dollar was a real dollar and we were not paying income taxes!
>
> Knowing how valuable Nimitz was to the Navy, I was gravely disturbed, but to my great relief Nimitz slowly replied, "No thank you, I do not want to leave the Navy." This was indeed wonderful to hear. There was some further

talk, and the man became more persuasive: "At any rate, money is no obstacle to us. Write your own ticket." By this time I was terribly concerned. Nimitz could have said, "That will be $40,000 a year and a ten-year contract." After a brief pause Nimitz reiterated, "No, I don't want to leave the Navy." The man from St. Louis departed.

I then hurried over to Nimitz and said, "Chester, I couldn't help hearing what went on. I'm the only one here to represent the Navy. That was wonderful of you. Thank God you refused that offer. We need you!"

It is not to be supposed that Lieutenant Nimitz spent all his time behind a desk. On the contrary, he superintended the design of the engines and the drafting of the plans and was involved in every step of their assemblage and installation, never hesitating to get into coveralls and dirty his hands. He was high up on one of the wooden platforms surrounding the engines one day when the scaffolding collapsed. Nimitz was knocked unconscious and was buried under a considerable weight of lumber. For several days afterward he was extremely sore, but no bones were broken, and he did not seem to have suffered serious injury. However, he attributed the severe back trouble of his old age to this fall in his youth.

As the building and installation of the engines neared completion, Lieutenant Nimitz was obliged frequently to explain and demonstrate them for the benefit of visiting naval and civilian engineers. He usually showed the visitors around in whatever he was wearing at the time, but on one occasion, when he was to give the grand tour to a convention of engineers from all over the country, he decided that it would be appropriate for him to dress up in his white uniform. Also, to keep his hands clean through the demonstration, he put on white canvas gloves.

The group this time was large and deeply attentive. Lieutenant Nimitz, lecturing and demonstrating, was putting on a star performance when one of the visitors interrupted to ask, "How can you tell whether the exhaust is clean or not?" Replied Nimitz, pointing, "Well, you see that place in there. . . ."

He got no further. He had pointed to that particular spot so often in past demonstrations that he did not bother to look, and he forgot that the fingers of the gloves he was wearing stuck out an inch beyond his own fingers. In "that place in there" were rotating gears, a pair of which caught his glove and pulled a finger in after it. The only thing that saved his hand was his class ring. As that struck the gears, he was able to pull his hand away. Nimitz was, of course, rushed to the hospital. A young sailor picked up the bloody glove that he had dropped. Out fell a piece of mangled finger, whereupon the sailor keeled over in a dead faint.

At the naval hospital, a doctor cleaned what was left of Nimitz's ring finger and sewed up the wound. No anesthetic was necessary because the hand was absolutely numb. After the sewing was finished, Nimitz said, "Thank you. Now I'll go back; I have a great many guests."

"Now wait, wait," replied the doctor. "Don't be hasty."

Chester pointed out that he had not concluded his demonstration and that the engineers would be expecting him.

"I'll tell you what," said the doctor. "You go into this room and you stay here, and if at the end of an hour you still want to go back, we'll see about it."

At the end of an hour, of course, Chester was in shock, his hand was hurting terribly, and he was more than willing to be put to bed.

By mid-1916 the *Maumee*'s engines had at last been completed and installed. On October 23 of that year, the oiler was commissioned under the command of Lieutenant Commander Henry C. Dinger. Lieutenant Nimitz did not have enough rank to command such a ship, but he was assigned as both executive officer and chief engineer. This he found an ideal combination. With a foot in each camp, he could mediate between the deck force, who tried to keep the decks spotless, and the engineers, who tended to leave oily footprints on the scrubbed decks.

After extensive trials and a shakedown cruise, in which the *Maumee*'s engines performed admirably, the oiler put into port for Christmas, which Nimitz spent in Brooklyn with Catherine and the babies. On December 28, 1916, the *Maumee*, with a crew of about forty-five, departed New York for Cuba. Their first task was to set buoys to mark channels in Guacanayabo Gulf, a deep indentation in the Cuban south coast. This was to be the temporary anchorage for the U.S. Atlantic Fleet while it underwent training maneuvers. The *Maumee* remained in the gulf, supplying bunker oil and fresh water to ships of all sizes, from destroyers to battleships. Such duty had its moments of interest, but the *Maumee*'s crew was distressed at the total absence in Guacanayabo Gulf of liberty ports and recreation areas.

Back in Brooklyn, Catherine Nimitz was considering a trip to Texas to introduce her babies to their paternal grandmother and step-grandfather and the rest of the Nimitzes and Henkes. She had, of course, taken them a good many times to visit her own parents in fairly-nearby Wollaston. It must have been with some trepidation that she contemplated the long train trip, more than half way across the continent, to an uncertain welcome, for she had not forgotten the bleak reception of her first visit. She was certain only that she would be warmly greeted by her mother-in-law, for in their brief acquaintance they had developed a real affection for each other. Since then all their contacts had been indirect because Anna Nimitz, who had grown up speaking, reading, and writing chiefly German, was never sure enough of her English to risk writing letters in that language.

In Kerrville, at the end of her exhausting journey, Catherine was joyfully received by her husband's family, particularly as she had brought a pair of new and very fine-looking junior Nimitzes. Anna Nimitz was delighted to see her daughter-in-law and the babies. Catherine said later of their second meeting, "Certainly nobody could have been sweeter to me than my mother-in-law. She was a very, very handsome woman with a lovely smile and a lovely laugh."

Catherine's visit was timed to coincide with the arrival of the *Maumee* to take on oil at Port Arthur, Texas, which was only a few hours by train from Kerrville. At Anna's insistence, Catherine left the children with her and made the journey alone for an all-too-brief visit with Chester. Afterward, on the voyage back to Cuba, which took from January 31 to February 4, 1917, Chester wrote his mother a kind of serial letter. He said in part:

> Dear Mother,
>
> I hope this reaches you in time for your birthday and I wish I could be there with the rest of my family to help you celebrate the day. However, Catherine and the babies will represent me. By now Catherine has probably written to you all about Port Arthur and about the trip. I am sorry that our stay there was so short that I couldn't get to Kerrville.
>
> We left early yesterday morning and by now are well along on the return trip. Catherine is probably boarding the train for Kerrville this very minute. How I wish I were with her! Did the babies behave well during her absence? I hope that you were not too tired as a result. The pictures Catherine brought along are fascinating. You can see for yourself why I'm so proud of my family.
>
> Port Arthur may be a good place to come for oil, but that is about the best that can be said for it. The mosquitoes, even at this time of the year, are terrible, and I'm all bitten up around the neck and ankles. The streets are continually afloat, and for two or three days after a rain, one needs a boat to get around the streets. Just before we left, we met some very nice people, and I know that if Catherine ever goes there again, she will have a good time. She is hoping to stop in San Antonio and order your birthday present from this part of the Nimitz family, and I hope it will be satisfactory to you. . . . I am enclosing a check for $25 to cover any expenses incident to the visit of Catherine and the babies. I don't want you all to be put to any extra expense, and please let me know if this check is too small. . . .
>
> We are finally near the eastern end of Cuba, and if our engines don't break down, we should be anchored in Guantanamo Bay by 5 p.m. this afternoon. The entire fleet will be there, and it will be quite exciting and busy for us all. This trip has been an unfortunate one for me, as we have broken a cylinder on my starboard engine. We can still run on eleven cylinders, and we are going to try to patch the broken one. . . .
>
> I hope you all managed to get by without colds. If the babies are to be indoors for several days, I feel sorry for you. They are quite a handful. Now, Mother dear, I will close, with best love to Father and Dora. I want to congratulate you on your birthday on February 14th and to wish you many happy returns. My babies kiss you for me.
>
> Chester

By the time the *Maumee* returned to Cuban waters, Germany, despite a pledge to the contrary, had resumed unrestricted submarine warfare. In the next few weeks, her U-boats sank several American merchant ships without warning and without providing for the safety of their crews. In response, the United States on April 6, 1917, declared war on Germany.

Not long afterward the *Maumee* was ordered to the mid-Atlantic, some 300 miles south of Greenland, to refuel U.S. destroyers en route to Ireland.

Nimitz later wrote of the operation: "Spring and early summer in this area is no time for a vacation. Icebergs are numerous and there is much drifting ice. Strong and bitter-cold winds prevail, and there are few days of smooth seas. This was the area where *Maumee* began the fueling-at-sea operations that gave our Navy the experience that was to prove invaluable in supplying mobile logistic support to our great fleets that crossed the Pacific in World War II and utterly destroyed the Japanese Navy."

In Guacanayabo Gulf the *Maumee* had remained at anchor to refuel small ships, which came to her, and she got underway and moored alongside battleships to deliver fuel to them. Commander Dinger and Lieutenant Nimitz had early discussed the advantages of underway refueling, if it could be done, and soon convinced themselves that it was indeed practicable. While the *Maumee* was undergoing overhaul, her officers studied destroyer deck plans that showed the location of fuel-filling valves, chocks, bitts, and strong points for towing. They designed towing rigs and drew up underway refueling plans, which they distributed to any destroyer that might need them.

The first ships ever to be fueled under way were the six destroyers of Commander Joseph K. Taussig's Division 8, which were also the first warships sent overseas by the U.S. Navy to participate in World War I. Sailing from Boston on April 24, they encountered tempestuous seas all the way. In the rough weather, the *Maumee* could not refuel a destroyer on either side while proceeding at 10 knots, as had been planned. She had to limit fueling to one destroyer at a time on her lee side while making only 5 knots. Nevertheless, Division 8 completed fueling in less than a day and resumed speed for Queenstown, Ireland, where it arrived on May 4 and soon went out on anti-U-boat patrol. By July 1917, thirty-four American destroyers had arrived at Queenstown, all refueled in mid-ocean by the *Maumee*.

As the wartime U.S. fleet expanded, the *Maumee*, in common with other naval vessels, was stripped of most of her regular crew so that they could share their know-how with the incoming reserves. By the end of 1917 only a handful of the *Maumee*'s regulars were left on board to train the new arrivals to operate the big diesel engines. The turnover proved too fast. Because the new men were not capable of keeping them in good repair, her engines gradually became inoperable. At last the *Maumee* was laid up in reserve at the Philadelphia Navy Yard. After World War I her diesels were replaced by a conventional steam power plant. She later served in the U.S. Navy through World War II, then was transferred to the Nationalist Chinese Navy, in which she bore the name *O Mei*.

Nimitz, promoted to lieutenant commander, was among those transferred from the *Maumee*. On August 10, 1917, he reported as engineering aide to Captain Samuel S. Robison, Commander, Submarine Force, Atlantic Fleet. The new billet proved in some respects the most fortunate of Nimitz's career, for in Robison he acquired a sage adviser, an influential patron, and a lifelong friend. Through the older man's influence, Nimitz shifted the direction of his career away from engineering, which could prove a dead end, and set his feet on the rungs of the ladder to high command. From this point on, he was concerned less with machinery than with people, less with construction and maintenance than with organization, and thus he found his true vocation.

Captain Robison's main duty was to get the U.S. Navy's infant submarine fleet ready and take it across the Atlantic to operate with the Allies. Late in 1917, accompanied by Nimitz, he established himself at the submarine base at New London, Connecticut, occupying quarters in the old cruiser *Chicago*, then anchored off State Pier. To be near Chester, Catherine and the children moved to New Haven. The reunion was brief, for in February 1918 Robison, now an acting rear admiral, left for Europe, taking Lieutenant Commander Nimitz along as his chief of staff.

Together, Robison and Nimitz toured British naval bases and shipyards, giving special attention to the famous submarine construction facilities at Barrow in Furness on the Irish Sea. For two such friendly, conversation-loving souls, it proved a lonely journey. At Belfast, on the opposite side of the Irish Sea, as they were sitting down to dinner in a restaurant one evening, they were surprised to see a group of young American and British submarine officers enter and take a table at the opposite side of the room.

Admiral Robison instantly brightened. "Let's go over and talk to these young officers," he said, and before Nimitz could stop him, he had started across the room. As he smilingly approached their table, the officers looked up, caught sight of his insignia, were on their feet, chairs flying in all directions, and were out of the room in a trice. Nimitz had an impression that a pair of them vaulted through a window. Robison, stupified, halted in his tracks. To Nimitz he said, "I don't think that's very nice."

"Admiral," said Nimitz, "they're off limits. They didn't want to see you." He reminded Robison that, with Ireland on the brink of a revolt against the British government, service personnel on regular duty there were restricted to their bases. "They shouldn't be in Belfast," he continued. "It's against the rules."

Their wanderings took Robison and Nimitz as far as the Mediterranean coast to inspect French antisubmarine devices. They spent the greatest part of their time, however, at Scapa Flow. There in the Orkney Islands, north of Scotland, Britain's Grand Fleet rode at anchor, with the U.S. dreadnoughts *New York*, *Wyoming*, *Florida*, and *Delaware* under the command of Rear Admiral Hugh Rodman, USN, serving as Battle Squadron Six. At Scapa Flow, Rodman, a gruff Kentuckian, had been something of a legend since his arrival in late 1917. On that occasion, reading a modest little speech, carefully prepared for him by the Navy Department, he offered the services of himself, his men, and his ships to Admiral Sir David Beatty, Commander in Chief, Grand Fleet. Replied Admiral Beatty: "Today marks an epoch in the history of England and America!" Rodman, who had stood next to bottom in the Naval Academy class of 1880, then somewhat marred the solemnity of the occasion by remarking to Beatty, "I don't believe much in paper work. Whenever you have anything to bring to my attention, come and see me."

Though Robison and Nimitz had friendly meetings with Rodman, Beatty, and other Grand Fleet officers, their real business here as elsewhere was with submarines and submariners. They held numerous conferences with submarine skippers, making notes on their tactics and their methods of eluding depth-charge and surface attacks. They inspected every type of British submarine, including the cumbersome K-boats, steam-turbine-driven craft designed to cruise with the Grand Fleet. The largest of these, the *M-1*, was a monster carrying a 12-inch gun on her deck. The *M-1*'s skipper, a commander, described the harrowing problem of getting all her water-tight doors closed before she dived. He had no clear notion of why such a vessel had been built but had heard that there was some thought of using her to bombard the Belgian coast.

Robison and Nimitz gathered a wealth of ideas and information for use by their own submarine service, but before the U.S. submarines could make any significant contribution toward victory, the war came to an end, and the Robison-Nimitz team was dissolved. In parting from his chief of staff, the admiral saw to it that Nimitz received a letter of commendation from the Secretary of the Navy for "meritorious service."

Through the fall and winter of 1918–1919, Lieutenant Commander Nimitz served in the office of the Chief of Naval Operations with special duty as Senior Member, Board of Submarine Design. This assignment was followed by a year's duty as executive officer of the battleship *South Carolina*, which made two round trips to Europe bringing back American troops. For a rising young officer this was a superb combination—six months in Washington, where his abilities could be observed by the high command, followed by a year of sea duty, indispensable to his career.

Chester's itinerant family joined him in Washington and spent Thanksgiving and Christmas of 1918 with him. He was saddened to be parted from them the following year, particularly when Catherine, on September 13, 1919, presented him with another daughter. They named her Anna, after her paternal grandmother, but it early appeared that little Anna, active, inquisitive, self-assertive, was nothing like the gentle, retiring lady for whom she had been named. So the family nicknamed her Nancy, and that is the name by which she has been known ever since.

From his mother, Chester received some socks that she had knitted for him. They probably did not fit, but nothing could have induced Chester to admit as much. From aboard the *South Carolina*, in the Norfolk Navy Yard, he wrote her on November 18, 1919:

> Today I received your letter and the three wonderful pairs of socks. I immediately sat down and pulled off my shoes and put on a pair of the black socks. They are most comfortable and acceptable. Thank you ever so much, Mother dear, and believe me, they are the most acceptable gift you could have

sent me. I like the black socks best, and I can wear them summer or winter. If you knit me any more, I think you had better make them just a little larger, as they might shrink in washing.

I am surprised that Otto's orders have not appeared in the papers. I am sure he must be on his way home, and I feel sure that he may yet arrive in time for Thanksgiving, and surely by Christmas. I would love to bring all of my family there for a reunion, but I'm afraid it can't be done this Christmas. But I know that we will have a reunion some Christmas before very long.

It was little Catherine who had to be taken out of school on account of her eyes, and not young Chester. He has nothing wrong with him except a tendency to catch cold easily. I am sure that Catherine's trouble can be fixed in a year or so. My sickness, bronchitis, has left me, and I feel very well. My only complaint now is that I can't find a place in this vicinity, not even two rooms and a bath, where I can have Catherine and the children come to stay. It is such a pity that I am tied down here in this war, and she can't come. It wouldn't be so bad if I were at sea. Then separations are to be expected.

Admiral Robison, under whom I served as chief of staff in the submarine service, is now commandant of the Boston Navy Yard, and he has offered me a job as his industrial aide, whatever that means, and I have told him I would be glad to go, providing he can get the Bureau of Navigation to send me there. I have not yet heard from him since my acceptance. If I go there, I will get a small house in the Yard and can at least have my wife and children together and close to my work. If I do go there, I can have Grandad come up for a visit, which would tickle me very much. Wouldn't you and Dad enjoy a trip up on the Mallory Line? We look forward now to Admiral Robison's luck in getting my orders to Boston Yard. We can also look forward to a visit from Dora whenever she is free to come. I'm so glad she likes her school.

We have not yet had ice here, but we have had some very cold and disagreeable weather. Just now it is warm and pleasant. We are still very shorthanded, only 200 in our crew where we should have a thousand. Everybody has five jobs instead of one.

I know Catherine and the children would join me in sending you all my best love, if they were here. I hope to see them on Thanksgiving Day. I hope you all keep well, and that Otto soon arrives.

Best love to you all, affectionately,

Chester

Nimitz did not get the transfer to Boston. Instead the Navy Department presented him with one of the most formidable challenges of his career. In June 1920 it ordered him to build a submarine base at Pearl Harbor, using salvaged World War I materials. For a 35-year-old lieutenant commander, this was quite an assignment.

Nimitz began his task with little more than a map of the Pearl Harbor area and the help of four chief petty officers. The chiefs, like most men who ever served under Nimitz, quickly developed for him a loyalty that made them redouble their efforts on his behalf.

Materials for the base, which was to include a machine shop and a complete foundry, were to be assembled from four East Coast shipyards. Nimitz, despite his orders, met with considerable resistance on the part of commandants and commanding officers, who were reluctant to declare surplus anything that their commands could conceivably make use of, then or later, and they did not hesitate to pull rank on a mere lieutenant commander.

Nimitz got partly around this impasse through sheer persuasiveness, at which he was already a master. His chiefs did the rest. Making contact with local chiefs and warrant officers, they managed to carry away—sometimes by truck at night—sorely needed materials that had been denied Nimitz. Usually the loot was removed so skillfully that the commanding officers missed it, if at all, only long after it had been installed at Pearl Harbor.

In later years Chester liked to say that the Pearl Harbor submarine base was built mostly with stolen materials. The description is not exact, of course, because, despite the transfer, the items remained U.S. government property. No one ever registered a complaint because all the victimized commanders had, at one time or another, been obliged to engage in this sort of in-the-family thievery, and they grudgingly admired an adroit and cheeky piece of legal larceny such as Nimitz and his chiefs had pulled. All had to admit that filching a whole submarine base from under the noses of its custodians ranked as at least a minor masterpiece of malfeasance.

The collected gear was trucked to Hampton Roads and loaded aboard ship for the long haul through the Panama Canal and across the Pacific to Pearl Harbor. The Nimitz family went more directly, across the country and out from the West Coast by passenger liner. Chester's first view of the base site was not encouraging. A peninsula jutting out into the Southeast Loch of Pearl Harbor, it was overgrown with cacti, some as much as twelve feet high, and where the cacti left off was dense jungle. The only sign of life was near the mouth of the loch where a few piers marked the navy yard, still fairly primitive in those days.

Men and equipment soon began arriving. The *Chicago*, in which Chester had berthed briefly at New London, was anchored off the peninsula. She was now to serve as living quarters for the bachelor officers. The old cruiser had once been commanded by the illustrious Alfred Thayer Mahan, but Nimitz felt no pride in being appointed her captain, because her engines were now inoperative and her propellers had been removed. The enlisted men were quartered in a wartime barracks, dismantled and brought from Europe. As quarters for himself and family, Nimitz rented a big old house in Minoa Valley.

Transportation between the Nimitz residence and the base site posed a problem which Chester's chief petty officers had foreseen. While collecting the materials in the United States, they had quietly "liberated" the navy car of a base commander from outside his office and, without reporting their acquisition to Nimitz, sent it on its way. When the car arrived at Pearl Harbor, Chester was astonished and demanded an explanation. On learning the shocking truth, he privately reprimanded the over-zealous chiefs but decided not to report the matter. After all, it would be far easier for a stateside admiral to have another car issued to him than for a lieutenant commander to persuade the authorities to ship a car out to the middle of the Pacific for his convenience. And, as the chiefs had anticipated, Nimitz certainly did need the transportation.

Merely clearing the base site proved a formidable task. Mastering one of the big cactus plants was a job for four men. They would loop chains over the branches and pull them down, then chop down the trunk with axes. The smaller cacti could be removed with machetes, but it was tough and rigorous work. So disagreeable was the task that Nimitz used it as a punishment. Anyone in need of discipline would be assigned twenty square feet of cacti to clear.

For the actual building of the submarine base, Nimitz of course had the assistance of construction engineers. He retained the full command responsibility, however, and that included foreseeing requirements and coordinating all activities. At the end of a year, the base was completed but Nimitz, now a commander, stayed on as its commanding officer. Seated in his new office, he little guessed that twenty years later he would be back at the same spot as wartime Commander in Chief, Pacific Fleet.

For additional duty Nimitz served as Commander, Submarine Division 14. Once again, as in the early days in Brooklyn, the Nimitzes played host and hostess to a battalion of young submarine officers. The hospitality dispensed in the big house in Minoa Valley soon became something of a legend.

Nimitz always retained pleasant memories of his first tour at Pearl Harbor. He worked hard there, as hard as he ever worked in his life, but he successfully met a severe challenge and left behind a completed base as testimony. Equally important to him was the fact that for a fairly extended period he had a real home where he could entertain his friends and enjoy his family.

Nancy was still a toddler, but Chet and little Catherine were approaching school age. Either Commander Nimitz or Mrs. Nimitz read to them every evening at bedtime. Once, when the two older children had chickenpox together, Nimitz found time to read to them both at considerable length. He thus helped them to forget their itching, but they never forgot his reading to them.

"I can remember my father sitting in a straight-back chair in the hall outside our two rooms on the ground floor of the house in the hills of Honolulu and reading *Robinson Crusoe* to us," Catherine said long afterward. "He read the whole thing from start to finish. The other book that he tried to read to us on this occasion was an adaptation of Maeterlinck's *The Blue Bird*, which my great aunt from Cambridge had sent us. And he got halfway—oh, not even halfway—into it and just couldn't stand it, and now that I'm grown up I think he had impeccable taste. I hate it myself."

In the late spring of 1922, Commander Nimitz was issued new orders. These he received with joy for they ordered him to report for instruction at the Naval War College. The War College, as Chester knew very well, was an important gateway to high command.

# CHAPTER 10

# TACTICIAN AND TEACHER

THE JOURNEY OF the Nimitz family from Honolulu to Newport proved something of an odyssey, which incidentally provided Commander Nimitz a much-needed vacation. The whole family—big and little Chester, big and little Catherine, baby Nancy, and Polly, a small Boston bulldog—traveled comfortably to San Francisco in the transport *Argonne*, occupying two rooms and a bath in the officers' quarters.

At the suggestion of the Navy Department, the Nimitzes remained with the *Argonne* during the two months she was undergoing overhaul and repair at the Mare Island Navy Yard. This unexpected stay proved a delightful, carefree interlude for all, enabling them to spend the spring of 1922 in the San Francisco area, where many of their friends lived. During this period Chester Junior wore small-size regular sailor suits and, when leaving the ship, merrily submitted to uniform inspection by the sailors of the watch. From time to time, the sailors would order him back for the correction of some such discrepancy as having his tie improperly tied. Chester Senior kept himself in good physical shape by taking long walks and playing tennis and golf.

When the *Argonne* got underway again, heading for the East Coast via the Panama Canal, several other naval families were aboard as passengers. Most of the officers were en route to the Naval War College. The long voyage provided leisure for much reading and conversation and innumerable games of cribbage, which was becoming one of Nimitz's favorite pastimes.

When the *Argonne* at long last reached Newport, Mrs. Freeman was on hand to greet the Nimitzes and take them home with her by car to Wollaston. Commander Nimitz soon returned to Newport on a house-hunting mission, no mean problem for a man with three small children and a pet dog. He finally rented a big old house that boasted eight bedrooms, a butler's pantry, a scullery, and a coal-burning kitchen range big enough to cook meals for a hotel.

For the Nimitz family the three-story dwelling with its spacious yard was pleasant enough during the summer. The coming of cold weather revealed, however, that the place had been constructed as a vacation retreat for the hot months only, and that it had been shoddily converted to winter use. Only three of the bedrooms were connected with the furnace, which was too small for the building it was supposed to heat. In freezing weather, the third floor and much of the rest of the house were uninhabitable.

Because of a strike, coal was in short supply that winter, and could be bought only in half-ton lots. All that was obtainable was soft and powdery.

When being ladled into the furnace or range, it formed clouds of dust that could have exploded but, instead, settled all over the house, its furnishings, and its occupants. The supply was continually running out, since furnace and range together consumed five tons a month. In the chilly, dust-laden atmosphere, the children suffered every childhood illness they had not been through before, and young Chester was once afflicted with such severe bronchitis that he had difficulty coughing, a situation that badly frightened his mother. Mrs. Nimitz and the children ever afterward remembered with a certain horror their winter at Newport, living in "that ghastly ark."

Chester Senior, on the contrary, always treasured the memory of his Newport duty, calling it "one of the truly important assignments of my career." To be sure, he fretted with Catherine over the sick children, and he lent a hand when he could with the dreadful problems of housekeeping, but for the most part his mind was absorbed in his studies. He spent most of his days at the War College, attending classes, participating in war games, or hidden away in his assigned little cubbyhole studying or working on his thesis. In the evening he immersed himself in books, reading rapidly as always—works on tactics and strategy, military and naval history, and biography. He always insisted that, more than any other experience, his eleven months in Newport prepared him for his wartime command. In a letter written some forty years later to Vice Admiral Charles L. Melson, president of the Naval War College, he explained the nature of that preparation:

> The enemy of our games was always—Japan—and the courses were so thorough that after the start of WWII—nothing that happened in the Pacific was strange or unexpected. Each student was required to plan logistic support for an advance across the Pacific—and we were well prepared for the fantastic logistic efforts required to support the operations of the war. . . . I credit the Naval War College for such success [as] I achieved in strategy & tactics both in peace & war.

Perhaps, stirred by the warmth of old memories, Nimitz was exaggerating a little, but basically the letter tells the truth. It is apparent that his War College studies brought into sharp focus his years of professional reading and that they also left him with a good, hard knowledge of the geography and the strategic and logistic problems of warfare in the Pacific Ocean.

Commander Nimitz's thesis, on which he labored diligently, concerned the Battle of Jutland, the last great conflict between surface warships, fought on the North Sea in 1916 by 250 ships of Britain's Grand Fleet and Germany's High Seas Fleet. Nimitz was by no means alone in his interest in Jutland. In the years following World War I, that battle was closely studied by naval officers everywhere on the erroneous assumption that it was the archetype of future battles at sea.

What particularly caught the attention of students of Jutland was the extraordinary complexity of the British battle formations and the difficulty of maneuvering them. In cruising formation, Admiral John Jellicoe's battle fleet consisted of twenty-four battleships in six columns abeam, with pairs of columns partly surrounded by destroyers to protect them against submarines. Lines of cruisers and destroyers extended twenty miles ahead, on the lookout for enemy surface forces. Merely turning this array of ships required complicated maneuvering-board calculations and a whole series of signals. Deployment of the battleships into single column for battle was so critical as to timing and direction that it was rightly considered the decisive maneuver in this or any other large-scale naval battle. One officer describing the deployment at Jutland recalled that "there was handling of ships ... such as had never been dreamt of by seamen before."

With the opposing battle fleets at times rushing at each other at express-train speed through smoke and mist, it was all Jellicoe could do to avoid crashes, sidestep torpedoes, and maintain contact with the enemy. What the harassed admiral obviously needed was better reconnaissance, earlier reports, and more far-seeing eyes than his light cruisers could give him. The Royal Navy's answer was the development of the aircraft carrier. The U.S. Navy, recognizing a good thing, followed suit by converting a collier into the small carrier *Langley*, which was commissioned in 1922.

It was soon obvious that the carrier with its planes was going to be not only a superior means of reconnaissance but a hard-hitting weapon of attack. General Billy Mitchell's flyers had already made that clear in 1921 by bombing and sinking the ex-German battleship *Ostfriesland* in trials off the Virginia Capes. To be sure, most naval officers had scoffed at Mitchell's demonstration, pointing out that the *Ostfriesland* had been at anchor, unattended, undefended, and without damage-control parties aboard. Not a few, however, drew the conclusion that the battleship had become obsolete. Even those who sharply disputed this point of view had to admit that protecting battleships from air as well as from subsurface attack was going to present a difficult problem, possibly requiring huge screens of cruisers, destroyers, and now carriers, more complicated and unwieldy than anything seen at Jutland.

Among the officers who had kissed the battleship goodbye was Rear Admiral William S. Sims, president of the Naval War College when Chester Nimitz arrived there in 1922 as a student. From Newport Sims was continuing a long and distinguished career of exasperating his fellow officers by being right, and being highly vocal about it, when many of them were wrong. Even before Mitchell sank the *Ostfriesland*, Sims had been staging on the game board at Newport war games that included carriers. In these he had demonstrated, at least to his own satisfaction, that the carrier had replaced the battleship as the Navy's capital ship. This was because the attack radius of the carrier's planes much outdistanced the range of the battleship's guns. Sims, far ahead of his contemporaries, as usual, foresaw naval battles in which the opposing fleets, out of sight of each other, indeed hundreds of miles apart, would attack and counterattack with only carrier planes.

Not all the officers at the War College agreed with Sims's interpretation of the war games. Some of them, wedded indissolubly to the tradition of the battleship as queen of naval battles, could not accept the proposition that the mighty dreadnought could ever be displaced by anything so novel and fragile-looking as an aircraft carrier. Nimitz has left us no record of his own reaction at the time, but judging from his subsequent actions, it would appear that he at least kept an open mind, determined to investigate the problem further.

From the Naval War College game board came also a possible answer to the problem of increasingly unwieldy formations. The innovator in this case was Commander Roscoe C. MacFall, Nimitz's classmate at the War College, as he had been at the Naval Academy. In setting up the board one day, MacFall placed the supporting cruisers and destroyers in concentric circles around the battleships. The obvious advantages of this arrangement were that it concentrated antiaircraft fire and that the direction of the whole formation could be changed by a simple turn signal, all ships turning together. Experiments showed, moreover, that deployment into a column was far less difficult and time-consuming from a circular formation than it was from a rectangular formation with echelons of supporting vessels thrust out ahead like exploratory antennae. Recalled Nimitz afterward, "We were all impressed with the things you could do from a circular formation." To Nimitz alone, however, fell the distinction of introducing the new formation to the fleet.

That came about because Admiral Robison had been appointed Commander in Chief, Battle Fleet, the next-to-most-senior operational command in the Navy and, in anticipation of assuming that lofty eminence, he had been able to pull a few strings to obtain once more the services of his favorite younger officer. Nimitz received orders, toward the end of his War College tour, to proceed to San Pedro and report for duty aboard the battleship *California*, flagship of the Battle Fleet.

After a brief leave at Wollaston, the Nimitz family was packed for the train trip to the West Coast when Chester Junior, nicknamed Calamity Joe for his succession of ailments and accidents, fell off a garage and cracked his skull. Commander Nimitz canceled the trip and stayed on in Wollaston until the crisis had passed. He then hastened alone across country in order to be present on June 30, 1923, when Robison hoisted his flag on the *California*, relieving Admiral E. W. Eberle. Robison appointed Nimitz his aide, assistant chief of staff, and tactical officer.

In 1920 the newer American battleships, together with cruisers, destroyers, and auxiliaries, had been ordered to base permanently on the West Coast as the Battle Fleet, on the assumption that their most likely potential enemy was the Japanese navy. Other cruisers and destroyers, plus two or three old battleships, made up the Scouting Fleet, which operated in the Atlantic Ocean and the Caribbean Sea. Together, the Battle Fleet and the Scouting Fleet constituted the U.S. Fleet or, informally, the combined fleet. The much smaller Asiatic Fleet was based on the Philippines.

When young Chester was well enough to travel, the family set out to join the commander. They did not travel to California by train but took the slow, roundabout way by sea, this time in the transport *Chaumont*. Not long out of port, Chester burned his ankle on an exposed steam pipe, and the burn refused to heal, evidently because the boy had expended his strength in recovering from the skull fracture. The burn was still festering when Mrs. Nimitz and the children reached San Pedro, then a dusty boom town with all sorts of construction going on.

Because the Battle Fleet spent a great deal of time at sea or at various ports up and down the West Coast, the burden of house-hunting as well as of tending her ailing son fell on Mrs. Nimitz. She rented a small furnished apartment not far from one occupied by Mrs. Robison. From there she took the boy frequently to the naval dispensary, whose staff had no success at all in healing his burned ankle. "It had gotten to where the child was discouraged and I was discouraged," said Catherine. Luckily a naval doctor living in an apartment adjoining that of the Nimitzes came up with a winning suggestion. "Let's put him to bed in that room where it's sunny," he said. "Let's take off all the bandages and everything and just let the sun start working." Within a week the ankle, thus treated, got well.

When the Battle Fleet put into port in the San Pedro area, the Robisons and the Nimitzes got together, renewing their friendship. Sam and Mary Robison, having no children of their own, became in fact surrogate grandparents to the Nimitz children. Admiral Robison and Commander Nimitz, during their brief periods ashore at San Pedro, took long walks together into the hills, often with their dogs. Unfortunately the Nimitzes' Polly and the Robisons' Mac, another bulldog, had both taken on too much weight, possibly overfed by the Nimitz children. The walks, which provided fine physical exercise for the men, sometimes proved too much for the fat dogs. "Very often," little Catherine afterward recalled, "either Mac or Polly would just simply pass out and have to be carried home."

Because of Commander Nimitz's frequent absences, Mrs. Nimitz more and more took over the management of the family's finances until, like many navy wives, she was handling it all. Possibly in reaction to memories of her spendthrift father, she developed a slight tendency to pinch pennies. Above all, she avoided debt like sin. During their whole married life the only thing the Nimitzes ever bought on time was a washing machine—an obvious and urgent necessity for a home with children.

As soon as Nimitz had established himself with his fellow officers, he proposed trying the circular formation. He was surprised at the resistance his suggestion encountered. "My greatest problem," he said, "was to convince the senior captains in the fleet that this was a proper cruising formation. I even had to persuade my own admiral to agree with me after he had had conferences with the captains, who did not like that cruising all alone out there by themselves on a point in the formation."

Nimitz was not disheartened. As he expected, Robison, an eager student of tactics and a born experimenter, mulled over the pros and cons a few days and then ordered his captains to try the circular formation. As first worked out on paper, the formation had the *California* at center serving as guide, surrounded by an inner circle of battleships and an outer circle of lighter vessels. Each ship was assigned bearing and distance from the guide.

The admiral and his captains were impressed with the ease and rapidity with which such a formation could maneuver. To evade a submarine contact the entire fleet could quickly reverse course or move off sideways, all ships turning together while maintaining constant bearing and distance from the guide. Thus the antisubmarine-antiaircraft screen remained at all times intact, and the fleet axis could be kept constantly in the assumed direction of the enemy. In deploying into line of battle, a designated battleship led the way out of the circle, and the cruisers and destroyers disposed themselves at either end of the battle line.

A major drawback of the circular formation was the difficulty in station-keeping. Except for the ships directly ahead, astern, or abeam of the guide, keeping on station was a delicate, time-consuming task that required almost constant changes not only of course but also of speed. At night, without radar, which was yet to be invented, keeping on station in concentric circles was considered impossible and an invitation to collision. It is safe to say that in the fall of 1923 few officers in the Battle Fleet foresaw that the circular formation would in time become standard, particularly for daylight cruising.

With the coming of winter, "Calamity Joe" fell ill again. This time his affliction was the aftermath of a bungled mastoid operation that had left him deaf in one ear. Now naval doctors discovered that the products of a continuing infection were draining inward. Since this condition could easily prove fatal, Chester Junior was sent to the Long Beach hospital and operated on. Chester Senior, to his deep chagrin, on the very day of the operation had to go to sea with the Battle Fleet. He could not learn until weeks later that the surgery was entirely successful. Not only was his son's dangerous condition cleared up; his defective hearing was completely cured. Thus, Nimitz's cherished objective of sending his son to the Naval Academy had again become possible.

The Battle Fleet had put to sea under radio silence in order to participate in joint Army and Navy Problem No. 2, designed to test the defenses of the Panama Canal, and through the winter joined with the Scouting Fleet in tactical exercises in the Caribbean Sea. The special features of the exercises were fleet-supported landings by marines in the Canal Zone and on the island of Culebra and the participation of the Navy's lone carrier, the *Langley*.

The little carrier engaged in defensive patrols and reconnaissance, and her planes simulated aerial combat and attacks on shipping and on the Canal. In order to be able to turn into the wind for flight operations, she had to leave the fleet, which was usually in rectangular formation, and she moved freely about within signal distance accompanied only by a pair of destroyers assigned to rescue aviators who landed in the water.

To Commander Nimitz this plan of operations was highly unsatisfactory. He believed that for maximum mutual protection from both submarines and aircraft, surface fleet and carrier needed to be closely integrated. He urged that the *Langley* be assigned to the Battle Fleet for extensive maneuvers.

Robison forwarded Nimitz's suggestion to the Navy Department over his own signature, but the Bureau of Aeronautics was not yet ready to release the carrier. Yet to be worked out were problems of plane design, takeoff and recovery, arresting gear and catapult, and rendezvous between carrier and planes following air strikes. In 1924 flyers were still communicating with their carrier by homing pigeon! Nevertheless, at Nimitz's insistence, Robison applied such pressure that in November 1924 the *Langley* reported for duty with the Battle Fleet. Some airmen contended, then and later, that the transfer was premature, that Nimitz had actually retarded naval aviation by drawing the Navy's lone carrier into the fleet too soon.

Nimitz, for his part, never doubted that the time had come to wed carrier and fleet. He tried the *Langley* in the circular formation and achieved perfect integration. When the carrier turned into the wind to launch and recover planes, the whole formation turned with her. At all times, the surface vessels had the close protection of the carrier planes, and the carrier had the protection of all the fleet's guns and depth charges. There were always destroyers aplenty nearby to pick up any aviators who might have splashed.

Admiral Robison was so favorably impressed by the exercises with the fleet-integrated *Langley* that he urged the Navy Department to rush to completion the big carriers *Saratoga* and *Lexington*, then under construction. Said Nimitz nearly forty years later: "I regard the tactical exercises that we had at that time as laying the groundwork for the cruising formations that we used in World War II in the carrier air groups and practically every kind of task force that went out."

During the spring and summer of 1925, the combined U.S. Fleet carried out maneuvers designed to test the defenses of the Hawaiian Islands. The Battle Fleet and a cruiser division of the Scouting Fleet then proceeded together on a practice and good-will cruise via Samoa to Australia, New Zealand, and Tasmania, returning to the U.S. West Coast in the latter part of August.

In October Robison was appointed to the Navy's top operational command as Commander in Chief, U.S. Fleet (CinCUS), retaining Nimitz as his aide, assistant chief of staff, and tactical officer. A year later both were assigned to shore duty. Thereafter the circular formation and the fleet-integrated carrier concept fell into disuse—either through negligence or because their merits were not recognized.

In 1930 Lieutenant Commander Forrest P. Sherman advocated the carrier-centered circular task-force formation that was later to become standard, but carriers were not assigned permanent screens of cruisers and destroyers until after the December 1941 Japanese raid on the battleships at Pearl Harbor. Then the carriers necessarily took over as the capital ships of the Pacific Fleet. The new fast battleships, when they became available, were relegated to the escort to protect the carriers. Before the end of World War II, all the warring navies had followed the U.S. Navy's lead in adopting the circular formation, at least for daylight operations. Subsequently, this formation was officially adopted for naval forces of the North Atlantic Treaty Organization (NATO).

The tactical innovations introduced into the U.S. fleet by Chester Nimitz are as epochal as the column formation that Oliver Cromwell's generals imposed on the English sailing fleet in the seventeenth century. Yet even Admiral Robison failed to perceive the true significance of the circular arrangement— or even of the carrier. After his retirement from the Navy he wrote, with Mrs. Robison's help, *A History of Naval Tactics from 1530 to 1930.* This huge book, published in 1942 and running to nearly a thousand pages, does not mention the circular formation. Robison quotes Nimitz at length but only on the subject of submarine warfare. Regarding aircraft carriers, he concludes with this ambivalent statement: "Aircraft carriers—a product of the last war, mounting guns for their own defense and carrying bombers, as well as fighters —are now units in all major navies. Their planes effectively attack the enemy on land as well as at sea. The ineffectiveness of planes from carriers, in both land and sea attacks, during the last war, has been referred to in Chapter L. In this war the plane is a major weapon."

Although Chester Nimitz Junior estimated that his father's duty as Admiral Robison's assistant chief of staff was one of the assignments most instrumental in fitting him for high command, Chester Senior found his next assignment more challenging. Commander Nimitz was one of six officers selected to establish the first units of the Naval Reserve Officers' Training Corps in American universities.

Advocated by the Navy Department as a national defense measure, the NROTC was authorized by Congress in March 1925 and funded by an appropriation available on July 1, 1926. Units were to be established at Harvard University, Northwestern University, the University of Washington, Yale University, Georgia School of Technology, and the University of California.

"An officer with the rank of captain or commander will be ordered to each of these universities and will be known as the professor of naval science and tactics," read the Bureau of Navigation announcement. "He will be in charge of the instruction of the students in the naval unit. One commissioned assistant will also be detailed to each university. The officers ordered to these universities will be members of the faculty and the professor of naval science and tactics will be given the status of a dean."

Some fifty or sixty students were to be assigned to each unit, where they would be taught seamanship, navigation, gunnery, military and international law, strategy and tactics, electricity, and engineering. Graduates would be eligible for commissions in the volunteer naval reserve.

Commander Nimitz was ordered to organize the NROTC unit in the University of California at Berkeley. The Navy Department had selected him for this duty on the recommendation of Captain William D. Puleston, one of the Navy's intellectuals and future biographer of Alfred Thayer Mahan. Puleston was one of a number of influential officers whose attention had been attracted to Nimitz's growing reputation.

Nimitz received the assignment with mixed feelings. This was not necessarily the sort of duty that would advance his career. On the other hand, a notable success at the outset of a new program would be bound to attract attention. Anyhow, handling personnel was becoming one of his chief professional interests, and here was for him a new and challenging means of dealing with people. In fact, the experience imbued him with a deep and abiding interest in education, and among his students he made lifelong friends whose careers he watched with paternal interest. For his family this three-year stretch of shore duty was an unqualified blessing. Nancy had only recently begun school, but Chester and Catherine were about to embark into their stormy teens, a period in which the guidance of a father's strong hand was especially needful.

Commander Nimitz established the Naval ROTC at the Berkeley campus of the University of California in the fall of 1926. Assisting him were Lieutenant Commander Ernest Gunther and four chief petty officers. The university assigned them classrooms and sparsely furnished office space. Government equipment, including typewriters, did not arrive until some time after the semester had begun.

Nimitz was at first fearful that he might not be able to attract enough students to form a unit. Those who enrolled in the NROTC would be furnished uniforms but would receive no scholarships, pay, or allowances. They would have to drill three times a week and take a heavy load of naval courses in addition to their regular undergraduate studies. On the other hand, they would participate in summer cruises, with pay at a dollar a day, and at the end of four years as midshipmen they would be commissioned ensigns in the U.S. Naval Reserve.

By the time the new crop of freshmen arrived, opening the fall semester, Nimitz and his aides had affixed notices proclaiming their offerings on all campus bulletin boards and in other appropriate places. The chiefs manned the NROTC office to receive applicants, while Nimitz and Gunther, in starched white uniforms, sat behind borrowed tables in a central passageway to attract students, answer questions, and try to enroll some good men. When business was slack at the tables, Nimitz cruised the campus on foot scouting for likely candidates. In front of Old North Hall, he espied and buttonholed Freshman James Archer and gave him a fast sales talk. Archer was interested but asked if it mattered that his father was an army colonel. Nimitz laughed and assured him that it did not. Archer not only signed up but talked his roommate Tracy D. Cuttle into signing up, too. "We certainly don't want to get in the Army," said Archer.

The chiefs were enrolling, also. When Nimitz counted up, he found he had an embarrassment of riches—eighty applicants. He carefully scrutinized the records of each and picked the sixty who appeared to be the best. Then, when the candidates assembled for the first time, he apologized for being unable to keep them all. Unfortunately sixty was the maximum established by law. "Gentlemen, I'm very sorry," he said, "but I will have to call out twenty names. They will have to go."

From that time forward, Nimitz found himself constantly in the company of professors, at home as well as at work, for he had rented a house at 1306 Bay View Place, where most of his neighbors were members of the faculty. This was the first time the Nimitzes had been associated with a group that was not predominantly Navy. They found it a refreshing experience. Their new associates were experts in a variety of subjects. Some were extremely narrow experts and some were wonderful eccentrics, but all were kind and friendly, and most proved to be good company.

A few of the faculty, to be sure, were at first a little resentful of Nimitz. They had earned their doctorates and, through years of teaching and publishing, had made the slow climb from instructor to assistant professor to associate professor, and had grown gray aspiring toward the rank of full professor. Now in came this 41-year-old commander with no degree at all—the Naval Academy did not grant degrees when Nimitz was a student there—and, by government fiat, he was added to the faculty as a full professor with the status of a dean—dean of the Department of Naval Science and Tactics. It was a little hard to take.

The resentment against the outsider came to a head when the chairman of the university's Astronomy Department learned that Nimitz proposed to teach nautical astronomy in connection with his navigation course. The chairman nearly broke up a meeting by thundering, "No one teaches astronomy at this university but people I pick!"

Nimitz, instead of returning the chairman's thunder, said, "Will you teach this course on astronomy such as they have to have for naval officers?"

The chairman replied grimly that his department would teach the course.

"This is wonderful," said Nimitz, "because we in the ROTC are allowed only a certain number of hours of a student's duty. If the astronomy course goes over to the university, that gives us so many more hours a week."

Nimitz never thought of himself as a naval officer thrust into an unfamiliar, faintly hostile environment but only as a member of the University of California faculty, and the faculty, attracted by his unfailing good humor and recognizing his wide-ranging knowledge, based on years of selective reading, at last accepted him fully as a colleague. Whenever Dean Baldwin Woods, head of aeronautical science, was called away, he asked Nimitz to take his classes. "You can give my students a lot they ought to know," he said.

Most remarkably, in recognition of his demonstrated ability at judging people, Nimitz was invited to join one of the university's promotions committees and also one of its search committees for selecting new faculty. He brought to both committees a fresh, not altogether scholastic set of criteria for weighing performance and probable achievement. He was puzzled by the decisive weight the professors, both in selecting and promoting faculty, gave to publications—the familiar "publish or perish" criterion. He could never understand why a master teacher should not be judged on the basis of his teaching skills alone, and he never quite accepted the argument that the mastery of material inherent in research, writing, and publishing provides a necessary background for teaching.

Nimitz took a paternal and individual interest in each of his students. He challenged them to handball and tennis matches, which he usually won. Most Saturdays he had some of the students out at his home for lunch. On those occasions, Mrs. Nimitz, with both the cost of food and youthful appetites in mind, specialized in casseroles, her chicken-noodle casserole being a great favorite.

The young men of the NROTC formed the Quarterdeck Club, and usually invited the Nimitzes to their dances. Both came when they could, Mrs. Nimitz dancing with the midshipmen, Commander Nimitz, with their dates.

Onnie P. Lattu, a young Finn who, through an oversight, had been allowed to join the NROTC before he got his American citizenship papers, became a great favorite of the Nimitzes. On one occasion, he invited both Nimitz and Gunther to his fraternity house, Sigma Phi Sigma, for a luncheon. The two officers, resplendent in white uniforms, arrived in Gunther's new roadster. At that moment the fraternity brothers were engaged in tossing bags of water at each other. One such bag was aimed at Lattu, who dodged, and the bag hit Commander Nimitz squarely in the chest. To the amazement of all, Nimitz said nothing. He neither changed his expression nor altered his pace. He walked into the fraternity house, chatted amiably with his hosts, and, still dripping wet, sat down to lunch, which he appeared to enjoy.

When at length some of the government equipment reached the NROTC offices, and Nimitz was supervising the unpacking, there arrived at his office an earnest young man, George S. Perkins. A former University of California student, he had just received the papers that, when completed, would make him a commissioned ensign, he said, and could not resist the opportunity to be sworn in at his alma mater by a regular naval officer. Would Commander Nimitz oblige? Perkins apologized for appearing sentimental.

Nimitz took the papers. "Perkins," he said, "don't you ever forget that sentiment is a big part of a naval officer's life." He explained that his typewriters had not been delivered yet. "Chief," he said to his yeoman, "I think we can prepare these papers without a typewriter." So, among the half-opened packing cases, the yeoman filled out the papers and Nimitz signed them and administered the oath of allegiance. Nimitz called it "the packing case oath" and in later life usually introduced Perkins as "Perkins of the packing case oath."

Anna was now always called Nancy, and the two elder Nimitz children were often called Kate and Chet to distinguish them from their parents. Their activity, together with sibling rivalry, led to some monumental brawls. These reached a bloody climax one afternoon when the Nimitzes were calling on the

Gunthers, and the children were playing in the Gunthers' back yard. Chet was experimenting on a protesting Nancy by squeezing the back of her neck, trying to make her lose consciousness. Nancy seized a rusty auto license plate that came to hand and whacked her brother behind the ear. "He bled—oh, how he bled!" recalled Nancy many years later. "The most satisfying occasion I can remember. Of course, he raced into the house bleeding and screaming. The call ended abruptly before twenty minutes were up, and we were all swept up and hurried home." Nancy, of course, was punished.

Kate recalls: "Both Dad and Mother have always given all of us the feeling they were enormously proud of us. They'd smack you down if you got out of line, but they were always very supportive and tried to give us self-confidence." On the record it appears there was far less "smacking down" by way of discipline than selective denial of privileges.

Nimitz continued to read aloud to the children, one of his choices in the early days at Berkeley being a translation of the *Odyssey*. He also took time to help them with their school lessons. On one occasion Kate felt that her father had been a little *too* helpful in this area. As they were clearing the dining-room table after dinner one evening, she happened to mention that she had to prepare a report on the Battle of Jutland—forgetting, if she ever knew, that her father had spent months at the War College researching and writing a thesis on that battle. "It was just like putting gasoline on a fire," she said.

When she returned with the J volume of the *Encyclopedia Britannica*, she found the dining-room table cleared except for quantities of salt and pepper shakers. This was unusual because after dinner her father normally left the table set for breakfast. "What's the matter?" she asked.

"Don't you have to do a report on the Battle of Jutland?"

"Oh, yes. Half a page."

"I'll tell you about the Battle of Jutland."

"All I could think of in later years," Kate recalled, "was the old story about 'Thank you for the book; it told me more about penguins than I cared to know.' We had saltcellars and pepper shakers, and the German High Sea Fleet was here and the British Fleet here. We went through the whole thing, and I was weakly saying, 'Half a page.' But I never forgot it, and I never brought up the Battle of Jutland again."

One welcome feature of duty at the University of California was genuine vacations. The leaves Nimitz had been granted between previous duties had generally been consumed in shifting the family from one home to another, often a continent or more apart. Now, several weeks were available every summer for presumably carefree vacationing, and, with the youngsters' tastes prevailing, the family decision was for camping trips. In the summer of 1927, the Nimitzes drove up the Pacific coast to the state of Washington. In 1928, they camped in the high Sierras, spending a week at Echo Lake and a week at Lake Tahoe.

Arrangements for these trips were made with the usual Nimitz efficiency.

Strapped to the outside of the 1926 Chevrolet sedan were a tent, a folding table, hammocks for the children. The car seats were convertible into a double bed for mother and father. The trunk let down into a little galley where Mrs. Nimitz could have supper cooking within half an hour of arriving at a camp site. The hammocks were the regular naval canvas sort, and to keep the children from falling out of them, Nimitz took a sailmaker's palm and needle and stitched the blankets to the hammocks.

The excursions would start off gaily, mother and father in the front seat, the children in the rear. Gradually, with enforced inactivity, the rear seat became the scene of altercations, then of fracases, and then of real fights, with the possible drawing of blood. The car would stop. One child would be ordered into the front seat. A parent would sit between the two battlers in the rear. A sort of uneasy calm would be restored, but the tension would remain until all could get out and let off steam. Once, on the way home, when the battlers on the back seat were not separated soon enough, Chet succeeded in breaking Kate's glasses. Nimitz, who was driving, merely said in even tones, "Chester, when we get home I'm going to spank you." And he did. Many years later, Nancy said, "As I look back on those happy excursions which were such pleasure to us children, I wonder how they could have been any pleasure to Mother and Daddy."

Nimitz gave his utmost to his NROTC appointment, and it certainly did not impede his career. In September 1927 he was commissioned ad interim captain from June 2, 1927, and the following January he was commissioned a regular captain from the same date.

To the vexation of some of his students, Nimitz corrected and graded their papers for English composition as well as for facts. With his feeling for the English language and his mastery of diction and syntax, he could hardly have brought himself to do otherwise.

Nimitz came to admire the University of California greatly. He hoped to enroll Chet in the Naval Academy, but he declared that if it proved practical he would certainly send the girls to the Berkeley campus. Nevertheless, he distrusted some of the academic freedoms of civilian universities, where the student, studying on his own schedule, needed to be prepared to meet only monthly, or perhaps semester, examinations. Harking back to his Naval Academy experiences, he tested his students at the beginning of each class on what they had been assigned for that day. "The average midshipman," he wrote to Admiral Robison, "acquires more information, works and studies more and harder, and accomplishes more than the average university student—and the reason for it *is that he is almost entirely on his own resources and must dig it out for himself or bilge.*"

On entering one of Nimitz's classes the midshipmen drew slips, each containing a different question on the day's assignment. Then, instead of manning the blackboards as at the Naval Academy, they took seats and wrote their answers on paper. At the end of twenty minutes Nimitz took up the answers and began a thirty-minute lecture, which the students were free to interrupt with questions. As soon as possible after class, Nimitz carefully graded the papers, placed them in pigeonholes for the midshipmen to pick up, and posted grades for the day.

The advantages of Nimitz's system over the Naval Academy system, as he saw it, were that written answers could be more carefully marked and graded, and the corrected papers could be retained for review by the midshipmen. Also a prepared lecture, based in part on his own or other service experience, was more effective than the somewhat haphazard discourse that resulted from the instructor moving from blackboard to blackboard correcting, grading, and explaining.

Robison, following his tour as CinCUS, reverted to his permanent rank of rear admiral and was assigned as Commandant of the 13th Naval District with headquarters at Seattle, Washington. From this vantage point, he watched with interest his protégé Nimitz's experiments in education and became convinced that his methods were ideal for instructing midshipmen. In the spring of 1928 Robison was appointed superintendent of the Naval Academy and proceeded to Annapolis determined to impose the Nimitz system. That Nimitz had some slight misgivings regarding the admiral's intentions appears from a letter he wrote to Robison on July 9, 1928:

> . . . My scheme for conducting recitations is not well adapted to instruction in *all* subjects. It best fits such subjects as Seamanship, Naval Engineering, Ordnance and Gunnery, Navigation and Piloting, where the instructor can give a class the benefit of his own experience. The scheme is not well suited for instruction in languages and mathematics, although I believe that an instructor can profitably spend a small part of each period in discussion, even in these subjects.
>
> When you lay the scheme before the Academy Board I hope you will make the above clear. The main idea is to make available to the students the service experience of the instructors. . . .

Though instruction at the Naval Academy had undergone some change since Nimitz was a midshipman, it had not evolved in the direction of the Nimitz plan. Experienced teachers resented having the teaching methods of an inexperienced outsider thrust upon them. Nimitz, after reading their objections, defended his scheme with less reserve than in his July 9 letter. In a letter to Robison dated May 30, 1929, he said:

> . . . It may be argued that [my plan] requires too much of an instructor's time. That may be but it certainly produces results in most subjects. It may also be argued that such a scheme cannot be used in every subject taught. That may also be—but even in languages, some modification of it can be employed and certainly the instructor should at least give the section a short discourse each day covering pronunciation, grammar, etc. etc.
>
> The above is *not* the University method—but a method we have had to come to in order to get the maximum amount of instruction out of the limited

time our students are available to us. We tried the regular university method of lectures with occasional problems or papers and we were not satisfied with the results. . . .

Some of the superintendents who succeeded Robison endeavored to impose Nimitz's teaching methods on the Naval Academy. This influence may account for the daily testing and daily grading that was prevalent at the Academy even after World War II. Gradually, however, the old lockstep gave way to established university procedures, for it was found that constant supervision and checking of the learning process did not make for self-reliance and independent thinking on the part of the students. By 1970 the U.S. Naval Academy was academically organized in the same way as a university and used university teaching methods—with the added advantages that classes were kept small and discussion was preferred over lecturing.

When Captain Nimitz in June 1929 handed over the Berkeley NROTC to his old friend Bruce Canaga, it had about 150 midshipmen enrolled and was run by six commissioned and six petty officers. For Nimitz the duty had been toilsome but memorable and rewarding. He never lost his interest in education or in the University of California, and the midshipmen with whom he had been associated there were among the men whose careers he followed most closely, lending a helping hand when possible.

# CHAPTER 11

# THE *RIGEL* AND
# THE *AUGUSTA*

In late 1929, when Captain Nimitz was Commander, Submarine Division 20, based on San Diego, he was surprised and gratified to receive a letter from his Naval Academy classmate William R. Furlong. Bill, it seems, was editing a 25th anniversary yearbook, *Class of 1905, United States Naval Academy*, to be published the following year. From each member of the class he wanted a photograph and a sketch of his career to be included in the book. Nimitz complied with a brief summary, which ended with the following paragraph:

> In looking backward at various phases of my life, I find it difficult to pick out any activity as having been more attractive to me than any other. I have enjoyed every one of my assignments and I believe it has been so because of my making it a point to become as deeply immersed and as interested in each activity as it was possible for me to become. My life in the Navy has been very happy and I know of no other profession for which I would forsake my present one. My oldest daughter, Catherine Vance, age 16, is almost ready for college and my boy, Chester William, Jr., age 15, hopes to enter the Naval Academy in the spring of 1931. My third and last child is a daughter, Anna Elizabeth, age 10. My wife, my children, my profession as a naval officer, and good health combine to make me a happy man.

The second sentence of that paragraph goes far toward explaining Nimitz's success and his satisfaction in his career. The next to last sentence he came to regret. Not long after his words "my third and last child" appeared in print, all his friends knew that a fourth little Nimitz was on the way, and he took a good deal of ribbing from his fellow officers. Mary Manson Nimitz was born June 17, 1931.

Mary's arrival coincided exactly with a change of duty for Captain Nimitz. He reported as commander of some thirty-five out-of-commission destroyers at the San Diego destroyer base. On June 16, 1931, the Nimitz family moved from an apartment in San Diego to the *Rigel*, a tender moored alongside the deactivated destroyers. She was to serve as living quarters for the Nimitzes as well as flagship for Captain Nimitz.

The *Rigel* proved a comfortable and attractive residence because the wife of the preceding commander had had the living spaces done over by a professional decorator. Captain and Mrs. Nimitz had their own bed, but the children had built-in bunks with curtains. The chart house was Chet's bedroom. The family was served by a staff consisting of a cook, a steward, and two messboys.

The elegance of the quarters, however, was somewhat marred by a deck clothes line usually displaying diapers and other infant wear for Mary.

Rats presented a problem. They somehow found their way aboard despite the rat guards on the mooring lines. As a result, the ship required periodic fumigation, whereupon the rats would die in the compartments, thereby strongly, if temporarily, offsetting the comforts of the dwelling afloat. As a further deterrent to the rats, the Nimitzes encouraged a cat named Curio, which lived on the base, to take up quarters on the *Rigel*. Curio did not prove a particularly effective ratter, but she distinguished herself by having seven kittens under the table during a dinner party.

The older children thoroughly enjoyed their novel setting, and Curio's kittens were Chet's especial joy. Chet and Nancy took pride in entertaining their friends, whom they would lead over deck after deck to the outboard destroyer or would invite to ride vessels being taken out of the water on the marine railway. On such expeditions they might be accompanied by the little bulldog Polly, now aging, who had the disconcerting habit of prying what Kate called "very, very defunct oysters" off the bottom of ships on the marine railway and concealing them about the living quarters of the *Rigel*, where they soon made their presence known.

Nancy's special joy was the machine shop or the carpentry shop, where she spent most of her time. The sailor workmen made her welcome, and to her mother's dismay she became very handy with tools. Once while Mrs. Nimitz was walking around the base with Mary, one of the petty officers, thinking to please her, stepped up and reported enthusiastically, "You know, ma'am, Nancy runs a better acetylene weld than any of the men in the shop." Mrs. Nimitz replied drily, "That's just lovely."

Somebody gave Nancy a Philippine dagger with a heavy blade and a light handle, just perfect for throwing, but the *Rigel*'s steel decks and steel bulkheads did not lend themselves to such sport. Looking about, Nancy came upon a box housing a refrigerator outside the galley. Perfect! The dagger penetrated as satisfactorily as one could wish, and Nancy had several highly gratifying sessions of tossing the knife against that box. Then came the day of the admiral's inspection. Captain Nimitz made a preliminary tour of his command to make sure that all was in order and came upon the refrigerator box disfigured with myriad punctures.

"Who did this?" he demanded.

The sailors, the steward, the messboys, all of whom were fond of Nancy, professed ignorance. All, including the cook, insisted, most improbably, that they had never noticed the punctures before. Captain Nimitz had his suspicions. When Nancy came home he said, "Come with me," and led her to the ice box. "Did you do that?"

"Yes."

"Do you think that was very smart?"

He walked away. No punishment. No scolding. "It was much better than a tirade," recalled Nancy. "It conveyed really almost contempt: How could anyone be so stupid? How could my own child be so stupid?"

"He's very strict," observed one of the messboys, "but those kids can get away with murder." The fact is that Nimitz now preferred to control the children by reasoning with them, and frequently they talked back. To the messboys, brought up in a different atmosphere, that sounded like gross disrespect, but Nimitz, esteeming his youngsters' intelligence, was permitting them the right of debate. There were limits, they knew, and these the captain sometimes laid down with the preamble, "Haven't you children any respect for your parents?" To Chet, he would begin: "At Annapolis, you won't be able to . . ." or "At Annapolis, you will have to. . . ."

One day at table the captain frowned a little and cleared his throat. Obviously the youngsters were in for a talking-to. Before he could begin, Chet inquired brightly, "Which is it going to be this time, Pop?"

"What do you mean?"

" 'At Annapolis'," replied Chet, "or 'Haven't you children any respect for your parents?' "

Captain Nimitz looked stern, but Mrs. Nimitz began to crack up. The captain rumbled a bit; then he too cracked up and, to the scandal of the messboys, the whole family roared with laughter. No Nimitz, not even the captain, was permitted to get away with stock phrases.

The older children had by this time come to realize that their parents were exceptional in several ways. For one thing, they never quarreled. It was not that they merely refrained from having their differences out in front of their offspring. The fact was that Chester and Catherine had reached such understanding and harmony of mind that they had no occasion for bickering. Another thing the children noticed was that their father never raised his voice and always used polite language, even when he was conveying intense dissatisfaction. And he never under any circumstances swore, yet he could put a miscreant in his place more effectively than most men could by using bluster and profanity.

The nearest Nimitz ever came to using off-color language was in the punch lines of the great hoard of stories that he collected, and sometimes invented, to illustrate points or to entertain his friends. In World War II, Nimitz's stories, tailored to fit all occasions and told with the skill of a true raconteur, became famous all over the Pacific.

During the San Diego days, the Nimitzes renewed many of their old Navy friendships and led as varied a social life as the presence of little Mary permitted. Captain Nimitz took long walks, as was his wont. A favorite hiking companion was Captain Raymond Spruance, then chief of staff to Commander, Destroyers, Scouting Force, and as great a walker as Nimitz. The two of them used to walk out on occasion to San Marcos Avenue for a visit with their mutual friend Commander James Fife, who would drive them back to the base.

The 1931–1932 San Diego social season ended climactically with the full-dress 11th Naval District ball. The affair was to be presided over by Mrs. Thomas Jones Senn, wife of the district commandant, a lady of austere dignity and imperial presence, "the personification of the admiral's wife," Mrs. Nimitz used to say.

Kate, home from her freshman year at the University of California at Berkeley, offered to baby-sit. Captain and Mrs. Nimitz dressed for the ball and had dinner before departing.

"I want you to know," said Nimitz, "this is my midshipman's full-dress uniform. I've just had the gold braid changed, and I don't think there are many captains who could get into their midshipman's full-dress uniform."

"That's wonderful," said Kate, and off went her parents to the ball. Presently Mary went to bed. Kate sat up reading a detective story and finally dozed off. She was awakened by the clang, clang of approaching footsteps on the *Rigel's* deck.

"I could hear my mother giggling as they came down the steps toward the cabin," said Kate. "They swept in the door, and Dad went right through the dining room and into the bedroom, and my mother was just absolutely in hysterics. I said, 'What's so funny?' Well, she could hardly pull herself together to tell me that Mrs. Senn had dropped her lorgnette early in the ball. My father had leaned over to pick it up and had split his trousers right up the rear and had spent the rest of the evening against the wall. Dad, well, he had enough of a sense of humor that the next morning he was thinking this was pretty funny, too, and at breakfast he said to Mother, 'I'm going to call up Mrs. Senn and I'm going to tell her that this gesture of chivalry has cost me $90.' "

In the fall of 1931 Chet crossed the continent to Annapolis, where he entered the Severn School to bone up on math in preparation for taking the Naval Academy entrance examinations. Successful in these, he was sworn into the Navy in the summer of 1932. With Kate away at the University of California and Nancy in school most of the day, the half-empty living quarters in the *Rigel* must have seemed strangely quiet. Even Polly left at last, succumbing to asthma. A true sailor's dog, she was taken out and buried at sea.

Captain Nimitz spent another year nurse-maiding his decommissioned destroyers. Of all the assignments of his career, this was the one in which he found it most difficult "to become as deeply immersed and as interested as it was possible for me to become." Relief came in the late summer of 1933 when he was ordered to take command of the new heavy cruiser *Augusta* and report with her to Shanghai, where she was to become flagship of the Asiatic Fleet. He was delighted to receive a command afloat and to return to the western Pacific, where he had served happily in his youth, but the new assignment brought about complications and disruptions for his family.

Mrs. Nimitz, intending to join her husband in the Orient, made a quick trip to Massachusetts to visit her sister, who had just undergone surgery, and to show Mary for the first time to her namesake, Grandmother Freeman. Chet, returning to the Naval Academy from summer leave, accompanied his mother eastward as far as Chicago, then continued alone back to Annapolis. It was a melancholy parting, for Chet knew that he would not be able to join his parents in the Orient. Kate could not join them until she had received her degree from California the following June. Thus, like all navy families, the Nimitzes had to make another in a series of such adjustments as most land-bound families are compelled to make only once or twice in a lifetime.

Mrs. Nimitz, after her trip to the East Coast, rejoined Captain Nimitz and Nancy in Berkeley. Then the captain proceeded to Bremerton, Washington, where on October 16, 1933, in the Puget Sound Navy Yard, he assumed command of his cruiser. The *Augusta* was accounted a lucky ship, and certainly she was fortunate in having capable skippers. Nimitz, the future CinCPac, her third commander, had been preceded by Captain James O. Richardson, the future CinCUS, and by Captain Royal Ingersoll, the future CinCLant. Nimitz relieved Ingersoll ahead of schedule because the latter, with serious illness in his family, had requested duty in American waters.

When Nimitz took command of the lucky *Augusta*, she was somewhat down in her luck. She had just undergone a nearly 100 per cent replacement of her crew, including a complete turnover of all her officers except five ensigns. Most of her other officers had come directly from extended shore duty, but a sixth ensign, James T. ("Junior") Lay, had, at his own request, transferred from the cruiser *Portland*, because he wanted duty in the Orient.

The prospects for the cruiser herself were not of the best. She had just undergone a bobtail overhaul, two months instead of the usual three, she was not scheduled for a shakedown cruise or for refresher training after the overhaul; she was assigned only a couple of days of port repair trial runs, and was destined for the China Station, where there were no proper navy yard facilities. The overhaul had, as usual, left the ship badly torn up, her paintwork dirty with greasy hand prints where piping had been removed and replaced. A stormy 21-day crossing by the great-circle route from Seattle to Shanghai was little conducive to improving the condition of the ship or the competence of her crew.

On the morning of November 9, the *Augusta* moored in the Whangpoo River, off Shanghai, and routine salutes and ceremonies were duly performed. The staff of Commander in Chief, Asiatic Fleet, then began shifting with their gear over from the heavy cruiser *Houston*, the outgoing flagship moored nearby. At 5:00 p.m., November 14, the commander in chief broke his flag on the *Augusta*. This was Admiral Frank B. Upham, an able and respected officer, known as "Stumpy" Upham because of his short stature. The four stars he was wearing represented only temporary rank, which enabled him to deal, socially and professionally, with other commanders in chief, particularly the British, in the Orient. In fact, Admiral Upham's fleet consisted only of his cruiser flagship, a squadron of destroyers, a squadron of submarines, a few auxiliaries, and some gunboats. The great majority of American warships operated out of U.S. West Coast ports in what was still called simply the U.S. Fleet.

The new arrivals aboard the *Augusta*, about a hundred officers and men, promptly began giving the *Augusta*'s crew a hard time by making invidious comparisons with the *Houston* regarding procedures, efficiency, and cleanliness. The *Augusta*'s officers determined to make the staff members eat their words, but that would take some time. Meanwhile they learned one of the *Houston*'s secrets for keeping immaculate: her officers were using coolie labor to chip and scrape steel decks, to shine the copper piping under the floor plates, and to clean the hard-to-get-at spaces of the ship. The beauty of it all was that the labor cost nothing. It was supplied in exchange for the ship's rubbish, which contained materials the Chinese could use or sell. Of course, in employing foreign labor aboard a warship, the *Houston*'s officers had broken U.S. law and defied naval regulations. It was an outrageous practice, and the *Augusta*'s officers resolved to do exactly the same thing at the earliest possible opportunity.

The function of the Asiatic Fleet flagship was to move up and down the China coast "showing the flag," which meant visiting ports, firing salutes, and exchanging calls with local officials and with officers of foreign vessels. Normally the ship operated out of Shanghai in the spring and autumn, out of Manila in the winter, and out of Tsingtao in the summer.

The families of the married officers generally moved with the flagship, but Mrs. Nimitz varied the plan somewhat. Because Tsingtao was expensive for foreigners and Shanghai is extremely hot in July and August, she and her girls spent the summer of 1934 in the little town of Unzen, Japan, in the hills behind Nagasaki. Mrs. Nimitz remained in Shanghai in the winter of 1934–1935 rather than take Nancy out of the Shanghai American School, where she was doing well. When the *Augusta* and Mrs. Nimitz were in the same port, Captain Nimitz lived partly afloat, partly ashore with his family. He played a good deal of tennis at such times and led a lively social life. The Nimitzes were particularly fond of having the junior officers, most of whom were bachelors, in to dinner, and Mrs. Nimitz mothered them as she had her husband's students at the University of California.

Under Captain Nimitz's command the *Augusta* was rapidly transformed from a slovenly tub into a crack and gleaming ship. Witnesses give most of the credit for the transformation to Nimitz himself, though certainly he could not have achieved it without a capable crew. However, the crew too was partly Nimitz's creation, for he never hesitated to replace an officer or enlisted man who did not measure up, and he had friends in Washington who saw to it that he got the sort of replacements he wanted. Nimitz made it clear that he expected every member of the crew to do his best. He did not broadcast his expectations but conveyed them subtly and individually to his officers, all of whom he quickly learned to know personally, and through the officers to his enlisted men. It was a demand for excellence, not for Nimitz's sake, and not altogether for the sake of the ship or the navy, but above all for the sake of the men themselves and their own pride and self-fulfillment.

In his drive to get his ship and crew into top condition, Captain Nimitz first zeroed in on his junior officers, particularly the six ensigns, all from the Naval Academy classes of 1931 and 1932. They, at least, were fresh from more than a year's sea duty, and he was determined as quickly as possible to make them efficient shiphandlers and effective division officers.

A principle of Nimitz's training plan was to give every man as much responsibility as he could handle, which was often a great deal more than the man thought he was capable of handling. By increasing the competence of his junior officers, he could give them responsibilities their immediate seniors were exercising and thus push the latter into higher responsibilities until, at last, he himself could confine his activities to those broad areas of command, administration, and ceremony that only he, as captain, could carry out. It was Nimitz's abiding rule that he should never do anything his juniors could do, least of all mere shiphandling. "Conning the ship," he said, "is ensigns' work."

In the early days of his command on the China Station, Nimitz from time to time had a box thrown overboard and then, under his personal supervision, required the junior officers to take turns bringing the ship alongside it as if it were a wharf. During these maneuvers he never raised his voice. If an ensign made a particularly egregious blunder, he might say, "Well, if I were doing it, I would have done it this way."

He next shifted from make-believe to the real thing. He kept a record and made sure that each of the junior officers had experience in entering and leaving harbors. An ensign or a lieutenant, junior grade, might hear himself ordered by name over the loudspeaker to report to the bridge. There Captain Nimitz would say, "Mr. So-and-so, take the ship and get her under way," or "Take the ship and bring her to anchor."

Once, coming in, Ensign Odale D. ("Muddy") Waters got rattled and failed to reduce speed. As a result he had to back the ship full power and lay out 90 fathoms of chain before he got her stopped, then had to heave back to 60 fathoms. Captain Nimitz remained silent until the ship was secure. Then he said, "Waters, you know what you did wrong, don't you?"

"Yes, sir, I certainly do," replied Waters. "I came in too fast."

"That's fine," said Nimitz, and that was the end of that.

Even in his own mistakes, Nimitz found lessons for his officers. Once in a strong, blustery wind the *Augusta*, requiring fuel, drew alongside the anchored oiler *Pecos*. In the circumstances and in that early period of the cruise, Nimitz had taken the conn himself.

"Another perfect Nimitz landing," remarked the acting first lieutenant, Lieutenant E. M. ("Tommy") Thompson, to the chief boatswain.

"I had all lines out," recalled Thompson, "when suddenly the wind shifted, catching the *Augusta* on the off bow and causing her to swing into the *Pecos*. The *Augusta*'s high, flaring bow proceeded to cut into the bridge structure and lifeboat davits of the *Pecos*. Captain Nimitz shouted from the bridge, 'Let go of everything, and I'll back away.'

"A little shaken by the experience," Thompson continued, "I shouted a reply that reverberated all the way back to the fantail, 'But, Captain, you can't back away. Your anchor is in the *Pecos*.'

" 'What do you propose to do?' queried the captain.

" 'Let me take a strain on the number 3 line,' I answered.

" 'You've got it,' came back the quick retort.

" 'I took a strain on the number 3 line and, perhaps with the fortunate help of a little shift of wind and a smidgen of divine guidance too, the *Augusta* swung clear, much to our relief and amazement. We had no more than secured alongside when the captain sent for me. 'Thompson, what did I do wrong?' he snapped.

" 'Well, sir,' I replied, 'you were overconfident and misjudged the effect the wind would have on a ship riding lightly on the water.'

" 'That is right,' he agreed. 'Now, Thompson, what should I have done?'

"Keeping the dialogue moving quickly, I answered, 'Probably the safe thing to have done, sir, would have been to have gone ahead, drop the starboard anchor, and to have backed down on it.'

" 'That's right,' " said Captain Nimitz, pointing his finger at me, 'and, Thompson, *don't you ever forget it*!' "

Captain Nimitz began gunnery practice shortly after his ship reached Manila. For the exercises the *Augusta* steamed over to Subic Bay and operated from there into the South China Sea, where target services were available for antiaircraft as well as surface guns. Available also was recording equipment to evaluate performances. Nimitz was one of the few American commanders at that time who insisted on night, as well as day, target practice. Because of the *Augusta*'s recent arrival in the Orient and her future cruising plans, she had to compress two gunnery-year training cycles into a short period. Nevertheless, she won the gunnery trophy for 1934.

The *Augusta* also won the Iron Man in athletics for cruisers. From the beginning Nimitz had encouraged his officers to get plenty of exercise and saw to it that teams were organized in various sports. One team even learned rugby in order to challenge the British at their own game. They did and won. Nimitz himself favored tennis and often played with his officers, for the sake of his own fitness as well as theirs.

Captain Nimitz was quick to capitalize on anybody's special talents. For example, when he learned that Junior Lay had won the sextant at the Naval Academy for standing number one in the navigation class, he promptly made him assistant navigator. Ensign J. Wilson ("Bill") Leverton, while officer of the deck one night, sent the bugler to bed and, to show off, blew tattoo and taps himself. It was a virtuoso performance, for Leverton had been bugling since his early Boy Scout days and had once been selected to play taps over the tomb of the unknown soldier in Washington. Nimitz sent for Leverton. "You're a fine bugler!" he said. "I tell you what. The rest of the buglers around here are not so good. I'll give you a month to make them just as good."

"So, damn it," recalls Leverton, "I had to get all of the buglers—there were only three or four of them—together and practice every day. Well that got to be rather noisy. They began to get me further and further aft and pretty soon we were practicing down in the steering engine room. Every day for an hour I'd practice with those darn buglers."

In the China ports, Captain Nimitz arranged a series of seminars to inform his officers about China. The officers would assemble in the wardroom of the *Augusta* to hear lectures, which would be followed by a discussion period. Among the speakers Nimitz secured were Nelson Johnson, U.S. minister and, later, first U.S. ambassador to China, Julian Arnold, U.S. commercial attaché, and the Republic of China's ministers of education and of finance, both of whom spoke English.

These sessions, which were Captain Nimitz's own idea and unheard-of in other vessels, aroused such interest in China among the *Augusta*'s officers that most of them devoted their leave periods to travel into the interior of the country. Many, including Admiral Upham and Captain Nimitz, together with their families, visited Peking. Some officers went as far north as Harbin, Manchuria, and returned to their cruiser via Korea by train and ship.

In June 1934 the *Augusta* paid a visit to Japan, arriving off Yokohama on the 4th. A great deal of powder was fired off that afternoon in the name of protocol: 17 guns for the Japanese light carrier *Hosho*, a 21-gun national salute for the Japanese battleship *Hiei*, 17 guns for Admiral Osami Nagano, and 17 for the French cruiser *Primauguet*. All salutes were duly returned.

The arrival of the *Augusta* in Tokyo Bay coincided with the death of Fleet Admiral Togo, victor over the Russian fleet at Tsushima in 1905. Nimitz, it will be recalled, in his first visit to Japan had met and admired Togo. On the day of the public funeral, June 5, the several foreign warships in Tokyo Bay sent delegations ashore to march in the procession. The *Augusta* sent a company of her most impressive bluejackets and marines, all over six feet tall. In the bay, the alien ships flew their own colors and the Japanese ensign at half-mast and fired 19 guns at one-minute intervals in honor of the dead admiral. Both Upham and Nimitz attended the service ashore. The next day they were present at the oriental funeral rites, held in Togo's home, a simple five-room cottage in the forest outside Tokyo.

That afternoon Captain Nimitz's serenity underwent a severe strain. The Republic of China ship *Ning Hai*, wearing a rear admiral's flag, stood in to Tokyo Bay. She and the *Hiei* properly exchanged gun salutes, but the atmosphere was tense because, as everyone present knew, China and Japan were enemies observing a temporary truce in an undeclared war. As the *Ning Hai* proceeded up the bay, the *Augusta* fired a salute of 17 guns. At the first gun, as custom required, a flag was broken at the *Augusta*'s fore. Her officers, looking up, were dumbfounded to behold not a Chinese but a Japanese flag. The flag, it seems, had the word *Chinese* stenciled on its border, a mistake made at the factory, but there was no excuse for the signalman and the officer of the deck confusing the rising sun of Japan's flag with the multicolored stripes of the Chinese, which they had seen every day in Shanghai on dozens of ships and buildings.

As soon as the 17-gun salute had been completed, another salute was fired with the Chinese flag at the fore. But the damage had been done. Both the Japanese and the Chinese were insulted, and the *Augusta* had been made to look ridiculous to every ship in the bay. An officer from the *Augusta* was promptly dispatched to both the *Hiei* and the *Ning Hai* to apologize and explain the mistake.

Captain Nimitz's calm was renowned, but this was too much. He instantly sent for the signalman and for the officer of the deck, Lieutenant (j.g.) Stuart McAfee, and, contrary to his custom, denounced them and their stupidity in choice words that carried far and wide. He then banished them from the bridge with orders never under any circumstances to return. Shortly afterward Lieutenant McAfee's application to enter the Supply Corps was approved. "It's a good thing," he observed, "because I think Captain Nimitz would have thrown me overboard."

On the way back to China, the *Augusta* on June 13 put into Kobe, Japan. Coincidentally, the liner *President Johnson* touched at the port at the same time. Aboard was Kate Nimitz, who had recently graduated from the University of California and was en route to China to join her mother and her sisters. At a reception aboard the *Augusta* she met Junior Lay, by then a lieutenant, junior grade. It is not recorded that they made any particular impression on each other. Certainly no one could have prophesied that Miss Nimitz would eventually become Mrs. Lay.

The *Augusta* reached Tsingtao on June 18. Not long afterward Captain Nimitz held mast, to assign punishment for minor infractions. One of Muddy Waters' men, a fire-controlman, third class, named Woolley, something of a character, was in trouble. While on shore-patrol duty he had been caught by his officer half-undressed in the upstairs apartment of a cabaret girl. He was charged with being out of uniform and with dereliction of duty while on shore patrol.

"Woolley," said Captain Nimitz sternly, "what have you got to say for yourself?"

"Well, Captain, it was this way," replied Woolley with great earnestness. "I was on shore patrol there and I was walking down the street and I snagged my uniform and tore it. I know that when you're on shore patrol you're supposed to be dressed completely in every way, and a snagged uniform is a very bad thing for anybody on shore patrol to have. This young lady happened to be a friend of mine and she offered, if I would come up to her room, to sew up the snag in my uniform. So that was why I was there with my jumper off. She sewed it up and that is why I was there."

"Captain Nimitz could hardly keep from laughing," Waters recalled, "but you could see that he thought that this was such an ingenious answer and good story that he had to give the man credit for it, so he dismissed the case."

At another mast one of marine Lieutenant Lewis Puller's men was called up. On such occasions the accused's division officer stood beside his man and usually opened with a good word for him, such as, "Captain, this man, who has been accused of such-and-such, has done a good job. He's a reliable man aboard ship. He sometimes gets into trouble ashore, but generally he behaves himself and is a credit to the ship."

Puller's man was charged with being asleep on watch. Captain Nimitz asked if Puller had any comment. To the surprise of Nimitz and everyone else, Puller shot back, "I certainly do, Captain. Get rid of the son of a bitch. He's not a marine if he goes to sleep on watch. I never want to see him again."

This reply, so utterly contrary to the usual pattern, left Captain Nimitz little choice but to court-martial the man. Lieutenant Puller was the *Augusta*'s third marine commander during Nimitz's command, the other two having been dismissed as unsatisfactory. He won the approval of Nimitz, who reported, "The work of Lieutenant Puller on board this vessel has been excellent." He later won fame on Guadalcanal as Colonel "Chesty" Puller and finally retired as a lieutenant general, one of the most illustrious marines in the history of the corps and the subject of Burke Davis's biography *Marine!*

In the autumn of 1934 the *Augusta* made a good-will voyage to Australia for the specific purpose of joining the citizens of Melbourne in celebrating their centennial. At all the ports the cruiser visited—Sydney, Melbourne, and Fremantle—the hospitality of the people reached such fantastic levels that Nimitz had to have a chart posted in the wardroom to enable his officers to accept as many invitations as possible. When not on duty, they were each scheduled for four social calls a day.

The return voyage carried the *Augusta* up through the Netherlands East Indies, touching at ports in Java, Bali, Celebes, and Borneo, and thence via the southern Philippines to Manila, where the cruiser arrived on December 23. When inspection followed a few days later, officers in ships and on stations in the Manila Bay area predicted that the *Augusta*, because of the long voyage she had just completed, would be found dirty and rated unsatisfactory. Instead she won an "outstanding."

That winter the *Augusta* again made a clean sweep of first-place awards in athletics and gunnery. Her carpenters were obliged to build a new case to hold all her trophies. Said Waters, "We were tops in everything we did. We were right at the top. It was a tremendous ship and a great experience." Vice Admiral Lloyd M. Mustin, recalling many years later his tour as a junior officer with Nimitz, added: "I think one can safely say that the *Augusta* had reached an absolutely unheard-of level of high morale, high pride, and competence at every level, down to the lowliest mess cook."

In Shanghai Mrs. Nimitz and her daughters were living in the French Concession. Because little Mary had a conscientious Chinese amah, Mrs. Nimitz could busy herself at painting in oils, at which she was gifted. Nancy was taking high-school classes at the American School. Kate was attending Farmer's Commercial College for Young Ladies. Her New England mother had insisted on her enrolling in a business course because, as she said, "an idle mind is the devil's workshop."

As always, Captain and Mrs. Nimitz kept in virtual daily correspondence. Because Nimitz's tour in the *Augusta* was to come to an end in the spring of 1935, they decided to send Kate and Nancy back to the United States, to the home of their Massachusetts grandparents, so that Nancy could have an unbroken second semester in high school. The girls left Shanghai in mid-February 1935 aboard the liner *President Pierce*. The *Augusta* arrived in Shanghai in March. The Nimitzes arranged to return to the United States in the liner *President Lincoln*.

The evening before Nimitz's relief by Captain Felix Gygax, the officers of the *Augusta* rented a whole club in Shanghai to give Nimitz a farewell party. There were a dinner and dancing but, above all, there were speeches of appreciation for the departing captain. It was an emotional send-off that brought tears to Nimitz's eyes. Muddy Waters called it "one of the greatest events I've ever gone to."

The next day, April 12, 1935, the crew of the *Augusta* was mustered on the quarterdeck. At 1:30 p.m. Captain Gygax formally relieved Captain Nimitz. When Nimitz started down the gangway, he was astonished and delighted to see awaiting him a whaleboat manned by twelve junior officers in frock coats, gold-striped trousers, epaulettes, and cocked hats, prepared to row him upriver to the *President Lincoln*, in which Mrs. Nimitz and Mary were waiting. Nimitz, acclaimed honorary coxswain, took the tiller and they rowed him to his ship.

When the whaleboat reached the liner, Captain Nimitz insisted that the oarsmen secure the boat and come aboard to have a drink with him. On their departure, they gave their former captain three cheers. This was not the end of their association with Nimitz. He retained a lifelong interest in these young men and took pleasure in advancing their careers. Some of them served with him again later, several made flag rank, and all, whenever opportunity presented, called on the Nimitzes to pay their respects. Chester and Catherine came to regard some of them almost as their own sons.

# CHAPTER 12

# FLAG RANK

ON ARRIVING on the east coast of the United States, Captain and Mrs. Nimitz and Mary paid a visit to Mrs. Nimitz's parents, then living at Wellfleet, on Cape Cod. Nancy was attending Sea Pines, a private school in nearby Brewster. Kate, rather to her mother's dismay, was merely loafing in her grandparents' home. The elder Nimitzes, after a brief stay at Wellfleet, were off to Washington, where Chester had been assigned to the Navy Department. Searching for a place to rent, they found what they thought they wanted in Chevy Chase, at 34 West Kirk Street, a house belonging to the journalist David Lawrence.

Chet, a second classman (junior) at the Naval Academy, joined his parents at their new residence on weekends. It was soon apparent that the two years' separation between father and son had built a psychological barrier between them. The young man who appeared in uniform before the recent captain of the *Augusta* was still the latter's son, to be sure, but he was also a junior officer. Though Captain Nimitz took a deeper and warmer interest in Chet than in any of the young men who had served under him in the cruiser, he unconsciously placed his son in somewhat the same category as the latter and held himself a little aloof, as a senior must when it is his duty to impose discipline upon a junior. Never again would Chet revive the easy familiarity with his father that he had enjoyed in the days when they lived together aboard the *Rigel*. The younger man reacted to the older officer's reserve with just a touch of resentment.

Captain Nimitz's new billet, Assistant to the Chief of the Bureau of Navigation, was essentially a desk job. For him it was a letdown from the happy tour in the *Augusta*. Instead of the camaraderie that bound the officers of the cruiser together, there was the tiresome political infighting of the Navy Department. Nimitz's relations with his bureau chief, Rear Admiral Adolphus ("Dolly") Andrews, a fellow Texan, were correct but distant. In contrast to Nimitz, Andrews was a man of lofty presence and senatorial utterance who made a practice of cultivating Presidents.

Since Andrews was frequently away from his desk, sometimes on errands for his great and good friend President Roosevelt, Captain Nimitz often served as acting chief of the bureau. And because Secretary of the Navy Claude Swanson was often ill, Nimitz from time to time acted in his place also. Such extra duties kept Chester working long hours, but they taught him details of the operations of the Navy Department that afterward proved invaluable.

To escape the brutal heat of the Washington summer, the Nimitz girls remained through August at Wellfleet with their grandparents. On their arrival in Washington, Mrs. Nimitz, abiding by her theory about "an idle mind," suggested that Kate either get a job or take more schooling. On this hint, Kate enrolled in the library science program at George Washington University. Nancy entered Chevy Chase-Bethesda High School, and Mary was placed in Miss Angel's nursery school in Chevy Chase. Mary was at first unhappy because her schoolmates thought the pidgin English she had picked up from her Chinese amah was marvelous and very, very funny.

In the late autumn the Nimitzes' tree-surrounded, rented house was inundated with leaves, which clogged the gutters and downspouts and kept the captain busy every weekend raking lawns. Before the last leaf had fallen, he was out looking for a less arboreal dwelling. He found what he wanted across the D.C. line at 5515 39th Street. The new house, into which the family moved in the winter of 1935–36, had the added advantage of being near the home of Chester's old friend Captain Bruce Canaga. Because both worked in the Navy Department on Constitution Avenue, they could share a motor pool. When the pool cars picked them up early enough, Chester and Bruce usually asked to be let off short of their-destination so that they could walk together the last mile or so.

For Captain and Mrs. Nimitz their stay in Washington was not without rewards. They met and associated with many old friends. They could get to Annapolis, 35 miles away, for football games and other sports. In Washington they could indulge their passion for good music by attending concerts. Catherine's musical tastes were eclectic, but Chester took pleasure chiefly in classical instrumental music. Much modern music annoyed him, and opera put him to sleep.

Captain Nimitz found the suburbs and environs of Washington superior hiking territory. Weekends provided opportunities for really long walks—eight or ten miles. On these hikes Nimitz was usually able to induce a friend or one or more of his children to accompany him. Sometimes Mrs. Nimitz would arrange to drive out and pick up the strollers at the end of their walk or, conversely, drive them out and let them walk back.

Nancy has commented on her father's hiking gear: "Long before it was common for American men to wear shorts, Daddy wore Bermuda shorts, and he wore socks that came just below the knees, and either a wool shirt or a knit shirt, and a rather cruddy-looking felt hat with a rather wavy brim or an old straw hat."

The strolls were occasions not only for exercise and good talk but also for flower- and mushroom-hunting. In residential areas Nimitz did not hesitate to step brazenly onto a front lawn to pluck an interesting specimen, while the residents, possibly seated on their front porch, watched with surprise. The trespasser would then turn on them a disarming smile, ask them if they were aware of what they had on their lawn, and soon have them engaged in a pleasant conversation. Said Nancy, "He was a person whom I think it would be impossible to resent."

Once while walking with a fellow naval officer, George W. Bauernschmidt, in Washington's Rock Creek Park, Nimitz's puckish sense of humor took over. "We got off the highway," recalled Bauernschmidt, "and were wandering on the bypath. There were two vestigial trails that went around a bend. As we came around the bend, we could see, just above the door of a parked automobile, the tops of two people's heads. Like almost everyone, I was for discreetly walking on by. Not so with Chester Nimitz. He walked up and stuck his head in the car and said, 'It's a nice day, isn't it?' and left two very startled people behind."

On his hikes Nimitz usually carried a walking stick, not necessarily as a stabilizing device. "It made a nice noise on the pavement," Nancy said, "and it could be used to point out objects, to part the grass to show a flower or something like that, and in crookneck fashion to drag down the branch of a tree to pick off the fruit. This was one of the things that used to embarrass my sister and me very much." Chester Nimitz Junior spoke of his father's "complete lack of conscience about stealing fruit if he could reach it over the fence."

In fact, Nimitz did not consider that helping himself to reachable fruit was larceny. For one thing, such sharing with the passerby is a Texas tradition, or at least a tradition in that part of Texas from which Nimitz came. He would have been glad to let passing strollers help themselves to fruit they could reach on any tree that he owned.

Of course, not all the tree-owners from whom he filched fruit were aware of the Texas tradition or were blessed with Nimitz's generosity. There was, for example, the case of the purloined cherries. Nimitz and a friend, while out walking, passed a yard in which was a tree full of ripe cherries, with a branch hanging over the fence. Without hesitation, Nimitz reached up with his cane and pulled the branch down. When he and his companion were engrossed in eating cherries, out came the lady of the house and began scolding them as common thieves.

As the lady thundered on, Nimitz assumed an expression of genuine regret. Then, when the scolding subsided, he stepped forward and began complimenting her on the excellence of her cherries. He went on to praise the appearance of her house and grounds. The lady's brow gradually became unfurrowed; her frown vanished. She began to smile, he smiled back, and presently she was offering to let him and his friend have all the cherries they wanted.

In June 1936 Chet was graduated from the Naval Academy and, after a period of leave, went to sea in the cruiser *Indianapolis*. Kate received her degree in library science and got a job in a branch of the District of Columbia Public Library. Nancy was awarded her high-school diploma, and Mary, having largely overcome her tendency to speak English with a Chinese syntax, ended her year in nursery school happily.

Shortly after the various graduations, sorrow visited the Nimitz family with the death of Catherine's mother, Mrs. Freeman. This event broke up the proposed celebrations and the comings and goings of Chet's classmates. Most of the family went off to Wellfleet, leaving Captain Nimitz and Kate at home to attend to their jobs. Left behind also was a colossal ham, intended for the canceled festivities. Kate, little experienced in cooking and unaware that a ham would keep, every evening put out slices of that ham with a simple vegetable and salad. Said Kate, "I just sliced and served it, every meal doggedly." Then the Canagas invited Kate and her father to dinner, and they served ham. Captain Nimitz, little concerned with food, made no complaint. "He was wonderful," continued Kate. "Whatever you served him was a wonderful dinner, absolutely the best meal." Nevertheless, the situation became so grim that Kate and her father sent Mrs. Nimitz a message: "Visit the old Nimitz Hamstead during Old Ham Week." Said Kate, "I never wanted to see another ham. Absolutely never."

In the fall of 1936, Nancy began her studies at George Washington University, and Mary entered kindergarten at the E. V. Brown School. Mary, however, soon contracted a series of ear infections and Mrs. Nimitz was obliged to teach her at home with Calvert School materials. The following autumn Mary, her health restored, entered the first grade of the Sidwell Friends School in Washington. Kate meanwhile had been transferred to the circulation department of the main public library at 8th and K Streets. Next she was appointed assistant chief of the music division, then acting chief, and finally permanent chief. On reaching this eminence she dashed delightedly home. Finding her father mowing the lawn, she exclaimed, "What do you think? I've been given the job permanently!"

Much gratified, Captain Nimitz reached in his pocket and pulled out a five-dollar bill. "Here," he said. "Run around the corner and get a bottle of gin and we'll celebrate."

The next day Kate's senior at the library, a prim New England type, inquired, "Oh, Miss Nimitz, what did your father say when you told him you were the new chief of the music division?"

Under the circumstances, Kate decided against a direct quotation. "Oh," she said demurely, "he was very pleased."

In the spring of 1938 Captain Nimitz was selected for rear admiral and learned to his delight that he was soon to have another seagoing command. As he contemplated flag rank, he regretted that he had no flight training in his record. He had applied for training at Pensacola, but an opening there and an opportunity in his schedule of duties never coincided.

In mid-May Nimitz received his orders. He was to report in early July to San Diego to take command of Cruiser Division Two. The timing was good in one respect, for Mary would have finished her first grade and could go to the West Coast with her parents. Her sisters would remain in Washington, where they found themselves a suitable apartment with the curious address 2222 Q Street.

In other respects the timing of the new command was extremely inconvenient, for Mrs. Nimitz had agreed to christen the new submarine *Sargo* at Groton on June 6. On June 18 Chet was to be married in the chapel at the Mare Island Navy Yard, near San Francisco. To pack, move, and keep all three dates required hard work and fast driving.

The *Sargo* was duly christened on the 6th. Said Mrs. Nimitz, "Poor Mary, aged seven, was so terrified by the sirens that she did not enjoy the affair very much—and also she wanted to 'get going'!"

"My chief recollection of the hasty trip across the continent," continued Mrs. Nimitz, "was when we were going through a cloudburst and the water was up to the hubs. As we wondered if we would get through, a small voice from the back seat came through the storm. We were passing a cemetery and the rain had made the flowers on the graves look fresh and lovely. Mary said, 'Isn't it nice to see the flowers on the graves because now we know that when we die we'll have flowers on our graves, too.' If the situation had gotten much worse, we could have had those flowers very soon. Both Chester and I laughed heartily and it relieved some of the tension."

Captain and Mrs. Nimitz and Mary made it to the wedding. Chet had waited just two weeks past the two years of bachelorhood then required of graduates of the Naval Academy. His bride was Joan Labern, a native of Jersey, Channel Islands, whom he had met at a cocktail party at Mare Island. She was then studying orthodontics at the University of California Dental School in San Francisco.

Chester and Catherine gave the newlyweds their heartfelt blessing and then hurried on to San Diego. There they met Lieutenant Preston Mercer, Nimitz's new flag secretary, who had also come from the East Coast. On July 9, 1938, Captain Nimitz, aboard his flagship *Trenton*, took command of his cruiser division, which was part of the U.S. Fleet, then commanded by Admiral Claude Bloch. On July 30 Nimitz was commissioned ad interim rear admiral dating from June 23.

At this moment of eminence in his career, Chester Nimitz was stricken with a hernia and had to undergo surgery. He was obliged to remain in the hospital a month and was not considered fit for duty for several weeks afterward. He became frustrated and irritable. The one thing he could not stand was inactivity. He felt that his physical weakness had cost him a golden opportunity.

But the Nimitz luck had not deserted him. He lost the cruiser command but, on his recovery, received instead the much more desirable Battleship Division One. He assumed command of the division on September 17 aboard his new flagship, the *Arizona*, at Long Beach. The Nimitzes, the Mercers, and Captain Isaac Kidd, skipper of the *Arizona*, all resided in the Ocean Boulevard area, where the Nimitzes had a waterfront apartment. Lieutenant Mercer and Captain Kidd soon learned that an inevitable hazard of serving with Nimitz was having to take long walks. Each morning when the division was in port, they joined him in a vigorous, extensive hike from their homes to the pier.

Nimitz, by this point in his career, had a well-earned reputation for never forgetting a name or face and for never failing to send cards or letters to his friends congratulating them on birthdays, anniversaries, and promotions. Those who marveled most not only at his kindliness but at his memory may not have known that Nimitz maintained a card file containing those important dates that he was credited with carrying in his head. At each station or command, some secretary, yeoman, or aide became the custodian of this file, with the collateral duty of keeping Nimitz posted on the dates and also on published notices of promotions or other honors that came to those listed on the cards.

However, Nimitz's ability to remember people really was extraordinary. Available sources record only one instance of his failure to recognize and immediately name an acquaintance. This was in the fall of 1938 when the Nimitzes were living in that waterfront apartment at Long Beach. Chet and his wife Joan, visitors for the weekend, had returned chilled from a swim, and the admiral was in the kitchen making a round of old-fashioneds for the family. A bell rang. At the door was an ancient, white-haired gentleman.

"Is this where Admiral Nimitz lives?" he asked.

"Yes."

"Well, I've come to pay a call."

In came the old fellow, not in the least perturbed at seeing the young people uncomfortable in wet bathing suits. The latter looked at Catherine, whose memory for names and faces was nearly as good as her husband's. Obviously she did not recognize the caller. Chet afterward wondered why he himself had not then and there asked the old boy what his name was. Somehow he was deterred by the awkwardness of the situation.

On invitation the visitor seated himself, very dignified, very taciturn. Catherine tried to engage him in conversation, without much success. Then in came the admiral carrying four drinks on a tray. The family was relieved. The mystery would now be resolved. Not so. Admiral Nimitz took a searching look at the visitor and clearly drew a blank. There followed an awkward silence.

Said the admiral at length, "Will you have an old-fashioned?" An affirmative reply gave him an opportunity to dart back into the kitchen—a strategic retreat to think this one over. But when he returned with the fifth old-fashioned and handed it to the guest, it was apparent to the family that the admiral was still mystified.

Ordinary people, accustomed to forgetting names, learn how to handle such situations. For Nimitz, however, this was a new and distressing experience. The family had never before seen him at a loss. To their embarrassment, instead of being his normal, cordial self, he just stood and stared at the old fellow. At last a light shone in the admiral's eyes.

"I know who you are!" he exclaimed. "You're Chief Crotchett. You were a bos'n on the fo'c'sle of the *Panay* when I was the skipper back in the Philippines in 1906."

"Yes, of course," said the old gentleman, as if the feat of recalling a name and face after 32 years was the most natural thing in the world.

In early January 1939 the greater part of the U.S. Fleet departed to conduct Fleet Problem XX in the Caribbean area. Admiral Nimitz was left behind as senior naval officer on the West Coast, commanding Task Force Seven, consisting of the *Arizona*, a large carrier, a cruiser, several destroyers and auxiliaries, and a tanker. This detachment had been left behind mainly to develop and train in underway refueling and in amphibious landings.

"It was my good fortune, as a newly made rear admiral," Nimitz afterward wrote, "to command Task Force Seven and to conduct fueling operations at sea with all types of ships and in all kinds of weather. Also—in the landing operations on San Clemente Island off the California coast—our amphibious Marines acquired valuable experience, not the least of which was the knowledge that ordinary ships' boats were entirely unsuitable for such work. The loss of several hundred ships' boats during these exercises brought about a completely new design of landing craft, which met the requirements of World War II landing operations."

Admiral Nimitz was pleased to note the advances in underway refueling that had been worked out since he and Lieutenant Commander Dinger had invented the art in 1917. He now devised some further improvements. "With accumulated experience," he wrote, "and with more reliable and sensitive speed and rudder controls and with skilled seamen on both ships, the manila lines between the tanker and the ship it was refueling could be eliminated. The tanker is put on a desired course, the ship to be fueled comes to the designated side, and both ships steam at the same speed with only the fuel lines connecting them."

Nimitz took a deep interest also in the landing operations, for he had long ago concluded that a main feature of any armed conflict between the United States and Japan would be a series of amphibious assaults to capture Pacific islands. Since the marines he ordered ashore at San Clemente were the Second Marine Brigade, nucleus of the First Marine Division, he was in fact preparing them for Guadalcanal, Cape Gloucester, Peleliu, and Okinawa.

At sea, Admiral Nimitz combined work and exercise by pacing the *Arizona's* decks, usually in earnest conference with one or more members of his staff. As was his wont, he lightened the most professional discussions with his endless fund of humorous stories. Officers made bets that no one could bring Nimitz a story he had not heard, and there is no record that any of them ever won the bet.

Admiral Nimitz threw himself into his labors with a kind of happy enthusiasm that proved contagious. Officers who served with him on this tour recall that they never worked harder or had more fun. The task force, no less than the admiral himself, was disappointed in the spring of 1939 when Nimitz received orders that required him to relinquish his command. He was to return to the Navy Department as Chief of the Bureau of Navigation.

The brevity of Nimitz's duty afloat was not uncommon, in that officers were at that time being rotated rapidly in and out of major fleet commands, none serving more than a year. It was widely believed that seagoing commands were being passed around among the most promising rear admirals to give them the experience that would be needed in the event, as appeared possible, that the United States should become involved in war. If command of Battleship Division One and of Task Force Seven was intended as a test of Nimitz's abilities, he passed with flying colors.

In June 1939 Admiral and Mrs. Nimitz, with Mary, were back in Washington. They considered themselves fortunate to find an apartment available at 2222 Q Street, where their two older daughters lived. Kate and Nancy, coming home from school and work, now usually had dinner with their parents. Admiral Nimitz was dismayed to find that in his absence Nancy had acquired strong leftist, even pro-Soviet, leanings. At George Washington University she had in fact applied for membership in the Young Communist League and to her consternation had been turned down because of her "bourgeois background." The admiral decided to raise no objections, trusting in Nancy's native intelligence to lead her back in due course to rationality. There were nevertheless moments of friction, as when, shortly after the outbreak of World War II, Nancy at dinner approvingly reported the rumor that the battleship *Royal Oak,* recently sunk by a German submarine, had in fact been destroyed by the British themselves as a means of enlisting sympathy for their cause. For Admiral Nimitz this was too much. With something like disgust, he laid down his fork and said coldly, "People who would believe that would believe anything."

During the same period the Nimitz family cruised one day on the Potomac River in the yacht *Sequoia* as guests of the Secretary of the Navy. On the way downstream, the *Sequoia* met the President's yacht *Potomac*, with the President's flag flying. "Of course," said Nancy, recalling the event several years later, "everybody on the *Sequoia* tumbled out on deck to stand at attention as the President's yacht went by. We had all been down in the cabin when the coxswain came down and reported that the President's yacht was passing, so Daddy went up on deck, and I said somewhat churlishly, 'I don't know whether I want to salute Roosevelt,' and he said, 'Whether you salute Roosevelt or not is your own business, but you are going to salute the President.'" Added Nancy, "It sank in."

When Admiral Nimitz took over as Chief of the Bureau of Navigation, the United States was embarked on the greatest naval race in history. The first Vinson Act, 1934, had authorized construction of more than a hundred ships, including replacements. The second Vinson Act, passed in 1938 in response to Japan's invasion of China and Germany's annexation of Austria, set up a billion-dollar-a-year naval building program. It was the job of the bureau to procure and train the needed sailors and assign them to duty in this rapidly expanding navy.

Nimitz prepared the way by clearing out red tape and simplifying procedures. At the same time he began the buildup. Since most of his proposed measures required congressional authority, he had frequently to appear before the House Naval Affairs Committee. There, he was fortunate to win the friendship and formidable support of the chairman, Carl Vinson.

To attract candidates, Nimitz placed advertisements and inspired stories in newspapers extolling the advantages of serving in the Navy. He expedited the supply of enlisted men by enlarging the training stations at San Diego, Norfolk, Newport, and Great Lakes and by shortening the basic course of recruit training from eight to six weeks.

At the Naval Academy, chief source of line officers for the Regular Navy, he enlarged the regiment, mainly by securing authorization for each congressman annually to appoint five instead of the usual four candidates. At the same time he temporarily reduced the academic course from four to three years. Graduates of the Naval ROTC were allowed to transfer from the Naval Reserve to the Regular Navy, and the number of NROTC units in colleges and universities was increased from 8 to 27. Permitted also to transfer to the Regular Navy line were reserve aviators and selected warrant and chief petty officers and ensigns.

With the outbreak of war in Europe, the President declared a state of limited national emergency and called up the reserves on a voluntary basis. After the fall of France, he proclaimed an unlimited national emergency and called to active duty all remaining reservists and graduates of midshipman schools, the Naval Academy, and the NROTC who had resigned.

A fruitful source of Naval Reserve officers was the Bureau of Navigation's new V-7 program, whereby candidates, mostly recent college graduates, were trained a month at sea and three weeks ashore and then commissioned ensigns in the Reserve. To help administer the shore establishment and thereby release regulars for sea duty, retired officers were brought back into the Navy and certain classes of specialists were commissioned directly in the Naval Reserve.

For clerical and other non-military jobs, Nimitz preferred to use Civil Service personnel. He refused to revive the World War I practice of enrolling men and women in the Naval Reserve for routine civilian work. During that war nearly 13,000 women, called yeomen (F) or yeomanettes, had been so enrolled to carry out purely clerical operations.

"While this plan met the needs of the Bureau and of the Department at that time," Nimitz reported, "it has proven, over almost a quarter of a century, to have been an expensive plan. These Yeomen (F) and others who enrolled for duties similar to those now performed by Civil Service clerks, became entitled to all of the benefits of the regular Navy men—bonus, pensions, hospitalization, etc., involving many thousands of dollars of Government funds after the services of the Reserves had terminated."

Nimitz was particularly opposed to the enrollment once more of the female yeomen. He concluded that they had been in general less effective than

Civil Service clerks. Another, more personal reason for his opposition to the yeomanettes was his strong distaste for seeing women in military uniform. It need hardly be said that he had nothing to do with the establishment in 1942 of the WAVES (Women Accepted for Volunteer Emergency Service).

In the period between Nimitz's assumption of duty as Chief of the Bureau of Navigation and May 15, 1941, the number of Civil Service personnel assigned to the Bureau rose from 280 to 950. Of these Nimitz reported: "It is a pleasure to perpetuate in these pages praise for the loyal work of most of the employees, both of the old line and of the new employees. There have been but few who were not imbued with the spirit of defense work and there has been much voluntary overtime which included not only time after usual office hours, but on Sundays."

Among the loyal "old line" employees was Mrs. Gorman, an ancient lady who hobbled about on a cane. Her apparel, which would have been fashionable in her girlhood, included high-buttoned shoes and a high, tight collar held up straight by strips of bone on each side. In short, she presented something of a caricature, but Admiral Nimitz was respectful and sympathetic. He told Mrs. Nimitz, "It's a tremendous thing for a woman of that age to go on supporting herself."

Mrs. Gorman, reciprocating the admiral's regard, used to waylay him in the corridor. When she noticed that he passed her office about the same time each day en route to the rest rooms, she made it her practice to get out her cane and water glass and head in the same direction, usually managing to intercept him on his return for a little conversation. "Doggone," said the admiral at last, apparently unaware that the meetings were contrived. "I'll have to change my eating and drinking habits because I just haven't got anything to talk to Mrs. Gorman about."

Admiral Nimitz, foreseeing that the Bureau would soon outgrow its allotted space in the Main Navy Building, early began pressing for larger accommodations. At last, in 1941, a spacious area in the newly acquired Navy Annex in Arlington, Virginia, was assigned. Nimitz himself delayed transferring from Main Navy until a specially ordered toilet-washroom had been built adjacent to his new Arlington office—a measure intended, it was said, to avoid his being waylaid in the corridors by any admiring old ladies. Nimitz thus found himself physically separated from his bureau at the time of the Pearl Harbor attack. He had to shuttle back and forth across the Potomac at a time when his labors concerned with rapid mobilization were complicated by problems related to the killed and wounded. It was an exhausted Chief of the Bureau of Navigation who, on December 16, 1941, received from Secretary of the Navy Knox the awesome tidings that he was to take command of the Pacific Fleet.

On arriving home, as we have seen, he revealed the news to Mrs. Nimitz. At dinner that evening, besides Kate, Nancy, and Mary, was Joan, who was visiting her parents-in-law while Chet was at sea in the submarine *Sturgeon*.

The admiral was uncharacteristically silent. The atmosphere was heavy with solemnity. At last Nimitz spoke, his voice grave. "Now I have some news," he said, "but this is not for publication."

Brightly, in unison, Kate and Nancy exclaimed, "You are going out to Pearl Harbor!"

The heavy atmosphere was at once dispelled. "I told you they would guess this," said Mrs. Nimitz, laughing.

At the end of the meal, the commander in chief designate took a pad and pencil. Expecting to be approached by the press as soon as his selection was announced, he was considering a statement to give out to the public. At last he wrote, "It is a great responsibility, and I will do my utmost to meet it."

He passed the pad around, "Does that sound all right?"

Everybody agreed that it was fine. When the pad reached Kate, she tore off the sheet. "I'm sure this is history," she said, sticking it in her pocket, "so make another copy."

Nimitz again wrote: "It is a great responsibility, and I will do my utmost to meet it."

Nancy tore that sheet off, saying, "I'll keep this one."

"My copy," demanded Joan, so the admiral wrote out the words again and handed the sheet to her.

Then at last the future Commander in Chief, U.S. Pacific Fleet and Pacific Ocean Areas, was permitted to write out a copy of the statement for himself and for the public.

# CHAPTER 13

# GUADALCANAL INVADED

Late Saturday afternoon, July 25, 1942, three junior CinCPac staff officers climbed Makalapa Hill toward the senior officers' residence area with mixed feelings of eagerness and apprehension. Lieutenants Arthur Benedict and John G. Roenigk, Japanese-language officers, and Lieutenant James Bassett, USNR, assistant public relations officer, were about to take their turn dining with the big boss in his quarters, a large clapboard house which Admiral Nimitz shared with Admiral Spruance, his new chief of staff, and with Captain Gendreau, the fleet surgeon.

Just as the young men turned toward CinCPac's house, a familiar long, black Buick drove up and Admiral Nimitz, in white uniform, stepped out. He was returning from a wedding. The lieutenants decided to stroll around for a while to allow their host time to freshen up and perhaps change his uniform. At length they mounted the triple flight of steps leading to the residence, were saluted smartly by a marine guard, and admitted by a Filipino messboy. Admiral Nimitz hurried across the room to greet his visitors, saying to the messboy, "Let me know when upstairs is ready."

Nimitz led his guests outside in back to inspect his livestock, a mongrel dog and four caged mongooses, the latter trapped for stuffing by Perez, the Filipino steward, an enthusiastic amateur taxidermist. The dog risked having his nose bitten off by barking and sticking his wet snout against the mongooses' cage while they chittered and snarled at him.

Back inside, the admiral pointed out a sample of the steward's art, a mongoose rather lumpily stuffed. He told how he once had three flag officers to dinner, and Perez had failed to get the word. The steward was distressed but promised to rustle up something, and he did.

"We ate it," said Nimitz. "Next morning the mongoose, stuffed, appeared on the sideboard. We never knew."

The messboy announced that "upstairs" was ready, whereupon the admiral asked the lieutenants if they would like a drink. They would indeed, and he led the way up the stairs. En route they passed the admiral's work table, charts of the Pacific area spread out on a drawing board supported by sawhorses. "It's a hobby," said Nimitz, laughing.

They entered a small, blacked-out room with five straight chairs and a desk on which stood two bottles of liquor, a bottle of bitters, fruit for old-fashioneds, a bucket of cracked ice, and a tray of hors d'oeuvres. "Bourbon or oke?" asked Nimitz.

"I'm a bourbon man," said Bassett. Benedict and Roenigk asked for oke, short for okolehao, a potent Hawaiian liquor. Nimitz chose bourbon and made old-fashioneds of both liquors, using generous portions. Later they had a second drink. "Strong as a mule's kick," Bassett remembered, "but swell."

Admiral Spruance soon joined them. He took a cup of tomato juice that was awaiting him. Nimitz offered to fortify it with a dash of oke. "No," said Spruance, "I don't think that would be good. Causative and curative in one drink. No, not good."

Nimitz mentioned that the United Services Organization (USO) wanted to bring theater and movie people out to Hawaii to entertain the troops. That notion collided with his prejudice against women in the war zone. "When Emmons gives out a signed statement that he figures this place is safe enough so that 'non-essential' people don't have to leave," he said, "then I'll okay those movie stars coming out, but not until."

"As an old submariner," Nimitz continued, "I tell you there's nothing in the world to stop a Japanese sub from surfacing some dark night off Honolulu and pumping 25 to 30 shells into installations and then submerging and running off at slow speed. We'd never catch her. Of course, I think they'd never get in *here*"—meaning into Pearl Harbor. "I'm not so sure *I* could do it."

Spruance agreed that enemy submarines were unlikely to penetrate the harbor. Nimitz grunted. "Hell, I don't know what their submarine motives are," he said. "I think they're more interested in reconnaissance than sinkings, right now at least."

Somebody mentioned the 9,000 young men of Japanese ancestry in the islands. Nimitz was of the opinion they should be drafted and sent to the front in Africa, where they would not have to fight Japanese. "They're good fighters," he said.

A Filipino messboy appeared at the head of the stairs and nodded. Nimitz nodded back and they tossed off the last of their cocktails and descended to the dining room. Nimitz proudly announced that they were having a special beef stroganoff prepared according to a recipe his daughter had sent him. The visitors agreed that the main course was delicious but had reservations about the dessert, which was avocado ice cream.

After dinner, Nimitz opened the fresh discussion with a few jokes, though he admitted that when he made captain his wife had told him that it was beneath his dignity to keep telling "those awful stories." Nevertheless he told them—about the Chinese wenches who wanted men with dragons on their chests, about the scared young marine facing his first parachute jump—a reasonably new story in 1942. The marine's sergeant had told him not to worry, just pull the rip cord. If the parachute failed to open, he was to pull the rip cord on the emergency chute. When he landed a station wagon would be there to take him back to camp. The marine jumped. When he pulled the first cord nothing happened. When he pulled the second, nothing happened. Looking down, he said, "I'll bet that damned station wagon won't be there either."

One of the lieutenants mentioned having been out to one of the army camps on Oahu and finding the troops bored and lonely.

"Soft, they're soft," said Nimitz. "They've got to learn to be hard. They're not having trouble. They only think they are. We're going to be here for a long time, and they'd better get used to it."

At about 9:00 p.m. the diners shoved their chairs back and Nimitz said, "Let's get a breath of fresh air"—his usual device for bringing a social evening to a close. They went out, the young men wearing their caps but Admiral Nimitz bareheaded, silvery-haired in the moonlight. They could hear the pumps sucking wet mud from the harbor to fill the extinct Makalapa crater. Nimitz said to Spruance, "Sounds like rain on a tin roof, doesn't it, Ray?" Spruance nodded.

Nimitz continued, "We'll sleep well with this going on, won't we?" Spruance nodded again.

As the three lieutenants were about to leave, Bassett had a question for Nimitz: "I understand you read a lot at night, sir. Do you?"

"Yes, I do," replied the admiral. "I read from three until five every morning."

"Three until *five*! When do you sleep, sir?"

"Well, I turn in at ten and I sleep till three, and then I catch another wink from five till 6:45."

Bassett, the future novelist and editor, that night wrote in his diary: "So that's what it's like to be the Admiral. The Admiral—a human, likable, hearty, zestful, kindly man—the best flag officer I've ever met, but preoccupied by the greater responsibilities on those broad but rounding shoulders. I noticed at the table when he was speaking of problems how he twisted his napkin into fine starched patterns. He's a good man. Grant him strength, God, and direct him. We need him."

Someone once asked Nimitz which period in the Pacific War caused him the greatest anxiety, to which he replied, "The whole first six months." Those months had passed, and mid-summer 1942 was a sort of breathing time for the admiral. The U.S. Pacific Fleet had turned back the Japanese in the Coral Sea and defeated them at Midway. Now the CinCPOA command faced the task of shifting to the offensive with inadequate forces. The prospect was filled with uncertainties, but the Japanese menace appeared far more manageable than before. The naturally optimistic Nimitz faced the future with confidence.

He had, moreover, by this time surrounded himself with the men with whom he worked most easily. His inherited staff had included able officers, to be sure, and some of them he would summon again to his service, but their replacements were men with whom he had a natural affinity. At their head was Spruance, a quiet, discreet, and companiable man who shared Nimitz's fondness for walking, swimming, and symphonic music. Nimitz found in Spruance a source of fresh ideas and a sounding board for his own. They conferred at breakfast, during their walks from quarters to headquarters and back, several times during the working day, and sometimes on their long hikes. In the evenings, when they usually entertained guests, their conversation was more casual and relaxed.

Spruance, before his Pearl Harbor duty, seems to have underrated Nimitz, whom he had encountered only socially and informally, contexts in which Nimitz's simple, even folksy, manner tended to conceal his keen, well-stocked, and determined intellect. Now, serving with him professionally, Spruance began to get a different picture. "The better I got to know him," he said, "the more I admired his intelligence, his open-mindedness and his approachability for any who had new or different ideas, and, above all, his utter fearlessness and his courage in pushing the war." On another occasion he remarked, "He is one of the few people I know who never knew what it meant to be afraid of anything. Typical of his character was his first reaction each time we thought of a way to hit the Japs. He always said, 'Let's go and do it!' "

In August Lieutenant Arthur Lamar arrived at Pearl Harbor to serve as Admiral Nimitz's personal aide. Nimitz was highly gratified to have his former flag secretary with him again. He had been asking for Lamar since January, but Admiral Jacobs was reluctant to let him leave the Bureau of Navigation, now called the Bureau of Naval Personnel. Lamar promptly began looking after his admiral, anticipating his needs and shielding him from time-wasters, with such complete devotion that he earned the ill will of some of the regulars, who, in any event, rather resented seeing a reservist so close to the throne.

Shortly after Lamar's arrival, a new CinCPac headquarters building, under construction on Makalapa Hill since the first of the year, was completed and occupied. It was a white, concrete, bombproof structure, with two stories above ground and one below. Both above-ground stories were encircled by wide verandas, or lanais, replacing corridors and giving access to offices and conference rooms. The below-ground deck, which housed the communications department, was equipped with air-pumping and water-pumping plants and was designed to resist a siege—considered not beyond the realm of possibility when the building was begun.

Admiral Nimitz was pleased to move from the steaming submarine base to the airy headquarters on the hill. His new office had two exposures, through which he could see, at the same time, part of Pearl Harbor, below, and the colorful Koolau Range in the distance. The admiral sat in a corner behind a flat double desk. His office was otherwise furnished with chairs made of split bamboo.

Just outside the building the marines, on Dr. Gendreau's recommendation, installed a pistol range. The doctor had noticed a slight tremor in his housemate's hands. When this was diagnosed as nervous tension, Gendreau consulted nerve specialists, who recommended target practice for relaxation, because in shooting a pistol one can think of nothing else but pulling the trigger. Directly after his morning conferences, Nimitz usually repaired to the pistol range, most often accompanied by Lamar. However, at any time of the day he might be heard firing away as a means of clearing his head while dealing with a troublesome problem. Spruance frequently joined Nimitz with the pistols but less often on the horseshoe court at their living quarters. "That game was never in my line," said Spruance. "He could always beat me with either hand."

One officer who was ready to join Nimitz at any game at any time was Jack Redman, Captain John R. Redman, who replaced Commander Curts as CinCPac communication officer. Redman, a hearty, fun-loving man, occupied quarters adjacent to CinCPac's, and Nimitz frequently called him over for a late-afternoon game of horseshoes. Redman, for his part, discovered a fine bowling alley in the naval hospital at Aiea on the hillside near Makalapa. Nimitz, Redman, and other CinCPac officers occasionally climbed the hill to bowl, challenging a team of doctors—the losing team paying for the Coca-Colas.

The first major concern of Nimitz and Spruance was the shift away from the defensive entailed in the forthcoming invasion of the Santa Cruz Islands and of Japanese-held Guadalcanal and Tulagi in the Solomons. Occupation of these South Pacific positions by American forces, it will be recalled, constituted Task I of the Joint Chiefs of Staff's plan for a drive on the Japanese base of Rabaul in the Bismarcks.

In overall strategic command of Task I was Nimitz's subordinate, Vice Admiral Ghormley, Commander, South Pacific Force and Area (ComSoPac). Nimitz intended, without interfering, to give the South Pacific command all possible support. He endorsed Ghormley's proposal to set up an air base at Espiritu Santo, in the New Hebrides, whence bombers under Commander, Air Force, South Pacific Area, Rear Admiral John S. ("Slew") McCain, would be able to reach Guadalcanal and its seaward approaches. Nimitz provided the fire support and air support forces, the latter including the *Enterprise* and *Saratoga* and the *Wasp*, which had just arrived from the Atlantic. To the *Enterprise* screen he added the new, fast battleship *North Carolina*, also just arrived in the Pacific. For the naval protection of Hawaii he retained only the *Hornet* force and Pye's old battleships.

Admiral Halsey being still unavailable, Nimitz ordered Frank Jack Fletcher to command the expeditionary force and at last obtained for him from Admiral King a promotion to vice admiral. Under Fletcher, but virtually independent of him, Rear Admiral Richmond Kelly Turner would command the amphibious force. The landing force was the 1st Marine Division, commanded by Major General A. Archer Vandegrift, USMC. Their transports would be escorted from New Zealand by ships from General MacArthur's Allied Naval Force, Southwest Pacific, which would include three Australian cruisers. General MacArthur would also provide additional air reconnaissance from New Guinea.

The invasion had been designated Operation Watchtower, but in view of the limited Allied forces available and the formidable opposition expected, its

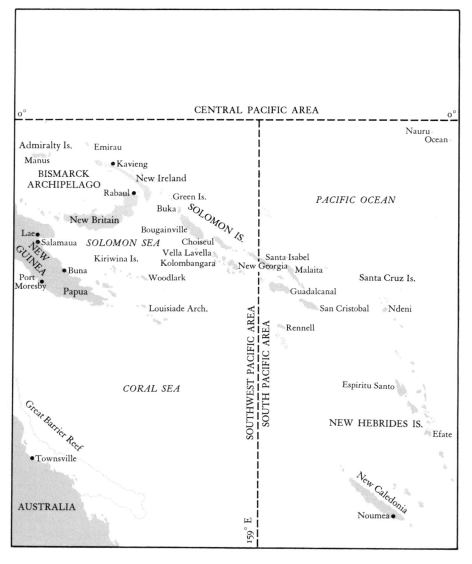

*Scene of Early Operations in the South and Southwest Pacific Areas*

baffled planners and participants began to refer to it as "Operation Shoe-string." Guadalcanal and Tulagi were within range of Japanese airfields at Rabaul and in the Upper Solomons. The Japanese fleet, despite its losses at Midway, was still powerful; besides destroyers, cruisers, and fast battleships, it included the fleet carriers *Shokaku, Zuikaku, Junyo,* and *Hiyo,* and the light carriers *Hosho, Zuiho,* and *Ryujo.* On Guadalcanal alone, there were believed to be more than 5,000 Japanese jungle fighters—tough troops such as had thrashed the Americans in the Philippines, the British in Malaya, and the Dutch in Java.

Admiral Ghormley and General MacArthur got together at Melbourne in the second week in July to compare notes and coordinate plans. Their confer-ence seems to have generated little more than funk. Speaking for himself and Ghormley, MacArthur protested to King and Nimitz against both the operation and the target date of August 1. To launch Operation Watchtower before building up greater Allied strength in the area was, he insisted, simply courting disaster.

King exploded. He said to General Marshall, "Three weeks ago Mac-Arthur stated that, if he could be furnished amphibious forces and two car-riers, he could push right through to Rabaul. . . . He now feels that he not only cannot undertake this extended operation but not even the Tulagi operation." Guadalcanal had to be taken, he contended, before the Japanese could make their airfield operational and use it to support a drive via the New Hebrides to New Caledonia, in order to cut the United States-Australia supply line. Ad-miral Nimitz and the Joint Chiefs of Staff concurred with King. Their only concession was to accede to Ghormley's request that the target date be de-ferred to August 7.

It was perhaps just as well that the pessimistic Ghormley remained in his headquarters flagship, the old naval auxiliary *Argonne,* at Noumea, far from the scene of action. The key officers in America's first full-fledged amphibious operation of the war were Fletcher, Turner, and Vandegrift. In view of the disparity of force, it was evident that their chief hope for success lay in sur-prise, by establishing footholds on Guadalcanal and nearby Tulagi before the enemy could react strongly. Santa Cruz would have to wait awhile. The prob-lem of attaining surprise and at the same time keeping track of enemy move-ments was immensely complicated by the fact that the Japanese on August 1 made a drastic change in their naval operational code, JN25, evidently scram-bling the code groups. That evening the keeper of the CinCPac Command Summary wrote: "We must depend almost entirely on traffic analysis to de-duce the enemy deployment."

Admiral Nimitz meanwhile had alerted Lieutenant Colonel Evans F. Carlson's Marine 2nd Raider Battalion to conduct a raid on enemy-held Makin Atoll, in the Gilbert Islands, using the 2,700-ton submarines *Argonaut* and *Nautilus* for transport and support. CinCPac's purpose was both to divert Japanese attention from the Guadalcanal-Tulagi operations and to discourage possible Japanese plans to advance from the Gilberts via the Ellices to Samoa or Fiji, in order to cut the United States-Australia communications at one of these points.

In the Fiji area, the Guadalcanal-Tulagi expeditionary force conducted landing rehearsals, and its senior officers held their sole conference. From Fiji the force was to shape course westward to the Coral Sea, then northward, approaching the target through the night hours. Shore bombardment of the islands was scheduled to begin at first light. The marines would probably start landing at 8:00 a.m., zone minus 11 time, on August 7, 1942, east longitude date. At Pearl Harbor that would be 10:30 a.m. August 6.

We may safely assume that CinCPac staff officers were in their offices early on August 6 awaiting news, but the hours passed without any reports from the South Pacific. CinCPac's far-flung radio listening stations picked up their first information not from Allied sources but from Radio Tokyo, which rebroadcast a call for help from the Japanese command at Tulagi. That island had been completely surprised by the American attack. Admiral Nimitz relayed the information to Admiral King in Washington, adding, "At last we have started!" At 4:00 p.m. Nimitz again radioed King: "No report from Ghormley. Our forces landed at Tulagi about 0830 and radio silent there since. Guadalcanal radio not heard. Enemy sent 18 bombers from Rabaul and apparently ordered subs to Tulagi." Traffic analysis revealed no major enemy units on the move. Evidently the Japanese assumed the Tulagi-Guadalcanal invasion to be nothing more than a hit-and-run raid. Radio intelligence, temporarily unable to read JN25, was nevertheless producing useful information.

Communications, on the other hand, left a great deal to be desired. On August 7,* the second day of the invasion, only fragments of dispatches reached CinCPac, but from these Nimitz concluded that the operation was proceeding satisfactorily. At the end of the day, however, two disconcerting reports came in: search planes had sighted an enemy naval force, composition uncertain, headed in the direction of Guadalcanal-Tulagi; Admiral Fletcher, citing the need to refuel, was withdrawing all three carrier groups from the area, leaving the marine landing force and the amphibious shipping without any air cover.

Not long after dawn on August 8, Fletcher's flagship *Saratoga*, by then far to the southeast of Guadalcanal, picked up a disturbing fragment of a radio message. It appeared to be from Turner, who was now senior officer at the scene of operations, and indicated that there had been a battle during the night in Savo Sound, the body of water north of Guadalcanal.

Throughout the day CinCPac's radio listening stations intercepted Ghormley's efforts on various frequencies and by various means to make contact with Turner. Ghormley's lack of success must have been caused by atmospheric conditions in the Guadalcanal area that were inimical to radio

---

* This account uses west longitude (Pearl Harbor) date, which is one day earlier than the east longitude (Guadalcanal) date on the far side of the date line.

transmission, by something wrong with the transmitter in Turner's flagship, or, as seemed most likely, by the disorganization of SoPac radio communications. Radio Tokyo came through clearly enough, however, with an announcement that, thus far in the Solomons campaign, Japanese forces had sunk or damaged eleven transports and seventeen "Anglo-American warships," including several cruisers. One witness recalls that Admiral Nimitz did a good deal of shooting on the pistol range that morning.

No doubt Nimitz did more shooting during the next three days, for not until the evening of August 11 did ComSoPac get around to relaying the report which Turner had originated in the early evening of the 8th, Pearl Harbor date. During the preceding night, according to Turner's report, in an action later called the Battle of Savo Island, a Japanese surface force, firing guns and torpedoes, had run through two formations of Allied warships that were guarding the entrances to Savo Sound. Turner added:

> Heavy running actions continued about 40 minutes. No knowledge of damage to enemy . . . . We lost [heavy cruisers] *Astoria, Vincennes, Quincy, Canberra*; [heavy cruiser] *Chicago* torpedoed in bow; [destroyers] *Ralph Talbot, Patterson* damaged. Heavy casualties, majority saved. Attack did not reach transports or shore forces.
>    Transports remained in area today to land more food and ammunition, probably 30 days (four units of fire on hand). Departed tonight via Lengo Channel in view impending heavy attacks.

In other words, an enemy force, later determined to have consisted of five heavy and two light cruisers, had made a nighttime attack, sinking one Australian and three American heavy cruisers and damaging three other American warships. The action amounted to the severest defeat in battle ever suffered by the U.S. Navy.

The following evening Turner had pulled out all the remaining Allied vessels from the Guadalcanal area and headed for SoPac headquarters at Noumea. Lacking air cover, he had little choice, but his departure meant that the marines had been abandoned with whatever supplies the transports were able, between air attacks, to unload in three days. It also meant that there was nothing whatever to prevent the Japanese from coming in with a superior force and retaking the islands, along with a sizable bag of American prisoners.

When Turner's evil tidings reached Pearl Harbor, Admiral Nimitz was in his office with members of his staff, awaiting news from the South. The duty officer, Commander Ralph Ofstie, brought the dispatch up from the communication department. Nimitz read it aloud. He displayed neither shock nor anger, but it was obvious to all present that his optimism had been shaken.

To the marines on Guadalcanal and Tulagi, Admiral Nimitz sent a message of encouragement. To Turner and his amphibious force he sent one of consolation and reassurance. Heads might fall later, but not until the dreadful defeat had been thoroughly investigated to ensure against injustice. To General MacArthur, Nimitz radioed: "Please express to the Australian government the

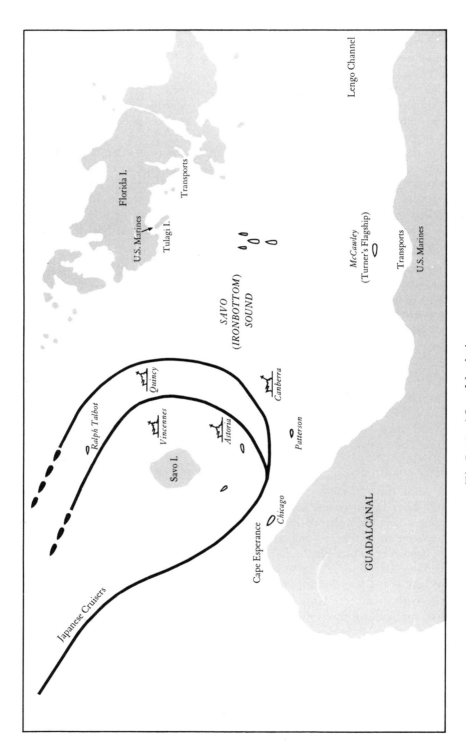

Florida I.

U.S. Marines

Tulagi I.

Transports

*SAVO*
*(IRONBOTTOM)*
*SOUND*

*McCawley*
(Turner's Flagship)

Transports

U.S. Marines

Lengo Channel

*Quincy*

*Ralph Talbot*

*Vincennes*

*Canberra*

Savo I.

*Astoria*

*Patterson*

Cape Esperance

*Chicago*

GUADALCANAL

Japanese Cruisers

*The Battle of Savo Island, August 9, 1942*

deep sympathy of the Pacific Fleet for the losses suffered by our Australian brothers in arms in the Watchtower Operation and also our admiration for the conduct and wholehearted cooperation of the entire Australian contingent."

The next few days at CinCPac were spent in reassessing and replanning on the basis of decreased strength. They were also a period of intense anxiety lest the Japanese discover and act upon the almost undefended state of the Americans in the Solomons. On top of the anxiety, there was the frustration of receiving from CominCh radioed demands for explanations and more information and having little of either to give. ComSoPac, it appeared, was both short on facts and plagued with wretched radio communications. Nimitz radioed King: "South Pacific messages passed to you give essentials situation there as now known to me. Intercepts indicate extreme communication difficulties."

Secretary Knox, more patient than King, wrote Nimitz: "Of course, we are waiting around with considerable anxiety for reports from Ghormley and yourself as to the progress in the Solomon Islands. The losses incurred to date, while heavy, are not out of proportion with those we must expect to incur as we pass from the defensive to the offensive."

After Turner arrived at Noumea on August 13, Ghormley was able at last to provide more details of Operation Watchtower to Nimitz, who forwarded everything as promptly as possible to King. It appeared that Guadalcanal was not as heavily defended as had been supposed, most of the Japanese there being construction workers. The U.S. marines had reached the airstrip the day after they landed, and they had quickly made it usable. Much-smaller Tulagi, 19 miles north of Guadalcanal, was heavily defended, but the marines had destroyed the enemy there and on adjoining islets. Enemy air raids had slowed unloading, set a transport fatally ablaze, and damaged two destroyers. Some 16,000 marines, meagerly supplied, had been left behind in the Guadalcanal-Tulagi area.

As for the night battle in Savo Sound, the causes of the Allied defeat seem to have been fatigue, inexperience, and, possibly, faulty deployment of forces. Another cause might have been the fact that, when the Japanese struck, the overall commander of the stricken ships, Rear Admiral V. A. C. Crutchley, RN, was in conference with Admiral Turner in the latter's flagship, the transport *McCawley*, 15 to 25 miles away from the scene of action. Allied casualties in the battle were estimated at 1,000 killed and 700 wounded.

None of the possible explanations satisfied Nimitz. He could not understand how his ships, with the benefit of radar and air reconnaissance, could have been so completely surprised or why they had reacted so tamely—but he intended to find out. As late as August 19, the CinCPac Command Summary was noting: "Our losses were heavy and there is still no explanation of why. The enemy seems to have suffered little or no damage."

Meanwhile, on August 16 Japanese radio was overheard reporting the arrival of the American raiders at Makin. Although the marines apparently encountered stiffer opposition than they had expected, on the 19th the submarine *Argonaut,* en route back to Pearl Harbor, reported by radio that the raid was a success. There was no indication, however, that the attack had influenced the Japanese to effect an immediate redistribution of their forces.

General MacArthur had been forewarned by radio intelligence of the Japanese intention to march over the Owen Stanley Mountains to seize Port Moresby, but he did not have enough troops to forestall the enemy move. In late July several thousand Japanese had landed at Buna, just across the mountains from Moresby. Hence MacArthur began calling on the Joint Chiefs to provide enough troops to enable him to hold his position in New Guinea at the same time that Turner was impressing on Ghormley the need for prompt reinforcements to retain the American foothold in the Solomons.

In the night of August 18, Japanese destroyers landed some 900 troops east of the American position on Guadalcanal and then briefly bombarded the U.S. marines on both Guadalcanal and Tulagi. On the 21st, shortly after midnight, the newcomers attacked, only to be wiped out in a daylong battle with the marines. The small size of the landing force implied that the Japanese had greatly underestimated the number of marines in the area. When they learned the truth, they could be expected to counterattack in far greater strength.

In mid-August, traffic analysis revealed to the Americans that a reconstituted carrier force had arrived at Truk, the Japanese Southwest Pacific island base 700 miles north of Rabaul. CinCPac staff speculated as to whether this shift of strength was intended to back up the Japanese landing at Buna or to reinforce and retake Guadalcanal, or both.

On August 15 four American destroyer-transports loaded with gasoline, ammunition, and ground crews darted into Savo Sound—or Ironbottom Sound, as it came to be called because of the many ships sunk there. On the 20th an escort carrier approached from the southeast and flew in planes to operate from the captured Guadalcanal airstrip, now named Henderson Field. Meanwhile, Admiral Fletcher with his three-carrier force, which included the *North Carolina* in the *Enterprise* screen, patrolled southeast of Guadalcanal, guarding the sea communications but remaining presumably beyond observation by enemy search planes.

Despite Fletcher's precautions, the Japanese evidently learned of his presence, for they brought down from Truk a segment of their carrier force to cover a new Guadalcanal-bound reinforcement group. The result was the Battle of the Eastern Solomons of August 24, in which Fletcher, having sent his *Wasp* group south for refueling, was embarrassed at being caught understrength. He nevertheless attacked promptly, sinking the light carrier *Ryujo.* Three of the bombs dropped by planes from the *Shokaku* and the *Zuikaku* struck the *Enterprise,* knocking out her elevators, wrecking compartments, blowing holes in her side plating, and killing 74 men. In spite of her damage, she was able to make it to Pearl Harbor under her own steam for repairs. Following this battle, Admiral Ghormley ordered the carriers to remain south of the 10th parallel, unless in pursuit of an enemy.

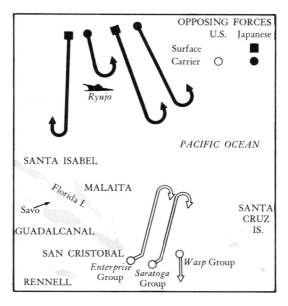

*The Battle of the Eastern Solomons, August 24, 1942*

On the last day of August the *Saratoga*, flagship of Admiral Fletcher, was patrolling east of San Cristobal when she was struck by a torpedo launched from a Japanese submarine—for the second time that year. She, too, proceeded to Pearl Harbor for repairs. Because Fletcher was slightly wounded, Nimitz had an opportunity to grant him leave so that he might get some much-needed rest. Fletcher left sea duty with a reputation for hard luck, which some observers, but not Nimitz, regarded as partly the result of ineptitude. Under his command two carriers had been lost and two heavily damaged. In his one unqualifiedly victorious battle, Midway, he had been obliged to relinquish the tactical command, and Admiral Spruance got most of the credit. Following his leave, Fletcher was to report to Washington for temporary duty in order, presumably, that a skeptical King might look him over.

Admiral Nimitz had already sent the *Hornet* south. She and the *Wasp* were, in September, the only operational U.S. carriers in the Pacific. Nimitz, in a letter to CominCh, expressed his conclusion that carriers should not be used in support of Tasks II and III of the drive on Rabaul. Such use, he pointed out, would confine them in the enclosed waters of the Coral and Solomon seas where they would be within easy reach of enemy airfields and where it would be easy for enemy submarines to locate them. Support for the coming operations should be provided by land-based air, he insisted, and he requested more planes, particularly dive-bombers, to operate from shore bases. He concluded, "There are too many other tasks ahead for our all-too-few carriers to allow them to be subjected to almost certain damage and destruction in an effort to accomplish a task which can be accomplished by other means."

In this gloomy September there were light moments, one of which came in the middle of the night. At three o'clock one morning, the officer of the watch at CinCPac headquarters called Lieutenant Lamar to ask whether Admiral Nimitz should be awakened and consulted in connection with a very puzzling message that had just arrived from General Vandegrift on Guadalcanal. The general was requesting a hundred gross of condoms, that is 14,400 contraceptives, an odd request indeed, for the only women on Guadalcanal were natives, and none of them were likely to be inside the marine defense perimeter. Since, in the Navy, contraceptives were controlled by the medical department, Lamar, instead of waking the admiral, telephoned Dr. Gendreau, who happened to be on duty that night.

Gendreau investigated and called back. There were not, he reported, a hundred gross of condoms on the island of Oahu, at least not in the Navy's possession. Anyway, what the dickens did the general want them for? Lamar, deciding the time for action had come, put on his uniform, went up to Admiral Nimitz's quarters, and awakened him with Vandegrift's message. Nimitz, not in the least perplexed, smiled and said, "General Vandegrift is probably going to use them on the rifles of his marines to keep out the rain."

September 1942 was for the high command a month of travel and inspection. Undersecretary of the Navy James Forrestal, in charge of the Navy's procurement, led the way, visiting the South Pacific to study the supply situation. En route back to the United States he stopped at Pearl Harbor for consultation. In the morning of September 6 Lieutenant Bassett saw a skinny little fellow with a flattened nose and wearing an open-neck sport shirt tapping at a typewriter at CinCPac headquarters and thought it was the typewriter repair man. It was the Undersecretary typing his own notes. That night Forrestal accompanied Nimitz and members of the CinCPac staff on a flight to San Francisco where Nimitz was going for another conference with Admiral King.

It may have been at this meeting that King showed up at the St. Francis Hotel in one of the new gray uniforms with black sleeve stripes and plain black visor and chin strap on the cap. This uniform, the austere King's own design, was generally disliked in the Navy and despised by Nimitz, who arrived as usual in blue and gold. When he and King left the hotel together, it was drizzling and both were wearing regulation raincoats, which in those days carried no insignia. News photographers were waiting for them. One of them said to King, who in his lackluster outfit looked like a chief petty officer, "Get out of the way, chief. I want to get a picture of Admiral Nimitz."

Admiral King had brought along Admiral Halsey, by this time completely cured of his dermatitis and anxious to return to duty. There were handshakes and heartfelt greetings all around, for the bluff and friendly Halsey was one of the most popular officers in the Navy. He was to participate in some of the forthcoming CominCh-CinCPac conferences, as was Undersecretary Forrestal.

Admiral King opened the first meeting in the morning of September 7 with an announcement that he was about to collect on that debt of gratitude that Nimitz owed him for transferring Admiral Bloch from the 14th Naval District. King was as eager to get Rear Admiral John H. Towers out of Washington as Nimitz had been to get Bloch out of Pearl Harbor. King now proposed sending Towers to Pearl. Nimitz must have groaned inwardly at the thought of having his old rival bureau chief on his hands. Rivalry was again causing trouble. Towers was still Chief of the Bureau of Aeronautics and still carrying on the struggle against the Bureau of Naval Personnel to get aviators into commanding positions. King had no control over Towers while the latter was a bureau chief, but he could offer Towers a tempting billet elsewhere and then put in one of his own men as Chief of BuAer. Thus King had offered Towers the post of Commander, Air Force, Pacific Fleet, which gave him administrative command over all Pacific Fleet carriers, a billet of great potential in view of the huge carrier fleet then building in U.S. shipyards. In recognition of the future responsibilities of ComAirPac, Towers was to be promoted to vice admiral. Rear Admiral Aubrey Fitch, the current ComAirPac, would relieve Rear Admiral McCain as Commander, Aircraft, South Pacific (ComAirSoPac), and McCain, a King man, would go to Washington as the new Chief of the Bureau of Aeronautics. All the participants in this merry game of musical chairs gained something, and King was relieved of a thorn in his side.

Admiral Halsey was to return to Pearl with Nimitz and then proceed south to resume his old post as commander of the *Enterprise* force. He would thus replace Fletcher as senior tactical officer and would command all American forces in any future carrier battles in the South Pacific. He would serve administratively under Vice Admiral Towers and strategically under Vice Admiral Ghormley. Since Halsey was himself a vice admiral, this situation could be awkward, but nobody had the heart to suggest that Bill Halsey should revert to two stars.

Command relations in the Aleutians were discussed. It was clear that there was strong dissension between Admiral Theobald and Generals Simon Bolivar Buckner, of the Alaska Defense Command, and William O. Butler, of the Army Air Forces. The latest in a series of controversies concerned whether Theobald's authority extended to the garrison of the Pribilof Islands, north of the Aleutians and west of Alaska. Nimitz drafted a dispatch stating that he and King interpreted the Joints Chiefs' directive as giving Theobald that authority. Nimitz and King decided to support Theobald, but they conceded that unless Army-Navy relations improved in the Aleutian theater, one or more transfers would be necessary.

King, Nimitz, and their staffs spent some time analyzing the Battle of Savo Island. They criticized the state of intelligence and alertness, the curious night deployment, and the absence of flag officers from the formation. Their discussion broadened into a review of the whole South Pacific command. King was beginning to wonder about Admiral Ghormley's command control. Was he well, able to stand up physically to the strain? Nimitz said that he would check on Ghormley's physical examination and let King know what he found.

The third day's conference, on September 9, was devoted to details, the most important of which was the possibility of using New Zealand troops. Any such troops that might be made available would serve under Ghormley as part of the SoPac force, just as Australians fought under MacArthur as part of the SoWesPac force. But most of New Zealand's soldiers were fighting in Egypt under General Montgomery. It was uncertain how many New Zealanders could be made available to Ghormley.

In conversation with Forrestal, Nimitz had said that while he was gratified to have the new fast battleships *North Carolina, South Dakota*, and *Washington* sent to the Pacific, he did not see how he could use them to replace the lost heavy cruisers as carrier escorts, since he did not have enough tankers to keep such "oil hogs" at sea. Forrestal said he understood and promised to do what he could to remedy that situation.

During the flight to San Francisco, some of the CinCPac staff had found Forrestal uncommunicative and put him down as aloof and surly, but they later had to admit that he lived up to his word and produced. Before he left the West Coast to return to Washington, the Undersecretary made use of his authority to shake loose the tankers that Nimitz needed. The staff would have been still more impressed had they heard Forrestal make his report orally to the President and cabinet. He urged in the most emphatic language that all possible assistance be rushed to the South Pacific. Secretary of War Henry L. Stimson, deeply immersed in the problems of the coming Anglo-American invasion of Northwest Africa, said, smiling, "Jim, you've got a bad case of localitis." Replied Forrestal hotly, "Mr. Secretary, if the marines on Guadalcanal were wiped out, the reaction of the country will give you a bad case of localitis in the seat of your pants."

Following the CominCh-CinCPac conference, Admiral Nimitz took a day off to allow his staff a bit of leave and himself a visit with Mrs. Nimitz. On September 11, Nimitz, staff, and Admiral Halsey were back at Pearl Harbor, where the *Enterprise*, Halsey's old flagship, had arrived for repairs. On the 12th Nimitz invited Halsey to accompany him on a visit to the carrier; CinCPac was to award decorations. All hands were lined up on the flight deck when the two admirals arrived aboard. As Halsey recalled the scene, "Chester stepped up to the microphone, beckoned me forward, and said, 'Boys, I've got a surprise for you. Bill Halsey's back!' They cheered me and my eyes filled up."

When Admiral Nimitz had finished presenting decorations, he again addressed the ship's company: "I know that you have been promised a rest and God knows that you deserve it, but you also know that we have lately suffered severe losses in ships and men. I have no recourse but to send you back into battle."

"Naturally," said an officer who was present, "this being a military organization, there was nothing but silence, but I know that they would have liked to cheer him if the situation permitted."

That afternoon, at a party at the Walter Dillinghams in Honolulu, Nimitz delighted Halsey by producing young Bill Halsey, an ensign in the Supply Corps reserves, who, unknown to his father, had recently arrived at Pearl Harbor.

On September 15 newspapers published the story of the transfers and new duties of Towers and McCain. Admiral Nimitz, aware that Mrs. Nimitz knew he did not approve of Towers' methods, hastened to assure her by letter: "I am to have a new air advisor. Never mind. We will get along fine." His confidence in his ability to deal with the new arrival is a measure of his increase in self-assurance since his early days at Pearl Harbor, when he was uncertain what to do about the advice-dispensing Bloch.

Meanwhile, the Japanese on Guadalcanal were being heavily reinforced. With American planes operating from Henderson Field, enemy ships dared not approach the island by day, but at night troop-carrying transports came down the Slot—the passage between the major Solomons—with such regularity that the disgusted marines called them the "Tokyo Express." In mid-September the Japanese staged a massive drive for Henderson Field. The resulting struggle, known as the Battle of Bloody Ridge, cost the attackers heavily, while the marine losses were comparatively light. Obviously the Japanese were still underestimating the American strength on Guadalcanal. The Japanese garrison on the island was believed to number no more than 6,000. There were 11,000 American marines there, plus another 5,000 on the islets to the north.

A thousand miles to westward, in New Guinea, Japanese troops, surging through a pass in the Owen Stanley Mountains and down the southern slope, had thrown back MacArthur's courageous Australians and come almost within sight of Port Moresby. Then, just as the fall of the base seemed imminent, the Japanese unaccountably retired over the mountains. One theory was that, having at last correctly estimated the American strength, they were going on the defensive in New Guinea in order to concentrate their forces for the recapture of Guadalcanal. This theory seemed confirmed when reinforcement operations by the Tokyo Express were suddenly increased.

As American transports were rushing the 7th Marine Regiment from Espiritu Santo to Guadalcanal, enemy submarines got in among the escorting vessels and within fifteen minutes torpedoed the *Wasp*, the *North Carolina*, and the destroyer *O'Brien*. The *Wasp*, fatally ablaze, was scuttled. The *O'Brien* broke up and sank. The *North Carolina*, a 32-foot underwater slash in her hull, headed for Pearl Harbor. Loss of the *Wasp* left the *Hornet* the only operational U.S. carrier in the Pacific.

On September 20 there arrived at Pearl Harbor on a fact-finding mission General Hap Arnold, Commander of the Army Air Forces and member of the Joint Chiefs of Staff. He was met by General Emmons who, having just returned from the South, was infected with the wave of pessimism that permeated the South Pacific and Southwest Pacific headquarters. Neither Ghormley nor MacArthur believed that Guadalcanal could be held, and they had so convinced Emmons.

Arnold found Nimitz just as sure that Guadalcanal *could* be held. Nimitz pointed out that the Japanese were already massing their full available strength against Guadalcanal and were losing men, ships, and, above all, aircraft far faster than they could replace them. Allied strength, real and potential, was only just beginning to be brought to bear on this point of contact. If the marines could hold out a little longer, the tide was bound to turn.

Could the marines hold out? Though they were in poor shape from combat fatigue, malaria, sleeplessness, and inadequate diet, their officers believed they could. The funk of Noumea and Brisbane had not seeped as far as Guadalcanal. Hanson Baldwin, of *The New York Times*, asked Vandegrift, "Are you going to hold this beachhead, General? Are you going to stay here?"

"Hell, yes," Vandegrift shot back. "Why not?"

Admiral Nimitz decided that it was time he personally headed south to look into the situation. On September 25 he departed Pearl Harbor in a Coronado flying boat accompanied by members of his staff, including Colonel Omar T. Pfeiffer, his senior marine officer; Captain Redman, his communicator; Commander Ofstie, his air officer; Commander William M. Callaghan, his petroleum and tanker expert; and Lieutenant Lamar, his aide.

Nimitz had radioed MacArthur inviting the general to join him at a conference at Noumea. MacArthur replied with an invitation to the admiral to extend his trip and join him at Brisbane, but neither felt that he could be away from his command long enough to cross the Coral Sea. The general said he would send a couple of senior staff officers to Noumea to represent him.

One engine of the Coronado burned out a bearing, thereby obliging Nimitz and company to spend the night on Canton Island while awaiting a substitute plane from Pearl. The time was not wasted because, by prearrangement, they were met here by Admiral Slew McCain, who was coming up from the South en route to his new duties in Washington. Nimitz was anxious to get McCain's views on conditions in SoPac. On Canton McCain and the Nimitz party were lodged in the luxurious Pan American Hotel, which had been built as a tourist attraction on the eve of the war. Each officer had a bedroom with an attached bath.

McCain, it will be recalled, had served with Nimitz in the gunboat *Panay* in the Philippines in 1906. He was only a year older than Nimitz but he looked ten years his senior, mainly because of his bony frame, his hooked nose, and his sunken cheeks.* He reported to Nimitz that Guadalcanal could be held only if enough fighter planes and pilots were provided to break up the persistent enemy bombing.

---

* Junior officers and enlisted men referred to McCain as "Popeye the Sailor Man," a cartoon character whom he superficially resembled.

That night an air raid alarm sent all hands on Canton scurrying to the shelter. When Admiral Nimitz got there, he asked where Admiral McCain was. A quick check showed him missing, whereupon Lamar hurried back to the blacked-out hotel and groped his way to the missing man's room. As Lamar recalled: "When I got there, I knocked on the door and asked Admiral McCain if he was all right. I could not understand his mumbled reply, so I opened the door and walked in. Admiral McCain had false teeth, which he had put in a glass on top of the toilet in his bathroom. In the excitement of getting out in the air raid, the teeth had gone into the toilet. I fished them out, and we went on to the air-raid shelter until the all-clear signal was sounded." The next morning McCain had the medical department thoroughly sterilize the teeth before he would put them in his mouth. Meanwhile, he was virtually incommunicado, being able to do little but munch and mumble.

Nimitz's seaplane arrived at Noumea in the afternoon of September 28, east longitude date. The small harbor there was crowded with no fewer than 80 cargo vessels, at a time when shipping was in desperately short supply for the coming invasion of North Africa. The ships at Noumea could not be sent to the forward area because at their points of origin, usually in the United States, they had not been combat-loaded; items used together, such as guns and their ammunition, were not stowed together, and in many cases were in separate vessels. The ships could not be reloaded at Noumea because the necessary piers, cranes, barges, trucks, and workers were lacking. The only recourse was to turn the ships around as fast as they arrived and send them to New Zealand for unloading and reloading—a process immensely complicated by a longshoremen's strike at Wellington. Ghormley was getting the blame for this situation, as well as for everything else that had gone awry, but the fault lay chiefly in Washington.

Nimitz found Ghormley haggard with fatigue and anxiety. He was occupying a small hotbox of an office in his headquarters ship, the *Argonne*, which had no air-conditioning. He had scarcely left the vessel since he arrived at Noumea just before the invasion of Guadalcanal. Nimitz wondered why Ghormley had not taken more comfortable and commodious headquarters ashore. It appeared that the local French authorities had offered nothing of the sort and Ghormley had not insisted.

A conference, a main reason for Nimitz's flight to New Caledonia, began aboard the *Argonne* at 4:30 that afternoon and continued until 8:00 p.m., the officers sitting around a green-baize-covered table in the wardroom. Present, besides Admirals Nimitz and Ghormley and members of their staffs, were General Arnold and his assistant, Brigadier General St. Clair Streett; MacArthur's chief of staff, Major General Richard K. Sutherland, and his air commander, Lieutenant General George C. Kenney; Admiral Turner; and Major General Millard F. Harmon, SoPac army commander. Colonels De Witt Peck and Pfeiffer represented the Marine Corps.

Admiral Nimitz opened the meeting. "The purpose of my visit," he said, "is to inform myself and members of my staff with conditions in the SoPac area; and to inform myself on the problems of Admiral Ghormley and General MacArthur. We will begin the conference by having Ghormley or Harmon outline the situation in this area."

Admiral Ghormley described the program and future plans of SoPac operations. General Sutherland presented General MacArthur's views. Admiral Turner talked about SoPac strategy. General Arnold discussed global strategy and plans for campaigns in the various theaters, stressing the fact that demands for airplanes, tanks, and ships were being made in all theaters. The essence of his remarks was that SoPac was only a small facet of the world military picture and had less claim to support than several others. Arnold was particularly critical of the stacking-up of aircraft in reserve that he had found, implying that no more army airplanes would be made available in this area until all those in reserve had been committed to combat.

Thereafter, the meeting turned into general discussion, with Nimitz asking numerous pointed questions. If there were doubts that the 1st Marine Division could hold Guadalcanal, why were troops of the army division in New Caledonia not sent to reinforce them? Had no investigation been made into the possibility of using New Zealand troops and planes? Why had naval forces not been used to derail the night-running Tokyo Express? Twice during the conference a SoPac staff officer brought in priority radio dispatches and handed them to Ghormley. Revealingly, instead of acting on the messages, Ghormley's reaction both times was to mutter, "My God, what are we going to do about this?"

The day following the conference, Nimitz presented the Navy Cross to Admiral Turner. Then with Major General Alexander Patch, the commander of the ground forces in New Caledonia, he inspected defenses in the Noumea area. That afternoon he flew in his seaplane to Espiritu Santo, where he awarded decorations, which included a Distinguished Service Medal to Jakey Fitch.

Nimitz's party was scheduled to fly to Guadalcanal the next day. Admiral Fitch provided a B-17 because there were no safe water landings at their destination. The Fortress took off from the army field piloted by a young captain who had no charts of the Solomons but pointed his plane in the right direction. When he got over Guadalcanal it was raining, visibility was poor, and he was unable to find Henderson Field. Commander Ofstie, who was riding up front with the air crew, remembered that Lieutenant Lamar had brought along a *National Geographic* map of the South Pacific. Lamar dug into his bag and gave it to Ofstie, who used it to navigate the B-17 onto the airfield.

The rain was pouring when Admiral Nimitz descended the ladder. He received a smart salute from General Vandegrift, and the general and the admiral shook hands. Despite the downpour, Nimitz that afternoon inspected flight headquarters, Bloody Ridge, and points in the marines' defense perimeter. At his own request, he was conducted also to the makeshift hospital where he chatted with the wounded and with those suffering from severe malaria and fungus infections who were awaiting transfer to the quiet islands to the south.

After dinner Nimitz conferred with Vandegrift and his senior officers, then with Vandegrift alone. He was glad to find in the latter a quiet determination to hold Guadalcanal and a strong conviction that he could do so. Nimitz noted, as Arnold had, that the nearer one got to the combat zone, the more confidence one found. Defeatism seemed confined mainly to the headquarters at Noumea and Brisbane.

Vandegrift was troubled because Kelly Turner was insisting that he go on the offensive from a number of points along the coast of Guadalcanal. Vandegrift believed that, with his limited forces, his wisest strategy was to maintain a defensive perimeter around Henderson Field. That landing strip was the key to the whole situation. Whoever held it, held Guadalcanal, and the enemy's tempo of reinforcement indicated that he was building up strength to make another grab at the field. In the circumstances, Vandegrift believed it would be a serious mistake to scatter his own forces. What he needed, above all, was more men to hold the defense line and more fighter planes to beat off the bombers that were persistently attacking the field and its defenses. At the time Admiral Nimitz was noncommittal, but his subsequent actions made it clear that he agreed with Vandegrift's strategy.

Late in the evening, over a drink, Nimitz said, "You know, Vandegrift, when this war is over we are going to write a new set of *Navy Regulations*. So just keep it in the back of your mind because I will want to know some of the things you think ought to be changed."

"I know one right now. Leave out all reference that he who runs his ship aground will face a fate worse than death. Out here too many commanders have been far too leery about risking their ships." Nimitz smiled. Perhaps he was recalling how, many years before, he had run the *Decatur* aground and been let off with the mildest of reprimands.

The next morning Nimitz again awarded decorations, including a Navy Cross for Vandegrift. As Lieutenant Lamar read the citations, he and the admiral moved down the line of gaunt figures, the latter pinning medals on chests. They came to a powerfully built, broad-shouldered sergeant, and Lamar read his citation: for outstanding bravery under fire. As Nimitz, medal in hand, reached for the sergeant's shirt, the intended recipient keeled over in a dead faint. Vandegrift was embarrassed. It turned out that the sergeant was scared to death at finding himself so close to a four-star admiral.

Because the Henderson Field runway was relatively short for heavy bombers, it was decided to lighten the takeoff load by dividing the Nimitz party between two B-17s. Admiral Nimitz was to be in the first plane. During the drive to the airstrip in the misting rain he promised Vandegrift "support to the maximum of our resources." Henderson Field at that time was a dirt strip, 2,000 feet of which were covered with metal matting. A 1,000-foot extension, added to accommodate B-17s, had no matting. This extension had been cratered by enemy bombs. The craters had been filled but, after two days of rain, the uncovered strip was mostly mire. Scarcely less forbidding than the muddy airstrip was the pilot the passengers found awaiting them. A major in the Army Air Forces, he was barefooted, had a black beard, and wore only a zippered coverall. After looking him over, several members of the CinCPac staff decided to wait for the second B-17.

Nimitz, less concerned with the state of the pilot than with the state of the airstrip, asked blackbeard how he planned to take off.

"Admiral," replied the pilot, "I thought I'd start at this end, even though it's downwind. I can get up to flying speed easy here on the metal matting. I'll probably be up to flying speed before I reach the dirt section."

"All right," said Nimitz and then surprised everyone by climbing up into the bombardier's area, the Plexiglas-enclosed nose of the plane. Evidently he wanted a good view. A couple of staff officers followed him, but the rest were content to ride in the cabin. Blackbeard climbed aboard, gunned the engines for all they were worth, and took off. When he got to the end of the matting, he decided he couldn't make it. He shut off the engine and hit the brakes. The bomber went slithering down the uncovered track, throwing up a geyser of mud. At the end of the field the plane did a ground loop and came to a stop with its tail hanging over a steep ravine that plunged down into a tributary of the Lungga River.

All the onlookers stood transfixed, their hearts in their throats, while the pilot switched on the engine, pulled the bomber off of its perilous perch, and taxied back down the strip. When the plane stopped, Admiral Nimitz climbed out and said, "Let's all go to the general's house and have lunch. We'll try this again after lunch."

The rain had stopped, so that by the end of lunchtime the airstrip had had time to dry a little. The delay, however, was dangerous because, the airfield at Espiritu Santo being unlighted and the whole island under blackout, it was vital that the planes reach their destination before dark.

Awaiting the first group of travelers were the same plane, same pilot. This time Lamar briskly conducted the admiral to the back part of the plane, where he belonged. Because there was now a little breeze from the opposite end of the runway, the pilot backed his plane up to the ravine, started in the dirt, and finally took off near the end of the matted strip. The second B-17 with the rest of the CinCPac staff took off twenty minutes later.

Nimitz's B-17 came down at Espiritu just as the sun was setting. An hour later, darkness was swiftly descending and the second plane had not arrived. It was obvious that her navigator was lost. Nimitz said to Fitch, "You tell the *Curtiss* to put her biggest searchlight up in the air, straight up in the air." Blackout or no blackout, Nimitz was determined to have his staff members back. Fitch not only had the searchlight turned on; he also had the airstrip outlined with gasoline drums containing oily waste ready to ignite.

Far out to the west, Commander Ofstie was the first to espy a slender vertical beam of light in the eastern sky. He had his plane swing to port and head for the beam. As it approached Espiritu, the drums alongside the airstrip were lighted and the pilot brought the plane in safely.

When Admiral Nimitz got back to Noumea, he and Admiral Ghormley conferred again. No doubt their conference was much concerned with the related problems of reinforcing Guadalcanal and stopping the Tokyo Express. It was probably at this time that Nimitz suggested rolling up the garrisons of the southern islands and feeding them in to Guadalcanal, thus relieving the 1st Marine Division according to the original plan. That division was still on Guadalcanal and Tulagi, and had been reinforced only by a single marine regiment. Denuding the southern islands of defenders was not too great a risk because, while the Japanese were fighting to hold Buna and recapture Guadalcanal, they would scarcely have sufficient forces available to stage an amphibious assault elsewhere.

In response to Nimitz's prodding, Ghormley dispatched to Guadalcanal a regiment of soldiers from his New Caledonia garrison. Turner commanded the convoy, the *Hornet* and *Washington* forces covered its flanks, and a cruiser-destroyer force under Rear Admiral Norman Scott advanced to derail a Tokyo Express which aviators had reported coming down the Slot. This particular Express, it turned out, was not composed of reinforcement transports but of cruisers and destroyers en route to bombard Henderson Field. In the night of October 11–12, Scott's force and this Express tangled northwest of Guadalcanal in the Battle of Cape Esperance. The Americans sank one cruiser and one destroyer and lost one destroyer, but Scott in his initial report mistakenly reported sinking "about 15" enemy vessels. He thus provided a terrific, if temporary, shot in the arm for the dispirited SoPac command.

The American reinforcements reached Guadalcanal on October 13, and the convoy that carried them there got safely away. That night, however, two Japanese battleships entered Ironbottom Sound and pounded the Henderson Field area with high-capacity shells that tore up the airstrip and destroyed half the planes on the island. Two bomber raids the next day and a cruiser bombardment the following night wrecked most of the remaining American aircraft. In the early hours of October 15, six Japanese transports arrived at Guadalcanal and disembarked soldiers almost with impunity. It was estimated that there were now as many Japanese as Americans on the island. Moreover, the Japanese were doubtless fresh and rested, while most of the Americans were malaria-ridden and battle-weary.

The struggle for Guadalcanal was obviously approaching a crisis. The CinCPac Command Summary expressed the unhappy appraisal of the situation shared by Nimitz and his staff: "It now appears that we are unable to control the sea in the Guadalcanal area. Thus our supply of the positions will only be done at great expense to us. The situation is not hopeless, but it is certainly critical."

In this extremity, repairs to the *South Dakota*, which had struck a pinnacle rock, and to the *Enterprise* were hastily completed and both ships headed

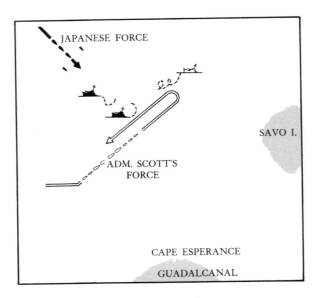

*The Battle of Cape Esperance, October 11–12, 1942*

for the South Pacific. By Nimitz's directive and with King's concurrence, the Central Pacific was stripped of planes for the defense of Guadalcanal, and the Army's 25th Division, on Oahu, was alerted to prepare to move south. Halsey, accompanied by members of his staff, took off by flying boat for Noumea to get ready to assume his carrier command.

In the evening of October 15, Nimitz called a special meeting, mainly of staff members who had accompanied him to the South Pacific. Those present recall that his eyes seemed to have changed from their usual sunny blue to a very icy gray. He opened with a brief lecture. "I don't want to hear, or see, such pessimism," he said. "Remember, the enemy is hurt too." The Japanese were obviously about to launch a major attack, and it was for this reason that he had called the group together to hear their impressions of the command situation in SoPac. Admiral Ghormley was an intelligent and dedicated officer, but was he tough enough to meet the approaching challenge? More important, did he have the personality to inspire his subordinates to heroic measures beyond their known capacities?

Each officer present expressed the opinion that ComSoPac did not have the required qualities and that the atmosphere at SoPac headquarters was intolerable. When one officer ventured on personal criticism of Admiral Ghormley, Nimitz promptly shut him up, calling such remarks "mutiny."

"All right," said Nimitz at last. "I'm going to poll you."

He then pointed to each officer in turn and put the question to him: "Is it time for me to relieve Admiral Ghormley?"

Every one of them replied, "Yes."

Nimitz discussed possible replacements. Turner came to mind. That grizzled and vociferous warrior was a leader, no doubt, but of the driving sort, a characteristic that had earned him the nickname of "Terrible Turner." His unresolved dispute with Vandegrift suggested that he needed the arbitrament of a more senior officer in his theater of operations. Halsey was a popular leader and had the necessary rank, but he was especially needed as a carrier commander. Besides, he had had little experience as an administrator and was believed not to be at his best behind a desk.

Without announcing any decision about relief or replacement, Nimitz thanked those present and closed the meeting.

That evening, after the admiral had undressed for bed, his orderly received a telephone call from one of a small group of staff officers who had not been at the meeting and did not know what had occurred there. Would the admiral hear them briefly on an unofficial basis? Nimitz said they could have five minutes.

In pajamas and dressing gown, he received the officers. The spokesman for the group pointed out that Admiral Halsey was en route to the South Pacific. He urged Nimitz to put aside any thoughts of sympathy or understanding for Ghormley, a brother officer, and order Halsey to take over the SoPac command on his arrival at Noumea. Nimitz said that he appreciated their coming and understood that only the best motives had brought them: he would give their suggestion every consideration.

In fact, he had already made up his mind. After the group had left he had a message sent to Halsey, then breaking his journey south at Canton Island, ordering him to cancel his proposed stop at Guadalcanal and to proceed as directly as possible to Noumea.

The next morning, October 16, Admiral Nimitz requested permission from Admiral King to have Halsey relieve Ghormley and received a prompt "Affirmative." Nimitz then composed a dispatch to Ghormley: "After carefully weighing all factors, have decided that talents and previous experience of Halsey can best be applied to the situation by having him take over duties of ComSoPac as soon as practicable after his arrival Noumea 18th your date. I greatly appreciate your loyal and devoted efforts toward the accomplishment of a most difficult task. I shall order you to report to Halsey for the time being, as I believe he will need your thorough knowledge of situation and your loyal help. CominCh has approved this change. Orders will follow shortly."

Admiral Nimitz next prepared the necessary dispatch orders to be handed Halsey on his arrival in Noumea. To Mrs. Nimitz he wrote: "Today I have replaced Ghormley with Halsey. It was a sore mental struggle and the decision was not reached until after hours of anguished consideration. Reason (private): Ghormley was too immersed in detail and not sufficiently bold and aggressive at the right times. I feel better now that it has been done. I am very fond of G. and hope I have not made a life enemy. I believe not. The interests of the nation transcend private interests."

# CHAPTER 14

# GUADALCANAL RECAPTURED

HARDLY HAD ADMIRAL HALSEY's Coronado alighted in Noumea Harbor at 2:00 p.m., October 18, when a whaleboat came alongside. As Halsey stepped aboard, Admiral Ghormley's flag lieutenant saluted and handed him a sealed envelope. Because Halsey would be aboard the *Argonne* in a few minutes, he realized that a message so delivered must have the highest priority. He opened the envelope at once, then tore open an inner envelope marked SECRET. Inside was a radio dispatch from CinCPac: "Immediately upon your arrival at Noumea, you will relieve Vice Admiral Robert L. Ghormley of the duties of Commander South Pacific Area and South Pacific Force."

Halsey, incredulous, read the message again. "Jesus Christ and General Jackson!" he exploded. "This is the hottest potato they ever handed me!"

Admiral Ghormley greeted Halsey as the latter stepped onto the quarterdeck of the *Argonne*. "He was cordial and friendly as ever," Halsey recalled, "but we were both ill at ease."

Ghormley said, "This is a tough job they've given you, Bill."

"I damn well know it," replied Halsey.

Such was Bill Halsey's reputation for aggressiveness that word of his succession to the SoPac command was received on ships and stations with wild enthusiasm. An officer on Guadalcanal recalled the effect on the men there: "I'll never forget it: One minute we were too limp with malaria to crawl out of our foxholes; the next, we were running around whooping like kids."

Halsey discovered that neither Ghormley nor any member of his staff could give him a firsthand description of the situation on Guadalcanal. All had been too bogged down with paper work to leave the *Argonne*. So Halsey radioed General Vandegrift to report to Noumea as soon as conditions permitted. Vandegrift arrived on the 23rd accompanied by Lieutenant General Thomas Holcomb, commandant of the Marine Corps, who had been visiting Guadalcanal. As soon as dinner was over, Halsey settled down with his visitors for a conference. Among those present at the meeting were Generals Patch and Harmon and Admiral Turner.

Halsey opened the proceedings by calling on Vandegrift to describe the situation on Guadalcanal. Vandegrift reviewed the campaign to date and told what he suspected concerning the enemy's strength and intentions. He stressed the poor state of his own men—weakened by malaria, restricted diet, and sleeplessness from night bombardment. He absolutely must, he said, have air and ground reinforcements without delay. Generals Harmon and Holcomb strongly supported his statement.

Halsey sat drumming on the desk with his fingers. Then he looked at Vandegrift and asked, "Can you hold?"

"Yes, I can hold," replied the general, "but I have to have more active support than I've been getting."

Kelly Turner protested that the Navy was already doing its very best. He was losing transports and cargo ships at an alarming rate, he said, because there were not enough warships to protect them. When Turner had finished his bitter recital, Halsey turned again to Commander, 1st Marine Division. "You go on back there, Vandegrift," he said. "I promise to get you everything I have."

At Pearl Harbor Admiral Nimitz was suffering from one of his rare periods of depression. He dreaded the arrival of Ghormley almost as much as he did the outcome of the approaching Japanese attack. His mood was somewhat lightened by a letter from Secretary Knox, which ended: "All of us here are very proud of the way you are handling your job." Nimitz relayed this complimentary sentence to Mrs. Nimitz. "Good news," he added. "Perhaps I can last out the year."

In a subsequent letter Knox supported Nimitz's action with respect to ComSoPac. "While I have the highest possible regard for Admiral Ghormley," he wrote, "I had had repeated reports of his physical condition, which gave me a good deal of anxiety and I am satisfied that you acted most wisely and with the most admirable initiative in ordering Halsey to relieve him."

When Nimitz received a report that Ghormley was about to leave Noumea, he wrote Mrs. Nimitz that the former ComSoPac would "be here in three or four days. It will be a tough time for G. and probably for me also but we both must face it."

As ill luck would have it, the story of Ghormley's relief was published in the newspapers the very day, October 24, that the superseded admiral reached Pearl Harbor. Ghormley and copies of the Honolulu *Star-Bulletin* headlining an account of his relief reached CinCPac headquarters at the same time. Respectfully but in deep dejection, Ghormley asked Nimitz for an explanation of his replacement.

"Bob," said Nimitz, his voice sympathetic, "I had to pick from the whole Navy the man best fitted to handle that situation. Were you that man?"

"No," Ghormley said. "If you put it that way, I guess I wasn't."

To Catherine that evening Nimitz wrote, "G. is taking it in fine style and his fine manner has saved me much embarrassment."

Nimitz invited Ghormley to remain at Pearl Harbor a few days as his house guest, but the latter chose to hurry on to assume his temporary duties in Washington. King had ordered him there in order, as was his wont, to "look him over."

"Ghormley left at 2 p.m.," Nimitz wrote Catherine, "and while he was not too cheerful, I am sure no one could have borne the disappointment better. What a tough break to have the matter announced on the day he arrived here—just in time to see it in the evening paper yesterday and this morning's paper. Fortunately the article was gentle in each case and as no catastrophe occurred while he was there it will die down soon."

This was a time of change for other officers who had by this time demonstrated their special skills and their shortcomings. Vice Admiral Pye was appointed president of the Naval War College. There he could exercise his strategic abilities and no one would have to question his aggressiveness. Vice Admiral Leary came up from the southwest to take over Pye's command of Task Force 1, the old battleships, and Vice Admiral Arthur S. Carpender replaced him as Commander, Naval Forces, Southwest Pacific, under MacArthur. Vice Admiral Fletcher requested a return to sea duty and Nimitz favorably endorsed his request, but King appointed him commandant of the 13th Naval District and Northwest Sea Frontier at Seattle.

When General Vandegrift got back to Guadalcanal from Noumea, Japanese soldiers had already launched their new drive for the airstrip, and Fitch's Catalinas had sighted a Japanese carrier fleet coming down from the north. The drive on the airstrip developed into the Battle of Henderson Field. The advance of the Japanese fleet led to the Battle of the Santa Cruz Islands.

On October 24 the *Enterprise* force, arriving in the South Pacific from Pearl Harbor, made contact with the *Hornet* force east of Espiritu. Though each carrier operated within its own screen, both forces came under the tactical command of Rear Admiral Thomas C. Kinkaid, a non-aviator who had commanded cruisers in the battles of Coral Sea and Midway. Halsey, disregarding Ghormley's restrictions, daringly ordered Kinkaid to sweep with his two forces around north of the Santa Cruz Islands so as to be on the flank of any enemy approaching Guadalcanal from the north or northwest.

The parallel with Midway cannot have been lost on Halsey. It was a closer parallel than he realized, for the commander of the Japanese striking force was the same Admiral Nagumo who had commanded the enemy carriers at Midway. In his striking force now were the fleet carriers *Shokaku* and *Zuikaku* and the light carrier *Zuiho*. In a detached advance force was the fleet carrier *Junyo*. As at Midway, it was essential for the outnumbered Americans to get the jump on the enemy. With this in mind, Halsey, shortly before dawn on the 26th, flashed to all his sea forces the stirring command: "Attack—Repeat—Attack!"

At about 6:30 a.m. the U.S. radio listening stations picked up the familiar Japanese aircraft contact report: TE-TE-TE, for *teki* (enemy), followed by grid position of the contact. Evidently the Japanese had sighted the Americans before they themselves had been sighted. CinCPac flashed this information to Admiral Kinkaid. Shortly afterward abbreviated Japanese plain-language contact-attack messages made clear to Admiral Nimitz that a carrier battle was in progress.

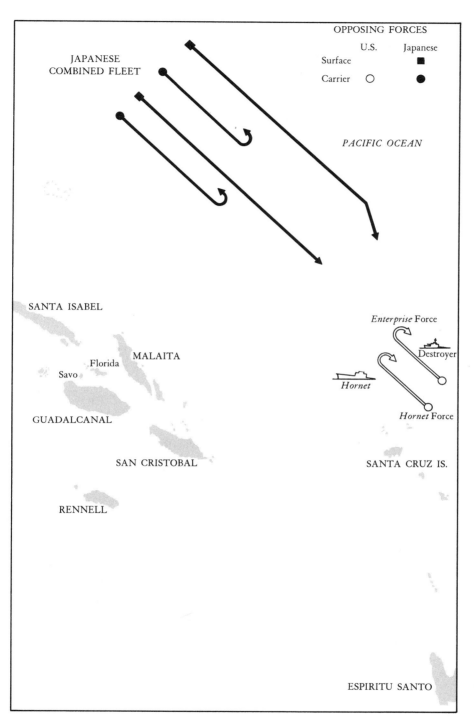

JAPANESE
COMBINED FLEET

*PACIFIC OCEAN*

SANTA ISABEL

MALAITA

Florida

Savo

GUADALCANAL

SAN CRISTOBAL

RENNELL

*Enterprise* Force

Destroyer

*Hornet*

*Hornet* Force

SANTA CRUZ IS.

ESPIRITU SANTO

*The Battle of Santa Cruz Islands, October 26, 1942*

In the afternoon Pearl Harbor learned that the *Hornet* was disabled and had been abandoned, and direction-finder stations reported that at least a part of the Japanese fleet was moving in her direction. This information also CinCPac passed to Admiral Kinkaid, who ordered the *Hornet* scuttled to keep her out of enemy hands.

As usual, several days passed before CinCPac had a full report of the battle. The report brought out the following additional facts. Japanese search planes had indeed made the first sightings when the opposing fleets came within combat-flight radius. Thus the Japanese got the jump on the Americans, who were obliged to accept battle over their own decks before their fighters attained altitude. The first Japanese attack had been directed solely at the *Hornet*, and she was put out of action by five bombs and two torpedoes.

In a second Japanese air attack, the *Enterprise* was heavily damaged by three bomb hits, and a torpedo plane crashed into a destroyer, setting her ablaze. A third attack damaged the *South Dakota* and a cruiser. The *Enterprise* force, after scuttling a destroyer that had been hit by a submarine-fired torpedo, retired to the southeast. Meanwhile, American carrier planes had done some damage to the *Zuiho* and a cruiser and had very heavily damaged the *Shokaku*.

The *Hornet*, left without fighter cover, became the target of several afternoon air attacks. After her crew had abandoned ship, Kinkaid ordered two destroyers left behind to sink her. These expended all their torpedoes and more than 400 shells without producing any effect other than starting new fires. The next morning U.S. aircraft, winging back over the battle area, saw only her superstructure still above the surface.

Though tactically the Americans had got the worse of the battle, there was some solace for them in their estimate that the Japanese had lost nearly twice as many planes as they. Part of the reason for the disparity was that the Americans had learned a great deal about fighter techniques and had vastly improved the accuracy of their antiaircraft fire, but it was also concluded that the Japanese had already expended their best-trained and most experienced carrier pilots and were not able to train replacements fast enough.

It was the American soldiers and marines on Guadalcanal who saved the immediate situation. They held firm while the enemy attack on land rose to a crescendo and finally died out on the 26th. Henderson Field remained in American hands, and Japanese casualties were roughly ten times those of the Americans. To General Vandegrift, Admiral Nimitz sent a message of commendation: "Reports of your successful land actions have thrilled all of us. Express my appreciation to your marines in the front lines and to your army troops for the way they have backed up and re-established the lines by their counterattacks. We feel that you have welded a combination that will be more than a match for the enemy."

Even during the height of the October crisis, Nimitz considered it essential that he carry out certain social and quasi-professional duties. On October 16 he attended a dinner the Walter Dillinghams gave for the Governor of

Hawaii and Mrs. Stainback. "I would have enjoyed it more," he wrote Mrs. Nimitz, "if my mind had not wandered too frequently to the Solomons. I went back to my headquarters and read dispatches until 11 p.m. The news was better and I came back to a reasonably good sleep." On the 21st he spoke at the inauguration of Dr. Sinclair as president of the University of Hawaii. "My address seemed to please," he wrote. "At least a number of people came to compliment me."

The crisis at Guadalcanal coincided with an outpouring of Allied military power all around the world. The Russians, having been supplied by Allied shipping via Murmansk and the Persian Gulf, were more than holding their own at Stalingrad. Three Allied expeditionary forces headed for the invasion of North Africa were at sea at the end of October. The Battle of the Atlantic was at its height—in October nearly 600,000 tons of Allied shipping were sunk, a figure that was topped in November. What Allied shipping remained was being stretched to the utmost to transport supplies via the Cape of Good Hope and the Suez Canal to the British in Egypt. There, General Bernard Montgomery was poised for the decisive Battle of El Alamein, which began October 23. Forces were being built up in the United Kingdom for a cross-Channel attack on Hitler's Festung Europa planned for 1943. General Arnold was concentrating Allied air power in England for the strategic bombing of Germany.

In the circumstances the harassed Joint Chiefs of Staff, with the exception of Admiral King, were inclined to overlook the portents of disaster in the South Pacific. It took the intervention of President Roosevelt to alert them to the perilous situation there. On October 24 he sent to the Joint Chiefs a memorandum indicating his desire "to make sure that every possible weapon gets in that area to hold Guadalcanal, and that having held it in this crisis, that munitions and planes and crews are on the way to take advantage of our success."

As a result, on the eve of the invasion of North Africa, more artillery and aircraft were brought to the beleaguered island, and Halsey was able to earmark 6,000 more soldiers and marines for early transport thither. All this was none too soon, for the Japanese were obviously determined to make good in November the victory they had missed in October. Nearly every night their destroyers steamed down the Slot bringing reinforcements for a renewed attack on Henderson Field.

Despite the labors attendant upon rushing the new supplies and men to Guadalcanal, the SoPac staff found time to move from the narrow confines of the *Argonne* into the city of Noumea. When the French authorities raised objections, Halsey simply bulled his way ashore and forced the governor to allot him space where his officers and men could live and work with greater comfort and efficiency. What he got for offices was a warehouse-like structure, and for residency the vacated Japanese consulate, which he eked out with Quonset huts.

Halsey also managed to make a quick trip to Guadalcanal to acquaint himself more intimately with the defense problems there and, more important, to raise morale by showing himself to the defenders. While on the island, he held a press conference and gave his recipe for winning the war: "Kill Japs, kill Japs, and keep on killing Japs!" One bumbling correspondent asked the admiral how long he thought the Japanese could hold out. Snapped Halsey, "How long do you think they can take it?" On the way back to Noumea, he paid a visit to the base hospital on Efate, and news of his visit spread throughout the South Pacific. In contrast to the earlier ComSoPac, it was said, the area now had a commander who cared.

Meanwhile Op-20-G was again reading the Japanese naval operational code with some facility. All intelligence from this source CinCPac promptly relayed to SoPac. Thus, when Halsey returned to Noumea on November 9, his chief of staff, Captain Browning, was able to present him with a timetable of forthcoming Japanese operations. There was to be a repetition of the October attack, but on a larger scale: aircraft would bomb Guadalcanal on November 11; ships would bombard Henderson Field during the night of the 12th; carriers would strike on the 13th, and at the end of that day a large contingent of troops would land on the island. Information from traffic analysis, coast-watchers, and aerial observation showed Japanese warships assembling in large numbers at Truk, Rabaul, and in the Shortland Islands in the Upper Solomons.

ComSoPac, not having time to send his damaged vessels to Pearl Harbor for repairs, had had them crudely patched up at Noumea. The *Enterprise* still had a damaged forward elevator and the *South Dakota* had an inoperable turret. Nevertheless, Halsey sent Kinkaid's *Enterprise* force north. Besides the *South Dakota* the force consisted of the *Washington*, one heavy and one light cruiser, and eight destroyers. Halsey, having learned caution from the Battle of the Santa Cruz Islands, directed Kinkaid under no circumstances to take the *Enterprise* into the waters north of the Solomons.

Meanwhile, the 6,000 reinforcement troops that Halsey had earmarked for Guadalcanal had reached the island in two convoys escorted by cruisers and destroyers. The convoys came under heavy bombing in Ironbottom Sound, but the last of the reinforcements had been safely disembarked by the late afternoon of November 12. At sunset Turner withdrew his convoys toward Noumea, but detached five cruisers and eight destroyers. These he sent back to Ironbottom Sound under the command of Rear Admiral Daniel J. Callaghan to break up an impending attack on Henderson Field by a Japanese bombardment group, including the battleships *Hiei* and *Kirishima*, which American planes had reported coming down from the north.

In the dark of a moonless night the two forces collided in the waters north of Guadalcanal. There ensued a furious midnight brawl in which all formations broke and both sides, at one time or another, fired on their own vessels. The Americans were saved from annihilation only by the fact that the Japanese battleships were provided with bombardment ammunition rather than with armor-piercing shells. At dawn one Japanese destroyer had been sunk, another was sinking, and the *Hiei*, riddled by more than 50 shells, was helpless north of

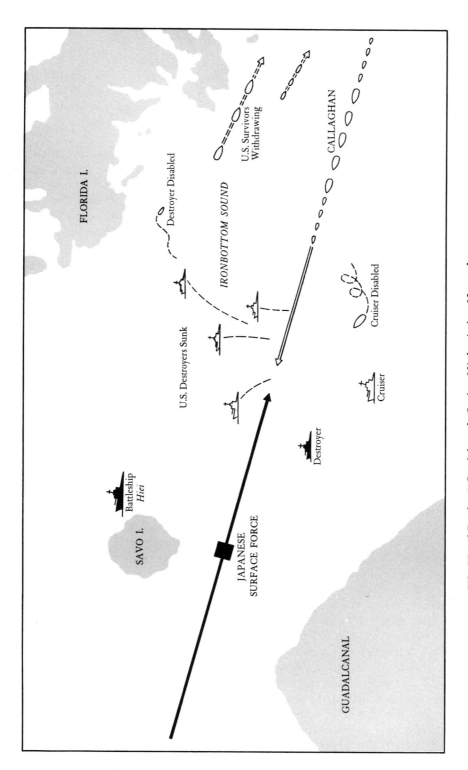

*The Naval Battle of Guadalcanal: Cruiser Night Action, November 12–13, 1942*

Savo Island, where aircraft from Henderson Field struck her again and again until she sank. Four U.S. destroyers and two cruisers were lost, and Admirals Scott and Callaghan and most of their staff officers had been killed. Despite overwhelming odds, the Americans had spoiled the enemy's timetable. They had turned away his battleships and forced his transports to return to base in the Shortlands.

Toward sunset on the 13th, a B-17 sighted a dozen Japanese destroyers escorting 11 transports, each capable of carrying at least 1,000 troops, leaving the Shortlands—obviously intending to get as far down the Slot as possible under cover of darkness. That night six cruisers entered Ironbottom Sound and bombarded Henderson Field, achieving considerably less damage than the *Hiei* and *Kirishima* might have done with their 14-inch guns the night before.

Daybreak on November 14 disclosed to American search planes two groups of Japanese ships: the cruisers that had bombarded Guadalcanal the night before, together with escorting vessels, were retiring on a westerly course south of New Georgia Island, in the Central Solomons; the transports that had left the Shortlands were in the Slot approaching Guadalcanal. Bombers from Henderson Field, from Espiritu Santo, and from the *Enterprise*, coming up from the south, struck repeatedly at both groups, sinking one cruiser of the bombardment group and damaging three others, and sending six of the troop-loaded transports to the bottom and forcing one to turn back.

Meanwhile, the *Washington*, the *South Dakota*, and four destroyers detached from the *Enterprise* group and commanded by Rear Admiral Willis A. Lee came up to protect Henderson Field from another night bombardment. That night, north of Guadalcanal, a Japanese bombardment force consisting of the *Kirishima*, four cruisers, and nine destroyers pounced upon the Americans, sinking two of their destroyers and putting the *South Dakota* and the other two destroyers out of action. The *Washington*, left alone, turned her guns on the *Kirishima* and reduced her to such helplessness that she had to be scuttled. The remaining warships departed, leaving only the four surviving transports, which steamed through the scene of the battle and beached themselves on Guadalcanal, where they were promptly attacked by a destroyer and by planes from Henderson Field. Thus ended the series of actions collectively known as the Naval Battle of Guadalcanal.

Early fragmentary reports of the three-day battle were received at Pearl Harbor and in Washington with some skepticism but, as confirmations came in, the mood changed to elation. Secretary Knox at last cast off his deep reservations and assured the press, "We can lick them. I don't qualify that. We'll defeat them." General Vandegrift, who had so long criticized the Navy for timidity, had nothing but praise for Admirals Scott, Callaghan, Kinkaid, and Lee and their forces. He radioed: "To them the men of Guadalcanal lift their battered helmets in deepest admiration." Admiral Nimitz expressed his opinion that the critical phase of the Guadalcanal campaign had passed. Recognizing that the new spirit of calculated risk in the South Pacific stemmed mostly from ComSoPac, he said of Halsey: "He has that rare combination of

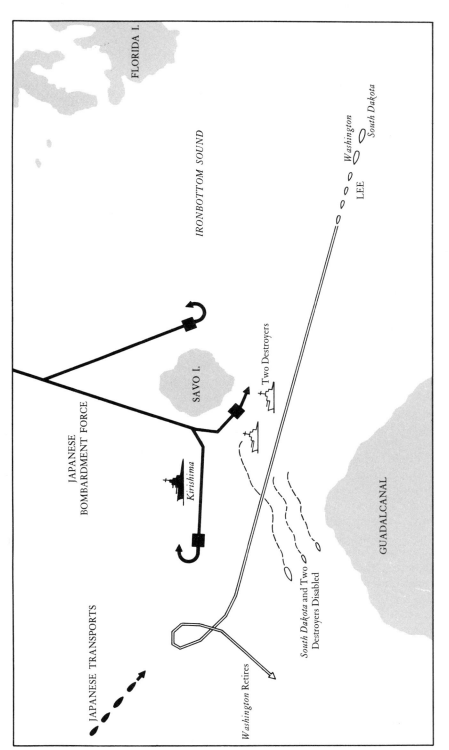

FLORIDA I.

IRONBOTTOM SOUND

JAPANESE
BOMBARDMENT FORCE

SAVO I.

*Kirishima*

Two Destroyers

*Washington*
LEE
*South Dakota*

JAPANESE TRANSPORTS

*Washington* Retires

*South Dakota* and Two
Destroyers Disabled

GUADALCANAL

*The Naval Battle of Guadalcanal: Battleship Night Action, November 14–15, 1942* intellectual capacity and military audacity, and can calculate to a cat's whisker the risk involved."

In eastern New Guinea also, 700 miles west of Guadalcanal, Allied forces had turned the tide. General MacArthur's troops had pursued the Japanese back over the mountains and were besieging them in Buna. On the other side of the world the Allies were likewise achieving victories. The Russians had trapped the German Sixth Army at Stalingrad. Montgomery had won his victory at El Alamein and was chasing Rommel across North Africa. The Americans and British had made good their landings in northwest Africa and obtained a cease-fire from the French. President Roosevelt said, "It would seem that the turning point of the war has at last been reached." Prime Minister Churchill described the situation as "the end of the beginning." Roosevelt, in recognition of Halsey's success and the growing importance of his command, nominated him for four stars, and Congress quickly approved the nomination.

After the Naval Battle of Guadalcanal, the Japanese in the Solomons appeared to go entirely on the defensive. When they were observed constructing an airfield at Munda Point on New Georgia Island, opinion was divided as to whether this presaged a renewed offensive or the creation of a new defensive line to replace Guadalcanal.

Whatever the enemy's intention, the Americans, as their strength increased, set out to cut off the supplies of the Japanese on Guadalcanal and to capture, destroy, or evict their forces. Then, at the end of November, as if to remind the U.S. Navy that it still had much to learn about night tactics, SoPac naval forces suffered a serious setback in the Battle of Tassafaronga. A U.S. group of five cruisers and six destroyers, hastily assembled to replace Callaghan's shattered force, entered Ironbottom Sound under Rear Admiral Carleton Wright, who was new to his command and to the area. The objective of this scratch team was to derail a Tokyo Express that had been detected approaching Guadalcanal, evidently on a supply mission. Unknown to the Americans, the Express on this night consisted only of eight destroyers. On making contact, the Americans set one of the destroyers fatally ablaze with gunfire, but the others, taking aim with reference to American gun flashes, fired torpedoes and sped safely away. The torpedoes sank the cruiser *Northampton* and heavily damaged the cruisers *Minneapolis, New Orleans,* and *Pensacola.* Luckily for their morale, the Americans did not realize the one-sidedness of their defeat, for CinCPac estimated that Wright's ships had sunk four enemy destroyers and damaged two or more others.

At a press conference held at Pearl Harbor on December 7, the anniversary of the surprise attack, a correspondent asked Admiral Nimitz for an "official guess" as to when the war would end. Nimitz replied, "By the calendar I wouldn't try to tell you. But I can tell you by the map." He gestured widely to the array of maps thumbtacked to the wall. "The war will end," he said, "when the Jap has been hunted down in all those regions and his striking power destroyed."

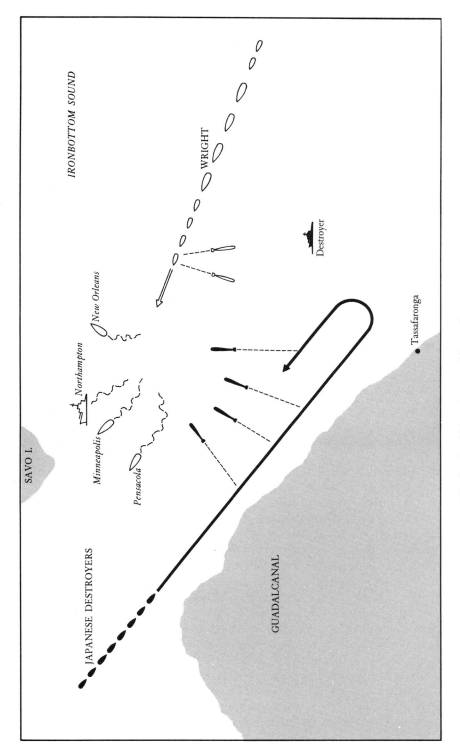

*The Battle of Tassafaronga, November 30, 1942*

SAVO I.

IRONBOTTOM SOUND

WRIGHT

New Orleans

Northampton

Minneapolis

Pensacola

Destroyer

JAPANESE DESTROYERS

GUADALCANAL

Tassafaronga

On December 9, General Vandegrift turned command of the American garrison on Guadalcanal over to General Patch, and the 2nd Marine and 25th Army divisions gradually replaced the malaria-ridden veterans of the 1st Marine Division, which was evacuated to Australia. By early January Patch had 50,000 soldiers and marines under his command, and in mid-month he launched a drive westward from the American defense perimeter in an effort to mop up what remained of the Japanese garrison.

Admiral King had grown impatient with the pace of the war in the South. He particularly opposed the phase of Task II that would see South Pacific forces moving step by step up the Solomons toward Rabaul. Such a strategy would continually shorten the enemy's line of communications, thrusting him back upon his sources of supply and reinforcement. Moreover, judging by the length of time it was taking to conquer Guadalcanal, securing each successive step would be a matter of months at least, giving the enemy time to build up strong points on the American line of advance—and the war would drag on interminably. King proposed a little outflanking. Specifically he recommended scrapping Tasks II and III, bypassing the Solomons and the Bismarcks, and seizing the Admiralty Islands. From there the Allies would be able to block the main line of supply to Rabaul and be in an excellent position to bomb that base into impotence and capture it.

Admirals Halsey and Nimitz wanted no part of King's plan. Nimitz put his objections and counterproposals into a memorandum, "Future Operations in the Solomons Sea Area," which he took to San Francisco for another series of meetings with King that was to begin on December 9. Nimitz pointed out that, with the limited Allied strength available, it would be fatal to attempt to bypass the numerous mutually supporting Japanese bases in the Bismarcks and upper Solomons, and that even if the Allies succeeded in capturing Rabaul or the Admiralties, their communications would be outflanked by Japanese bases at Kavieng, Buka, Kieta, Buin, and Gasmata.

Admiral Nimitz believed that the advance had to be made step by step and that no step beyond the cover of land-based fighter planes should be taken. The extreme first step would be to Buin, on Bougainville, 300 miles from Henderson Field. A more practical jump would be to seize the enemy airfield building at Munda Point, 180 miles from Henderson. No advance, however, could be contemplated until the Japanese had been cleared from Guadalcanal, the Guadalcanal-Tulagi area had been developed into a naval and air base, and considerably more Allied ground forces, particularly amphibious forces, became available. He predicted that the Allied advance would accelerate as it went along, mainly because of the growing superiority of American air power. Lastly, Nimitz recommended that the SoPac command structure, only now attaining maximum efficiency, be retained intact.

Admiral King fully accepted Nimitz's proposals and promised to make every effort to get him and MacArthur the additional military force to maintain and speed up the momentum of their campaigns. Specifically he would endeavor to have the 15 per cent of total Allied resources then allotted by the Combined Chiefs of Staff to the Pacific theater raised to between 20 and 35 per cent.

Admiral Nimitz had brought to the meeting another memorandum, "Review of the Aleutian Situation," in which he recommended that the Army occupy Amchitka in order to establish airfields closer to the enemy-occupied Aleutians, and that sufficient troops be trained in amphibious warfare for operations against these islands. Nimitz had invited Admiral Kinkaid to the conference, because Kinkaid had been selected to take over the North Pacific command, relieving Admiral Theobald, who continued to bicker with the Army. Theobald, reputed to have one of the best minds and one of the worst dispositions in the Navy, was to go to Boston as Commandant, 1st Naval District. Kinkaid, diplomat as well as warrior, was expected to heal the Navy's relations with the Army, and to prepare for offensive operations against Kiska, with a target date of March 1, 1943.

King and Nimitz talked about the Pacific Fleet of the future. The twenty-two U.S. carriers that were on the ways or nearing completion would, with their screens and associated amphibious vessels, form a force of unprecedented power that would require thirty more flag officers. Nimitz had foreseen this and had a list of candidates ready to submit.

Both CominCh and CinCPac were unwilling to see the great new carrier-spearheaded fleet tied to MacArthur's intended advance along the north coast of New Guinea. They proposed to revive the "Orange Plan," which for nearly thirty years had been the projected U.S. strategy for recapturing the Philippines in the event they were taken by Japan. It envisaged a drive straight across the Central Pacific, via the Marshall and Caroline islands. Once recaptured, the Philippines would provide bases whence the vital Japanese "oil line" from the East Indies could be blocked. After securing a foothold on the China coast, the Allies would be in a position to invade the Japanese homeland. King and Nimitz also looked at the southern Marianas as islands to be captured in addition to, or instead of, say, Truk in the Carolines. From the Marianas the Americans would be able to block Japanese north-south communications east of the Philippines and prevent the ferrying of planes southward from Japan, via her chain of island airfields.

King, to Nimitz's dismay, was determined to replace Station Hypo with a large joint Army-Navy intelligence center. King had been annoyed by the bickering between Hypo and the Communication Security Section in Washington over who deserved the most credit for making the Midway victory possible. In October 1942 he transferred Rochefort to non-cryptographic duties on the mainland. Nimitz objected to King's proposal for a joint center, on the grounds that a large, possibly bureaucratic organization was unlikely to forward intelligence as fast as he had been getting it under the old, simpler arrangement, but King said the decision had been made, and that ended the discussion.

On his return to Washington, King took up with General Marshall the question of command relationships. In Task II an awkward situation would arise: Nimitz's subordinate, Admiral Halsey, commanding ships, troops, and planes provided by Nimitz, would be advancing into and operating in Mac-Arthur's command area. Various solutions were proposed, ranging from putting the whole Pacific theater under one commander to extending the South Pacific Area westward at the equator and then southeastward so as to enclose the Admiralties, the Bismarcks, and the Solomons. The first solution was not considered feasible because there would be too much high-placed opposition, military and political, to putting MacArthur under Nimitz or Nimitz under MacArthur. General Marshall was perhaps the only American officer with sufficient prestige to be put over or to replace both, but Marshall was Army Chief of Staff and a member of the Joint and Combined Chiefs of Staff and could not be spared. As to the second solution, MacArthur could be expected to fight tooth and nail against any whittling-down of his command area, and Marshall would doubtless back him up. In the end, the Joint Chiefs returned to their original plan: Halsey would be subject to general strategic directives from MacArthur, and would handle his own tactics.

General Marshall pointed out that the Japanese position in the Solomons, New Guinea, and the Bismarcks resembled an inverted V with Rabaul at the apex. Against the left, or western, leg of the V, MacArthur had placed his Southwest Pacific Forces. Against the right, or eastern, leg, Halsey had placed his South Pacific Forces. "Skillful strategic direction, coordinating the employment of the two strong Allied forces available," said Marshall, "appears mandatory to offset the Japanese advantages of position and direction."

In January 1943, at the Casablanca Conference, Admiral King laid the problems of the Pacific theater before the Combined Chiefs of Staff, President Roosevelt, and Prime Minister Churchill. Though the United States was pledged to join England in beating Germany first, King had some convincing arguments to support his contention that a greater proportion of Allied military resources should be allotted to the Pacific war. In the first place, the British had greatly underestimated Japanese military prowess. With minimum force and extraordinary valor the Allies, chiefly the Americans, had put the Japanese on the defensive. They now needed more power if they were to take advantage of this favorable situation. In the European theater, the Americans had shelved their cherished plan to seize at least a foothold in western Europe in 1942 and had accepted the British strategy of invading North Africa. Now the British wanted the Americans to join them in invading Sicily, which would require postponing the invasion of western Europe till 1944. Thus far the Americans had sidetracked their own strategy in favor of British strategy. They had no intention of abandoning their agreement to beat Germany first, but King insisted that the time had come for a little compromise. The British reluctantly agreed to some stepping-up of the war against Japan, but the Combined Chiefs were not prepared to accede to King's demand that the military resources allotted to the Pacific be increased to a full 35 per cent.

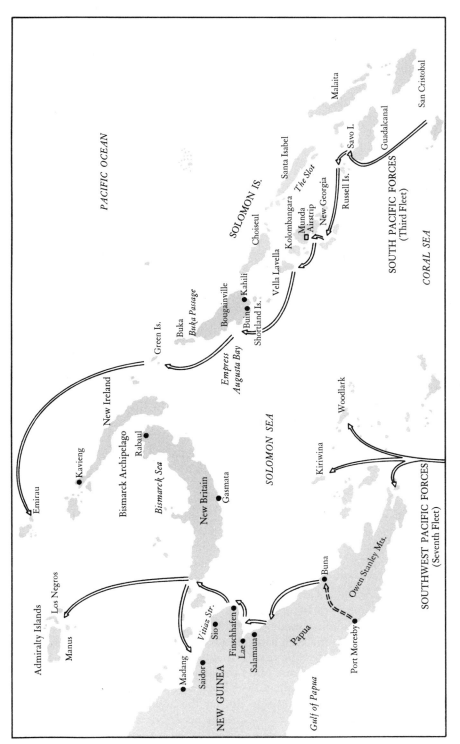

*Rabaul Neutralized and Bypassed*

At Pearl Harbor Admiral Nimitz concluded that the time was propitious for him to make another inspection of the forward area and of the South Pacific. Since Secretary Knox was due at Pearl on January 12 and would accompany Nimitz on his inspection tour, Nimitz suggested to General MacArthur that he meet and confer with them at Noumea. If MacArthur objected to coming there, Nimitz, Halsey, and, doubtless, Knox, would fly to MacArthur's headquarters at Brisbane. MacArthur replied with a long dispatch describing his situation and his strategic plans, the latter closely paralleling those advocated by Nimitz. "I have given the above facts and have expressed my views," he concluded, "in order that you may have a clear picture of the situation here. An exchange of views may preclude the necessity for an immediate conference that requires long journeys and prolonged absence of higher commanders." In other words, MacArthur saw no advantage in a summit conference at that time.

Secretary Knox, accompanied by his special assistant, Adlai Stevenson, and a couple of aides, arrived by air at Pearl Harbor and, together with Admiral Nimitz and some of his staff, departed on January 14 for Midway. The party took off from Pearl in a four-engine seaplane, which had been furnished as a flag plane and was loaded with steaks and other choice provisions, including the admiral's china and silverware, to alleviate the possible hardships of the forward area.

Hardly had the plane taken off when the pilot, Lieutenant Commander McLeod, sent word to his passengers that two of his engines were out. He could dump the gasoline and attempt a landing in the canefields, he said, or make a dead-stick landing in the water. Which should it be? A quick survey in the cabin produced a consensus that a water landing would certainly be softer and probably less dangerous. Admiral Nimitz so ordered. McLeod brought his plane down expertly into Pearl Harbor, but he could not prevent it from striking the water with such impact that a hole was ripped in its bottom and it began to sink.

The only possible escape was through a hatch up onto a wing. Several of the party climbed out without difficulty, but Knox, who was a bit broad across the hips, got stuck in the opening. A combination of pulling by those on the outside and pushing by those still in the cabin finally freed the Secretary. The passengers and crew kept the plane afloat by standing on one wing until rescue boats sent by Admiral Towers arrived from Ford Island.

On reaching Ford Island, Admiral Nimitz asked Towers for another plane so that the party might resume its flight to Midway. Towers could offer only an amphibian, one of four that had just arrived from the mainland with green crews. Nimitz asked that the best of these planes be sent immediately, adding that he would keep Commander McLeod as adviser to the crew.

When the substitute plane had been in the air several hours, Admiral Nimitz, who had kept his cap on during the accident and afterward, called Lamar aside and asked him to look at his head. Nimitz removed his cap and the aide was shocked to see that the admiral's white hair was clotted with blood. An inspection revealed an inch-and-a-half cut in his scalp. Lamar warmed some water, washed the blood from the wound, and cut away some of the hairs. The only antiseptic the first-aid kit provided was iodine, which was obviously too strong, so Nimitz suggested diluting it with water. Lamar, not realizing that iodine and water do not mix, followed the suggestion. When he applied the solution to Nimitz's head, the admiral let out a roar of pain and almost took off through the roof of the plane. After the party arrived at Midway, several stitches were taken in the wound and it was properly dressed.

The island commander and his staff entertained the Knox-Nimitz group at dinner. At last, all seemed to be going well, but the jinx was still there. The meal was interrupted by the dismal news that a fueling boat had torn a hole in one of the amphibian's pontoons. The party would not be able to take off the following morning, as scheduled.

January 16 demonstrated that the Midway Islands were much too small for two such active men as the Secretary of the Navy and the Commander in Chief of the Pacific Fleet and Pacific Ocean Areas. They inspected the island defenses, interviewed the defenders and, when these chores had been completed, watched the antics of the gooney birds. Long before the day was over SecNav and CinCPac were bored with each other and with Midway and were suffering from an acute attack of island claustrophobia.

At last another plane arrived from Pearl Harbor and the party headed south, with island stops, around the Japanese-held Marshalls and Gilberts. When the crew of the plane found that Stevenson had not before crossed the equator, they asked Nimitz's permission to initiate this polliwog into the Ancient Order of Shellbacks, and the admiral consented. Stevenson took the abbreviated initiation good-naturedly. He even had a few sips of a proffered King Neptune cocktail, which consisted of motor oil, catsup, tabasco sauce, salt, and pepper. He was sick as a dog for the rest of the day.

On January 20, east longitude date, the Knox-Nimitz party arrived at Espiritu Santo. There they were met by Admirals Halsey and McCain, who had flown up from Noumea to join them. Slew McCain, now chief of the Bureau of Aeronautics, had come from Washington to assess the South Pacific's need for naval airmen and aircraft. Halsey was just back from New Zealand, where he had paid an official visit and inspected American personnel and equipment. His confident, not to say bellicose, personality and his salty and cocky statements had delighted the New Zealanders. He had repeated his earlier-published opinion that the Allies would be in Tokyo inside of a year. This time he added: "When we first started out against them, I held that one of our men was equal to three Japanese. I have now increased that to twenty." The Navy Department was aghast at Halsey's public prediction of an imminent end to the war and, when he publicly referred to the Japanese prime minister and emperor by scarcely printable names, the State Department was shocked because it might eventually have to make use of these personages to bring the war to a close.

In view of the criticism Halsey had already received for the loose language he used in public, Nimitz probably did not at this time add any strictures of his own. He did intervene mildly, however, in a running feud Halsey was having with the Bureau of Naval Personnel over obtaining the services of his old friend Commander Oliver Owen ("Scrappy") Kessing, with the temporary rank of captain, to command the naval base at Tulagi. After an exchange of snappish radio messages, Scrappy finally arrived, but without the requested temporary rank. Halsey told Nimitz that he was fed up and that if the promotion had not been confirmed by the time he returned to Noumea, he would send Scrappy a message, with an information copy to the Bureau of Naval Personnel: "You will assume rank, uniform, and title of captain, U.S. Navy."

Nimitz threw up his hands. "No! For God's sake, don't do it!" he exclaimed. "You'll foul up everything."

"You wait and see," replied Halsey.

Fortunately confirmation of the promotion came through in time to prevent a showdown between ComSoPac and the bureau.

At Espiritu both parties were lodged aboard Admiral Fitch's flagship *Curtiss*. Hardly had they turned in for the night when enemy bombs started falling. The attack did not last long and the result was only a few craters on the beach, but since this was Espiritu's first raid in several weeks, there was speculation as to whether the enemy had some information about a high-ranking assemblage being present.

The next day the group, including Halsey and McCain, flew to Guadalcanal. The island, to be sure, was still far from being a resort, but Admiral Nimitz perceived at once that the installations and the condition of the men themselves had improved enormously since his last visit. Henderson Field had become a respectable, all-weather airstrip and was supplemented by a fighter strip not far away. Malaria was still very much of a problem, but the men Nimitz saw little resembled the weary wraiths of the preceding September. Though Guadalcanal was still being bombed from time to time, it could be said that the Americans had won substantial command of the air over and the sea around the Guadalcanal-Tulagi area.

That night the Japanese bombed the American installations on Guadalcanal from 8:30 p.m. till daybreak. This "coincidence" convinced almost everybody that the Japanese were after big game—and knew where it was to be found.

"I have very little stomach for bombs," said Halsey. "There were no foxholes on the *Curtiss*, but there were plenty on Guadalcanal. When I heard the first *boom*!, I left my comfortable hut and dove into the ground, with Mr. Knox and 'Slew' McCain. But not Chester. He said he hadn't had any sleep the night before; he was going to catch up; besides, he said, he was scared of mosquitoes. Chester spent the night under a sheet, behind screens. The other three of us spent it half-naked, out in the open. And Chester was the only one who caught malaria!"

The next day the travelers took off for Noumea, and the Guadalcanal communication officer prepared to file the routine departure dispatch. "Do me a favor, will you?" said his shaken assistant. "Send it in Japanese. I want 'em to know for sure that the high-priced hired help has left here!'"

In the afternoon of January 23, Admiral Nimitz, Secretary Knox, and Admiral Halsey took seats at a conference table at Halsey's headquarters in Noumea. Present also were Admiral McCain and De Witt Peck, now a marine brigadier general, and members of the CinCPac and ComSoPac staffs. General Harmon joined the group a little later.

Admiral Nimitz opened the meeting at 3:20 p.m. "The object of this conference," he said, "is to review the situation in the South Pacific and to exchange views. No decision will be reached. Indeed, we may not agree on all points. First, as to Guadalcanal. What is ComSoPac's view as to progress, approximate date Japs will be eliminated? Shall we need more troops? What number should be left as a garrison on completion of the operation?"

Halsey, who had done a good deal of talking on the trip to Guadalcanal, now let his subordinates do the answering for SoPac. General Peck estimated that the Japanese would be eliminated from the island by April 1; there were already enough U.S. troops on Guadalcanal; two divisions plus service troops should be sufficient to garrison the base until the next advance.

Nimitz said he believed the island could be secured quite a bit earlier than April 1. Peck replied that his estimate was based on the possibility that the Japanese might use delaying tactics. He outlined a scheme the SoPac staff had hatched during Halsey's absence: to occupy the small Russell Islands, thirty miles northwest of Guadalcanal, chiefly as a PT-boat base and as a staging point for landing craft.

"It seems reasonable to me," said Halsey.

The question of the aircraft supply came up. McCain promised more naval planes and offered to help put pressure on the Army to provide more army aircraft. They talked about improving the airfield facilities on Guadalcanal. Admiral Nimitz asked when the new airstrip, then under construction, would be finished.

"It should be ready for heavy bombers by the end of February," replied Halsey, "but in emergency it could be used by the middle of February."

Admiral Nimitz asked how Guadalcanal would be used next.

Peck replied, "It will be used as a supporting base for further advancing movements in the Solomons."

"It is my idea," said Nimitz, "that no permanent installations should be erected there. The only construction should be that necessary, and there should be a reduction in the rear areas. Everything should be based on a forward movement."

Most of the rest of the conference concerned implementing Task II. The South Pacific Force was assigned the task of invading Bougainville, in the upper Solomons, in order to establish airfields within easy range of Rabaul, but first it would have to seize the new Japanese field at Munda Point, on New Georgia.

"When do you think you can move against Munda?" asked Nimitz.

"April first," said Peck, but the move would depend, he added, on the readiness of a division of amphibious troops.

General Harmon being present, the conference went into details concerning setting up surface and air-base facilities in the Guadalcanal-Tulagi area and concerning the proposed invasion of the Russells and the capture of Munda.

Those who had been present at both CinCPac-ComSo-Pac conferences could not have failed to note the sharp contrast between the harried, anxiety-ridden atmosphere of the September meeting and the confident, optimistic tone of the January meeting. The difference was not merely the result of a vastly improved military outlook; there was clear evidence of the much better administration that had resulted mainly from Halsey's delegating of authority to able men and backing them wholeheartedly. Admiral Nimitz had helped not a little by lending Halsey two of his ablest experts, Captain Redman and Rear Admiral William L. Calhoun, CinCPac service force commander, the former to straighten out the South Pacific's communications, the latter to unsnarl the logistic tangle.

Secretary Knox, who had not been present at the September conference, came away from the South Pacific with reservations concerning Halsey's abilities as an administrator but none at all concerning his high qualities as a fighter and leader. Back in Washington he liked to tell a story about two SoPac enlisted men who were ambling down a passageway talking about Halsey. "I'd go to hell for that old son of a bitch," said one of them.

Just then he felt a stiff finger jab his back. It was Halsey. "Young man," said he, "I'm not so old."

The SoPac officer who made the poorest impression upon Secretary Knox was Halsey's temperamental chief of staff, Captain Miles Browning. That saturnine character had succeeded in offending Knox as he had so many others. At any rate Knox decided that Browning was ineffective and began a campaign to have him relieved.

Knox noted the poor air transportation with which CinCPac was provided. He promised Nimitz a decent flag plane and, in due course, there arrived at Pearl Harbor a gleaming R-5D with a private cabin for the admiral and suitable accommodations for staff and for VIPs.

On his return to Pearl Harbor on January 28, Admiral Nimitz was saddened to learn that a Pan American Clipper en route to San Francisco with several Pacific Fleet officers aboard had disappeared. The wreckage was eventually found in the mountains of California. There were no survivors. Perhaps most keenly felt was the loss of Admiral English, whose death necessitated several shifts of command. Rear Admiral Charles A. Lockwood came to Pearl Harbor from Australia to replace English as Commander, Submarines, Pacific Fleet. Captain Ralph Christie was promoted to rear admiral and replaced Lockwood as Commander, Submarines, Southwest Pacific (ComSub-SoWesPac).

The onset of malaria, not yet fully manifest, may account for Nimitz's sharp reaction to the sinking of the *Chicago* south of Guadalcanal the day after his return to Pearl. On the other hand, he had good cause for anger, for her loss appeared to be the result of sheer ineptitude on the part of her defenders. Torpedoed at night by Japanese planes using parachute flares and floating lights, she was under tow the next day when enemy planes struck again and sent her down. At the time of her sinking, she was surrounded by six destroyers and covered by a combat patrol of ten Wildcat fighters from the nearby *Enterprise*. All the ships involved were provided with the new, supersecret proximity-fuzed shells, which were deadly to aircraft.

However much the sinking shocked and angered Nimitz, nothing could be done to bring the *Chicago* back, but he was determined, if possible, to conceal the fact of her loss from the public and from the enemy. He had been intensely annoyed when CominCh had informed the press of the loss of the *Wasp* before the next of kin of those killed could be notified. He was dismayed when the President—so as not to be accused of withholding bad news before the November elections—prematurely announced the loss of the *Hornet*. The President's announcement may have achieved its political purpose, but Nimitz believed it also informed the Japanese that the Americans were left with only one even partially operational carrier in the Pacific. Following the loss of the *Chicago*, in one of his rare outbursts of anger, he told his morning conference, "I've never said this in my life before, but if any man lets out the loss of the *Chicago*, I'll shoot him!" Not long afterward he succumbed to malaria and entered Aiea Hospital.

Though the admiral's hospitalization was no secret to his staff, he ordered his flag kept flying at CinCPac headquarters. He feared that if the fact that he was ill became generally known, somebody would pass the word to the South Pacific, and the unpredictable Halsey, the only other four-star American admiral in the Pacific, might conceivably exercise the prerogative of his seniority and declare himself temporary Commander in Chief, Pacific Fleet and Pacific Ocean Areas. The result could be chaos.

Nimitz's incapacity made him impatient and irritable. Lamar and Mercer visited him in the hospital and took along a pot of flowers to cheer him up. The admiral received the flowers with thanks but, it seemed to his visitors, rather coolly and with a bilious eye. After they had left, the two visitors returned to the corridor leading to the admiral's room to have a look. As they suspected, the offending pot of flowers had been deposited on the floor outside his door.

Good news arriving at Pearl Harbor on February 9 did much to put Nimitz on his feet again. General Patch's troops, in their westerly penetration of Guadalcanal, found nothing but signs of a hasty evacuation. There was no longer a single living Japanese on the island.

In eastern New Guinea also the fighting was over. There General MacArthur had at length committed nearly 30,000 troops, half of them Australians and half Americans, to dislodge some 12,000 enemy, but the Japanese held

Buna until late January 1943. Then, at last, their defenses collapsed, as much from starvation and disease as from outside pressure. In recapturing eastern New Guinea, 3,095 Allied troops had lost their lives, nearly twice as many as were killed on Guadalcanal.

Admiral Halsey in widely publicized pronouncements called the Japanese "bastards" and "monkeys" and continued to predict an early end to the war. General Kenney, in a report to General Arnold, more accurately reflected the Allied fighting man's estimate of his formidable foe:

> I'm afraid that a lot of people who think this Jap is a "pushover" as soon as Germany falls, are due for a rude awakening. We will have to call on all our patriotism, stamina, guts, and maybe some crusading spirit or religious fervor thrown in, to beat him. No amateur can take this boy out. We have got to turn professional. Another thing: there are no quiet sectors in which troops get started off gradually, as in the last war. There are no breathers in this schedule. You take on Notre Dame, every time you play!

# CHAPTER 15

# CINCPAC AND
# CINCPAC STAFF

AFTER BREAKFAST and a brisk walk, Admiral Nimitz was usually at his desk
by 7:30 a.m., reading dispatches that had come in during the night. Messages
requiring his attention, or those he might wish to see, would have been routed
to oo (Zero Zero), his CinCPac designator. In the admiral's light and airy
office, the flowered cushions of the split-bamboo visitors' chairs matched the
drapes. Maps were fastened to the walls with thumbtacks, and a barometer was
attached to a pipe behind the admiral's desk. Under the desk, at his master's
feet, usually lay Makalapa, a schnauzer, a breed Admiral Spruance had introduced to Nimitz. Makalapa was widely considered a surly fellow, but he
adored Nimitz and generally stayed close to him.

Above Nimitz's outer door was a maxim: "Nations, like men, should
grasp time by the forelock instead of the fetlock." On an inside wall he had a
sign bearing three questions that he expected his subordinates to answer in
connection with any proposal they put forward:

1. Is the proposed operation likely to succeed?
2. What might be the consequences of failure?
3. Is it in the realm of practicability of materials and supplies?

On the admiral's desk were a pen set, several souvenir ashtrays, a miniature machine gun, and a metal bumblebee, symbol of the Seabees, whom he
valued and admired. On the desk also was a framed picture of General Mac-
Arthur, apparently clipped out of a rotogravure.* To some observers, this last

---

* Whatever Nimitz thought privately of MacArthur, he never permitted at CinCPac headquarters the overt censure of the general and his strategy that was common in the Navy Department.
Rear Admiral Raymond D. Tarbuck has described the contrast he found in 1943 when, en route
from Washington to join MacArthur's staff, he stopped at Pearl Harbor and called on Nimitz to
pay his respects.

"A very strange thing happened to me when I was in Washington for the briefing," Tarbuck
told Nimitz. "People tried to prejudice me against General MacArthur with their left hand, and
with their right they were issuing me orders to be a member of his staff."

Nimitz asked Tarbuck to explain. The latter continued: "They told me not to have too much
confidence in MacArthur, that the big blue fleet, the Central Pacific, was the one that was fighting
the war. . . . To put it in plain language, I've been brainwashed to prejudice myself against the
man to whom I'm supposed to be loyal."

Nimitz leapt from his seat behind the desk and, pointing a finger at Tarbuck, said sharply,
"Young man, that never came out of this office, and I want that strictly understood!"

was puzzling, for Nimitz, in common with other CinCPac officers, was thought to deplore the general's obvious glory-seeking and habit of dramatic utterance. To a friend Nimitz once confided that he kept the picture on his desk merely to remind himself not "to make Jovian pronouncements complete with thunderbolts."

Under the glass top of Nimitz's desk were several cards bearing military slogans, and in a central position one small card with a list: "Objective, Offensive, Surprise, Superiority of Force at Point of Contact, Simplicity, Security, Movement, Economy of Force, Cooperation." Some people call such lists "principles of war," but Nimitz thought of his merely as reminders, a check-off list of things to be considered before launching an operation, beginning with a clearly defined objective and ending with full cooperation among forces involved—this last being particularly important in a theater of operations in which there were two separate commands, his and MacArthur's.

Admiral Nimitz was prompt in writing replies to letters or dispatches, or guides for staff members to do so. Short items he wrote by hand. For longer letters or memoranda he might call in Adams, his hotshot yeoman, winner of a medal for shorthand, former court reporter, and probably the most expert scribe in the Pacific.

In the early morning Nimitz received staff members who had reports and problems requiring his immediate attention. Commander Layton usually called with intelligence items that were too secret or too urgent for the general briefing.

The CinCPac morning conference began at nine o'clock, in Nimitz's office or in a nearby conference room, depending on how many were attending. For office conferences there were folding chairs available. Senior officers visiting or stationed on Oahu were welcome. General Emmons attended often. After February 1943 Admiral Ghormley also was frequently present. At Nimitz's request he had been returned to the Pacific as commandant of the 14th Naval District and thus was CinCPac's near neighbor. He was found to have been suffering from abscessed teeth, possibly the main cause of his shortcomings as ComSoPac. With all his teeth drawn, he was in excellent health.

Expected to attend the morning conferences were key members of the CinCPac staff, visiting fleet and task force commanders, and senior participants in recent or forthcoming operations. Commander Layton opened the proceedings with an intelligence briefing. Visitors from combat areas were called on to make reports. Discussion followed under Nimitz's general guidance. Since these were informational rather than planning or decision-making meetings, the atmosphere was informal, and Nimitz might rise and close the proceedings at any time.

At 10:00 a.m. Nimitz often knocked off for a while and, with Lamar, Mercer, or other officers, or perhaps alone, did a little shooting on the pistol range. He then returned to his office for more desk work or conferences.

Eleven o'clock was visiting time, with CinCPac acting as the genial host.

After he moved to his cement fortress headquarters, Nimitz remarked one day that he rarely had visitors anymore. "I would like to see, as *Navy Regulations* specify," he said, "the commanding officer of any ship that joins the command." His aides thereupon telephoned all the type commanders at the base and made the necessary arrangements. Commanding officers of all vessels, from lieutenants (j.g.) commanding LSTs to senior captains from new battleships as they arrived at Pearl Harbor reported at eleven o'clock and stayed fifteen minutes. "Some of the best help and advice I've had," said Nimitz, "comes from junior officers and enlisted men."

At precisely eleven Lamar would conduct the visitors into Nimitz's office and try to introduce them, but as often as not the officers would introduce themselves: "I'm John Smith, or whatever, of the USS So-and-so." "Glad to have you with us," Nimitz would reply, shaking hands, and motioning them to chairs.

Admiral Nimitz would open each meeting with a few remarks about what he was thinking of doing or planning to do. His visitors would listen, fascinated at hearing high strategy from its source. "Now tell me what you are doing," he would say and look at the man he wanted to hear from. Thus he would go around the circle, listening to informal reports. He would ask if any of them were unhappy, if there was anything he could do for any of them. When the allotted time was up, he would rise, go to the door, and shake hands again with the officers as they filed out.

The story of the commander in chief's morning receptions spread through the fleet and the stations, giving assurance that the big boss was interested in everyone and was their active partner. The calls gave Nimitz a feel for the operational front which he found invaluable. Moreover, they introduced him to future leaders. "There's an officer we must watch," he would say to Lamar when the visitors had left. "He's going to be one of the good ones."

"He wanted a chance to size them up," another staff officer recalled, "and for them to know they had an identity with the fleet commander. It was an important element in morale."

When, at a morning or other gathering, a visitor stayed beyond his allotted time, Nimitz might, if the subject was important, hear him out; then he would give some polite indication that the interview was at an end. If that didn't work, and the visitor deserved special consideration, Nimitz would lead him into the chief of staff's office and turn him over to Spruance. In this office few visitors lingered long, for it contained no chairs. Spruance rarely sat during the daytime and did all his paper work at a stand-up desk.

In general, anyone who had legitimate business could get in to see Nimitz at his regular eleven o'clock receiving time or at any other time when he was not in conference. A few callers got past Lamar even when their business was less than legitimate. There was, for example, the bluejacket from the *Enterprise* who showed up at CinCPac headquarters to "pay his respects" to the commander in chief. The marines reported his arrival to Lamar. "It had been a rough morning," said Lamar. "Things hadn't gone well, so I thought this would divert him. I was always looking for something to break the monotony, so I went in and told him this young fellow was out there, and the admiral said, 'Send him in.'"

In the admiral's presence the sailor quickly broke down. The visitor admitted that he had bet his shipmates that he could get in to see the commander in chief. They had said he could not and contributed a pool of several hundred dollars to back their conviction.

"Well," said Admiral Nimitz, "in order to collect your money you've got to have some evidence." So he buzzed for Lamar and said, "Get the staff photographer here."

The admiral had his picture taken with the young sailor and gave him several copies to take back to the *Enterprise* as proof that he had won his bet.

Then there was the case of Radarman McCaleb of the destroyer *Shaw*. While the *Shaw* was undergoing extensive repairs at Pearl Harbor, leave parties were sent to the mainland, and McCaleb went home to Kerrville, Texas. There, at his aunt's house, he met a caller who turned out to be Admiral Nimitz's half sister Dora. When Dora learned that the radarman had come from Pearl Harbor, she asked, "Mr. McCaleb, have you seen Chester?"

"No, ma'am," replied McCaleb, shocked at hearing the commander in chief called by his first name and bemused at the notion of a petty officer meeting a four-star admiral.

"Dear me," said Dora. "You've been out there in the Pacific for more than a year and you haven't seen Chester! That's terrible! Now when you return to your ship, I want you to go and see him. Furthermore, I will write and tell him to expect you."

On McCaleb's return to Pearl Harbor, he duly wrote to CinCPac. His letter was intercepted by the censor, and he was called in by his commanding officer, to whom he told the whole story. "So you see," McCaleb concluded, "she's got me over a barrel. I've got to write this note. I'm really embarrassed, but I don't know what else to do."

So the skipper approved the letter, off it went, and a few days later McCaleb received the answer that Admiral Nimitz would be delighted to see him at 10:00 a.m. three days hence. The *Shaw*'s executive officer succeeded in borrowing a car and driver in order to send the radarman up to Makalapa in style. As he went over the brow, his shipmates spontaneously manned the ship's sides. "Well," said McCaleb, "at least maybe I can find out where the *Shaw* is going when she completes her overhaul."

Arriving at CinCPac headquarters, McCaleb was promptly escorted into the commander in chief's presence. Admiral Nimitz warmly shook his hand. "McCaleb," said the admiral, "where are they going to send the *Shaw* after she completes overhaul?"

For Nimitz lunch was often an occasion for further conference, though by

1943, in order to overcome a new, slight tendency to overweight, he was frequently skipping the midday meal altogether, resting or walking or sunning himself instead.

Most afternoons were left unstructured, though there was usually plenty for Nimitz to do, including intensive planning sessions with staff members and with officers involved in forthcoming operations. It was in the planning stage that the admiral was most thorough. He would pick drafts of war plans to pieces, especially the parts dealing with amphibious operations, and send them back for revision.

At the planning sessions, Admiral Nimitz acted like a chairman of the board, guiding and being guided by others. This does not mean that the war was being run like a town meeting. Nimitz made the final decisions, sometimes despite contrary advice, but first he heard the advice and weighed it carefully. He knew that World War II was far too complex for any one man in any theater of operations to do all the high-level thinking, keeping his own counsel and at last handing down Napoleonic decisions.

On quiet afternoons, Nimitz might stroll about headquarters, dropping in on staff members to inquire into their operations and make suggestions. Or he might visit naval and marine operations around Oahu. If the visit was formal, he would probably go with his driver in his big black official Buick with his flag flying. Otherwise, he was likely to travel in a smaller, unmarked car with Lamar doing the driving.

On official and social calls, Admiral Nimitz insisted upon strict punctuality. "He was the most punctilious man that I've ever done business with," said Lamar, "in that, where the commander in chief was involved, he had to have things exactly to the letter. If he was to visit a new ship coming into Pearl Harbor whose arrival was at 10 a.m., I always sent the barge out early in the morning to time the thing exactly. If we were invited to the Governor of Hawaii's palace and were to be there at 6:45, he wanted his car to drive up at 6:45, not a minute before or a minute after."

The admiral expected others also to adhere strictly to schedules and regulations. Once, in full uniform, he was being driven down Beretania Street in Honolulu in his official sedan with his stars flying. He passed hundreds of bluejackets, and not one saluted. Much annoyed, on his return to Pearl Harbor, he sent for Admiral Ghormley, under whose jurisdiction such matters came, and suggested that he send officers with buses into town and load aboard every enlisted man who failed to salute, pick up his liberty pass, and return him to his ship. This was no very severe punishment, merely loss of part of a day's liberty, but it was sufficient. After several days of busloads of bluejackets being hauled out of Honolulu, the word got around, and saluting again became a habit.

On quiet days Nimitz knocked off at 4:00 or 4:30. This was the time for a long walk, often with Spruance, possibly up to Aiea Hospital and back—or for a fast game of tennis, perhaps followed by a horseshoe match. Then a bath and dinner. Almost invariably when Nimitz did not go out to dinner, he had guests in. He expected punctuality, and when his guests were officers, he got it. Later in the war, when numerous civilian VIPs visited the Pacific and had to be entertained, Nimitz was distressed at their frequent carelessness about being on time for their appointments.

Before dinner, Nimitz had two cocktails served, never more, and had two himself, usually old-fashioneds. Spruance, who often mixed the drinks, would take for himself no more than a thimbleful of liquor, perhaps mixed with ginger ale, in an old-fashioned glass and nurse it through the cocktail hour. He was not opposed to social drinking but, as a young man, he had learned the hard way that he could not hold liquor and he was taking no chances.

The dinner that followed was usually worth waiting for. The admiral's steward was an excellent cook and he got the best cuts of meat, filet mignon being a favorite. He had a garden in which he grew fresh vegetables and salad greens for the admiral's table. For dessert he served tropical fruits, pineapple, avocado, papaya, and Chinese gooseberries flown in from New Zealand; and ice cream, often in such exotic flavors as mango and avocado. On the table at the end of the meal were fresh local lichee nuts. After dinner Nimitz joined his guests in smoking cigarettes, but Spruance abstained.

Sometimes following the meal, Nimitz would show a movie, or, more often, to the acute boredom of some of his guests, he would play records of classical music with the lights turned out and the blackout curtains thrown open. After a conversation period, Nimitz, Gendreau, or Spruance usually suggested everyone take a short walk for "a breath of fresh air," and said good night to their guests on the return. When important operations were taking place, Nimitz would go to his headquarters and read the latest dispatches before turning in.

One evening, returning from a dinner in Honolulu with Lamar, Nimitz saw a very intoxicated sailor standing on the side of the road thumbing a ride. The admiral had his driver stop and sent his orderly back to invite the sailor to ride with him. The enlisted man, who turned out to be a Seabee, climbed gratefully into the car, having not the slightest notion with whom he was riding, for the road was unlighted, all structures were blacked out, and the only light was from a pair of crossed slits in each of the car's headlights.

On being questioned by the admiral, the Seabee poured out his grievances about his camp—it was dirty, ill-run, provided poor food, and was presided over by a martinet of a commanding officer. Nimitz let the man off near the entrance to his camp, and the fellow, not in the least aware to whom he had made his report, went stumbling off.

The next morning Nimitz called in Lamar and told him that he intended to inspect the Seabee battalion in question at eleven o'clock that day. Lamar accordingly called the senior officer of the Seabees at ten. This of course did not give the battalion much time to get ready, which is what Nimitz wanted. He arrived at the Seabee camp precisely on time and found conditions just as the drunken sailor had described them: foul, confused, and the men brow-beaten and ill-fed. Nimitz made his displeasure clearly known to the command-ing officer and saw to it that he was properly disciplined.

About once a week, when things were quiet, Admiral Nimitz organized an expedition across to Kailua on the eastern shore of Oahu for an afternoon of hiking and swimming. The group went over in a big, seven-passenger sedan and changed to swimming gear in a waterfront home, the "Damon property" (or "Prostate Rest"), which the Navy had rented for the use of senior officers between tours of sea duty but was rarely used by them because it was too isolated for men who preferred to socialize while they were on shore.

In a letter to Catherine, Nimitz described one such excursion from his point of view: "Yesterday afternoon Spruance and I filled our car with Lamar, [Captain Tom R.] Hill, Gendreau and [Commander Ernest M.] Eller and went to the beach house for a walk on the beach and a swim. G. wore a blister on his bare foot but otherwise enjoyed the health trip."

The outing consisted mainly of a hike along the beach in bathing trunks—two miles, according to Admiral Spruance, who always went, five miles accord-ing to the recollections of the more tenderfooted officers—followed by a swim. Mell A. ("Pete") Peterson, then a commander, recalls grimly the results of hiking on sand: "You lose a layer of skin on the bottoms of your feet [which] are sensitive for two or three days." At the end of the hike, Nimitz, Spruance, and Lamar usually swam back part of the way, probably a mile. The less fit swimmers came ashore exhausted after a quarter of a mile or so.

Certainly these brisk afternoons were healthful and invigorating, but they were not as popular among his staff as Nimitz seemed to believe. The outings always came as a surprise because, for security reasons, no pattern was main-tained, that is, they rarely came the same day in successive weeks. As soon, however, as the marines or the admiral's aide started along the verandas, or the latter started telephoning, to issue invitations, the word spread like a forest fire and staff members quickly made themselves scarce. Jack Redman says some hid in closets or under desks.

The CinCPac staff worked seven days a week, often well into the eve-nings, but no objection was raised if officers knocked off work in the middle of the day and went out for a game of tennis. Certainly Admirals Nimitz and Spruance never hesitated to stop for exercise or relaxation when the pressure was not too great. If Nimitz, Spruance, or anybody else was needed to answer a question, an orderly might be sent out to the tennis courts with the question written and a blank pad for the answer.

Admiral Nimitz believed in maintaining a hard-working staff, kept as small as possible. But he also wanted a healthy, efficient staff. He expected his people to work around the clock when necessary, but when duties permitted he wanted them to keep body and nerves in shape by taking exercise and relaxing. He could not forget the harassed look and manner of the SoPac staff in the early days aboard the *Argonne*, when they were bogged down in detail and infecting the whole area with defeatism.

One of Admiral Nimitz's favorite means of relaxation was his Saturday evening visits with his dear friends the Alexander Walkers, who had a vacation home on the far side of Oahu. Nimitz was invited to bring along another officer and he usually took Lamar or Spruance. They put on shorts and aloha shirts, had a steak dinner, and then listened to symphonies, while watching the stars come up over the ocean. The conversation might be about anything—orchids, trivia. Only war and military problems were taboo.

They spent the night at the Walkers', as was customary in Hawaii during the war on account of the blackout, but Nimitz always returned to Makalapa Sunday morning and was in his office by 10:00 a.m., because, beginning at that time, an hour of classical music was beamed out from San Francisco. One could always tell which officers had especially pleased him during the week; Nimitz would plug them in on the intercom and let them hear the music— loudly because of the admiral's slight deafness. When Major General Edmond Leavey came out to represent the Army, he was startled, on one of his first Sundays on the job, to have his office suddenly flooded with music. He called up Lamar with great excitement. "What the hell's going on?" he demanded. "Where's all this music coming from?"

Lamar told him. "The admiral is actually paying you a compliment," he said, "letting you enjoy his Sunday morning concert."

Nimitz could match any man on his staff in ability to work hard and put in long hours, but he refused to let himself get involved in details that others could handle. As during his tour as commanding officer of the *Augusta*, his aim was to do nothing officially that anybody else could do. He reserved his energies for those activities of decision-making and ceremonial and social obligations that were appropriate only to the commander in chief. As always, he delegated as much authority to his subordinates as he believed they should be able to handle. If they showed they could not, out they went—discreetly if they had seniority, roughly if they were young and needed a shock. "Young man," he would say, "you fail to cut the mustard, and I hereby dispense with your services."

Though Admirals Nimitz and Spruance thought alike, particularly in matters of strategy, their personalities were decidedly different. Spruance was no less warmhearted than Nimitz, but he found it difficult to communicate with people. Mell Peterson called him "prim," and some junior officers referred to him as "Old Frozen Face."

Said Peterson, "Admiral Nimitz was rather easygoing, amiable, sort of old shoe type. Admiral Spruance was the neat, rigid, down-to-earth type of person who was always all business." Spruance's close association with Nimitz and their evenings together appear to have had a salutary effect on the chief of staff. At any rate, in his later relations with people, Spruance was less stiff and formal.

Admiral Spruance had two functions at Pearl Harbor—directing the CinCPac staff and advising Admiral Nimitz. In his first capacity he was not the bright, harassed, nail-biting chief of staff of the stereotype. Bright he was, *brilliant* is probably a better word, but he never let himself become harassed. He was, by his own admission, inclined to be lazy—the kind of smart, indolent character said to make the best commanding officer. When Nimitz passed details down to Spruance, Spruance promptly passed them on down the chain of command. Like Nimitz, he was a master organizer, who organized himself as much as possible out of the staff picture. Also like Nimitz, he was adept at picking men, delegating authority to them, then leaving them alone to perform.

Spruance was of the greatest value to Nimitz as a source of ideas and as a sounding board for Nimitz's own ideas. Practically all such exchanges were oral, for Spruance was at his best when he was talking, thinking aloud he called it, and he liked to be on his feet. In spoken words, he could spin the most ingenious and intricate strategic plans, but he was repelled by the tedium of spelling out complicated details on paper. That sort of thing he turned over insofar as possible to others. What he could not delegate, he performed rather perfunctorily at that stand-up desk.

One of the earliest ideas Spruance sold Nimitz resulted from the shock of the heavy losses of American aviators in the Battle of Midway. As some of the survivors pointed out to Spruance, they were in a calling that had little or no future: if they kept flying in one operation after another, percentages and fatigue would continually lessen their chances and they would all eventually be destroyed. What Spruance recommended and Nimitz accepted was a rotation plan whereby aviators in reserve would relieve those on the front line. The plan gave each squadron periods of rest and recreation between combat tours. Thus, all aviators remained fresh and alert and had better hopes of survival.

When Spruance joined Nimitz in 1942, the CinCPac-CinCPOA staff numbered forty-five officers. Though Spruance as well as Nimitz believed in keeping the staff as small as possible, it kept growing until, in mid-1944, it numbered about 250 officers. The main reason for the growth was the planning and servicing of the Central Pacific Force's drive across the Pacific, particularly in the areas of supplying and maintaining the force and garrisoning the islands it captured.

The nature of the war in the Pacific posed the unique problem of freeing the fleet from dependence on rearward bases, so that it could move across the ocean, capturing islands as it went, without having to turn back for replenishment and upkeep. Only thus could it maintain the strategic momentum needed to keep the enemy off balance.

Most important in freeing the naval forces were the roving service squadrons of Vice Admiral Calhoun's Service Force, Pacific Fleet. One service squadron had the duty of refueling the fleet at sea, an operation in which Admiral Nimitz, as co-inventor of the process, took the keenest interest. Naval attack forces were accompanied by oilers, each carrying up to 80,000 barrels of fuel oil, 18,000 barrels of aviation gasoline, and nearly 7,000 barrels of diesel oil. Other oilers cruised on a set schedule in geometric patterns near the scene of action, so that ships knew where and when they could meet them for refueling, as needed. Underway replenishment groups were available to transfer to ships at sea ammunition, food, stores, aircraft, and personnel. Tenders delivered mail to ships at sea and evacuated serious casualties to hospital ships. Squadrons of tenders, repair ships, and floating dry docks became bases afloat in the lagoons of atolls or other enclosed waters and were prepared to render any service to the fleet, except major repairs.

During the Guadalcanal campaign, when ships were piling up in Noumea Harbor, Admiral King turned to the Army for advice in solving the South Pacific's supply problems. Lieutenant General Brehon Somervell, head of the Army's service forces, sent his chief planner, Major General Leroy Lutes, to investigate. Among other useful suggestions, Lutes urged the establishment of an interservice logistical organization to control supply activities.

As a step toward carrying out Lutes's suggestion with respect to all the Pacific Ocean Areas, Somervell sent to Pearl Harbor his assistant, General Leavey, but Nimitz merely attached Leavey as an adviser to Admiral Calhoun's staff. Leavey protested to Somervell that this was not at all what was needed. The Service Force, he pointed out, was for fleet supply only. There should also be a theater supply headquarters, he said, with a staff of naval, air, and ground officers, and it should be directly under the area commander in chief, Admiral Nimitz.

General Marshall endorsed Leavey's suggestion, adding as a corollary that in the Pacific Ocean Areas the fleet command and the area command should now be separated. Admiral Nimitz, as CinCPOA, would command the areas, just as Generals Eisenhower and MacArthur commanded theirs, but another officer, probably Halsey, should become CinCPac and command the fleet. King and Nimitz agreed that the idea of a joint staff had merit, but King was opposed to separating CinCPac and CinCPOA, since that would interrupt the chain of command between himself and the fleet. "I plan," he told Nimitz, "to keep command of the Pacific Fleet and command of the Pacific Ocean Areas vested in one person—you."

After months of study, including review of the supply and planning systems in Eisenhower's and MacArthur's areas, Admiral Nimitz on September 6, 1943, finally announced the formation of a Joint Staff at Pearl Harbor. It initially had four sections: Plans (J-1), Intelligence (J-2), Operations (J-3), and Logistics (J-4). General Leavey headed the Logistics Section, which cooperated closely with Service Force. Till the end of the war, the Logistics Section remained in the CinCPac-CinCPOA headquarters building, where General Leavey many times again found himself plugged in to the commander in chief's Sunday morning concerts, but Service Force grew so big that it had to move into a separate building erected for it next to the CinCPac-CinCPOA building.

The new Intelligence Section collaborated closely with the Joint Intelligence Center, Pacific Ocean Areas (JICPOA), which had been formed at the behest of Admiral King. JICPOA occupied a building just north of the headquarters building. It normally reported to Admiral Nimitz through Commander Layton, who remained CinCPac intelligence officer. Layton had asked for sea duty, but Nimitz turned him down. "You can kill more enemy working at your desk," said Nimitz, "than if you commanded a division of cruisers."

Next to JICPOA headquarters was another, similar building that housed the Fleet Radio Unit, Pacific Fleet (FRUPac). This was nothing more nor less than the Combat Intelligence Center, Station Hypo, which had not been superseded after all. Headed since the departure of Rochefort by Captain William B. Goggins, it had changed its name and moved out of its basement into more spacious quarters, at length employing more than a thousand operators.

FRUPac was concerned almost solely with enemy naval radio communications. As before, its operations included traffic analysis, cryptanalysis, and the translation of Japanese naval messages. Its cryptanalysts had gradually learned to cope with Japan's wartime call-sign and code changes, especially the frequent substitutions of new random additive numbers, and they had broken down other Japanese codes. For the Americans, one of the most fruitful of these was a system used by Japanese naval shipping-control officials, who not only routed convoys but assigned in advance their noon positions. This vital information was transmitted by direct, secure wire to the operations officer of Commander, Submarines, Pacific Fleet, who sent pertinent parts to appropriate U.S. submarines, thereby greatly increasing their opportunities for attacks and sinkings.

This advantage, however, was more than offset by flaws in the American torpedoes, whose warheads tended to explode prematurely, if at all. The problem was complicated by the fact that the Mark-6 exploder used in the torpedoes carried by the fleet-type submarines was supposed to be activated either by direct impact or by a magnetic impulse as it passed under or near the steel hull of a vessel. Submariners were early advised to make use of the magnetic impulse feature, because an explosion under a keel could be devastating and because head-on, "down the throat," shots were presumably less likely to miss their targets when their exploders were activated by a ship's magnetic field.

Unfortunately the exploder often failed to operate, particularly when the torpedo had been set to pass under a vessel. Admiral Lockwood, while still in Australia, discovered part of the trouble. By firing torpedoes through a submerged net, he proved that they were running eleven feet deeper than they were set. When this flaw had been corrected, there were fewer duds but more premature explosions.

At the time of his transfer to Pearl Harbor, Lockwood was received warmly but somewhat wanly by Admiral Nimitz, who was still in the hospital suffering from malaria. Lockwood and Nimitz worked closely together, forming a friendship that lasted the rest of their lives. Nimitz, who had contributed so much to developing the submarine, was convinced that it could prove decisive against an island nation such as Japan—provided the Americans could get the bugs out of their torpedoes.

Lockwood fired off a whole series of complaints, endorsed by Nimitz, to the Bureau of Ordnance but got no effective result. On a visit to Washington, he aroused the wrath of the Bureau by sounding off before an audience of submarine officers. "If the Bureau of Ordnance," he said, "can't provide us with torpedoes that will hit and explode, or with a gun larger than a peashooter, then, for God's sake get Bureau of Ships to design a boat hook with which we can rip the plates off the target's sides!"

The Bureau of Ordnance blamed the failures on the submarine commanders, who manned the periscopes and provided the data for maneuvering the submarines and aiming the torpedoes. Crews lost confidence in their captains, and some of the captains, embarrassed and discouraged, concluded at last that handling submarines was not their cup of tea and asked for other duty.

Lockwood, however, remained convinced that the trouble was with the Mark-6 detonator. Also convinced was Captain Tom Hill, CinCPac gunnery officer. Together they went to Admiral Nimitz, who, after hearing their arguments, directed Lockwood to issue orders deactivating the magnetic impulse feature of the detonators. Henceforth submariners would fire directly at their targets to obtain explosions on impact. The number of premature explosions declined, but the percentage of duds increased sharply. "See," said the Bureau, in effect, "the whole trouble is the result of poor aiming." More frustrated submarine captains applied for transfer.

Not so Lieutenant Commander Lawrence R. Daspit. In his submarine *Tinosa* he stopped an enemy tanker with two torpedoes fired from an unfavorable track angle. He then worked his way abeam of the motionless tanker and, from this perfect position, fired nine carefully checked and aimed torpedoes. All nine hit and not one exploded. Daspit took his one remaining torpedo back to Pearl Harbor and wrathfully demanded that it be examined and the defect corrected.

An examination of Daspit's torpedo found everything apparently in order, so with Admiral Nimitz's permission Lockwood led a party out and fired three torpedoes against a cliff that rose vertically from the sea. Two exploded and the third failed. This last they fished out and took back to Pearl. Then at last the final cause of failure was revealed. On impact, the firing pin was released and, by a spring, pushed athwartships between a pair of guides against the fulminate cap. When the impact was directly head-on, inertia tended to drive the firing pin so hard against the forward guide that it never reached the cap. Lightening the pin and thereby decreasing the friction against the guide corrected the trouble. At last American submarines had reliable torpedoes. But it was already September 1943, nearly two years after the declaration of war.

FRUPac's most striking interception occurred in the early hours of April

14, 1943. The decrypted and translated Japanese dispatch was promptly transmitted to Commander Layton, who hastened with it to Admiral Nimitz's office, arriving at 8:02 a.m. Layton was admitted by Lamar, who announced, "Zero Zero is in and will see you now."

Entering the inner office, Layton handed the dispatch to Nimitz. "Our old friend Yamamoto," he said. The admiral glanced at the message and sat suddenly erect. It read: "The Commander in Chief Combined Fleet will inspect Ballale, Shortland, and Buin on April 18.... 6 a.m. depart Rabaul in medium attack plane escorted by six fighters.... 8 a.m. arrive Ballale...." There followed Admiral Yamomoto's complete itinerary for the day.

Nimitz turned and studied the wall chart. The tour would bring Yamamoto within 300 miles of Henderson Field. The Japanese admiral's well-known passion for punctuality guaranteed that he would follow the itinerary to the minute.

"What do you say?" asked Nimitz. "Do we try to get him?"

"He's unique among their people," replied Layton, adding that he was idolized by younger officers and enlisted men. "Aside from the Emperor," he continued, "probably no man in Japan is so important to civilian morale. And if he's shot down, it would demoralize the fighting navy. You know Japanese psychology; it would stun the nation."

"The one thing that concerns me," said Nimitz, "is whether they could find a more effective fleet commander."

After discussing the senior Japanese admirals, Layton concluded, "Yamamoto is head and shoulders above them all." Then he drew an interesting parallel: "You know, Admiral Nimitz, it would be just as if they shot you down. There isn't anybody to replace you."

Nimitz smiled. "It's down in Halsey's bailiwick. If there's a way, he'll find it. All right, we'll try it."

Taking a pad, Nimitz wrote out a dispatch for Halsey, repeating Yamamoto's itinerary and suggesting, in order to protect the code break, that the information be attributed to Australian coastwatchers around Rabaul. He concluded: "If forces your command have capability shoot down Yamamoto and staff, you are hereby authorized initiate preliminary planning."

Because the assassination of so eminent a personage might have political repercussions, Admiral Nimitz took the precaution of checking with Washington and received the go-ahead from Secretary Knox and President Roosevelt. From Guadalcanal, via Halsey's headquarters at Noumea, came the assurance of Rear Admiral Marc A. ("Pete") Mitscher, Commander, Air, Solomons, that his aviators would be ready to carry out the ambush on April 18, using long-range P-38 fighters. At that, Nimitz gave final orders for the attempt, adding as a personal note to Halsey, "Good luck and good hunting."

April 18! Nimitz must have been struck by the coincidence. Exactly a year earlier Mitscher, as commanding officer of the *Hornet*, and Halsey, the task force commander, had participated in the bombing of Tokyo.

In the afternoon of the 18th, Palm Sunday, Mitscher sent his report to Halsey, who relayed it to Nimitz:

> P-38 led by Major John W. Mitchell, USA, visited Kahili area about 0930. Shot down two bombers escorted by Zeros flying close formation. One shot believed to be test flight. Three Zeros added to the score sum total six. One P-38 failed return. April 18 seems to be our day.

Halsey replied: "Congratulations to you and Major Mitchell and his hunters. Sounds as though one of the ducks in their bag was a peacock."

That night, which happened to be April 17 at Pearl Harbor, the CinCPac Command Summary noted: "It seems probable that CinC Combined was shot down in a plane over the Buin area today by Army P-38s."

The Americans were not sure of their success until May 21, the day Admiral Yamamoto's ashes reached Japan in the superbattleship *Musashi*. Then a Japanese newscaster on Radio Tokyo announced in a voice choking with emotion that Yamamoto "while directing general strategy on the front line in April of this year, engaged in combat with the enemy and met gallant death in a war plane."

# CHAPTER 16

# LAUNCHING THE
# CENTRAL PACIFIC DRIVE

THE PERIOD FOLLOWING the recapture of Buna and Guadalcanal in early 1943 was one of relative inaction in the Pacific theater. For all Allied Pacific commands it was mainly a time of planning and preparation for further offensives.

In the Aleutians, where Admiral Kinkaid had established excellent relations with the Army, the Americans constructed on the far-western islands of Adak and Amchitka airfields from which bombers soon cut off Kiska from all surface contact with Japan. Undertaking similarly to isolate Attu, a cruiser-destroyer force under Rear Admiral Charles McMorris, CinCPac's erstwhile planning officer, in late March ran into a Japanese force of twice its firepower and there ensued the Battle of the Komandorski Islands. This was mainly a chase in which the fleeing Americans, steadily returning the enemy's fire, saved themselves by use of smoke, expert shiphandling, and a certain amount of bluff. The Japanese, fearing air attack, at length broke off action and retired. The battle turned out to be an American victory after all, for thereafter the Japanese used only submarines to supply Attu.

Kinkaid, anxious to get going but starved for ships and men, decided to bypass Kiska for the time being and attempt to recapture the more distant but less strongly held Attu. He awaited only the assembling of his meager forces and the go-ahead from Admiral Nimitz and the Joint Chiefs of Staff.

In the early months of 1943, the war in the South and Southwest Pacific areas consisted mainly of mutual aerial bombings and of South Pacific surface forces launching night bombardments against Japanese airstrips on New Georgia and Kolombangara islands. The Japanese destroyed some ships and installations by their air attacks, but they lost planes at a clearly unacceptable rate. Some of their attacking aircraft were found to be carrier planes, a dubious use of such craft, which underscored Japan's growing shortage of air power.

An attempt by the Japanese in early March to reinforce their footholds at Lae and Salamaua in New Guinea resulted in the Battle of the Bismarck Sea, which consisted of attacks by General Kenney's Fifth Air Force on the troop convoy. The Allied planes sank all eight transports and four of eight escorting destroyers and shot down twenty-five escorting aircraft. After a few more of their vessels were sunk in the next few days, the Japanese stopped routing convoys to New Guinea, and limited themselves to sending in trickles of reinforcements and supplies by barge and submarine.

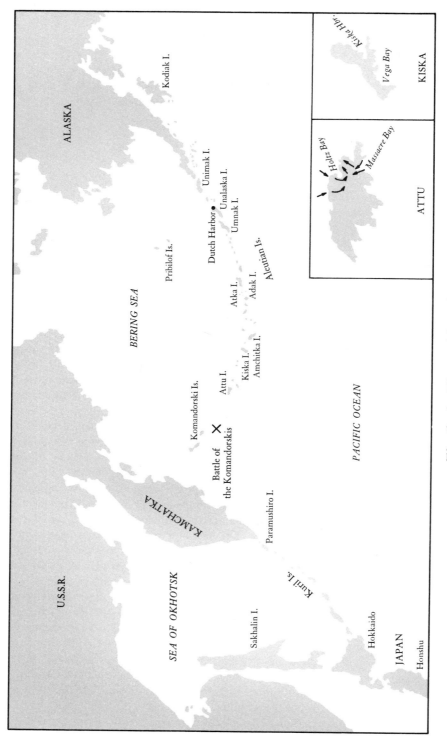

*The Aleutian Theater of Operations*

Doubts about the effectiveness of the odd command arrangements in SoPac that had Halsey looking to Nimitz for troops, ships, and supplies and to MacArthur for strategic direction, were completely resolved in April when Halsey went to Brisbane to confer with the general. He was immediately captivated by the famous MacArthur charisma. "Five minutes after I reported," he said, "I felt as if we were lifelong friends. I have seldom seen a man who makes a quicker, stronger, more favorable impression." Thereafter there was no friction between the two men, and their differences were easily settled.

Admiral King meanwhile was fretting over the relative inactivity on the Pacific front. In February he summoned Nimitz to San Francisco to talk about ways to speed up the war. The minimum objective for 1943, he said, must be to keep Allied communications intact and disrupt those of the Japanese. When Halsey's forces had been adequately built up, should he not, King asked, go right for Buka Passage at the northwest end of Bougainville? Nimitz pointed out that an attack there would be beyond the range of Allied air support and that it would bypass two strongholds of Japanese land-based air. Allied, not Japanese, communications would be blocked.

King was of the opinion that the Japanese had withdrawn from Guadalcanal in hopes of doing better elsewhere. Frustrated in their drive for New Caledonia, might they not yet offer a threat to U.S. communications southward by advancing from the Gilberts via the Ellices to Samoa? He suggested that Nimitz might put an end to this danger by recapturing the Gilberts. Nimitz replied that even if he landed in the Gilberts he would not be able to hold them with the forces available, since they were within easy range of powerful Japanese air bases in the Marshalls. There was no point, he said, in capturing positions only to be forced off with heavy losses. He reminded King that he had put marines on Funafuti Atoll in the Ellices and was building an airstrip there to block any Japanese advance in that direction.

Thus Nimitz, the advocate of daring measures and calculated risk, was put in the unhappy position of repeatedly counseling caution, and King, who had hoped to stimulate the Pacific theater into greater activity, let himself be convinced that for the time being nothing more could be done. However, King was pleased to point out that before many months there would be a reasonable supply of the weapons least needed in the European theater—*Essex*-class carriers, *Iowa*-class battleships, dive-bombers, and torpedo planes. These were precisely what was needed to spearhead a drive across the Central Pacific. Enough troops could be found for the new drive by redistributing ground forces already assigned to the Pacific theater. Nimitz said he needed heavy bombers, and King promised to get them.

In March the Joint Chiefs invited Nimitz, Halsey, and MacArthur to send representatives to Washington for a Pacific Military Conference. Admiral Spruance headed the CinCPac delegation. The main subjects were the division of U.S. forces between the European and Pacific theaters and the conduct of the advance on Rabaul. All the old arguments favoring unified command in the Pacific and again shifting the South Pacific-Southwest Pacific boundary were brought up, and all were discarded. The only change made was to slow down proposed operations. For lack of supplies, troops, and planes, Rabaul was not to be taken till early 1944. In 1943 MacArthur would advance only as far as Cape Gloucester, New Britain; Halsey, only as far as Bougainville. King pointed out that it might not be necessary after all to undertake the storming of heavily manned, well-defended Rabaul. At less cost in troops and weapons, the base could be surrounded with airfields and bombed into impotence.

Nimitz had instructed Spruance to secure approval from the Joint Chiefs for the recapture of Attu and Kiska; and Nimitz, Spruance, and King wanted to put in a word for the Central Pacific drive. Since neither the North nor the Central Pacific was on the conference agenda, King and Spruance eased them in by indirect means. If Rabaul was not to be taken, or at least not taken in 1943, said King, there was no point in keeping any major part of the Pacific Fleet tied down in the South Pacific, the implication being that the fleet could be used more profitably in the Central Pacific.

Spruance, picking up this cue, spoke of the danger to Pearl Harbor of a Combined Fleet, no longer committed to the Guadalcanal campaign, being on the loose. He argued that U.S. ships transferred from the South Pacific, plus those released by recapture of the Aleutians, plus new construction would form a force capable of seizing the Gilberts and Marshalls, thereby permanently removing the threat of a Japanese attack on Hawaii. The Joint Chiefs could make no ruling about an attack on the Gilberts and Marshalls without a clearer commitment from their British counterparts, but they could and did authorize Nimitz to recapture Attu and Kiska.

On his way back to Pearl, Admiral Spruance stopped at San Diego to observe the troops undergoing amphibious training for the assaults on the enemy-occupied Aleutians and to confer with their commander, Major General Holland M. Smith, USMC. Spruance had earlier met and developed a high regard for the hard-driving Smith, whose reaction to a sloppy or inept performance had earned him the nickname "Howling Mad" Smith. At San Diego, Spruance was so favorably impressed with the general's knowledge of amphibious warfare and his ability to command that he filed him away in his mind for future reference.

On March 15, Admiral King, anticipating the expansion of U.S. task forces to fleet strength, instituted a uniform numbering system, fleets in the Pacific being assigned odd numbers. Thus Halsey's South Pacific Force was designated U.S. Third Fleet, warships in the Central Pacific were to constitute U.S. Fifth Fleet, and MacArthur's Naval Forces, Southwest Pacific, became U.S. Seventh Fleet. For the time being Admiral Nimitz declined to dignify the few old battleships and supporting craft at Pearl Harbor with a fleet title, calling them instead Task Force 50.

To officers who had an inkling of King's and Nimitz's plans, Task Force

50 held tremendous interest. It was evidently the nucleus of a far-striking fleet that could become the mightiest in the history of the world. Its commander would wield immense power, possibly be the chief victor over Japan and thus earn an unassailable place in history. It was a command an ambitious officer would sacrifice almost anything to attain. Since the principal punch of the new fleet would presumably be provided by carriers, most naval aviators assumed that the appointment would go to one of themselves. At the forefront of those who considered themselves competent and deserving of the command was Admiral John Towers, Commander, Air Forces, Pacific, and chronologically the Navy's number 3 aviator.

Scarcely less appealing than the fleet command were the immediately subordinate commands: heading the carrier forces, heading the amphibious forces, and heading the amphibious troops. There was no question that the carrier commander should be an aviator and the commander of the amphibious forces should be a regular line officer, but since soldiers would make at least half the landings in the Central Pacific, there was pressure to appoint an army officer to command the amphibious troops.

Nimitz had his own ideas about who was to command what. While walking with Spruance from their quarters to headquarters one morning, he said, "There are going to be some changes in high command of the fleet. I would like to let you go, but unfortunately for you, I need you more here."

"Well," replied Spruance philosophically, "the war is the important thing. I personally would like to have another crack at the Japs, but if you need me here, this is where I should be."

Spruance put the subject out of his mind until the next morning. As they were again coming down from their quarters, Nimitz said, "I have been thinking this over during the night. Spruance, you are lucky. I decided that I am going to let you go after all."

On April 8 Nimitz wrote to King: "When Task Force 50 is strengthened . . . it is my intention to nominate Spruance as the task force commander with the rank of Vice Admiral." In the same letter he listed, as relief for Spruance, the names of five officers "arranged in the order of their desirability and possible availability," with Admiral McMorris named first.

When it at last dawned on the astonished Spruance that he was going to command the whole Central Pacific Force, he asked for Admiral Kelly Turner to head the amphibious force, "if I can steal him from Admiral Halsey," and General Holland Smith to command the amphibious troops. To himself he promised to secure as his own chief of staff his old friend Captain Charles J. ("Carl") Moore, an officer who would willingly and capably relieve him of the toil of drafting operation plans.

Turner had served with Spruance for three years on the staff of the Naval War College and had strongly impressed him with his intelligence and energy. Turner's reputation had been tarred for a while by the Savo Island defeat, but he had been exonerated by the findings of Admiral Arthur Hepburn, former

Commander in Chief of the Fleet, who had been ordered by Secretary Knox to analyze the battle and fix the blame. Though Hepburn had not yet submitted his report, he was known to have concluded that blame for Savo Island "was so evenly distributed that it would be unfair to censure any particular officer," and King and Nimitz concurred. Nimitz agreed to submit Turner's name to King for the amphibious force command. He wanted to think a while about recommending Smith.

Admiral Nimitz had set a target date of May 7 for the assault on Attu, with Rear Admiral Francis W. Rockwell commanding the North Pacific amphibious group. From Task Force 50 he sent to the North Pacific Force three old battleships for extra gunfire support and an escort carrier for close air support. After two postponements because of heavy surf, 3,000 troops of the 7th U.S. Army Division stormed ashore on May 11. Because the defenders were holed up in the mountain passes, 11,000 troops, the entire U.S. reserve, had to be put ashore to pry them out. At last on May 29 the thousand surviving Japanese staged a suicidal banzai charge that practically ended the campaign.

On June 1 Nimitz was again in San Francisco conferring with King. Admiral Rockwell and General Holland Smith, fresh from the Aleutians, were on hand to report on what they had learned at Attu. Rockwell was sharply critical of intelligence, which had grossly underestimated the number of enemy on the island and had provided incomplete hydrographic data. The training of the assault troops he considered inadequate. The old battleships and the escort carrier had proved useful, but Rockwell believed that bombardment "should be done more intelligently." Smith was satisfied with the landings but found fault with the campaign ashore. The soldiers moved so slowly, he said, that the retreating enemy had time to regroup and consolidate his defenses. King and Nimitz listened with intense interest. Attu was only the third amphibious operation the Americans had undertaken in World War II. Many more were doubtless ahead of them, and thus far they had not assaulted a strongly defended beach.

King reviewed for Nimitz the decisions reached at a recent conference, code-named Trident, of the Combined Chiefs of Staff held in Washington. This time the American chiefs were far better prepared than they had been at Casablanca, where the British largely had their way. At the Trident Conference the Americans reluctantly agreed to an Allied invasion of Italy, but their agreement had a price tag attached. At American insistence the British firmly committed themselves to a cross-Channel attack into western Europe in 1944, and they accepted a "Strategic Plan for the Defeat of Japan" drawn up by the U.S. Joint Chiefs of Staff and their subordinate committees.

The "Strategic Plan" assumed that Japan was to be defeated by (1) blockade, especially the cutting-off of Japan's access to the oil and other strategic products of the East Indies area, (2) by sustained aerial bombardment of Japan's cities, and (3) by invasion of Japan's home islands. To acquire a base for carrying out these operations, all Allied forces were to converge on Hong Kong and the China coast.

Since, as it turned out, neither the British nor the Chinese were able to carry out their assignments, the drive would have to be made by the Americans, assisted by such limited forces as the Australians, the New Zealanders, and the Canadians could provide. In 1943–44, the Allies, besides ejecting the Japanese from the Aleutians, would advance along two lines toward Mindanao, southernmost of the Philippines: after the conquest or neutralization of Rabaul by South Pacific and Southwest Pacific forces, the Southwest Pacific Force, under the command of General MacArthur, would advance toward Mindanao along the north coast of New Guinea; the Central Pacific Force, under the command of Admiral Nimitz, would advance across the Pacific by way of the Marshall and Caroline islands and support MacArthur's reconquest of the Philippines.

With the Central Pacific drive assured, King and Nimitz considered the advantages of beginning with the Gilberts instead of the Marshalls. King said that the British chiefs had tacitly turned over control of the Pacific war to the American Joint Chiefs. He said that Nimitz was free to move troops about the Pacific without advance authority from the Joint Chiefs.

Admiral King accepted the nominations of Spruance to command the Central Pacific Force and of Turner to head the amphibious force, and he agreed to Spruance's promotion to vice admiral. He was willing to accept Holland Smith to lead the amphibious troops, if Nimitz should decide to nominate him.

When Admiral Nimitz mentioned that he planned to pay a visit to the South Pacific after he returned to Pearl, General Smith hinted broadly that he would like to accompany the admiral to see where the marines he had trained had fought and to inspect those who were again about to go into action. Nimitz at once extended the general a cordial invitation to go along. No doubt he was pleased to have an opportunity to look over this officer whom Spruance had recommended.

Before leaving the States, Nimitz briefly visited Seattle for a conference with Frank Jack Fletcher, whom King had shunted off to the Northwest Sea Frontier because he had doubts about his aggressiveness. Fletcher felt that King had added insult to injury by ordering him, in connection with the recent Attu invasion, to place himself and his forces at the disposal of CinCPac. Fletcher had promptly made available his ships and planes but not himself. To have done so would have placed him, a vice admiral, in the embarrassing position of taking orders from Rear Admiral Kinkaid. Nimitz soothed Fletcher's ruffled feelings, and told him that the arrangement had worked satisfactorily and that the same would do very well for the forthcoming assault on Kiska. Later, Fletcher swallowed his pride and fruitlessly offered to take a demotion to rear admiral in order to get back to sea.

Admiral Nimitz and General Smith arrived at Pearl Harbor on June 7.

There the admiral's spirits were gladdened by the sight of the 27,000-ton *Essex*, first of the new carriers to reach the Pacific. She had arrived during his absence.

The admiral and the general departed for SoPac on the 10th, flying via Fiji to Noumea, where they discussed plans for the coming invasion of New Georgia with Halsey and his staff. Halsey was ready and marking time, but MacArthur had decreed that the South Pacific assault should be timed to coincide with Southwest Pacific's invasion of Kiriwina and Woodlark islands, and this could not take place until Rear Admiral Daniel E. Barbey's Seventh Amphibious Force received more ships. The dual operation was scheduled for June 30.

Halsey accompanied Nimitz and Smith on an inspection of Espiritu Santo and Guadalcanal. Nimitz was particularly gratified to note at Noumea and Espiritu the improvement in handling cargo and the resultant quick turnabout of ships. Only Guadalcanal still presented serious cargo-handling problems because of enemy air attacks and the open roadstead.

When Halsey and Nimitz discussed the desirability of relieving the commanding general of the I Marine Amphibious Corps, Smith listened intently. He wanted above all to lead in combat the men he had trained. He hoped that he might be considered as the replacement, but his name was not even mentioned. Apparently for him it was back to his training chores in the States.

In deep depression Smith headed back toward Pearl Harbor in Admiral Nimitz's plane. Thinking somber thoughts, he was watching cloud formations when Nimitz called him over to the other end of the cabin.

"Holland," said the admiral, "I am going to bring you out to the Pacific this fall. You will command all marines in the Central Pacific Area. I think you will find your new job very interesting."

When the party got back to Pearl Harbor on June 18, awaiting Nimitz were formal orders from the Joint Chiefs of Staff directing him to plan for an invasion of the Marshall Islands with a target date of November 15. For this operation he was allocated the 1st and 2nd Marine Divisions and all the amphibious shipping and most of the naval forces from the South Pacific.

General MacArthur lost no time in protesting, for this reallocation of forces clearly implied that the Central Pacific drive was henceforth to be the main effort in the Allied westward advance. He argued that his own proposed advance, on what he called the New Guinea-Mindanao Axis, would be far less risky. His army, carried forward along the north coast of New Guinea in a series of amphibious operations, would be able to bypass enemy strong points, and would be supported all the way by "utterly essential" land-based air. He pointed to the Japanese defeat at Midway as an example of what could happen to a force that attacked strongly defended islands.

Proponents of the Central Pacific drive argued that a force spearheaded and supported by carrier-based air could take tremendous leaps, bypassing enemy positions far more effectively than could an army that must keep within the attack radius of its own shore-based fighters. A Central Pacific advance would have shorter, more direct communication lines, with a consequent saving in shipping, and by threatening all of Japan's island empire, it would impel the enemy to disperse his forces all over the Pacific to defend each position.

The means for the new drive were assembling. By fall Nimitz would have 11 fast carriers, 8 escort carriers, 5 new battleships, 7 old battleships (useful for shore bombardment), 8 heavy cruisers, 4 light cruisers, 66 destroyers, 27 attack transports and cargo carriers, and 9 merchant ships suitable for use as transports. He was to have an expanded Seventh Army Air Force and all Pacific Fleet aircraft not assigned to the South Pacific.

With these means the Central Pacific Force was to capture the Marshalls. The first question to be decided was: Which Marshalls? CinCPac planners proposed simultaneous landings on five atolls: Kwajalein, Maloelap, Wotje, Mili, and Jaluit. Spruance quashed that proposal at once. The Central Force did not have enough amphibiously trained troops to seize five heavily defended points at the same time. And splitting the U.S. fleet five ways to support the landings would expose each of its segments to destruction by the concentrated Japanese fleet.

Every discussion of the Marshalls came around to the fact that they were out of reach of American land-based planes. This meant that the invasion would have to get its air support solely from carrier planes, and nobody was sure that, by November, the Pacific Fleet carrier force would be strong enough and its aviators experienced enough to do the job. Then there was the problem of photoreconnaissance. It was imperative that aerial photographs be taken to show defense installations, water depths, coral reefs, and beach gradients. Only land-based planes, it was then believed, could carry out the extensive photography that was needed.

Captain Forrest P. Sherman, Admiral Towers' brilliant chief of staff, made the less-than-brilliant proposal that Wake Island should be captured to provide an airfield from which the Marshalls could be photographed. Spruance came down hard on that suggestion, for Wake was otherwise worthless as a base: it led nowhere, it had no usable anchorage, it was not so placed as to offer protection to any current or foreseeable Allied communication line.

The planners both in Washington and at Pearl Harbor kept coming back to consideration of the Gilbert Islands. Aircraft based there could easily photograph and support assaults on the Marshalls. The Gilberts themselves could be reached by bombers based on Funafuti, in the Ellice Islands, and on Canton, in the Phoenix Islands. Funafuti could be supplemented by fighter bases to be built on Nukufetau and Nanumea islands; Canton, by a fighter strip on Baker Island. All these bases and the Gilberts themselves were well placed for supporting communications from Hawaii southward.

What decided the Washington and Pearl Harbor planners almost simultaneously to recommend invading the Gilberts before tackling the Marshalls was the Joint Chiefs' decision to let General MacArthur retain the veteran 1st

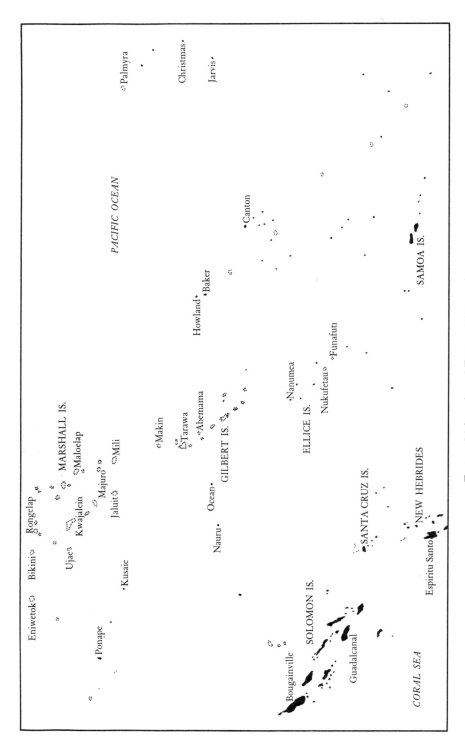

*Eastern Melanesia and Eastern Micronesia*

Marine Division, which he had scheduled to land at Cape Gloucester. Only thus could the Allied advances be mutually supporting, with MacArthur and Halsey applying pressure on the enemy in the Rabaul area while forces under Nimitz applied pressure in the Central Pacific. Assigning the 2nd Marine Division to Nimitz meant that Rabaul would have to be neutralized, not captured, but that was the solution Admiral King had favored for some time.

Admiral Nimitz in early July accepted the Gilberts-before-Marshalls plan and forwarded it for approval to the Joint Chiefs. The main target in the Gilberts would be the island of Betio in Tarawa Atoll, for there the Japanese were known to have an airfield. A possible secondary target was Butaritari Island in Makin Atoll, where they had established a seaplane base.

On July 20 the Joint Chiefs of Staff gave their approval to the CinCPac plan, but they added a clinker. They ordered Nimitz also to capture Nauru Island, which the Japanese had at last occupied. "Capture, occupy, defend, and develop bases on Nauru and in the Gilberts," read the new order. Unfortunately Nauru was nearly 400 miles from Tarawa, to the southwest. Neither Spruance nor Nimitz favored undertaking simultaneous assaults so far apart.

Meanwhile, at the end of June, Halsey's South Pacific Force had begun making landings in the New Georgia group in the Central Solomons, and MacArthur's Southwest Pacific Force went ashore on Woodlark and Kiriwina islands and at Nassau Bay, on the northeast coast of New Guinea. These operations were uncontested except for some light air raids on the forces attacking New Georgia. Shortly after the assault phase at New Georgia was completed, Kelly Turner turned over the command of his Third Amphibious Force to Rear Admiral Theodore S. Wilkinson and headed for Pearl Harbor to organize amphibious forces for the Central Pacific.

On New Georgia the Americans had to face the problem the Japanese never succeeded in solving on Guadalcanal—how to seize an airfield inside a strong defensive perimeter. It required a month of jungle fighting for 32,000 U.S. soldiers and 1,700 marines to wrest the Munda airstrip from 5,000 defenders. Among the Americans killed in the New Georgia operation was Admiral Nimitz's friend and housemate Dr. Gendreau, whom CinCPac had sent to the South Pacific to inspect facilities for the care of the wounded.

At Nimitz's suggestion, Halsey took a leaf out of Kinkaid's Aleutian plan and bypassed the strongly defended island of Kolombangara in favor of a landing on lightly held Vella Lavella Island, farther up the Slot. On August 15, Wilkinson's Third Amphibious Force, under cover of Allied planes operating from the Munda field, put a landing force ashore on Vella Lavella without opposition from ground forces. Assisted by New Zealanders, the Americans destroyed the small Japanese garrison and built a fighter strip to cover Halsey's next invasion, scheduled for November 1 on Bougainville.

During Halsey's march up the Solomons, small U.S. cruiser and destroyer forces fought a series of after-sunset battles with a revived Tokyo Express and gradually, with the help of improved radar and the development of the combat information center, outfought the Japanese at their own night-fighting specialty. The first unqualified victory by American surface forces fighting the Japanese in darkness was achieved in the Battle of Vella Gulf, August 6–7, in which an American destroyer task group sank three enemy destroyers with torpedoes and gunfire and came away unscathed.

On August 15, as South Pacific forces were invading Vella Lavella, Kinkaid's North Pacific Force was assaulting Kiska. To seize this island an amphibious fleet of nearly a hundred ships brought 29,000 U.S. and 5,300 Canadian troops. After a tremendous bombardment, the troops headed for the beach in scores of landing craft. In the greatest anticlimax of the war, they encountered no opposition whatever—it was found that under cover of fog the Japanese had evacuated the island. There were some red Allied faces but also general relief at the saving in lives.

With the Aleutians cleared of the enemy, Kinkaid, who had been promoted to vice admiral, wondered what was next in store for him and his command. Feeling it would not be proper for him to send a message to CinCPac requesting information on the subject, he decided instead to make inquiry through his flag secretary, Commander Bill Leverton. Leverton, it will be recalled, had served as an ensign aboard the *Augusta* when Nimitz was her commanding officer. He had subsequently been aide to Nimitz, and there had grown up between them an almost father-son relationship. Through the years they had exchanged letters every three or four months. Kinkaid suggested to Leverton that in his next letter to Nimitz he make a discreet inquiry about the future operations of the North Pacific Force.

"Just ask him what's in prospect for our area," said Kinkaid. "What are we going to do?"

Leverton asked the question and back came an answer from CinCPac. "Tell Kinkaid," wrote Nimitz, "I'm sending him a package, and it will tell him what he's going to do."

In due course the package arrived and the whole North Pacific staff gathered around as Leverton opened it. It contained nothing but a cribbage board.

Kinkaid remained idle in the Aleutians, possibly playing cribbage, until late November when, at General MacArthur's request, he was transferred to Australia to command the Seventh Fleet. He was succeeded as Commander, North Pacific Force, by Vice Admiral Frank Jack Fletcher, who presumably fell heir to his cribbage board.

In the summer of 1943, Admiral Nimitz received a letter from President Roosevelt. "Dear Chester," it began, "Eleanor has decided she's got to come to the Pacific. I don't approve of the visit. If you want to turn her down, go ahead and do so." Her main purpose was to visit, as a representative of the Red Cross, the sick and wounded in the South and Southwest Pacific military hospitals. Admiral Nimitz, of course, cordially invited Mrs. Roosevelt to come.

She came out in great secrecy, landing at Hickam Field at 6:00 a.m., August 23. Major General Walter O. Ryan, who commanded there, anticipating her dawn arrival, arranged to entertain her at breakfast at his house and invited all the local senior officers, including Admiral Nimitz. He also asked Lamar to send over some of the admiral's messboys to assist with the serving. Among those Lamar sent was Pedro, Admiral Spruance's messboy.

Nimitz went directly from the breakfast to his office, where the first thing he did was to ask Lamar to send for Pedro. Lamar called the quarters and learned from the chief steward that Pedro had gone in to Honolulu on liberty. There followed eight anxious hours of waiting for Pedro to return. It seems that during the breakfast several guests had presented their short-snorter bills for Mrs. Roosevelt to sign. Pedro, who had no short snorter, offered his liberty pass and she signed that. Had Pedro been picked up by the shore patrol, her presence in the Pacific would quickly have become common knowledge.

That evening Mrs. Roosevelt dined at Admiral Nimitz's quarters. Nimitz's reaction, as expressed to Catherine, has been lost, but we have Admiral Spruance's letter to Mrs. Spruance, in which he wrote: "I had the pleasure of sitting next to her. She is very simple, charming, and has a delightful sense of humor. Whatever we may think of the possibility of achieving her ideals, she certainly has them and she has a deep faith in the underlying goodness of the ordinary human being. She is certainly a very fine person."

At Noumea Admiral Halsey received Eleanor with some misgivings, but he was completely won over by her tirelessness in visiting each bed in several hospitals, having words of comfort for each patient, and taking down his name and address in order to write to his family, which she did.

On her return to Hawaii, Mrs. Roosevelt was taken by Admiral Nimitz on a tour of Pearl Harbor in his fine, dark-blue admiral's barge. The crew, who went to immense pains and took great pride in keeping the barge in apple-pie order, had repainted its mahogany deck especially for this occasion. Mrs. Roosevelt, unaware of the preparations the crew had made, arrived aboard in high-heel shoes and promptly wrecked the paint job. Nimitz tried to distract her attention when he noticed the coxswain and crew giving her murderous glances.

On August 5, 1943, Admiral Nimitz formally established the Central Pacific Force, or U.S. Fifth Fleet,* and named Admiral Spruance its commander. "The admiral thinks it's all right to send Raymond out now," a CinCPac staff officer is said to have remarked. "He's got him to the point where they think and talk just alike." Relieving Spruance as CinCPac chief of staff was the Phantom of the Opera, Rear Admiral Soc McMorris, recently returned from the Aleutians. As had Spruance, McMorris shared Nimitz's quarters.

The appointment of Admiral Spruance to command the Fifth Fleet

---

* Initially the title *U.S. Fifth Fleet* was applied only to the *ships* of the Central Pacific Force. Early in 1944 it was extended to include the amphibious troops and land-based planes, and the name *Central Pacific Force* was dropped. For simplicity, this account uses the title *Fifth Fleet* in its extended meaning from this point on.

dashed Admiral Towers' hopes in that direction. He still aspired to the senior carrier command, but on August 6 Nimitz announced the selection of Rear Admiral Charles ("Baldy") Pownall to be Commander, Fast Carrier Forces, thus leaving Towers high and dry.

The amphibious component of the Fifth Fleet was established on August 24 as the Fifth Amphibious Force, with Rear Admiral Turner in command. In an invasion, this force would control the transports, cargo vessels, landing craft, and such supporting vessels as old battleships, cruisers, destroyers, escort carriers, and minesweepers. The amphibious troops of the Fifth Fleet were designated V Amphibious Corps, which was established on September 4 with Major General Holland Smith in command. Lastly, the Fifth Fleet had its own land-based air arm, the Defense and Shore-Based Air Force under Rear Admiral John H. Hoover. This command, which included army, navy, and marine planes, was to supplement the carriers by carrying out pre-invasion photo-reconnaissance and by making raids on or about the targets.

Admiral Nimitz's selections for these high commands brought immediate and prolonged criticism. He had picked the men he considered best fitted for their tasks without overriding regard for their service connections. Critics noted that only two naval aviators, Pownall and Hoover, had been included and that not one army officer had been appointed, though the 27th Army Division had been assigned to assault Nauru, substituting for the 1st Marine Division. At Pearl Harbor the principal spokesman for the naval aviators was of course Admiral Towers; for the army it was Lieutenant General Robert C. Richardson.

General Richardson had relieved General Emmons as Commanding General of the Hawaiian Department, a defense-oriented command. As the Central Pacific geared itself to the new offensive, Admiral Nimitz obtained for Richardson an additional appointment as Commanding General, U.S. Army Forces, Central Pacific. In this capacity, Richardson was responsible for the administration and training, but not the operations, of all U.S. Army units, whether ground or air, in the Central Pacific Area.

What fretted Richardson was that army air forces were serving under Hoover, a naval officer, and army ground forces were serving under Holland Smith, a Marine Corps officer. Neither officer, he believed, was likely to be familiar enough with army doctrine. Richardson finally induced Nimitz to appoint an army officer, Major General Willis Hale, to command, under Admiral Hoover, a task group composed of army air units. Nimitz saw no reason to make any adjustment for the 27th Division, which of course had its own commander, Major General Ralph Smith, USA.

Admiral Nimitz was particularly nettled when Admiral Harry E. Yarnell, retired but recently recalled to active duty in the Navy Department, bypassed CinCPac and sent to Pacific force commanders and naval aviators a form letter requesting their opinions concerning the appointment of commanders and the use of carriers. Predictably the aviators replied that CinCPac's plan for the use of carriers were too defensive and that there should be aviators in all major commands, or at least in all major command staffs. Rear Admiral Frederick Sherman,* commander of Halsey's carrier force, went all out in his criticism, calling the current organization and methods of naval warfare antiquated. He recommended that King, Nimitz, Spruance, and all non-aviator commanders of mixed forces that included air be forthwith replaced by active aviators.†

Just at this time Admiral Towers turned in a recommendation on fast-carrier policy that Nimitz had requested. The carriers, Towers had written, were to spearhead the fleet, attacking the enemy on land and sea, and were to provide air support for the rest of the fleet and for amphibious operations. So far so good, but Towers then went into the matter of command. Fleet commanders, he asserted, should be aviators or have aviators in senior positions on their staffs. Either Towers himself or some other senior naval aviator, such as Fitch, should be commanding the Fifth Fleet, or else Spruance's chief of staff should be an aviator.

Towers' comments on command, coming on the heels of Yarnell's form letter, annoyed Nimitz. He sent for Towers and with some asperity told him that his reasoning was faulty and that Spruance, and no other, was the right man to command the Fifth Fleet. "To put it bluntly," Towers wrote to Yarnell, "his reaction was to the effect that I did not know what I was talking about."

But Nimitz was nothing if not amenable to reason, and, besides logic, Towers had on his side a particularly good reasoner, his chief of staff, Captain Forrest Sherman, whom Nimitz liked and respected. Whether or not Sherman acted as go-between at this point is uncertain but, a few days after the dressing-down, Nimitz invited Towers to join him and Spruance in a discussion concerning carrier admirals and appointments. Thus ComAirPac was admitted into a planning role. He would have liked again to press his request for a seagoing command suitable to his rank, but he was beginning to suspect, probably correctly, that King had instructed Nimitz to keep him ashore.

The first practical step Spruance took toward preparing for the Gilberts-Nauru operation, code-named Operation Galvanic, was to make an extensive tour of Pacific bases with Captain Carl Moore, a non-aviator, whom he had succeeded in recruiting as his chief of staff. They visited Upolu Point, Canton Island, and Funafuti Atoll to study the sort of fringing coral reefs the amphibious troops would have to cross to reach the islands of the Central Pacific. At Noumea they consulted Admiral Halsey and his new chief of staff, Rear Admiral Robert B. ("Mick") Carney. From New Caledonia they flew to New Zealand to visit the 2nd Marine Division, earmarked for Tarawa, and to confer with its commanding officer, quiet, impressive Major General Julian C. Smith. Smith's marines, veterans of Guadalcanal, sorely needed amphibious craft of various sorts for training and rehearsal, and they were particularly anxious to

---

* No kin to Captain Forrest P. Sherman, mentioned above.
† Admiral King had had flight training, but he was not an *active* aviator.

get more amtracs (LVTs), versatile, treaded landing craft that could swim through the water, climb up over a reef, and make 15 miles an hour on dry land. On the way back to Pearl, Spruance and Moore visited Guadalcanal and stopped at Espiritu Santo to confer with Rear Admiral Harry W. Hill, who was to command the attack force at Tarawa.

When General Holland Smith arrived in Hawaii from the States on September 5, he was welcomed at the airport by Admiral Turner. On such an occasion as this, Turner was the essence of old-world courtesy, and Smith could be almost equally gracious. As soon, however, as these tough-minded, blunt, vociferous warriors started working together, they began living up to their nicknames of "Terrible" and "Howling Mad." Each had his own notion of how an amphibious assault ought to be conducted and who should command, and at first neither was prepared to budge an inch.

Smith's long experience in amphibious training and exercises finally enabled him to win from Turner grudging acceptance of Marine Corps methods, but deciding who was to command what, and when, brought them almost to an impasse. Turner insisted that while the troops were in his ships and in his landing craft they were under his command, and that applied to amphibious training and rehearsals as well as to an actual assault. General Richardson complicated the situation by pointing out that *he* was charged with training all soldiers in the Pacific. He asserted moreover that he should have control of the 27th Division right through the invasion. Irked by these arguments, Smith was further frustrated because his marines were in far-away New Zealand, and the 27th Division struck him as a sorry outfit with elderly officers and homesick men. At one point he threw up his hands in disgust. "All I want to do is kill some Japs," he roared. "Just give me a rifle. I don't want to be a commanding general. Just give me a rifle and I'll go out there and shoot some Japs. I'm not worrying about anything else around here."

Richardson turned to Nimitz for a decision on how far his command extended. CinCPac replied that all troops assigned to Operation Galvanic were under the command of Holland Smith and were to be trained by him. Richardson, not satified with this answer, appealed over Nimitz's head to General Marshall. Marshall upheld Nimitz. "The exact determination as to when such training responsibilities will pass from you to CinCPac," said Marshall's dispatch, "must, in all cases, be decided by CinCPac after consultation with you as his army adviser."

Turner and Holland Smith, with the help of Carl Moore, finally worked out a rough solution to their conflicts. During the training period, they shared responsibilities and command. During an assault, while the men were afloat and throughout the amphibious phase, Turner would exercise operational control. When Smith had established headquarters ashore, he would take command of the men who had landed. It worked well enough, but between two such hot-headed characters as Turner and Smith there were bound to be many stormy scenes.

General Richardson could never reconcile himself to the notion of a marine general exercising command over soldiers. He regarded the V Amphibious Corps as just another echelon to be dealt with. Its elimination, he believed, would not affect operations in the least. He regarded his own headquarters as better fitted to command and control the expeditionary troops. Despite differences of opinion, his relations with Nimitz remained cordial, but Richardson continued to watch General Holland Smith's actions with a critical eye. Questions of command and interservice relations thus became a sort of time bomb, likely to explode at any time.

When General Holland Smith saw pictures and charts of Nauru, he took an instant dislike to the place. It was an almost-circular island, not an atoll, with a narrow beach surrounding cliffs. Its interior was hilly and pocked with easily defensible holes and caves resulting from the excavations of phosphate rock. Smith doubted that the 27th Division was capable of taking it. Anyway, there were not enough transports available to carry both the whole of that division and the 2nd Marine Division, all of which was needed to take Tarawa.

Turner for once agreed with Smith and the two went to Spruance with their objections. In him they found a ready listener because Commander, Fifth Fleet, could see no way adequately to cover such widely separated targets as Nauru and Tarawa. The Japanese might strike his ships at Nauru from Truk while the rest of his ships were supporting the assault on Tarawa, 380 miles away. Spruance went to Nimitz with a suggestion that they cancel Nauru and substitute Makin, which was less than 100 miles from Tarawa, but Nimitz refused to recommend so important a change before his forthcoming conference with King.

In preparation for the next bimonthly CominCh-CinCPac conference, due to begin at Pearl Harbor on September 25, Spruance had Smith put his recommendations and arguments into a carefully prepared memorandum which both Turner and Spruance endorsed. When Admiral King had arrived and settled down with Admiral Nimitz and his staff members in the CinCPac conference room, Spruance passed Smith's memorandum to Nimitz, who read it and passed it to King. When the latter had finished reading it, he said to Spruance, "What do you propose to take instead of Nauru?"

"Makin," replied Spruance, who then went on to produce additional arguments that might impress King. Makin, big enough for a bomber base, is 100 miles nearer the Marshalls, their next objective, than is Tarawa. Nauru would be of no use whatever to the Americans and, after the Americans had captured the Gilberts, it would be of little value to the Japanese, because American aircraft from the Gilberts would be able to keep it pounded down.

King gave Spruance the old fish eye but said he would recommend the change of objective to the Joint Chiefs.

The second day of the conference was devoted to planning for the seizure of the Marshalls. The Joint Chiefs had scheduled the assault for early 1944 but had not yet directed which Marshalls were to be invaded. CinCPac and his staff favored Kwajalein, Maloelap, and Wotje; and Nimitz had warned his officers to present before King a united front on this choice, in order to be more convincing and to avoid protracted debate or the introduction of one of King's little surprises that could spoil CinCPac's planning.

Spruance was not altogether sold on the CinCPac plan. He wanted the strongest possible land-based air support for help in taking Kwajalein, the biggest atoll in the Pacific. He desired therefore first to take the little atoll of Ujae, near Kwajalein, in order to provide an additional airfield. Knowing that it would be difficult to crack the carefully contrived CinCPac façade in private, Spruance decided to spring his idea before Admiral King during the conference. As it turned out, Spruance could not be present on the 26th, so he sent Captain Moore to sit in for him and bring up his recommendation.

The conference was humming along to Nimitz's satisfaction, with all the CinCPac staff in perfect agreement, when Kwajalein was brought up. At this point Moore announced that Spruance wanted to seize Ujae. Silence fell among the CinCPac staffers, and Nimitz turned upon Moore a withering look—that icy blue stare that could make a strong man shudder. In measured tones he expressed his indignation at Moore's deviation from conformity. "Now," he concluded, "you come up and bring up a perfectly strange proposition here." Moore replied that he was only carrying out Spruance's orders.

King's features creased into an unaccustomed grin. He was beginning to get suspicious of the beautiful unanimity among the CinCPac staff officers. Now he had an opportunity to take a few digs at Nimitz.

To Spruance Moore reported CinCPac's sharp reaction. "That's all right," said Spruance. "I'll fix it up," and he headed for Nimitz's office.

Nimitz never brought the matter up again. In all probability he began to see the humor in the situation and was quietly amused at his own discomfiture. Anyway, nothing was lost. King accepted Kwajalein, Maleolap, and Wotje, and on the 27th a dispatch arrived from the Joint Chiefs of Staff approving the substitution of Makin for Nauru. As noted earlier, the target in Makin Atoll would be Butaritari Island. King and Nimitz spent the 27th sloshing about Midway in the pouring rain, inspecting submarine, air, and defense facilities.

With the decision to take Makin instead of Nauru, revised planning reduced the participation of the 27th Division to one regiment, the 165th, which would be reinforced to 6,500 assault troops to form a regimental combat team. That certainly seemed sufficient to take such a small island as Butaritari, which was estimated to be garrisoned by between 500 and 800 men, less than half of whom would be combat troops. This vast disparity of strength was intended to ensure a one-day conquest of the island so that the supporting fleet could be quickly released.

Admiral Turner had originally assigned himself and his attack force to Nauru, which looked tougher than Tarawa and was much closer to Truk, where the Japanese Combined Fleet was based. When Makin was substituted for Nauru, he decided that he would not disturb Admiral Hill in his preparations to assault Tarawa and would, instead, give his personal attention to Makin.

Planning went into high gear to meet the target date of November 19 (Pearl Harbor date). All echelons worked simultaneously, and JICPOA labored to speed production of an "Intelligence Book" containing everything it could find out about the Gilberts—from charts, histories, former residents, and submarine and air reconnaissance.

A singularity about the CinCPac command was that much of its planning was done orally, by officers standing before wall maps or gathered in corridors or seated in Nimitz's office or around conference tables. This unusual system no doubt grew out of the preference of both Nimitz and Spruance for vocalizing their thoughts before committing them to paper. On the basis of such initial discussions, teams prepared studies on "how to do it." They then explained their studies to Admiral Nimitz, who selected the one he considered best and issued it to his top participating subordinates. These subordinates assigned the various phases of the planning—strategic, tactical, and logistic—to *their* subordinates, who prepared written plans and submitted them back up the chain of command for criticism, suggested changes, and, finally, coordination with the other plans.

The officers often worked till midnight. Nimitz and Spruance had their normal busy days, but they mainly kept aloof from the planning drudgery. They took their long walks as usual, and in the evening read, listened to music, or entertained guests. They thus kept their minds clear for their regular duties and for the stresses to come. Nimitz was thinking ahead to the attack on the Marshalls and beyond, but he kept himself available for consultation on the planning in hand. Even when he was hospitalized in late October with acute prostatitis, a stream of officers came to consult him in his sick bed.

Final amphibious training for the expeditionary troops was conducted by the division commanders, that of the 27th Division under the general direction of Commander, Fifth Amphibious Force, and Commander, V Amphibious Corps. Since these commanders were too busy to go to New Zealand, General Julian Smith and members of his staff came to Pearl Harbor for indoctrination by Turner and Holland Smith. Admiral Hill, Commander of the Southern Attack Force, went to New Zealand. He later conducted the 2nd Marine Division to Efate, in the New Hebrides, for final landing rehearsals.

In late August Admiral Pownall led a three-carrier task group in a raid on Marcus Island, destroying seven aircraft and causing heavy damage to installations. On September 18 and 19 planes from another three-carrier group joined Seventh Air Force bombers from Canton and Funafuti in a series of raids on the Gilberts. An important result of the Gilberts raid was that the Japanese evacuated all their planes from Tarawa and all but four amphibians from Makin. Moreover, the defenders shot off a good deal of ammunition they could not replace, and the attacking aircraft got some useful oblique photographs of the landing beaches. On October 5 and 6, a six-carrier force blasted Wake with six strikes, and the atoll was shelled by cruisers and destroyers.

A major purpose of these raids was to give the carrier personnel warm-up and training against live targets. The attacks were also tests of the new Hellcat fighters and Dauntless dive-bombers, and they were trials of the new multicarrier groups. The theory being put into practice with the new groups was that it was advisable to operate several carriers within a single ring of escorts and to depend for defense not on maneuver, as in the past, but on concentrated combat air patrols and massed proximity-fuzed antiaircraft fire.

At a meeting at CinCPac headquarters on October 9, movies of the Marcus and Wake attacks were shown. Admiral Nimitz and his staff were impressed with the power of the carrier forces both to inflict punishment and to protect themselves. The aviator-commanders of the carriers and the carrier forces had shown surprising skill in handling ships as well as in handling aircraft.

Three days after the film demonstrations, Nimitz asked Towers to remain behind following the morning conference. The CinCPac planning officer, Captain James M. Steele, was being rotated out to sea duty, said Nimitz, and he asked Towers to nominate an air officer for his replacement.

An air officer! Towers was agreeably surprised at this concession to the aviators. He named Rear Admiral Arthur W. Radford, Captain Forrest Sherman, and Captain Donald Duncan. Nimitz eliminated Duncan, saying he needed more sea experience. He then asked Towers which of the other two was preferable. Towers, hedging, said that he had named them in order of seniority.

"If you were CinCPac, which would you take?" asked Nimitz.

Towers reluctantly named Sherman, his own chief of staff. Then he added that if Sherman was taken, he wanted one of the other two to replace him. Nimitz agreed, and orders went out that immediately following Operation Galvanic, Sherman would become CinCPac plans officer and Radford would be chief of staff to Towers. Meanwhile, Radford would command one of the carrier groups in the assault on the Gilberts.

The carrier raids had demonstrated to skeptical officers the power of the carrier force to pound down enemy bases. The aviators insisted that the carrier forces should be free to cruise about, striking the source of any land-based or carrier planes that might interfere with the American assault forces. Turner, on the contrary, wanted the carriers to remain near the landing beaches. Spruance felt compelled to support Turner. Towers, frustrated, considered sending Pownall and Radford to appeal to Nimitz, then in the hospital. Spruance compromised. He would let the carriers lead off by attacking the Japanese air bases, but once the assaults on Makin and Tarawa began, they were to keep the amphibious shipping and beachheads closely covered.

Nimitz and Spruance expected, and rather hoped, that the assault on the Gilberts would spur the Combined Fleet to sortie from Truk and give battle. In his "General Instructions to Flag Officers," Spruance wrote:

> If . . . a major portion of the Japanese Fleet were to attempt to interfere
> with GALVANIC, it is obvious that the defeat of the enemy fleet would at once

become paramount. . . . The destruction of a considerable portion of the Japanese naval strength would . . . go far towards winning the war. . . . We must
be prepared at all times during GALVANIC for a fleet engagement.

Because of the threat to Operation Galvanic from sea and air, Spruance proposed to seize the target islands with "lightning speed" and quickly withdraw
his ships from the beachheads. To attain maximum celerity, he wanted every
ship he could get, including Ted Sherman's carrier group in the South Pacific.
Slated for the assault on the Gilberts, not counting service and garrison groups,
were 5 new and 7 old battleships, 6 fleet carriers, 5 light carriers, 8 escort
carriers, and 100 other vessels. Grumbled Admiral Towers, "Spruance wants a
sledgehammer to drive a tack."

At last the operation plans were drawn up and coordinated. The overall
Fifth Fleet plan, organized mainly by Captain Moore and running more than
300 pages, was presented in its essential features in the CinCPac war-game
room before Admiral Nimitz and his staff. The presentation was a long and
intricate process, interrupted frequently by questions and criticisms, but when
it ended, CinCPac and CinCPac staff knew what the Fifth Fleet intended to do,
and the Fifth Fleet had benefited from the comments of CinCPac and CinCPac
staff. The plan could now undergo final revision and be mimeographed and
distributed.

Just when plans for Operation Galvanic seemed firm and settled, the
situation down south almost wrecked its timetable. Halsey, about to invade
Bougainville Island at Cape Torokina, only 200 miles from Rabaul, asked
Nimitz to let him retain Sherman's carrier group a little longer and also to lend
him another carrier group. Nimitz granted both requests provided the two
groups could be scheduled to reach the Gilberts in time to participate in
Galvanic. Halsey's Third Amphibious Force invaded Bougainville on November 1. Sherman's carriers hit Rabaul on the 5th. The borrowed carrier group,
under Rear Admiral Alfred Montgomery, joined Sherman's group in a second
raid on Rabaul on the 11th. In these operations, so many Japanese carrier
planes were shot down that the Americans suspected that lack of air cover
would make it impossible for the Combined Fleet to oppose the forthcoming
assaults on the Gilberts.

Because there was no certainty that the two carrier groups loaned to
Halsey would get to the Central Pacific in time, Nimitz on November 5 directed Spruance to prepare an alternate plan based on the assumption that only
the two remaining groups would be available for Galvanic. To allow a little
extra time for the borrowed ships to join Spruance, he postponed D-day by 24
hours, to November 20.

Despite the tumult of moving aboard ship, the Fifth Fleet staff produced
the alternate plan at breakneck speed. If the borrowed carrier groups did not
return in time, the amphibious forces would seize Tarawa first, then Makin,
supported at each assault by the two groups on hand. Since Spruance would

not know before putting to sea how many groups he could count on and he was determined not to reveal his approach to the target by breaking radio silence, he left it to Nimitz to announce to the fleet by radio which plan it should use.

The day before the main body of the Fifth Fleet sailed from Pearl Harbor, Nimitz called together the senior commanders, navy, army, marine, and laid down the law for nearly an hour. Officers accustomed to the genial Nimitz were astonished at his severity on this occasion. He was not only severe but deadly serious. "If I hear one case of a naval officer not giving required help to the Army ashore," he said, "I will immediately relieve him."

As he finished his lecture, he snapped, "That's all, gentlemen." Then, breaking into a broad smile, he said, "By the way, have you heard the one about two male squirrels racing around a chestnut tree?"

As Nimitz doubtless expected, his admirals and generals repeated the applicable parts of his lecture to their subordinates, not failing to conclude with the "Old Man's" latest story, which sifted down till it had been heard by every man in the fleet.

By mid-November the whole Fifth Fleet was at sea. From Pearl Harbor came the Northern Attack Force, under the direct command of Admiral Turner and destined for Makin. From Pearl Harbor also came two carrier groups, commanded by Admirals Pownall and Radford. Spruance's flagship, the heavy cruiser *Indianapolis*, sailed with the Northern Attack Force. Nearby steamed the *Pennsylvania* with Admiral Turner and Generals Holland Smith and Ralph Smith aboard. From the New Hebrides came the Southern Attack Force, heading for Tarawa with the commander, Admiral Hill, in the *Maryland*. From the Solomons, via the New Hebrides, and strictly on time, came Sherman's and Montgomery's carrier groups. Sherman's carriers blasted Nauru and Pownall's raided the southern Marshalls. At dawn on November 20 all forces were at their targets in the Gilberts.

# CHAPTER 17

# GALVANIC AND FLINTLOCK

ADMIRAL NIMITZ DIRECTED the principal officers of Operation Galvanic to make CinCPac an information addressee on all important radio messages passing between their commands. From this source and from an occasional direct report from Spruance, he early recognized that the assault on Makin had got off to a good start, while that on Tarawa was hitting snags.

In mid-morning, November 20, Turner, off Makin, notified Spruance, "Troops landed Red Beach Makin on schedule at 0830 and are advancing. No opposition." A little later Spruance, who was in the *Indianapolis* off Tarawa, informed Nimitz that the first wave had not got ashore at Betio until 9:13 a.m., nearly three quarters of an hour late.

Shortly after 1:00 p.m., Hill, also off Tarawa, reported to Turner: "Successful landing Beach Red 2 and Beach Red 3. Toehold on Beach Red 1. Am committing one landing team from division reserve. Still encountering strong resistance throughout." Committing reserves so early implied serious trouble. Half an hour later, in a message that concluded with the ominous words "Issue in doubt," Hill relayed to Turner General Julian Smith's request for release of the corps reserve. Turner quickly approved the release.

Hill's message came as a shock to CinCPac headquarters. The staff officers recalled that "Issue in doubt" was the phrase used by the commanding officer at Wake in his next-to-last message before the island fell to the Japanese. Admiral Nimitz sat quietly, showing no emotion, but it was obvious that he was deeply disturbed. At last he said softly, "I've sent in there everything we had, and it's plenty. I don't know why we shouldn't succeed."

A little after 7:00 p.m. Turner reported to Spruance the situation on Makin at day's end: "Progress satisfactory. Junction made between forces from Red and Yellow beaches. About half Butaritari Island in our hands. Resistance still to eastward.... Casualties light." In fact, the progress was not at all satisfactory. Nimitz had ordered the amphibious forces to "get the hell in and get the hell out." In view of the invaders' immense advantage in numbers, Nimitz had expected the conquest of little Butaritari in a single day and the consequent release of the fleet to safer waters.

Narrow, two-mile-long Betio in Tarawa Atoll was known to be far more heavily garrisoned and defended than Butaritari, but with a whole division of battle-hardened marines available to take it, CinCPac had anticipated that it

257

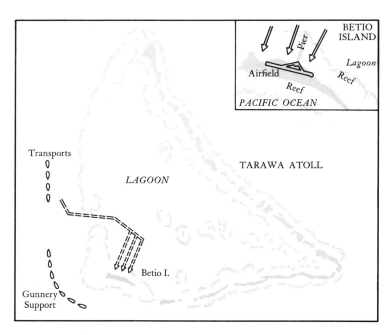

*The Assault on Tarawa, November 20, 1943*

too might be conquered in one day. Hill's evening report to Turner revealed that the island was still far from conquered: "At no time during the day have tide conditions permitted any boats to land on beach. Damage to LVTs [amtracs] heavy, resulting in difficult reinforcement of beachhead beyond shallow foothold on all Red beaches. Small gap still exists between Beaches Red 1 and 2. Two combat teams committed. No artillery or supplies yet landed."

Obviously CinCPac's intelligence about Tarawa's tides had been incorrect. Turner had not worried much about the fact that he did not have enough amtracs to land the whole force and would have to use LCVPs as well, because the invaders expected to go in on a high tide that would float the latter over the reef to the beach. However, the tide was apparently so low that the men in the LCVPs had been obliged to disembark at the edge of the reef and wade to the beach in the face of enemy fire.

Despite the formidable defenses and determined opposition the Americans were meeting on Betio, by nightfall CinCPac had grounds for guarded optimism. "The progress made during the day was small," said the Command Summary, "but as about 5,000 troops have been landed the capture is believed sure."

At 7:00 p.m. Pearl Harbor radio had intercepted a message from Admiral Montgomery to Spruance stating that Montgomery's carrier group had just been subjected to an air attack in which an enemy torpedo plane had struck and disabled the light carrier *Independence*. A cruiser and two destroyers were standing by to take her in tow while the rest of the group fled southward.

The next day, following the CinCPac morning conference, Admiral Nimitz at Admiral Towers' request called a meeting of CinCPac staff officers to discuss the implications of the torpedoing of the *Independence*. The Japanese had succeeded in finding the carrier groups, said Towers, because the carriers were tied closely to the beachheads. Supported by Soc McMorris and Forrest Sherman, he asked that Spruance be instructed to give the carriers more freedom. Spruance's restrictions, after all, were based mainly on fear of attack by enemy carriers. Now the basis for that fear had about evaporated. The Combined Fleet, still anchored snugly at Truk, showed no signs of coming out.

Towers wanted the American carriers to go north at once to pound those air bases in the northern Marshalls that Pownall had not struck. Nimitz would not give any such order before the Gilberts had been secured, but he had McMorris and Sherman draft a "despatch of instructions" to Spruance that gave the carrier groups a little more freedom of maneuver:

> Reaction by enemy to Galvanic clearly indicates opposition by submarines and by air attack from Marshalls and Nauru. Use of surface craft unlikely. In the circumstances, operating areas for carrier groups prescribed in Galvanic order are too restrictive. If carriers continue too long in such narrow confines, they become subjected to progressively greater torpedo hazard. Take corrective action to insure them greater freedom of movement consistent with their mission.

This was less than Towers had hoped for, but it was a clear step toward his goal of freeing the carriers so that they could protect the beachheads not by close support but by striking at enemy fleets and bases that were the chief sources of counterattack.

The battles for Makin and Tarawa continued through November 21 and 22. The enemy fleet was still at Truk, but all the participants in Galvanic were sure that Japanese submarines were converging on the Gilberts from bases in the Carolines and Marshalls. The fast carriers had been given a greater margin of safety through their newly permitted mobility, but the amphibious forces, which included the escort carriers, were still tied to the beachheads, providing close support and sending munitions and other supplies ashore.

Shortly after noon on the 23rd Admiral Spruance reported to CinCPac that enemy resistance had ended on both Butaritari and Betio. Admiral Nimitz and General Richardson flashed back to all hands: "Congratulations on a well done job."

On Butaritari the occupation forces had numbered about 800 men, of whom 284, all naval infantry, were combat troops. Only one of these permitted himself to be captured. The Americans with a 23-to-1 superiority had suffered 64 killed and 152 wounded.

CinCPac intelligence had estimated that there were about 2,500 Japanese on Betio. That estimate was not far short of the number of combatants, but there were also about 1,000 construction troops and some 1,200 Korean laborers. As usual at a captured Japanese island base, nearly all the defenders were killed. Of the 18,300 Americans, Marine Corps and Navy, committed to the conquest of the island, more than 3,000 became casualties, and of these a third were killed or died of their wounds.

Although the islands were in American hands, the amphibious forces could not leave until all the cargo vessels had been unloaded, the assault troops had been reembarked, and the garrison troops disembarked. Before dawn on November 24, Japanese submarines began to arrive. Off Makin one fired a torpedo into the escort carrier *Liscome Bay*, which simply blew apart as her magazine exploded, killing nearly 650 officers and men of her crew of about 900. Her loss strongly confirmed the CinCPac planners in their belief that speed was vital in an amphibious assault.

Admiral Nimitz decided that he ought to go to Tarawa to study the defense that had taken such a heavy toll of American lives. In preparation, he had Lamar type on filing cards the names, ranks, and titles of the principal officers he would be meeting for the first time. He would memorize these details during the flight down and thus would be able quickly to establish rapport with the men.

On November 25 he took off from Pearl Harbor in the staff Coronado and flew non-stop to the Ellices accompanied by, among others, General Richardson, Admiral Forrest Sherman, the indispensable Lamar, and Captain Redman, who would advise on radio communications for Tarawa. Each of the officers whiled away the hours in the air in his own way; Nimitz, when he was not memorizing names, played cribbage with Redman. At Funafuti he found awaiting him a message from Spruance advising him to postpone his visit to Tarawa. Mopping up, said Spruance, was still going on, the airfield was not ready to receive large planes, and the dead had not been buried.

Nimitz disregarded Spruance's advice. After inspecting the installations at Funafuti, he took off in a Marine Corps combat paratroop plane provided by Admiral Hoover. Although the marines on Betio worked manfully to get the airfield ready in time to receive him, his plane was obliged to circle over the island for nearly an hour while bulldozers scraped and extended the strip. From the air, little Betio looked like a wasteland of rubble from which projected the seared and blasted trunks of palm trees mostly stripped of fronds. At last the signal to land was made and the plane came down and bounced and bumped to a rough stop. As the door was opened, the nostrils of the men inside were assailed with the stench of burnt and rotting flesh. Burial details had interred most of the American corpses in shell holes or bulldozer-dug trenches, but there were still thousands of burned and dismembered Japanese bodies to be disposed of.

The Nimitz party was met by Admiral Spruance, General Julian Smith, and officers of their staffs. Together the three groups made an inspection of the island. Among the ruins were bodies and parts of bodies, sometimes in heaps. Carl Moore kicked a shoe and discovered there was a foot in it. Along the beach among the shattered amtracs, the bodies of marines who had died on the reef were still washing ashore. "It's the first time I've smelled death," murmured Nimitz.

On the living marines the party encountered, the last few days' struggle had left its mark. Their uniforms were filthy, and they themselves were sunkeneyed, unshaven, obviously bone-weary, and almost expressionless. Some were mere boys, but all looked like old men.

Nimitz's attention was caught by the fact that, among the palm-tree skeletons and fire-blackened remains of barracks, the basic defenses of the island were almost intact. These consisted of half-buried pillboxes and blockhouses of heavy concrete or of many layers of sandbags or green-coconut logs held together by angle irons and corrugated sheet metal. Some had guns with diameter of bore up to eight inches protruding from them. Most were piled high with soft coral sand, which simply absorbed the impact of aerial bombs and the shells of the two-hour naval bombardment that preceded the ship-to-shore movement. Eventually the marines had had to disable the defenders the hard way: they used the bayonet, tossed grenades or TNT charges into the structures, and, in some instances, poured gasoline down the air vents, then dropped grenades after it. One of the few Japanese taken alive reported that the island commander had boasted that a million men could not take his island in a hundred years.

Admiral Nimitz and his party, despite warnings by the marine officers, peered into one of the half-submerged structures. All they could see was about fifteen half-burned bodies. Some of the onlookers turned away, nauseated by the stench. The marine officers' warnings were well advised, for among the bodies was concealed a still-living Japanese. A few days later, crazed with thirst, he came out firing a machine gun and was promptly shot down.

In one of the less damaged structures in a well-cleared and scraped area of the island, General Julian Smith had established his command post, and there he invited the visitors to have lunch. Tables, chairs, white cloths, and food had been brought ashore from one of the ships. The food looked attractive, but the visitors had little appetite after what they had seen and in their awareness that the marines around them were still eating K and C rations out of cans.

On Canton Island, last stop on the way back to Pearl Harbor, Admiral Nimitz wrote Mrs. Nimitz a letter, in which he said in part:

> I have never seen such a desolate spot as Tarawa. Gen. Richardson, who saw the battlefields in France last war, says it reminded him of the Ypres field, over which the battle raged back and forth for weeks. Not a coconut tree of thousands was left whole. The Japs had prepared a magnificent defense and fought to the last man, except that a few wounded and dazed Japs were taken. The stench was terrific from bodies yet unburied, even though our troops were working hard to bury the dead. I was relieved when we left the place for a

neighboring island in the atoll—to eat supper and to sleep. Even there we could get occasional whiffs when the wind shifted. But enough of that. We are all working hard to consolidate our gains and to prepare for the attacks which we know are inevitable. With the Lord's help we will not only hold on to what we have got but will use the new places to attack the Japs when we get the fields ready for planes.

At some point during his trip, Nimitz heard the welcome news that another atoll in the Gilberts, Abemama, with an island big enough for an airfield, had fallen into American hands. A company of marine scouts had been put ashore there by the big submarine *Nautilus* to reconnoiter in preparation for a later assault. When the marines learned that the atoll was defended by only 25 Japanese, they called on the submarine for gunfire support and captured it themselves.

Nimitz and party got back to Pearl on November 30. They found Holland Smith already there, shaken by the ordeal "his" marines had undergone at Tarawa, which he had visited, and indignant at the shortcomings of the soldiers on Makin. He had fully expected the 27th Division troops to take lightly defended Butaritari in a single day. At the end of the second day, Howling Mad went roaring ashore and spent, he said, one of the worst nights of his Pacific campaigns. Jittery troops were shooting at every shadow and rustling leaf. They drilled holes in the command post tent and shot coconuts off trees. The next day he found a company of soldiers firing at phantoms where there was not a Japanese within thousands of yards. Smith yelled to their captain, "If I hear one more shot from your men in this area, I'll take your damn weapons and all your ammunition away from you."

Admiral Turner, after studying the assault on Betio, prepared a paper titled "Lessons Learned at Tarawa," dated November 30, and had it flown to Pearl Harbor from the flagship *Pennsylvania*. He pointed out that Kwajalein, principal atoll of the Marshalls, was almost certainly as strongly fortified as Tarawa had been. The Japanese, anticipating an early attack there, would strengthen it further. To tackle such a stronghold, more of everything was needed: more photoreconnaissance, more amtracs, more LCI gunboats, more bombardment vessels, more ammunition, more aerial bombing. He wanted sustained shore-based bombing of the Marshalls to begin as soon as practicable. He also wanted several days of bombing by carrier planes and of bombardment by battleships, cruisers, and destroyers to precede the assault.

The CinCPac staff, joined by Turner and Spruance on their arrival from the Gilberts, minutely studied the problems of Tarawa, beginning with Turner's "Lessons." Nimitz had pillboxes and blockhouses similar to those he had seen on Betio built on the small Hawaiian island of Kahoolawe, then had them bombed and bombarded to discover what could penetrate them. It became clear that a general pouring-in of unaimed fire could not destroy this type of fortification. Such area fire raised great clouds of smoke and dust which merely gave the attackers the false notion that they were achieving destruction. What was needed was precision bombing and accurate, aimed gunfire sustained over

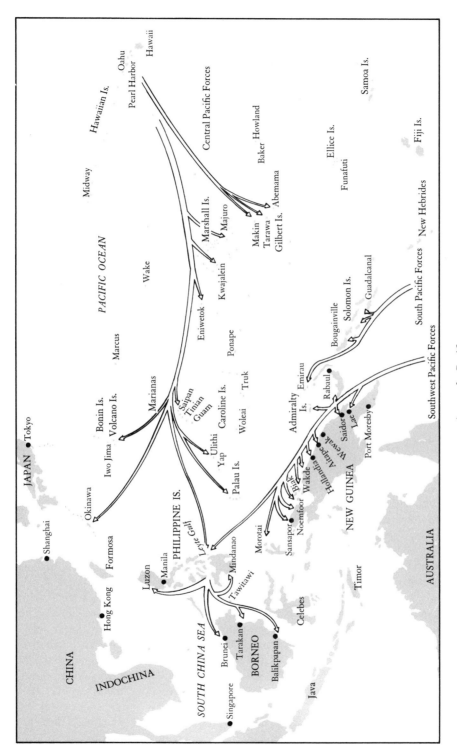

*Across the Pacific*

a considerable period of time. Penetration could be assured only by plunging fire, using major-caliber, armor-piercing shells.

When the casualty report of the Gilberts campaign was released to the newspapers, the Pacific Fleet command became the object of sharp criticism by public and press. Distraught relatives of the men killed wrote personal, accusatory letters to Admiral Nimitz. One bereaved mother began her letter: "You killed my son on Tarawa." Nimitz insisted that every piece of mail be answered. When Lamar saw that the quantity of such letters was beginning to get on the admiral's nerves, he passed on only a few of them, and he, Mercer, and other volunteers answered the rest.

A nation shocked by the cost in lives of the brief Gilberts campaign could not be reconciled by pointing out that it was not nearly so costly as the six-month Guadalcanal campaign had been, yet it achieved comparable advantages: the bases acquired safeguarded vital Allied lines of communication and provided airfields for bombing and photographing the next objective. To those within the services who, like General Holland Smith, began to argue that Tarawa should have been bypassed, the answer was obvious: if the lessons of amphibious assault had not been learned at Tarawa, they would have to be learned elsewhere, probably at greater cost.

General Richardson had his own explanation for the heavy casualties at Tarawa. It was that the marines had been in command and they, clearly, were not competent to direct such operations. He put his conclusions into a memorandum to Admiral Nimitz, which also recommended that the V Amphibious Corps be replaced by an army corps that would be in command of all army and marine operations in the Central Pacific and would, of course, be under Richardson's own control. Nimitz disregarded the recommendation.

Spruance, Turner, and Holland Smith, made cautious by the heavy casualties at Tarawa, reviewed the plans for their forthcoming assault on the Marshalls. They concluded that they did not have enough amphibious troops and support for the proposed simultaneous assaults on the atolls of Wotje, Maloelap, and Kwajalein. Consequently, they advocated a two-step campaign, first capturing Wotje and Maloelap, which lay between Kwajalein and Pearl Harbor, and then using the bomber strips on those atolls to support a subsequent assault on Kwajalein, the Japanese headquarters at the heart of the archipelago.

Immediately following the Gilberts operation, Admiral Pownall with two carrier groups had raided and photographed Wotje and Kwajalein. The evidence thus obtained revealed growing enemy power on the latter and reinforced the argument of Spruance, Turner, and Smith that the Marshall Island objectives should be taken in two bites. The pictures showed that, in addition to the airfield on Roi Island, at the northern end of Kwajalein Atoll, the Japanese were building a second field on Kwajalein Island at the southern end.

Admiral Nimitz concurred in canceling the triple attack, but he had devised a different alternative. The Joint Chiefs of Staff had ordered him, upon completion of the Marshalls assault, to send his fast carriers to the South Pacific to support Halsey's amphibious operations. Nimitz, therefore, in consultation with McMorris and Forrest Sherman, decided to bypass Wotje and Maloelap and assault Kwajalein alone. The capture of that atoll would yield him two airfields and a first-rate anchorage. Sherman assured Nimitz that before the assault the carriers would be able to knock out the airfields on the surrounding atolls and that afterward aircraft from the Kwajalein fields and from the Gilberts could keep them pounded down.

Spruance, unimpressed with Sherman's assurances, was shocked at Nimitz's plan. He had no doubt that he could take Kwajalein, but he wondered whether he would be able to hold on to it after the carriers had been withdrawn. To him the surrounding airfields constituted a first-class menace, and those on Wotje and Maloelap would be athwart the supply line from Pearl Harbor. All these fields could be endlessly supplied with aircraft staging out of Japan through the Marianas, the Carolines, and Eniwetok, the westernmost atoll of the Marshalls.

Spruance tried to convince Nimitz that if any objective was to be omitted it had better be Kwajalein, not the outer islands, and Turner and Smith supported him. Nimitz refused to be persuaded. His decision was confirmed by new radio intelligence showing that the Japanese were strengthening their outer islands at the expense of Kwajalein. Evidently it was against one or more of the outer islands that the enemy expected the attack to come.

At last, at a meeting on December 14, Admiral Nimitz polled the Fifth Fleet flag and general officers concerning where they should hit.

"Raymond," he asked, "what do you think now?"

"Outer islands," replied Spruance.

"Kelly?"

"Outer islands," replied Turner.

"Holland?"

"Outer islands," replied Smith.

And so it went around the room, every one of the commanders recommending an initial assault on the outer islands of Wotje and Maloelap. When the poll was completed, there was a brief silence. Then Nimitz said quietly, "Well, gentlemen, our next objective will be Kwajalein."

When the meeting was adjourned, Turner and Spruance stayed behind to argue some more. Turner insisted to Nimitz that the decision to go straight in to Kwajalein was dangerous and reckless. He argued and argued. He raised his voice. Spruance asserted that Kelly was right.

When Ray and Kelly had exhausted their arguments, Nimitz said calmly, "This is it. If you don't want to do it, the Department will find someone else to do it. Do you want to do it or not?"

Kelly Turner frowned for a moment, then relaxed his knitted brows and smiled: "Sure I want to do it."

Subsequently Carl Moore came up with an idea that was acceptable to all: the occupation, concurrently with the assault on Kwajalein, of Majuro, an atoll in the Marshalls which radio intelligence revealed to be very lightly held, if at all. This atoll would provide a large lagoon that could be used as an anchorage and, on the surrounding islands, there was space for airfields within supporting range of Kwajalein.

The photographs that Baldy Pownall brought back from the Marshalls showed more than enemy airfields and installations. They revealed also that at Kwajalein there was a large number of Japanese long-range bombers that the American carrier planes had not hit. Pownall had planned to launch two strikes against Kwajalein, but he changed his mind after the first. When he learned from his aviators that there were numerous undamaged planes still on the atoll, he decided to make a run for it, away from the Marshalls—as if ships could outrun planes. That evening, in the moonlight, the neglected enemy bombers caught up with the fleeing fleet and one put a torpedo into the stern of the new carrier *Lexington*, which however was able to limp to Pearl Harbor.

In the carrier raids preceding Operation Galvanic, some officers had questioned Pownall's aggressiveness. His retreat from Kwajalein convinced most of them that he was not fitted for the top carrier command. Not the least vocal of these officers was Captain Joseph J. ("Jocko") Clark, skipper of the *Yorktown*, who assisted in the preparation of a "white paper" describing what had happened during the Marshalls raid and recommending more aggressive use of the carriers and more aggressive leadership at the top. Clark passed the paper to Admiral Towers, who concurred with its recommendations. To Admiral Forrest Sherman he showed one of the aerial photographs of Japanese ships and planes that the American carriers had missed at Kwajalein. Sherman gasped and called to Admiral McMorris in the adjoining office, "You want to see the fish that got away?"

On December 23 Nimitz called Towers, McMorris, and Sherman into conference to discuss the fast carrier command. Towers recommended that more vigorous use be made of the carriers and asked that Pownall be relieved by Rear Admiral Marc A. Mitscher, who at that time was Commander, Fleet Air, West Coast. Sherman, seconding Towers, pointed out that Mitscher was available and that his experience with naval aviation extended back to the *Langley*, the first American carrier.

McMorris, at Nimitz's suggestion, sounded out Spruance about the recommended relief. Spruance was opposed to it. Knowing only vaguely the fine points of carrier-group command, he had found nothing wrong with Pownall's handling of the carriers in Operation Galvanic. On the other hand, he had not been favorably impressed with Mitscher's conduct in the Battle of Midway. There Mitscher had commanded the *Hornet* and had achieved very little. Nimitz, taking into account the high standards of Mitscher's overall career, ordered him to Pearl Harbor anyway, without consulting Spruance.

After the morning conference of December 27, Nimitz asked Pownall, along with Spruance, Towers, McMorris, Sherman, and Vice Admiral John H. Newton, Deputy CinCPac, to remain behind. In a kindly but serious voice, he told Pownall that he was being criticized by his subordinates as being too cautious and, without revealing its source, he referred to the white paper that Clark had had a hand in preparing. Nimitz said he was disappointed with the results of the Kwajalein raid. In operating with carriers, he pointed out, one often had to take calculated risks in order to inflict maximum damage on the enemy. Pownall was so obviously distressed and dumbfounded that Nimitz softened his criticism by mentioning that Spruance had praised his performance in Operation Galvanic. Pownall attempted to defend his hasty departure from Kwajalein but without much success.

Admiral Halsey, who was pausing at Pearl en route to the States, concurred in the appointment of Mitscher. Final arrangements, however, had to await the forthcoming CominCh-CinCPac bimonthly conference, when Admiral King's opinion would be sought.

Admirals King, Nimitz, and Halsey met in San Francisco on January 3 and 4, 1944. A major task on their agenda was solving CinCPac's command problems, one of which arose out of Undersecretary of the Navy Forrestal's insistence that aviators, particularly Admiral Towers, be given more authority in the Pacific Ocean Areas. So far as the Pacific Fleet was concerned, that presented a difficulty, for many naval aviators had attained senior rank almost exclusively through aviation activities. Officers who had never had command at sea of anything larger than a minesweeper were now candidates for the command of capital ships and seagoing task forces.

King and Nimitz decided, by way of placating Forrestal, who himself had been a naval aviator in World War I, to appoint Admiral Towers Deputy CinCPac-CinCPOA. Thus, Towers would relieve Admiral Newton, who would go south as deputy to Halsey. They slated Admiral Pownall to succeed Towers as Commander, Air Forces, Pacific, a post that would be reduced to administrative and logistic duties, since Towers would carry his operational duties with him to his new command. Admiral Mitscher would relieve Pownall with the carriers, but only as senior carrier division commander. In this capacity, Mitscher would be in temporary command of the Fast Carrier Task Force. If he failed to measure up in the Marshalls operation, he could be quietly shunted aside from the overall carrier command. Since Mitscher had never commanded more than a single carrier, Pownall was to be Spruance's aviation adviser in the Marshalls operation.

In this new game of musical chairs everybody got some enhancement of dignity, if only on paper. Poor Pownall acquired a high-sounding title without inheriting the full authority his predecessor had wielded. As for Admiral Towers, he would have much preferred to command the carriers, but he could hardly complain, for he was not only chief representative of the naval aviators but also second in command to the Commander in Chief, Pacific Fleet and Pacific Ocean Areas.

King and Nimitz adopted the principle that all major commanders in the Pacific Fleet who were non-aviators must have aviators as their chiefs of staff or seconds in command, and all major commanders who were aviators must have surface officers in the second position. By this principle, Mitscher would have to have a surface officer as his chief of staff, and, after the Marianas operation, Spruance would be obliged to replace his hard-working friend and assistant, Carl Moore, with an aviator.

With the command questions settled, the discussion turned to operations. Halsey proposed to seize Green Islands, east of Rabaul, and then take Emirau Island, to the northwest, while MacArthur invaded the Admiralty Islands, to the west. By these conquests the Allies would have completely surrounded Rabaul and the nearby Japanese base at Kavieng, both of which could then be kept pounded down and neutralized by air attacks. It would not be necessary to invade either.

In that case, said Nimitz, CinCPac need not send his fast carriers to the support of Halsey. Instead he would send Spruance with the fast carriers and new battleships to attack Truk, destroy or force out the Combined Fleet, and make Truk as useless to the Japanese as Rabaul and Kavieng would be. King, pleased with the concept, said that submarines should be stationed in the waters off Truk ready to torpedo enemy ships fleeing from the carrier attack.

King, as at earlier conferences, emphasized that the key to the western Pacific was the Marianas. Through or alongside these islands flowed supplies, munitions, and planes to the Carolines and, from there, to the Marshalls, the Bismarcks, and New Guinea. American seizure of the major Marianas and the establishment there of submarine and air bases could materially diminish the flow and thus dry up the Carolines and the bases beyond. The Army Air Forces wanted Saipan, Tinian, and Guam, in the Marianas, for bases from which their new, long-range B-29 bombers would be able to raid Japan, but King regarded this objective as decidedly secondary to cutting Japan's southbound communications.

All current operations, King pointed out, were also part of a drive to the China coast to exploit China's manpower and to obtain bases for the bombing and eventual invasion of Japan. En route the Americans would seize a position, Luzon or Formosa, from which they would be able to block Japan's northbound communications and prevent the oil and raw materials of the East Indies area from reaching the home islands.

Plans for the assault on the Marshalls, code-named Operation Flintlock, were taking final form. D-day, twice unavoidably postponed, was set finally for January 31. As in Operation Galvanic, Admiral Spruance would command the Fifth Fleet and Admiral Turner would command the amphibious force. Admiral Hill, in the attack transport *Cambria*, was to direct the occupation of Majuro by one battalion landing team of the 27th Division. Rear Admiral Richard L. Conolly, in one of the new amphibious command ships, the AGC *Appalachian*, would command the Northern Attack Force in its assaults on Roi and the adjacent island of Namur. Assigned for these targets was the newly organized 4th Marine Division, led by Major General Harry Schmidt,

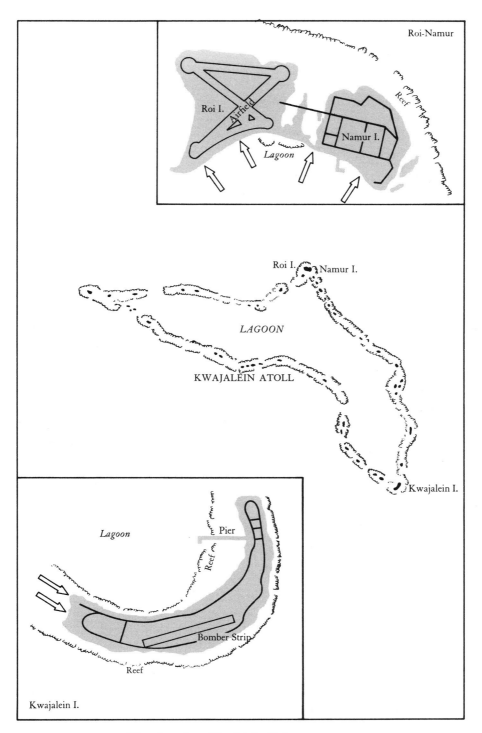

Roi-Namur

Roi I.

Airfield

Lagoon

Namur I.

Reef

Roi I. Namur I.

*LAGOON*

KWAJALEIN ATOLL

Kwajalein I.

*Lagoon*

Pier

Reef

Bomber Strip

Reef

Kwajalein I.

*The Assault on Kwajalein, February 1, 1944*

USMC. Across Kwajalein Lagoon, 40 miles to the south, Admiral Turner, in the AGC *Rocky Mount,* would command the Southern Attack Force's assault on Kwajalein Island. The ground force for this assault was the 7th Infantry Division, veterans of Attu, headed now by Major General Charles H. Corlett, USA. The corps reserve, a regiment of marines and two more battalion landing teams of the 27th Division, was to stand by during the assault on Kwajalein Atoll. If they were not needed there, they were to proceed, under Admiral Hill, to take Eniwetok.

General Holland Smith's name, to his intense irritation, was simply left out of the CinCPac directive for Flintlock. Shortly before Galvanic, Smith found that his name had disappeared from the directive for that operation and learned that it was Admiral McMorris who had removed it. It is a fairly safe guess that it was the chief of staff who had done the same thing to the Flintlock directive. McMorris's reasoning is not hard to follow: since the two participating divisions in each of the operations were too far apart for coordination, and each had its own commanding general at the scene, there seemed no particular point in having a corps commander present.

Each time Smith found his name removed, he complained loudly to Spruance, who saw to it that his name was put back into both directives. For Flintlock, as for Galvanic, Smith, with his staff, was assigned to Turner's flagship. General Corlett also rode in the *Rocky Mount,* and it was rumored that Corlett threatened to put General Smith under arrest if he went ashore at Kwajalein and interfered. Corlett may have been joking, but the fact is that Holland Smith remained afloat throughout Operation Flintlock.

It took a good deal of presumption for the chief of staff to change a CinCPac directive, but presumption was what McMorris had in abundance. It grew out of a blend of rigor and well-justified self-confidence. McMorris had the reputation of being one of the brainiest officers in the Navy, the ugliest, and maybe the harshest. Once when he flatly refused an Army colonel's request for a Navy jeep, the colonel demanded to know why. "Because," replied McMorris, "I'm a born sonofabitch and I'm going to stay one."

It was fortunate that Admiral Nimitz had McMorris to handle the big, heterogeneous CinCPac staff of 1944. Spruance was perfect for the small, all-Navy staff of 1942, but he was perhaps too much of a gentleman to deal with the crowd of officers who eventually came to roost on Makalapa Hill. He could be the scourge of a distant and faceless enemy, and, excellent administrator that he was, he could be severe when necessary, but severity he exercised chiefly by proxy. Knocking heads together was not his line.

Admiral McMorris saw himself as the principal buffer for his commander in chief, shielding Nimitz from routine matters and, indeed, from anything else that he could handle himself, and he took it on himself to handle a great deal—more, some said, than he had the authority to handle. So many communications sent up the chain of command to Nimitz were stopped by the chief of staff that the latter's office became known as Bottleneck Bay. Nimitz, far from resenting McMorris's presumption, called it initiative and appreciated the fact that it relieved him of many burdens. He did, however, suggest to key staff officers that when they felt strongly that a memorandum should be brought to CinCPac's personal attention, they might pass the original directly to him and send the copy through channels.

Planning for Operation Flintlock brought the aviators and amphibians once more into conflict. Admiral Towers, spokesman for the former, did not share the extremists' view that the carrier forces should be allowed to roam freely, with no other responsibility than to raid Japanese bases until the enemy fleet came out and offered itself for destruction, thus paving the way for Japan's final defeat. Admiral Spruance, for his part, did not believe that the carriers' one and only function was the close support of amphibious operations. Still, the differences between the two men were substantial. Each learned from the other, but, unfortunately, in reaching a meeting of minds, they developed a real antipathy for each other. Each regarded the other as a strategic amateur, and Spruance came to think of Towers as a self-serving opportunist. "If you were not an admirer of Towers and did not play on his team," Spruance once wrote, "your path was not made smooth if he could help it.... Towers was a very ambitious man."

The record is not complete, but it appears that Admiral Nimitz remained above the dispute. The final operation plan had to have his approval, but so far as possible he followed the sound rule of telling his subordinates *where* and *when* to operate, but never *how*.

Two weeks before Operation Flintlock Admiral Nimitz staged his famous Texas picnic in Honolulu's largest park. All Texans in uniform were invited and it is estimated that some 40,000 soldiers, sailors, and marines showed up. What started as a little friendly socializing turned into a Texas-size, that is to say gargantuan, beer bust. There was a ruinous overrunning of flower beds and a widespread scattering of lunch baskets, C-ration cans, leis, and, as the afternoon and the beer warmed up, khaki shirts. This one-day revolt against military decorum left the park in a state of devastation like the aftermath of a typhoon. The Honolulu police retrieved 120,000 bottles and quantities of other debris from the grass and shrubbery.

Brigadier General S. L. A. Marshall has left us a description of Admiral Nimitz's participation in the affair:

> Nimitz, the Tall Texan among them all, came striding into this scene in mid-afternoon, followed by a few members of his staff. Apace with him, but separated by about 30 yards, was my old friend, General Robert C. Richardson, Army Commander of the Central Pacific Area, followed by members of his staff.
>
> As one man, the soldiers in this melee quit whatever they were doing to form behind Admiral Nimitz and march the length of the park, forward and then back again, whooping it up like a pack of Comanches. They had nothing against General Richardson, who was an able and considerate leader; it was

simply that they loved Nimitz more. Amid the vast disorder, Nimitz was not only fully at ease, but enjoying himself hugely, laughing, waving to all hands, and submitting to the few autograph hunters in the crowd while moving at a pace that nearly winded the merry mob.

On the eve of the departure of the Fifth Fleet for Operation Flintlock, Undersecretary Forrestal went out to Pearl to have a look. As procurement chief, he must have been gratified to see how tremendously the fleet had grown since his last visit. It had expanded even since the Gilberts operation.

After Forrestal had viewed the Fast Carrier Task Force, now designated Task Force 58, and the Southern Attack Force, both of which were at Pearl Harbor and Honolulu, Admiral Nimitz conducted him by destroyer over to Lahaina Roads, off the island of Maui, to have a look at the Northern Attack Force, which had arrived the day before from San Diego.

As they approached the roadstead, the young commander who was skipper of the destroyer asked Commander Lamar to find out what the admiral would like to do. Nimitz replied that he wished to pass up and down the row of anchored transports and supply ships. The destroyer captain made his run along the line a little too fast, so that his wake caused the anchored ships to rock. The flagship of the transport squadron flashed a scolding message: "I do not like your sea manners." When Nimitz was shown the message, he smiled and asked the skipper to break his four-starred flag at the peak. When this was done, the commodore of the squadron sent a prompt apology. Nimitz was not mollified. The commodore's nasty message amounted to a public reprimand of a fellow officer. Nimitz decided to see what sort of flagship that sort of officer would maintain. At Nimitz's order, the destroyer stopped and he and the Undersecretary, accompanied by their aides, went over in a small boat to inspect the transport.

The young ensign who was the officer of the deck did not realize that the Undersecretary of the Navy and the Commander in Chief of the fleet were coming to make a call. Lamar and the aide assigned Mr. Forrestal tried to make him understand, holding up eight fingers and shouting "Undersecretary" and "Fleet." It was all to no avail. The party arrived at the gangway and was given no recognition whatever. When the admiral reached the quarterdeck and found neither the commodore nor the captain there to greet his party, he was indignant. The Undersecretary did not quite grasp the situation, but he could see that something was very wrong indeed.

Presently the commodore and the captain appeared, red-faced and out of breath, still putting on their uniforms, evidently having been aroused from an afternoon nap. Admiral Nimitz inspected the ship, found things in considerable disarray, and made an appropriate report to the task force commander.

Ships of the mighty Fifth Fleet, which sailors were beginning to call the big blue fleet, were so packed into Pearl Harbor that it appeared almost paved with steel. In the night of January 22, 1944, the ships sailed away for the

Marshalls and Operation Flintlock. The next morning, Admiral Nimitz, at his headquarters on Makalapa Hill, looked down on a harbor that was nearly empty. Task Force 58, the fast carriers and their numerous escorts, did not return to Pearl Harbor until the end of the war. Individual ships, chiefly those requiring extensive repair, came back, but the task force as a whole remained at sea where it was supplied, fueled, and otherwise serviced by the mobile service squadrons.

Since early January the 475 planes of Admiral Johnny Hoover's Defense and Shore-Based Air Force, operating mainly from the Gilberts, had been pounding the Marshalls. Photoreconnaissance showed that the invasion targets, Roi-Namur and Kwajalein Island in Kwajalein Atoll, were not nearly so heavily fortified as Betio had been, yet they received far more bombing.

Spruance's Fifth Fleet heading for the Marshalls comprised 375 ships carrying 53,000 assault troops—of whom half were soldiers and half were marines—and 31,000 garrison personnel. Mitscher's Task Force 58 consisted of 6 fleet carriers, 6 light carriers, 8 fast battleships, 6 cruisers, 36 destroyers, and 700 carrier aircraft. It was a far more powerful array of force than had been sent against the Gilberts, but this time Admiral Towers said nothing about Spruance wanting a sledgehammer to drive a tack.

According to the carefully worked-out schedule, Task Force 58 was to reach the Marshalls on January 29. While Hoover's aircraft were neutralizing the airfields on the atolls of Jaluit and Mili, nearest the Gilberts, one carrier group would strike the field on Wotje, another would attack that on Maloelap, and the other two would attack Kwajalein. That night the Task Force's gunnery ships were to move in and bombard the airfields to prevent the Japanese from flying planes in from Eniwetok. On the 30th one carrier group would cover both Wotje and Maloelap, two would work over defense installations at Kwajalein, and one would move out and strike Eniwetok to destroy any aircraft banked up there.

The Northern and Southern Attack Forces were due at the Marshalls on January 30 to begin a three-day bombardment of the target islands, each of which, it was estimated, would be pounded with four times the weight of bombs and shells that had been hurled against Betio. On the 31st a force under Admiral Hill was scheduled to occupy Majuro, and forces under Turner and Conolly would land on islets adjacent to the main targets and site artillery there to cover landings. D-day for Roi, Namur, and Kwajalein was February 1.

During the passage of the fleet to the Marshalls, there was doubtless a good deal of nail-biting at CinCPac headquarters. Had the Pacific Fleet really absorbed and profited by the lessons of Tarawa, or were the soldiers and marines in for more bloody Betios?

The news when it came in was all good. At 9:50 a.m. on January 31, Hill notified Spruance that Majuro had been secured. Somewhat later Turner and Conolly reported that the islets were captured, "Casualties few." In the afternoon of February 1, Turner reported to Spruance that the 7th Division was on

Kwajalein Island. "Troops landed on schedule Beaches Red 1 and 2 after adequate bombing and bombardment by ship and shore artillery," his intercepted message read. "No opposition at beach. Troops advanced rapidly eastward against slight opposition."

Conolly's reports were even more favorable. The 4th Marine Division had gone ashore against little or no opposition, and by the end of D-day had captured Roi Island, which consisted of little more than an airfield. The more heavily built-up Namur they had secured by the following afternoon.

Before nightfall on February 4, Turner announced that all effective resistance on Kwajalein Island had ended. The slower rate of that conquest did not reflect any ineptitude on the part of the soldiers; they were delayed by the fact that beach conditions required them to land at one end of the narrow island. Thus they had to advance its entire length.

The 7th Division was slowed also by the continental-style warfare favored by some army commanders. They advanced under a barrage, repeatedly pausing until the enemy had been forced back by artillery. The marines, on the other hand, advanced if possible on the run in order to keep the enemy off balance and prevent him from digging in. They bypassed isolated pockets of resistance, leaving them for the rear echelons to clear up. Such tactics, they believed, were particularly suitable for fighting on small islands where there was little danger of physical exhaustion or of outrunning supply. The greatest advantage of this marine-style fighting was that it speedily released the supporting fleet from dangerous waters.

Army tacticians pointed out that bypassing pockets of resistance was an excellent way to get shot in the back, to which the marines replied that their method cost fewer casualties than the deliberate army advance. In fact, at Kwajalein the marines suffered 196 killed and about 550 wounded; the soldiers, 177 killed and nearly 1,000 wounded. By comparison, of the roughly 8,000-man occupation force in the islands at the beginning of the air raids, 100 Japanese and 165 Korean laborers were captured, and the rest were killed.

All hands agreed that Operation Flintlock was as nearly perfect an amphibious assault as could possibly be carried out, and that it should serve as a model for future assaults. Clearly, the lessons of Tarawa had been learned and properly acted upon. Everyone was pleased with the support provided by the eight escort carriers attached to the attack forces. Their success assured greater freedom in the future for the fast carriers. Majuro Lagoon proved to be the ideal anchorage for a floating base. Into the lagoon, soon after Majuro was captured, came Service Squadron 10 to service the fleet. An invaluable dividend of Operation Flintlock was the discovery on Kwajalein of a batch of hydrographic charts of all the islands the Japanese were occupying.

Even before Kwajalein had been secured, Nimitz radioed Spruance asking what he thought about going ahead with the capture of Eniwetok. Spruance found both Turner and Holland Smith ready to go. He so informed Nimitz, who sent back an order to proceed with the assault.

That evening, February 4, Admiral Nimitz departed Pearl Harbor for Tarawa in a B-24 Liberator. Accompanying him were members of his staff, including Captain Thomas C. Anderson, who had replaced Dr. Gendreau as fleet surgeon and also as Nimitz's housemate. Nimitz, as on his previous trip to the Gilberts, amused himself by playing cribbage with Jack Redman. He had become the owner of a new cribbage board, of blue-tinted lucite, made as a gift for him by the Seabees, who also had provided a carrying case for it. Redman didn't especially try to win; he thought it might even be poor policy to win from the boss, but he had a winning streak and ran up a big score at a penny a point. In one game he double-skunked the admiral for four dollars. Nimitz, who prided himself on his skill at cribbage, was noticeably shaken.

Finally, the admiral said it was time to turn in. Unable to find his cribbage-board carrying case, he asked Redman to put the board in his own overnight bag. When Redman opened the bag, Nimitz saw and admired a hunting knife that lay on top.

"Would you like it, Admiral?" said Redman. "There's plenty of them around. I'll get another one."

"Oh, no," replied Nimitz. "I wouldn't take yours."

Nimitz and Redman then lay down in their clothes, as most of the others in the cabin had already done, and pulled blankets over themselves. The next morning at about seven o'clock they landed at Hawkins Field, the old Japanese airstrip on Betio, which had been extended and renamed for a marine officer killed at Tarawa.

Nimitz was much gratified at the striking recovery of the island that he had last seen in a state of devastation. Except for the damaged palm trees, there was little to show that the grimmest of battles had been fought there a few weeks before. The Seabees had done their work well. Nimitz conferred with Admiral Hoover and General Hale, and that night he and his party got a good night's sleep in the tender *Curtiss*, Hoover's flagship, which had earlier served Admiral Fitch.

The next day Nimitz and party took off in a seaplane for Kwajalein, flying over Makin en route in order to observe Starmann Field, the new bomber strip on Butaritari. As the seaplane passed over Kwajalein Island, the passengers looked down in wonder. Every tree seemed to have been stripped away, and only the foundations of buildings, blockhouses, and pillboxes could be seen. Absolutely nothing appeared to be left standing.

The plane landed in the lagoon. When Nimitz went ashore he was immediately accosted by correspondents.

"What do you think of the island?" was the first question asked.

"Gentlemen," replied Nimitz, "it's the worst scene of devastation I have ever witnessed—except for the Texas picnic."

The size of Kwajalein Atoll, the largest atoll in the world, was impressed upon Nimitz when, during this visit, he traveled from Kwajalein Island to Namur Island by destroyer. Making better than 20 knots, the destroyer took two hours to cross the lagoon. The northern islands, Roi and Namur, joined by a strip of beach and also by a causeway, Nimitz found as utterly devastated as the southern island. Apparently the Fifth Fleet had discovered the way to prepare for an amphibious assault.

Spruance and Turner had nothing but praise for the way Admiral Mitscher had handled Task Force 58. Its greatest achievements were destroying every plane in the Marshalls and keeping the airfield on Eniwetok so churned up that no planes could be ferried through that way station.

Nimitz talked with his commanders about the forthcoming assault on Eniwetok. Admiral Hill, as has been noted, was to command the amphibious force, and Brigadier General Thomas E. Watson, USMC, would command the 8,000 assault troops, the reserve that had not been committed at Kwajalein. Since Eniwetok was only 669 miles from Truk, Task Force 58 would support the assault in two ways. One of its task groups would stand by the atoll to give direct support, while the other three steamed away to raid Truk. It was hoped that the threat to Truk would force the Combined Fleet to come out and fight. Spruance, with nine carriers and six battleships, had no doubt he could defeat anything the Japanese could send against him. Lastly, if practicable, part of Task Force 58 was to make a run to the southern Marianas. Its planes would bomb these islands, of course, and destroy as many aircraft as possible, but their main purpose would be to photograph the next objectives of the Central Pacific drive—Saipan, Tinian, and Guam.

Having much to discuss with his staff, Nimitz found no time for cribbage on the journey back to Pearl. When he and Redman arrived by car at their quarters, which happened to be next door to each other, Nimitz called out, "Redman, send over my cribbage board with your bill."

Redman did so, and the next day a marine orderly came to his office and laid $6.25 on his desk.

"What's that?" asked Redman.

"Admiral Nimitz told me to give this to you."

CinCPac was paying his cribbage bill.

Redman, feeling a little embarrassed about "taking" the boss for that much, thought of his hunting knife that Nimitz had admired. Having been told that similar knives could be bought in Pearl Harbor, he sent out for one, which turned out not to be exactly like the one he had carried to Kwajalein.

Later in the day, in answer to a summons, Redman went to Nimitz's office, taking both knives with him. After they had discussed the official problem, Redman said, "Admiral, you admired that knife I had in my bag the other night. Here's two of them, and you can have either one. It doesn't make a bit of difference. There's no sentiment attached to mine, so far as I'm concerned."

"No, I wouldn't take yours," said Nimitz. "I'll take the other one." After a moment, he added, "Where did you get this?"

Redman's hesitation gave him away. "You bought it, didn't you?"

"But it didn't cost anything, Admiral. Please accept it from me." At that point the jovial Redman saw an opening he couldn't resist. "Anyway," he added, "I'll get it back at cribbage."

"You get the hell out of my office," said Nimitz, his eyes twinkling with mirth.

As February 16 (west longitude date), the day of the assault on Eniwetok and the opening attack on Truk, approached, there was little of the nervousness at CinCPac headquarters that had preceded the assaults on the Gilberts and Kwajalein. Hope of destroying the Combined Fleet, however, had begun to fade. On February 4 a Marine Corps B-24 from Bougainville had snooped the Truk anchorage and observed plenty of targets afloat, but subsequent traffic analysis indicated that the Combined Fleet was abandoning Truk and pulling back to the Palau Islands, westernmost of the Carolines. The fact was that Admiral Mineichi Koga, Yamamoto's successor, felt uneasy when the Americans invaded Kwajalein, and, alerted by the snooper, he had begun to withdraw westward.

Typically, Admiral Hill kept CinCPac well informed of the operations at Eniwetok, while Admiral Spruance made no report at all concerning his raid on Truk until it had been completed and the results carefully assessed. Most of the information CinCPac received about Truk on February 16, 17, and 18 came from the enemy. Japanese headquarters on the atoll sent out a stream of encoded reports and FRUPac read them. Truk reported that a U.S. carrier group had been sighted to the northeast, that U.S. carrier planes had attacked, and that a detached surface force that included battleships and heavy cruisers had approached the atoll and taken Japanese surface units under fire. At nightfall on the 16th, Truk reported one of its cruisers afire, five destroyers damaged, and three freighters sunk.

Later that evening the cruiser *San Francisco* notified Admiral Turner, with CinCPac as information addressee, that the carrier *Intrepid* had just been damaged by a Japanese torpedo plane.

At 8:30 p.m. on the 17th, Admiral Lockwood broadcast a cautious report to his submarines, ten of which were operating off Truk: "With the big show still continuing today no box scores have been received from Truk stadium. However all indications appear optimistic." The CinCPac Command Summary noted: "Although reports from our task force are lacking, intelligence sources indicate that the carrier air strikes on Truk were continuing on the 17th according to schedule. Considerably less reaction on the enemy's part was noted, suggesting the probable expenditure of the majority of his air strength, including available trained reinforcements."

At last, on February 19, Admiral Spruance made his accounting. Skeptical of aviators' reports, he understated his force's achievements. The raid actually sank 15 naval vessels, including 2 light cruisers and 4 destroyers, sent 19 cargo vessels and 5 tankers to the bottom, and destroyed about 200 enemy aircraft. On the 16th Spruance had detached 2 battleships, 2 heavy cruisers, and 4 destroyers and led them around the atoll in a counterclockwise sweep in which they sank a cruiser and a destroyer, both of which had been damaged by planes and were escaping through the reef. They also sank a cargo vessel and a submarine chaser.

Admiral Mitscher led two carrier groups toward the southern Marianas, deep in Japanese territory, 1,500 miles from Tokyo. Having been detected on the approach, the groups became the targets of a series of night air attacks. By use of radar and proximity-fuzed ammunition, they took a heavy toll of the attacking planes, while suffering no damage whatever to their ships. In attacks on Saipan, Tinian, and Guam on February 22, the carrier planes destroyed 168 enemy aircraft; Mitscher, as little given to overstatement as Spruance, reported 135. More important, the carrier planes fulfilled their primary mission by taking a batch of fine photographs for the operational planners to study.

Meanwhile Eniwetok Atoll had been secured. Because for this operation the Americans had only a 3-to-1 numerical advantage over the defenders (as compared to a 6-to-1 ratio at Kwajalein), the three occupied islands of the atoll had to be taken one at a time. It took the marines one day each to secure Engebi and Parry islands, but the Army became so bogged down on Eniwetok Island that a marine landing team had to be rushed in to take over the brunt of the fighting. The 27th Infantry Division, which provided the soldiers for Makin as well as for Eniwetok, was beginning to get a reputation for being poorly trained and poorly led.

Of all the Fifth Fleet's February exploits, the raid on Truk got the biggest headlines in most stateside newspapers. That is doubtless because of the exaggerated billing the atoll had been getting as "Impregnable Truk," "the Japanese Pearl Harbor," and "Gibraltar of the Pacific." Kate and Nancy Nimitz, much impressed by the news stories, cabled their father:

> Like Carrie Nation guzzling booze,
> When man runs over Truk, that's news.

While the assault on Kwajalein was still in progress, Admiral Nimitz sent a dispatch to Admiral King which said, in part: "In view of the marked capabilities and devotion to duty of Rear Admiral Richmond Kelly Turner, his proficiency in amphibious operations as demonstrated in the South Pacific, the Gilberts, and currently at Kwajalein, I recommend his immediate promotion to the grade of vice admiral."

Admiral King radioed back, "What are your views about also promoting Spruance, which seems fitting to me?"

Nimitz replied immediately, "Yes."

Spruance's promotion to four-star admiral met with no opposition. It was confirmed by the Senate on February 16, 1944, to date from February 4. Turner's promotion ran into some difficulty in the Senate: the Savo Island defeat and the heavy casualties at Tarawa were mentioned. Nevertheless, he was confirmed as vice admiral on March 7. One week later Holland Smith was promoted to lieutenant general. On March 21 Marc Mitscher became vice admiral and was appointed Commander, Fast Carrier Forces, Pacific Fleet.

# CHAPTER 18

# LEAP TO THE MARIANAS

AT THE END of 1943 the concept of a dual Allied advance across the Pacific was firmly established. It had the blessing of the Combined Chiefs of Staff, of President Roosevelt, and of Prime Minister Churchill. This strategy would require General MacArthur's Southwest Pacific force to proceed along the northern coast of New Guinea and enter the Philippines at the southern island of Mindanao—a line of advance that MacArthur called the New Guinea-Mindanao Axis. Admiral Nimitz's Central Pacific force, the Fifth Fleet, was to take the Marshalls, Truk, and possibly another of the Caroline Islands, and Saipan, Tinian, and Guam in the southern Marianas. Both lines of advance would converge on the Luzon-Formosa-China triangle, from which Japan could be bombed, blockaded, and, if necessary, invaded. If the Marshalls invasion and a subsequent raid on Truk demonstrated the capacity of carriers to support and carry out such operations, then the Fifth Fleet might bypass the central Carolines and make the thousand-mile leap from the Marshalls straight to the Marianas. Admiral King, as we have seen, wanted the Marianas taken mainly in order to block southward-flowing Japanese supplies and reinforcements.

General MacArthur had not strongly objected to the proposed invasions of the Gilberts and Marshalls because these assaults would remove a threat to his communications with the United States and also engage hostile forces that might otherwise be used against his Southwest Pacific operations. Any further advance along the Central Pacific Axis, however, he sharply opposed, for he believed that an approach to Japan without land-based air support would prove costly in men, ships, and planes, and might well be defeated. Moreover, the inevitable buildup of Nimitz's force at the center would withhold supplies from his own force and thus slow down his movement across the south. Indeed, should the drive at the center pick up momentum, it might render MacArthur's roundabout advance via New Guinea and the Philippines superfluous. He therefore began a campaign to divert the direct advance of the Central Pacific force and make it merely supportive of his own offensive.

The bloody battle for Tarawa confirmed MacArthur in his objections to the Central Pacific drive and also gave him the ammunition he wanted. He promptly dispatched General Sutherland to the Joint Chiefs, in Washington, to urge that Nimitz, after taking the Marshalls, be directed to abandon his central drive and switch his Central Pacific force southward to support MacArthur in his advance to Mindanao.

When the Joint Chiefs rejected MacArthur's suggestion, the general decided that he had no recourse but to bypass them. His opportunity came in mid-January 1944 when Brigadier General Frederick H. Osborn, of the War Department staff, visited the Southwest Pacific Area. MacArthur handed Osborn a statement of his views, and asked him to bring them to the attention of Secretary of War Stimson and, through him, of the President. In his statement, MacArthur pointed out what he considered the advantages of his own strategy in bypassing and bottling up the enemy and in saving lives. He said that, using such means, he confidently planned to have his own forces in Mindanao by the end of the year, provided he was given control of the ships, men, and equipment in the Pacific. He continued:

> I need only that; what is now in the Pacific is sufficient if properly directed. . . . I do not want command of the Navy, but must control their strategy, be able to call on what little of the Navy is needed for the trek to the Philippines. The Navy's turn will come after that. These frontal attacks by the Navy, as at Tarawa, are tragic and unnecessary massacres of American lives. . . . The Navy fails to understand the strategy of the Pacific, fails to recognize that the first phase is an Army phase to establish land-based air protection so the Navy can move in. . . . Mr. Roosevelt is Navy minded. Mr. Stimson must speak to him, must persuade him. Give me central direction of the war in the Pacific, and I will be in the Philippines in ten months. . . . Don't let the Navy's pride of position and ignorance continue this great tragedy to our country.

Admiral Nimitz had invited senior officers of the Pacific theater to meet at Pearl Harbor on January 27 and 28, 1944, to discuss strategy. He expected to head his own delegation, which would include Admirals McMorris, Forrest Sherman, Towers, and Calhoun, and General Richardson. Admiral Halsey, who was detained in the United States, was to be represented by his chief of staff, Admiral Carney, and his army commander, General Harmon. General MacArthur planned to send his chief of staff, General Sutherland; his air force commander, General Kenney; and his naval commander, Admiral Kinkaid. MacArthur's delegation was prepared to argue for a single line of advance, via New Guinea and the Philippines.

Admiral Nimitz was himself inclining toward the single-line strategy. This change of view resulted in part from the shock of the heavy American losses at Tarawa. He had not opposed the forthcoming assault on the Marshalls, because these small islands with their bomber fields had to be taken, or the nearby Gilberts would be untenable. Conquering them would no doubt present about the same problems that invading the Gilberts had presented. Conquering the big, rugged islands of the southern Marianas, however, would probably be much more difficult and costly. The Marianas were far beyond the range of Allied land-based air support. If it had cost a thousand lives to take flat, two-

mile-long Betio with land-based air support, what might it cost to take moun-
tainous, twenty-five-mile-long Guam without such support?

Nimitz's staff also was questioning the advisability of seizing the southern
Marianas. Admiral Towers had sent Nimitz a memorandum opposing the
Marianas operation because of their vulnerability to air attack from Japan. He
pointed out that the Japanese, who had airfields on Iwo Jima and Chichi Jima,
halfway between Japan and the southern Marianas, could attack the latter with
medium bombers accompanied by fighters. Bombing of Japan from the Marianas would be ineffective, he reasoned, because fighters would not be able to
accompany the bombers so far. He thought that without protection the bombers would be obliged to bomb from such altitudes that precision would be
impossible. He recommended that the Pacific Fleet bypass all the Central
Pacific islands, most of which were heavily defended, and proceed via the
Admiralties, the Palaus, and the Philippines. Thus, he agreed precisely with
what MacArthur had been recommending. Admirals McMorris and Forrest
Sherman endorsed the memorandum. Nimitz wrote "Concur" beside Mc-
Morris's endorsement and forwarded the recommendation to Admiral King.
He was thus proposing to abandon the concept of a Central Pacific offensive
that he had earlier espoused.

The strategy conference met on the 27th at Pearl Harbor, as scheduled.
In preliminary talks, Richardson and Kenney proposed pooling all forces for a
move along the New Guinea coast to the Philippines, and they easily won the
agreement of Towers, Sherman, and Carney to this concept. Calhoun said that
supply and construction would be much easier along the New Guinea route
than in going through the enemy-held island groups.

At the first formal meeting, Sutherland argued in favor of concentrating
all Allied resources in MacArthur's area. "If Central Pacific will move against
Palau in the next operation after the Marshalls," he said, "and make available
to the Southwest Pacific Area the amphibious force now contemplated for
Truk, we can take all of New Guinea, the Kai and Tanimbars, and Halmahera
in time to join you in amphibious movement to Mindanao this year."

Nobody spoke in favor of invading the Marianas. Kenney expressed the
opinion that bombing Japan with B-29s based on them would be "just a
stunt." McMorris doubted that such long-range bombing could make Japan
capitulate. Sherman pointed out that invading the Marianas would be costly
and that they could provide harbors of only limited usefulness. Kinkaid said
that "any talk of the Marianas for a base leaves me entirely cold."

Everyone agreed that the Philippines should be invaded and reoccupied,
and all except McMorris were in accord that the advance should be via New
Guinea and Palau. Supported by the unanimous opinion of the assembled
officers, whose judgment he respected, Nimitz stated that he would recommend
a single line of advance, along the New Guinea-Mindanao Axis. General Kenney wrote afterward, "The meeting finished with everyone feeling good and
ready to work together and get the war over." At a luncheon on the 28th,

following the conference, Admiral Nimitz "spoke about now seeing an end to the war." He appointed Admiral Sherman to go to Washington and present the opinions of the conferees to the Joint Chiefs of Staff.

General MacArthur was elated at the results of the conference. To General Marshall on February 2 he dispatched a message urging that, in accord with the conference opinions, all Pacific forces following the Marshalls operation be concentrated on his New Guinea-Mindanao Axis, the shortest and most direct route to the Philippines. He requested that all available B-29s be assigned to his Southwest Pacific Area and that all naval forces be placed under Admiral William F. Halsey as his Allied naval commander. He asked that the British be invited to assign to him any available Royal Navy task forces. Because speed was essential, he concluded, he was sending General Sutherland to Washington to present his requests.

What MacArthur was urging was a good deal more than the conference had contemplated. He was apparently intent on making himself the overall commander of the Pacific war against Japan. The outright transfer of forces he requested would have relegated Admiral Nimitz to a subordinate position. That the Joint Chiefs were not likely to consent to such a wholesale transfer of power in the midst of a war seems not to have occurred to him. When Halsey arrived in Brisbane, he found the general talking as if his requests had already been granted.

"I'll tell you something you may not know," said MacArthur. "They're going to send me a big piece of the fleet—put it absolutely at my disposal. And I'll tell you something else: the British are going to do the same. I want my naval operations to be in charge of an American. Whoever he is, he'll have to be senior enough to outrank the Britisher, or at least equal him. How about *you*, Bill? If you come with me, I'll make you a greater man than Nelson ever dreamed of being."

Halsey said he was flattered but was in no position to commit himself; however, he would certainly tell King and Nimitz about MacArthur's offer.

In Washington, Sherman and Sutherland, bearing the conference's opinions and MacArthur's requests, ran into a stone wall named King. In his opposition to bypassing the Marianas and assigning the B-29s, King was sturdily backed by General Arnold.

The complete success and relatively light losses of the Marshalls assault, which took place shortly after the Pearl Harbor strategy conference, were immensely cheering to Admiral Nimitz. He took another look at the map. The short, straight drive across the Pacific again began to look attractive to him, even though it might require conquest of the southern Marianas.

Before Nimitz could communicate his revised opinion to Admiral King, he received from the latter a stern letter. After congratulating the Pacific Fleet commander in chief for the happy outcome of the Marshalls operation, King got to his main subject. "I have read your conference notes with much interest," he wrote, "and I must add with indignant dismay." He continued:

Apparently, neither those who advocated the concentration of effort in the Southwest Pacific, nor those who admitted the possibility of such a procedure, gave thought nor undertook to state when and if the Japanese occupation and use of the Marianas and Carolines was to be terminated. I assume that even the Southwest Pacific advocates will admit that sometime or other this thorn in the side of our communications to the western Pacific must be removed. In other words, at some time or other we must take out time and forces to carry out this job. . . .

A number of conferees, particularly Towers, stated, and his statements were allowed to go unrefuted, that the object of taking the Marianas was to provide for B-29 bombing attack against the Japanese Empire. Of course, that was never the object. That was merely one of the results that would ensue from this operation, which was to be taken to dry up the Carolines, facilitating the capture or neutralization of the Carolines, and to speed up the clearing of the line of communications to the northern Philippine area. . . .

The idea of rolling up the Japanese along the New Guinea coast, throughout Halmahera and Mindanao, and up through the Philippines to Luzon, as our major strategic concept, to the exclusion of clearing our Central Pacific line of communications to the Philippines, is to me absurd. Further, it is not in accordance with the decisions of the Joint Chiefs of Staff. . . .

When Nimitz received this scolding letter, he was already planning his next move along the Central Pacific Axis, but it was to Truk, not the Marianas. It might be dangerous, Nimitz reasoned, to bypass this major fleet anchorage, leaving it in enemy hands. Possibly Truk might be neutralized, but to Nimitz it seemed desirable, if only for psychological reasons, that the American flag be raised over Japan's largest and most important naval base outside the home islands. Such a gesture, offsetting the raid on Pearl Harbor, would raise American spirits and correspondingly cast down those of the Japanese.

When Admiral King got wind of what Nimitz was planning, his ire was again aroused, because he had long since written off an assault on Truk. Also, intensely secretive and suspicious of the press, King thought that Nimitz was giving out too much information. He concluded that Nimitz had better come to Washington in order to achieve a meeting of minds with the Joint Chiefs of Staff concerning forthcoming operations. The timing of the visit would have to be carefully selected, because Admiral Towers was soon to be installed in his appointed post as Deputy CinCPac-CinCPOA and, consequently, would be acting Commander in Chief in Nimitz's absence. Neither King nor Nimitz wanted him to be in command when far-reaching decisions were to be made. King put these thoughts into a letter to Nimitz dated February 17, 1944, this time avoiding the wrathful tone of his previous letter:

Dear Nimitz:

I am sorry to say that the impression prevails here—rightly or wrongly— that you seriously contemplate taking Truk by assault. I am sure you will agree that we should not do so unless and until all other measures have been fully examined.

Personally, I feel that our best method is to occupy the Marianas-Palaus line which should have the effect of pinching off Truk, as was so well done in the case of Wotje, Maloelap, Mili.

I am aware of the "deficiences" of the Marianas as bases for the operating forces. However, the occupation of Eniwetok should enable close photo coverage of the Marianas to be made, to supplement the information made available by the capture of the up-to-date hydrographic charts—which was a fine windfall!*

Then there is the further measure—conveyed to you by despatch and orally via Forrest Sherman—of organizing for the quick development of sheltered-waters areas such as Apra Harbor (Guam) *plus* the use, perhaps, of artificial-harbor expedients such as are now in hand for the crossing-the-channel operation from England to France.

Further, with Eniwetok only about 1000 miles from Guam-Saipan, there will be available a good main advanced base which will tend to reduce the minimum requirements for the forward base (Guam-Saipan) to a "detachment" status.

*Another subject.* You may be surprised to know how widely you are quoted as the basis for comment and speculation as to what we are going to do next in the Pacific Ocean Areas. In fact, you said nothing much but what would be obvious to military men of high status—but—the use made of it has, I fear, verged on "giving aid and comfort to the enemy." You must watch your step in dealing with the press, etc.—basically, they care for nothing except their own "kudos"—or interpretation of news—that will enable them to peddle more papers! I am sorry to have to make mention of this matter, as there has been nothing but praise—perhaps too much!—from the press re the handling of releases during the progress of the Marshalls' operations. However, press and radio here can have left no doubt in the minds of the enemy that our next objectives were Eniwetok and Ponape.

I still contemplate having you come to Washington on your next trip to the mainland—timing will, of course, be premised on what you have in hand in POA, "complicated" by the fact that you will have to leave matters in the hands of the new deputy.

In the meantime, "remain cheerful"—and keep up the splendid work you are doing.

Sincerely yours,

King

Discussions among officers at CinCPac headquarters revealed that General Richardson was determined to get soldiers removed from Marine Corps control and army airmen from naval control. More specifically, he was intent on shooting down General Holland Smith and Admiral John Hoover. Having achieved no success in these aims with Admiral Nimitz, Richardson and his right-hand man, General Hale, decided to bypass CinCPac and take the matter to Washington. Nimitz on February 18, before receiving King's letter opposing the invasion of Truk, sent King a letter of warning:

* *See* page 274, above.

Dear King:

Lieutenant General Richardson and Major General Hale are about to leave for Washington for conferences in the War Department. I feel that you should be informed of certain matters that they may discuss with General Marshall and General Arnold and which may, therefore, be discussed with you during their visit.

Richardson has informed me that he proposes to organize an Army Corps under Major General Corlett who now commands the Seventh Army Division. He apparently visualizes use of such a corps in amphibious operations in the Central Pacific Campaign as an entity separate and distinct from the Fifth Amphibious Corps. I told him that the creation of a corps command for army purposes was an army matter to which I could interpose no objection, but that command arrangements for future operations would not be settled now.

I oppose the establishment now of another amphibious corps in the Central Pacific, and reserve the right to employ army divisions as components of the Fifth Amphibious Corps. If two or more army divisions are employed in a single operation such as the capture of Truk, the existence of an Army corps command may have some advantages, but I would insist on having all troops in the operation under one general officer who would, initially at least, be the Commanding General of the Fifth Amphibious Corps.

Richardson expressed the very emphatic view that if one general officer should command all five divisions that might be engaged at Truk it should be an Army officer; and that he would strongly protest both to CinCPOA and to General Marshall against a Marine officer exercising such command. The matter, however, was not further discussed at this time.

Richardson then proceeded to indict in a courteous manner, but in extremely positive terms, the competence of Holland Smith in particular, and of senior marine officers in general, to command large bodies of troops. He also alleged lack of discipline and superficial training among the Marines in this area. I invited him to submit his views to me in writing. He complains of the extent to which naval officers are in command in the forward area and expresses his opinion that all island commanders should be army officers.

Both Richardson and Hale may bring up the question of command of shore based air forces in the forward area. Richardson is critical of Hoover's methods in spite of our recent successes. Sherman brought me your pencilled notations on the papers shown you. He did not discuss the question in Washington outside your headquarters. I intend to defer any action and retain the present arrangements for the time being, at least until the CATCHPOLE [Eniwetok] operation is completed.

I propose to handle all the foregoing matters locally and bring them to your attention only as a precautionary measure in case they are broached in Washington. They are, for the most part, outcroppings from the clash of difficult personalities and will not be removed by changes in organization.

Although Richardson is frequently critical of naval or marine personnel organization and methods it is not to be inferred that our personal relationships do not continue friendly. We meet almost daily and he frequently gives verbal assurance of his wholehearted cooperation. He is encouraged to discuss any matter with me with great freedom and he does so. This final paragraph is added that you may not gain an impression of strained relationships between Richardson and myself; but will understand that the letter is solely to acquaint you in advance with certain of his views that may come to your attention while he is in Washington.

With kindest regards and best wishes.

Sincerely,

C. W. Nimitz

On February 15 Admiral Halsey's South Pacific forces landed nearly 6,000 New Zealand and American troops on Green Islands, 115 miles due east of Rabaul. When the invaders had defeated the small Japanese garrison, Seabees moved in and built a fighter strip on the main island.

Two weeks later Americans in General MacArthur's Southwest Pacific forces staged a thousand-man reconnaissance-in-force of Los Negros, easternmost of the Admiralty Islands. Though the invaders were outnumbered more than 4-to-1, they were able, with the aid of ample air and naval support, to maintain their grip on the island while reinforcements were rushed in to take and hold Los Negros and the much larger neighboring island of Manus. In a sense, the Admiralties were a substitute for bypassed Rabaul and its fine harbor, for adjoining Manus and Los Negros was Seeadler Harbor, fifteen miles long and four wide.

Long before MacArthur's forces invaded the Admiralties, the Joint Chiefs of Staff had noted the great advantages of Seeadler Harbor. Los Negros, on one side of the harbor, had flat land suitable for airfields. Planes from there could reconnoiter as far as the Palaus and the Marianas and help to neutralize Truk and other bases in the Carolines and support operations in New Guinea. Larger and more rugged Manus, on the other side, provided ample room for a naval base. The harbor would be a perfect staging point for seaborne attacks on New Guinea, the Palaus, the Philippines, and Formosa.

The Joint Chiefs wanted the Admiralties developed as a major base that Nimitz's Fifth Fleet as well as MacArthur's small Seventh Fleet would be able to use. Since CinCPOA had the necessary Seabees and service troops, General Marshall suggested to General MacArthur that he delegate the development of the Manus-Los Negros base facilities to Admiral Halsey. Admiral Nimitz then sent a message to Admiral King, with a copy to MacArthur, recommending that, to facilitate command problems, the boundary of the South Pacific Area be extended to enclose the Admiralties.

MacArthur exploded. He chose to regard Nimitz's recommendation as a sinister attempt to encroach upon his territory. In a letter to General Marshall, he declared that the recommendation reflected upon his capacity to command, and insisted that his professional integrity, indeed his "personal honor," were involved. If this, he wrote, was an endeavor to infringe upon his control, he demanded that he "be given early opportunity personally to present the case to the Secretary of War and the President."

In reply General Marshall wearily told MacArthur that he "should retain command of all base facilities in your area unless you yourself see fit to turn over control of them.... Your professional integrity and personal honor are in no way questioned.... However, if you so desire I will arrange for you to see the Secretary of War and the President at any time on this or any other matter."

The Joint Chiefs agreed that the time had come to summon MacArthur and Nimitz to Washington to straighten out their differences and make definite decisions on strategy. General MacArthur, as always, declined to leave his theater of operations, sending in his stead General Sutherland. Admiral Nimitz, with Admiral Sherman and other officers of his staff, left Pearl Harbor for the United States on March 2. At San Francisco Mrs. Nimitz and Mary joined the party for the flight to Washington in order to have a brief family reunion.

Admiral Nimitz, during his stay in Washington, was provided with an office in the Navy Department and with a secretariat. The latter was composed entirely of Waves and Women Marines, some of the prettiest and most efficient to be found. It was not by accident that women of high quality were assigned to Nimitz. The commander of the Waves and the commander of the Women Marines were anxious to have some of their officers and enlisted personnel assigned to the forward area in the Pacific. Nimitz, who disliked seeing women in uniform and anywhere near the war zone, was adamant against receiving them in the Territory of Hawaii. In Washington, as a gentleman of the old school, he could not get used to women jumping up and snapping to attention when he entered a room. No Wave or Woman Marine was assigned to Pearl Harbor until after Nimitz had moved his headquarters forward to Guam, and none served on Guam during his stay there.

Nimitz found planning and decision-making in Washington much more formalized than at Pearl Harbor. The Joint Chiefs and their subordinate committees usually opened the planning process with the writing and submission of memoranda, which became the basis for the discussion that followed. Nimitz was asked to submit several extensive memoranda and to revise them after conference.

The matter of Manus was easily disposed of. General MacArthur, on the advice of his staff, had already agreed to let Halsey develop Seeadler Harbor into a major base. It was necessary only to give MacArthur assurances that the boundaries of his Southwest Pacific Area would not be meddled with. However, the general having requested that the problem be carried to the top, it seemed wise to get the concurrence of Secretary Stimson and President Roosevelt.

The main purpose of the series of conferences was to plan strategy for getting Allied forces to the Luzon-Formosa-China triangle. General MacArthur had requested permission to cancel his proposed advance to Hansa Bay and, instead, take a 400-mile westward leap to Hollandia, on the north coast of New Guinea. To advance that far beyond the radius of his fighter planes, he would require the support and cooperation of the Fifth Fleet carriers, which were already earmarked for an assault on Kavieng. Nimitz objected that, if his fast carriers were to support both operations, they would all be tied up and his invasion of the Marianas would be delayed until the typhoon season. The Joint

Chiefs' solution was to cancel the Kavieng assault. Instead, they ordered Halsey to put troops ashore and build an airstrip on the unoccupied island of Emirau, 70 miles northwest of Kavieng. Thus, both Kavieng and nearby Rabaul would be surrounded by a ring of Allied air bases that would keep them pounded down and neutralized.

By March 11, the Joint Chiefs' strategic plan was ready. Hollandia was approved for April 15. Truk was to be neutralized and bypassed. Nimitz's forces would invade the Marianas on June 15 and the Palaus on September 15. Beginning November 15 they would support the invasion of Mindanao by MacArthur's forces. The decision whether to invade Luzon or Formosa was left open, but a target date of February 15, 1945, was selected.

On the morning of the 11th, Admirals Leahy, King, and Nimitz went to the White House to get the President's approval for the Joint Chiefs' strategic plan and for the command arrangements in the Southwest Pacific. Roosevelt received them in the Oval Office. He was obviously not well. His face was ashen and his hands trembled. Yet he smiled and turned on the Roosevelt charm for his visitors. He listened with attention to the briefing and approved the strategy. He said he was glad to see that the drives were directed toward the China coast, for he was determined to keep China in the war. Roosevelt noted that the plan did not carry through to the actual overthrow of the enemy and reminded his callers that in the Pacific war his objective was the defeat of Japan as soon as the Allies had enough forces. With regard to Manus, Roosevelt said he did not even know exactly where it was and it was a matter for the Joint Chiefs to handle.

Lunch was served in the office, and afterward Roosevelt brought out a packet of enormous cigars, very dark in color, that Prime Minister Churchill had accidentally left in the White House. The President offered them around, but all his guests, like himself, were cigarette-smokers. Admiral Nimitz said, however, that he'd like to take one to his housemate, Dr. Anderson, who smoked cigars. He'd have the doctor keep it for some special occasion.

The President began asking irrelevant questions and making random comments. He was probably getting tired. He asked Nimitz why, after the daring raid on Truk, he had sent his carriers to raid the Marianas. Since Roosevelt prided himself on keeping abreast of the progress of the war, he obviously knew the answer.

This question provided an opportunity for Nimitz to end the visit on a light note. Grinning, he said the question reminded him of the case of the elderly, fat hypochondriac who wanted to have his appendix removed. Because of his age and obesity, no local surgeon was willing to perform the operation. At last the hypochrondriac obtained the services of an eminent surgeon from out of town, and the appendectomy took place. When he regained consciousness, the patient, anxious about the operation, sent for the surgeon and asked about his condition.

"You're doing fine," said the surgeon.

"But, doctor," the patient said, "there's something I don't understand, I have a terrible sore throat which I didn't have when I entered the hospital. What causes that?"

"Well," said the doctor, "I'll tell you. In view of the circumstances, your case was a very special one, as you know. A big group of my colleagues came to watch the operation. When it was over they gave me such a round of applause that I removed your tonsils as an encore."

"So you see, Mr. President," said Nimitz, "that was the way it was. We just hit Tinian and Saipan for an encore."

Roosevelt threw back his head and laughed, and the visit was at an end.

The next day, March 12, the Joint Chiefs' directive was formally published by radio to the commands involved, and Nimitz and party started back to the West Coast. At San Francisco Admiral Nimitz took leave of Mrs. Nimitz and Mary and he and his staff went on to Pearl Harbor.

When Nimitz arrived at Pearl on the 15th, he learned that before dawn that morning eleven B-24s from Kwajalein, in compliance with the JCS order to neutralize Truk, had pounded the base with sixty-six 500-pound bombs, setting ablaze hangars, ammunition dumps, and oil-storage tanks.

Awaiting Nimitz was a newly arrived radio message from MacArthur: "I have long had it in my mind to extend to you the hospitality of this area. The close coordination of our respective commands would be greatly furthered I am sure by our personal conference. I would be delighted therefore if when you are able you would come to Brisbane as my guest. I can assure you of a warm welcome."

This was the general who only a short time before had accused Nimitz of trying to purloin a piece of his operational territory. Nimitz knew that MacArthur resented having to share with him the glory of directing the war against Japan. He had never been able to induce MacArthur to attend a Pacific Ocean Area conference, even at Noumea, which was just across the Coral Sea from Brisbane. But, with the Fifth Fleet about to support MacArthur's operations, a meeting of the two commanders in chief was imperative, and, if the general would not come to Pearl Harbor, the admiral would go to Brisbane. Nimitz sent his reply to MacArthur that day: "Your very kind invitation which is greatly appreciated was awaiting me on my return to Pearl from Washington this morning. It will give me much pleasure to avail myself of your hospitality in the near future. I am certain that our personal conference will insure closest cooperation in the coming campaign. Within the next few days I shall acquaint you with the time it will be feasible to leave here."

Nimitz summoned Spruance from Kwajalein and gave him the details of the Joint Chiefs' new strategic plan. The two men decided, in conference with the CinCPac staff, to support MacArthur's Hollandia invasion in two stages. On April 1 Task Force 58 would raid the Palaus and adjacent bases in the Carolines. On the 15th the carriers would provide direct support to the Hollandia landing and strike other Caroline bases, including Truk.

Halsey was asked to have his planes photograph the Palau anchorages and deliver the photos by air to Task Force 58 as it passed Green Islands. The raid on the Palaus was to be mainly a covering operation for Hollandia, but it was also a reconnaissance to obtain information for the scheduled assault by the Central Pacific forces. With luck, Task Force 58 would catch the Combined Fleet in the Palau anchorages. Or the Combined Fleet might come out and offer battle. That seemed unlikely, however, for there was evidence that the Japanese carriers still did not have enough planes and trained aviators to deal with an opposing carrier force.

Should the enemy elect to fight, Vice Admiral Willis A. Lee was to pull out of the carrier screens 6 battleships, 13 cruisers, and 26 destroyers to form battle line. As at Truk in the February raid, Pacific submarines that had been sent ahead would take station off the openings in the archipelago to attack any enemy vessel that came out for fight or flight.

Spruance returned to Majuro on March 20. On March 23 Nimitz and some of his staff departed Pearl Harbor for Brisbane. The admiral had taken steps to ingratiate himself with the general. From Hawaiian friends he got fine specimens of rare orchids, which he took as a gift for Mrs. MacArthur. He sent Commander Lamar into Honolulu to have silk playsuits made up in Hawaiian prints for little Arthur MacArthur and to purchase several boxes of Hawaiian candy for the MacArthur family.

As the CinCPac seaplane was approaching Brisbane on the 25th, its estimated time of arrival was radioed ahead. When it taxied up to the wharf, Nimitz and party were gratified and somewhat surprised to see General MacArthur and members of his staff waiting to greet them. After formal greetings and introductions, the Pearl Harbor party was conducted to its quarters. Admiral Nimitz was made comfortable in a suite in the elegant Lennons Hotel, which was across the square from the Queensland Supreme Court building.

MacArthur's aide presently appeared at the Nimitz suite with an invitation to a banquet to be held that evening in the ballroom of the hotel. Before going to the banquet, Nimitz, accompanied by Lamar, called at the MacArthurs' penthouse atop the hotel to present the gifts they had brought from Hawaii.

The general and his lady were obviously delighted with the magnificent display of orchids that Admiral Nimitz presented to Mrs. MacArthur. When the admiral asked to be allowed to give Arthur his gifts, the general explained that the little boy had gone to bed.

"General," said Mrs. MacArthur—she always addressed her husband as General, "You should let him come out for just a minute."

MacArthur somewhat reluctantly gave his permission, and the boy was brought out and given his playsuits and a big box of candy.

The next day, while the conference was in progress, Lamar was left to his own devices. He was impressed when at 11:00 a.m. the street in front of Lennons Hotel was cleared by military police, whereupon Arthur MacArthur and his Chinese amah paraded across to the enclosed grounds surrounding the

Supreme Court building. The gates were opened, Arthur and his amah entered, and the gates were locked behind them. Lamar learned that this was a daily occurrence and that the child and his nurse strolled about the grounds for about an hour.

At the conference, held in General MacArthur's office, the Supreme Commander and his staff accepted Nimitz's plan for supporting the Southwest Pacific's invasion of Hollandia. Nimitz said that Task Force 58 should not remain off the beachhead past noon of the second day following the landing. General Kenney commented that if by that time he did not have an airdrome ready in the area to receive his fighter planes, he would not be able to cover the unloading of the Seventh Amphibious Force supply vessels. Nimitz had already agreed to lend the Seventh Fleet eight escort carriers which, he said, could remain in the area for as long as eight days after the landing to fill in on fighter cover.

Admiral Nimitz was concerned about the threat to his big carriers. He said he didn't want to send the Task Force 58 carriers to Hollandia while 200 or 300 Japanese planes were there, ready to pounce on them. He was assured that bombers out of Darwin would take care of the enemy aircraft based on the Vogelkop Peninsula, western New Guinea. As for the Japanese planes based on the Hollandia area, General Kenney promised to wipe them out with his long-range P-38s. All those present, except MacArthur, looked skeptical.

Nimitz found MacArthur highly intelligent, with a magnetic personality, but also with an unfortunate tendency to strike poses and to pontificate. The general's sometimes pompous manner impressed some people and irritated others. Nimitz it seems to have amused. This reaction crept into his report to Admiral King. MacArthur, Nimitz wrote, "seemed pleased to have the J.C.S. directive covering the entire calendar year of 1944 because it definitely provided for his entry into the Philippines via Mindanao—a plan which is very close to his heart." Nimitz continued:

> His cordiality and courtesy to me and my party throughout my visit was complete and genuine, and left nothing that could be desired. Everything was lovely and harmonious until the last day of our conference when I called attention to the last part of the J.C.S. directive which required him and me to prepare alternate plans for moving faster and along shorter routes towards the Luzon-Formosa-China triangle if deteriorating Japanese strength permitted. Then he blew up and made an oration of some length on the impossibility of bypassing the Philippines, his sacred obligations there—redemption of the 17 million people—blood on his soul—deserted by American people—etc., etc.— and then a criticism of "those gentlemen in Washington, who, far from the scene, and having never heard the whistle of pellets, etc., endeavor to set the strategy of the Pacific War"—etc. When I could break in I replied that, while I believed I understood his point of view, I could not go along with him, and then—believe it or not—I launched forth in a defense of "those gentlemen in Washington" and told him that the J.C.S. were people like himself and myself,

who, with more information, were trying to do their best for the country and, to my mind, were succeeding admirably.

When Admiral Nimitz got back to Pearl Harbor on March 29, Task Force 58 was approaching the Palaus. Spruance, who was with the force, notified Nimitz by aircraft message that, having been snooped by enemy planes, he was advancing his attack on Palau by 48 hours in hopes of catching the Combined Fleet before it could escape. On April 1 (Pearl Harbor date), CinCPac received a preliminary report from Spruance. Task Force 58 had raided Palau, Woleai, and Yap: many enemy aircraft destroyed, all ships in anchorages sunk or destroyed, three small enemy ships sunk at sea, 27 American planes lost, no American ships damaged.

After that, silence. Nimitz, under pressure from Secretary Knox, who was eager to publicize the raid, asked repeatedly for details and even ordered Spruance to break radio silence. The latter suspected that the source of the pressure was newspaperman Knox. "I'm not going to tell them anything," Spruance told Captain Moore. "My job is to report to my superiors precisely what I have accomplished. When I have an accurate assessment, then I will report. If they want somebody to come out here and fight a publicity war, then they can relieve me."

Task Force 58 entered Majuro Lagoon on April 6 and Mitscher sent Spruance his estimate of damage achieved, which Spruance then forwarded to Nimitz: 29 auxiliary ships sunk, 17 damaged; 160 planes destroyed, 29 probably destroyed. The submarine *Tunny* reported inflicting torpedo damage on a battleship which turned out to be the giant *Musashi*. It was clear, however, that the rest of the combat vessels of the Combined Fleet escaped from the Palaus unscathed.

Admiral Nimitz and some of his staff arrived at Majuro two days later to discuss the forthcoming Hollandia operation, which had been postponed to April 21. Whether Nimitz had any sharp words for Spruance for ignoring his orders to break radio silence is not known. At any rate, Spruance did not stay around. With his staff he headed for Pearl Harbor to plan the Marianas operation. Nimitz was back at Pearl on the 9th. Task Force 58, with Mitscher in tactical command, departed Majuro for the Southwest Pacific on the 13th.

The Fast Carrier Force operated off Hollandia from the 21st to the 24th, but it was not needed, after all. General Kenney had made good his promise. In a series of raids, his bombers and fighters had completely knocked out Hollandia as a Japanese air base. On the return passage, the carrier aircraft gave Truk another pounding, which left it so helpless that aircraft from the Marshalls and the Admiralties had no trouble keeping it neutralized. Before returning to Majuro, Task Force 58 detached nine heavy cruisers to bombard the island of Satawan, and Admiral Lee's six battleships shelled the island of Ponape.

On April 23 Frank Knox died. James Forrestal was appointed his successor as Secretary of the Navy. Nimitz probably had mixed feelings about the change. Forrestal no doubt would prove a more vigorous administrator than Knox had been, particularly during the latter's period of declining health. But Knox had always supported Nimitz, his choice for CinCPac. Between Nimitz and Forrestal, however, there existed a tension that went back to Nimitz's incumbency as Chief of the Bureau of Navigation. At that time, Nimitz had opposed Forrestal's efforts to get his Wall Street friends commissioned and appointed to major commands in the naval administration. When Forrestal tried to get a commission for a civilian with a prison record, Nimitz vigorously blocked the effort on the grounds that *Navy Regulations* forbade it.

During the war, Forrestal was offended by what he regarded as Nimitz's reluctance to appoint aviators to important commands. Nimitz was, in his own opinion, moving them up as fast as they were prepared to assume responsibility. It was mainly to placate Forrestal that Nimitz and King appointed his protégé, Admiral Towers, Deputy CinCPac-CinCPOA. During the planning stage of the Central Pacific drive, Forrestal used his influence to encourage, induce, or force Admiral King to take direct command of the Pacific Fleet. In this maneuver, however, the Undersecretary was probably more interested in getting King out of Washington than in having Nimitz superseded.

The next ComInCh-CinCPac meeting took place at San Francisco on May 5 and 6, 1944. Admiral King brought Rear Admiral Charles M. ("Savvy") Cooke, his top planning officer. Admiral Nimitz brought his chief planner, Rear Admiral Forrest Sherman. Admiral Halsey was there, accompanied by his chief of staff, Rear Admiral Mick Carney.

King, as was his custom, explained the plans and decisions of the Combined and Joint Chiefs of Staff as they affected operations around the world. Most important of the forthcoming operations at that time was the cross-Channel invasion of Normandy, just a month away, to be followed by an Allied invasion of southern France and a drive into Germany. Since the Combined Chiefs aimed at ending the war with Japan within a year of the defeat of Germany, plainly the Pacific commands had better hustle.

Much of the discussion at this conference concerned plans for invading China and bringing the Chinese army more fully into the war, objectives that were never attained. As it turned out, the most pivotal achievement of the meeting was the decision to adopt in the Pacific Fleet the two-platoon system of rotating fleet commands.

The two-platoon system grew out of the question of what to do with Halsey. His South Pacific Area, left far behind in the war, was gradually being reduced to garrison status. His combat soldiers and a few of his ships were being allotted to MacArthur; his marines and most of his naval forces were going to Nimitz. In such a reduced command, an officer with Halsey's experience, skill, and rank would be wasted.

Savvy Cooke had already put forward a solution. He proposed separating the South Pacific and Third Fleet commands. Let Admiral Newton take over the former. Admiral Halsey, as Commander, Third Fleet, would transfer with his staff to Pearl Harbor, where they would plan the Palau operation. Following the conquest of the Marianas, Halsey would take command of the Fifth Fleet. Ray Spruance, Kelly Turner, Holland Smith, and Marc Mitscher would all be replaced and go to Pearl Harbor to plan future operations. Their former commands would then be called Third Fleet, Third Amphibious Force, III Amphibious Corps, and Task Force 38.

In due course, Spruance and his subordinates would rotate back into their former commands, and the old fleet and force numbers would be restored. As Halsey explained it: "Instead of the stagecoach system of keeping the drivers and changing the horses, we changed drivers and kept the horses. It was hard on the horses, but it was effective. Moreover, it consistently misled the Japs into an exaggerated conception of our seagoing strength." Obviously such a relief system would have been unwise had not the Pacific Fleet enjoyed a plethora of able commanders.

Back at Pearl Harbor, Spruance resumed his regular walking and swimming with Nimitz, rather to the disgust of Carl Moore, who felt that his boss should devote more time to planning. McMorris, Spruance's successor as Nimitz's chief of staff and housemate, did not share Spruance's enthusiasm for exercise: he wouldn't walk across the street if he could get a ride. Nor did McMorris emulate Spruance's temperance. It was suspected that he sometimes violated Nimitz's rule of no more than two drinks before dinner, but since his imbibing didn't affect the quality of his work and he never made a spectacle of himself, Nimitz was tolerant. Nobody could figure out where he got the booze.

One evening when Admiral Nimitz had a tableful of guests, he said to Anderson at the end of the meal, "Doctor, I think this is the special occasion when you should smoke the Prime Minister's cigar." While Anderson went to get it, Nimitz told how it came into his possession. The doctor returned with the outsize stogie, took his seat, and lighted it while the others watched appreciatively.

After a few puffs Anderson remarked, "Gee, it's getting hot around here." A few more puffs and the doctor, wiping perspiration from his forehead, excused himself and hastily left the room. All agreed that Prime Minister Churchill must be quite a man.

In mid-May planning and rehearsal for the Marianas campaign were in high gear. The assaults on the islands were to be carried out by marines, the 2nd and 4th Divisions for Saipan and Tinian, and the III Amphibious Corps (comprising the 3rd Division and the 1st Provisional Brigade) for Guam. There was no possibility that these islands could be virtually disarmed, as Kwajalein had been, by preliminary bombardment, for they were sizable bodies of land, Guam being 25 miles long; the other two, more than 10 miles. They would have to be taken by regular land campaigns, which would inevitably involve the two reserve divisions, the 27th and the 77th, both army. Regiments of the 27th, it will be recalled, had bogged down on Makin and Eniwetok; the 77th was going into battle for the first time.

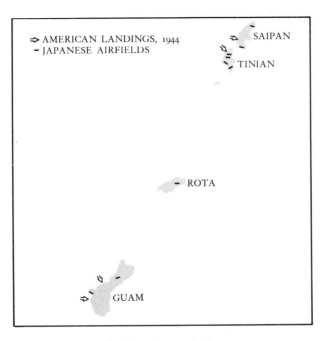

AMERICAN LANDINGS, 1944
JAPANESE AIRFIELDS

SAIPAN

TINIAN

ROTA

GUAM

*The Southern Marianas*

Despite the efforts of General Richardson to displace him, Lieutenant General Holland Smith was to command all the troops. His deputies, both marines, would be Major General Harry Schmidt on Tinian and Major General Roy S. Geiger on Guam. Thus marines were to command soldiers, with the added complication that marines and soldiers, presumably using different tactical doctrines, would be fighting shoulder to shoulder. Some hot arguments on the subject erupted at the planning conferences. Admiral Nimitz is said to have calmed one outburst with a particularly apropos story.

"This all reminds me," said Nimitz, "of the first amphibious operation—conducted by Noah. When they were unloading from the Ark, he saw a pair of cats come out followed by six kittens. 'What's this?' he asked. 'Ha, ha,' said the tabby cat, 'and all the time you thought we were fighting.'"

Admiral Nimitz was learning some interesting facts about the enemy. Admiral Koga, in command of the Combined Fleet, had disappeared. His plane had taken off from the Palaus at the time of Task Force 58's attack on the islands, and American flyers thought they had shot him down, as they had his predecessor, but it is more likely that his plane went down in a storm at sea.

Another plane, bearing some of Koga's staff officers, crashed in a storm near the island of Cebu, in the Philippines. Several of the survivors, including the chief of staff, were captured by guerrillas. They were soon retaken by the

Japanese occupation force, but the guerrillas kept the chief of staff's briefcase containing top-secret documents and notified General MacArthur by radio that they had it. MacArthur sent a submarine, which brought the briefcase to Australia. One of the documents contained an outline of "Operation Z," evidently a naval attack plan. General MacArthur had the plan translated into English and sent the gist of it by radio to Admiral Nimitz, but Captain Layton and his staff could make no sense of it because it had been translated by a nisei who was not familiar with naval terminology. Layton asked MacArthur's headquarters to send a photostatic copy of the original Japanese document to Pearl Harbor.

On May 5, the Japanese radio announced that Admiral Soemu Toyoda had been appointed Commander in Chief, Combined Fleet. A few days later Nimitz received word that most of that fleet, including all of the fast carriers, had arrived at Tawitawi, between the Philippines and Borneo—evidently to be near a source of fuel, Borneo's oil wells. Nimitz and MacArthur promptly ordered submarines to the waters off Tawitawi. By sinking a few ships, including destroyers, the submarines so convincingly announced their presence that the carriers dared not emerge for flight operations. As a result, the newly trained Japanese aviators could not practice their skills and were likely to lose their fighting edge.

At the end of May the amphibious forces destined for the Marianas, having departed Pearl Harbor and Ironbottom Sound, were at sea, en route to join Task Force 58 in the Marshalls. At the same time the photostatic copy of "Operation Z" was being flown from Australia to Hawaii. When the copy arrived at Pearl Harbor, Layton and his Japanese-language experts stayed up all night translating it. The plan called for decisive action by the Japanese Navy against any enemy force that penetrated as far west as the Marianas-Carolines-New Guinea line. By this time it was known at Pearl Harbor that "Operation Z" had been superseded by something called "Operation A-Go," but the latter was believed to be only a more detailed version of the former. When Admiral Nimitz was shown the translation of "Operation Z," he ordered copies run off and flown out to all the flag officers assembling in the Marshalls.

Apparently the long-awaited opportunity for the Americans to engage and destroy the Japanese carrier fleet was approaching. Admiral Nimitz was gratified to learn that among the carriers that would soon be offering themselves for destruction were the *Shokaku* and the *Zuikaku*, the last of the Pearl Harbor raiders. "Holland," he had once said to General Smith, "the happiest day of my life will be the day when I reach my office and find a message on my desk reporting that we have sunk these two carriers."

On June 6, 1944, the date of the Normandy invasion on the opposite side of the globe, Task Force 58 led the way out of the Marshalls. It was followed by the Fifth Amphibious Force, comprising 535 ships carrying 127,000 troops. The simultaneous involvement of American forces in the invasion of France and the Marianas constituted the most titanic military effort put forth by any nation at any one time in history.

So far as CinCPac headquarters was concerned, the next few days were a period of waiting while the Fifth Fleet steamed westward under radio silence. On June 11 Japanese garrisons in the southern Marianas reported that they were under air attack—evidently from the approaching Task Force 58.

On the 13th, Admiral Lee's fast battleships, detached from the Fast Carrier Force, bombarded Saipan and nearby Tinian. On the 14th, the old battleships and other fire-support vessels relieved Lee's battleships and began the pre-landing bombardment of Saipan's west coast. The bombardment continued through the 14th and was resumed at first light on the 15th, while aircraft from escort carriers bombed shore defenses.

Admiral Turner reported that the marines began landing on Saipan on the 15th at 8:44 a.m. They immediately came under massed fire. By the end of the day, 20,000 marines had landed. Casualties had been heavy, and the invaders had penetrated only about halfway to the D-day objective. It was a hard beginning, but no American doubted that the islands would be taken.

# CHAPTER 19

# OF GENERALS, ADMIRALS, AND A PRESIDENT

THE AMERICAN ATTACK on the Marianas in June 1944 resembled the Japanese attack on Midway in June 1942 in that in both operations the attacking force crossed a great stretch of the Pacific Ocean to assault a target inside the enemy's inner defense perimeter. A major difference was that in 1942 the Japanese did not know where the U.S. fleet was and thus were taken by surprise, whereas in 1944, the attacking force knew very well where the enemy ships were. The Americans were aware that the Mobile Fleet, which comprised 90 per cent of the Japanese Combined Fleet, was at Tawitawi in the Sulu Archipelago. They were eager for it to come out into the Pacific and thus offer itself for defeat, but they were determined that it should not get away from base without being detected and should, if possible, be kept under observation.

Three American submarines were covering the exits from the Tawitawi anchorage. To observe the Japanese fleet should it pass through the Philippines, three U.S. submarines were stationed north of Luzon, three more were south of Mindanao, one was off the eastern exit from San Bernardino Strait, and another was off the eastern exit from Surigao Strait. Other U.S. submarines patrolled the Philippine Sea, the part of the Pacific Ocean that lies between the Philippines and the Marianas.

Since April 1, 1944, naval air-search operations extending out to 1,000 miles had been conducted from the Admiralties. As MacArthur's forces leapt westward along the New Guinea coast in a series of amphibious assaults, they organized air patrols at the bases thus established. After the assault on Saipan, seaplanes from that island and carrier planes from Task Force 58 searched south, west, and north. It was, however, impossible for Allied air search to cover the entire Philippine Sea.

In the evening of June 10 the submarine *Harder* sighted a battleship-cruiser force departing Tawitawi on a southerly course and radioed a warning to Allied commands. This departure was rightly assessed to be in reaction to General MacArthur's invasion of the island of Biak, near the western end of New Guinea. The sortie was considered a matter for concern since MacArthur's Seventh Fleet had no battleships. On the 13th the submarine *Redfin* saw 6 carriers, 4 battleships, 8 cruisers, and numerous destroyers heading north from Tawitawi. After dark the *Redfin* surfaced and flashed the word by radio to Rear Admiral Ralph Christie, ComSubSoWesPac. From there the warning was passed to Brisbane and Pearl Harbor and so on to Admiral

Spruance, off Saipan. This Japanese move was judged to be in response to Task Force 58's air attack on the Marianas. In Operations Plot at CinCPac headquarters, the plotting officers had begun drawing their blue and orange lines on the chart overlays.

On the 15th the submarine *Flying Fish* reported the Mobile Fleet debouching from San Bernardino Strait. An hour later the submarine *Seahorse* sighted a battleship-cruiser force on a northerly course 200 miles east of Surigao Strait. CinCPac concluded that this was the force the *Harder* had observed leaving Tawitawi on the 10th, and estimated that it had changed course in reaction to the air attack on the Marianas. It appeared to be heading for a rendezvous with the main body of the Mobile Fleet, but because the Japanese, traditionally favoring complicated entrapment tactics, tended to operate their ships in several divisions, nobody could be certain that that was their destination. In any case, Spruance, anticipating a major battle, signaled that the invasion of Guam, scheduled for June 18, was to be postponed.

Two contacts by the submarine *Cavalla* on June 17 in the Philippine Sea indicated that the Japanese were advancing on the Marianas and, as they did so, cannily keeping beyond the reach of Allied scout planes out of the Admiralties and New Guinea. Admiral Lockwood, ComSubPac, who had four submarines patrolling a 60-mile square, 500 miles west of Saipan, ordered this "invisible trap" moved 250 miles southwestward, where it would be in the path of the oncoming Japanese. He also radioed all his submarines: "Now that contact with enemy forces has been made, shoot first and report later. Due to presence own surface forces, identify targets as enemy before firing."

Through intelligence sources, the Americans knew quite a bit about the Mobile Fleet. Its commander was Vice Admiral Jisaburo Ozawa, reputed to be one of the ablest officers in the Japanese navy, and it was estimated to include 9 fast carriers; by way of comparison, Task Force 58 had 15. Ozawa was believed to have between 50 and 60 ships and more than 400 planes. In the forthcoming battle Mitscher would have twice as many of each, and his aviators would be far better trained.

Ozawa nevertheless had certain advantages. Steaming into the easterly trade wind, he would be able to launch and recover planes while advancing on his enemy. He could expect assistance from Japanese planes based on Guam, Rota, and Yap. He would be able, with luck and skillful calculation, to stand off beyond the range of the American carrier aircraft while he attacked the carriers, for the Japanese planes, not encumbered with the weight of armor and self-sealing fuel tanks, had greater range than the American. Ozawa's planes could search out to 500 miles and attack at 300. Mitscher could search only to 350 miles and could not attack much beyond 200.

Admiral Towers noted another possible advantage for the Japanese. If Ozawa were permitted to get within 600 miles of Guam and Task Force 58 were between him and the Marianas, he would be able to shuttle-bomb the Americans; that is, his planes could attack the American force, go on to Guam or Rota for refueling and rearming, and attack the task force again on the way back to their own carriers. All this time the Mobile Fleet might be too far out for American planes to reach it.

Towers urged that Nimitz order Spruance to send Task Force 58 west to seek out the enemy before the enemy got too close to the islands. Nimitz refused, considering it poor practice to tell a commander on the scene how to fight his battle, but he did have McMorris send Spruance a dispatch pointing out the possibility of shuttle-bombing.

Japanese radio broadcasts had begun intimating that a major naval battle was impending. When newsmen asked Nimitz about this, the admiral replied, "I hope they stick to that idea. I don't know anything more we can do to provoke those people into a fleet action." In fact, Nimitz, along with every other informed American officer in the Pacific, was confident that, in view of the American advantages and proved leadership, the Fifth Fleet was about to deal the Mobile Fleet a crushing defeat.

Unfortunately, after the *Cavalla* contacts, the Americans lost track of the oncoming enemy. Japanese planes had snooped Task Force 58, which was standing off to westward of the Marianas in a covering position, but no American plane sighted the Japanese fleet and no more observations were made by American submarines. At last in the evening of June 18, Ozawa broke radio silence, whereupon CinCPac's arc of high-frequency direction-finder stations obtained a fix. Nimitz promptly passed the word to Spruance: the Mobile Fleet was at latitude 13° north, longitude 136° east, within 600 miles of Guam.

Task Force 58 was evidently caught somewhere within that less-than-600-mile stretch, where it was sure to be shuttle-bombed. To the officers studying the CinCPac plot, it seemed that Mitscher's best bet was to steam westward through the night so that he would be close enough to the Mobile Fleet to attack it at dawn. If Mitscher had half the luck Spruance had at Midway, the shuttling Japanese planes would have no flight decks to return to.

Radio intercepts during June 19 indicated to Pacific Fleet headquarters that a daylong battle was in progress. At dusk Admiral Spruance, who was with Task Force 58, sent his report to CinCPac:

> Task Force 58 made 325-mile search from 185 degrees, launching at 0530 in latitude 14-35 north, longitude 143-40 east with no contacts. Air attack on Task Force 58 commenced at 1045 coming in initially from westward and continued for several hours. Some enemy planes landed at Guam and Rota but these fields were hit by Task Force 58 planes several times to prevent their use. Over 300 enemy planes are reported destroyed by our planes and AA fire. Own aircraft losses not yet reported. Only known damage to our ships: 1 bomb hit on *South Dakota*, which does not affect her fighting efficiency. Believe enemy may have made long strikes depending on Rota and Guam fields for reservicing. If so, his plane losses may be greater than reported.

The report was received at CinCPac headquarters with a mingling of relief and dismay—relief that Task Force 58 had suffered so little damage, dismay that the Japanese carriers had apparently received none at all. Spru-

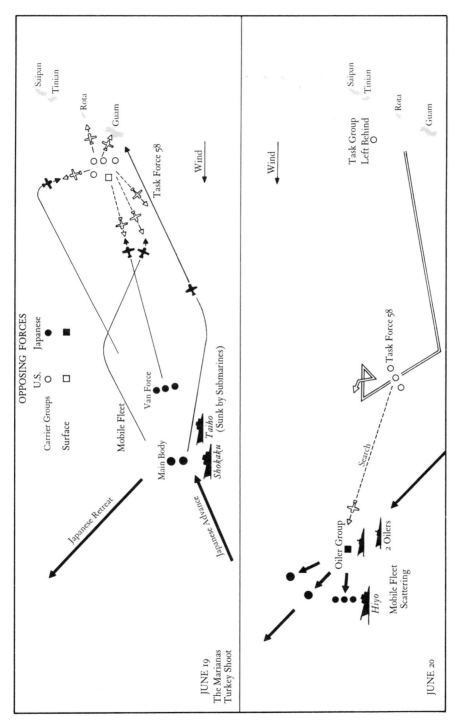

The Battle of the Philippine Sea, June 19–20, 1944

OPPOSING FORCES

| | U.S. | Japanese |
|---|---|---|
| Carrier Groups | ○ | ● |
| Surface | □ | ■ |

Mobile Fleet

Van Force

Main Body

*Taiho* (Sunk by Submarines)

*Shokaku*

Japanese Retreat

Japanese Advance

Task Force 58

Wind

Saipan
Tinian
Rota
Guam

JUNE 19
The Marianas
Turkey Shoot

Wind

Task Group
Left Behind

Saipan
Tinian
Rota
Guam

Task Force 58

Search

Oiler Group

2 Oilers

*Hiyo*

Mobile Fleet
Scattering

JUNE 20

ance's reported 5:30 a.m. position placed him 90 miles northwest of Guam and Rota, 125 miles southwest of Saipan. Evidently he had kept the fast carriers tied to the beachhead as he had in the Gilberts operation, though this time close-in support of the beach was assigned to the old battleships and escort carriers of the Fifth Amphibious Force.

Possibly, Spruance was worried lest a portion of the Mobile Fleet get between him and the beachhead and attack the amphibious shipping. However, as he certainly must have known, most of the American shipping was out of reach, having retired to eastward of Saipan. If any part of the Japanese fleet did arrive off the beachhead, it would have encountered Turner's seven old battleships and seven escort carriers and would have been destroyed or, at least, damaged sufficiently for Mitscher's returning carriers to finish it off.

Nimitz refused to criticize Spruance without having full knowledge of the circumstances under which he and the Japanese were operating. Spruance's orders had specified that he was to "capture, occupy and defend Saipan, Tinian and Guam." They said nothing about going on the offensive against an enemy fleet. Remaining close enough to the Marianas to keep the enemy airfields on Guam and Rota unusable may have been the surest way to prevent Task Force 58 from being shuttle-bombed or attacked by planes coming down from Japan via the Jimas.

That evening CinCPac and his staff were cheered by a dispatch from the submarine *Cavalla*, relayed by ComSubPac: "Hit *Shokaku*-class carrier with three out of six torpedoes.... Heard four terrific explosions in direction of target two and one half hours after attack.... Believe that baby sank." From Spruance came a report that, having virtually stripped the enemy carriers of planes, TF 58 was headed westward to attack the Mobile Fleet itself.

At CinCPac headquarters the battle of June 20 was pieced together from Spruance's and Mitscher's radioed reports. According to these, Task Force 58 pursued a retreating Mobile Fleet through the night of the 19th and most of the following day without making contact. At last, in the late afternoon of the 20th, one of Mitscher's scouts sighted the fleeing enemy and reported his position. Mitscher promptly launched a deckload strike. His planes found the Japanese, "6 carriers, 6 cruisers, 4 battleships present, carriers without planes on deck and only few airborne," and attacked at 6:42, which would have been shortly before sunset. Mitscher's aviators reported sinking "1 *Hiyo*-class carrier, 2 destroyers, 2 large oilers," and leaving two other carriers in flames.

Later CinCPac learned that many Task Force 58 planes landed in the water as a result of the long flight back and night recovery. Some of the downed aviators were rescued that night, others not until the next day. Ultimately all but 49 of the 209 aviators who had participated in the June 20 battle were recovered. On the 21st, long-range Avengers from Mitscher's carriers sighted the Mobile Fleet, still in flight. Because Task Force 58 had been moving at slow speed to facilitate rescues, it became increasingly evident that it had no chance of overtaking the enemy. At the end of the day Spruance called off the chase, and the battle was over. Officially, the action was named the Battle of the Philippine Sea, but to the American sailors who on June 19 had witnessed hundreds of Japanese planes falling like autumn leaves or streaking like comets into the sea, it would always be "the Marianas Turkey Shoot."

Admiral Mitscher, it was learned, had in the early hours of June 19 strongly recommended heading westward "in order to commence treatment of the enemy at 0500," but Admiral Spruance had restrained him. After the battle, Mitscher's official action report ended with a bitter note: "The enemy had escaped. He had been badly hurt by one aggressive carrier air strike, at the one time when he was within range. His fleet was not sunk."

Spruance himself expressed disappointment that he had not attacked the Mobile Fleet on the 19th. "As a matter of tactics," he wrote, "I think that going after the Japanese and knocking their carriers out would have been much better and more satisfactory than waiting for them to attack us; but we were at the start of a very important and large amphibious operation and we could not afford to gamble and place it in jeopardy."

Admiral King defended Spruance's decision. "As the primary mission of the American forces in the area was to capture the Marianas," he wrote, "the Saipan amphibious operations had to be protected from enemy interference at all costs. In his plans for what developed into the battle of the Philippine Sea, Spruance was rightly guided by this basic obligation."

Though Admiral Nimitz always stoutly defended Spruance's tactics, a little of the dissatisfaction at Pearl Harbor, particularly among the aviators, crept into CinCPac's summary for June 1944:

> There may be disappointment to some in the fact that in addition to the successful accomplishment of our purpose—the occupation of the Southern Marianas—there was not also a decisive "fleet action," in which we would naturally hope to have been victorious, and to have thereby shortened the war materially.
>
> It may be argued that the Japanese never had any intention of evading Task Force 58 with part or all of their forces, and making their major attack against our shipping at Saipan. From this premise it can be proved that our main body of carriers and gunnery ships could have pushed to the westward without concern for the expeditionary forces, and that had it done so, a decisive fleet air action could have been fought, the Japanese fleet destroyed, and the end of the war hastened.

Among the naval aviators at Pearl there was little doubt that Spruance had muffed the opportunity of the century. "This is what comes of placing a non-aviator in command over aviators," was the common complaint.

Not until the end of World War II were Admiral Spruance's tactics fully vindicated. Then, when the Japanese records became available, it was revealed that, through luck or intuition, he had placed Task Force 58 in the best possible position on June 19.

First of all, Ozawa did divide his Mobile Fleet, but not in the way his opposition anticipated or realized. What he did was to form his most powerful antiaircraft vessels into three circular groups, each surrounding a light carrier, and send them out a hundred miles ahead of his heavy carriers, which were in two groups and lightly screened. Mitscher's planes, in order to attack Ozawa's heavy carriers, would have had to pass through the intense antiaircraft fire and air attacks of the van force, fly a hundred miles farther to the main force, attack it and defend themselves there, fly back another hundred miles, and again pass over the enemy van force before returning to their own carriers. Had Mitscher attempted such an attack, his aircraft losses would probably have been catastrophic.

If Task Force 58 had advanced westward to bring its planes within range of the Mobile Fleet, it might have sunk some Japanese carriers, but the Japanese would have had a better chance of sinking some American carriers, for Mitscher would have had to divide his air strength, using some planes for defense and some for attack. By remaining on the defensive on June 19, he was able to use all his fighter planes, as well as his antiaircraft fire, to achieve the spectacular success of the Marianas Turkey Shoot. Had his flyers and gunners shot down fewer enemy planes on the 19th, they would have had more of them to contend with on the 20th. Also, by sticking close to the Marianas, Mitscher was able to use his bombers to destroy planes on Rota and Guam and to keep the airstrips on those islands so cratered that Ozawa's attempts at shuttle-bombing were frustrated.

Because Ozawa's heavy carriers were weakly escorted, both the *Albacore*, one of the submarines of Lockwood's "invisible trap," and the *Cavalla* managed to penetrate their screens. The *Cavalla* did indeed sink a carrier, the *Shokaku* herself, next to last of the Pearl Harbor attackers to survive. The *Albacore* got even bigger game, the new *Taiho*, Ozawa's flagship and the largest carrier of the Imperial Navy. The captain of the *Albacore* fired a spread of six torpedoes and dived. Because he believed he had missed, he made no report. In fact, one of his torpedoes had penetrated the *Taiho*'s hull, releasing explosive vapors that caused the great carrier simply to blow apart, but not before Ozawa and his staff had transferred to a cruiser, from which they later shifted to the carrier *Zuikaku*.

In the twilight attack of June 20, Mitscher's planes sank the carrier *Hiyo* and two oilers, set two more carriers afire, and damaged a battleship and a cruiser. At the end of this battle, the Mobile Fleet had only 35 carrier aircraft.

Thus, the Mobile Fleet was left with fewer planes than the Combined Fleet had been left with at the end of 1943. This time there was no chance of training replacement pilots. The American submarines, provided at last with dependable torpedoes, were getting into high gear. Their slaughter of tankers coming up from the East Indies had created a desperate shortage of fuel in Japan, and the lesson they had taught at Tawitawi had demonstrated the folly of the Japanese taking their carriers to the oil wells. The best Ozawa could do was to operate his carriers within the narrow confines of Japan's well-guarded Inland Sea, using the trickle of oil that reached him there. This recourse proved not good enough. The Japanese carriers had been rendered offensively harmless and defensively helpless. Sinking a few more of them would have achieved less toward Japan's ultimate defeat than the destruction of planes and aviators that actually took place in the Marianas Turkey Shoot.

Hardly had criticism of Spruance's tactics begun to subside when Admiral Nimitz received a profound shock. On June 23 (Pearl Harbor date), he was informed that General Holland Smith had summarily relieved General Ralph Smith, commander of the Army's 27th Division. Ralph Smith was by no means the first general to be relieved in the course of the Pacific war, but he was the first army general to be relieved by a marine general. Because the Army, particularly in the person of General Richardson, had long complained about the practice of having marines command soldiers, there was bound to be an outcry, more probably an explosion.

The 27th Division had bogged down on Saipan, as it had on Makin and Eniwetok. This time it was dangerously exposing the flanks of the marine divisions alongside it. General Holland Smith concluded that the main troubles with the division were lack of offensive spirit and poor leadership and that, therefore, its commander had to be relieved. Major General Sanderford Jarman, commander-designate of Saipan and the senior army officer on the island, agreed and offered to take command of the division until a replacement for Ralph Smith could be sent out.

Map in hand, Holland Smith went aboard the amphibious command ship *Rocky Mount* to talk over the problem with Admiral Turner. After a long and thoughtful discussion, Smith and Turner went to the cruiser *Indianapolis*, in which Admiral Spruance had just returned from the Battle of the Philippine Sea. There, more soul-searching was done. At length Captain Moore wrote a memorandum addressed to Holland Smith: "You are authorized and directed to relieve Major General Ralph Smith from command of the Twenty-seventh Division, U.S. Army, and place Major General Jarman in command of this division. . . ." Admiral Spruance signed it.

This was one story Admiral Nimitz would have given a great deal to keep from public knowledge, but that was obviously impossible. People on various errands were constantly flying between Pearl Harbor and Saipan. General Ralph Smith had been seen at Fort Shafter, army headquarters on Oahu, where General Richardson, in high dudgeon, was organizing an army board of inquiry headed by General Buckner to look into Smith's relief.

Richard Haller, of International News Service, went to see Commander Kenneth McArdle, assistant CinCPac public relations officer, and asked, "When are you going to release the fact that Ralph Smith has been relieved as commander of the 27th Division?"

McArdle replied that he had no official knowledge of any such relief and asked where Haller had heard the rumor.

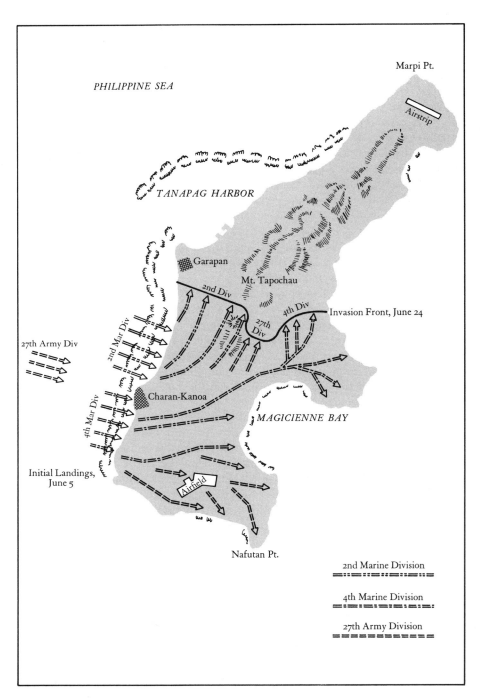

PHILIPPINE SEA

Marpi Pt.

*Airstrip*

TANAPAG HARBOR

Garapan

Mt. Tapochau

2nd Div

4th Div

27th
Div

Invasion Front, June 24

27th Army Div

2nd Mar Div

4th Mar Div

Charan-Kanoa

MAGICIENNE BAY

Initial Landings,
June 5

Airfield

Nafutan Pt.

2nd Marine Division

4th Marine Division

27th Army Division

*Opening Stages of the Saipan Campaign*

"It's all over town," said Haller. "I heard it from one of the general's close friends."

McArdle, realizing that concealing the story had become impossible, added to the end of the communiqué on which he was working a straightforward paragraph reporting the relief, and took the communiqué to the chief of staff.

"No!" shouted McMorris when he came to the final paragraph, and he scratched it out.

"It's all over Honolulu," said McArdle.

"Who told 'em?"

"Fifty thousand men on Saipan know it. You can't keep a thing like that quiet."

"The answer is no," said McMorris with finality.

The time-honored, if slightly irregular, way around McMorris's frequent and definitive negatives was through the assistant chief of staff, now Captain Bernard L. ("Count") Austin, who had recently relieved Preston Mercer in that capacity. McArdle took the story to Austin and the latter agreed that it was a mistake to sit on it. Better publish the plain facts than have them leak out in some sensational form.

Austin went to Nimitz's office to discuss the situation with the boss. In ten minutes he was back.

"The answer is still no," he said. "The admiral is going to say nothing of the incident; the War Department can make such announcement as it cares to. You see, the admiral doesn't want to do anything to hurt Ralph Smith."

As McArdle had feared, the story broke wrong in the American press. Some newspapers said that Holland Smith, "the butcher of Tarawa," was again ruthlessly sending boys to certain slaughter. Others implied that Ralph Smith's soldiers simply refused to fight. The *San Francisco Examiner* accused the Marine Corps of incurring excessive casualties and called for unified command in the Pacific theater under General MacArthur, whose "difficult and hazardous military operations...have been successfully carried out with little loss of life in most cases." *Time* and *Life* came out with stories supporting Holland Smith. The *Time* article concluded: "When field commanders hesitate to remove subordinates for fear of interservice contention, battles and lives will be needlessly lost."

General Richardson did nothing to relieve interservice tensions by storming out to Saipan, where he arrived on July 12. Without so much as a by-your-leave to Spruance, Turner, and Holland Smith, he reviewed the 27th Division, awarded decorations, and, for his board of inquiry, took depositions from the division's officers, including Major General George Griner, who had relieved General Jarman. Admiral Spruance, foreseeing trouble, extracted from Holland Smith a promise that he would control his temper. Kelly Turner was unwilling to give any such assurance.

Following the decoration-award ceremony, Lieutenant General Holland Smith and Major General Harry Schmidt, commander of the 4th Marine Division, called on Lieutenant General Richardson in his quarters. Richardson, in the presence of Schmidt, proceeded to upbraid Holland Smith.

"You had no right to relieve Ralph Smith," said Richardson. "The 27th is one of the best trained divisions in the Pacific. I trained it myself. You discriminated against the Army in favor of the marines. I want you to know that you can't push the Army around the way you've been doing. You and your corps commanders aren't as well qualified to lead large bodies of troops as general officers in the Army. We've had more experience in handling troops than you've had, and yet you dare remove one of my generals.... You marines are nothing but a bunch of beach runners anyway. What do you know about land warfare?"

To the incredulous amazement of all who heard the story, Howling Mad Smith managed to hold his tongue through this torrent of abuse. When Richardson visited the *Rocky Mount*, however, Kelly Turner sharply reminded him of the chain of command and the requirements of protocol. Richardson replied that he was in no way accountable to any officer in the Marianas. At that, Terrible Turner let loose a blast that caused the visiting general to turn white with anger. Restraining his wrath, Richardson went at once to the *Indianapolis* to complain to Spruance. The latter tried to make light of the situation. "That's just Kelly Turner's way," he said, "and no one takes him seriously."

Holland Smith prepared an official report of Richardson's conduct as he had observed it, and Harry Schmidt certified it in writing. Kelly Turner incorporated Smith's report in a scorching one of his own titled "Reporting unwarranted assumption of command authority by Lieutenant General R. C. Richardson, Jr., USA." Spruance forwarded Turner's report to Nimitz. General Richardson, on his return to Fort Shafter, sent Nimitz a report accusing Turner of gross discourtesy to himself. He later sent Nimitz the report of his Buckner Board, which predictably concluded that Ralph Smith's relief was unjustified.

Admiral Nimitz simply disregarded the whole silly dispute. When he received Spruance's official report of the Marianas campaign, he personally deleted all disparaging statements concerning the 27th Division. On learning that General Richardson had sent a copy of the Buckner Board report to General Marshall, Nimitz labeled his own copy of that report "Exhibit 1" and the Turner and Richardson reports "Exhibit 2," and sent them both to Admiral King by officer messenger with a top secret classification. In his cover letter to King he said:

> Exhibits 1 and 2 are being made available to you at the present time without official forwarding simply in order that you may have full information on the subjects discussed therein. It is my belief that General Marshall has received from General Richardson a copy of the Buckner Board which forms part of Exhibit 1, and that he may have received biased and one-sided stories regarding the controversial matters between Turner and Smith on the one hand and General Richardson on the other.

I am particularly not bringing these matters to your official attention because I still have hope of effecting settlements locally, even if such settlement consists only in filing the papers. If I forward them to you officially, it may become necessary for you to take the matter up with the War Department, which might result in unpleasant and unnecessary controversy at a time when we need all our energies to win the war.

I am anxious that you should be fully informed on these matters should Marshall ever bring up the subject with you. It is my belief that Marshall feels that Army troops should not be placed under the command of Marines. I hope I am wrong in this belief, for I can not accept the idea that Army troops can not serve under Marine leadership or that Marines can not serve under Army leadership.

The Joint Chiefs were already aware of what was going on. The War Department, in an effort to ease frictions, transferred General Ralph Smith out of the Pacific theater and gave him a command in Europe. Luckily, the Navy had another slot for Holland Smith. He was ordered to take command of the newly created Fleet Marine Force, Pacific. This promotion, which was in the works before the fracas, assured that Smith would not again command soldiers. Nor would he be in direct command of any combat units.

General Marshall did bring the Buckner Board to Admiral King's attention, and King asserted that General Richardson had no business setting up an all-army board to pass on the decision of a marine officer. Marshall replied that Richardson was within his rights since the board had no judicial authority and was set up merely to furnish advice to Richardson. Marshall then, taking aim at Nimitz as well as at Richardson, suggested that the senior officer of each service in the Pacific Ocean Areas be instructed that "the prevention of such a state of affairs is squarely his own responsibility, as is also the task of remedying it should it be found to exist." King replied that the proposed instruction might cause more trouble than good. "I can foresee no benefit," he wrote, "in encouraging him [Richardson] to make a further investigation along the lines he appears to consider appropriate." There the matter rested until several years after the war when Holland Smith reopened the controversy with his rather choleric memoir, *Coral and Brass.*

In mid-1944 CinCPac and the Joint Chiefs of Staff reexamined their strategy to determine how the war against Japan might be accelerated. That an increase of tempo was possible seemed assured by the striking success of the Fast Carrier Force in neutralizing the Marshalls and raiding Truk and the Palaus.

The most daring strategy advocated by the Joint Staff planners involved a carrier-supported advance north from Saipan, via the Bonins, for an invasion of Japan itself. Admiral Nimitz opposed this plan as too risky. A surer route to Japan would be an extension of the Joint Chiefs' plan of the preceding March, that is, an advance through the Philippines, Formosa, and the Ryukyus, to Kyushu and Honshu.

MacArthur, of course, espoused the latter plan. Nimitz at first agreed with him because, by that route, land-based air forces, ground troops, and naval forces would be able to advance together.

Early in July MacArthur submitted a detailed schedule for carrying out plan number 2. His forces would advance via the Vogelkop Peninsula and the island of Morotai and, with support from the Pacific Fleet, land on Mindanao on October 25 and on Leyte on November 15. With Leyte secured, Central Pacific forces would go ashore in northern Luzon on January 15, 1945. Southwest Pacific forces would land in southeast Luzon and on Mindoro in February. Then, again supported by the Pacific Fleet, Southwest Pacific forces would swing around north of Luzon, from east to west, to land six divisions at Lingayan Gulf on April 1, 1945, for an advance on Manila.

Hardly anybody liked the complicated MacArthur plan. General Kenney pointed out that it did not provide for enough air support. The consensus was that it was far too slow. April 1 for the main assault on Luzon was not acceptable. Admiral Nimitz came forward with an alternate plan: let MacArthur's Southwest Pacific forces, with Pacific Fleet support, land on Mindanao, establish airfields there to keep Japanese air power on Luzon neutralized, and then join the Central Pacific forces in a drive on Formosa and China.

MacArthur was shocked. He was bitterly opposed as strategically unsound and morally wrong to any plan that would mean bypassing, even temporarily, so many Philippine islands and so many Filipinos. He sent a message to the Joint Chiefs: "I request that I be accorded the opportunity of personally proceeding to Washington to present fully my views."

President Roosevelt thought he had a better idea. Since he was planning to make an inspection tour of bases on the Pacific coast and in Hawaii after the Democratic National Convention, which was to start on July 19, he would meet General MacArthur and Admiral Nimitz on Oahu and attempt to smooth out their differences. Contrary to his past practice when traveling overseas, he would not be accompanied by all the Joint Chiefs of Staff. Only Admiral Leahy would go, and not as the senior member of the Joint Chiefs but in his capacity as chief of staff to the President.

Admiral Nimitz seems to have first learned of the President's impending visit when Mike Reilly, chief of the White House Secret Service detail, arrived at Pearl Harbor to inspect and provide security measures. Reilly chose for the presidential quarters a palatial residence at Waikiki Beach which the Navy had leased for the use of pilots on rest and recreation leave. Nimitz radioed MacArthur an invitation to come to Pearl Harbor. For security reasons, perhaps recalling Yamamoto's fate, he did not mention that the President was coming. MacArthur returned courteous regrets, saying that he was too busy.

A meeting between Mr. Roosevelt and General MacArthur was liable to produce complications. Though they had become well acquainted when MacArthur was army chief of staff, the general was no admirer of the President, and until lately had been his political rival. He had permitted his name to be entered in Republican primaries, opposing Wendell Willkie and Thomas E. Dewey. He came in second in Wisconsin but picked up three delegates. Running against a political unknown in an Illinois preferential primary, he had received 300,000 votes.

MacArthur appeared to be gaining strength until he spoiled his chances through sheer political naïveté. He fell into correspondence with a little-known congressman from Nebraska, who had a weakness for overstatement. In his letters to the general, the congressman sounded off with such extremist pronouncements as: "If this system of left-wingers and New Dealism is continued for another four years, I am certain that this monarchy which is being established in America will destroy the rights of the common people." To the letter containing this outburst, MacArthur felt he had to return a polite reply. "I appreciate very much your scholarly letter," the general wrote. "Your description of conditions in the United States is a sobering one indeed and is calculated to arouse the thoughtful consideration of every true patriot."

When the congressman released this supposedly confidential correspondence to the press, MacArthur was assumed to share his extremist views. Public reaction was so unfavorable that the general and his backers knew that his candidacy was wrecked, and MacArthur discreetly bowed out of the race.

On July 13 Admiral King arrived at Pearl Harbor for one of the periodic CominCh-CinCPac conferences and a tour of inspection. He was in a bad humor. He was convinced that the President's visit to the Pacific without the Joint Chiefs was a politically inspired grandstand play. Just two days before, Roosevelt had notified the chairman of the National Democratic Party that he would accept the party's nomination for a fourth term: "If the convention should . . . nominate me for the Presidency, I shall accept. If the people elect me, I will serve. Every one of our sons serving in this war has officers from whom he takes orders. Such officers have superior officers. The President is the Commander in Chief and he, too, has his superior officer—the people of the United States."

A few weeks earlier President Roosevelt had passed the word to Admiral King, through Admiral Leahy, that he would like the Navy to shorten the titles Commander in Chief, U.S. Fleet; Commander in Chief, Atlantic Fleet; and Commander in Chief, Pacific Fleet, to Commander, U.S. Fleet; Commander, Atlantic Fleet; and Commander, Pacific Fleet. Thus there would be only one commander in chief, the President, who was Commander in Chief of the Army and the Navy. King told Leahy that he would act only if Mr. Roosevelt ordered or definitely requested the change. Leahy replied that the President preferred not to issue a definite order but would simply like to have it done. At that, King disregarded the matter and no change was made.

In his conference with Admiral Nimitz, Admiral King said that the Army Air Forces had requested authority to set up twelve groups of B-29s in the Marianas for the long-range bombing of Japan. King, who had little faith in what the bombers could contribute, had succeeded in getting the authorization cut down to four groups. To him, the servicing of so many additional bombers in the Pacific risked diverting support from the fleet and thus from "getting on with the war." He recognized the desirability of securing in the Bonin or Volcano islands, north of the Marianas, a base whence short-ranged fighters would be able to escort the bombers to their targets, but he believed the operation should not be carried out unless an invasion of Japan became necessary. He directed Nimitz to look into the feasibility of taking Chichi Jima or Iwo Jima and to prepare plans.

With the need for major warships in the struggle against Germany about ended, the British had proposed that part of the Royal Navy be transferred to the Pacific to operate against the Japanese. The proposal annoyed King. He called it an "intrusion" into an area where the Americans had already broken through the enemy's main defenses. He opposed having another fleet come in to share the credit for the final conquest. Moreover, a British fleet in the Pacific, lacking means of underway replenishment, would be a burden on the American logistic system. For the latter reason, King had obtained an agreement from the Combined Chiefs of Staff that the Royal Navy should not operate north or east of the Philippines.

King believed that the British might contribute by supporting the Australians in the recapture of Borneo and Sumatra, as sources of oil for operations in the far western Pacific. On the other hand, he was uneasy about having the British enter the East Indies at all, lest they make their contributions to the area's conquest a basis for claims on what had been Dutch territory.

King had heard that Lord Louis Mountbatten was being considered as British Far Eastern commander in the Southwest Pacific Area that the Allies had assigned to MacArthur as Supreme Commander. He believed that this possibility would so alarm the general that he would be glad to discuss it. Accordingly he sent the general an invitation to join him at Pearl Harbor. MacArthur again returned regrets, again saying that he was too busy.

General Marshall, who had been kept informed of the invitations and the general's regrets, then took action. He *ordered* MacArthur to report to Hawaii to meet "Mr. Big."

Admiral King did some inspecting while at Pearl Harbor. He visited a submarine about to put to sea and some others newly arrived from war patrols, and had a long conference with Admiral Lockwood. He was keenly aware that German submarines had nearly defeated the island kingdom of Britain by sinking ships bearing supplies to her, and believed that American submarines, which were now destroying huge tonnages of enemy tankers and cargo ships, could make a major contribution to the defeat of the island empire of Japan.

On July 14 King and Nimitz took off for Kwajalein, where they inspected the new installations and spent the night. Having lost July 15 by crossing the date line, they arrived on Eniwetok on the 16th. The atoll was crowded with planes and supplies because not only was it the American way station nearest to the Marianas, but it was also being used as a bomber base for keeping Truk neutralized. The travelers, after inspecting, dined and spent the night aboard the *Curtiss* as guests of Admiral Hoover.

Early on the 17th the King-Nimitz party took off from Eniwetok for the six-hour flight to Saipan. Their plane was escorted by several flying boats and, as it neared Saipan, a squadron of fighter planes flew out to accompany it in, a necessary precaution because the Japanese still held the rest of the Marianas. The party was met at the airfield by Admiral Spruance, Admiral Turner, General Holland Smith, and several other officers. King's first words as he stepped from the plane were addressed to the Commander, Fifth Fleet. "Spruance, you did a damn fine job there," he said, obviously referring to the Battle of the Philippine Sea. "No matter what other people tell you, your decision was correct."

The party and their hosts proceeded by various conveyances to the battered village of Charan-Kanoa, on the west coast, where General Smith had established a rough corps headquarters and was able to serve lunch. During the meal the visitors heard firsthand accounts of the suicidal fury of the final struggle, in which hundreds of Japanese threw away their lives in the hope of carrying a few Americans with them. American casualties had not been finally determined but were believed to exceed 16,000, killed and wounded.

After lunch the party headed up the west coast to examine the beaches where the marines had stormed ashore. Holland Smith, waxing eloquent over the combat efficiency of his marines, suddenly said to King, "Give me three marine divisions and I'll take Luzon."

CominCh growled, "What kind of meat have you been eating?"

"The same kind you've been eating for the last forty years," replied Smith.

Afterward King remarked, "The trouble with Holland Smith is that he's like Stilwell in China. All he wants to do is fight."

King and Nimitz proposed going to the top of Mount Tapochau, whence they would be able to observe the whole island and study the military problems involved in its capture. Holland Smith put his foot down sternly on that project. He explained that, though the island had been declared secure and the U.S. flag had been raised on July 12, there was still plenty of mopping up to be done. Japanese soldiers were everywhere, hiding in caves, ravines, and canefields, ready to snipe at any opportunity. Mount Tapochau was swarming with them. CominCh and CinCPac agreed to bypass the mountain but insisted upon making a circuit of the island. Smith protested that this too was extremely dangerous, but the visitors had their way. Later, Smith remarked, "Nobody has ever accused Ernie King or Chester Nimitz of lack of guts or equilibrium."

The tour of the island was made in jeeps. Riding in one were King, Nimitz, Spruance, and Smith. In the others were marines, with rifles at the ready. The procession stopped at Marpi Point, at the northern tip of the island, where hundreds of Japanese civilians had hurled themselves from cliffs onto the jagged rocks below to avoid being taken by the Americans. To King and Nimitz this riot of self-destruction and the suicidal banzai charges of the Japanese soldiers were a miniature preview of what an invasion of the Japanese home islands would be like. They determined if possible to starve Japan into surrender by means of a naval blockade.

As the party drove past the canefields of the east coast, the escorting marines were on the alert for snipers, but no shooting occurred. The visitors saw the ridge where several of the senior Japanese officers had killed themselves rather than face inevitable defeat. Among these was Admiral Chuichi Nagumo, who had commanded the Japanese carriers in the Battle of Midway. They also saw troops of the 2nd and 4th Marine Divisions and the Army's 27th Infantry Division, the warriors who had conquered the island.

When the tour was over, the officers boarded a landing craft and chugged out to the *Indianapolis*. Because the weather was hot and the cruiser could show no light in these dangerous waters, dinner was served in the late afternoon, while the ports could be left open to admit a little fresh air. Unfortunately the open ports also admitted swarms of enormous black flies that kept alighting on the diners and buzzing the food. Some of the officers were sickened by the thought that the flies had probably been gorging on dead Japanese on nearby Saipan.

After dinner the senior officers conferred, their chief topic being strategy. King asked Spruance what he would recommend for their next objective.

"Okinawa," said Spruance.

"Can you take it?" King asked.

"I think so," said Spruance, "if we can find a way to transfer heavy ammunition at sea." He explained that the Fast Carrier Force would have to remain at sea between Okinawa and Japan to "run interference" until the island had been secured. Nimitz said he would take the matter up with Vice Admiral Calhoun.

Privately, King reminded Spruance that Captain Carl Moore, the latter's chief of staff, would soon have to be replaced. Moore was not eligible for his current billet both because, like Spruance, he was a non-aviator and because he was a captain, whereas a four-star admiral rated at least a rear admiral as chief of staff. Moore had been allowed to remain with Spruance as long as he had only because he was helping to plan the Marianas campaign. In March Mitscher had reluctantly accepted as his chief of staff the famed destroyerman Captain Arleigh Burke, in place of Captain Truman J. Hedding. Spruance asked King to promote Moore to rear admiral but King would not hear of it. Moore had once run a cruiser aground and that was a blunder that King would not forgive.

After a hot night in the closed-up, stationary ship, King and Nimitz went ashore, mainly to survey the supply situation. They visited the southwest shore where all available artillery, nearly 200 field pieces, was placed hub-to-hub, ready to begin the bombardment of nearby Tinian. The assault on Tinian was scheduled for July 24, with the 2nd and 4th Marine Divisions comprising the landing force. Guam was to be invaded on July 21 by the 3rd Marine Division and the 1st Provisional Marine Brigade, the Army's 77th Infantry Division being held in reserve. The 27th Division was to be transferred to the New Hebrides for retraining.

Shortly before noon the King-Nimitz party took off to return to Oahu. They stopped en route at Eniwetok and Majuro and arrived at Pearl Harbor on July 20 in time for breakfast.

Admiral King and his staff spent two days reviewing plans that the CinCPac staff had worked out during his absence. CinCPac staff wanted the invasion of the Palaus, scheduled for September 15, to be followed by an assault on the island of Yap and the occupation of Ulithi, an atoll with an excellent anchorage that Nimitz had "discovered" while studying his Pacific charts. Rear Admiral Carney ventured to argue against King's preference for bypassing the Philippines.

King snapped, "Do you want to make a London out of Manila?"

"No, sir," replied Carney. "I want to make an England out of Luzon."

During his last evening at Pearl Harbor, King talked with Nimitz about the latter's forthcoming conference with the President and General MacArthur. They agreed that there was much to be said for taking Luzon, but Formosa was strategically better situated with respect to both China and Japan. King gave Nimitz no definite orders about what arguments he was to use or even which of the alternate strategies he was to espouse. He merely asked him to think over very carefully what he ought to propose.

King then wrote a letter to leave behind for MacArthur. In it he outlined the discussion that had taken place in London between the U.S. and British chiefs of staff concerning proposed British participation in the war against Japan. On July 22 he and his party left for Washington. King's plane, eastbound, passed over the heavy cruiser *Baltimore* bearing President Roosevelt toward Pearl Harbor.

The President had crossed the country by special train, pausing to confer with political leaders in Chicago, where the Democratic Convention was about to meet. On July 20, the Convention overwhelmingly nominated him for a fourth term, and he broadcast his speech of acceptance by radio from his train as it stood on a siding in the naval reservation at San Diego. The next day Senator Harry S. Truman, of Missouri, with presidential blessing, was nominated Vice President. The following midnight, Roosevelt sailed in the *Baltimore* from San Diego. Admiral Nimitz and General MacArthur were informed of his estimated time of arrival at Pearl Harbor.

Nimitz had invited MacArthur to stay in his quarters at Makalapa during the latter's forthcoming visit to Hawaii. General Richardson, an old friend from West Point days, had asked him to stay with him at Fort Shafter. Because garbles made Nimitz's radio message unintelligible, MacArthur accepted Richardson's invitation before he realized that he had also been invited by the admiral.

CinCPac headquarters tried to keep the President's approaching visit secret, but so many people had to know about it in order to make preparations that the word leaked. Nimitz took the precaution of ordering all mail outgoing from Hawaii held up until after the President had departed. On the eve of Roosevelt's arrival, CinCPac put out an order requiring white uniforms to be worn in the afternoon of July 26 by all officers and men on ships in Pearl Harbor, in the waterfront area, and on the main street of the base.

In the early afternoon of the 26th the *Baltimore* rounded Diamond Head. Off Fort Kamehameha she slowed down to receive the pilot. Admiral Nimitz, General Richardson, and other dignitaries went aboard from the pilot's tug. As the cruiser stood up the channel, the presidential flag was hoisted to the main. Inside the harbor every ship manned rails.

The cruiser was eased alongside a pier and the landing stage was rolled up. On the pier, with Soc McMorris in charge, was a line of senior officers in gleaming whites—General Leavey and Admirals Towers, Lockwood, Pownall, Carney, and Forrest Sherman, and more than a dozen others. Soc ordered, "Right Face!" It had been so long since these middle-aged officers had engaged in close-order drill that two of them faced left, evoking a gleeful cheer from the sailors on the *Baltimore*. With pipings, ruffles, and flourishes, the formation marched on board to be presented to the President in the flag cabin. When all except Admirals Nimitz and Leahy had departed, Mr. Roosevelt asked for General MacArthur.

MacArthur had landed about an hour earlier, but instead of joining the other officers to greet the Commander in Chief, he had gone to General Richardson's quarters at Fort Shafter. The President, after waiting for some time, was about to disembark, when from the direction of Honolulu could be heard cheers, police whistles, an automobile siren, and the roar of a motorcycle escort. Presently onto the pier, preceded by police on motorcycles, rolled a long army car showing the four stars of a general and driven by a chauffeur in khaki. Alone in the back seat was General MacArthur.

The car stopped at the gangplank and out stepped the general clad in khaki trousers, brown leather air force jacket, and Filipino field marshal's cap. Halfway up the gangplank he stopped and turned to acknowledge the applause of the crowd. At the gangway, against a background of boatswains' pipes, he smartly saluted the quarterdeck. Intentionally or not, the general had upstaged the President—and everyone else. In the cabin Mr. Roosevelt greeted him warmly.

"Douglas," said Admiral Leahy, a friend of almost forty years, "why don't you wear the right kind of clothes when you come up here to see us?"

"Well," replied MacArthur, "you haven't been up there where I came from, and it's cold up there in the sky."

After a brief conference, photographers were called and pictures were taken of the President with General MacArthur and Admiral Nimitz, seated together on chairs on the deck.

The presidential party left the cruiser at 5:00 p.m. and proceeded past crowds of cheering civilians and uniformed men to Roosevelt's assigned residence in Honolulu. Nimitz went to Makalapa. MacArthur went with General Richardson to Fort Shafter. Once inside Richardson's quarters, the normally self-controlled MacArthur gave vent to his vexation. He felt humiliated, he said, at being ordered to leave his command in order to participate in a picture-taking junket.

The general, pacing up and down, continued to fulminate. He denounced the conference as a piece of political play-acting, set up and timed to display the Commander in Chief, immediately upon his nomination, advising his Pacific commanders how to defeat the Asian foe. He was handed Admiral King's letter. He took it as a warning, as no doubt King intended, that when he moved into the Philippines an independent British command would move into his Australia-East Indies territory.

At dinner MacArthur confided to Richardson that he was shocked at the appearance of the President, whom he had not seen in seven years—his cheeks were sunken and his frame was so shrunk that his clothes hung loose. Then came an invitation from Roosevelt to MacArthur to join him for a tour of inspection in the morning. It revived the general's mood of denunciation—more picture-taking, more publicity for the political campaign!

General Richardson, who had arranged the next day's inspection, a passing-in-review parade followed by a visit to several military installations, had difficulty finding an open car such as the President preferred. Only two were available: a red, five-passenger vehicle that belonged to Honolulu's fire chief, and a more sedate seven-passenger car that belonged to the madam of one of Honolulu's better-known bawdy houses. Richardson, realizing that the larger car would be readily identified, perforce selected the smaller red one. Nimitz, squeezed in the back seat between the President and General MacArthur, found himself almost left out as "Douglas" and "Franklin" exchanged observations.

That evening, after dinner at Roosevelt's quarters, the President, MacArthur, Leahy, and Nimitz repaired to the living room where an enormous map of the Pacific had been erected. Roosevelt, as he rode past the map in his wheelchair, pointed to Mindanao and said to MacArthur, "Douglas, where do we go from here?"

"Leyte, Mr. President, and then Luzon!"

The discussion that followed was conducted in a friendly, quiet tone, Nimitz and MacArthur rising from time to time to point with a bamboo pole at areas on the big map. Roosevelt would intervene occasionally to narrow the area of disagreement. Nimitz spelled out the strategic advantages of Formosa: it was ideally situated to block the flow to Japan of the oil, tin, rubber, quinine, and other vital materials of the East Indies area; it was close to China, where the Americans hoped to have the cooperation of the Chinese army in establishing a base on the mainland for the bombing and, if necessary, the invasion of Japan; or, if the establishment of a base in China proved impossible, Formosa itself could be used, and it was closer to Japan than Luzon. Nimitz was at a disadvantage in pressing the move to Formosa, however, because he had been thinking carefully, as King had suggested, and had come to the conclusion that bypassing Luzon might not be the best idea after all.

MacArthur based his arguments heavily on humanitarianism. "You cannot abandon 17 million loyal Filipino Christians to the Japanese in favor of first liberating Formosa and returning it to China," he insisted. "American public opinion will condemn you, Mr. President. And it would be justified."

The people of the Far East, MacArthur went on, would react even more sharply to such abandonment. They would take it as proof that Japanese propaganda to the effect that we were unwilling to shed American blood to save our friends in the Orient was right. He spoke of the 3,700 American prisoners of war in Luzon hoping for an early deliverance. By taking Formosa to the north and Mindanao to the south, we should be cutting off the rest of the Philippines from all outside sources of supply. The occupying Japanese would surely feed themselves with what was available and leave the Filipinos and the American prisoners to starve.

The general turned to the military problem. The Japanese airfields on Luzon, he said, could not be neutralized from distant Mindanao. American airfields would have to be established on Leyte or Mindoro, or both. Once that was done, MacArthur's forces would be able to land at Lingayen Gulf and be in Manila in five weeks.

"But, Douglas," the President said, having in mind recent reported Japanese ground and air reinforcements in the Manila area, "to take Luzon would demand heavier losses than we can stand. It seems to me we *must* bypass it."

"Mr. President," replied MacArthur, "my losses would not be heavy, any more than they have been in the past. The days of the frontal attack are over. Modern infantry weapons are too deadly, and direct assault is no longer feasible. Only mediocre commanders still use it. Your good commanders do not turn in heavy losses."

Admiral Nimitz might have replied to the obvious insinuation that, had not the Central Pacific drive held Japanese forces from massing on MacArthur's more easily predictable drive across the south, the general's losses would have been far heavier. But Nimitz chose to disregard MacArthur's bad manners. He listened intently, interested only in devising the most effective, least costly strategy for defeating the enemy.

General MacArthur pointed out that Americans landing on Formosa could expect no help from the populace because the island had been a Japanese possession for half a century. In the Philippines, on the other hand, we could expect every possible assistance from the Filipinos against the hated Japanese occupation forces. In some areas, indeed, powerful Filipino guerrilla groups had already made substantial progress toward ousting the conqueror.

The discussion lasted till midnight and was resumed the next morning. It was soon apparent that MacArthur had won his argument, convincing not only President Roosevelt but Admiral Nimitz as well. He then turned to a matter that was very much on his mind, British entry into the Pacific war. Now that the Americans, with the help of other Allied Pacific powers, were about to win the war, he could see no reason why any U.S. command should be superseded by a British command, so that the British might reap the benefits of the peace. MacArthur feared they would withdraw from him his Australian and New Zealand troops and would not only provide no logistic support but would themselves require Lend-Lease. A British command in the Far East, he said, would damage American prestige in that area. He would welcome British contributions to the war in the Southwest Pacific but only under the existing command structure. The President appeared sympathetic but did not commit himself.

At noon the meeting broke up and all climbed into waiting cars and rode out to Pearl Harbor to lunch as guests of Admiral Nimitz. When they reached Makalapa, Nimitz hardly recognized his quarters. Under the direction of Mike Reilly, the Seabees had been working on them all the preceding afternoon and all morning. They had temporarily removed palm trees in order to run a road around to the back, where the President could be removed from his car to his wheelchair without being seen, for he was sensitive about such matters. They had built a ramp up to the back door, which they had rehung to permit the wheelchair to pass through. They had practically rebuilt the downstairs bathroom for Mr. Roosevelt's convenience. Finally, they had painted over all their alterations and dried the paint with blow torches.

Before lunch the President had three strong martinis. There were thirty-six guests, a glittering assemblage of flag and general officers. The senior officer after MacArthur, Leahy, and Nimitz was Admiral Halsey, recently recalled from the South Pacific. Lamar counted 146 stars on the collars of those present. The main dish was the famous Hawaiian fish mahimahi, which had been examined and approved by the President's personal physician, Vice Admiral Ross McIntire.

After lunch, General MacArthur made his farewells. He assured Mr. Roosevelt that he and Admiral Nimitz had cleared away all disagreements. "We see eye to eye, Mr. President," he said; "we understand each other perfectly." The general's plane was waiting at nearby Hickam Field. When it was airborne MacArthur turned to his aide and joyfully exclaimed, "We've sold it!"

That afternoon the President had himself taken to Aiea Naval Hospital to visit the wounded. He made a point of being pushed slowly through the wards where there were young men who had lost limbs. He wanted to show them that he knew what it was to have dead legs and that he had been able to rise above his affliction.

The next day, July 29, Mr. Roosevelt watched while the wounded from Guam were being unloaded from planes at Hickam Field. He inspected the

Pearl Harbor Navy Yard. He made a speech from his open car to administrative officers, enlisted men, and civilian workers assembled before the 14th Naval District headquarters building. At dusk he sat in his car on the pier alongside the *Baltimore* and chatted with Nimitz, Richardson, and Ghormley. He thanked them for three enlightening and constructive days, shook hands, and was wheeled aboard the cruiser, which after dark steamed away on course 354 degrees for Adak in the Aleutians.

The following day, while the Seabees were replanting Nimitz's palm trees and restoring his quarters, Halsey and his staff were in the JICPOA building making preliminary plans for the conquest of the Palaus, Yap, and Ulithi. Halsey was grumbling. Ulithi would provide a useful anchorage, but the rest of the operation, he believed, would be a waste of time and lives. Enemy air power in the Carolines was no longer a threat and, with the Americans in the Marianas, it could not be reinforced from Japan.

The Marianas campaign was drawing to a close. The 2nd and 4th Marine Divisions, with the aid of bombardment from land, sea, and air, swept over the plain of Tinian in a single week. They were held up for a while by the cliffs and escarpments at the southern end, but on August 1 General Harry Schmidt was able to announce that Tinian had been secured. It took a little longer to secure the big island of Guam. Before the landings on July 21, the fleet subjected it to thirteen days of sustained, methodical bombardment. In the fighting ashore, troops of the 3rd Marine Division and the Army's 77th Division fought side by side, using similar tactics and fully supporting each other.

By mid-August, 1944, all organized resistance to the reconquest of Guam had ended, and the greater Marianas were securely in American hands. The cost had been great: in taking Saipan, Tinian, and Guam, more than 5,000 American lives had been lost, while nearly 60,000 Japanese had been destroyed. But the United States had penetrated the enemy's last defense line and acquired logistic bases for further conquests, submarine bases for stepping up attacks on Japanese communications, and air bases from which B-29s could blast the industrial concentration in the Tokyo area. The fearful impact of these events on Japan was evidenced by the fall of the Tojo government, which had initiated the war against the United States.

# CHAPTER 20

# RETURN TO THE PHILIPPINES

PRESIDENT ROOSEVELT HAD no intention of imposing the MacArthur-Nimitz Honolulu agreement on the Joint Chiefs of Staff. His only communication to them on the subject was through Admiral Leahy, who reported the details at a special meeting of the Joint Chiefs. "They may have been somewhat surprised," wrote Leahy later, "to learn that Nimitz and MacArthur said they had no disagreements at the moment and that they could work out their joint plans in harmony."

On the basis of Leahy's report, the Joint Chiefs were to make a recommendation to the President. Unfortunately they could not reach agreement. General Marshall was won over to MacArthur's strategy, chiefly by the general's arguments that the national honor was at stake and that, with Filipino assistance, the Americans could conquer Luzon more readily than they could win and maintain a foothold on Formosa. Admiral King, disdaining the national-honor argument as mere sentiment, stuck to his Formosa strategy. An invasion of Formosa, he insisted, would win the war sooner than would the reconquest of Luzon and thus probably free the Philippines more quickly. He ordered Admiral Nimitz to plan for invading Formosa and also Amoy, on the coast of China. Accordingly, Nimitz directed JICPOA to prepare an intelligence book on Formosa.

The Joint Chiefs did agree to order General MacArthur to occupy Leyte, in the Central Philippines, so that it could be used either as a stepping-stone to Luzon or as an air base from which enemy air power on Luzon could be neutralized. The invasion of Leyte they scheduled for December 20, six weeks following the invasion of southern Mindanao.

Nimitz, aware that his orders from King were only tentative, sent Forrest Sherman to Washington to urge the Joint Chiefs to make up their minds. Sherman pointed out to them that the invasion of the Palaus was only two weeks away. The Central Pacific forces needed to know where to go after that. A bad decision, he said, might be better than no decision at all.

The Joint Chiefs turned the problem over to their planners who, in spite of Sherman's urging, suggested that the choice between Luzon and Formosa might well be deferred. Working with General MacArthur's representatives, they devised a timetable of operations for presentation at the conference of the Combined Chiefs of Staff with the President and the Prime Minister, which was to open at Quebec on September 11:

September 15: Southwest Pacific forces occupy the island of Morotai, halfway between New Guinea and southern Mindanao; Central Pacific forces occupy Peleliu and Angaur in the Palau Islands.

October 5: Central Pacific forces occupy Yap and Ulithi.

October 15: Southwest Pacific forces occupy the Talaud Islands, halfway between Morotai and southern Mindanao.

November 15: Southwest Pacific forces land in southern Mindanao.

December 20: Southwest Pacific forces land at Leyte.

Southwest Pacific and Central Pacific forces combine to land either (1) on Luzon on February 20, or (2) on Formosa and at Amoy on March 1, 1945.

On September 11 Admiral Halsey in his flagship, the 45,000-ton battleship *New Jersey*, joined the Fast Carrier Force off the Philippines. While he was en route from Pearl Harbor, the Fifth Fleet had become the Third Fleet, the Fast Carrier Force changed its designation from Task Force 58 to Task Force 38, and Admiral Spruance left Saipan and headed for Pearl in the *Indianapolis*. There was no opportunity for any sort of change-of-command ceremony.

With Spruance was his new chief of staff, Rear Admiral Arthur C. Davis. Also in the *Indianapolis*, riding as a passenger, was Spruance's ex-chief of staff, Captain Carl Moore. Moore, heading for a staff job in Washington, was relaxing for the first time in months.

As the *Indianapolis* entered East Loch at Pearl Harbor, the signal station flashed a message of congratulation from CinCPac. When the flagship had moored, Spruance proceeded to Makalapa and reported to his commander in chief. Nimitz greeted him warmly, then said, "The next operation is going to be Formosa and Amoy. You just hop in a plane, go back to California to see your family, and be back here in a couple of weeks."

Spruance reacted unexpectedly. "I don't like Formosa," he said.

"What would you rather do?" asked Nimitz.

"I would prefer taking Iwo Jima and Okinawa."

Spruance saw Iwo Jima as not merely a way station from which fighters could escort the Marianas-based B-29s over Tokyo, but as the focus of an arc extending from Okinawa through the Japanese home islands of Kyushu, Shikoku, and Honshu to Tokyo. Bombers would be able to fuel at Iwo Jima and, from there, with fighter escort, reach any of these areas. Fighters based on Iwo would be able to support a fleet operating in Japanese waters, as fighters from the Solomons in late 1943 had supported the carrier groups attacking Rabaul. From Okinawa, the Americans would be able to intercept ships en route to Japan bearing oil and other materials from the south and also block direct contact between Japan and China. As a bomber base Okinawa was superbly situated for attacks on southern Japan.

"Well," said Nimitz, having in mind Admiral King's order, "it's going to be Formosa."

Normally Spruance would have set his staff to work at once drawing up plans. Instead, he was so convinced that King would eventually see the light and drop Formosa that he told his staff to take leave and not waste their time on an operation that would never take place. He then headed for home.

On September 12 (Pearl Harbor date) Nimitz received a startling radio message from Halsey. As the result of Task Force 38's attacks in the Central Philippines, it said, the Japanese had few serviceable planes remaining in the area, most of their oil storage had been destroyed, and there was "no shipping left to sink." The "enemy's non-aggressive attitude was unbelievable and fantastic," the message continued, and "the area is wide open." One of his downed aviators, Halsey reported, had been told by the Filipinos who rescued him that there were no Japanese on Leyte. Halsey strongly recommended that intermediate operations—against the Talauds, Mindanao, the Palaus, and Yap —be canceled and all the shipping and ground forces thus released be used to invade Leyte as soon as possible. Task Force 38 would cover the landings until airfields could be established ashore.

Nimitz was not willing to cancel the Palau operation, believing that an airfield on Peleliu and the Kossol Passage anchorage would be useful for staging into Leyte. He did, however, forward Halsey's recommendation by radio to the Joint Chiefs of Staff, then meeting at Quebec, together with an offer to place at MacArthur's disposal the Third Amphibious Force and the XXIV Army Corps, then loading at Pearl Harbor for Yap.

General Marshall referred Halsey's proposal and Nimitz's offer to General MacArthur, asking his opinion regarding the proposed changes. Mac-Arthur was at sea, en route to Morotai, observing radio silence, but General Sutherland, at Hollandia, replied in his name. He said the information about there being no Japanese on Leyte was false, but that with the additional forces offered by Nimitz, the intermediate operations could be eliminated and an early attack made on Leyte. General Marshall in his official report describes the effect Sutherland's reply had at Quebec:

> The message from MacArthur arrived at Quebec at night and Admiral Leahy, Admiral King, General Arnold, and I were being entertained at a formal dinner by Canadian officers. It was read by the appropriate staff officers who suggested an immediate affirmative answer. The message, with their recommendations, was rushed to us and we left the table for a conference. Having the utmost confidence in General MacArthur, Admiral Nimitz, and Admiral Halsey, it was not a difficult decision to make. Within 90 minutes after the signal had been received in Quebec, General MacArthur and Admiral Nimitz had received their instructions to execute the Leyte operation on the target date 20 October, abandoning the three previously approved intermediary landings. General MacArthur's acknowledgment of his new instructions reached me while en route from the dinner to my quarters in Quebec.

At the Quebec conference it soon became apparent that Prime Minister Churchill was by no means satisfied with the Combined Chiefs' agreement that the Royal Navy was not to operate north or east of the Philippines. The British, with many political and economic interests in the Far East, needed a victory in that part of the world to erase from the minds of the Orientals the effect of their crushing defeats in 1941 and 1942. Churchill was not content with the prospect of minor successes in some out-of-the-way corner of the Pacific theater. He wanted British forces clearly and visibly involved in the final defeat of the Japanese homeland. At a plenary session he offered the British fleet for operations in the Pacific under Nimitz's command.

"I should like," replied President Roosevelt, "to see the British fleet wherever and whenever possible."

Churchill's offer made Admiral King shudder. Already the logistic services of the Pacific theater were strained to the utmost to provide for the swelling inflow of American vessels from shipyards and from the European theater, where large naval forces were no longer needed. British ships, moreover, posed special problems in that they were short-legged, not built or manned to operate far from base or for long periods at sea. King interposed to say that a paper had been prepared for the Combined Chiefs, who had the matter under active study.

Churchill was offended. To him it was inconceivable that an offer of the fleet of Drake and Hawke and St. Vincent and Nelson should not be instantly and gratefully embraced.

"The offer of the British fleet has been made," growled Churchill. "Is it accepted?"

"Yes," said Roosevelt.

Out in the Pacific Ocean, ships bearing the XXIV Army Corps, originally intended for Yap, on orders from Nimitz shaped course instead for Manus. The attack force assigned to make landings in the Palaus and at Ulithi continued toward its original objectives, but Nimitz ordered its fire-support vessels, escort carriers, transports, and escorting ships to report to MacArthur as soon as they could be released. Thus the U.S. Third Fleet was to be stripped down virtually to Task Force 38. Everything else was being transferred to the Southwest Pacific Force for the forthcoming assault on Leyte. Meanwhile, the four task groups of Task Force 38 deployed to support the Southwest Pacific landing on Morotai and the Central Pacific attack on the Palaus.

The preliminary bombing and naval bombardment of Morotai sent the 500 or so Japanese on the island scampering to the hills, and the Seventh Amphibious Force put 28,000 troops ashore without opposition. On this island engineers had two bomber fields and a fighter strip ready in time to cover the left flank of the Leyte invasion.

On Angaur, in the Palaus, two regiments of the Army's 81st Division had no difficulty subduing the 1,600 Japanese occupation troops. Here two 6,000-foot runways were ready for use by October 17. Ulithi proved to be unoccupied by the enemy. This atoll provided the Pacific Fleet with an anchorage and logistic base of major importance.

Among the mid-September invasions, the only difficult one was that of Peleliu. Conquering this little island was in some respects the toughest operation of the war. Most of its 10,000 defenders had concealed themselves and their guns in a labyrinth of more than 500 caves dug into a series of ridges. The 1st Marine Division, assisted by a regiment of the 81st Division rushed over from Angaur, fought a month trying to clear the ridges of enemy by using bazookas, demolition charges, and tank-mounted, long-range flame throwers. On October 15, the two remaining regiments of the 81st Division took over the struggle. Organized resistance on the island did not end until November 25. Long before that date, American planes were operating from the bomber strip on Peleliu, and Allied ships were using Kossol Passage, but the capture of Peleliu had cost 10,000 American casualties, including nearly 2,000 killed. It is questionable whether the advantages gained offset the terrible cost.

The Joint Chiefs of Staff and CinCPOA headquarters were much concerned about coordination among the forces going against Leyte. Though two separate fleets, the beefed-up Seventh and the stripped-down Third, were to support the invasion, there would be no overall commander at the scene. Admiral Kinkaid, Commander, U.S. Seventh Fleet, took his orders from General MacArthur, who would be present, and General MacArthur took his orders from the Joint Chiefs in Washington. Admiral Halsey, Commander, U.S. Third Fleet, took his orders from Admiral Nimitz, who would be at Pearl Harbor, and Nimitz took his orders from the Joint Chiefs. In such a situation of divided command, there was the obvious danger that the fleets might be operating at cross-purposes, with no officer at hand authorized to restore order.

In an effort to achieve cooperation and mutual support, representatives of the forces involved met at MacArthur's new headquarters at Hollandia. Nimitz sent a delegation headed by Forrest Sherman. Halsey sent one headed by his chief of staff, Mick Carney. On Sherman's return to Pearl Harbor on September 22, the CinCPOA staff completed Operation Plan 8-44, which Nimitz signed on September 27. This plan directed forces of the Pacific Ocean Areas to "cover and support forces of the Southwest Pacific in order to assist in the seizure and occupation of objectives in the Central Philippines." It ordered the Third Fleet, that is, Admiral Halsey, to "destroy enemy naval and air forces in or threatening the Philippine Area."

The order to "destroy" enemy forces could have been interpreted as going beyond and even conflicting with the general order to "cover," which implies merely preventing the enemy from interfering with the landing forces. A separate directive to the Third Fleet went even further: "In case opportunity for destruction of major portion of the enemy fleet offer or can be created, such destruction becomes the primary task." This directive, unlike the others in the Plan, was not headed by either a number or a letter designation, which made it appear to have been added later—possibly by aviation officers who wanted to make sure that Halsey would feel free to do what Spruance had refused to do the preceding June. Yet it did not cancel the order to "cover." It did not say that destruction was the *sole* task. In short, it did not authorize Halsey to abandon the beachhead.

While some of the CinCPac-CinCPOA staff were planning POA participation in the forthcoming Leyte campaign, others were looking ahead to future operations. These officers drew the conclusion that Admiral King's cherished plan to invade Formosa was impracticable. The scheduled date of March 1, 1945, was based in part on the widely held belief that Germany would surrender in the fall of 1944, thus releasing all the troops needed to bring the war against Japan to a quick end. But it was becoming apparent that the fanatical will of Hitler would keep the Germans fighting past all hope. Hence the Pacific commanders needed to reconsider their objectives.

The CinCPOA planners liked Spruance's suggestion of taking Iwo Jima and Okinawa, but those islands were too close to Japan to be assaulted until Japanese air power had been further reduced. Meanwhile MacArthur had offered, using the force he had and relying on support from the Third Fleet, to invade Luzon on December 20, the date originally assigned for the invasion of Leyte. The planners accepted that date and tentatively scheduled a target date of January 20, 1945, for Iwo Jima and a target date of the following March 1 for Okinawa.

Admiral Nimitz, summoned to San Francisco for another CinCPac-CominCh conference, took with him Admiral Forrest Sherman; General Harmon, who had come up from SoPac headquarters to command the Army Air Forces in the Central Pacific; and General Buckner, who had been appointed to command the new Tenth Army. To Spruance, Nimitz sent word not to leave California but to join him at San Francisco. Nimitz, preparing for the ticklish chore of talking King out of his Formosa project, had the arguments carefully marshaled and then summarized on a single sheet of paper.

When Spruance arrived in the Federal Building on September 29, he found CinCPOA and CominCh staff members chatting in the conference room while awaiting the arrival of Nimitz and King. Sherman handed him the summary sheet. "Read it carefully," he said, "and tell me what you think of it."

Spruance studied the sheet with obvious satisfaction. "I wouldn't change a word of it," he said, giving it back to Sherman.

Admiral Nimitz came in, presently followed by Admiral King, and the meeting came to order. Nimitz took the paper from Sherman and handed it to King, who frowned as he read it. In the discussion that followed, Nimitz and Sherman did most of the talking, very tactfully pointing out why King's proposed strategy should not be adopted. King turned to Spruance, who had been sitting quietly. It was Spruance, King recalled, who had first suggested Okinawa. What did he have to say now? Spruance replied that Nimitz and Sherman were presenting the case very well; he had nothing to add.

Nimitz called on Harmon for the air force view and on Buckner for the army view. Both opposed Formosa. Buckner pointed out that the crack Japanese Kwantung army had gone into garrison on Formosa. Judging from recent American experience in attacking elite troops, Buckner concluded that at least nine divisions would be needed to conquer Formosa and that, even with that large a force, the invaders might well suffer 50,000 casualties. King at last gave in. He agreed that Iwo Jima and Okinawa should be attacked instead of Formosa, and said that he would so recommend to the Joint Chiefs.

In subsequent discussions a good deal of ground was covered. King and Nimitz agreed that Japan could and should be defeated by blockade, bombing, and submarine warfare. King said that if the Army insisted on invading Kyushu, it should be prepared to push on smartly, without delay, to the Tokyo plain. King approved Nimitz's plan to use Guam as his Pacific Fleet advanced headquarters. He directed Nimitz to see that the Fast Carrier Force provided all possible aid to MacArthur in his Philippine landings. He said that Halsey should begin without delay to pound the airfields on Formosa and Luzon and in the Central Philippines.

In contrast to the rather furtive early CinCPac-CominCh conferences, this one, outside of business hours, was almost festive. The officers from Pearl Harbor and Washington entertained and were entertained at receptions and dinners by local army and navy commands. Ladies were present. Catherine joined Chester. Spruance sent for his wife Margaret. On October 2 the conference ended. The next day the Nimitz party, including Spruance, was back at Pearl Harbor.

Awaiting Nimitz was a letter from Halsey, in which Halsey made it clear that he did not intend to fight the sort of battle that Spruance had fought off the Marianas:

> . . . I intend, if possible, to deny the enemy a chance to outrange me in an air duel and also to deny him an opportunity to employ an air shuttle (carrier-to-target-to-land) against me. If I am to prevent his gaining that advantage I must have early information and I must move smartly.
>
> Inasmuch as the destruction of the enemy fleet is the principal task, every weapon must be brought into play and the general coordination of these weapons should be in the hands of the tactical commander responsible for the outcome of the battle. . . . My goal is the same as yours—to completely annihilate the Jap fleet if the opportunity offers. . . .

On October 4, Nimitz received dispatch orders from the Joint Chiefs of Staff directing him to seize Iwo Jima and Okinawa.

Though General MacArthur did not keep Admiral Nimitz informed concerning the movement of his forces, CinCPac headquarters was aware, beginning in early October, that elements of Admiral Kinkaid's Seventh Fleet were moving out of Manus and Hollandia toward the Philippines. This formerly modest naval force, by temporarily absorbing a large part of the U.S. Pacific Fleet, had suddenly become the largest fleet in the world, with 738 ships. Included were the Pacific Fleet's escort carriers and old battleships and the amphibious vessels of Admiral Wilkinson's Third and Admiral Barbey's Seventh Amphibious Force. The former carried the XXIV Corps, on loan from General Buckner's Tenth Army; the latter carried the X Corps, part of Lieutenant General Walter Krueger's Sixth Army. About 145,000 troops were scheduled to land on Leyte in the first five days, with more than 55,000 to follow.

As a result of Nimitz's loan of ships to MacArthur, the U.S. Third Fleet was reduced to Task Force 38, the Fast Carrier Force, which consisted of 17 fast carriers, 6 fast battleships, 17 cruisers, and 58 destroyers. Admiral Mitscher, in the *Lexington*, was to retain command of the force until after the Leyte landings had been completed. He would then turn it over to his alternate, Admiral McCain, who meanwhile was commanding Task Group 38.1, one of the four component parts of Task Force 38. Because, as combat units, Third Fleet and Task Force 38, had become identical, Halsey and Mitscher were commanding the same force. Halsey, in the *New Jersey*, frequently took over tactical command—a practice that Mitscher found disconcerting.

Halsey's initial objectives were to sever communications between Japan and the Philippines and to destroy as many enemy aircraft as possible. He reported his operations to Nimitz whenever the situation permitted him to break radio silence and often when it did not. From Halsey's reports Nimitz learned that Task Force 38 raided Okinawa on October 10, strafed Luzon airfields on the 11th, and on the 12th began three days of attacks on Formosa, striking at shipping, airfields, and installations and shooting down quantities of enemy planes, many of which were observed to be carrier types. Japanese aircraft succeeded in torpedoing the *Canberra* and *Houston*, and Halsey ordered the crippled cruisers towed toward Ulithi.

Radio Tokyo, apparently on the basis of this modest success and of erroneous reports by Japanese aviators, announced that the American carrier fleet had been almost annihilated and that a Japanese fleet was en route to destroy the remnant, then retiring. The radio described victory celebrations in Japanese cities and quoted congratulatory messages from Hitler and Mussolini. To counter this propaganda, Halsey sent a dispatch to Nimitz: "The Third Fleet's sunken and damaged ships have been salvaged and are retiring at high speed toward the enemy," whereupon Nimitz released a communiqué: "Admiral Nimitz has received from Admiral Halsey the comforting assurance that he is now retiring toward the enemy following the salvage of all the Third Fleet ships recently reported sunk by Radio Tokyo."

Halsey hoped his damaged cruisers might serve as bait to lure out a Japanese fleet for destruction. An American submarine reported that a cruiser-destroyer force had indeed sortied from the Inland Sea, but Japanese long-range planes must have sighted Halsey's main body, obviously unimpaired, for the force soon turned around and prudently withdrew. Halsey was deprived of his chance for a naval battle, but between October 11 and 16, his carrier planes had destroyed about 500 enemy aircraft at the cost of 79 of his own. The *Canberra* and the *Houston* made it to Ulithi and ultimately reached shipyards in the United States for repairs.

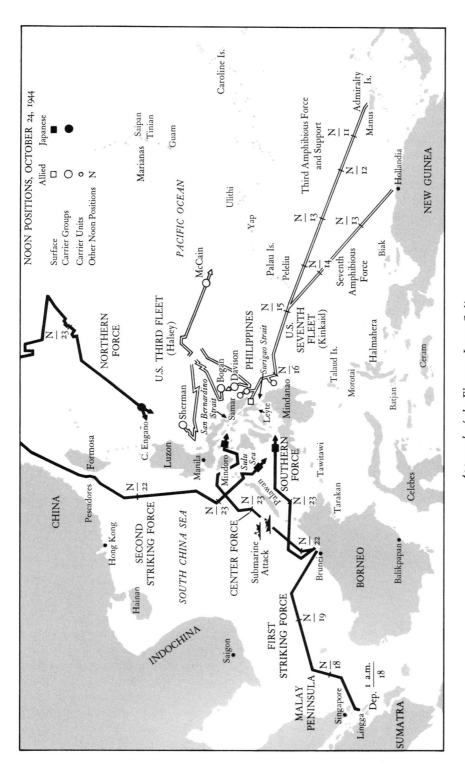

Surface
Carrier Groups
Carrier Units
Other Noon Positions

Allied    Japanese

N

CHINA

Pescadores

Hong Kong

Hainan

SECOND
STRIKING FORCE

N
22

SOUTH CHINA SEA

N
23

CENTER FORCE

Submarine
Attack

N
23

Palawan

N
23

Brunei

N
22

BORNEO

Balikpapan

FIRST
STRIKING FORCE

N
19

INDOCHINA

Saigon

N
18

MALAY
PENINSULA

Singapore

Lingga
Dep.

1 a.m.
18

SUMATRA

N
18

Tarakan

SOUTHERN
FORCE

N
23

Tawitawi

Sulu
Sea

Mindoro

Manila

Luzon

C. Engaño

NORTHERN
FORCE

N
23

Formosa

U.S. THIRD FLEET
(Halsey)

Sherman

San Bernardino
Strait

Bogan

Davison

Samar

PHILIPPINES

Surigao Strait

Leyte

Mindanao

N
16

N
15

PACIFIC OCEAN

Marianas    Saipan
Tinian

Guam

Ulithi

Yap

Palau Is.
Peleliu

Caroline Is.

McCain

U.S.
SEVENTH
FLEET
(Kinkaid)

N
14

Seventh
Amphibious
Force

N
13

N
13

Third Amphibious Force
and Support

N
12

N
11

Admiralty
Is.

Manus

Hollandia

NEW GUINEA

Biak

Morotai

Talaud Is.

Halmahera

Batjan

Ceram

Celebes

*Approach of the Fleets to Leyte Gulf*

The first word from the Southwest Pacific forces came from Rear Admiral Jesse Oldendorf, Commander, Seventh Fleet Bombardment and Fire Support Group, who reported by radio on October 17 and 18 that advance units of the Seventh Fleet had put troops ashore on islands guarding the entrance to Leyte Gulf and that his fire-support ships had entered the gulf and begun the bombardment of the beachheads. On the 20th General MacArthur announced that all landings on Leyte had been made on schedule with extremely light losses.

What the Americans did not realize was that the Japanese had abandoned the costly and hopeless policy of trying to defend beaches under battleship fire. The defenders were ordered to dig in beyond the easy reach of fleet marksmanship and let the invaders come to them.

In the afternoon of October 20 MacArthur went ashore accompanied by Sergio Osmeña, President of the Philippines. On the beach the general delivered into a microphone his speech of liberation, which was repeated several times by high-power radio for all Filipinos to hear:

> This is the voice of freedom, General MacArthur speaking. People of the Philippines! I have returned. By the Grace of Almighty God our forces stand again on Philippine soil—soil consecrated in the blood of our two peoples.... Rally to me. Let the indomitable spirit of Bataan and Corregidor lead on. As the lines of battle roll forward to bring you within the zone of operations, rise and strike. Strike at every favorable opportunity. For your homes and hearths, strike! For future generations of your sons and daughters, strike! In the name of your sacred dead, strike!

Some of the officers at Pearl Harbor considered the speech a bit on the melodramatic side, but all agreed that it might be just the thing to stir into action a tyrannized people longing for freedom.

President Roosevelt sent General MacArthur a heartfelt message of congratulations. Then, not forgetting who had paved the way for the invasion and whose ships had taken the invaders to the target, the President sent a separate message addressed to Admirals Nimitz and Halsey:

> The country has followed with pride the magnificent sweep of your fleet into enemy waters. In addition to the gallant fighting of your fliers, we appreciate the endurance and super seamanship of your forces. Your fine cooperation with General MacArthur furnishes another example of teamwork and effective and intelligent use of all weapons.

At CinCPac headquarters it was known that most of the heavy units of Japan's Combined Fleet had steamed down to the East Indies area, undoubtedly to be closer to the oil wells of Borneo, Java, and Sumatra. Ozawa's carriers had remained in the Inland Sea together with a small cruiser-destroyer force. Here they would be safe from American submarines. Evidently Ozawa's bitter experience at Tawitawi, where his flyers grew stale from enforced inactivity, made him decide to do what flying he could with what oil he could get in the Inland Sea rather than go south again. American capture of the Luzon bottleneck would prevent oil and aviation fuel from reaching Ozawa in the north, and ammunition resupply from reaching the heavy surface force to the south.

Following Halsey's attacks on Formosa, as we have seen, the Japanese cruiser-destroyer force made a sortie from the Inland Sea and then quickly retreated, evidently taking refuge behind the Ryukyu chain of islands. This mild and timorous reaction, plus the absence of any visible fleet response to MacArthur's invasion of Leyte, convinced some CinCPac officers that the Combined Fleet was again paralyzed by loss of planes and flyers, as it had been at the time of the American invasions of the Gilberts and Marshalls, and that it would not dare to make another sortie.

If the Combined Fleet should refuse to come out and fight, that would be good news for the sailors and aviators of Task Force 38. As Admiral Mitscher reported: "No other period of the Pacific War has included as much intensive operating. Probably 10,000 men have never put a foot on shore during this period of ten months. No other force in the world has been subjected to such a period of constant operation without rest or rehabilitation.... The spirit of these ships is commendable. However, the reactions of their crews are slowed down. The result is that they are not completely effective against attack."

Task Force 38 refueled some 300 miles east of Luzon. Admiral Halsey, tired but as bellicose as ever and not caring a fig about keeping radio silence, asked Admiral Kinkaid whether the two openings in the Philippines, Surigao Strait, south of Leyte Gulf, and San Bernardino Strait, north of the gulf, were being swept of mines. He had to know since he contemplated passing through one or the other to reach the South China Sea. If the Japanese fleet would not come to him, he was going to go after the Japanese fleet.

When this radio message reached CinCPac, it produced something of a shock. Admiral Nimitz quickly reminded Admiral Halsey that he was still governed by CinCPOA Op Plan 8-44, which required him to "cover and support forces of the Southwest Pacific." Further, continued Nimitz's message, "movement of major units of the Third Fleet through Surigao and San Bernardino straits will not be initiated without orders from CinCPac."

Having been forbidden to go looking for the Japanese fleet and the Japanese fleet being apparently unwilling to come to him, Halsey decided to do the next best thing: send his carrier groups to the nearest anchorage to reprovision and rearm and get some rest for his men. He notified CinCPac of his intention, and at 10:30 in the evening of October 22 he ordered McCain's Task Group 38.1 to retire to Ulithi. Rear Admiral Ralph Davison's Task Group 38.4 was to follow the next day. Upon the return of these groups on October 29, Rear Admiral Gerald F. Bogan's 38.2 and Rear Admiral Frederick Sherman's 38.3 would retire. The choice of McCain's group to lead the retirement parade proved unfortunate, for it had more carriers, more planes, and, hence, more punch than any of the others.

After midnight on October 23, the American submarines *Darter* and *Dace*, in company off the southern end of Palawan Passage, on the opposite side of the Philippines, sighted what appeared in the darkness to be eleven heavy ships and six destroyers in two columns on course 040°. The *Darter* flashed word of the contact to Admiral Christie at Fremantle, and Christie relayed it to Admirals Nimitz and Halsey at 6:20 a.m. on the 23rd. Halsey promptly canceled his order for Davison to retire but permitted McCain's group to continue on a southeasterly course for Ulithi.

By about the time Nimitz and Halsey were getting the word, the *Darter* and the *Dace* had worked into position to attack the enemy force. Torpedoes from the *Darter* sank one heavy cruiser and put one out of action. Those from the *Dace* sank another heavy cruiser. Thus was drawn the first blood in the Battle for Leyte Gulf, the greatest naval battle in history.

The Battle for Leyte Gulf was also observed by more distant commands than any other battle had ever been. The forces involved did much reporting and much communicating by radio. Because the weather was clear and there was little static, CinCPac's network of listening stations picked up nearly all the messages and relayed them to CinCPac, who relayed them to CominCh. Nimitz at Pearl Harbor and King in Washington followed the action closely. So did Kinkaid in Leyte Gulf; his communicators were breaking everything, whether intended for him or not. Yet, because of human error, messages were delayed, sent in wrong sequence, obscurely worded, misinterpreted, and, in one famous instance, accidentally corrupted. As a result, all through the hours of crisis nobody knew quite what was going on.

When the three remaining groups of Task Force 38 finished refueling on October 23, Admiral Halsey ordered them to move in closer toward the Philippines. After fanning out to westward during the night, the groups by dawn on the 24th had reached positions 125 miles apart. Sherman's group 38.3, with Mitscher in the *Lexington*, was off Luzon; Bogan's group 38.2, with Halsey in the *New Jersey*, was off San Bernardino Strait; and Davison's group 38.4 was off Leyte Gulf. By 6:30 a.m. scout planes from all three groups were searching the inland seas of the Philippines.

The amphibious and fire-support vessels of the Seventh Fleet were off the beachheads, inside Leyte Gulf, with General MacArthur in the cruiser *Nashville* and Admiral Kinkaid in the amphibious command ship *Wasatch*. To the east, just outside Leyte Gulf, were 16 escort carriers. These ships, screened by destroyers and destroyer escorts, were divided into three task units whose voice radio calls were Taffy 1, Taffy 2, and Taffy 3. They were on antisubmarine, antiaircraft, and ground-support patrol.

Early in the morning Task Force 38's search planes sighted two groups of eastbound enemy ships. One group was in the Sulu Sea and seemed to be headed for Leyte Gulf via Surigao Strait. The other group, much larger, was entering the Sibuyan Sea, apparently en route to Leyte Gulf by way of San Bernardino Strait. As the battle progressed, the Americans referred to these groups as the Southern Force and the Center Force, respectively. To all appearances, the two forces intended to make a pincer attack on the shipping in the gulf.

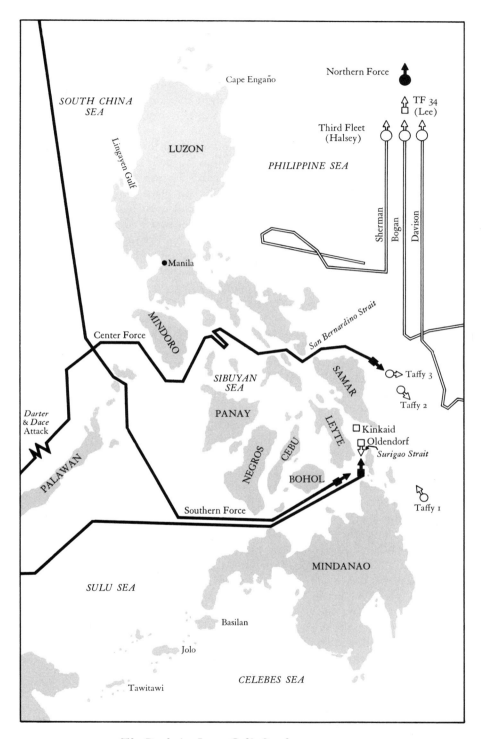

*The Battle for Leyte Gulf, October 23–25, 1944*

Admiral Halsey, reacting to the presence of the Center Force, which consisted of 5 battleships, 9 cruisers, and 13 destroyers, ordered McCain, then 600 miles east of the Philippines, en route to Ulithi, to reverse course and refuel in order to be ready for whatever might develop. He ordered Sherman and Davison to close on Bogan's group, off San Bernardino Strait, and gave all three groups their combat orders in one word, "Strike!"

Davison's search planes discovered and attacked the Southern Force. The plotting officers at CinCPac headquarters, drawing their blue and orange lines on the chart, noted that, by closing on Bogan, Davison would be in the optimum position to attack the Center Force, but his planes would no longer be able to reach the Southern Force. Admiral Kinkaid must have noted the same thing, for he took it on himself to engage the Southern Force with his surface units. He sent Admiral Oldendorf, commanding his fire-support ships, a message, listing Halsey, Nimitz, and King as information addressees: "Prepare for night engagement. Enemy force estimated 2 battleships, 4 heavy cruisers, 4 light cruisers, 10 destroyers reported under attack by our carrier planes in eastern Sulu Sea at 0910, 24 Oct. Enemy can arrive Leyte Gulf tonight."

Sherman, commanding Task Group 38.3, could not comply with Halsey's order to close on Bogan because an enemy air attack had left his light carrier *Princeton* afire and dead in the water. The damage to the *Princeton* was bad news, indeed, but to Halsey it was no excuse for neglecting the attack mission he had assigned. He radioed Mitscher, who was with Sherman's group: "Assume ComTaskGroup 38.3 is striking large enemy force near Mindoro. Advise results of strike earliest possible."

To Nimitz it was obvious that a piece of the Japanese puzzle was missing: the enemy would hardly commit so much surface strength in an area guarded by an American carrier force unless he intended to use his own carriers. Those carriers were known to have been training in Japan's Inland Sea, and Nimitz assumed that they were coming down from the north under Ozawa to form a Northern Force which, together with the Southern Force and the Center Force, would attempt a triple attack on Leyte Gulf. Halsey evidently had come to the same conclusion, for at 1:34 p.m. he radioed Mitscher: "Enemy carrier strength not located. Keep area to north under observation."

At 3:12 Halsey, listing ComInCh and CinCPac as information addressees, sent his task group commanders a message that Nimitz found highly gratifying. Headed "Battle Plan," it announced that a Task Force 34 would be formed, consisting of 4 battleships, including his flagship *New Jersey*, 2 heavy cruisers, 3 light cruisers, and 14 destroyers—all drawn from Bogan's and Davison's task groups. Vice Admiral Willis A. Lee was to command the new task force, which would "engage decisively at long ranges," while the carriers kept clear of the surface fighting.

CinCPac and his staff judged this the proper tactic to meet the situation—pulling out of the carrier screens a surface force to engage an enemy surface force, while retaining supporting air power in the background. Although Kinkaid was not an addressee of Halsey's message, he knew about it because his communicators had intercepted it and shown it to him. Naturally, he, Mitscher, Nimitz, and King all assumed that Halsey would order his plan executed— possibly by short-range voice radio since the two task groups involved were close together.

At about 4:00 p.m. Mitscher notified Halsey that a magazine in the burning *Princeton* had exploded, damaging the cruiser *Birmingham* and two destroyers that were alongside fighting the carrier's fires. The *Birmingham's* casualties were severe, estimated at 150 killed and 400 wounded. Nimitz wondered why Sherman had risked such a valuable and heavily manned vessel as a cruiser to do the sort of rescue work ordinarily assigned to destroyers.

In the late afternoon Mitscher radioed Halsey that Sherman's search planes had located the Northern Force, evidently in two sections, and that the carrier section was some 180 miles east of the northern tip of Luzon. In the circumstances he recommended scuttling the *Princeton*, whose flames might serve as a beacon for enemy planes after dark. Halsey told him to use his discretion about the *Princeton*. After a further exchange, in which Mitscher reported the *Princeton* scuttled, Halsey informed Nimitz and MacArthur that the enemy carrier force had been sighted—information that Nimitz had already obtained through intercepts.

At 8:24 p.m. Halsey sent a message to Kinkaid, with ComInCh and CinCPac as information addressees. He gave the location, course, and speed of the Center Force, which suggested that it was headed for San Bernardino Strait and could pass through in a few hours. Strike reports, however, indicated that the Center Force had been heavily damaged. Halsey concluded: "Am proceeding north with three groups to attack enemy carrier force at dawn." At Pearl Harbor it was assumed that this meant three carrier groups, Task Force 34, the surface group, being formed and left behind.

Nobody at CinCPac headquarters was surprised at Halsey's northward dash. Given a choice of objectives, he could always be expected to go after carriers, the warships with the longest reach and the hardest punch. He was frustrated at having missed a chance to get at the carriers in the Battle of the Coral Sea and again in the Battle of Midway. He had condemned Spruance's failure to go after the carriers on the night of June 18–19. Lastly, he could hardly do otherwise than go charging off after the toughest enemy force, because he had come to identify himself with the ferocious character invented by the press: "Bull" Halsey, Nemesis of the Japs. It was predictable, too, that he would not head north until it was dark, so as not to reveal his intention to any snooping enemy planes, and then he would steam toward the enemy carriers through the night, in order to cancel the enemy's advantage in outranging the Americans with their planes.

Of course, the Japanese Center Force, damaged or not, also had to be considered, for unless something stopped it, it would soon have passed through San Bernardino Strait and be in the Pacific, heading along the east coast of

Samar for Leyte Gulf. Admiral Spruance, looking at the chart, placed his hand on it just to east of the strait and said softly, as if to himself, "If I were there, I would keep my force right there." It is not likely that many naval aviators would have agreed with him. To remain so near enemy airfields could invite shuttle-bombing by an enemy carrier force. While fighting a battle, Spruance could hardly have cratered the complex of airfields on Luzon, as he had cratered the few on Rota and Guam during the Battle of the Philippine Sea.

Certainly it was comforting to know that Halsey had had the wisdom to leave Task Force 34 behind to guard San Bernardino Strait. One nagging question, however, was whether he was wise to lead all three of his available carrier groups against the Northern Force. That move left Admiral Lee without any air support, as he opposed an enemy that might be supported by planes from Luzon. Nimitz must have considered this problem, but he kept hands off. In the first American carrier counterattack of the war, he had learned from Halsey himself the wise practice of not interfering with the man at the scene.

Toward dawn on October 25, two messages came into CinCPac headquarters almost simultaneously. One was from Halsey, who, still disregarding radio silence, reported that one of his night snoopers had contacted the enemy carrier force 100 miles north of his own northbound force. Halsey had succeeded in canceling the enemy's advantage by bringing him before dawn well within the attack range of the American carrier planes.

The second message was from Kinkaid. At anchor in Leyte Gulf, he had no need to observe radio silence. Reporting on Oldendorf's operations, the dispatch read: "Our surface forces are engaging enemy surface forces in Surigao Strait and southern Leyte Gulf." Subsequent dispatches from Kinkaid described the progress of the battle. Sent at 4:12 a.m.: "Enemy force sighted in strait by PT boats about 0200 I,* arrived entrance gulf about 0300 I. Consists of 2 battleships, 3 cruisers, and destroyers. Question: Is TF 34 guarding San Bernardino Strait?"† Sent at 6:23: "About 0500 I, 25 enemy surface vessels Surigao Strait pursued by our light forces." Sent at 7:03: "At 0645 I 25th, our forces closing to polish off four Nip cripples near Kanihaan Island, Surigao Strait."

Obviously the Seventh Fleet gunnery vessels had won a resounding victory over the enemy's Southern Force. This was cheerful news indeed. Still, Nimitz was worried. The course and speed of the Center Force, as given in Halsey's 8:24 message to Kinkaid, should have carried it through San Bernardino Strait a little after midnight. If Task Force 34 had been waiting outside the strait, there should have been a night battle. On the other hand,

---

* Zone Item time (Greenwich minus 9 hours), then used in the Philippines. Noon, October 25, in the Philippines was 4:30 p.m., October 24, at Pearl Harbor.

† At 7:04, in reply to this message, Halsey signaled: "Negative. TF 34 is with carrier groups now engaging enemy carrier force"–an answer that appalled Kinkaid. Halsey's answer is not in the microfilmed CinCPac file and evidently was not received at Pearl Harbor. As will be seen, Nimitz asked Halsey a similar question at 9:44 a.m.

Admiral Lee, as Nimitz knew, had developed a distaste for night combat in the battleship night action of the Battle of Guadalcanal. Perhaps Lee had managed somehow to hold off till dawn. Now the sun had risen over the Philippines, but there was still no word from him. If the Center Force had met no opposition, it could be east of Samar heading straight for Leyte Gulf. The only ships that might challenge it in that area were the three little escort carrier units, Taffy 1, 2, and 3.

A suspicion was growing in Nimitz's mind that Task Force 34 had not been formed after all, or that, if it had been formed, it had not been left behind on October 24. Halsey in his battle plan had assigned his own flagship *New Jersey* to that force, yet in the 8:24 dispatch he had said: "Am proceeding north with three groups." That he personally had gone north with three groups was indicated by his contact report, which concluded, "Own force in three groups concentrated." Nimitz knew that he was not alone in his concern; Kinkaid's inquiry about Task Force 34 showed that he too wanted assurance.

Nimitz buzzed for his assistant chief of staff. When Captain Bernard Austin entered his office, Nimitz asked him if there were any dispatches regarding the situation off the Philippines that he had not seen. Austin replied that he knew of none and added, "Will you tell me in particular what you are looking for?"

"I'm very concerned," replied Nimitz, "because nothing I have seen indicates that Admiral Halsey has left San Bernardino guarded against Japanese units coming through there and getting our ships off Leyte."

"Well, Admiral," said Austin, "that *is* an unclear point in dispatches, and several other people are wondering the same thing."

"If anything comes in," said Nimitz, "let me know right away."

"Aye, aye, sir," said Austin and left the room.

Admiral Nimitz sounded a good many buzzers that morning in his search for information and opinions. About the third time he called in Austin, the latter got up his courage sufficiently to suggest that Nimitz ask Halsey if he had left any force to guard San Bernardino. "That's what you want to know," said Austin. "Why don't you ask him?"

Nimitz thought a moment and then gave Austin the expected answer—he did not want to send any dispatch that would directly or indirectly influence the responsible tactical commander in the tactical use of his forces.

Out in the Philippine area about this time, communicators were startled to intercept a dispatch in plain English. The sender was Rear Admiral Clifton A. F. Sprague, the commander of Task Unit 77.4.3, known as Taffy 3, northernmost of the three Seventh Fleet escort carrier units stationed outside Leyte Gulf. This message, addressed to Commander, Third Fleet, and Commander, Task Force 34, read: "Enemy battleships and cruisers 15 miles astern this unit and firing on it. My position is 80 miles bearing 060 from Homonhon Island." Taffy 3's bearing and distance from Homonhon, which is at the mouth of Leyte Gulf, placed it due east of Samar.

Taffy 3's call for help was not heard at Pearl Harbor. It was soon followed, however, by an encoded message from Kinkaid to Halsey. Sent by the *Wasatch*'s powerful transmitter, this message was read by both Admiral Nimitz and Admiral King: "About 0700 CTU 77.4.3 reported under fire from enemy battleships and cruisers in position 11-4, 126-25. Evidently came through San Bernardino Strait during the night. Request immediate air strike. Also request support from heavy ships. My old battleships low in ammunition."

Kinkaid followed this message almost immediately by another to Commander, Third Fleet, this time in plain English—evidently intended as much to frighten the Japanese as to prod Halsey into action. This message read: "Enemy force attacking our escort carriers composed of 4 battleships, 8 cruisers, and other ships. Request Lee proceed top speed cover Leyte. Request immediate strike by fast carriers."

Kinkaid continued to call on Halsey and Lee for help. "Fast battleships are urgently needed immediately at Leyte Gulf," he cried by radio. Nearly an hour later, he was signaling, "My situation is critical. Fast battleships and support by carrier strikes may be able to keep enemy from destroying escort carriers and entering Leyte."

Evidently these cries for help were not reaching the *Lexington*, for Admiral Mitscher was notifying Admiral McCain that Task Force 38 was attacking four enemy carriers. They were reaching the senior commands, however. At Pearl Harbor the usually serene Nimitz was pacing the floor. In Washington Admiral King was pacing, too—and swearing.

Finally at 8:48 a.m. Halsey indicated his awareness of the situation off Samar. It was later learned that Kinkaid's dispatches had reached him after much delay and confusingly out of sequence. Halsey's response was to order McCain to proceed at best possible speed toward Samar and strike the enemy force, whose position he gave. To Kinkaid he signaled: "Am now engaging enemy carrier force. Task Group 38.1 with 5 carriers and 4 heavy cruisers has been ordered to assist you immediately." He gave McCain's estimated position, which was nearly 300 miles northeast of the beleaguered Taffy 3, and his own, which was more than 350 miles due north. The implication was that help from McCain's Task Group 38.1 would be considerably delayed and that timely help from the rest of Task Force 38 was out of the question.

Halsey's message to McCain answered the main question in Nimitz's mind. Had Task Force 34 been anywhere near Samar, Halsey would have ordered Lee to attack the enemy that was attacking Taffy 3. He would probably have ordered McCain to attack also, but he would certainly have signaled Lee. That he did not implied that Lee was with Halsey. There was a possibility that Task Force 34 had never been formed, but Nimitz conjectured otherwise. Knowing Halsey, he was convinced that Halsey had formed it that morning and was now in it, forging out ahead of the carrier groups to fight an old-fashioned surface battle with stragglers and with the cripples left by Mitscher's carrier planes.

Austin, who had brought the latest dispatches to Nimitz, was several miles behind his chief's thinking. He could see that the admiral was perturbed, and he concluded that he was still wondering where Task Force 34 was. Trying to be helpful, he suggested, "Admiral, couldn't you just ask Admiral Halsey the simple question: Where is Task Force 34?"

Nimitz thought for a minute and then said, "Go out and write it up. That's a good idea."

Austin thought the question was intended as a simple inquiry, but Nimitz was using it as a nudge. What Nimitz meant was: "Where *ought* Task Force 34 to be—and hadn't it better get the hell there as fast as possible?" He was sure that Halsey would take the hint. Now, in Nimitz's considered opinion, these were extraordinary circumstances that justified his interfering with the man on the scene.

Because Nimitz's Task Force 34 message became famous, or notorious, and because it produced a remarkable effect on Halsey, it is interesting to trace its progress to the addressee. Captain Austin went to his office and dictated the message to his yeoman: "Where is Task Force 34? From Admiral Nimitz to Commander Third Fleet, with information to Admiral King and Admiral Kinkaid."

The yeoman, having caught a certain emphasis in his boss's voice and feeling that he ought to indicate the emphasis in the message, stuck in the words "RPT [repeat] where is." He then took the message down to the communication department, Jack Redman's domain, and handed it to an ensign on duty. The ensign prepared the dispatch for transmission. He changed the words Admiral Nimitz to CinCPac, Admiral King to CominCh, and Admiral Kinkaid to CTF 77, added padding, and assigned a date-time group, 250044, meaning 44 minutes past midnight, Greenwich time, on the 25th of the month (9:44 a.m. in the Philippines).

Padding consisted of nonsense phrases placed at both ends of encrypted radio messages to bury the opening and closing words which, because they tended to be stereotyped, might provide easy points of attack for enemy cryptanalysts. The rules for padding specified that it may not consist of familiar words or quotations, it must be separated from the text by double consonants, and it must not be susceptible to being read as part of the message.

At this point we shall digress to point out that October 25 is no ordinary day in military history. For one thing, it is Saint Crispin's Day, the date of the Battle of Agincourt (1415). It is also the date of the Battle of Balaklava (1854). The latter was marked by the magnificent, futile charge of the Light Brigade, of which Tennyson wrote:

> When can their glory fade?
> O the wild charge they made!
>     All the world wonder'd.
> Honour the charge they made!
> Honour the Light Brigade,
>     Noble six hundred!

Did the ensign who prepared Nimitz's dispatch remember that this was Balaklava Day and recall the lines of Tennyson? It would not be too surprising if he did, for English professors and students of literature tend to be attracted, or assigned, to communications. If our anonymous ensign did remember the Light Brigade, he must have compared its charge into the teeth of the Russian guns with Taffy 3's combat with the battleship force, the story of which had been coming in over his desk in dispatches all that morning. The padding he wrote at the beginning of Nimitz's message, "Turkey trots to water," was nonsensical enough, but his end padding, "The world wonders," echoed Tennyson. Perhaps it was an unconscious echo, because when he was called on the carpet about it, he said, "It was just something that popped into my head."

Admiral Halsey had a standing order that, when he was in his flagship *New Jersey* and a "hot" message came in addressed to him, the communicators were not to take time transferring it to a dispatch form but were to rush it to flag country as quickly as possible by the pneumatic tube. When Admiral Nimitz's message was deciphered in the *New Jersey*'s communication department, a yeoman tore the strip off the ciphering machine and handed it to Ensign Burton Goldstein, who realized at a glance that this was a message that should go to Halsey without delay. He routinely ripped off the opening padding, but the end padding puzzled him. Although it was separated from the rest of the dispatch by a double consonant, it read devilishly like a part of the message. Goldstein showed the strip to his superior, Lieutenant Charles Fox, who advised him to send it on with the words attached. The liaison officer in flag country, said Fox, could point out to the admiral that the concluding phrase was probably padding.

So up the tube went the strip. The liaison officer plucked it out of the holder, noted that it was addressed to Commander, Third Fleet, and immediately handed it to Halsey. It read:

FROM CINCPAC ACTION COM THIRD FLEET INFO COMINCH CTF SEVENTY-SEVEN X WHERE IS RPT WHERE IS TASK FORCE THIRTY-FOUR RR THE WORLD WONDERS.

Halsey, not accustomed to seeing padding, took the final phrase to be part of the message. It looked to him like heavy-handed sarcasm, with King and Kinkaid called in to witness his humiliation.

"I was stunned as if I had been struck in the face," recalled Halsey. "The paper rattled in my hands. I snatched off my cap, threw it on the deck, and shouted something that I am ashamed to remember. Mick Carney rushed over and grabbed my arm: 'Stop it! What the hell's the matter with you? Pull yourself together!'

"I gave him the dispatch and turned my back. I was so mad I couldn't talk. It was utterly impossible for me to believe that Chester Nimitz would send me such an insult."

Admiral Nimitz's surmise was correct. Halsey had formed Task Force 34 that morning; it included all six of his fast battleships, and with it he had forged ahead to attack stragglers and finish off cripples. After brooding for an hour over the supposed insult from CinCPac, Halsey angrily ordered Task Force 34 to reverse course from due north to due south. "For me," he later wrote, "one of the biggest battles of the war was off, and what has been called 'the Battle of Bull's Run' was on."

As Halsey passed Task Force 38, which was still northbound, he picked up Bogan's Task Group 38.2 to provide air cover for Task Force 34 and detached from Task Force 34 four cruisers and ten destroyers to provide additional surface support for the carriers remaining under Mitscher. To CinCPac he reported: "Your 250044. TF 34 with me engaging enemy carrier force. Am now proceeding with TG 38.2 and all fast battleships to reinforce Kinkaid. 1 enemy carrier sunk. 2 carriers dead in water. No damage own force.... TG 38.1 already ordered assist Kinkaid immediately."

To Kinkaid, Halsey radioed: "I am proceeding toward Leyte with Task Group 38.2 and 6 fast battleships. My position, course, and speed later, but do not expect arrive before 0800 tomorrow."

Meanwhile, Kinkaid continued to sound off by radio. First, he reported that the Center Force had turned away, then that it was threatening Leyte Gulf again. The enemy force was, in fact, retiring. To intercept it, Halsey detached his fastest ships, 2 battleships, 3 cruisers, and 8 destroyers, and with these sped ahead. When Halsey reached the vicinity of San Bernardino Strait a little past midnight, the only ship of the Center Force that had not passed back through the strait was a destroyer that had lingered behind to pick up Japanese survivors of the battle with Taffy 3. Halsey's cruisers and destroyers darted ahead and sank this lone vessel with gunfire and torpedoes. His fast battleships had steamed 300 miles north and 300 miles back south between the two main enemy forces without making contact with either.

Afterward, when U. S. naval officers reviewed the Battle for Leyte Gulf, they gave each of the four main actions a name. They called the air attacks made on the Center Force as it plowed its way eastward on October 24 toward San Bernardino the Battle of the Sibuyan Sea. In this phase, Halsey's carrier planes put a heavy cruiser out of action, damaged several other ships, and sank the superbattleship *Musashi*.

The Southern Force was actually two enemy groups that never got together. The first group, consisting of 2 battleships, 1 heavy cruiser, and 4 destroyers, was nearly annihilated in the Battle of Surigao Strait, fought before dawn on October 25. Oldendorf had set a trap for it by lining the sides of the strait with his destroyers and PT boats and placing his battleships and cruisers on T-capping courses across its northern end. The second Japanese group, seeing what happened to the first, prudently withdrew.

The action, fought a few hours later, between the Center Force and Taffy 3 was named the Battle off Samar. The Center Force opened fire on the six jeep carriers of this unit, sinking the *Gambier Bay* and heavily damaging two others. The unit's destroyers and destroyer escorts made smoke and courageously counterattacked with torpedoes. Three of these vessels were sunk by gunfire, but the enemy was thrown into confusion. Planes from the Taffies and from Leyte struck at the Center Force, sinking three of its cruisers and inducing the remainder of the force to retire. In the afternoon of October 25 aircraft from McCain's Task Group 38.1 attacked the Center Force but did little damage. Striking from extreme range, they were hampered by wing tanks and were obliged to carry bombs instead of the heavier torpedoes. That same afternoon Japanese pilots, flying land-based planes, crashed into five carriers of Taffy 3 and nearby Taffy 1, heavily damaging all and causing one to sink. These suicide, or kamikaze,* attacks were the beginning of a development that was ominous for the Americans.

Task Force 38's attack on the Northern Force was called the Battle off Cape Engaño. In this operation, U.S. carrier planes sank the fleet carrier *Zuikaku*, last of the Pearl Harbor raiders, three light carriers, and two destroyers. They also damaged a cruiser, which was sunk by an American submarine as she limped homeward.

Because the Northern Force made no counterattack and its carriers appeared almost bare of planes, some officers concluded that it was as helpless as the Combined Fleet had been two years earlier and was being used merely to lure Halsey away from Leyte so that the Southern and Center forces could close in on American shipping in the gulf. After the war the Japanese confirmed that this conclusion was correct. Their carriers had lost most of their planes in the Battle of the Philippine Sea. Any Japanese fleet aviators who had attained proficiency after that time had been sacrificed in trying to protect the Formosan bases from Halsey's carrier attacks.

As long as he lived, Admiral Halsey rejected all evidence and every assertion that the Northern Force was bait. The notion that he had been lured away to the north did not sit well with him.

During the cocktail hour and at dinner in Admiral Nimitz's quarters on the evening of October 25 (east longitude date), discussion of the day's battles was lively and sometimes caustic. In addition to high-ranking officers present on this occasion, there was a lieutenant commander who, having just relinquished command of a submarine, was en route to the United States for leave. This young man was by no means awed into silence by the age and rank of the other guests. He felt free to express his opinions in such lofty company for the very good reason that his name happened to be Chester W. Nimitz, Jr.

Chet was amazed that CinCPac and his staff had let hours pass while they wondered whether Task Force 34 was covering San Bernardino Strait. Why, he asked, had they not asked Admiral Halsey point-blank where it was and told

---

* *Kamikaze* ("divine wind") is the name given to a typhoon that, in 1274, scattered Kublai Khan's fleet, thereby saving Japan from invasion.

him to send it forthwith to wherever they wanted it to be. Patiently Admiral Nimitz explained that he and his staff were thousands of miles away from the operational area, and it was his policy to avoid like the plague interfering with the judgment of the tactical commander at the scene of action.

Later in the evening someone read or quoted the directive in Op Plan 8-44 specifying that if Halsey saw an opportunity to destroy a major portion of the enemy fleet, such destruction would become his primary task. Chet was again surprised. In signing such an order, he said brightly, Admiral Nimitz was practically giving Admiral Halsey carte blanche to abandon the beachhead. He said it was a mistake to offer Halsey any alternative whatever to supporting the landings in Leyte Gulf. "It's your fault," he concluded, looking at his father.

The room fell silent. This was too much. The elder Nimitz turned a bleak gaze upon his impertinent offspring. "That's your opinion," he said, ending the discussion.

At a little after 7:00 p.m. (Philippine time), Kinkaid, by then reasonably sure that the Center Force was retiring, expressed his appreciation to the Taffies by radio: "For your magnificent performance of today my admiration knows no bounds. You have carried a load that only fleet carriers could be expected to carry. Well done. Kinkaid."

At 9:26 p.m., Halsey, still southbound with Task Force 34, radioed Nimitz (date-time group 251226): "It can be announced with assurance that the Japanese navy has been beaten, routed, and broken by the Third and Seventh Fleets." Nimitz passed the message to the Navy Department, and King told him not to release it because Halsey had not had sufficient time or opportunity to evaluate the situation completely. Secretary Forrestal concurred with King but nevertheless informed President Roosevelt.

The Navy's hand was forced by MacArthur, who, on his own, released a victory communiqué to the Reuters news agency. Harry Hopkins, special assistant to the President, called Forrestal and suggested that Halsey's message be given to the press. Forrestal was, he said, dubious about releasing good news without being absolutely certain of the facts. Hopkins thought it was worth taking a chance. Consequently, at six o'clock on the evening of October 25 (Washington time), the President called in the White House reporters and read them a paraphrase of Halsey's victory message to Nimitz.

When the facts became known, they more than justified Halsey's optimism. Not only had the Japanese been thwarted in their scheme to sink American shipping in Leyte Gulf, but they had lost 306,000 tons of their own combat ships—3 battleships, 4 carriers, 10 cruisers, and 9 destroyers. The Americans, at a cost of 37,000 tons of warships—1 light carrier, 2 escort carriers, 2 destroyers, and 1 destroyer escort—had utterly destroyed Japan's capacity to wage another fleet battle. In short, they had won uncontested command of the Pacific Ocean.

At 10:17 in the evening of the 25th, Halsey sent a top-secret message (date-time group 251317) to Nimitz and King explaining his tactics:

Searches by my carrier planes revealed the presence of the Northern carrier force on the afternoon of 24 October, which completed the picture of all enemy naval forces. As it seemed childish to me to guard statically San Bernardino Strait, I concentrated TF 38 during the night and steamed north to attack the Northern Force at dawn. I believed that the Center Force had been so heavily damaged in the Sibuyan Sea that it could no longer be considered a serious menace to Seventh Fleet.

In a letter to King, dated October 28 and marked PERSONAL and TOP SECRET, Nimitz observed:

I am greatly pleased with the Fleet operations of the past week with two exceptions. My first exception and regret is that so valuable a unit as the BIRMINGHAM was taken alongside the damaged PRINCETON instead of relying on destroyers for the rescue, salvage, and fire fighting operation. My second exception and regret is that the fast battleships were not left in the vicinity of Samar when Task Force 38 started after the striking force reported to be in the north end of the Philippines Sea, and composed of carriers, two battleships, cruisers and destroyers in support. It never occurred to me that Halsey, knowing the composition of the ships in the Sibuyan Sea, would leave San Bernardino Strait unguarded, even though the Jap detachments in the Sibuyan Sea had been reported seriously damaged. That Halsey feels that he is in a defensive position is indicated in his top secret despatch 251317.

That the San Bernardino detachment of the Japanese Fleet, which included the YAMATO and the MUSASHI, did not completely destroy all of the escort carriers and their accompanying screen is nothing short of special dispensation from the Lord Almighty; although it can be accepted that the damage the Japs had received the day before in the Sibuyan Sea undoubtedly affected their ability to steam and shoot when they attacked Sprague's escort carriers.

Nimitz was careful not to criticize Halsey publicly or to permit criticism of him in any records that might subsequently be made public. When Captain Ralph Parker, head of the CinCPac's Analytical Section, sharply condemned Halsey's tactics in the official CinCPac report of the battle, Nimitz refused to sign the report. He sent it back with a note written across it: "What are you trying to do, Parker, start another Sampson-Schley controversy? Tone this down. I'll leave it to you."

Halsey reported in person to Admiral King the following January, and his first words were, "I made a mistake in that battle."

King held up his hand. "You don't have to tell me any more," he said. "You've got a green light on everything you did."

In his autobiography, however, King criticized both Halsey and Kinkaid. He attributed "the element of surprise in the Battle of Samar not only to Halsey's absence in the north but also to Kinkaid's failure to use his own squadrons for search at a crucial moment."

Rarely in military history have two successive battles presented more similar tactical problems than those of the Philippine Sea and Leyte Gulf, and rarely have the commanders responded so differently. Long afterward Halsey sadly suggested that it might have been better if he had commanded in the Philippine Sea and Spruance at Leyte Gulf.

One reason why historians have treated Halsey's blunder so gently is that his earlier advice had led to the speeding up of the timetable for action against the Philippines. Had the Leyte invasion taken place on December 20, as originally scheduled, Ozawa would have had time to train his aviators enough to give the Americans a real fight. Since Halsey was responsible for the speed-up, his strategic insight more than offset his tactical lapse.

# CHAPTER 21

# THE PHILIPPINES CAMPAIGN AND THE MOVE TO GUAM

THE MORE ADMIRAL NIMITZ learned about the enemy from intelligence sources, the more he appreciated the truth of Admiral Halsey's announcement that the Japanese navy had been "beaten, routed, and broken." It became obvious that the Battle for Leyte Gulf was the last stand-up naval battle of World War II. The U.S. Navy, however, still had plenty to do in helping the marines and the army ground and air forces to attain the objectives assigned to them in the Pacific.

Following a period of badly needed rest and replenishment at Ulithi, Task Force 38's first scheduled support mission was to join the B-29s of the Army's 21st Bomber Command in a raid on Tokyo. Halsey's carriers were to provide fighter escorts that would permit the Marianas-based bombers to attain precision by bombing at low altitudes, taking aircraft factories as their chief targets. This mission, dear to Halsey's heart, had to be canceled because General MacArthur's forces on Leyte badly needed the support of Task Force 38.

Following the Battle for Leyte Gulf, MacArthur had ordered General Kenney's Far Eastern Air Forces to relieve the battered Seventh Fleet escort carriers of the responsibility of supporting his ground forces. This task proved beyond the capacity of Kenney's land-based planes because Tacloban Field, the only serviceable airstrip on Leyte, could not accommodate enough aircraft for the job. U.S. Army engineers tried to enlarge the airfield at Tacloban and to construct others, but their efforts were defeated by a combination of torrential monsoon rains and unsuitable subsoil. The Japanese, however, could and did stage in planes from Japan via Formosa to their all-weather airdromes on Luzon. They thus gained such command of the air over Leyte that MacArthur was obliged to call for help. Nimitz ordered Halsey to strike the Luzon airfields and otherwise support the U.S. troops on Leyte. At the same time he requested MacArthur "to release the forces of the Third Fleet as soon as the situation permitted." Vice Admiral "Slew" McCain had replaced Vice Admiral "Pete" Mitscher as Commander, Task Force 38, the latter having flown to the United States for some much-needed leave.

Task Force 38 aviators spent a month supporting MacArthur's forces, during which time they destroyed about 700 planes and sank 3 cruisers, 10 destroyers, and numerous transports and other auxiliaries. They sent one complete Leyte-bound convoy to the bottom, drowning nearly 10,000 Japanese. Nevertheless, the Americans could not regain complete command of the air in the Leyte area. Kamikazes damaged 7 of the task force's carriers and in the

Seventh Fleet they hit 2 battleships, 2 cruisers, 2 transports, and 7 destroyers. One of the destroyers sank. After a particularly severe suicide raid on November 25, Task Force 38 withdrew to Ulithi. It had been at sea and in combat almost continuously for three months.

At the end of November 1944, Admiral Nimitz and members of his staff met at San Francisco with Admiral King and a delegation of officers from Washington and elsewhere. King and Nimitz agreed that Halsey and his subordinates needed a long stateside leave. Nimitz said he planned to turn the fleet back to the Spruance team as soon as Task Force 38 and the Third Amphibious Force could be released from supporting MacArthur. The operation was taking longer than expected because the Japanese command of the air and the foul weather at Leyte had obliged the general to shift his target date for the invasion of Luzon from December 20, 1944, to January 9, 1945. This shift meant that the target date for Iwo Jima had to be postponed from January 20 to February 19 and that for Okinawa from March 1 to April 1. Any delay beyond that date would push the Okinawa operation into the typhoon season and thus imperil the supporting fleet.

The Army planned to stage an invasion of Kyushu in the fall, following the Okinawa campaign. King and Nimitz believed that an invasion of Japan, which would certainly be costly in lives, would not in fact be necessary. They were convinced that the Japanese could be defeated by blockade and bombing and that for those operations a base on the Chinese coast opposite Japan was desirable. Nimitz proposed invading China in the vicinity of Hangchow Bay, south of Shanghai.

The conference took note of the acute shortage of carrier fighter pilots. This situation resulted from an ill-timed cutback in pilot-training followed by an unforeseen increased need for fighters to support troops, to protect bombers, and to defend the carriers from air attack, particularly by kamikazes. A proposal to assign marine fighter pilots with swift-climbing Corsairs to the fast carriers was approved by the conference.

Admiral King announced that a British fleet, with carriers, would arrive in the Pacific in 1945 to participate in the war against Japan. The commander in chief of that fleet, Admiral Sir Bruce Fraser, would have administrative control over it, but would report to Nimitz for operational orders. The British were to share the American advanced bases at Manus, Leyte, and Ulithi, but were expected to be otherwise self-sustaining. They were to adopt American tactical and communication procedures but, because they were not experienced in handling large carrier forces, King suggested that they should operate independently rather than in maneuvers with American ships.

This British fleet was in fact already on its way to the Pacific. On December 10, Admiral Fraser established headquarters at Sydney, Australia. A flurry of top-secret dispatches from London and Sydney to CinCPac headquarters requested a conference between Admiral Fraser and Admiral Nimitz and then announced the approach to Pearl Harbor of Fraser and his staff. Nimitz wrote King: "I do not need Paul Revere (with his three lanterns) to tell me that the

British are coming. The attached paraphrase of six Top Secret dispatches reads like an operation order for an occupation force. Perhaps it is intended to be an occupation force."

Fraser and his staff arrived at Pearl on December 16. Nimitz and the British admiral renewed their acquaintance, and Nimitz invited Fraser to be his house guest. They had met ten years earlier when Nimitz was commanding officer of the *Augusta* on the Far Eastern station, and both he and Fraser were captains.

The British Pacific Fleet included 4 fleet carriers, 2 battleships, 5 cruisers, and 15 destroyers—about the strength of one task group of Task Force 38. Though the British carriers had nearly the same displacement as an American *Essex*-class carrier, they could accommodate only about half as many planes, and their closed-in hangars slowed operations and would probably prove uncomfortable in tropical waters. Their armored flight decks gave them a special advantage, however, rendering them less vulnerable to kamikaze attack than the American carriers with wooden flight decks and armored hangar decks.

At the first of the Anglo-American conferences, Admiral Nimitz inquired about the problem that gave him the most concern, the sea-keeping capacity of the British fleet. He was told that the fleet had its own train, including tankers, and that, although they did refuel at sea, they had not mastered the swift underway-alongside refueling techniques used by the Americans. Admiral Nimitz asked for something more specific. Fraser estimated that his fleet could remain at sea eight days out of a month. Nimitz said that would not do at all. As he afterward told the story, "Admiral Fraser and I had a long conference.... He felt he could operate for eight days a month, and we compromised on twenty."

It was arranged for an experienced American carrier captain and several small American communication teams to be assigned to the British fleet. Admiral Fraser suggested that Commander Harold Hopkins, RN, who had served for a year as British liaison officer on Nimitz's staff, should be replaced by a vice admiral.

"What's wrong with Hopkins?" asked Nimitz, who liked the young man and thought he was doing a fine job.

Admiral Fraser explained that, with the British fleet coming into the theater, the Admiralty felt it would be appropriate to assign a more senior officer.

"Make Hopkins an admiral," suggested Nimitz.

The Admiralty compromised. They made Hopkins an acting captain and left him with CinCPac another six months.

Nimitz refused to make any commitments to the British concerning operations. He suggested that they raid the Japanese-held oil installations on Sumatra and implied that, for the time being, the British Pacific Fleet could make its best contribution by attaching itself to Kinkaid's Seventh Fleet for operations in the Southwest Pacific Area.

This was distinctly not what the British had in mind. When they objected, Admiral Nimitz said that he might be able to make use of their fleet in connection with the scheduled assault on Okinawa. He then turned them over to Admiral Spruance so that he and his staff could consider that possibility.

On December 11 the U.S. Senate approved a House bill authorizing the appointment of four fleet admirals and four generals of the army—five-star ranks that presumably would enable senior American officers to deal more effectively with five-star British officers. The President at once appointed Marshall, MacArthur, Eisenhower, and Arnold generals of the army, and Leahy, King, and Nimitz fleet admirals. The Senate confirmed these appointments on the 15th.

Many persons, including congressmen, were surprised that Halsey did not get the fourth appointment to the new naval rank. Eventually he did, but King, reluctant to see Halsey promoted while Spruance was not, postponed making any recommendation for the fourth five-star appointment. He did, however, recommend four stars for Kinkaid to bring him into line with Halsey and Spruance, the other fleet commanders in the Pacific.

When Nimitz took the oath of office as fleet admiral on December 19, he was surprised and gratified to learn that his sailor metalsmiths had new collar insignia ready for him. Apparently they had taken stars from the insignia of lesser flag ranks and mounted them by fives in circular formation.

News from the Philippines was both good and very bad indeed. On December 15 MacArthur's forces had successfully invaded the island of Mindoro in order to establish airfields on the western side of the Philippines, near Luzon and outside the monsoon rain belt. During the passage of the Mindoro invasion convoy via Surigao Strait and the Mindanao and Sulu seas, Task Force 38 had kept its fighters over the Luzon airfields around the clock to prevent enemy planes from taking off. No kamikazes reached the fast carriers because McCain had greatly increased the proportion of fighters to bombers and because he had stationed radar picket destroyers to give early warning of approaching enemy aircraft. American planes returning from a strike were required to make a turn around a picket destroyer so that any kamikazes that might have joined the returning planes as a means of locating the carriers could be weeded out by the pickets' own combat air patrol.

The Mindoro invasion convoy, enjoying no such system of protection, was struck by kamikazes from the Central Philippines. Worst damaged was the convoy flagship *Nashville* which, with 133 killed and 190 wounded, was obliged to turn back. Task Force 38, which had successfully defended itself against human attack, became a victim of foul weather. In the morning of December 18 a typhoon struck the carrier force in full fury. At the height of the storm three destroyers capsized and went down. Seven other ships were heavily damaged; 186 planes were jettisoned, blown overboard, or broke from their lashings and crashed; and nearly 800 officers and men were lost. Admiral Nimitz said, "It was the greatest loss that we have taken in the Pacific without compensatory return since the First Battle of Savo."

Because the weather continued foul, Task Force 38 withdrew to Ulithi, where it arrived on the 24th. Admiral Nimitz flew in the next day. He had already appointed a court of inquiry, but he wanted to find out for himself the reasons why the carrier force had let itself be caught by the typhoon. He took along with him a decorated Christmas tree for the *New Jersey*'s wardroom and was a little piqued to notice that the ship's officers were much prouder of a tree that her crew had fashioned out of nuts, bolts, and metal scraps.

The court of inquiry, presided over by Vice Admiral John Hoover, put most of the blame for the force being caught in the storm on Admiral Halsey. The findings of the court confirmed to some extent what Halsey's officers were saying—he lacked the skill to command a body of ships as complex as the Third Fleet. His casual methods and impetuous changing of plans were widely known. They had not mattered too much in early 1942 when he was commanding small carrier groups, but in 1944, when he was commanding a force comprising scores of ships, his sudden improvisations created confusion.

Hoover was of the opinion that Halsey should be court-martialed, but Nimitz and King thought he had been punished enough by being made to bear the principal blame for the typhoon damage. Nimitz, in his endorsement to the Court of Inquiry's Record, said that Halsey's mistakes "were errors of judgment committed under stress of war operations and stemming from a commendable desire to meet military requirements." King softened this endorsement by changing "commendable desire" to "firm determination" and after "judgment" adding the phrase "resulting from insufficient information."

Nimitz sent out orders that any commanding officer who found his ship endangered was to break radio silence at once and notify CinCPac. He also put out a Fleet Letter of advice for dealing with severe storms. "A hundred years ago," he wrote, "a ship's survival depended almost solely on the competence of her master and his constant alertness to every hint of change in the weather." Nimitz compared the sailing master's limited sources of meteorological information with those of "seamen of the present day, [who] should be better at forecasting weather at sea." The safety of a ship, he pointed out, "is always the responsibility of her commanding officer; but this responsibility is also shared by his immediate superiors in operational command." Nimitz continued:

> It is most definitely part of the senior officer's responsibility to think in terms of the smallest ship and most inexperienced commanding officer under him. He cannot take them for granted, give them tasks and stations, and assume that they will be able to keep up and come through any weather that his own big ship can; or that they will be wise enough to gauge the exact moment when their task must be abandoned in order for them to keep afloat. . . .
>
> In conclusion, both seniors and juniors must realize that in bad weather, as in most other situations, safety and fatal hazard are not separated by any sharp boundary line, but shade gradually from one into the other. There is no little red light which is going to flash on and inform commanding officers or higher commanders that from then on there is extreme danger from the

weather, and that measures for ships' safety must take precedence over further efforts to keep up with the formation or to execute the assigned task. This time will always be a matter of personal judgment. Naturally no commander is going to cut thin the margin between staying afloat and foundering, but he may nevertheless unwittingly pass the danger point even though no ship is yet *in extremis*. Ships that keep on going as long as the severity of the wind and sea had not yet come close in capsizing them or breaking them in two, may nevertheless become helpless to avoid these catastrophes later if things get worse. By then they may be unable to steer any heading but in the trough of the sea, or may have their steering control, lighting, communications and main propulsion disabled or may be helpless to secure things on deck or to jettison topside weights. The time for taking all measures for a ship's safety is while still able to do so. Nothing is more dangerous than for a seaman to be grudging in taking precautions lest they turn out to have been unnecessary. Safety at sea for a thousand years has depended on exactly the opposite philosophy.

From Ulithi Nimitz flew to Leyte to confer with MacArthur concerning Task Force 38 support of the forthcoming invasion of Luzon. The general was in a jovial mood, having just announced the end of organized Japanese resistance on Leyte. He was instantly irked, however, when he perceived that Nimitz was wearing his five-star insignia while he did not yet have any. That evening he ordered his aides to see to it that he had his own five-star insignia by early the next morning.

On December 28 Nimitz, en route back to Pearl Harbor, stopped again at Ulithi to pass on to Halsey the agreements he had reached with MacArthur. Halsey requested permission to take Task Force 38 into the South China Sea in order, primarily, to attack the Japanese carrier-battleships *Ise* and *Hyuga*, refugees from the Battle for Leyte Gulf, that had been sighted in this area; secondarily, so far as Halsey was concerned, to safeguard the supply line to the Luzon beachhead in Lingayen Gulf. Nimitz consented but stipulated that Halsey should not make his foray behind the Philippines until the fast carriers had finished supporting the Lingayen landings.

Halsey brought to Nimitz's attention the illegal and misleading padding at the end of CinCPac's "Where is Task Force 34?" message—padding that had caused Halsey such distress during the Battle for Leyte Gulf. Nimitz was shocked, and promised to find out who was at fault and take appropriate action. According to Halsey in his autobiography, "Chester blew up when I told him about it; he tracked down the little squirt and chewed him to bits." The facts are somewhat different. On his return to Pearl Harbor, Nimitz had Jack Redman look into the matter and make a report. When he learned that the author of the offending padding was an ensign, he said to Redman, "If that ensign can't keep his thoughts out of operational dispatches, you'd better transfer him to a less sensitive spot." The ensign was transferred.

On December 30 Task Force 38 departed Ulithi to support the impending landings at Lingayen Gulf by raiding airfields on Luzon and Formosa. Kamikazes struck furiously at MacArthur's approaching attack forces, which were spearheaded by Admiral Oldendorf's bombardment and minesweeping groups from Leyte Gulf. By the time Barbey's and Wilkinson's amphibious forces approached the landing area, a combination of Third Fleet fast carriers, Seventh Fleet escort carriers, and army air force planes had very nearly put Luzon airfields out of operation. After January 7 there were no more organized air attacks on the invasion forces, but individual pilots attacked Allied shipping from time to time. In ten days Japanese aircraft, mostly kamikazes, damaged 43 Allied vessels, 18 severely, and sank 5, including an escort carrier; and they killed 738 men of the invasion forces and wounded nearly 1,400. Nevertheless, on January 9, the assault troops made their landings, on schedule, against virtually no opposition.

That night Halsey led Task Force 38 through Luzon Strait, north of Luzon, into the South China Sea. The *Ise* and the *Hyuga* had prudently departed southward, but the carrier planes still found plenty of targets to attack. They raided the coast of Indochina, southern Formosa, and the Hong Kong area, sinking 44 ships and destroying large numbers of aircraft. As the task force slipped out through Luzon Strait on the 21st, its planes again struck at Formosa. This time kamikazes struck back, damaging two carriers and a destroyer.

On January 25, Task Force 38 steamed into Ulithi Lagoon. Admiral Spruance and his staff were waiting to take command. The officers of the Third Fleet, which was about to become the Fifth Fleet again, viewed the changeover with mixed feelings. Captain George C. Dyer, commanding officer of the light cruiser *Astoria*, expressed one view: "My feeling was one of confidence when Spruance was there and one of concern when Halsey was there. . . . When you moved into Admiral Spruance's command from Admiral Halsey's . . . you moved from an area in which you never knew what you were going to do in the next five minutes or how you were going to do it, because the printed instructions were never up to date. . . . He never did things the same way twice. When you moved into Admiral Spruance's command, the printed instructions were up to date, and you did things in accordance with them."

Admiral Halsey, despite his shortcomings, which were few compared to his virtues, was liked by all and revered by the enlisted men of his fleet. Always approachable, always solicitous, always daring, he operated not in the spirit of "Go!" but of "Let's go!" He asked no man to face dangers that he would not face himself. He passed no bucks, he shirked no responsibilities. Always appreciative, he never left a command or ended a campaign without words of thanks or commendation for his subordinates. Few of his officers or men ever forgot the substance of his message when he took leave of them at Ulithi:

> I am so proud of you that no words can express my feelings. This has been a hard operation. At times you have been driven almost beyond endurance but only because the stakes were high, the enemy was as weary as you were, and the lives of many Americans could be spared in later offensives if we did our work well now. We have driven the enemy off the sea and back to his inner defenses. Superlatively well done!

After the operations in Lingayen Gulf, the Central Pacific forces and the Southwest Pacific forces parted company. While the former moved north toward Iwo Jima, Okinawa, and perhaps the China coast, General MacArthur and his Southwest Pacific forces moved south to capture Manila, then the rest of the Philippines, and finally the major ports of Borneo.

The disentanglement of Nimitz's Pacific Fleet and MacArthur's Seventh Fleet that this parting involved was no simple operation. Nimitz had for several days been trying to get back the ships he had lent to MacArthur. He needed them to build up the Fifth Fleet for the imminent assaults on Iwo Jima and Okinawa. Admiral Kinkaid, on the other hand, felt he needed all the vessels then under his command to protect communications to Lingayen and the Lingayen beachhead.

Nimitz pointed out that the Japanese certainly had not enough force available to menace the Philippines and at the same time defend themselves against the forthcoming American Central Pacific offensive, which would threaten Japan itself. If the Philippines, which were already being protected by land-based air, required also the protection of a naval defense force capable of meeting all the heavy ships left in the Japanese fleet, then there would be no further major Allied offensives in the Pacific for an indefinite period.

In the end, Nimitz allowed Kinkaid to keep four old battleships, but he recalled the *New Mexico* and the *California*, which were in serious need of repair from kamikaze-inflicted damage. He also approved the temporary retention by the Seventh Fleet of 2 heavy cruisers and 22 destroyers of the Pacific Fleet. He was able, but barely, to dispense with those vessels because a number of warships, including four old battleships, had recently arrived from the European theater. The exchange of dispatches between MacArthur on behalf of Kinkaid on one side and Nimitz on the other, though sometimes insistent, remained courteous and restrained and thus left no bitterness behind.

At about this time, Admiral Nimitz received a welcome and not altogether unexpected piece of news. Commander James Lay had sent Nimitz's daughter Kate an engagement ring. Ever since Jim had served under Nimitz in the *Augusta*, Admiral and Mrs. Nimitz had taken an interest in him and observed with approval the growing friendship between him and Kate. The young couple had not seen each other often in the past three years because Jim had spent most of the war in the Pacific, but they had corresponded regularly. Admiral Nimitz sent them his heartfelt blessing.

Nimitz had for some time been preparing to move out to Guam. His stated reason, and no doubt his major one, was to establish a forward headquarters nearer the combat area. A scarcely secondary reason was to get away from the increasingly crowded conditions at Makalapa and the massive routine involved in servicing constantly expanding armed forces. An additional story had been built atop CinCPac headquarters, but still the building was ever more crowded with desks and with men doing mostly repetitious work from which CinCPac could not entirely divorce himself.

Nimitz was taking with him only a small staff, such as he preferred, and

they were to be concerned, insofar as possible, only with planning and directing combat operations. The staff left behind would be encumbered mostly with
administration and logistics. At their head and loudly protesting, was Nimitz's
deputy, Admiral Towers, who all along had wanted a fighting command.
Left behind also, to handle training and routine business for the army, was
General Richardson.

Because the bombardment of Guam and the ensuing battle had turned the
few towns and settlements on the island into rubble, CinCPac headquarters
and all associated structures had to be built from the ground up. During a visit
to Guam the preceding August, Nimitz had selected a site for his new headquarters on top of a bluff, later known as CinCPac Hill. As soon as CominCh
gave the green light for the forward move, Seabees with bulldozers went to
work leveling out a space for the headquarters complex.

Nimitz rejected several designs for the advanced headquarters and then
himself prepared the design that was actually used. The building was a two-
story wooden structure, nothing like the bombproof fortress at Makalapa. Not
far away was a circle of cottages for flag and general officers and visiting
dignitaries. Nimitz, Admiral McMorris, and Dr. Anderson shared a white,
clapboard house that had four bedrooms, a large living-dining room, and a
porch that provided a view of the harbor at Agaña. Next door was a large staff
cottage where Admiral Sherman and other senior staff officers lived. At first,
the rest of the officers and the enlisted men lived in quonset huts, but by the
time the Pacific Fleet advanced headquarters had become operational, the
officers were housed in two-storied bachelor officers' quarters.

In preparation for the move, CinCPac had all important documents dup-
licated and shipped the 3,500 miles out to Guam in huge crates. The selected
CinCPac staff and subordinates, divided into five groups, began moving forward by plane, one group at a time, in January 1945. Nimitz arrived at his new
quarters and headquarters on the 27th, just as Spruance was taking command
of the Fifth Fleet at Ulithi.

For Nimitz the routine at Guam was much the same as it had been at
Pearl Harbor, but conduct and relationships were somewhat more relaxed.
Neckties, de rigueur at Pearl, were not worn at all at Guam, and shortly after
his arrival Nimitz announced that uniform shorts were acceptable and often
wore them himself. Captain Harold Hopkins, who arrived from a visit to
Sydney on February 2, found most of the CinCPac staff in shorts. "The concession coming as a surprise," he wrote his wife, "nobody had any stockings
except me, and some of the long, hairy legs one sees walking about the place in
bobby socks, are amusing or nauseating depending on the state of one's
health."

Admiral Nimitz had brought out with him his schnauzer Makalapa,
commonly known as Mak. Overbred, Mak was as mean as ever and growled at
everybody but his master and one or two others. He was a walker, however,
and at Guam he developed a fondness for swimming. So far as Nimitz was

concerned, no creature that liked walking and swimming could be all bad. Anyway, for him there was no such thing as not having a dog.

Sometimes in the morning before breakfast, Nimitz combined exercise and soaking up the sun by running down the road shirtless and in shorts. This was a degree of public informality he had not permitted himself at Makalapa because of the female clerks and typists in the CinCPac offices and because topless running seemed out of place in an area that, with trees and spreading shrubs, looked like a prosperous residential neighborhood. On rough, rugged Guam it seemed eminently in place, but on one occasion it almost cost the fleet admiral some embarrassment.

Early one morning over at the fleet hospital, a "disturbed" patient slipped out of the quonset hut for psychiatric cases clad only in his undershorts. He climbed the fence and when last seen was heading at a gallop in the general direction of Agaña. Commander Robert Schwab, MC, in charge of neuropsychiatry, collected two corpsmen and an armed marine—there were still Japanese soldiers loose on Guam—and with this posse set out in pursuit. Presently they espied a man in shorts hotfooting it down the road. They were about to grab him, when around the bend there appeared a jeep with five stars on it and a marine guard inside.

"Our posse took a good look at the five stars and slunk off," Dr. Schwab recalls. "Had the jeep not arrived at that moment, the man in the shorts would have been unceremoniously carried off to the psycho hut. And we would have been certain that we had our missing patient had he proclaimed, 'But I'm Chester Nimitz.' "

Admiral Nimitz was of course guarded at all times. His personal bodyguard consisted of eight husky marine sergeants who took turns. Day and night they were with him, outside his door, or following him at a discreet distance. Such protection was particularly necessary on Guam because Japanese soldiers roamed the jungles until the end of the war and afterward. One night, a Japanese soldier, probably looking for food, came up into Nimitz's front yard. He was seen by the sentries and there was much shooting, but he got away.

Some accounts of Japanese on Guam may be apocryphal, but it seems well established that Seabees attending a Dorothy Lamour movie one night suddenly discovered Japanese in the background watching the show. The Seabees took off after the interlopers, and there was a great deal of wild firing and fruitless beating about the brush. Hopkins wrote his wife: "There's a story going around of a Jap who got hold of a marine uniform and who, until he was apprehended the other day, had been lining up in the chow line and living well for weeks. I don't know if it's true, but it's quite likely."

CinCPac-CinCPOA advanced headquarters necessarily kept in constant touch with CinCPac-CinCPOA Pearl Harbor. The two headquarters often communicated by teleconference, which was achieved by a combination of radio and cryptography. In the presence of one set of conferees, an operator would tap out a query or statement on a typewriter keyboard; and 3,500 miles away, where the other conferees were assembled, a teletypewriter would instantly spell out the message. Exchange of information could thus be almost as swift as conversation. The words were automatically enciphered and deciphered by identical one-time tapes, which produced radio messages that were immune to cryptanalysis.*

Admiral Nimitz sought and maintained special relationships with two Marianas-based commanders, Vice Admiral Hoover and Major General Curtis E. LeMay, USA, both hard-nosed, authoritarian officers with reputations for being difficult but efficient. Between them, Hoover and LeMay controlled all American aircraft operating from the Marianas.

Hoover, as Commander, Shore-based Air, and Commander, Forward Area, had moved in his flagship *Curtiss* from Eniwetok to Saipan shortly after the latter was secured. In the U.S.-controlled Marianas he commanded shore personnel and shore facilities as well as most shore-based air. A perfectionist, harsh and demanding, he was jestingly referred to throughout the Pacific as "Genial John." In a calm, almost-silken voice he would blisteringly assail any subordinate whose command failed to meet his exacting standards. To the disgust of General Richardson, this naval officer's wrath sometimes fell upon Major General Willis Hale and his Seventh Army Air Force. Admiral Nimitz, aware that Hoover was doing his utmost and achieving outstanding results in a fairly thankless job, protected him from Richardson's attacks.

The Army Air Force's General LeMay was the only Allied flag or general officer in the Pacific Ocean Areas who was not under Admiral Nimitz's command. LeMay headed the independent 21st Bomber Command. This and the China-based 20th Bomber Command comprised the Twentieth Army Air Force, which controlled all the B-29s and was directly under General Arnold of the Joint Chiefs of Staff. Though the 21st Bomber Command was thus a separate kingdom within the CinCPac-CinCPOA empire, a Joint Chiefs of Staff directive gave Admiral Nimitz the right to direct the employment of the Marianas-based B-29s in a tactical or strategic emergency. Any exercise of that right, however, could cause an explosive reaction on the part of a stubborn, hotheaded officer such as LeMay.

Nimitz sought to head off explosive reactions and encourage teamwork among the local officers by having them in from time to time for dinner and an evening of friendly conversation. He hoped to promote cooperation by helping each to know the others and to understand the others' problems.

Many visitors to the Marianas, official or merely social, enjoyed the Nimitz hospitality. One notable guest was Archbishop Francis Spellman, of the see of New York, who went as apostolic vicar to the U.S. armed forces. Commander Lamar, who met him at the airfield and conducted him to the guest

---

* Because the enciphering elements on the tapes were random with no sequences repeated, and the tapes were never reused. Obviously, one-time tapes could not be used for general traffic because the volume of communication would require more tapes, and more time to prepare them, than could possibly be made available.

house, helped him off with his jacket and was shocked to note that, in the heat of Guam, the archbishop had sweated so much that his shirt was dyed from his purple vest.

"Your Excellency," Lamar said, "you can't wear this sort of uniform on Guam. Let me get you some khakis."

"Fine," replied Spellman.

Thus at a merry dinner at Admiral Nimitz's quarters that evening, the archbishop was dressed like the officers present, except that he had no collar insignia.

Spellman asked Nimitz if he could help him in any way. The next morning the admiral had Lamar explain to the archbishop how he could indeed be of assistance. It seems that in December 1941 the bishop of Guam had fled to Australia just ahead of the conquering Japanese, leaving a young Guamanian priest as the sole religious authority and spiritual leader on the island. Nimitz had heard quite a bit about this runaway bishop, a worthy man in many respects but a bungler, certainly no administrator, and he had made up his mind that the man should not return.

In the period of confusion following the reconquest, however, the bishop did return, and Nimitz wanted him out. What was needed was a man not only of spiritual devotion but an organizer, a man of real executive ability. The Guamanians, most of whom were devout Catholics, had built their lives around their church. Now there was scarcely a church left standing on Guam and the religious organization was a shambles. Agaña, the seat of government, formerly a city of 12,000 inhabitants, had been reduced by the bombardment to ruins. The island commander, Major General Henry L. Larsen, USMC, was making important strides toward reconstruction and rehabilitation of the people, but he needed at his side a strong man of the church.

Archbishop Spellman grasped the situation and understood the need at once. He paid a call on the bishop and got nowhere except to reach the conclusion that Nimitz had already reached—that he was not the man for the task at hand. Spellman therefore took out a little book, prepared a message in code, and asked that it be sent to the Roman Curia. The Navy's communication system was up to the challenge. Spellman's encoded message went to Washington, thence to the naval attaché at the American Embassy in Rome, and the American ambassador delivered it to the Vatican. A week later Admiral Nimitz was informed that the incumbent bishop was being relieved and that one from Rochester, New York, was being sent to Guam.

The evening following Archbishop Spellman's visit to CinCPac's quarters, Admiral Nimitz had as his dinner guest his old friend and walking companion of Washington days, Captain George Bauernschmidt. At the table and afterward the admiral told one delightfully humorous story after another and had the diners in a roar. As he was leaving, Bauernschmidt commented on this fund of funny stories, an unusually large repertoire even for Nimitz.

"Oh," said Nimitz, "these aren't mine. I told mine last night to Archbishop Spellman, and these are the ones he told me."

# CHAPTER 22

# IWO JIMA AND OKINAWA

On February 2, 1945, Fleet Admiral Nimitz flew from his headquarters on Guam to Ulithi and boarded the Fifth Fleet flagship *Indianapolis* to discuss the forthcoming Iwo Jima operation with Admiral Spruance. The Fast Carrier Force, again designated Task Force 58 with Vice Admiral Mitscher in command, was assembled at anchor in the lagoon. Ships were being replenished; several were undergoing minor repair. The sailors and airmen, exhausted by the long-drawn-out Philippines campaign, were enjoying a few days' respite—swimming and playing softball ashore, or drinking beer and just loafing.

When Spruance had first proposed capturing Iwo Jima, he and Nimitz had assumed that the operation would pose no special difficulties. They had learned better. Photoreconnaissance revealed that this barren mass of lava and ashes might prove extraordinarily defensible. General Holland Smith, after studying the aerial photographs, had pronounced it "the toughest place we have had to take" and somberly predicted 20,000 American casualties.

The campaign to soften up the target had proved disappointing. B-24s had begun raiding Iwo the preceding August, and since early December they had struck the island daily. Five times cruiser-destroyer groups had bombarded its defenses. Through it all the Japanese garrison had maintained two airfields and begun construction of a third. Aerial photographs at first revealed some 450 major defense installations on Iwo. They now showed more than 700, and there were doubtless numerous others that could not be seen. Evidently the defenders were burrowing into the lava, and the overlying black volcanic ash simply absorbed the shock of bomb and shell.

Major General Curtis LeMay had visited the *Indianapolis* the preceding week to confer with Spruance on how the Army Air Forces could support the assault on Iwo Jima. Spruance first put to the general the question that had been troubling him: Just how valuable would Iwo be in American hands? LeMay replied at once that it would be of tremendous value—as a staging field, as an emergency landing field for B-29s in distress, as a base for air-sea rescue, and as a base for fighter escorts. "Without Iwo Jima," he said, "I couldn't bomb Japan effectively."

"This took a load off my mind," said Spruance. "LeMay's opinion was reassuring to me."

Spruance proposed to protect the U.S. ships off Iwo from air attack by using Task Force 58 to neutralize the complex of air bases in the Tokyo area. This would be the first carrier raid on Japan since Doolittle's "ten minutes over Tokyo" in April 1942. Spruance planned to spread his attacks over two days. The fast carriers could complete replenishing at Ulithi and be off Japan by

February 16. On that date therefore the naval bombardment of the island could safely begin.

After his conference with Spruance, Nimitz flew to Saipan to witness the final landing rehearsals of the Iwo Jima attack force, which had just arrived from the Hawaiian Islands. Three marine divisions were assigned to the operation: the 4th and 5th for the assault and the 3rd as floating reserve. Together they constituted the V Amphibious Corps, which was now commanded by Major General Harry Schmidt, USMC.

Holland Smith accompanied Nimitz to Saipan, but for what purpose is not altogether clear. Although in his new capacity as Commanding General, Fleet Marine Force, he was senior to General Schmidt and also to Major General Roy Geiger, USMC, who headed the III Amphibious Corps, earmarked for Okinawa, he was expected, and apparently ordered, not to intervene in corps tactics. This was a melancholy restriction for Smith, of whom King had said, "All he wants to do is fight."

The fact is that even Smith's most ardent partisans had to admit that he had not used the best possible judgment on Saipan. He should not have placed the Army's 27th Division, known for slowness, where it would have to advance while covering the flanks of two swift-moving marine divisions. Nor should he have positioned the laggard 27th atop a rugged ridge with the marines on each side along the shores. Such demonstrated misjudgment had given Smith's critics the ammunition they sought.

On February 14, Rear Admiral William H. P. Blandy's Task Force 52, composed of bombardment ships, escort carriers, and minesweepers, shoved off for Iwo. The assault craft and transports would later depart Saipan in groups, the slower vessels first.

Admiral Kelly Turner, a victim of obsessive overwork who had been suffering from a bad back, now succumbed to a virus. On the 15th, however, by sheer effort of will he hauled himself out of his bunk and joined Nimitz, Holland Smith, and the island commander, Major General Sanderford Jarman, USA, at Saipan's Isely Airfield to meet a plane bringing the Secretary of the Navy. Forrestal was coming out to witness the assault on Iwo Jima. After the Secretary had landed and shaken hands with the reception committee, Jarman conducted him and Nimitz on a motor tour of the island, the same circuit King and Nimitz had made six months earlier. They could hear guns. Jarman explained that his garrison troops were shelling a Japanese position that was still holding out at the center of the island. At the end of the tour Nimitz flew back to Guam.

That evening aboard the *Eldorado*, Turner's new flagship, Forrestal was briefed on the background of the forthcoming operation. General Schmidt, he learned, had requested ten days of naval bombardment preceding the landing of his marines on the island. Admiral Turner had replied that this was impossible, and not merely because of the concurrent raid on Tokyo airfields by Task Force 58. The gunnery ships simply could not carry enough ammunition to bombard for ten days, or even half that many. The only way they could

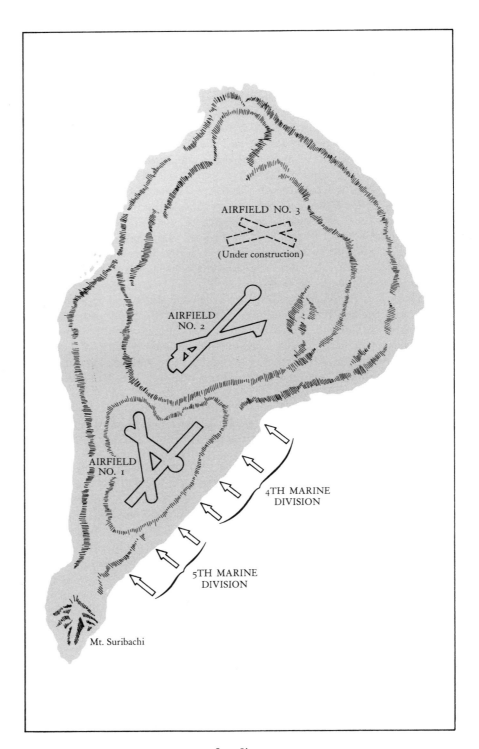

*Iwo Jima*

obtain a resupply of ammunition was by steaming 900 miles to Ulithi or 650 miles to the Southern Marianas. Gunfire-support ships that might have served as a reserve were either still with MacArthur or were undergoing repair from damages received in the Philippines campaign. Methods of transferring ammunition at sea from replenishment vessels were under study, as Admiral Spruance had requested, but the process was still in the experimental stage.

The alternative of delaying the Iwo Jima assault until MacArthur could release more ships was out of the question, because the naval vessels that were to be used in the Iwo operation were scheduled also for the Okinawa assault on April 1. Planning for a massive invasion of Japan in the fall was already under way, and the success of that invasion depended in large measure upon long-sustained air operations involving planes launched from both Iwo Jima and Okinawa. In the circumstances, the Fifth Amphibious Force could give Iwo Jima only three days of preliminary naval bombardment, but Turner had assured Generals Schmidt and Smith that three days was enough for a target with an area of only eight square miles. Any defenses that the naval guns had not destroyed by that time, he said, would have to be taken out by infantry and tanks on the island.

At dawn on February 16 on Guam, Admiral Nimitz was anxiously awaiting news. He knew that the Navy Department expected him to issue a communiqué that day on both the bombardment of Iwo Jima and the carrier raid on Tokyo. He would have no trouble doing the former. Admiral Blandy had been instructed to make an early report and he would do so. But one never knew about Spruance. He would not report until he was good and ready and not until he was reasonably sure of his facts.

Nimitz got his first word on the Tokyo raid from the Japanese. Radio Tokyo went off the air at 7:00 a.m. More than an hour later it was back in operation with a news bulletin stating that an air-raid alarm had sounded because "small enemy planes" were attacking Tokyo airstrips. Enemy ships, the broadcast reported, had been observed off the coast.

By this time CinCPac had been informed that the naval bombardment of Iwo Jima had begun at 7:07 and that B-24s were winging north, toward Iwo, for their daily raid. Admiral Nimitz took a sheet of paper and wrote out Communiqué No. 259:

> Vice Admiral Marc A. Mitscher is in command of a powerful task force of the Pacific Fleet which is now attacking enemy aircraft, air bases and other military targets in and around Tokyo.
>
> This operation has long been planned and the opportunity to accomplish it fulfills the deeply cherished desire of every officer and man of the Pacific Fleet.
>
> Surface units of the Pacific Fleet are bombarding Iwo Jima. Aircraft of the Strategic Air Force, Pacific Ocean Areas, are bombing Iwo Jima and nearby positions in the Bonins. The fleet forces are under the tactical command of Admiral R. A. Spruance, Commander of the Fifth Fleet.

*The New York Times* responded with banner headlines:

1,200 Planes of U.S. Fleet Attack Tokyo
as Ships and Fliers Bombard Iwo Isle

The *Times* story concluded: "The carrier strike against the Japanese home island with our greatest concentration of sea strength close enough for Hellcats, Hell Divers and Corsairs to sweep the streets of Tokyo with strafing attacks is the most daring operation of the Pacific war to date."

Because of worsening weather, Admiral Spruance broke off the raid on Tokyo before noon on the 17th and hastened south with Task Force 58 to lend direct support to the assault on Iwo Jima. At dawn on the 19th he made his first report on the Tokyo raids to CinCPac: "Task Force approach completely undetected and target area was not alerted until strikes neared targets. Weather conditions both days low clouds and squalls over task force.... Bad to unsatisfactory over target with much of target area completely closed in. Result of two days strike: 332 enemy aircraft shot down, 177 destroyed ground, many others probably destroyed or damaged, including 150 first day. Hangars, shops, and installations destroyed at many airfields and air depots."

A little before 11:00 a.m. on the 19th, Admiral Turner, apparently recovered from the virus, reported the progress of the Iwo assault: "Following intense naval gunfire and air bombardment, 5th Phib Corps landed as scheduled. Eight battalions supported by tanks landed by 1020. Little opposition was met initially though some mortar and artillery fire at LSTs and boats. Mortar and artillery fire developed on all beaches...Regimental reserves being landed. Personnel casualties moderate."

General Schmidt had estimated that it would take ten days to secure Iwo Jima, but Admiral Turner's report of February 19 seemed to support the more optimistic estimate that the island could be taken in four days. On the evening of the 20th Turner made a report that was scarcely less encouraging. He stated that a night counterattack by about a thousand Japanese had been repulsed; that during the morning the 5th Marine Division, on the left, had secured its half of the main airfield and thrust to the slopes of Mt. Suribachi, a dormant volcano at the southwest end of the island; that the 4th Division had secured the other half of the airfield but was receiving heavy mortar and artillery fir, from the high ground to the northeast; and that after noon neither division had made any substantial progress.

By the evening of the 21st the nature of the Iwo Jima campaign was becoming apparent. The marines held the narrow middle of the island and were not likely to be dislodged, but their conquest of Suribachi on the left and the rugged plateau on the right could be achieved only by means of a yard-by-yard advance, using flamethrowers, grenades, and satchel charges to blast the concealed enemy from his holes and caves. In the late afternoon suicide planes from Japan had struck at the support ships, sinking the escort carrier *Bismarck*

*Sea,* heavily damaging the fleet carrier *Saratoga,* and inflicting some damage on three other vessels.

Thus far CinCPac communiqués had reported that no estimate of casualties was available. However, that of February 22 stated: "At 1800 (6 P.M.) as of February 21, our casualties on Iwo were estimated at 644 killed, 4,108 wounded, and 560 missing." Newspapers were quick to note that this was worse than Tarawa. A Washington paper recommended: "Give our boys a break—gas the Japs." The idea was not new to the U.S. armed forces. Ever since the planning for Iwo began, it had been apparent that poison gas would be the most practical way of getting at the Japanese in the holes and caves of the island, and might be more merciful on the defenders than bullets, napalm, and flame. Neither President Roosevelt nor Admiral Nimitz, however, was willing to violate the Geneva Convention outlawing gas warfare, even though the United States and Japan were not signatories. Nimitz's scruples, he afterward confessed, "cost a lot of good marines."

Early in the morning of the 25th, Secretary Forrestal, returning from Iwo, arrived by ship at Guam's Apra Harbor. Notified of his approach, Admirals Nimitz and Hoover and General Larsen were on hand to meet him. Nimitz conducted the Secretary to the CinCPac morning conference, where Forrestal gave his impressions of the fighting on Iwo Jima. He had gone there in the *Eldorado* with Turner, Smith, Schmidt, and Harry Hill, Turner's second-in-command. Hill had expected to have to substitute for his ailing chief, but by D-day Turner had somehow snapped out of his illness and taken over command of the bombardment from Blandy.

Forrestal described how the most powerful assault of the Pacific war, expected to carry well into the interior, had been virtually stopped at the water's edge. The steep-rising shore was composed of volcanic ash so soft that the treads of the amtracs failed to take hold. These and conventional landing craft piled up in a mass of wreckage along the coast. As the marines scrambled ashore, they sank up to their knees in the ash, but nevertheless crawled up a series of terraces in the face of enemy fire.

On the morning of the 23rd, Forrestal reported, he went to the island with Holland Smith and other officers to witness the last stage of the fight for 550-foot-high Suribachi. Just as their boat touched shore, voices shouted, "There goes the flag!" Looking up, Forrestal saw, at the crest of the volcano, a tiny rectangle of red, white, and blue break and flutter. He turned to Smith. "Holland," he said, "the raising of that flag on Suribachi means a Marine Corps for the next five hundred years." The following day the Secretary had departed Iwo, leaving behind the message, "The operation is in good hands."

At Guam Forrestal was shown a photograph of marines raising a second flag on Mt. Suribachi, larger than the flag that had caught the Secretary's attention. Associated Press photographer Joe Rosenthal took the photo without realizing that he was catching a breathtaking example of pictorial composition. When his negatives were developed on Guam, this picture captured everyone's attention. CinCPac immediately sent to Iwo for the names and home towns of the marine flag-raisers. The Associated Press forwarded the photograph to the United States, where it became the most famous picture ever taken, and for all Americans a symbol of victory.

Forrestal had lunch with Nimitz, Larsen, Hoover, McMorris, and Sherman. Somebody remembered that the day before had been Nimitz's 60th birthday. Thereupon the luncheon was turned into a party in his honor. There was something else to celebrate, for Radio Tokyo had announced that the American carriers were again off Japan, sending in planes to raid the Tokyo airfields. The next day Forrestal departed to return to the United States by easy stages, stopping at hospitals across the Pacific and talking to the wounded.

Even Schmidt proved too optimistic about the length of time it would take to secure Iwo. Ten days after the initial assault, the CinCPac Command Summary described the situation: "At Iwo Jima during the night 28 Feb.-1 March enemy artillery blew up the ammunition dump of the 5th MarDiv. During the day of D-plus-10 gains were limited along the entire front; however, the 3rd MarDiv was able to seize a portion of airfield #3. Airfield #1 is now reported operational for emergency landings of fighter aircraft, 1 carrier plane having landed on the field already."

It was time for Admiral Nimitz to turn his attention away from the bloody battle on Iwo and consider future operations. On March 1, accompanied by Admiral Sherman and Commander Lamar, he departed for Washington, with stops at Pearl Harbor and San Francisco. At San Francisco Nimitz learned that the Rosenthal photograph had created a sensation across the country when it appeared in the newspapers the previous Sunday. On the following Thursday, however, the *San Francisco Examiner* had come out with another blast, in the form of a front-page editorial implying that the heavy losses on Iwo Jima were the result of inept leadership. This, said the editorial, was the sort of thing that happened at Tarawa and Saipan, but never in General MacArthur's campaigns. It concluded:

> GENERAL MacARTHUR is our best strategist.
> He is our most SUCCESSFUL strategist.
> He wins all his objectives.
> He outwits and outmaneuvers and outguesses and outthinks the Japanese.
> HE SAVES THE LIVES OF HIS OWN MEN, not only for the future and vital operations that must be fought before Japan is defeated, but for their own safe return to their families and loved ones in the American homeland after the peace is won.
> It is our good fortune to have such a strategist as General MacArthur in the Pacific war.
> Why do we not USE him more, and indeed, why do we not give him supreme command in the Pacific war, and utilize to the utmost his rare military genius of winning important battles without excessive loss of precious American lives?

For the marines on leave in San Francisco this was too much. About a hundred of them stormed into the *Examiner* building and confronted the managing editor, William Wren, with a demand for an apology or an opportunity to reply.

"Look," said Wren, "I only take orders from my commanding officer, just like you do." The offending editorial, he explained, had come directly from William Randolph Hearst. On the marines' demand, he put in a call to San Simeon but was told that Mr. Hearst was too busy to be disturbed.

Mrs. Nimitz left Mary at her convent school and joined her husband for the flight to Washington. Here the party was provided quarters in the Fairfax Hotel, on Massachusetts Avenue, near DuPont Circle, Admiral and Mrs. Nimitz occupying the hotel manager's top-floor apartment.

Nimitz spent most of Monday, March 5, with the Joint Chiefs of Staff. Just back from the Yalta conference, they were of the opinion that the last major strategic decisions had already been made for the war in Europe, which appeared about over. That was the war that had been absorbing their main attention, and they had left the direction of the war against Japan largely to King and Nimitz, and MacArthur, who was running his own show. Now they were prepared to give operations in the Pacific closer scrutiny.

The Joint Chiefs listened while Nimitz and Sherman described plans for the forthcoming invasion of Okinawa. The invasion forces were to consist of the army's XXIV Corps, enlarged to four divisions since it invaded Leyte, and the III Amphibious Corps, consisting of the 1st, 2nd, and 6th Marine Divisions. Together, these forces would form the Tenth Army, to be commanded by Lieutenant General Simon Bolivar Buckner, USA. Task Force 58 would provide cover between Okinawa and Kyushu, and the British Pacific Fleet would provide cover between Okinawa and Formosa. Because the carrier forces would have to remain in these highly vulnerable positions until the campaign had been completed, Nimitz was insisting on speed ashore, despite any army doctrine to the contrary.

Though most naval leaders continued to believe that Japan could be defeated by sea power and air power alone, King and Leahy had reluctantly given in to the Army's insistence that plans be drawn up for the invasion of the home islands. The landing on Kyushu, Operation Olympic, was scheduled for November 1, 1945. The invasion of the Tokyo plain, Operation Coronet, was tentatively scheduled for the following March. Nimitz, commanding all naval forces, would establish the beachheads, whereupon MacArthur would take command of the ground forces. Nimitz, though he privately had little expectation that either Olympic or Coronet would ever take place, discussed with the Joint Chiefs how he proposed to collaborate with MacArthur.

One of the main reasons for invading the China coast, to supply the Chinese army, was no longer valid, because the growing confusion and disintegration of the Chinese government had left its army incapable of putting up an effective fight. King, however, pointed out that on the Asiatic mainland alone there was space for enough airfields to accommodate all the aircraft that would be needed to support the invasion of Kyushu. He also spoke of a nebulous plan to capture the southern tip of Korea and the nearby Tsushima Islands. From those two bases ships and planes could establish an absolute blockade of Japan, and bombers would be able to make precision attacks on all the country's industrial centers. From there also, American forces would be able to cooperate with those of Russia, for Stalin had pledged at Yalta that his forces would enter the Pacific war by attacking Japanese troops in Manchuria and Korea.

Monday evening was family night in the Nimitz suite at the Fairfax Hotel. With the Nimitzes was Commander James Lay, on temporary duty in Washington on the staff of Vice Admiral Theodore Wilkinson. Kate and Jim had had a brainstorm. Why not get married while Admiral Nimitz was in town? Everybody thought that was a splendid idea—except perhaps Lamar, who knew that he would have to make most of the arrangements. It was agreed that the wedding should take place Wednesday or Thursday so that Admiral and Mrs. Nimitz would have plenty of time to get back to the West Coast where, on the following Sunday, March 11, thirteen-year-old Mary was scheduled to christen the destroyer *Buck*.

On Tuesday Kate and Jim went to get their marriage license and were confronted with the fact that in the District of Columbia there is a mandatory three-day wait between the application and the ceremony. That meant no wedding before Friday, which was the day Admiral Nimitz planned to fly to California. The admiral telephoned some high-ranking officials but found that there was no getting around the law; he had to wait or else miss the wedding. "I remember thinking," said Kate afterward, "that this was the first instance I had encountered since living in the District, of something that couldn't be 'fixed'—no matter *who* might ask." When signs began to point toward bad weather over the weekend, Chaplain Everett Wuebbens, a family friend, told Admiral Nimitz that he stood ready to perform the ceremony at one minute after midnight Thursday, if that would help him to get out of the area ahead of a storm.

On Thursday President Roosevelt had Secretary Forrestal and Fleet Admiral Nimitz to lunch at the White House and spent an hour and twenty minutes with them discussing the war and the approaching defeat of Japan. Nimitz saw that the President's health had deteriorated since the preceding summer. He was slack of jaw, he slurred his words, and his hands trembled. (In point of fact, he had only five more weeks to live.)

The weather improving, the wedding was set for 5:00 p.m. Friday in the Nimitz apartment at the Fairfax. Lamar had the catering done by nearby Napoleon's Restaurant. Nancy Nimitz was maid of honor and a classmate of Jim's was best man. Admiral and Mrs. Wilkinson and Bill Leverton were there. Most of the rest of the guests were Kate's friends from the D.C. Public Library. Two colleagues, on the staff of the Navy School of Music, played the Bach and Handel that Kate had always planned for her wedding.

Admiral and Mrs. Nimitz reached California Saturday evening. They found Mary disconsolate because she wanted her three favorite teaching sisters at her convent school to come to the christening of the *Buck*, but the convent's rules forbade their attending. Admiral Nimitz, who had got nowhere trying to circumvent a law of the District of Columbia, had better luck with the Roman Catholic hierarchy. Not a Catholic himself, he telephoned the archbishop, and three sisters showed up at the 8:00 a.m. christening—though only one of the three was on Mary's list.

The Nimitz party proceeded back across the Pacific with a stop at Pearl Harbor and reached Guam on March 15. At the end of the following day, General Schmidt announced that organized resistance by the defenders of Iwo Jima had ended. In fact, there was a great deal of fighting on the island after that date. Admiral Nimitz concluded his communiqué announcing the securing of the island with the memorable statement, "Among the Americans who served on Iwo Island uncommon valor was a common virtue."

To Mrs. Nimitz, Admiral Nimitz wrote: "I am delighted with the news that Iwo has finally been conquered and I hope that I will not get too many letters cursing me because of heavy casualties. I am receiving two or three letters a day signed 'a Marine Mother' and calling me all sorts of names. I am just as distressed as can be over the casualties but don't see how I could have reduced them."

General Holland Smith had had a miserable time. "His" marines had been taking heavy casualties and he was forbidden to participate in the fighting. Admiral Turner kept him aboard the *Eldorado* and permitted him to go ashore only for "inspections." When Hill relieved Turner on March 8, Smith merely shifted to Hill's flagship, the *Auburn*. Deeply depressed, he spent most of the time in his cabin. Hill liked and sympathized with the general and occasionally went down and played cribbage with him to relieve his self-imposed loneliness. Smith knew that this was his last operation. Invasions in the Pacific Ocean Areas from then on would be army-sized and army-commanded. On March 17 he left Iwo Jima. He paused a few days at Guam and then proceeded to Pearl Harbor. Though marines fought in the Okinawa campaign, Smith did not leave his headquarters at Pearl until the campaign was over. He then turned the Fleet Marine Force over to General Geiger and went back to his old training command in the States. The following year, having reached the age for mandatory retirement, he left the Corps, sad and embittered, convinced that he was a victim of interservice rivalry.

On March 24, 1945, Admiral Nimitz and members of his staff visited Iwo Jima. As usual on such occasions, Lamar had prepared for Nimitz's study a set of filing cards with the names, ranks, and commands of all the principal officers he would meet. On arriving at Iwo, the admiral was gratified to learn that 65 B-29s had already saved themselves from destruction by using the island for emergency landings. He later described his visit to Mrs. Nimitz:

Some fighting was still going on in a small gorge or ravine at the N.W. end where a pocketful of Japs—estimated to number 200 or more— were putting up a final last gasp resistance rather than surrender. By now they are all dead or sealed up in caves where death will come soon. Iwo must be seen to appreciate the character of the terrain and the defenses and the volcanic *dust.* We all looked like coal heavers within a few minutes after starting. The entire island is a thermal region with steam coming thru the ground at numerous points. There are some hot water wells—sulphur of course and brackish but very hot and fresh enough for bathing with soap. They are very popular with the men. There *was* some vegetation and a few trees before the attack but now there is nothing growing.

The battle for Iwo was extremely bloody. More than 22,000 of the Japanese defenders were killed. A record 1,083 were taken prisoner. On the island and in the fleet, 19,000 Americans were wounded and nearly 7,000 were killed or died of their wounds. On the bright side, by the end of the war, the island had served as an emergency landing site for some 2,400 B-29s, whose crews numbered about 27,000. Costly as the conquest of Iwo Jima was, it therefore saved more American lives than it took.

In fact, Iwo's greatest and most valuable use was as an emergency landing field and a station for rescue activities, rather than as a base for fighter planes. General LeMay soon shifted emphasis from low-level precision bombing, which produced meager results, to night operations without fighter escort. One such operation, LeMay's own project, was the incendiary bombing of Japanese cities. This type of warfare proved more effective than it had been in Europe, largely because of the inflammable materials with which Japanese houses were built. The first of the fire raids, against Tokyo in the night of March 9–10, 1945, destroyed 250,000 houses, burned to death 83,793 persons, and left a million homeless. This was actually somewhat more destruction than was achieved by either of the atomic bombs.

Another operation, devised at CinCPOA headquarters and vigorously pushed by Admiral Nimitz, was the mining of Japanese ports and waterways. Japanese shipping had disappeared from the Pacific altogether, but a vigorous commerce with the Asian continent continued, some of it from Japan's few west coast ports but most of it via the Inland Sea and Shimonoseki Strait. The Navy provided the mines, and the B-29s, operating singly, dropped them at night by radar. The first of the mining operations was directed against Shimonoseki Strait in preparation for the assault on Okinawa. From the strait, operations were expanded to other strategic waters, the bombers sowing mines faster than they could be swept.

In planning the Okinawa operation, Admiral Nimitz's biggest worry was what enemy air power might do to the invasion forces before American airfields could be established on the target island. There were 55 fields on Kyushu, to the northeast, 65 on Formosa, to the southwest, and, in between, airstrips all along the chain of the Ryukyus, including Okinawa. Since the Japanese were not engaged in combat anywhere but in the Central Philippines, and there they were cut off from the homeland and its resources, they might be counted on to hurl every plane in Japan, maybe 3,000 or 4,000, against the invasion forces, using the deadly kamikaze tactics.

In mid-March, according to plan, Task Force 58 with Mitscher in tactical and Spruance in strategic command departed Ulithi to do something about this dangerous situation. On the 18th and 19th it launched a series of raids on Kyushu airfields. The Japanese struck back, damaging five carriers, one of which, the *Franklin*, lost more than 700 of her crew and was out of the war for good. Nimitz then exercised his right to call on the B-29s for help. General LeMay complied, reluctantly, because he believed that fire-bombing industrial centers was a more effective way for his big bombers to wage war. On the 27th B-29s raided air installations on Kyushu, that night they sowed mines in Shimonoseki Strait, and on the 30th they struck again at the Kyushu air bases. Task Force 58 had moved south to give direct support to the invasion.

By this time, the British Pacific Fleet, under the tactical command of Vice Admiral Sir H. Bernard Rawlings, RN, had entered the Pacific Ocean and reported by radio for duty. Nimitz replied: "The United States Pacific Fleet welcomes the British Carrier Task Force and attached units which will greatly add to our power to strike the enemy and will also show our unity of purpose in the war against Japan." He added the British force to the Fifth Fleet, designating it Task Force 57, and sent it to patrol the islands between Okinawa and Formosa.

While the Fifth Amphibious Force's gunnery vessels were pounding away at Okinawa's Hagushi beaches, an amphibious attack force that included the 77th Infantry Division seized the lightly held Kerama Retto, a group of islands surrounding a roadstead 15 miles west of southern Okinawa. Into this anchorage on March 27 steamed Service Squadron 10, which was to serve as a floating base for replenishment and light repairs right in the area of operations.

Individual suicide planes were already striking at the American ships off Okinawa. On March 31 a kamikaze crashed into Spruance's flagship *Indianapolis*, releasing a bomb that penetrated several decks and blew holes in her hull. Spruance sent her to Mare Island Navy Yard for repairs and shifted his flag to the *New Mexico*.

In the early hours of April 1, Easter morning, the transports arrived off the Hagushi beaches, and at 6:00 a.m. Admiral Turner assumed command of the invasion and support forces. At Guam, 1,400 miles to the southeast, CinCPac and his staff were awaiting information. Turner's report did not come in until after noon: "Preceded by intense naval and air bombardment, troops of Tenth Army began landing Hagushi beaches at 0830 I(-9). Troops landed on all beaches against very light opposition. Practically no fire against boats, none against ships. Considerable number of tanks and artillery landed. Regimental reserve now landing. Troops are advancing inland standing up."

The lightness of the Japanese resistance was puzzling. The Hagushi

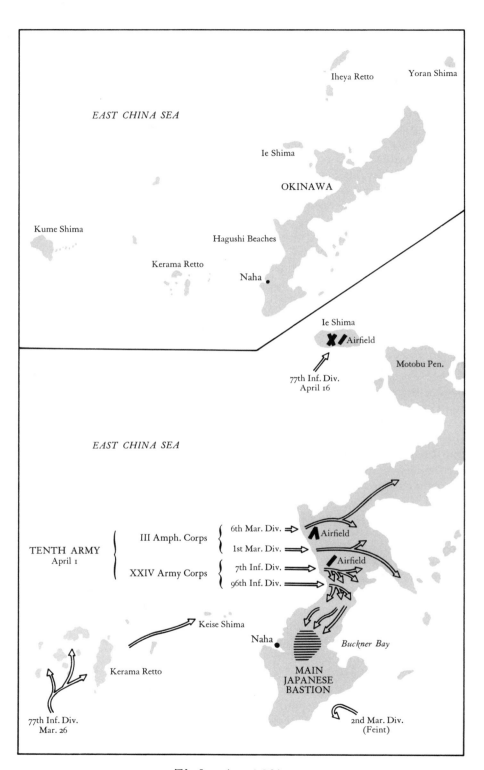

*The Invasion of Okinawa*

beaches had been chosen, in part, because they were close to two airstrips. It was incredible that the Japanese were letting their airfields go by default to an invader who would be sure to make use of them as soon as possible. In the days that followed, the marines went racing up the northeast peninsula, and in the south the Army advanced slowly against light resistance. The enemy launched some air attacks but nothing the fleet and antiaircraft batteries could not handle.

General LeMay went to see Admiral Nimitz. "We've finished now," said the general. "There's not another thing we can do for you. May we go back to hitting our strategic targets? We'll do a lot more good there."

"Yes, LeMay," Nimitz answered, "you've done a very fine job. *Very* good. I guess it's about time you go back on your own type of operation. But let me check with Sherman."

Nimitz called for Rear Admiral Forrest Sherman, now deputy CinCPOA chief of staff, and explained the situation. Sherman was strongly opposed to releasing the B-29s. The Kyushu fields had been knocked out, no doubt, but only temporarily. The Japanese were sure to make repairs, bring in more planes, and, before long, strike in force. Nimitz accepted this line of reasoning and sent LeMay back to his headquarters to plan for another strike against Kyushu.

The big raids predicted by Sherman came on April 6 and 7, when probably 700 planes from Kyushu struck at ships of the Fifth Fleet. Then and later they most often attacked the destroyer types on picket duty in rings around Okinawa because they were usually the first ships the enemy pilots saw. In this two-day blitz, 3 destroyer types and an LST were sunk, 2 ammunition ships were blown up, and a minesweeper and 12 destroyer types were heavily damaged, some beyond repair. Suicide planes also crashed into the carrier *Hancock* and the battleship *Maryland*, killing hundreds of sailors and leaving many others hideously burned.

The Combined Fleet joined the suicide attack. Out from the Inland Sea came the superbattleship *Yamato*, a cruiser, and 8 destroyers. This force tried to slip past Task Force 58 in the darkness and head for Okinawa, but Mitscher had been alerted by a picket submarine. His carrier planes found the enemy ships a little after noon on the 7th and worked over them for two hours with bombs and torpedoes. The *Yamato*, the cruiser, and 4 destroyers went down. The other 4 destroyers, severely damaged, headed at best speed back to Japan.

Neither at this time nor later did CinCPac communiqués make any mention of the kamikaze raids, and CinCPac censors let no word of them pass through. Since most of the planes made one-way trips, the Japanese had no way of estimating their achievements and Admiral Nimitz had no intention of letting the enemy know how successful they were. The sinking of the *Yamato* and the other vessels, however, he joyfully announced both in a communiqué and in the Army Day speech he broadcast to the forces in the Pacific.

By this time the marines on Okinawa's northeast peninsula and the soldiers in the south were meeting stiffer resistance. Enemy air raids were formidable but apparently less skillfully controlled than the kamikaze attacks in the Philippines had been. The feeling among some U.S. commanders on the scene was that Japanese resistance was about to crack. At noon on April 7, Admiral Turner radioed, "If this is the best the enemy can throw against us, we shall move forward." After the sinking of the *Yamato*, he signaled Nimitz playfully: "I may be crazy but it looks like the Japs have quit the war, at least in this section."

To the second message, CinCPac replied, "Delete all after 'crazy'!" To Nimitz the pattern of Japanese island defense was becoming apparent. As he had done at Peleliu, Leyte, and Iwo Jima, the enemy had avoided trying to defend the beaches in the face of naval gunfire; he was holing up in the interior and preparing to meet the invader there. Fortunately for the Americans, no area in Okinawa was beyond the reach of supporting naval guns.

On April 8, the B-29s again struck at Kyushu airfields. General LeMay, studying air photographs of the areas attacked, became more convinced than ever that the efforts of the big bombers were being wasted. The Japanese, he concluded, were successfully concealing the poor crates intended for suicide attack and learning to repair their churned-up airfields in record time. Again LeMay called on Nimitz and argued with him. Again Nimitz, on Sherman's advice, refused to release the B-29s from support of the Okinawa campaign. This time General LeMay fired off a message to General Arnold in Washington, expressing his opinion that Admiral Nimitz was hampering the war effort. When Arnold mentioned this complaint to Admiral King, King suggested that if the army air forces were not willing to support the Navy off Okinawa, the Navy might well pull out and let the army ground forces on the island try to protect and supply themselves. After that, nothing more was said in Washington about LeMay's complaint.

Admiral Nimitz finally released the B-29s on May 11 with thanks and warm words of praise. "Personally," said General LeMay, "I don't know why we should have received much in the way of thanks. The B-29 is not a tactical bomber and never pretended to be. No matter how we socked away at those airdromes, we could not reduce the kamikaze threat to zero."*

The big bombers went back, full time, to the business of igniting cities and burning up hapless civilians, a form of warfare Nimitz privately deplored. He had apparently expected the B-29 attacks to be restricted to the precision bombing of military and military-industrial targets in daylight, as was the American practice in the European war.† He pinned his hopes for victory, however, mainly on the blockade, which became almost complete when Amer-

---

* They could not, but LeMay underestimated the effect his bombers had on the airfields of Kyushu. Since the war the Japanese have stated that, by using demolition and fragmentation bombs, the B-29s not only cratered the runways, parking stands, and taxiways, but they so cut up shops, hangars, and even tools that keeping the planes operational required a major effort.

† But the Germans, and later the British, did make night incendiary raids in Europe.

ican submariners had learned how to penetrate Japanese minefields and get into the Sea of Japan, thereby cutting Japan off from continental Asia.

Task Force 58 was obliged to remain between Kyushu and Okinawa until June 10. By that time there had been nine mass raids on the American ships, with individual suicide planes attacking nearly every day. Sometimes half a dozen planes came streaking down on a single unlucky vessel. Kamikazes slammed into the armored flight decks of three of the British carriers without inflicting serious damage. But when they crashed into the wooden flight decks of the *Bunker Hill* and the *Enterprise*, they knocked these successive flagships of Admiral Mitscher out of the war for good.

In the morning of April 13 Admiral Nimitz had been shocked to learn of President Roosevelt's death at Warm Springs, Georgia. "I for one feel a deep sense of personal loss," he wrote Mrs. Nimitz. "Whether or not we liked *all* the things he did, and stood for—he was always for a strong Navy and was always most cordial and friendly to me. I have just sent a message of sympathy to Mrs. Roosevelt as coming from all of us in the Pacific Ocean Areas."

The marines by mid-April had reached the tip of Okinawa's northeast peninsula, but the soldiers were just coming up against the main Japanese defenses in the south—a system of caves, entrenchments, and concealed guns resembling those of Iwo Jima but on a larger scale. Admiral Nimitz was beginning to wonder whether the Army was deliberately using slow, methodical tactics to save the lives of its soldiers at the expense of the supporting Navy, whose sailors were being slaughtered by enemy aircraft. He was torn between an urge to investigate and his self-imposed rule of not interfering with the commander at the scene.

On April 16, Archer Vandegrift, who had become Commandant of the Marine Corps and a four-star general, arrived at Guam with two members of his staff. They had been in Hawaii visiting the 4th Marine Division, sadly depleted by its fighting on Iwo. General Vandegrift informed Admiral Nimitz that he proposed visiting his marines fighting on Okinawa, and was shocked and angered when Nimitz told him flatly that he would not permit him to go.

"Things are very active up there now," the admiral wrote Mrs. Nimitz that evening, "and I am not willing to have my agents there interfered with— even by me—although God knows I would like nothing better than to go up for a visit."

"I thought I knew what was bothering him," wrote Vandegrift afterward. "It was the Saipan controversy and was probably the main reason Holland Smith was sitting back at Pearl Harbor. In Nimitz' mind, I concluded, a senior Marine general by barging into Okinawa might upset the applecart of command relations. I subtly tried to quiet his fears, but at the same time I let him know I intended to visit my Marines."

On Guam General Vandegrift inspected the 3rd Marine Division, veterans of the Iwo Jima battle. Next, at Nimitz's suggestion, with his two staff members he visited Iwo Jima, where he climbed Mt. Suribachi and watched army troops unsealing caves and trying to persuade Japanese soldiers inside to surrender. Finding, as he said, "the official climate on Guam still temporizing," Vandegrift visited Saipan. There he found the 2nd Marine Division, Tenth Army reserve for Okinawa, ready and itching for combat, on an alert status, their transports loaded and prepared to sail on a few hours' notice.

On returning to Guam on Saturday, April 21, Vandegrift was surprised and gratified to be greeted cordially by Nimitz, who invited him to accompany himself and Forrest Sherman on a trip to Okinawa. Either Nimitz had communicated with Washington and been informed that he had no right to deny the marine commandant the privilege of visiting his troops in the field, or he had concluded that the fact that the Army in southern Okinawa had not moved forward for several days constituted the "extraordinary circumstances" that justified intervention.

The next morning the CinCPOA flag plane, with Nimitz, Vandegrift, Sherman, Lamar, and Vandegrift's chief of staff, General Gerald Thomas, took off for Okinawa escorted by a dozen fighter planes. During the flight Sherman began discussing service unification. Vandegrift, to whom the whole subject was anathema, was startled to find that Sherman favored it and that Nimitz generally agreed with him. This should not have surprised the marine general, for the CinCPOA command was a model of unification, and many of Nimitz's troubles had arisen from officers who refused to accept that fact.

A few minutes after 6:00 p.m., as the CinCPOA plane was landing at Yontan Airfield, near one of the Hagushi beaches, sirens on Okinawa began announcing Condition Red. Before the horrified gaze of the new arrivals, a single enemy plane spun out of the sky and crashed into a nearby cargo ship with a flash and a blast, followed by fire and black smoke. In the distance other ships, including a destroyer, were hit by planes, and a minesweeper was sunk.

Admiral Nimitz and his party were conducted by boat to the *New Mexico*, where they were guests of Admiral Spruance. Just as they were about to sit down to dinner, the Japanese staged a conventional air raid. "On that occasion," Nimitz wrote Catherine, "no planes reached the anchorage where we were. Some 53 were shot down by our planes or gunfire from screening ships and we in the visiting group were deprived of the excitement of seeing falling Jap planes."

The next day, April 23, the Nimitz party, joined by Admiral Spruance, traveled by jeep around the part of Okinawa then in American possession and conferred with the commanders. The engineers had concluded that Okinawa could accommodate 18 airfields and that nearby Ie Shima, just captured by the Army's 77th Division, could hold four more. These fields could handle all the Allied air power that would be transferred from Europe, and some were big enough to take B-29s. Since Okinawa also afforded several excellent harbors, there no longer appeared any need for more bases in the Ryukyus or in China to support the invasion of Japan.

General Buckner seemed to have a chip on his shoulder that day. When

Admiral Nimitz remarked on the need to speed up operations ashore in order to release the supporting fleet, Buckner pointed out that this was a ground operation. The implication was that tactics on Okinawa was strictly army business and he would thank the Navy to keep its hands off and its opinions to itself. Here it was again, that persistent and irritating interservice resistance to clearly established lines of authority. Nimitz glanced icily at Buckner.

"Yes, but ground though it may be," said the admiral, measuring his words, "I'm losing a ship and a half a day. So if this line isn't moving within five days, we'll get someone here to move it so we can all get out from under these stupid air attacks."

Later, at a conference at General Geiger's command post, General Buckner said that he planned to transfer the 1st and 6th Marine Divisions south to the main combat area in the next few days. General Vandegrift said that was what the marines were on Okinawa for—to fight. But what about the 2nd Marine Division, waiting on Saipan? Instead of merely slugging it out with the enemy in a single frontal attack on his main defenses, why not use the 2nd Division to make an amphibious assault on the enemy's flank or rear? Admiral Sherman objected that it would take too long to load out the division from Saipan, but Vandegrift assured him that it could be under way in six hours.

To Buckner, this was an old proposal, already rejected. Major General Andrew D. Bruce, USA, had recommended that his 77th Division make such an end-run following its conquest of Ie Shima. The Tenth Army staff had studied that plan long and carefully and concluded that no beaches behind the enemy lines were suitable for assault and that all were exposed to strong enemy attack. Buckner had decided that any attempt to land on the south or southeast coasts would be prohibitively costly, "another Anzio, but worse." He believed that with massed artillery, fleet support, flame-throwing tanks, and the fresh troops from the north, he would be able quickly to blast the enemy out of his stronghold. Nimitz listened attentively to the arguments and then said that he would accept Buckner's tactics "provided they produced early results."

In fact, it took the Tenth Army a month to crack the enemy's main defenses. Newspapers began to ask questions. Unfortunately someone had leaked the suggestion of a second landing to correspondents on Okinawa, and newsman Homer Bigart revealed it in the New York *Herald Tribune.* "Our tactics were ultraconservative," he wrote. "Instead of an end-run, we persisted in frontal attacks."

Admiral King asked Admiral Nimitz for an explanation of the leak. Nimitz said he thought General Vandegrift must have released the information. King called in Vandegrift and told him what Nimitz had said.

"I'm sorry to hear that," said Vandegrift. "I regard Nimitz as a personal friend and he should know better than to think I operate like that."

Vandegrift then told King that, in his candid opinion, Buckner's tactics were time-consuming and unnecessarily exposed the Navy to repeated kamikaze attack. King frowned and said that he would attend to the matter. A couple of days later, King asked Vandegrift to discuss it with the columnist David Lawrence, who subsequently wrote:

> Certain high Navy officers here feel that a major mistake was made in handling the Okinawa campaign. . . . Did the Army officers who handled the campaign adopt a slow course? Were there other landing places that could have been used? Why were the Marine Corps generals who had had far greater experience in handling amphibious operations not given opportunity to carry on another type of campaign that might, perhaps, have meant larger land casualties at the outset, but in the end a quicker all-around result for the armed forces as a whole?

Alarmed, Secretary Forrestal and Admirals Turner and Mitscher issued statements supporting the Army's tactics. Lawrence warmed to his subject. In a later column he called the Okinawa campaign a fiasco, "a worse example of military incompetence than Pearl Harbor."

Here was the basis for another interservice wrangle, just when the Army and Navy should be coordinating as never before for the forthcoming invasion of Japan. Nimitz now broke precedent by discussing the campaign with 76 newsmen on Guam. Calling the Okinawa campaign a "magnificent performance," he praised the Army's tactics and pointed out that an amphibious outflanking of the Japanese would have been more costly and time-consuming than the frontal drive that had been made. Such was the general confidence and trust in which Nimitz was held that the threatening controversy simply vanished.

Because of the strain caused by operating under kamikaze attacks, Nimitz had all three top naval commanders at Okinawa relieved before the end of the campaign. In mid-May Harry Hill, promoted to vice admiral, took over from Kelly Turner, who received four stars. Toward the end of the month on successive days, Halsey relieved Spruance and McCain relieved Mitscher. The Fifth Fleet again became the Third Fleet and Task Force 58 became Task Force 38. All the relieved commanders got some much-needed rest, after which Spruance and Turner began planning for Operation Olympic. Mitscher went to Washington to relieve Admiral Fitch as Deputy Chief of Naval Operations for Air.

Halsey, anxious to break away from close support of Okinawa, suggested to the Army that completion of the radar network on the island should be expedited, and on his recommendation a marine air group was ordered up from the Philippines to operate from Okinawa's airfields. Nimitz then took Hill's amphibious force and Buckner's Tenth Army under his direct command, thereby freeing Task Force 38 as a striking force. Halsey promptly advanced on Japan and sent air strikes against Kyushu on June 3 and 4. On June 5, for the second time, a typhoon struck Halsey's force, wrenching off the bow of the cruiser *Pittsburgh*, damaging 32 other ships, and destroying 142 planes. Three days later Task Force 38 struck again at Kyushu. Then, leaving Hill's escort carriers and army and marine pilots to provide air cover for Okinawa, the task force withdrew to prepare for a series of attacks against the Japanese home islands in July. When the force arrived at Leyte Gulf on June 13, it had been at sea 92 days.

Halsey's second typhoon came near ruining his career. Another court of inquiry, this one also presided over by Admiral Hoover, put most of the blame on Halsey and on Admiral McCain, pointing out that they had not followed Admiral Nimitz's Fleet Letter of advice for dealing with severe storms. The court recommended that Admirals Halsey and McCain be assigned to "other duty." Secretary Forrestal was on the point of retiring Halsey, but Nimitz and King argued him out of his intention on the basis that Halsey was a national hero whose removal would impair American morale and boost that of the enemy.

Gunfire support ships and escort carriers remained off Okinawa until after the island was declared secured on June 21. Of about 100,000 defenders, 11,000 had been taken prisoner and all the rest had been killed. Twenty-six American naval vessels had been sunk by air attack and 368 damaged, many beyond salvage. In the Tenth Army, 7,613 soldiers and marines had been killed and nearly 39,000 wounded. In the fleet 4,900 sailors were killed and nearly as many wounded. This campaign, the most costly of the Pacific war for the Americans, had purchased a position from which the bomber campaign against Japan could be intensified, the blockade of the home islands could be tightened, and invasion forces could be launched against Kyushu, but its most important result from the American point of view was that it forced Japan to face the inevitability of defeat and the advisability of an early surrender.

# CHAPTER 23

# VICTORY

DURING THE FIRST two years of the Pacific war, General MacArthur's Southwest Pacific Area was the most active theater of operations. His subsequent advance along the coast of New Guinea had a far less decisive impact. This advance was, as the general had feared, rendered almost superfluous by the rapid drive of Admiral Nimitz's forces directly across the Central Pacific. MacArthur's capture of Luzon provided a useful base for blockading Japan. But after Luzon, his forces, still confined within the Southwest Pacific Area, could only head south, to the southern Philippines and Borneo, operations that contributed nothing toward the defeat of Japan.

By 1945 the War Department as well as MacArthur had become increasingly dissatisfied with the restriction on the general, particularly since it would prevent him from participating in the invasion of Japan. The War Department was unwilling to see MacArthur shunted off to the south while Nimitz, with his navy-centered headquarters, commanded the assault on the home islands. In Washington all the old arguments for establishing unified command over the whole Pacific theater were again brought forward, and each met with insurmountable opposition. At last, in late March, MacArthur was informed indirectly by the President that the high command had found a solution. Roosevelt said to General Kenney, who was visiting Washington, "You might tell Douglas that I expect he will have a lot of work to do north of the Philippines before long."

The compromise solution ordered by the Joint Chiefs of Staff on April 3 was deceptively simple-looking: for the invasion of Japan, MacArthur would command all army ground and air forces in the Pacific except the Twentieth Army Air Force in the Marianas and units in certain inactive areas; Nimitz was to command all naval forces in the Pacific. By supplementary directive, the Joint Chiefs ordered MacArthur and Nimitz to complete their current campaigns under the old command structure. The transition to the new structure was to be by degrees and by mutual consent.

On April 13, a party of officers headed by General Sutherland flew from MacArthur's Manila headquarters to Guam to meet with Admiral Nimitz and his staff in an effort to implement the Joint Chiefs' directives. Sutherland, deceived by Nimitz's gracious manner, assumed a magisterial tone and began setting forth what he called General MacArthur's ideas. The general, he said, proposed as soon as possible to take complete control of army forces under Nimitz, including the garrisons of island bases in the Pacific Ocean Areas. In the process, he would break up Nimitz's unity of command, which Sutherland called "an unworkable shibboleth." In the future, he asserted, no army troops would be allowed to serve under any admiral.

If Sutherland thought that Nimitz was going meekly to accept such terms, he was quickly undeceived. The admiral told him that he expected to relinquish to MacArthur the operational control of army units only as they were released from operations, that the essential garrisons of all positions in the Pacific Ocean Areas had to remain under Nimitz's control as long as he was responsible for those areas, and that abolition of unity of command in the subareas and outlying islands would produce chaos and retard the prosecution of the war. He concluded: "I shall not therefore accede now to his assuming operational control of army forces—ground, air, or service—which are essential to the defense and functioning of the Pacific Ocean Areas."

Sutherland said that MacArthur wanted Okinawa as a base for General Kenney's air force and for launching Operation Olympic, the invasion of Kyushu, scheduled for November 1, 1945. Nimitz was willing to turn all of the captured Ryukyus over to MacArthur as soon as the conquest of Okinawa had been completed, or earlier if the Joint Chiefs issued a firm directive for the invasion. He declined a suggestion that he assume operational control of, and responsibility for, naval operations in the Southwest Pacific Area. Were he to do so, he would necessarily be acting as MacArthur's subordinate. If he started taking orders from the general, the latter might insist on controlling the movements of the fast carrier force, an outcome that would be anathema to the Navy Department and to Admiral King in particular. Nimitz said that, while he would not take command of naval forces involved in Southwest Pacific amphibious operations, he would, as he had in the past, provide naval cover for such operations and allocate naval forces for direct participation under MacArthur.

Since the Sutherland party had come to Guam almost exclusively to present what Sutherland represented as MacArthur's proposals for immediate action, they left on the morning of April 16 fairly empty-handed but aware that under Nimitz's gracious demeanor there was an iron will. Nimitz reported to King: "Very little useful discussion has taken place concerning invasion plans and preparations and the SWPA party was apparently not prepared for such discussion."

That evening Admiral Nimitz wrote to Mrs. Nimitz:

> I have had a very tough day commencing with the departure early this morning of my friends from the far west. I do not believe either side convinced the other but at least my side *so far* has lost nothing and the other side knows we are tough and no push-overs. More conferences must follow—I am sure of that—and perhaps we can make progress then.

More conferences did in fact take place, involving much flying of staff members between Manila and Guam. Nimitz found divorcing Army from Navy a brain-cracking and exhausting exercise. In the midst of one day devoted to this and other tedious problems, he dashed off to Mrs. Nimitz a confused letter: "...Believe me—the directive of the Joint Chiefs of Staff to separate the Army and the Navy certainly requires a lot of work and talk to unscramble the closely knit teams.... If my disconnected or incoherent remember that I am under great pressure these days that does not originate with the Japs."

In his labors to untie the Gordian knot of unified command, Nimitz gradually convinced himself that there were limits to unification—that its success depended on circumstances, and on who was commander in chief. He never again recommended unification of armed services on a national scale.

Since MacArthur refused to go to Guam for discussions, and his sense of protocol forbade him from reaching final agreements with Nimitz's representatives, Nimitz on May 15 flew to Manila to confer directly with him. The general received the admiral with his usual courtesy and invited him to stay in his own quarters, the Bachrach mansion, one of the few suitable houses in the war-shattered city that had not been reduced to rubble. Face to face, Nimitz found MacArthur eminently reasonable. They jointly endorsed the plans worked out in the previous meetings and, in two days of talks, settled most of the remaining problems and laid the basis for cooperation in the invasions of Kyushu and Honshu, in the home islands.

Nimitz and MacArthur quickly discarded the notion that no army troops would be allowed to serve under any admiral. They rejected the old British amphibious assault plan, which provided for two coequal commanders throughout, a general and an admiral; and chose instead to adhere to the American system, first introduced at the invasion of North Africa in November 1942. In the American amphibious assault plan, the landing force was commanded by only one officer at a time, first an admiral, then a general. The essence of the assault plan for Kyushu was set forth in a top secret CinCPac/POA serial of May 19, 1945:

> Commander Fifth Fleet will control the amphibious movement and landing through Commander Amphibious Forces Pacific Fleet, who in turn will control the Attack Force or Group Commanders who are responsible for the amphibious operations of their respective objectives.
> Control of forces ashore will pass to the Commander of each Assault Division or each separate Landing Force, after his arrival and establishment ashore, and upon his notification to the commander of the corresponding Naval Attack Group that he is ready to assume command of the forces ashore....
> Control of forces ashore will pass to each Corps Commander with his respective area of operation after his arrival and establishment ashore....
> Control of forces ashore will pass to Commanding General, Sixth United States Army, upon his announcement to the Commander Amphibious Forces, Pacific Fleet, that he is ready to assume command of forces ashore.

The growing size of the Central Pacific Force at last enabled Admiral Nimitz to separate the Fifth and Third fleets. The Fifth Fleet, commanded by Admiral Spruance, was to open Operation Olympic by supporting and controlling the landing on Kyushu. This fleet included Admiral Turner's amphibious forces and part of the fast carrier force, designated Task Force 58, under Vice Admiral Frederick Sherman. Admiral Halsey's Third Fleet now existed in fact as an entirely separate organization. It consisted of the rest of the fast carrier force, as Task Force 38, plus the British Pacific Fleet, designated Task Force 37. With amphibious forces added, the Third Fleet was to open Operation Coronet by supporting and controlling the landing on Honshu. Vice Admiral Rawlings, RN, was operational commander of Task Force 37. Vice Admiral McCain, who was in declining health, was to be relieved as Commander, Task Force 38, by Vice Admiral John H. Towers.

Had the relief of McCain worked out as planned, Jack Towers would at last have had the fighting command he longed for. As it turned out, however, he did not get it until after the fighting was over. Nimitz never warmed to Towers' personality, but he recognized the man's ability and the general correctness of his professional thinking. Moreover, Towers had carried out his essentially tedious duties faithfully and competently. Nimitz had recommended him for the carrier command, and King had reluctantly consented.

The final defeat of the European Axis, marked by the German surrender on May 8, 1945, took nobody at CinCPac headquarters by surprise. The only wonder was that the Germans had held out so long. All the Pacific commanders were, of course, immensely gratified by the Allied victory, but Nimitz saw it as having little effect upon his own problems. A year earlier he would have hailed it because it meant that more manpower and more air power would be available for defeating Japan. He was now convinced that the blockade and the bombing would force the Japanese to surrender before the Allied forces in Europe could be redeployed to the Pacific.

Admiral Nimitz's conviction that Japan would surrender before long was based also on a piece of solid information. In February a young officer, Commander Frederick L. Ashworth, had arrived at his headquarters in khakis so wrinkled and sweaty that Lamar was hesitant to admit him to the inner sanctum. Ashworth, a naval weapons specialist, explained that he had just flown out from the United States and had encountered unaccustomed heat and humidity at the island stops. It was imperative that he see Admiral Nimitz. With misgivings, Lamar explained the situation to Nimitz, who told him to let the commander in.

When Lamar had departed, Ashworth looked about with a conspiratorial air that made Nimitz smile, then opened his shirt, exposing a sweat-covered money belt from which he drew a damp and crumpled envelope and handed it to the admiral. Nimitz slit open the envelope and found a second envelope marked TOP SECRET, which he also opened. Inside was a letter from Admiral King.

King's letter stated that an atomic bomb was under development and was expected to have an energy yield equivalent to about 20,000 tons of TNT. The bomb should be available in the Pacific theater about August 1, 1945. King directed Nimitz to disclose the contents of his letter to no more than one officer on his staff, and told him that if he had any specific technical questions about the bomb, the bearer of the letter would be able to answer them.

Admiral Nimitz buzzed for Soc McMorris and handed him the letter to read. He also let Ashworth read it. Ashworth explained briefly the technology of the bomb, but Nimitz did not appear interested. His mind seemed to Ashworth to be filled with the awesome thought of a single bomb that could destroy a whole city and kill all, or nearly all, its inhabitants.

"Young man," he said, "this is very interesting, but August is a long time from now, and in the meantime I have a war to fight. Furthermore, please tell Admiral King that I cannot abide by his requirement to inform only one officer on my staff if he expects me to provide the support I am sure will be needed. You tell him that I must inform my combat-readiness officer, Captain Tom Hill, who will have the responsibility to see that the support is provided."

Nimitz turned in his chair and gazed out of the window for a moment, then rose and said to Ashworth, "Thank you very much," adding softly, almost as if to himself, "You know, I guess I was just born a few years too soon."

Commander Ashworth next explored the Marianas in search of a suitable place from which the B-29s of the 509th Composite Group that were to drop the atomic bombs on Japan might fly. He selected the northwest corner of Tinian. Accordingly, long airstrips were laid out there, B-29s were brought in, a village of Quonset huts arose, and the new base was surrounded by barbed wire and closely guarded. On June 27 the officers of the 509th Group, following extensive exercises in Utah and Cuba, arrived to continue their training. The subsequent activities of the 509th, flying out over the ocean and flying back again, mystified and aroused the resentment of the other B-29 aviators on Tinian, who were regularly risking their lives in bombing and mining flights to Japan.

In the midst of the busy spring of 1945, the publicity-minded Secretary of the Navy decided that CinCPac should publish a daily newspaper, or at least a Pacific Fleet magazine. Nimitz admitted that he had a good public relations staff and that they could do the job, but, he said, "the work of distribution, etc. is just too much when we are trying to run a war and, besides, we get daily press and radio and plenty of magazines." Even the most forward areas received miniaturized, overseas editions of *Time* and *Newsweek*, and Nimitz had no desire to compete with these.

"The publicity side of the war is getting so large," said Nimitz, "it almost overshadows the fighting side." The more Mr. Forrestal insisted that Nimitz go into the publishing business, the more the admiral dug in his heels and refused to do anything of the sort. At last the Secretary gave up, having concluded that, with the possible exception of Ernie King, Nimitz was the most stubborn officer he had to deal with.

General Hap Arnold, in a visit of inspection to the Pacific, undertook to crack the renowned Nimitz obstinacy. The army air forces, including LeMay's

21st Bomber Command, had been complaining to Arnold that the CinCPac command was putting unnecessary obstacles in the way of their getting what they wanted when they wanted it. Arnold barged into CinCPac headquarters and repeated the complaints to Nimitz himself. Nimitz listened courteously and readily agreed to all changes suggested by the general.

"After this conference with Admiral Nimitz," Arnold wrote later, "it finally dawned on me that most of the Air Force problems, difficulties, and complications were a result of junior officers' magnifying something of relative unimportance and making it a great matter. Everything pointed to my getting my people together and giving them a talk." Arnold learned, as many another officer had done, that Nimitz was stubborn in opposition only to what was irrational, time-wasting, or unjust.

Operations on Guam in the spring and summer of 1945 were complicated not only by efforts to divorce the army and navy commands, but by an endless stream of visitors, most of them civilians, who were there on the invitation of the Secretary of the Navy or by his authority. Congressmen, labor leaders, publishers, executives of defense industries—anybody, it seemed, who could dredge up even a remote reason for visiting forward bases and conferring with senior officers, found his way out there. It was the duty of CinCPac's public relations officer and his assistants to greet these visitors and plan their itineraries, but Nimitz himself met with most of them and invited a good many of them to dinner.

Among the congressmen who visited Guam was Nimitz's Texas neighbor, Lyndon B. Johnson. Among the publishers was Douglas Southall Freeman, editor of the Richmond, Virginia, *News Leader*. Nimitz had looked forward to making Freeman's acquaintance, because he had recently read and enjoyed his four-volume biography *R. E. Lee*.

Other officers considered the time-consuming callers an unqualified nuisance and treated them coolly. Some of the travelers complained about such treatment to Forrestal, who complained to King, causing the latter to write to Nimitz: "The number of prominent visitors to your area will increase, and it is important that they be treated with courtesy."

Hardly had King got this admonition in the mail when he received another, sharper complaint from the Secretary. The offenders this time were the two reputedly most impatient officers on Guam, Soc McMorris and "Genial John" Hoover. King promptly fired off a memorandum to Nimitz: "It is the view of SecNav that *Hoover* and *McMorris* should have as little to do with 'visitors' as possible—unless and until they have been indoctrinated—and it 'takes'!"

Nimitz had other problems with his officers. Halsey announced to the press that he wanted to ride Emperor Hirohito's horse. "Bull" Halsey and the emperor's white horse made headlines. The saddles, bridles, lariats, and spurs that Halsey began receiving from his admirers were good for more newspaper stories. Nimitz lost no time in shutting Halsey up. The Japanese were beginning to put out peace feelers, this was no time to ridicule their "divine" emperor, particularly since he alone had the authority to order his subjects to stop fighting.

At Leyte Gulf a show-off army pilot making dives and dummy runs on the ships of Ted Sherman's task group crashed into the flight deck of the *Randolph,* killing eleven men. Sherman thereupon in a rage issued dispatch orders to his captains to shoot down any plane whatever that buzzed their ships. Nimitz canceled those orders and did what he could to cool down the hotheaded Sherman.

At the end of June, Admiral Nimitz flew to San Francisco for what proved to be his final wartime meeting with Admiral King. At this conference, which lasted only one day, King informed Nimitz that President Truman had approved Operation Olympic and that the Joint Chiefs recommended that preparations be made for the subsequent Operation Coronet. The briefness of the meeting may well have reflected the near-conviction in the minds of both Nimitz and King that neither Olympic nor Coronet would ever take place.

During July Spruance was on Guam planning Operation Olympic with his and Nimitz's staffs. The more he studied the proposed invasion, the deeper became his foreboding that the losses in ships and men would be heavy. Turner was at Manila planning the amphibious phase of Operation Olympic with General Walter Krueger's Sixth Army, which was to be the landing force.

The reconstituted Third Fleet was parading with impunity up and down the east coast of Japan, bombing and bombarding. Halsey's carrier planes raided airfields, factories, and naval bases and sank or heavily damaged the remnants of the Imperial Japanese Fleet in the Inland Sea. The failure of the Japanese to retaliate against this indignity suggested to Allied leaders that the enemy was hoarding his remaining aircraft to throw against any attempted invasion.

Bombers from Okinawa and the Marianas were appearing over Japan in waves of 500 or more, burning out vast areas in Japan's major cities. Submarines and mine-bearing planes were drawing the blockade of the home islands ever tighter.

When cryptanalysis of Japanese radio messages revealed that Japan was attempting to extend peace feelers through the Soviet government, CinCPac and Commander, Fifth Fleet, began to shift their emphasis from planning for Operation Olympic to preparing for a possible Japanese surrender. Washington was shifting too. Experts in fields ranging from civil government and war crimes to reconstruction joined the CinCPac staff.

On July 25, a plane carrying Captain William S. Parsons, a naval ordnance expert, landed on Guam. Parsons had with him films of the world's first man-made atomic explosion, which had occurred at Alamogordo, New Mexico, on the 16th. Before an awed audience that included Admiral Nimitz, Admiral Spruance, General LeMay, and selected officers of their staffs, Parsons showed his movies of the great fireball rising over the desert. The next day he flew on to Tinian, where the cruiser *Indianapolis,* repaired from the damage she received off Okinawa, had just arrived with a heavy but subcritical mass of uranium 235 for the atomic bomb.

On the 26th the governments of the United States, Britain, and China issued the Potsdam Declaration, which set forth peace terms for Japan: the Japanese army must surrender unconditionally; Japan was to be stripped of all her territorial possessions except the four home islands; points in Japan would be occupied until a "peacefully inclined and responsible government" had been established by free election. The alternative to acceptance of these terms was "prompt and utter destruction."

After unloading the uranium at Tinian, the *Indianapolis* proceeded to Guam, whence she departed on the 28th with orders from CinCPac to report to Leyte Gulf. There her crew would undergo two weeks' training before rejoining the fleet.

At Tokyo on the 28th, Prime Minister Kantaro Suzuki held a press conference in which he was asked about his government's action on the Potsdam Declaration. Because his government had not yet decided how to reply, Suzuki answered with an ambiguous statement which the Allied governments took to be a rejection of the Declaration.

At the end of July there arrived at Guam Brigadier General Thomas Farrell, deputy to Major General Leslie R. Groves, commander in chief of the Atomic Bomb Project. Farrell conferred with Major General LeMay and with General Carl Spaatz, the new Commanding General, U.S. Strategic Air Forces, concerning orders from the War Department that required the 509th Composite Group to "deliver its first special bomb as soon as weather will permit visual bombing after about 3 August."

Farrell next visited Admiral Nimitz to request the Navy's assistance in setting up some means of rescuing the atomic-bomb flyers, should they be forced to bail out or ditch. Specifically, he wanted submarines to be stationed in waters along the route the flyers would take and navy flying boats to be in readiness at nearby bases.

After agreeing to have these precautions taken, Nimitz called Farrell over to a window and pointed to a speck on the northern horizon.

"That island over there," he said, "is Rota. There are about 3,000 Japanese on it. They bother us a great deal. They have radios. They know what we are doing. They are sending out information. Haven't you got a small bomb you can drop on Rota? I don't feel it warrants an amphibious invasion at this time. But they do bother us."

"Unfortunately, Admiral," replied Farrell, "all our bombs are big ones." He then proceeded to Tinian to take command of the 509th Group's base.

Admiral Nimitz was becoming impatient with the inability of the Japanese government to face facts. To him it was perfectly apparent that Japan was defeated. Samurai tradition, however, made it impossible for the Japanese to acknowledge defeat. The peace feelers they had put out through the Soviet government were designed to achieve two things at the same time—to get terms short of unconditional surrender from the Allies and to keep Russia out of the Pacific war. Russia obviously was not going to be kept out of a war in which she had little to lose and quite a bit to gain. The Soviet government was stalling.

Nimitz considered the atomic bomb somehow indecent, certainly not a legitimate form of warfare. He hoped the Americans would not have to use it. He discussed the situation with Captain Edwin Layton, who had devoted much of his adult life to the study of Japanese psychology. Layton thought the dropping of the atomic bomb was virtually a necessity. He pointed out, as he had often done before, that only the Emperor had the prestige to make the Japanese stop fighting, and even for him it would be no easy thing. "If he told all the women to cut off their hair, or for everyone to walk on their hands, they would do it," said Layton. "If he told all the men to castrate themselves, 99 per cent of them would do it." But, said Layton, to tell the Army to stop fighting was something else again. Even if His Imperial Majesty did so, the result might not be decisive, unless he could prove to his people that the alternative was indeed the destruction of Japan. The atomic bomb might provide that proof. Nimitz listened carefully. He had come to the same conclusion, but he wanted to hear it from his Japanese expert.

By August 2, via ship and plane, the component parts of two atomic bombs had been delivered to Tinian. All that was needed then was for the weather to clear up a bit and the first of the bombs would be on its way to Japan.

In the early hours of the 3rd, the news reached Guam that shortly before midnight on July 29, the *Indianapolis*, en route to Leyte, had been sunk. Her survivors, after four days on rafts and in the water, had just been found. Why had the failure of the cruiser to arrive in Leyte Gulf not been noted and reported? Admiral Nimitz promptly ordered a court of inquiry to convene at Guam.

In the evening of August 4, Captain Parsons, observing B-29s taking off to raid Japan, was horrified to see four of them crash at the end of the runway and burn. If that sort of thing happened to a plane bearing a fully armed atomic bomb, the resultant explosion could just about blow Tinian off the map. Parsons resolved that the assembling of the bombs should not be completed until the planes were aloft and some distance from land.

Sunday, August 5, dawned clear. Because the forecast was for at least two days of fair weather over Japan, General Farrell scheduled the dropping of the first atomic bomb for the morning of the 6th. Captain Parsons spent the day practicing assembling and disassembling the bomb.

Word got around in the Marianas that something special was in the offing. Perhaps it resulted from observation of the unusual activity that was taking place at the 509th Group base. More likely one or more of the people who were in on the secret of the bomb could not refrain from hinting that something was about to happen that would end the war sooner than anyone suspected. At any rate August 5 was a day of growing tension in the islands.

At 2:45 on the morning of August 6, the *Enola Gay*, the B-29 that was carrying the first atomic bomb, and two observer B-29s took off from Tinian. In the hours that followed, none of the officers they left behind at the base did much sleeping. They kept repeating to each other the questions that troubled them most. Would Captain Parsons get the bomb reassembled? Would it live up to expectations? Would it prove to be a dud and reveal its secrets to the enemy? Others watched through the night at General LeMay's, General Spaatz's, and Admiral Nimitz's headquarters.

The *Enola Gay* was scheduled to drop its bomb on the city of Hiroshima, on the Inland Sea, at 9:15 a.m. The time came and went, with all hands at 509th Group headquarters watching the clock. At 9:20 two words in plain English spanned the 1,500 miles from the air over Japan to Tinian: "Mission successful!" Captain Parsons presently followed this up with a fuller report in code. General Farrell passed the news on to General LeMay, to General Spaatz, to Admiral Nimitz, and to General Groves for relay to President Truman, then en route home from the Potsdam Conference in the cruiser *Augusta*, the same *Augusta* that Nimitz had commanded in the Orient.

Washington kept demanding more details, but Farrell could not supply any until the *Enola Gay* arrived back at Tinian at 3:00 p.m. Then, the flyers were interrogated one by one, *New York Times* reporter William Laurence taking copious notes. When the interrogation was over, Laurence dashed for a typewriter and began writing his story:

> The first atomic bomb ever used in warfare, a small, man-made fireball exploding with the force of 20,000 tons of TNT, dropped from a B-29, today wiped out the great industrial and military center of Hiroshima.
>
> At exactly 9:15 this morning Hiroshima stood out under the clear blue sky. One tenth of a millionth of a second later, a time imperceptible by any clock, it had been swallowed by a cloud of swirling fire as though it had never existed. The best watches made by man still registered 9:15.
>
> If any air-raid wardens below became aware of the approach of the great silver ship high overhead, they gave no sign of it. No flak. No alarm of any kind. The 400,000 inhabitants of Hiroshima, it appeared, were going about their business as usual. . . .

In the United States, Secretary of War Stimson released to the press Truman's previously prepared statement. It announced that an atomic bomb, "harnessing the basic power of the universe," had been dropped on Hiroshima. "The force from which the sun draws its power has been loosed against those who brought war to the Far East." The United States, it continued, was prepared to obliterate all the factories, docks, and communications in Japan. "It was to spare the Japanese people from utter destruction that the ultimatum of July 26 was issued at Potsdam. Their leaders promptly rejected that ultimatum. If they do not now accept our terms, they may expect a rain of ruin from the air, the like of which has never been seen on this earth."

The Japanese government remained silent.

On Wednesday, August 8, the Navy's hospital ship *Tranquillity* arrived at Guam with the survivors of the *Indianapolis* who had originally been landed by rescue vessels at Peleliu. Among the survivors was the *Indianapolis'* commanding officer, Captain Charles Butler McVay. It was now believed that the cruiser had been sunk by one or more torpedoes from an enemy submarine. Some 350 to 400 crewmen had gone down with the ship, nearly 500 had survived the sinking but died while awaiting rescue, and only 316 were picked up alive. Admiral Spruance went to the hospital to visit his former shipmates and award Purple Heart medals to the men, who were suffering from exposure and dehydration. "You'll never know how happy I am to see you made it," said Spruance, "and I'm only sorry we had to lose so many men I had come to think of as my family."

That evening the Soviet Union declared war on the Japanese Empire, and invaded Japanese-occupied Manchuria. At 3:50 the following morning, August 9th, B-29 *Bock's Car* took off from Tinian with the second bomb. At 11:01 a.m. it dropped the bomb and devastated the city of Nagasaki, on Kyushu.

Admiral Nimitz had been nominated to receive from the British crown the Order of Knight Grand Cross of the Bath, and the Duke of Gloucester had been appointed to do the honors. But with the war obviously rushing toward its conclusion and the duke detained in Australia, Admiral Sir Bruce Fraser was assigned the duty of investing Nimitz. The ceremony took place on August 10 aboard Admiral Fraser's flagship, the battleship *Duke of York*, off Guam. Nimitz, accompanied by several officers of his staff, arrived aboard just before 11:00 a.m. Fraser read from an impressive document, then draped the broad scarlet ribbon of the order from Nimitz's shoulder across his chest. Nimitz requested drinks for the crew, paid a brief social visit, and returned to his headquarters to struggle anew with problems of the coming occupation.

Early on the 11th Nimitz received from Admiral King a message that began, "This is a peace warning," and went on to say that the Japanese had notified Washington through the Swiss government that they were willing to accept the terms of the Potsdam Declaration, on the understanding that it would not prejudice the prerogatives of the Emperor as sovereign. The United States agreed that the Japanese might keep their Emperor but his authority would have to be subject to decisions of the Supreme Commander for the Allied Powers until a responsible government had been established in Japan by the freely expressed will of the Japanese people. The U.S. State Department was seeking the concurrence of Britain, China, and the Soviet Union with this concession.

Some of President Truman's advisers recommended a cease-fire pending final negotiations, but Truman insisted upon keeping up the pressure lest the Japanese be emboldened to demand more concessions. Accordingly LeMay's 21st Bomber Command began loading the B-29s for another fire raid. Halsey flashed a radio order to his Third Fleet, which was pounding targets in northern Honshu, to move in and attack the Tokyo area. Nimitz countermanded that order; then, when no further word came from Japan, told Halsey to go ahead. The raid was carried out on August 13 and Third Fleet planes destroyed several hundred enemy aircraft. On the morning of August 15, Halsey ordered another raid on Tokyo and notified Nimitz that he had done so. Two hours later he received a high priority dispatch from CinCPac: "Suspend attack air operations."

Early that morning Captain Layton had been summoned by automatic electric bell to his office at CinCPac headquarters. A special teletype that only he was permitted to operate had started clicking in its cage. Layton put in the appropriate one-time tape, and the machine typed out its message in plain English. The sender was Op-20-G acting for the Chief of Naval Operations. The body of the dispatch was Japan's message, sent via the Swiss and Swedish governments, accepting the provisions of the Potsdam Declaration.

As soon as the transmission ended, Layton hit the acknowledge key. He then called his communications technician and said, "Send a plain-language acknowledgment by serial number and keep the copy." He tore off the top sheet of the dispatch and dashed for Nimitz's office. It was about 7:20 a.m.

As he strode past Lamar, Layton said, "This is the hottest thing we've had," and entered Zero Zero's inner office unannounced.

Admiral Nimitz was at his desk. "What is it?" he asked.

"Here it is," replied Layton and handed him the dispatch.

Nimitz glanced at the paper and smiled. "I've just got one from Admiral King." Apparently King's message was a bare statement that the Japanese had capitulated.

Admiral Nimitz, Layton said afterward, "didn't get jubilant or jump up and down like I saw some other officers do. He merely smiled in his own calm way ... as if he'd known all along this was going to happen and as if he'd expected it, and I'm sure he did. He knew that they were defeated. He had said this several times recently."

After the President's official statement that he deemed the Japanese reply "a full acceptance of the Potsdam Declaration, which specifies the unconditional surrender of Japan" had been broadcast, Admiral Nimitz broadcast an order to his forces in the Pacific Ocean Areas: "Cease offensive operations against Japanese forces. Continue searches and patrols. Maintain defense and internal security measures at highest level and beware of treachery or last moment attacks by enemy forces or individuals."

When Admiral Halsey, off Japan, learned that the war was over, he yelled, "Yippee!" and pounded the shoulders of everybody around him. He ordered battle flags hoisted on his flagship, the *Missouri*, and his four-star flag broken at the main, and had the whistle and siren sounded for one minute. The rest of the fleet followed his example. He ordered the flag hoist "Well Done" run up. However, he took the precaution of maintaining a combat air patrol, lest some kamikaze make a last-minute attack for the honor of his ancestors. To the pilots in the air he signaled, "Investigate and shoot down all snoopers—not vindictively, but in a friendly sort of way."

Later in the day Nimitz broadcast another message to the forces under his command:

> With the termination of hostilities against Japan, it is incumbent on all officers to conduct themselves with dignity and decorum in their treatment of the Japanese and their public utterances in connection with the Japanese. The Japanese are still the same nation which initiated the war by a treacherous attack on the Pacific Fleet and which has subjected our brothers in arms who became prisoners to torture, starvation, and murder. However, the use of insulting epithets in connection with the Japanese as a race or as individuals does not now become the officers of the United States Navy. Officers in the Pacific Fleet will take steps to require of all personnel under their command a high standard of conduct in this matter. Neither familiarity nor abuse and vituperation should be permitted.

It was announced over the radio that President Truman had appointed General MacArthur Supreme Commander for the Allied Powers and directed him to arrange for and conduct surrender ceremonies and the subsequent occupation of Japan. "Well, this does it!" muttered Admiral Nimitz, obviously annoyed. It was not that he wanted to command the occupation. He wanted to return to the United States and be Chief of Naval Operations. What he opposed was bringing an army officer front and center at the hour of victory when the Navy had borne the brunt of the war against Japan. Giving MacArthur the spotlight implied that it was his forces that had been chiefly responsible for defeating the Japanese.

The Secretary of the Navy came to the Navy's rescue with the suggestion that, if the surrender ceremony was to be conducted by an army officer, it should take place aboard a naval vessel. He further proposed that that ship should be the battleship *Missouri*, named after President Truman's home state and christened by his daughter, Margaret. Forrestal also won an agreement from the Secretary of State that if MacArthur was to sign the instrument of surrender for the Allied powers, Nimitz would sign it for the United States.

Admiral Halsey was delighted to learn that his flagship was to be the scene of an event of such historic moment. He sent a message to the Naval Academy Museum requesting the loan of the American flag that Commodore Matthew Calbraith Perry had flown when he entered Tokyo Bay in 1853. The request was granted and a special messenger took the flag to Halsey, who had it mounted on a bulkhead overlooking the veranda deck where the instrument of surrender was to be signed.

General MacArthur summoned Japanese government officials to Manila for the purpose of giving them instructions on receiving the occupation forces. General Sutherland represented General MacArthur and Admiral Forrest Sherman represented Admiral Nimitz. At the request of the Japanese delegation, the arrival of the occupying forces was postponed until August 28 in order to give army hotheads in Japan time to cool off and realize the futility of further resistance.

Admiral Nimitz invited Admiral Sherman, a senior army officer, a senior marine officer, and a senior army air force officer to accompany him to the surrender ceremony. He also planned to take Commander Lamar, his general factotum; his communication officer, to handle the special five-star systems; and Captain Layton. He told Layton that he was taking him to the surrender as some recompense for having so many times refused his requests to leave the CinCPac staff and go to sea.

Layton suggested to Nimitz that if he intended going ashore in Japan he had better take along his best marine bodyguard.

"What's the matter with you?" said Nimitz. "Can't you shoot?"

"Yes, I can," replied Layton, "and I think I could recognize, better than your marine, a situation involving a risk of an attack on you by a Japanese. I could challenge him in vernacular Japanese, which your marine can't."

"Well," said the admiral, "let's go out on the pistol range and see how good you are."

After they had shot at targets for a while, Nimitz said, "All right," and forthwith appointed Layton his interpreter and bodyguard.

As scheduled, the first American occupation troops landed at Atsugi airfield, near Yokosuka, on August 28. On the 29th part of the U.S. Third Fleet, including the *Missouri*, the *South Dakota*, and Admiral Fraser's flagship *Duke of York*, entered Tokyo Bay and dropped anchor. A little after 4:00 p.m. that day Nimitz arrived in Tokyo Bay by seaplane, and broke his flag on the *South Dakota*. Almost immediately, he was visited by Admiral Halsey, who had a problem. He had learned of sickness and inhumane conditions in prisoner-of-war camps in the Tokyo area. General MacArthur had directed that there was to be no recovering of POWs until the Army was ready to participate. Nevertheless Halsey had sent a task group, including the hospital ship *Benevolence*, up the bay to Tokyo with orders to stand by for a possible landing and rescue operations.

"Go ahead," said Nimitz. "General MacArthur will understand." Halsey gave the order, and by midnight nearly 800 prisoners had been brought out.

On the 30th the 11th Airborne Division landed at Atsugi and its band was playing when General MacArthur's plane landed at 2:19 p.m. the same day. MacArthur descended the stair smoking his famous corncob pipe and, at the foot, shook hands with General Robert L. Eichelberger, commander of the Eighth Army, who had preceded him to Atsugi by several hours. "Bob," said MacArthur, grinning, "this is the payoff."

The Third Fleet had begun landings at ten o'clock that morning. U.S. marines occupied Yokosuka Air Base and U.S. bluejackets occupied Yokosuka Naval Base. At 10:30 a.m. Vice Admiral Michitare Totsuka formally turned over the Yokosuka facilities to Admiral Carney, who was acting as

Admiral Halsey's representative. Headquarters of the Third Fleet and of the landing force were established there, and Halsey's flag was raised over the station.

Admiral Halsey and Admiral Nimitz went ashore for the raising of the American flag. Captain Layton, who carried a .45 in a shoulder holster, stayed close to Nimitz. When Nimitz saw Halsey's four-star flag flying at the base, he sharply ordered it hauled down and reminded Halsey of the impropriety of breaking his flag ashore in the presence of an officer senior to himself.

But there were no hard feelings. Together that afternoon, in a limousine provided by the Japanese, Nimitz and Halsey toured the shipyard and inspected the dry dock, the officers' club, and the hospital. They passed through cheering lanes of U.S. sailors and marines. The two admirals were gratified to see that bomb damage to the base was so slight that facilities could be quickly restored for American use during the occupation. On the other hand, it was obvious that the Japanese had made little effort to comply with orders specifying that "on delivery to the Allies, all facilities will be cleared of debris, scrupulously clean, and in full operating condition." In fact, the place was filthy, and much of the equipment was in poor shape or inoperable. Nimitz told newsmen that there was no evidence that Japanese had made any effort to clean the place or get the machinery working. "Most of Admiral Halsey's remarks," said *The New York Times*, "were unprintable." The disgust of the two admirals reached some sort of climax when their limousine ran out of gas and left them stranded.

In the days before the surrender ceremony, Admiral Nimitz not only wrote daily to Mrs. Nimitz, but he wrote to each of his children so that they might have a letter of historical interest. To Kate he told about a visit he made to General MacArthur on Saturday, September 1:

> Today in the pelting rain and rough water, I boarded a destroyer in Lower Tokyo Bay and went to Yokohama to call on the Supreme Commander of the Allied Powers (SCAP, for short), General MacArthur, at his quarters in the New Grand Hotel in Yokohama. His headquarters are in the customs-house building.
>
> Yokohama is like a dead city with very little activity. There are Japanese police and gendarmes on duty at SCAP quarters, and they act as if we were not in sight. They are not sullen or amazed, as one might expect. They simply do not see us.
>
> So far, the occupation has gone ahead with no violence or signs of it. When Junior [Lay] arrives tomorrow, his gang will walk ashore as they would in San Francisco, but without the welcome they would receive in San Francisco.
>
> The Allied POWs in the Japanese camps are the only ones who delightedly welcome us to Japan. I understand that there are some 38,000, including civilians, of which number about 8,000 are American.
>
> After leaving SCAP about noon today, we boarded a naval hospital ship, *Benevolence*, in the bay, where some 450 ex-POWs were recovering from their bad treatment, and they were badly treated, too, beatings, starvation rations,

solitary confinement, and so forth. They will be sent home as rapidly as their condition and transportation permit.

Tomorrow is the big day, and 9 A.M. is the hour when the Japanese emissaries sign the formal terms of surrender. I suspect there will be a rash of suicides after that.

You should see the ships in the bay, hundreds of U.S., with a few British ships. We have a huge fleet outside ready to fly in planes if necessary. In a few minutes I will go to call on Admiral Fraser, RN, on the *Duke of York*, anchored close by—partly on official business, partly because I like him, and mostly to get a Scotch and soda before dinner because our ships are dry.

It may be a day or so before I can join you so I'm sending you this in the mail now, hoping it finds you well and happy. Worlds of love to you and Nancy from your Dad.

Admiral Nimitz must have recalled that he had sent the girls a bottle of scarce liquor, for he added a postscript: "Hope you saved some of the bourbon for V-J day."

Wishing to please General MacArthur, Nimitz had had his Seabees at Guam fix up a landing boat to look like an army version of an admiral's barge. The Seabees' boat was painted red, had red and white seat covers, and had five stars on the bow. It was an elegant-looking craft and, with considerable effort, the Navy transported it to Tokyo Bay to take MacArthur out to the *Missouri*.

Nimitz's gesture was well-meant, but he had not realized that MacArthur would be quartered at Yokohama, twenty miles away from the *Missouri*, which was anchored off Yokosuka, or that most of the other officers would be going to the *Missouri* in a destroyer. Reporters, photographers, and, as it turned out, even the Japanese envoys were to be taken to the battleship in destroyers.

When Lamar proudly presented Nimitz's "general's barge" to MacArthur, the general took one look at it and said, "It's too small. I'm not going 20 miles in that thing."

Crestfallen, Lamar said, "General, what would you like to come out in?"

"I want a destroyer, and I want a new destroyer."

Later, through one of his staff officers, MacArthur informed Lamar that he had never flown his flag from a ship, and he would like to fly it from the *Missouri*. The general's wish presented something of a problem because, according to regulations and by tradition, the flag of the senior *naval* officer aboard, in this case Admiral Nimitz, should be broken at the main. Neither MacArthur's nor Nimitz's flag could be shifted to the fore peak because one was not senior to the other.

Baffled, Lamar asked Nimitz, "What do we do now?"

The admiral was amused. "You're the flag lieutenant," he answered, "That's your problem."

Together with other officers, Lamar came up with a solution. He had MacArthur's red flag and Nimitz's blue flag prepared for breaking side by side at the mainmast. "That's the first time in naval history," said Lamar, "that there have been two five-star flags on the same mast."

On September 1, the surrender ceremony was rehearsed aboard the *Missouri*, with scores of sailors representing the dignitaries who would arrive the next day. A mess table covered with a green baize cloth was set up on the starboard veranda deck to hold the two copies of the instrument of surrender, one in Japanese, one in English.

Shortly after 7:00 a.m. on September 2, correspondents and photographers of all nationalities, including Japanese, arrived by destroyer and took their assigned places aboard the *Missouri*. At morning colors the flag raised at the flagstaff was the one that had flown over the capitol in Washington on December 7, 1941. At 8:03 high-ranking officers and officials arrived in the destroyer *Nicholas*. A few minutes later Admiral Nimitz and his party arrived by barge from the *South Dakota*. Nimitz's five star flag was broken at the main, he was piped aboard, the "Admiral's March" was played over the amplifiers, and he was welcomed by Admiral Halsey, who was having a marvelous time as the genial host.

There followed a long wait. At last General MacArthur arrived with staff officers in the destroyer *Buchanan*. When his flag had been broken alongside Nimitz's, and honors had been duly rendered, he stepped quickly to where Nimitz, Halsey, Carney, and others were awaiting him. "Chester! Bill! Mick!" he exclaimed, happily shaking hands. To Mick Carney he said, "It's grand having so many of my sidekicks from the shoestring SoPac days meeting here at the end of the road!"

Halsey, Nimitz, and MacArthur retired to the flag cabin to await the arrival of the Japanese envoys, who were nearby in the destroyer *Lansdowne* awaiting a summons. On being signaled, the *Lansdowne* approached and the envoys and their aides boarded the *Missouri*. Leading the delegation was Foreign Minister Mamoru Shigemitsu, in formal morning dress complete with black silk hat. He was limping on an artificial limb, having long before lost a leg to an assassin's bomb. Next, in uniform, came General Yoshijiro Umezu, chief of the army general staff. They were followed by three officials of the Foreign Office, three army officers, and three naval officers.

On the veranda deck, besides representatives of the Allied nations, were senior American army and naval officers who had played important roles in the defeat of Japan.* Happy to be together and exhilarated by the occasion, the officers were shaking hands, slapping backs, and sounding off with enthusiastic conversation. Presently the *Missouri*'s gunnery officer, Commander Horace V. Bird, hastened onto the scene and shouted, "Gentlemen, General MacArthur and Admiral Nimitz are approaching!" His words were drowned out by the

---

* Admiral Spruance was in his flagship *New Jersey*, off Okinawa. Admiral Nimitz did not invite him to the ceremony, possibly because he wanted there to be somebody to take command of the Pacific Fleet in the event the Japanese treacherously attacked the *Missouri* in Tokyo Bay and killed the officers aboard her.

happy chattering. In desperation, Bird filled his lungs and bellowed, "Attention, all hands!" Instantly the admirals and generals fell silent, snapped to attention, and took their assigned places.

The chaplain gave the invocation, the band played "The Star-Spangled Banner," and presently General MacArthur and Admiral Nimitz strode briskly onto the veranda deck, Admiral Halsey following. General MacArthur took his place behind the table and addressed the assemblage. "We are gathered here," he began, "representatives of the major warring powers, to conclude a solemn agreement whereby peace may be restored." He concluded his remarks with these words:

> It is my earnest hope—indeed the hope of all mankind—that from this solemn occasion a better world shall emerge out of the blood and carnage of the past, a world founded upon faith and understanding, a world dedicated to the dignity of man and the fulfillment of his most cherished wish for freedom, tolerance, and justice.

MacArthur then pointed to the chair at the opposite side of the table and said sternly, "The representatives of the Imperial Japanese Government and the Imperial Japanese Staff will now come forward and sign."

Foreign Minister Shigemitsu limped to the table, sat down, took off his hat and gloves, dropped his cane, picked it up, fumbled with his hat and gloves, and felt in his inside pocket for a pen. A Foreign Office aide stepped forward and handed him one and held his cane. Shigemitsu then seemed confused about where to put his name. "Sutherland," MacArthur snapped to his chief of staff, "show him where to sign." Sutherland pointed, and Shigemitsu affixed his signature "by command and in behalf of the Emperor of Japan and the Japanese Government." General Umezu then stepped forward stiffly and without sitting scrawled his name on the two documents "by command and in behalf of the Japanese General Headquarters."

General of the Army MacArthur beckoned Lieutenant General Jonathan Wainwright and Lieutenant General Sir Arthur Percival to stand behind his chair as he signed the acceptance of the surrender on behalf of all the Allied powers. Wainwright, who surrendered the Philippines, and Percival, who surrendered Singapore, both in 1942, had been flown from prisoner-of-war camps in Manchuria.

Fleet Admiral Nimitz, with Admiral Halsey and Rear Admiral Forrest Sherman behind his chair, signed for the United States. He was followed, in order, by General Hsu Yung-chang, signing for China, Admiral Sir Bruce Fraser for the United Kingdom, Lieutenant General K. Derevyanko for the Soviet Union, General Sir Thomas Blamey for Australia, Colonel L. Moore Cosgrave for Canada, General Jacques LeClerc for France, Admiral Conrad E. L. Helfrich for the Netherlands, and Air Vice Marshal Sir Leonard M. Isitt for New Zealand.

When all the representatives had signed, MacArthur again addressed the assemblage: "Let us pray that peace be now restored to the world and that God will preserve it always. These proceedings are now closed."

At that moment the sun came from behind the clouds and a massed flight of several hundred U.S. planes, carrier aircraft and B-29s, swept over Tokyo Bay and the British and American ships.

As the Japanese were turning to depart, one of their Foreign Office aides came forward to pick up the Japanese copy of the surrender document. He glanced at it and hurried off, calling out to the Japanese delegates, who stopped. There followed among them an excited conversation.

MacArthur said to Lamar, "Go over and find out what's going on."

In English, the aide explained to Lamar that their copy of the surrender instrument was not valid; there was a blank space in the column of acceptance signatures. The Canadian representative, it seemed, had skipped his space and written his name where the French representative should have signed. The rest had followed, all one line too low, and the New Zealand representative had perforce signed in the margin at the foot of the column, which made him, as he afterward said, "an humble footnote to history."

"Change the thing," MacArthur said to Sutherland.

Lamar placed the document back on the surrender table. Sutherland then, in the words of *The New York Times,* "ran two strokes of his fountain pen through the names of the four countries above the misplaced signatures and wrote them in below. The Japanese gravely accepted the corrected document, and peace became a reality."

As the Japanese envoys approached the gangway, they were given the customary honors to betoken the fact that they were no longer enemies. Nimitz revoked Halsey's order to the commanding officer of the *Lansdowne* not to offer coffee, cigarettes, or other courtesies to the delegation. When the Japanese had left, Admiral Halsey entertained the Allied signatories in his cabin, regretting that he had only coffee and doughnuts, but no champagne, to offer them.

As soon as Admiral Nimitz had returned to the *South Dakota,* he released a statement he had prepared for broadcast throughout the Pacific and the United States:

> On board all naval vessels at sea and in port, and at our many island bases in the Pacific, there is rejoicing and thanksgiving. The long and bitter struggle . . . is at an end. . . .
>
> Today all freedom-loving peoples of the world rejoice in the victory and feel pride in the accomplishments of our combined forces. We also pay tribute to those who defended our freedom at the cost of their lives.
>
> On Guam is a military cemetery in a green valley not far from my headquarters. The ordered rows of white crosses stand as reminders of the heavy cost we have paid for victory. On these crosses are the names of American soldiers, sailors and marines—Culpepper, Tomaino, Sweeney, Bromberg, Depew, Melloy, Ponziani—names that are a cross-section of democracy. They

fought together as brothers in arms; they died together and now they sleep side by side. To them we have a solemn obligation—the obligation to insure that their sacrifice will help to make this a better and safer world in which to live.

Now we turn to the great tasks of reconstruction and restoration. I am confident that we will be able to apply the same skill, resourcefulness and keen thinking to these problems as were applied to the problems of winning the victory.

Before lunch, Nimitz retired to his cabin to write his daily letter to Catherine. He wrote it on the back of the printed program of the surrender ceremony:

Best beloved, The big moment is over and the Japs have signed the formal terms of surrender. Everything clicked in a minute-by-minute schedule, and the ceremony started at exactly 9 A.M., Tokyo Time. The press came off in a transport destroyer before 8 A.M., followed by another destroyer carrying all the guests except the Supreme Commander's private party, which came alongside as did all the destroyers at 8:30. I don't see how I can describe this scene or why I should attempt it, because there were present at least 200 correspondents who have by now written and broadcast thousands of words of description, which even as I write at 11:30 A.M. is either being read or heard by you and all our children, wherever they may be. Many of our officers from the ships still at sea were present, they having flown in by plane. Among those was Shafroth, who particularly asked that I include in this letter his best wishes to you and Mary. Fortunately the bad weather for the last two days passed on, and we were blessed with dry, though overcast, skies.

Last night I was tremendously pleased and surprised to receive your fine letters of the 23rd and 24th of August with the enclosures, which were brought up from Guam by one of our officers who brought up important mail. This is rapid time for your 24th of August letter, written on my 25th, with only seven days from Berkeley to Tokyo Bay.

Now I must close. All my heart's devotion. Love and kisses to my sweetheart.

On the opposite side of the page, under the printing, Nimitz added:

Every turret top, every point of vantage was occupied by newsmen, cameramen, including local Japanese papers, and officers and men from the ship who could get a foothold. When it came time to sign, I confess to nervous excitement, but I did sign in the correct places. One signer did not. First copy signed with the Woo gold gift pen, and the second copy signed with my old green Parker pen.*

After lunch Admiral Nimitz and his party went ashore for a final visit. They boarded the *Mikasa*, Admiral Togo's flagship, in which in 1905 he virtually annihilated the Russian fleet in the Battle of Tsushima. The battleship, encased in concrete at the Yokosuka Naval Base, was preserved as a

---

* Explanation by Mrs. Nimitz: "The pen which he called the Woo pen was given to him by our friends Y. C. and Eching Woo, great friends of ours. And the other was a 50-cent Parker pen that he bought from a bumboat in our travels. That is now in the Naval Academy Museum."

national monument. Halsey had already been there and commandeered her flag, which he sent to Admiral King to be presented to the Russians as a trophy.

Nimitz reacted somewhat differently. He recalled the time, many years before, when he met the victorious Togo, his admiration for the old sea dog, and his attendance at the admiral's funeral. He ordered a marine guard permanently placed aboard the *Mikasa* to prevent her being damaged or looted by occupying sailors and marines in search of souvenirs. Before he left the ship, Nimitz induced some veteran sailors who were stationed aboard her to talk with him through Captain Layton.

With several jeeploads of marines ahead and several behind, the party set out by car down the road to view the countryside and visit the colossal bronze Buddha at Kamakura. Every time the lead jeep sounded its horn, the peasants along the highway would fall on their knees and cover their eyes.

"Why are they doing that?" asked Nimitz. Nobody in the car knew, so he stopped the caravan and had Layton get out and inquire. He was told that in Japan only the Emperor had an electric horn such as the marines were sounding. It was used as a signal that the God-Emperor was coming, whereupon devout citizens knelt and hid their eyes.

When the party came to a military hospital, Nimitz decided he would visit the sick and wounded Japanese service men, as he had often visited hospitalized American soldiers, sailors, and marines. The admiral's friendly gesture backfired. The patients, informed that the American head man was coming to see them, were struck dumb with fear.

The next morning, September 3, Admiral Nimitz and his party headed by air back toward Guam. As their plane gained altitude, they could see, first, the scores of American and British vessels in Tokyo Bay, then the scores more, including numerous carriers, outside in Sagami Bay. Hours later they looked down on the military bastion of Guam, transformed in less than a year from a ravaged battleground into a bustling and vibrant base, crisscrossed with many miles of new highways linking Apra Harbor with the airfields.

The fleet and the base were spearheads of the military force that extended back to and drew most of its strength from the continental United States. That force, having attained its goal in the defeat of Japan, must now necessarily begin to contract. Admiral Nimitz led the way back. After a few days needed to wind up his affairs at Guam, he returned to Pearl Harbor. He never saw Guam again.

# CHAPTER 24

# FROM CINCPAC TO CNO

SECRETARY FORRESTAL, ever alert to see that the Navy received proper recognition, pulled wires to get for Admiral Nimitz a homecoming at least as impressive as those the Army had earlier arranged for Generals Dwight D. Eisenhower and Jonathan M. Wainwright. Largely through Forrestal's efforts, October 5, 1945, was designated "Nimitz Day" in Washington. On that date the admiral would address a joint session of Congress, be honored by a parade, and be decorated by the President. Invitations for the admiral to attend ceremonies poured in from elsewhere, and Nimitz accepted those from San Francisco and New York and from the Texas cities of Dallas, Austin, Kerrville, and Fredericksburg.

When the *Missouri*, en route from Tokyo to Norfolk, stopped at Pearl Harbor, Nimitz had the fireproof paint scraped from her weather decks to reveal again the handsome teak. He also had the CinCPac staff design a circular plaque and sent it home with the ship to be cast in bronze and embedded in her veranda deck where the surrender table had stood. As part of his homecoming, Nimitz was expected to board the battleship at Norfolk, ride her up the coast, and steam into New York Harbor with his flag flying at the main. When President Truman learned of this project, he promptly vetoed it. The President himself, in connection with a big Navy Day show at New York on October 27, planned to review the fleet from the deck of the *Missouri* and broadcast a speech from her bridge. He had no intention of letting Nimitz steal his thunder.

Admiral Nimitz undoubtedly had mixed feelings about the triumphal homecoming and the proposed *Missouri* stunt. Though he liked to have his accomplishments appreciated, he was not a publicity-seeker. For example, in early 1945 when the Navy's Public Relations Office had suggested building up Nimitz personally to offset the publicity the colorful MacArthur was getting, Nimitz would have none of it. "Any plan for a publicity buildup for me," he said, "is absolutely contrary to my ideas for the conduct of the war in the Pacific and meets with my disapproval, as well as the disapproval of Mr. Forrestal."

When, however, the publicity spotlight was turned full on MacArthur as commander-designate for the invasion of Japan, as conductor of the surrender ceremony, and as commander in chief of the occupation forces, Nimitz and Forrestal decided that the American public needed to be forcefully reminded that the defeating of Japan was mainly a naval victory. Nimitz intended to make it clear that he was taking part in the parades and accepting other honors only as a representative and symbol of the victorious U.S. Navy. He thought it particularly important that the *Missouri* arrive at the American metropolis wearing only an admiral's flag at the main. When former artillery captain Truman ordered him to keep off the *Missouri*, Nimitz was exasperated.

Admiral Nimitz's plane from Pearl Harbor arrived at Oakland, California, on Tuesday, October 2. With him were Commander Lamar, on whom Nimitz had grown increasingly dependent for personal services, and Rear Admiral Forrest Sherman, on whom he had leaned so heavily for advice that he believed Sherman should share the spotlight. Waiting at the airport was Mrs. Nimitz. Anticipating that Chester's next assignment would take them to Washington, she had sent Mary ahead to join her sisters there and be entered in the National Cathedral School.

At San Francisco there was no formal parade, but the route Admiral Nimitz's escorted car would be taking was well advertised, and thousands of people turned out to applaud as it passed. At the City Hall, before a large crowd, Dan Gallagher, president of the board of supervisors and acting mayor, handed Nimitz a key to the city. "What wouldn't Yamamoto have given for this?" said the admiral.

In reply to a speech of welcome by Governor Earl Warren, Nimitz sounded the four themes he was to repeat again and again during his homecoming: the major role played by the Navy in defeating Japan, the fact that the Japanese were suing for peace before the atomic bombs were dropped, the need for research in new naval weapons, and the imperative necessity of maintaining a powerful Navy. "New weapons such as the atomic bomb," he said, "may change the character of warfare but it will not change the fact we must have control of the sea. We have it now. We have the power and the resources now. We must keep them."

Mrs. Nimitz joined the homecoming party for the flight to Washington, where they landed at Anacostia naval air station shortly before noon on Friday, October 5. Awaiting them were Nancy, Kate, and Mary. Mary had been granted the day off by her school so that she could participate in her father's honors. From the air station Nimitz was driven to the capitol to address Congress. When the Secretary of the Navy entered the House chamber, the senators and representatives rose and cheered him. Forrestal, looking neither to right nor left, walked directly to his seat. This was Nimitz's day; the Secretary was not accepting any plaudits for himself.

Before Congress, Nimitz sounded his themes. Neither the dropping of the atomic bomb nor the entry of Russia had defeated Japan, he insisted. The Japanese were suing for peace before either of those events took place because Japan, "a maritime nation, dependent on food and materials from overseas, was stripped of her sea power." The United States, possessing the world's mightiest sea power, must not "pat it on the back and let it die.

"Let us go forth in all friendliness," he concluded, "but let us make certain that our olive branch is planted firmly in a rich soil with a high content of uranium 235. This, I maintain, is not cynicism, but what we in Texas and in the Navy call 'savvy'."

After delivering his address, Nimitz, sitting high in the back of a car, began his parade along Pennsylvania and Constitution avenues to the Washington Monument. Cheering him were a half a million Washingtonians, released for the occasion from shop, school, and government office. The Navy had seen to it that this should be the biggest of the victory celebrations. The city was plastered with 2,000 posters of Nimitz. Nine ships, veterans of the Pacific war, were anchored in the Potomac and were thrown open to the public. A thousand navy fighters and bombers flew over the parade, one squadron trailing red, white, and blue smoke streamers. In the line of march, which included tractors towing captured Japanese planes, were units of midshipmen, marines, navy nurses, Spars, Waves, and veterans of every naval operation from the Java Sea to Okinawa.

The President had denied Nimitz a ride to New York in the *Missouri*, but the Navy saw to it that he was provided with a reasonable facsimile of the *Missouri*'s deck as a reviewing stand at the Washington Monument. There he made his second speech of the day. "Perhaps it is not too much to predict that history will refer to this present period not as the ending of a great conflict," he said, "but as the beginning of a new atomic age."

From the Monument Nimitz proceeded to the White House rose garden, where President Truman presented him his third Distinguished Service Medal. That evening Nimitz was honored at a dinner attended by many of the country's war leaders. The Admiral remarked, "We've got everything we need here for a small war."

The next morning Admiral Nimitz visited the Navy Department to pay his respects to Secretary Forrestal and to find out what plans the Secretary had for his future. He told Forrestal that he would like to succeed Admiral King as Chief of Naval Operations. Forrestal respected Nimitz as a person and valued him as a representative of the Navy, but to take him on as CNO would be something else again. He had spent a year and a half battling King, and now had no wish to acquire another CNO who might be less blunt than King but would be no less stubborn in defense of his own convictions.

Forrestal told him he thought it would be a mistake for Nimitz to become Chief of Naval Operations, because he would risk impairing the prestige he had won as a successful commander. He suggested that he take the chairmanship of the General Board or continue as Commander in Chief of the Pacific Fleet. Nimitz said he held to his original preference.

Forrestal tried a new tack. He said that in his view there were ways in which Nimitz could be of greater use to the Navy than being tied down to the routine of such an exacting post as CNO. Nimitz replied that he was fully aware of how exacting it would be but he still wanted the billet and was confident that he could do a good job. Since neither man would back down, the interview ended in a polite standoff.

That evening Nimitz spent with his family at his daughters' apartment at 2222 Q Street, talking and listening to symphony records. During the next two days, a weekend, he called on old friends, most of them naval officers, and asked them, if the opportunity arose, to put in a good word for him with Forrestal. His talks with the officers completed his conversion from supporting unification of the armed services, which the President and the Army favored, to strongly opposing it.

Unification of the services under himself in the Pacific Ocean Areas had drawn some criticism—from Admiral Towers and Generals Richardson, Marshall, Arnold, and a few others—but it had demonstrably been an unqualified success. The unified Central Pacific Force, comprising navy surface, submarines, and air, marines, and army ground and air forces, had effaced the threat to U.S.-Australian communications, charged across the Pacific taking bases, isolated Japan, and, at last, blockaded and bombed the Japanese into submission.

Nimitz had achieved a model of unification. Why not have it on a national scale? In December 1944 he had in fact recommended just that to a Joint Chiefs of Staff committee: "I favor a single Secretary of the Armed Forces with a complete elimination of civilian secretaries for Army, Navy and Air Force...it will be better to have a single Commander of Armed Forces who has all the authority and responsibility for issuing a directive."

The move in the preceding spring toward separating the services and the possibility that MacArthur might assume the dominant strategic role in the Pacific, caused Nimitz to rethink his point of view. The general had neither appreciated nor understood the King-Nimitz strategy of driving across the center. Had he taken over the top command, he would probably have reduced Pacific Fleet operations to a mere supporting role. To Nimitz, that possibility exemplified the chief danger of overall unification. An all-powerful secretary or commander would be likely to understand one service and its functions better than he did the others and hence favor it at the expense of proper balance. It was better, Nimitz concluded, for the services to remain separated; thus they served to correct one another. Anyway, why change a warmaking organization that had just demonstrated its effectiveness by defeating Italy, Germany, and Japan?

On Tuesday morning, October 9, the Nimitz party flew to New York. At La Guardia Airport they were greeted by, among many others, Commander Chester W. Nimitz, Jr. The admiral was taken by car along East River Drive to the south end of Manhattan. From there, perched on the back of an open automobile, he led a motorcade of veterans who had won the Medal of Honor under his command. The canyon of lower Broadway was lined with 4,000,000 New Yorkers roaring him welcome. From overhead in the buildings along the street, other New Yorkers poured down a veritable snowstorm of 274 tons of ticker tape and other paper. "It's just overwhelming," said Nimitz. "I think I'm in a dream."

At City Hall, the admiral was piped aboard a huge replica of a ship's bow. Mayor Fiorello La Guardia welcomed him to New York and presented him with the city's gold medal of honor and a certificate of honorary citizenship. To the estimated 350,000 people gathered in City Hall Plaza, Nimitz repeated his plea for "adequate sea power to ensure that we do not lose the peace."

"We must make certain now and for the future," he said, "that the peace is secure. We must remain strong. Never again should we risk the threat which weakness invites. We owe this to the men who have fought and to the youngsters who are growing up today."

Following the parade, Admiral Nimitz, the Medal of Honor winners, and a number of the admiral's Naval Academy classmates were guests of Mayor La Guardia at a buffet luncheon. That evening in the ballroom of the Waldorf-Astoria, 2,000 dinner guests, who had paid $15 a plate, honored the admiral. Introduced by Nelson Rockefeller, Nimitz prefaced his serious remarks by reciting some verses written by a naval captain, William Gordon Beecher, about the claims of an imaginary sailor named Patsy McCoy:

> Me and Halsey and Nimitz
> Have sure got the Japs on the run.
> We're driving them wacky
> In old Nagasaki. . . .
>
> Me and Halsey and Nimitz
> Are havin' a wonderful time.
> What we ain't uprootin'
> By bombin' and shootin'
> Would fit on the face of a dime. . . .
>
> Me and Halsey and Nimitz
> Are anchored in Tokyo Bay.
> The place is just drippin'
> With American shippin'. . . .
>
> We're warnin' them never
> To start it again.
> For we've got a country
> With millions of men
> Like Nimitz and Halsey and me.

The following morning Admiral Nimitz made a televised speech, his first, for broadcast to wounded veterans in hospitals. He and his party then flew back to Washington, where, the next day, the admiral encountered the Secretary of the Navy and found him in a more receptive mood. The Secretary's changed attitude seems to have been induced mainly by support Nimitz had won in making his round of weekend calls. Representative Carl Vinson, the powerful chairman of the House Naval Affairs Committee, had had a few words with Forrestal, probably by telephone. Admiral King had sent the Secretary a written endorsement, declaring Nimitz "the officer clearly and definitely indicated" to be the new Chief of Naval Operations. This was the sort of pressure Forrestal could not resist. His diary has the following paragraph among the entries for Wednesday, October 10:

I spoke to Admiral Nimitz today about our conversation of last Saturday with reference to his future duties. I said that if he wished to succeed King I would so recommend to the President, with these qualifications: (1) that his staff would be mutually agreeable to the two of us, and (2) that his term would be limited to two years, and (3) that he subscribe in general principle to the conception of the Navy Department organization as expressed in the new chart.

Admiral Nimitz readily accepted Forrestal's qualifications. He said he did not want to hold the office for more than two years, that he certainly would submit his choice of staff members to the Secretary, and that he fully subscribed to the new organization, by which the CNO would not also be CominCh and was no longer permitted to bypass the Secretary of the Navy and deal directly with the President, as Admiral King had done regularly.

On Thursday evening, Commander Lamar was packing Nimitz's things for the flight to Dallas, where another victory celebration was to take place, when Representative Lyndon Johnson telephoned to ask if he might fly down with the Nimitz party. Nimitz welcomed him aboard. The plane, with the Nimitz party and Johnson, took off at midnight.

In Dallas, Admiral Nimitz was welcomed by Mayor Woodall Rogers and Texas Governor Coke Stevenson. After a ceremony, lunch, and a parade, the Nimitz party, accompanied by Congressman Johnson and Governor Stevenson, flew to Austin. There the city fathers, anticipating that the planned parade would last until after dark, had had some 10,000 Christmas lights hung along the route two months ahead of time to illuminate the admiral's procession. That evening Johnson introduced Admiral Nimitz to a mass meeting on the campus of the University of Texas.

On Saturday the 13th, the Nimitz group, still accompanied by Governor Stevenson, headed for Kerrville in an undertaker's limousine. A couple of miles out of Kerrville, they were met by a welcoming party of mounted cowhands and ranchers and citizens riding ancient buggies and other vehicles, who insisted that Nimitz come into town as he might have done 50 years earlier—in a buckboard pulled by two strawberry roans. Grinning, Nimitz got out of the limousine and climbed aboard the wagon along with Governor Stevenson, who took the reins. Mrs. Nimitz seated herself in the back seat, flanked by Rear Admiral Sherman and Rear Admiral Harold B. Miller, the Navy Department's public relations officer. Nimitz was fulfilling a promise made when he left for Annapolis in 1901, that he would return some day as an admiral.

At a public ceremony Admiral Nimitz was welcomed by, among others, two of the mentors who had coached him for the Annapolis examination, Susan Moore and John Toland, both long since retired. He shook their hands warmly and expressed his appreciation for their help. The admiral was gratified to be presented at last with the high-school diploma that he had missed by leaving town before being graduated. "He earned it," remarked 80-year-old Toland. "He was and is a fine student and a positive character."

Fredericksburg, Admiral Nimitz's birthplace, opened all the stops to give its favorite son a blast of a homecoming. At the Gillespie County line he was met by county officials and relatives. At the town boundary, where he arrived on schedule at 2:00 p.m., he was welcomed by Mayor Joe Molberg and other city officials, and the small daughter of an officer who had died in a Japanese prison camp presented him with a key to the city. In front of the rebuilt Nimitz Hotel, the admiral seated himself on the back of an open Buick, then, flanked by an honor guard of naval students from the University of Texas, led the parade down Main Street. Among the many units following the admiral's car were no fewer than seven bands, including the naval band from Corpus Christi Naval Station and the army band from Fort Sam Houston. Overhead, planes from the Corpus Christi Naval Station formed a roaring canopy. Everywhere were flags and bunting bearing the words: WELCOME HOME CHESTER.

Nimitz reviewed the parade from a platform constructed over the steps to the courthouse. In the formal ceremony that followed, Governor Stevenson introduced the admiral and concluded by handing him a framed certificate appointing him "Admiral of the Texas Navy." In his address Nimitz stated: "During the surrender negotiations at Tokyo, one of my principal worries was ... that I would not be able to persuade Texans to stop fighting. However, a satisfactory agreement was arrived at between Tokyo and Austin...."

After the ceremony, Nimitz laid a wreath in front of the Pioneer Memorial Building at the shrine which honors the dead of World War II, and, with close relatives, he visited his birthplace on East Main Street. There he professed that he was disappointed not to find in the kitchen the old stone cookie jar filled with Pfeffernuesse. At 5:30 he and his party joined the visiting dignitaries and his uncles, aunts, and first cousins at a dinner at the Nimitz Hotel. Lamar was a little shocked to hear, in Fredericksburg and elsewhere, farmers and small tradesmen addressing "his" admiral by his first name, but Nimitz seemed delighted. At 8:00 p.m. Nimitz and his party left for Austin, where they boarded the admiral's plane for an overnight flight to San Francisco.

Though Admiral Nimitz spent four days in the San Francisco area, he managed to keep mention of his presence out of the newspapers. Admiral Halsey and a part of his Third Fleet arrived there from the Pacific on October 15. Nimitz was anxious not to divert any attention whatever from Bill's welcome home.

On the 18th Nimitz was back at Pearl Harbor. During his absence a board of officers that he had appointed had been hard at work preparing a report to Admiral King. King believed in a balanced fleet, that is, a fleet balanced as to types of ships. But because he was uncertain about what characteristics each type should possess, he had asked CinCPac headquarters to advise him, basing their advice on combat experience in the Pacific War.

In preliminary discussions Nimitz and his appointed board had reached general agreement. By the time Nimitz returned from his victory tour, the board had completed a rough draft, which Nimitz carefully studied, making marginal notes, chiefly of a technical nature. Curiously, with Nimitz's concurrence, the board recommended that *Essex*-class as well as the *Midway*-class carriers be retained, though the former, with their wooden flight decks, had not stood up well to kamikaze attack at Okinawa. The board and Nimitz, moreover, expressed a conviction that the *Iowa*-class of fast battleships was essential as escorts for carriers. Concerning the versatile cruisers and destroyers, the report advised that the Navy should avoid the obvious temptation toward overly complex equipment. These types, said the report, should be kept as simple as possible so that they could serve as prototypes for ships that might be built later for actual combat.

Special emphasis was given to submarines, not because they were likely to become the backbone of the fleet, but because in World War II they had fallen far short of their potential, mainly through lack of speed and endurance when submerged. In fact, the submarine then in use was not accurately named; it was a submersible surface vessel, which was slow and vulnerable during its relatively brief periods of submergence. The Germans had made some progress toward developing a true submarine, first by use of the snorkel breathing tube to supply air to the diesel engines, and then by a closed system that used hydrogen peroxide instead of air to supply oxygen for fuel combustion. The CinCPac report urged further research to streamline and strengthen hulls for greater speed and protection underwater and more experiments directed toward permitting the submarine to operate submerged for longer periods.

Nimitz, King, and Forrestal released Navy Day statements calling for maintenance of "the greatest naval forces the world has ever known." Nimitz afterward learned that President Truman had not made use of the *Missouri*, after all. He had reviewed the fleet from the deck of a destroyer and delivered his Navy Day address before a huge audience in New York's Central Park. His address was a major foreign policy speech, which had little to say about, much less anything in praise of, the Navy. It was becoming clear to Nimitz and other naval officers that the Navy no longer had in the White House a friend such as the late Franklin Roosevelt had been. Harry Truman, in praising General of the Army George Marshall, had recently gone out of his way to take a crack at the men in blue and gold. Marshall, he said, "succeeded in getting the Navy to cooperate with the Army." It was a bad sign.

About this time word reached Pearl Harbor that Secretary Forrestal was reneging on his promise to recommend Admiral Nimitz for Chief of Naval Operations. A brief story in *The New York Times* of November 1 seemed to confirm this information: "The Army and Navy Bulletin predicted tonight that Admiral Nimitz would succeed Admiral King as Chief of Naval Operations. The service journal said that a move was underway in Congress to give Admiral Nimitz the post. It added that Admiral R. S. Edwards, deputy CNO, was the choice of Secretary Forrestal, while Admiral King supported Admiral Spruance, Fifth Fleet Commander." Since Nimitz was convinced that King was not recommending anybody but himself, Nimitz, as his successor, he was puzzled how much credence to give to the story that Forrestal had changed his mind.

At any rate, Nimitz was not one to let events drift if he could control them. As luck would have it, a few days after the *Times* story appeared, William Waldo Drake arrived in Honolulu. Drake, who had been Nimitz's public relations officer early in the war, was now on the staff of Edwin Pauley, President Truman's representative on the Allied Reparations Commission.

Drake accepted Nimitz's invitation to come out to Pearl Harbor and pay him a visit. In the course of their conversation, the admiral mentioned that he had told Forrestal that he wanted to be Chief of Naval Operations. "I haven't got much enthusiasm out of the Secretary," he concluded. "I'd like to know if you have any ideas that might help."

"Just by chance, I do, Admiral," replied Drake. "My friend Ed Pauley is arriving to join the airplane that is taking us to Japan tomorrow, and he's the man who put Harry Truman in the White House. He succeeded in having him nominated at the Chicago convention and he later became Vice President. He's the only man who, I think, could help you."

"Well," said Nimitz, "bring him out."

The next day Drake returned to Pearl Harbor, this time accompanied by Pauley. The latter, an astute politician and businessman, former treasurer of the Democratic Party, wanted a private conference with Nimitz before endorsing him, so he and the admiral drove over to the Damon property on the beach at Kaneohe where they could be alone. In the course of an extended conversation, Nimitz convinced his visitor that he deserved the post of Chief of Naval Operations and was uniquely qualified to hold it. Pauley reached for the telephone and did something few other men could have done. He put a call straight through to the President of the United States in the White House. Pauley vigorously described to Truman the claims and competence of Nimitz. "You can talk to him yourself, if you want to," he concluded. Truman declined. Then after a further brief exchange, he said: "Well, I'd like to help him, Ed, but Forrestal insists he's just a stubborn Dutchman and he doesn't rate the job and he doesn't want him to have it."

In a final bid, Pauley said: "I know him pretty well, and I've had a long talk with him. I think he should have it."

Truman remained noncommittal, and the conversation ended. Nimitz was disappointed, but at least the Pauley endorsement could not have hurt his chances.

In Washington, the army seemed to be making its case for merging the services. General Eisenhower was scheduled to testify before the Senate Military Affairs Committee on behalf of the merger. Lieutenant General James Doolittle appeared before the committee on November 9 and let loose a blast that shook the Navy Department from top to bottom. Doolittle, terming air power the first U.S. line of defense, called for a defense organization in which air forces would have a position "at least" equal to that of the land and sea forces.

"Admiral Nimitz and Admiral Mitscher are great commanders," said Doolittle, "but this war has been won by teamwork. Each of the three agencies did its best. No single agency was responsible. I do feel very strongly that it was not sea power that compelled Japan to sue for peace, and that it was not carrier strength that won the war. Our B-29 boys are resting uneasily in their graves as a result of these two comments."

The first lesson of World War II, continued Doolittle, "is that you can't lose a war if you have command of the air, and you can't win a war if you haven't." He agreed that carrier-based naval planes should remain under naval control but he insisted that the carrier itself was "going into obsolescence, having reached the peak of its usefulness." The carrier, he said, had two attributes—"first, it can move about, and second, it can be sunk. When we get aircraft with sufficient range, we will not need carriers." A few days later, as if to emphasize Doolittle's last remark, a B-29 flew non-stop the 8,198 miles from Guam to Washington, D.C.

Naval leaders concluded that Admiral Nimitz was sorely needed in Washington as spokesman for the Navy. On Navy Department summons, he hastened back from Pearl Harbor and on November 17 appeared before the Senate committee. He opposed a single Department of the Armed Forces, he said, because a merger of the War and Navy departments might impede the Navy and reduce the vital role of sea power in the nation's defense. He saw no point in having a separate Air Force; it was no more warranted, he said, than a separate Submarine Force. After all, the Navy had 250 submarines, and they had played an indispensable, and fairly independent, role in defeating Japan.

Admiral Nimitz said that his earlier opinion, favoring a merger, had been formed without opportunity for adequate study and that he had no apology for having changed his mind, since the view he was now upholding "represents my conviction based on additional experience and further study of the proposal and its current implications." He concluded:

> It is also clear that the defeat of Japanese sea power, and the preponderance of our own sea power, played a tremendously important part in the result. I feel that the successes which led to this result are convincing evidence of the merit of the system under which they were accomplished. Our successes were more rapid than I had believed possible a year ago. I believe we should have very good reasons—better reasons than any offered so far—before we change a system that has proved itself so effective. Certainly in our conduct of the war I can see no fault so grave that only a drastic reorganization can correct it—a reorganization undertaken when many other complex problems are facing the country.
>
> Our people must be shown that a single department will improve upon the record of the past year's operations in the Pacific. For my part, I am convinced that a single department will not work as efficiently as two separate departments have proved they can work in producing the kinds of forces required for modern war. I am also convinced that the merging of the War and Navy departments into a single department cannot help, and may hinder, the adequate provision and efficient use of our sea power.

Following his appearance, Nimitz met briefly with representatives of the press. Asked where he was going next, he replied that he was going to the

White House to pay "a very personal call" on the President. Apparently Mr. Truman had invited him in for a conference. What passed between them is not recorded, but evidently they made a favorable impression on each other. Each saw the other as honest, competent, and without pretense, and a warm friendship sprang up between them. After Nimitz's death, Truman, then in retirement, wrote: "I came to regard Admiral Nimitz from the outset as a man apart and above all his contemporaries—as a strategist, as a leader and as a person. I ranked him with General George Marshall as military geniuses as well as statesmen."

After his visit to the White House, Admiral Nimitz went to Chicago, where, on Monday, November 19, he addressed the American Legion convention. Concerning the war against Japan, he said, "the Navy had to blaze the way, because it was a war in the Navy's element," but the capturing of bases was the job of "unified force."

"For the principle of unity of command in a theater of operations I have nothing but the most enthusiastic support," he went on. "It makes sense. It works. That has been demonstrated."

To the convention Nimitz presented a three-part plan to preserve the "unity of command" that had brought victory in the Pacific: (1) Continue the Joint Chiefs of Staff. (2) Set up a national security council to include the secretaries of State, War, and Navy, and representatives of the Federal agencies that administer the national resources both in personnel and material. (3) Create a non-partisan board of prominent citizens to study at length the pros and cons of the proposed merger. "Remember that the only controversy," he concluded, "should be how our country can best be guaranteed."

The next day, November 20, President Truman announced his appointments in the armed forces. General Eisenhower was to succeed General Marshall as Army Chief of Staff. Admiral Nimitz was to succeed Admiral King as Chief of Naval Operations. General Joseph T. McNarney was to succeed Eisenhower as commanding general of occupation forces in Europe. Admiral Spruance was to succeed Nimitz as Commander in Chief of the Pacific Fleet. The Senate confirmed all four appointments without a dissenting vote.*

---

* The full details of Nimitz's accession to the billet of Chief of Naval Operations may never be told. Theodore Taylor opens his biography, *The Magnificent Mitscher*, with a story of how on Sunday, November 18, 1945, Secretary Forrestal "abruptly offered Mitscher the position of Chief of Naval Operations," but how Mitscher declined the appointment. It would appear that in this account the date, if nothing else, is wrong.

In *Fleet Admiral King*, of which King is listed as coauthor along with Walter Muir Whitehill, we find (p. 636) this account: "As Mr. Forrestal would not agree that Nimitz should relieve King, King endeavored to force his hand by writing, on 23 November 1945, a letter to the President via the Secretary of the Navy, asking to be relieved by Fleet Admiral Nimitz, and passing the letter to Secretary Forrestal for transmission to President Truman. When the Secretary refused to endorse the letter, and send it to the White House, King went to the White House in person and discussed the matter with Mr. Truman, who agreed without hesitation that Nimitz should have the post." Here again the date is obviously wrong.

It has been said that Admiral King told the President that if he did not appoint Nimitz Chief of Naval Operations, he would have to explain his failure to do so to the American people.

For Nimitz, shifting from CinCPac-CinCPOA to CNO, the Navy's two top commands, would be a huge undertaking. He would need plenty of time to clean up details of the first and prepare for the second. Admiral King, fully aware of the situation, told Nimitz he might delay as much as two months before assuming his new duties. "But Mr. Forrestal," wrote King. "was sufficiently irritated about the whole matter to order the change of command to be moved up to 15 December 1945." More likely, Forrestal, who had carried on a kind of running feud with King ever since he took office as Secretary, could not wait to jettison his hard-nosed Chief of Naval Operations.

Nimitz hastened back to Pearl Harbor. There Admiral Spruance, having been relieved as Commander, Fifth Fleet, on November 8 in Tokyo Bay by Admiral Towers, was awaiting orders.

Admiral Nimitz had assumed command of the Pacific Fleet on the deck of a submarine, and he so relinquished it. Though there were in Pearl Harbor plenty of other decks on which the simple ceremony could have taken place, Nimitz chose to use a submarine as a salute to his fellow submariners for a job well done. On November 24 on board the submarine *Menhaden*, he turned over to Spruance the responsibilities of CinCPac and CinCPOA. He promised Spruance that he would do his best to get him the post in which he aspired to end his naval career, the presidency of the Naval War College.*

In San Francisco, Catherine Nimitz was once more making preparations to cross the country, this time by car with Admiral Nimitz. Old "Chrissy," the family Chrysler, was packed for another transcontinental trek. Bought on the West Coast in 1938, Chrissy had taken the family to Washington the following year when Nimitz was appointed Chief of the Bureau of Navigation. Mrs. Nimitz, Nancy, and Mary had driven to the West Coast in her in 1942.

The evening before Admiral Nimitz was due to arrive from Pearl, Catherine went to her room in the Fairmont Hotel, shut the door behind her, and, without turning on the light, walked over to a window and looked across to the Claremont Hotel in Berkeley, which was lighted up for the first time since the early days of the war. "Well," she said to herself, "the next few years are going to bring lots of problems, but we'll get through them all faithfully."

She stood at the window a long time. She thought of the four years she had been on the West Coast working. She thought of what Chester had gone through and of what she knew was going to be an exasperating time when he got to Washington. Out there in the Pacific he had been supreme commander, making quick decisions that no one questioned. He was going to find it irksome working again in the Navy Department where his every move would be subject to scrutiny.

---

* Because Vice Admiral William S. Pye retired as President of the Naval War College earlier than expected, Spruance's tour as CinCPac-CinCPOA was curtailed. On February 1, 1946, he was again relieved by Admiral Towers, and on March 1 he took over the presidency of the war college. Spruance had to take the presidency then or not at all, for he was approaching retirement age.

She thought about the next morning at nine o'clock, when she would meet Chester at the plane. She had seen so many men come home after years of fearful pressure, men who needed to unwind and needed somebody with them to help them unwind. Chester would not be able to unwind. He was relinquishing one set of pressures only to submit to another. She only hoped she would be able to help him. Luckily, their marriage was a tremendous success, each continually calming and comforting the other.

This time, Admiral Nimitz arrived home without any fanfare. Soon after his plane landed, he and Catherine were headed eastward in Chrissy, just another American family making a long, wearisome trip. Catherine longed for Nancy to spell her and Chester with the driving, for they could feel the difference in years since their last drive across together. As for Chester, he obviously missed Commander Lamar, the ever-efficient aide, hitherto always at Nimitz's elbow, anticipating his every need. But, at war's end, Lamar had a "wild idea" that he wanted duty in China and Nimitz had obligingly arranged for him to be sent there.

When at last the Nimitzes arrived, very tired, in Washington, they found little opportunity for relaxation. She and Chester prepared to move into the big house on the grounds of the Naval Observatory where Chiefs of Naval Operations were customarily quartered.*

Admiral Nimitz called on Admiral King, who assured him that the job of Chief of Naval Operations was to be entirely his, that he, King, would not interfere in any way. If, moreover. the Secretary of the Navy should ask for King's advice on anything, King would promptly inform Nimitz both what had been asked and what the answer had been.

On December 15, 1945, in a simple change-of-command ceremony at the Navy Department, Admiral Nimitz became Chief of Naval Operations. Admiral King started reading from a sheaf of papers, then, as if to speed up the proceedings, began omitting parts of his prepared speech. When he had finished, Nimitz took the oath.

Said King: "In turning over the job of CNO to Admiral Nimitz, I'm sure it will be in good and safe hands. I'm sure you will render him the same kind of loyalty and teamwork that you have given me." As he turned to shake hands with Nimitz, King dropped his sheaf of papers and the pages scattered.

"Well," said Secretary Forrestal to the assembled staff officers and families, "I'm not going to call this a sad occasion. It's quite the contrary." Then, to assure his hearers that he did not really mean that he was joyful to be bidding goodbye to the outgoing chief, he made a little speech praising King.

Nimitz repeated what he had told the press when he was appointed CinCPac in December 1941: "I have just taken on a great responsibility and I will do my utmost to meet it."

---

* In 1974 Observatory House was assigned as residence to the Vice President of the United States.

# CHAPTER 25

# CHIEF OF
# NAVAL OPERATIONS

WHEN ADMIRAL NIMITZ took office as Chief of Naval Operations, the court-martial of Captain Charles McVay, of the *Indianapolis*, was in progress. Not in more than a century had an officer of the U.S. Navy been tried by court-martial for losing his ship to enemy action. Nimitz and other high-ranking officers had strongly advised against the trial, but Secretary Forrestal had felt obliged to order it as a means of quieting the press and satisfying the families of the men who were lost. The press, thus appeased, found new cause for complaint when the Navy brought Commander Mochitsura Hashimoto, skipper of the Japanese submarine that sank the cruiser, to Washington to testify in the case.

Captain McVay was charged with (1) hazarding the safety of his ship by neglecting to zigzag, and (2) failing to issue timely orders to abandon ship. He was acquitted of the latter charge but found guilty of the former, even though Hashimoto testified that he could have hit the *Indianapolis*, whether she had been zigzagging or not.

On the morning of February 23, 1946, Admiral Nimitz received newsmen in his office in the Main Navy Building on Constitution Avenue to inform them of the final disposition of the *Indianapolis* affair. After copies of the Navy's "Narrative of the Circumstances of the Loss of the U.S.S. *Indianapolis*" had been handed out, Nimitz opened the conference by declaring, "We have no desire or intention to deny any of our mistakes." He announced that the members of the court-martial and the judge advocate had recommended Captain McVay to the clemency of the reviewing authority and that this recommendation had been seconded by senior officers who were well acquainted with the captain's professional background. The Secretary of the Navy, said Nimitz, "has approved these recommendations and has remitted the sentence of Captain McVay in its entirety, releasing him from arrest and restoring him to duty."

This was about what the newsmen had expected. One of them asked if, despite the remission of the court-martial sentence, the case would hurt McVay's career. "Has there ever been a court-martialed officer in the history of the U.S. Navy who was later promoted to flag rank?"

Pointing to himself, Nimitz grinned and said, "Here's one." To the amusement of the reporters, he then told how he had run the destroyer *Decatur* aground in 1908, had been court-martialed, and had received a "reprimand."

So far as the newsmen were concerned, the big news of the day was the disclosure in the "Narrative" that four officers, the acting commander of the Philippine Sea Frontier and his operations officer and the acting port director at Leyte and his operations officer, had received letters of reprimand in connection with the *Indianapolis* case. Since Captain McVay had been exonerated, the assumption was that the reprimanded officers must be the guilty parties, that out of sheer neglect they had failed to report the nonarrival of the cruiser.

The assumption was unjustified. Port directors had been instructed by fleet letters *not* to report the *arrivals* of combatant vessels. The inference was that the movements of warships were none of the port directors' business. Consequently, when the *Indianapolis* failed to arrive at Leyte, the port director there assumed that she had been detained at Guam or diverted to another command. After the loss of the *Indianapolis*, port directors were ordered to report as missing any naval vessel sailing independently that failed to appear within eight hours of her estimated time of arrival.

After a careful and somewhat belated study of the case, Secretary Forrestal withdrew all four letters of reprimand. Captain McVay did make rear admiral, but only on his retirement from the Navy in 1949 at the age of 51.

Admiral Nimitz had rarely in his life worked harder than during his first months as Chief of Naval Operations. He arrived early each morning at his office and often remained until well into the evening, seven days a week. He found little time for long walks or other exercise. This was the period of "bringing the boys home" and of demobilizing the armed services, a reduction of force carried out so swiftly and unsystematically that President Truman aptly called it "disintegration." Loss of experienced naval personnel made constant reorganization necessary. The Navy was kept going by makeshifts and short cuts. Reserve officers and enlisted men were being released from service so fast that it was sometimes difficult to get ships to port for decommissioning.

Congress, complacent because of the American monopoly of the atomic bomb, cut defense appropriations so drastically that office workers were in short supply even in the Navy Department. Civil Service secretaries and filing clerks in the office of the Chief of Naval Operations, out of devotion to their new boss, worked overtime without extra pay until their fellow employees began taunting them as "scabs." Nimitz thereupon transferred his Civil Service employees to departments where they could keep regular working hours and brought in Waves to replace them.

Luckily for Nimitz, he had a star team of helpers. Admiral DeWitt C. Ramsay, former Chief of the Bureau of Aeronautics, was his vice chief. His deputy chiefs were Vice Admirals Forrest Sherman, for operations; Louis E. Denfeld, for personnel; Richard Conolly, for administration; Robert Carney, for logistics; and Arthur Radford, for air. Vice Admiral Charles Lockwood, who had been Commander, Submarines, Pacific Fleet, was Inspector General.

As useful to Nimitz's peace of mind and well-being as these high-ranking offiers were three commanders, his aides. Two of these, H. Chester Bruton and Neil K. Dietrich, he inherited from Admiral King. Bruton's primary concern was keeping track of the Joint Chiefs of Staff papers; Dietrich was flag secretary but on occasion served Nimitz as personal aide. Nimitz's regular personal aide, his own selection, was Eugene B. Fluckey, a World War II submarine ace and holder of the Medal of Honor. Fluckey soon learned to anticipate the admiral's needs as thoroughly as had Lamar. To this list of Nimitz's faithful helpers should be added Master Sergeant George E. Cozard, his driver. Gradually Cozard took on extra duties until he, too, rated as an aide. With one interruption, he remained with Nimitz until 1961, when he retired from the Marine Corps.

A nuisance Admiral Nimitz now encountered was the attention resulting from his fame. Because in the early postwar period officers were still required to wear uniform, he was easily recognized and was frequently stopped and asked for his autograph. To save time, he had Fluckey accompany him with a pocketful of cards that he had previously signed, ready to be handed out. On several occasions when he ventured into a public place, he found himself virtually mobbed, mostly by admiring women. He found that if he and Mrs. Nimitz wanted to go to the movies, for example, he had better wear civilian clothes with a slouch hat that covered most of his hair and could be pulled down over his eyes.

The worst case of mobbing that Nimitz endured was at Kansas City, where he made a speech at a governors' conference. As he was leaving the convention hall with Fluckey, the crowd recognized him, broke through the police lines, and dashed up the steps toward him. Police charged forward and formed a circle around the admiral, but the mob broke through that, clawing at him. By this time, Fluckey was almost dragging his boss back into the building. With a crowd following, they sped down a corridor, and Fluckey pushed the admiral into a men's room and closed the door.

That stopped the crowd, most of whom were women, but only for a moment. They shoved Fluckey aside and swarmed into the washroom, where Nimitz had prudently locked himself in a stall. Fearing that the crowd might break into that, Nimitz stood on the toilet seat. His head appeared over the top of the partition, and he made a polite little speech to the ladies standing there among the urinals.

Suddenly everybody present began laughing and, as the story was repeated down the corridor, the laughter spread until it circulated through the building and broke up the governors' conference for the afternoon. Nimitz and Fluckey finally managed to slip out through a basement door and make good their escape.

During his tour as Chief of Naval Operations, Admiral Nimitz was in constant demand for speeches. He was not a spellbinder, but he made intelligent talks, usually salted with humor. Sometimes he was called on to make two or three speeches in a day. This demand kept his speech-writers busy, but they were disconcerted by the admiral's habit of glancing over a prepared address, then laying it aside and improvising. In fact, Nimitz often did not call for a prepared speech, but only for a few cards with notes about the organization he was to address and other pertinent facts, figures, or ideas. He would glance over the cards and speak largely from memory.

Despite the admiral's remarkable power of recall, such a loose system was bound eventually to result in a mishap. The slip-up occurred when Nimitz was speaking to a meeting of one of the volunteer organizations serving the needs of members of the U.S. armed forces. This one happened to be the arch rival of the more famous United Services Organization (USO).

Nimitz had to make three speeches that day. An executive session with a congressional committee ended just in time for him to get to a nearby hotel where he was to deliver his first speech, to the service organization. Cozard had the car ready, and Nimitz and Fluckey jumped in and sped away. Fluckey gave the admiral the speech cards to put in his pocket and began to make a few remarks about the organization's objectives and what it was currently doing. "Gene," said the admiral, "you don't need to tell me about that organization. I was granddaddy of it when I was Chief of the Bureau of Navigation."

So they talked about other things. When they got to the hotel, the program was about to start. Besides national representatives of the service organization, other notables including senators and congressmen were present.

Because Admiral Nimitz had to make a luncheon speech elsewhere, and hence could remain only about 20 minutes, the scheduled first speaker was asked if he would mind postponing his speech until Nimitz had spoken. This he was glad to do and, after a brief introduction, Nimitz began to speak, without taking his cards out of his pocket.

In two minutes it dawned on Fluckey, seated on the platform behind the admiral, that Nimitz was talking about and praising, not the organization whose officers he was addressing, but its rival, the USO. Fluckey started to rise and tell the admiral to take his cards out of his pocket and look at them, but he felt a hand on his shoulder gently pressing him back into his seat. He looked around. The hand belonged to a lady, the president of the organization. She had tears in her eyes.

The admiral finished speaking. There was applause and he sat down. He could remain only a couple of minutes longer, but he waited for the next speaker to be introduced and start speaking. Hardly had the latter begun when it dawned on Nimitz that he had made a dreadful mistake. He turned red. Fluckey decided he'd better get him out of there. "Admiral," he said softly, "it's time to go."

Nimitz leaned over to the president and asked her in a whisper to please forgive him. He guessed, he said, that he was just too busy. "I know your organization," he said. "It's a wonderful organization, and I just so deeply apologize."

The president kissed Nimitz on the cheek. "Admiral," she said, her eyes glistening, "we're just so happy to have you here. We know your real feelings."

Back in the car, Fluckey knew that he would have to start coaching Nimitz for his next speech. He had the cards ready but he thought he had better let the admiral settle down a few minutes before he said anything. It was Nimitz who broke the silence. "Gene," he said, slapping his aide on the thigh, "the next time I say to you that I'm the granddaddy of any organization, will you just say, 'Shut up and take these cards and listen'?"

Admiral Nimitz would not accept compensation for any of his speeches or for anything he wrote for publication. He would either refuse to accept the honorarium or ask the organization tendering it to send the check directly to some charity or other cause that he would name. His explanation was that everything he published or said in public was derived from his experiences in the Navy, and the Navy had already paid him.

While Nimitz was Chief of Naval Operations, Fluckey made out his tax returns. He found it a very simple task because the admiral's only source of income was his salary and he always took the standard deduction although, had he itemized his deductions, he could have saved himself thousands of dollars. When Fluckey protested, the admiral replied that he never minded paying taxes.

The $15,000 annual salary that Nimitz depended on was static and thus, in the postwar period of galloping inflation, it was continually shrinking in purchasing power. Other officers were getting raises to offset the inflation, but a certain congressman put on each of the pay bills a rider that denied pay increases for the five-star officers.

This situation made it difficult for the Nimitzes to meet their social obligations. They had, of course, an allowance that was intended to cover official dinners and receptions at Observatory House, but it was never enough. They solved the problem by cutting official entertaining to a bare minimum and limiting the stewards to preparing only three courses for dinner, which gave everybody enough to eat with no waste. This thrifty example was especially appreciated by those foreign representatives in Washington who were restricted by tight budgets. "You are making it so much easier for us," they would tell the Nimitzes privately. "We can't afford to give the dinners that the people are giving in Washington, and when you do this, you make it so much simpler for us. Now *we* can do it."

Frequently Mrs. Nimitz would call guests and ask them: "Do you want an official dinner, or would you rather bring your children?"

Almost invariably they would reply that they would just love to bring their children. Usually the result was a jolly sort of picnic dinner, after which the Nimitzes might conduct their guests to the observatory to look at the moon and stars through the big telescope, an adventure the children particularly appreciated.

"Neither Chester nor I have ever been interested in money," said Mrs. Nimitz. "So long as we had enough to pay our bills and see our children through college, we never cared a darn. We didn't entertain very much. I had very few clothes. I mean to say I didn't have dozens of evening gowns when he was CNO."

During this period, Commander James Lay had duty in the Washington area, and he and Kate were living in nearby Maryland. As a result, they were to some extent caught up in the Nimitzes' official life. Various embassies and legations in Washington were presenting the admiral with postwar decorations awarded by their governments. The Lays were sometimes invited to these ceremonies, and they were expected to attend. They did so faithfully, even though in the hot summer of 1946 it was sometimes a chore, particularly for Kate, who was in the last stages of pregnancy. In July there came an invitation from the Greek embassy. Nimitz was to be awarded the Grand Cross of the Order of George I, Greece's highest military decoration. The ceremony was scheduled for the 31st, the very day that Kate expected to go to the hospital to have her baby.

In distress she telephoned her mother. "What will I do?" she wailed. "I know enough to send formal regrets, but obviously we received this invitation because they knew we're daughter and son-in-law, and we're living right here. What are they going to think? They're going to be insulted."

"Well," said Mrs. Nimitz after thinking over the problem, "I would send the formal regrets today and then tomorrow call the embassy and explain to the secretary who you are and why you sent the regrets."

So Kate sent the formal regrets and the next day telephoned, expecting somebody to answer in heavily accented English. Instead she heard a very American female voice, somebody she could picture chewing gum. "This is Mrs. James Lay," she said. "I sent a regret and I want to explain why." She identified her father and told what order he was to be awarded and on what date. "That is the date," Kate concluded, "that I am due to go to the hospital to have our first baby."

There was a minute's silence; then the voice at the other end replied sympathetically, "Oh, honey, that's a shame. I knew I should have gotten those invitations out earlier."

"Yeah," said Jim when Kate told him the story, "last October would have been a good time."*

The sort of party the Nimitzes never stinted on was the small, intimate gathering with close friends. Such parties were always occasions for one or more of the admiral's stories, of which he had a new set, dealing mostly with soldiers and sailors. One of his favorites, he got from General Omar N. Bradley. It was a long story, which the admiral narrated with great showmanship and in masterly detail. In brief summary, it tells of a young soldier who took advantage of the G. I. Bill of Rights to take a course in, of all things, midwifery. Having earned his diploma, he returned to his small home town, rented an office, bought a doctor's satchel with instruments, and hung out his shingle.

---

* James T. ("Jimmie") Lay, Jr., arrived on time, July 31, 1946. He was Fleet Admiral and Mrs. Nimitz's third grandchild. Chester, Jr., and Joan had presented them with Frances Mary, born May 19, 1940, and Elizabeth Joan, born January 26, 1946.

After about a week in which no patients appeared, an excited farmer rushed into the G.I.'s office looking for the midwife. Astonished at finding a man claiming to be the midwife, he was finally convinced by being shown the diploma. "You'll have to do," said the farmer, "because our only doctor has gone about 90 miles away and my wife's in labor."

In the farmer's car they rattled out to the farm at top speed. Here the G.I. donned his white jacket, told the husband to take it easy and read a magazine, and then, with his black satchel, entered the bedroom. In ten minutes he cracked the door, asked for a screwdriver and closed the door again. The astonished farmer fetched the screwdriver and tapped on the bedroom door, which the G.I. cracked open. "Fine," he said, "just what I need. Now you go read your magazine and don't worry. Everything's going to be fine."

Twenty minutes later, the G.I. was at the door again, looking somewhat worried. This time he asked for a putty knife "with a limber blade." When the farmer brought it, the soldier repeated his assurances and again closed the door.

Another twenty minutes passed. Again the G.I. cracked the bedroom door. "Say, mister," he said, his voice a bit shaky, "I wonder if you'd have a piece of wire about five or six inches long—a good, stiff piece of wire, with a hook in the end of it."

The farmer didn't have anything quite like that, but he brought a wire coat hanger. The G.I., cracking the door again, said, "Fine, fine. Now don't you worry. Just go and sit down."

The farmer couldn't stand it any longer. He noticed that there were beads of sweat on the soldier's forehead and a sort of wild look in his eye. "Look here," he said. "What's going on? First you want a screwdriver, then you want a putty knife, then you want a coat hanger. What's the matter? I just have to know. Are there complications?"

"Complications!" the G.I. burst out. "Are there complications! Hell, yes. I can't get my damned satchel open!"

Another favorite story of Nimitz's told of a British gun instructor, a sergeant, who was addressing a class of student officers. " 'Eretofore," said the instructor, "we 'ave used 'ard woods for gun stocks—hoak and hash and hoccasionally 'ickory—but 'ard wood is becoming hincreasingly rare."

From the rear of the room came a voice with an Oxford accent: "Do you by any chaunce mean oak and ash and hickory?"

Replied the instructor: "Hi means hoak and hash and 'ickory; them is the 'ard woods Hi uses for my stocks. Now there is lignum vitae—a very 'ard wood, and water-resisting to boot. In fact, hit is hextensively used for piles for piers—and for the benefit of that hover-heducated bastard in the back row, when Hi says piles for piers, Hi doesn't hintend to convey the hidea of 'emmeroids for haristocrats."

President Truman, simply brushing aside Forrestal's rule that the Chief of Naval Operations could make contact with the President only through the

Secretary of the Navy, frequently summoned Nimitz to the White House for official as well as social reasons. In private the President and the admiral, who were about the same age, began to call each other by their first names. Whenever possible, Bess Truman got Catherine Nimitz off to herself, in order to hear some of the latter's stories, for Mrs. Nimitz, like her husband, was no mean raconteur. Whenever the Trumans and the Nimitzes planned to attend the same concert or other public function, the Secret Service would arrange to have them seated in adjoining boxes as an added security measure in protecting the President.

The Trumans accepted an invitation from the Nimitzes to come out to Observatory House to pitch horseshoes. The day before the visit, Secret Service men arrived to look over the grounds. "This is the most wonderful thing," said the leader of the group to Mrs. Nimitz. "We don't have to do a thing. For a few hours tomorrow afternoon we can relax. You have marines at all the gates and nobody's going to get in."

When the Trumans arrived, Chester took Harry upstairs and loaned him a pair of his old khaki pants to wear. Then they went down to the horseshoe court, where Harry teamed up with Catherine and Chester with Bess. Because Harry was the least expert of the four pitchers, Bess and Chester won, but all had a good time. After the game they walked around the grounds of the Observatory, the Trumans remarking what a sense of freedom it gave them to be left alone, with nobody, not even Secret Service men, following them about.

Chester showed the Trumans a magnificent oak of which he was very fond. On the side lawn they stopped under an apple tree and plucked and ate apples. When the Trumans remarked on their fine flavor, Catherine summoned the messboys and had them fill a large bag with the fruit. The Nimitzes and their guests then went inside and had highballs.

As the Trumans were getting into their car to leave, one of the boys brought out the bag of apples and gave it to the chauffeur. Mrs. Truman leaned over and said to the latter, "Now I want it understood this bag of apples is not to go into the kitchen. It's to go up to our bedroom. We're going to eat these apples."

Not long after that a man showed up in the Chief of Naval Operation's outer office and, exhibiting proofs, identified himself as the world's champion horseshoe pitcher. He asked if he might possibly get an autographed picture of Admiral Nimitz.

"You're not going to get just an autographed photo," replied Fluckey. "I'm sure he's going to want to see you."

The admiral did indeed want to meet the champion. After they had engaged in a long conversation, during which his appointments were sidetracked, Nimitz picked up the White House telephone and easily got through to the President. "Hey, Harry," he said, "I've got the champion horseshoe pitcher of the world over here. Let's come over to the White House and show you how he can pitch horseshoes."

Truman had *his* appointments canceled, and in fifteen minutes he, Nimitz, Fluckey, and the champion were in the garden behind the White House observing and attempting all sorts of trick horseshoe-pitching.

Admiral Nimitz took advantage of his friendship with President Truman to educate the latter regarding the Navy and sea power. To help Truman to forget his artillery days, Nimitz set up for him as a vacation spot a Little White House at the Key West Naval Base. From there he arranged for Truman to take submarine rides, including trips in at least one U-boat that the United States had taken over. He escorted the President out on some of the carriers to demonstrate to him what the carriers could do. Truman's affection for the Army never diminished but, under Nimitz's tutelage, he acquired considerable respect for the Navy.

Mrs. Nimitz was surprised one day to get a telephone call from Lady Balfour, wife of the acting British ambassador. "Mrs. Nimitz," she said, "Winston Churchill has just arrived in town from Florida, where he's been vacationing, and he wants very much to talk to your husband. He's never had the privilege. I asked who he wanted to meet, and he said, 'Just Admiral Nimitz. I want to meet Admiral Nimitz. Can you arrange so that I can?'" There was a slight pause; then she added, "Will you come to dinner tonight?"

"Well, this is a problem," said Mrs. Nimitz, "because we were going to dine somewhere else." However, she concluded, she would see what she could do because she knew that Admiral Nimitz wanted above everything to meet Winston Churchill. Catherine called their intended hosts of the evening and explained the situation. They said it was perfectly all right. Thus it was that the Nimitzes dined at the British embassy. There were only a few people at the table because Churchill had said, "I don't want a dinner party because I want to talk to Nimitz."

After dinner, when they all returned to the drawing room, Churchill sipped his brandy and soda and smoked one of his potent cigars, the sort that had floored Dr. Anderson. He then drew Nimitz aside, and they sat down to have a good talk.

"What," asked Churchill, "was your lowest point in the war?" When Nimitz had replied, Churchill told Nimitz what *his* lowest point in the war was. That exchange opened a lively and earnest conversation that lasted for an hour and a half, the two men hugely enjoying each other.

Admiral Nimitz was, of course, offered honorary degrees by many universities and he found time to accept a number of them. Probably he enjoyed no such occasion more than that in which the University of Richmond conferred on him a doctor of laws degree. General Eisenhower, Nimitz's opposite number on the Joint Chiefs of Staff, received the same degree at the same university in the same ceremony. The affair had been arranged by Douglas Freeman, rector of the University of Richmond and an editor-historian whose books both Eisenhower and Nimitz admired. After the ceremony Freeman honored the general and the admiral with a garden party at his home. The two five-star officers agreeably posed together for a news photographer while sipping high-balls. When their picture, thus enjoying themselves, was published, the local bluenoses bombarded the newspapers with letters of outrage, much to the amusement of the two new doctors of law.

The Chief of Naval Operations traditionally serves as president of the U.S. Naval Institute and is a member of its board of control which, in Admiral Nimitz's day, acted as an editorial board. Nimitz was expected to read many manuscripts of books considered for publication by the Institute and of articles under consideration by the monthly periodical *United States Naval Institute Proceedings*. He was counted on moreover to attend board meetings at the Institute's offices in the grounds of the Naval Academy at Annapolis. In a sense this was just another burden for the overburdened Chief of Naval Operations, but in fact this was one job that Nimitz especially enjoyed. He read rapidly and was a good judge of what naval officers wanted to read and of what was worth reading in naval literature. Much concerned with language, he was an enemy of circumlocution and fuzzy expression. He would run a ruthless blue pencil through unnecessary or misleading verbiage in the manuscripts he reviewed for the Naval Institute.

Although Secretary Forrestal had campaigned to prevent Nimitz from becoming Chief of Naval Operations, once the admiral was in office, the Secretary and he worked amicably and effectively together. Part of the reason for this was Forrestal's habit of making the best of a situation he had not been able to avert or could not change. Another part was Nimitz's cooperativeness and general agreeableness, for, as Nancy said, "he was a person whom I think it would be impossible to resent." Most important, perhaps, was the fact that they usually saw eye to eye on problems that arose.

Neil Dietrich, who served as aide to both King and Nimitz, said: "I know Admiral Nimitz had great respect for the Secretary, and I happened to be present on a few occasions when he would sit back with Mr. Forrestal and tell a story that would reinforce his point in some discussion. And Mr. Forrestal on occasion would make some humorous remark in their conversation.... I had occasion to observe a feeling of relaxation in their conversations and in their discussions, and not as much difference in viewpoint, or at least nothing approaching the degree of stiffness and formality, that existed between Admiral King and Secretary Forrestal."

Despite the cooperation between the Secretary and the Chief of Naval Operations and the air of relaxation that Dietrich observed in their conferences, Nimitz afterward testified that there always existed between them a degree of tension. Nimitz recognized the Secretary's brilliance but was perplexed by his introverted, taut, and enigmatic personality. Forrestal could never be fully at ease with Nimitz because, half-buried in his consciousness, there was a neurotic streak that was hostile to authority, particularly as symbolized by high military rank.

Nimitz was perhaps most useful to Forrestal as a representative of the

Navy before congressional committees. The admiral was meticulous in the preparation of his testimony. His manner was honest and forthright. His opinions, always clearly expressed, carried authority and conviction. "Admiral Nimitz was very well treated by the committees when he appeared on the Hill," Chester Bruton recalls, "because of his prestige. He didn't talk down to them, nor did he talk up to them."

Forrestal and Nimitz early concluded that it would be useless to continue fighting unification of the services, because unification was strongly favored by the President, by leaders of the army ground and air forces, and, apparently, by a majority in Congress, which would have to make the final decision. It also appeared futile to argue against the establishment of a separate air force, an idea whose time seemed to have come. What the Secretary, the admiral, and other naval leaders sought was to prevent a complete merger of the services, a situation in which an all-powerful civilian Secretary would distribute appropriations and set policy and an all-powerful military chief of staff would direct operations. They strove moreover to retain for the Navy its Marine Corps and naval air arm.

During the months of debate and deliberation over the shape of the American defense organization, when Forrestal turned to naval officers for ideas, he most often consulted Admirals Nimitz, Radford, and Sherman. Characteristically, however, he relied more often on civilians, particularly Ferdinand Eberstadt, a Wall Street financier, whose background was much like his own. It was Eberstadt who prepared the report that formed Forrestal's basic concept of a national establishment for defense.

After innumerable conferences, meetings with congressional committees, and bouts with the President, Forrestal and the naval leaders got most of what they wanted in the National Security Act that was signed into law by Truman on July 26, 1947. Under a National Military Establishment there were to be subordinate but separate departments of the Army, the Navy, and the Air Force. Heading the Establishment was a Secretary of Defense, who was a member of the President's Cabinet. Each department had a secretary who was not of Cabinet rank. The Joint Chiefs of Staff were retained to direct operations, and the Navy kept its carrier aviation, its shore-based reconnaissance wing, and its Marine Corps. President Truman appointed Forrestal first Secretary of Defense and, on the latter's recommendation, named John L. Sullivan to be the new Secretary of the Navy.

While Nimitz was Chief of Naval Operations, Admiral Karl Doenitz, former commander of the German submarine force, was tried before the International Military Tribunal in Nürnberg for, among other offenses, conducting unrestricted submarine warfare. At the request of Doenitz's attorney, Nimitz provided an affidavit stating that, on orders from Washington, submarines under his command had conducted the same sort of warfare: "In the interest of operations against Japan, the Pacific Ocean was declared an operational area. On December 7, 1941, the Chief of Naval Operations had ordered unrestricted submarine warfare against Japan." Though the tribunal found

Doenitz guilty of conducting unrestricted submarine warfare, it imposed no sentence for that particular offense.

A major project involving the office of the Chief of Naval Operations during Admiral Nimitz's incumbency was testing the effect of atomic weapons on warships. The Navy needed to know what changes should be made in ship design, in tactical formations, and in the spacing of ships in harbor. Army ground forces wanted to expose on the decks of the test ships equipment that might require redesign. Army air forces wanted to find out to what extent an enemy's vessels would be profitable targets for atomic bombs.

The experiment was under the direction of Vice Admiral William H. P. Blandy, who, before participating in amphibious assaults from Kwajalein to Okinawa, had been Chief of the Bureau of Ordnance. Now, as head of the Division of Special Weapons under the Chief of Naval Operations, he organized a joint army-navy task force to conduct the tests, which were to be staged at Bikini Atoll in the Marshall Islands in the summer of 1946.

In February, 1946, the President summoned Admiral Nimitz to a meeting at the White House to discuss the forthcoming tests. Others present were James F. Byrnes, Secretary of State; Robert P. Patterson, Secretary of War; Secretary of the Navy Forrestal; General Eisenhower; and Admiral Leahy. Mr. Truman referred to suggestions that the tests might be conducted in such a way as to establish whatever conclusions the military wanted to establish, and he read from an accusatory letter written by Secretary of Commerce Henry A. Wallace. He recalled how in 1921 General Billy Mitchell had rigged a test of the effect conventional bombs would have on warships, and thus made the experiment prove what he wanted it to prove. The President said he trusted his army and naval leaders to be objective, but that was not enough—the public must be convinced that they were objective.

Forrestal told Truman that Admiral Blandy was planning to invite a civilian group to observe the tests. Out of the ensuing discussion among those present came the suggestion that this group, with additions from the House and Senate, might be the basis for a commission appointed by the President to report directly to him. This solution, satisfactory to all, was accepted by Mr. Truman.

Involved ultimately in the Bikini tests were 42,000 men, 150 planes, and 200 ships. Two atomic bombs were exploded, and these sank eleven old ships and burned and battered several others. The tests provided the information wanted by the armed forces. It is noteworthy that no one later accused the conduct of the experiment of not being entirely honest.

In March 1946 the Naval Research Laboratory distributed a report recommending the construction of a nuclear-powered submarine. To attain extended high-speed underwater operations, an advanced hull design, such as that devised by the Germans for their hydrogen peroxide system, would be used. With all-out effort, said the report, a submarine of this type could be in operation within two years. The proposal attracted wide attention among naval officers because such a submarine was certainly what the Navy wanted and because the report had been prepared under the guidance of the respected physicist Philip H. Abelson.

Though the Bureau of Ships was intensely interested in developing nuclear propulsion, and a nuclear-propelled submarine in particular, its personnel lacked the nuclear technology to superintend such developments. Accordingly, Rear Admiral Edward L. Cochrane, chief of the bureau, sent a small group of engineering officers to the Manhattan District's plant in Oak Ridge, Tennessee, to study the fundamentals of the subject. Heading the group was Captain Hyman G. Rickover.

Rickover had an excellent technological background, but he also had a prickly personality that sometimes cost him friends and support. A perfectionist, he was a remorseless critic of defects and shortcomings, even of those that lay outside of his sphere of responsibility. But he had a reputation for competence and drive. Any objective in which he strongly believed he would promote with bulldog determination. Rickover took as his special project the attainment as soon as possible of the submarine Abelson had proposed.

In his campaign to get the work started, Rickover encountered discouragements that would have daunted a less determined man. He met opposition even in the office of the Chief of Naval Operations. There, Rear Admiral William S. Parsons, Nimitz's director of atomic defense, insisted that the Navy should give first priority to naval weapons. Working toward nuclear propulsion should take second place, he maintained, to general studies for producing power by nuclear means. Prematurely confining the search for engineering solutions to those applicable to submarines, he said, might actually delay the production of nuclear submarines.

Admiral Nimitz had from the first favored the development of a nuclear-powered submarine, but he was in no position to dispute the opinion of Parsons and other nuclear experts who agreed with him. Nimitz tackled the problem from another angle. In September 1946, he appointed a board of experienced submarine officers to study antisubmarine techniques and new submarine designs. These officers concluded that, with inevitable improvement in surface and near-surface detection, the submarine would have to run so deep that air-breathing engines for submarines would become impractical. In its final report, submitted in January 1947, the board urged the gradual replacement of existing submarines by diesel models capable of greater submerged speed and endurance, experiments with the hydrogen-peroxide submarine to attain still greater submerged speed, and the design and development of "nuclear-power plants for eventual installation in submarines to give unlimited submergence at high speed." Nimitz at once approved these recommendations.

Rickover knew that Nimitz favored early development of the nuclear submarine and, unless he got massive opposition from the nuclear experts, would give it his full support. But Nimitz's tour as Chief of Naval Operations would end in December 1947. No one could predict what the attitude of the next Chief would be. There was no time to spare.

By the fall of 1947, Rickover believed the progress that had been made toward nuclear propulsion would lessen the opposition he might expect from the physicists, who continued to recommend general studies before specific applications. With the help of his assistants, Rickover began preparing a memorandum that he hoped he could persuade Admiral Nimitz to forward to Secretary of the Navy Sullivan. The memorandum pointed out that only nuclear power could provide the Navy with submarines of high speed and unlimited endurance that current developments urgently demanded. It stated that, if suitable effort were applied, an atomic submarine capable of launching a guided missile with a nuclear warhead could be completed by the mid-1950s. The memorandum urged the Secretary to bring "the strategic and tactical importance of a nuclear-powered submarine" to the attention of the Secretary of Defense and the Research and Development Board. It took weeks of negotiation and meticulous revision of the memorandum before Rickover could obtain the necessary endorsements from nuclear experts and veteran submariners. He then sent it to Admiral Nimitz.

Nimitz, convinced by Rickover's arguments and the endorsement of the experts, approved the memorandum. As almost his last official act, he signed it and sent it to Secretary Sullivan. Sullivan, equally convinced, signed it and promptly forwarded it to Secretary of Defense Forrestal, to Vannevar Bush, Chairman of the Research and Development Board, and to Admiral Cochrane, Chief of the Bureau of Ships. Though there were to be more obstacles along the way, Rickover and his assistants were thus given status, and their project was given top priority.

When Nimitz began his tour as Chief of Naval Operations, he was determined not to continue indefinitely working in the evenings and on Sundays. By reorganizing his office and expanding his base of operations, he again approached his ideal of having as his official duties only those that no one else was called upon or had the authority to do. He began walking the three and one-quarter miles to work in the morning and back to Observatory House in the afternoon, nodding to everyone he met. He would sometimes telephone Mrs. Nimitz, who would come out part way to meet him, and they would walk back together. The admiral kept up his walking habit through the heat of summer and the coldest days of winter.

Once, on a late mid-winter afternoon, Nimitz came out of his office at the usual time in blue uniform and gloves but no overcoat and, though it was snowing heavily, started to walk home. "Admiral," said Commander Fluckey in some alarm, "let me order your car." Nimitz grunted and walked out.

Commander Fluckey and Commander Bruton talked over the situation. Fluckey did not have his car at the Navy Department, and the admiral's car had been dismissed. The snow was coming down harder than ever. Bruton decided to refer the problem to higher authority. "I'm going to call Mrs. Nimitz," he said.

"Mrs. Nimitz," said Bruton on the telephone, "the admiral started walking home in this heavy snow. I hope you're not going to go out and meet him."

"Of course not," she said.

"I think I'd better go out and pick him up."

"You do just that," said Mrs. Nimitz.

So Bruton got out his car and proceeded along the route that Nimitz usually took. He had driven more than a mile when he caught up with the admiral, striding along through the ankle-deep drifts, with snow piling up on his cap and shoulders. Bruton pulled over, flagged his boss down, opened the door, and asked him to get in. "I called Mrs. Nimitz and she said to come pick you up." The admiral got in reluctantly and Bruton took him home.

Admiral Nimitz at length found time to indulge his writing hobby. For *American Federalist* he wrote "Labor, We *Thank* You," a salute to the workers who, during the war, had kept the armed forces provided with ships, munitions, and other necessities. Most of his writing at this time, however, was to combat the widespread simplistic notion that warships exist only to fight warships and that, since no potential enemy at that time had a fighting fleet of any consequence, it was a useless extravagance for the United States to support a navy.

For *Sea Power*, published by the influential Navy League, he wrote "Is the Navy Obsolete?" and answered his own question in the negative: "Your Navy is not obsolete. The A-bombs which fell on Japan were themselves the apex of the spear of sea-air power. The bombs were transported on naval vessels, over sea lanes made safe by naval power. They were delivered to an island in the western Pacific that sea power forced the enemy to surrender. There they were placed aboard a plane which could not have left the ground if naval power had not been able to deliver the gas to that spot." He reminded his readers of the continuing responsibilities of the Navy:

> We must remember that one of the important responsibilities of the Navy is the support of American forces on shore in overseas positions. During the recent global war, the U.S. found it necessary to send forces into many foreign lands. Remnants of our forces are still serving in outlying positions in Germany, Italy, India, China, Korea, and Japan.
>
> Wherever our troops remain, and wherever they must be sent, units of our fleet are required to go. That they appear in waters adjacent to areas where we have forces on shore constitutes no threat to anyone and should cause no concern. Its significance is primarily the integration and coordination of the services, in the interest of mutual support and also united support of our national policies.
>
> The Navy has approximately seven functions: to protect the coasts of the U.S.; to maintain lifelines for our merchant marine; to transport troops; to protect the troops in landing; to maintain an unbroken pipeline of supplies to the troops; to operate against the enemy naval forces and his shipping; and to implement the foreign policy of this nation.
>
> Another Navy function is to bring the troops back home after they have

defeated the enemy on his home grounds. Without the fleet, the contest would be on our own home grounds, and war is one contest in which it is best to be on the visiting team.

*National Geographic* carried Nimitz's article "Your Navy as Peace Insurance," with numerous pictures, most of them of ships, and most of them in color. "Now that the war is over, and everybody seems to be eager to shove all reminders of the conflict out of sight," Nimitz wrote, "one hears the question: 'Why do we need a powerful Navy today, in peacetime?'" After marshaling his replies to that question, he took a look into the future and described a monster submarine which "would approach an enemy coast and, remaining a hundred fathoms down, bombard the shore with self-guided atomic missiles." He continued his campaign in *Nation's Business* with "The Navy: Investment in Peace," and in the Washington *News Digest* with "Seapower Still Indispensable."

Admiral Nimitz avoided writing about World War II operations, lest in giving credit to one officer or force he might imply that another was less deserving. He believed that in the victory of Allied arms there was glory enough for all, and that the distribution of credit and blame should be left to posterity. To him the dangers of prematurely rushing into print were well illustrated by "Admiral Halsey Tells His Story,"* which was serialized in *The Saturday Evening Post*. In explaining away his own abandonment of the beachhead at Leyte Gulf, Halsey implied that Admiral Kinkaid had been somewhat derelict. Then, in a transparent attempt to eat his cake and have it too, he added: "I have attempted to describe the Battle for Leyte Gulf in terms of my thoughts and feelings at the time, but on rereading my account, I find that this results in an implication grossly unfair to Tom Kinkaid.... Had I been in his shoes, I might have acted precisely as did he." Kinkaid was not appeased by the disclaimer. Friendship between the two men was destroyed, never to be resumed.

Despite Nimitz's campaigning, which was done not only by written word but also on the public platform and before congressional committees, the Navy was ever more starved for appropriations. More and more ships were scrapped or mothballed. Nimitz had planned a streamlined navy of seven fleets, but those fleets existed mainly on paper. The most powerful navy in the world, an armada that had played a major part in defeating Italy, Germany, and Japan, became so whittled down that it lacked the force to protect American overseas interests, let alone to support American foreign policy.

Fluckey, observing the admiral testifying before the House Naval Affairs Committee, thought he was "absolutely magnificent," but in the long run the admiral's performance was to no avail. "They would end up the session on, say, the Navy's budget for the next year," Fluckey recalled, "asking him, 'Are

---

* Published in book form as *Admiral Halsey's Story*.

you sure you have enough, Admiral?' And he would assure them that's all the Navy needed at this particular time, with what he could see coming up in the next two or three years. Of course, this was just an educated guess, but they were always very friendly and offered him more. Nimitz was astute enough that in the car on the way back from the Congressional hearing, he would say, 'Well, now we go back and start our cutback plan.'

"I would say, 'What do you mean? They accepted everything. They offered you even more.'

"He'd say, 'No, the party line this year is out to cut, and cut they will. There they are reasonable while they're listening to you, but the minute you're away, they'll go back and adopt the party line. So now we'll go back and plan for the cuts.' Three weeks later, in would come the cut, and we'd have the plan all prepared for it."

On November 12, 1947, a month before his tour as Chief of Naval Operations was to end, Nimitz issued his last official warning. Testifying before the President's Air Policy Committee, he stated that the Navy needed all 5,793 of the planes it was authorized to have and warned that its strength was "dangerously low." The next day President Truman announced the appointment of Admiral Louis E. Denfeld, then CinCPac, to succeed Nimitz as Chief of Naval Operations.

As he prepared to leave office, Admiral Nimitz was sick at heart to see the national defense being endangered by political considerations—for such appeared to him to be the case. He was almost equally disturbed by an apparent change in the character of the U.S. Navy. He had expected that in wartime, with the great influx of reservists, the Navy would undergo change. But somehow he expected that, after the war, it would again become the almost intimate association of friends he had known in, say, his *Augusta* days.

He gradually realized that, so far as he was concerned, the Old Navy had gone forever. The Navy Department seemed to him now less like an association than like a corporation. In his own class of 1905, 144 midshipmen had been graduated. Even the immediate prewar classes never produced as many as 500 graduates. By 1947 the Naval Academy was turning out graduates by the thousand, and to these was added an increasing influx of officers from the NROTCs. The Navy was acquiring more potential commanders than there were ships to command. Nimitz, walking the corridors of the Navy Department building, was continually encountering officers he had never seen before.

Above all, Nimitz was tired. For six years he had been carrying heavy burdens and had had no leave to speak of. There had been times when he regretted and rather resented Secretary Forrestal's having cut his tenure as Chief of Naval Operations from the usual four years to two. But, as December 1947 approached, he could hardly wait to lay down his burdens and get out of Washington.

Congress had conferred permanent rank on all the five-star officers. None would retire except at his own request. It had been announced that, when

Nimitz was relieved as Chief of Naval Operations, he would become a special aide to the Secretary of the Navy. Admiral King had been given the same duty, and, in that capacity, had occupied an office in the Navy Department. As time went on, he had been more and more left alone. Some officers held that this neglect, following years when practically his every waking moment was required in the service of his country, was the cause of his declining health.

Nimitz was determined not to stay around. "When it comes time for me to give up my job here," he said, "we get out on that day. We're not going to stick around and breathe down the next man's neck." He would be available, but at a distance. He and Mrs. Nimitz had long since decided to take up residence on the West Coast when the admiral's active duty terminated.

On the morning of December 15, 1947, at Observatory House, the Nimitzes breakfasted as usual at seven o'clock. During the meal, the admiral called in his stewards and messboys, made a little speech of appreciation and good wishes, and handed each of them an envelope containing Christmas money. He then left for the Navy Department. Mrs. Nimitz prepared to drive to 2222 Q Street to pick up Nancy, who was then living alone there. As she was leaving Observatory House, she noticed that the boys were washing finger marks off doors and otherwise sprucing up the house for the Denfelds, who would move in at the end of the day.

The brief change-of-command ceremony took place in the Secretary's office in the Main Navy Building at 10:00 a.m. Mrs. Nimitz and Nancy were present and, to Nimitz's special gratification, so were Admiral Spruance, now president of the Naval War College, and Admiral Blandy, who had become Commander in Chief of the Atlantic Fleet. After the reading of orders and brief speeches by Secretary Sullivan and Admirals Nimitz and Denfeld, the Secretary led the way into a large office where movie- and still-cameras photographed a repetition of highlights of the ceremony.

The Nimitz family then proceeded through the corridors, past throngs of applauding officers, enlisted men, and civilians. At the main entrance, on Constitution Avenue, a navy band and a marine guard gave the prescribed honors, and the Nimitzes climbed into Chrissy, the family Chrysler, now nearly ten years old and looking her age. Nancy took the wheel and, with a cough and a wheeze, Chrissy left the curb. Among the cheering crowd on the sidewalk, Nimitz recognized several senators and representatives before whom he had frequently testified on Capitol Hill.

Nancy was going along, as she had in 1942, to help with the driving. Mary Nimitz was already in California, attending the Dominican Convent Upper School. Admiral and Mrs. Nimitz, Nancy, and Freckles, the aging cocker spaniel, made it in Chrissy on December 15 from Washington to within nine miles of Raleigh, North Carolina, where they all checked into a motel. That evening Catherine and Chester began keeping their first diary, a composition book bearing the title *Life Begins at One Hundred Seventeen* (their combined ages). The first entry was made by Catherine, and it began:

This has been a momentous day. The great event has taken place and tonight, despite rain and cold air, we are happy! For the first time in many years Chester has little responsibility. Nancy, Freckles, Chester and I are headed south, then west to California and our hearts are young and gay.

Chester, after describing the change-of-command ceremony and the departure from the Navy Building, concluded the entry with:

I feel as if a great burden has been lifted from my shoulders and that Catherine & I are just beginning to live. With a wonderful family of children and grandchildren—and with that world before us—how can we fail to have a full and happy life?

# CHAPTER 26

# FROM THE NAVY DEPARTMENT TO THE UNITED NATIONS

THE NIMITZ FAMILY'S cross-country trek, following the admiral's retirement as Chief of Naval Operations, ended on December 21, 1947, at the Lay residence in San Diego, home port of Commander James Lay's destroyer *Orleck*. On hand to greet the new arrivals, besides Jim and Kate, were Jimmie Lay, now a 17-month-old dynamo, and Mary Nimitz, just down from her convent school at San Rafael and proud of her report that showed excellent grades. Poor Freckles had to be boarded out because nobody was sure how he and Dopey, the Lays' cocker spaniel, would get along. Of the 1938 Chrysler, Mrs. Nimitz wrote: "Chrissy made a splendid record on the time out. How proud I am of our old car: Not a murmur of complaint on all the 2,940-mile journey."

In the following days Granddaddy Nimitz took Jimmie on several walks, and newsmen came out to interview the admiral and take dozens of pictures of him and Jimmie together. On Christmas morning Jimmie was, of course, the center of attention, his father taking movies as the youngster opened his presents. "All of us had lovely gifts," Mrs. Nimitz wrote, "and it was a happy day." The admiral gave Mrs. Nimitz an evening bag of Chinese brocade in rust and beige. There came pouring in for the Nimitzes hundreds of letters and telegrams with greetings and good wishes.

Kate was pregnant again and tired easily. Her mother realized that a week of entertaining guests, even members of her own family, was quite enough for her. So on the morning of December 28, the travelers boarded Chrissy again and, with Mary as an additional passenger, headed for San Francisco. There, on the afternoon of the 29th, they checked into the Fairmont Hotel.

The next day Admiral Nimitz reported in at 12th Naval District headquarters in the Federal Building, where he found an office and quantities of mail awaiting him and learned that his personal aide was to be Lieutenant Lennon T. Paige of the Naval Reserve. On New Year's Day he and Mrs. Nimitz took Nancy to the Oakland ferry for the eastbound train that would carry her back to her library post in Washington. A week later the Nimitzes, using the navy car and driver that had been assigned to the admiral, drove to San Rafael to return Mary to school. They next visited Oakland Naval Hospital, where Catherine had worked during the war.

The Nimitzes were delighted to see again their friends who were then living in the San Francisco Bay area. Of the many invitations extended to them, one of the first they accepted was from Vice Admiral and Mrs. Jesse B. Oldendorf. As commandant of the Western Sea Frontier, Oldendorf occupied Quarters One, an imposing house on Yerba Buena Island, in San Francisco Bay. The Nimitzes little dreamed that eventually they would themselves be residents of Quarters One.

Chester soon began to display the restlessness of a man who, after a busy career involving important responsibilities, has nothing much to do. Tiring of the idle life in San Francisco, he moved with Catherine across the bay to the Claremont Hotel in Berkeley. There they had many friends, notably Bruce and Margaret Canaga and Y. C. and Eching Woo. Since Chester and Bruce, as classmates, had sailed to the Orient together in 1905 aboard the *Ohio*, their paths had crossed many times and their friendship had grown ever closer. Catherine met the Woos during World War II. From distinguished Chinese families, they had come to the United States shortly before the war. Y. C. Woo was a banker. Catherine called Eching "the most beautiful, brilliant woman I have ever known."

Chester and Catherine began seriously hunting for their hearts' desire, a house of their own, something they had never had. Chester specified only two requirements for the house. It must have three bathrooms, because he didn't want to share a bathroom with his grandchildren, who, he hoped, would be visiting them often, and it must have a long view—preferably of the sea.

Before the end of January, Admiral and Mrs. Nimitz were again heading for San Diego in the old Chrysler, which was beginning to disintegrate. The occasion for this trip was to look after Kate. She was expecting twins, and Jim had been ordered to Japan. So as to be in a position to help without putting extra strain on the Lay household, the Nimitzes took residence in a San Diego hotel.

The twins, Chester Nimitz Lay and Richard Freeman Lay, arrived on March 18, 1948. The newspapers made quite a story of the event and, as soon as practical, news photographers were at the Lay residence to take pictures of Granddaddy Nimitz with Jimmie and the twins. Kate wrote disgustedly to Jim: "You didn't even get a by-line. These were the admiral's twins. They had to mention my name, but they didn't mention your name at all."

During this period, Admiral Nimitz received large quantities of mail, most of it forwarded from Washington or San Francisco, and numerous invitations to speak and to participate in various ceremonies. He was particularly pleased to receive from Earl Warren, Governor of California, an invitation to become a regent of the University of California. He accepted at once. "Chester's news that he has been made a Regent of the University," wrote Mrs. Nimitz, "pleases me more than words can express. It somehow solidifies our place in the Bay area!"

Another letter reaching San Diego at this time proved less pleasing to the admiral. It was from an obviously virtuous but confused woman who had belatedly come upon the opening installment of "Admiral Halsey Tells His Story" in *The Saturday Evening Post.* What particularly caught her attention and shocked her was Halsey's statement: "There are exceptions, of course, but as a general rule, I never trust a fighting man who doesn't smoke or drink."

Somehow the good woman got it into her head that the author was Admiral Nimitz, and she was writing to upbraid him. "Dear Admiral," she began, "I have always admired you, but I am very much disappointed in you. I have just finished reading an article in the Saturday Evening Post in which you said that you never trust a fighting man who doesn't smoke or drink." She went on to say that she had seen his picture in the newspaper "with those darling little twins" and had understood that he was supposed to be a good influence. Now he had spoiled it all by making that awful statement.

Ordinarily such crank mail merely amused Nimitz, but this letter annoyed him, possibly because he disapproved of the Halsey memoir and did not like being credited with writing it. Without delay, he sat down and wrote a reply: "Dear Madam, you have obviously confused me with another naval personage. I did not write that article, and I am sure that a woman of your obvious rectitude would want to correct the mistaken impression."

Shortly afterward Admiral Nimitz, accompanied by Mrs. Nimitz, went off to fill a speaking engagement. In their absence, Kate was instructed to open all mail. "About a week later," Kate recalls, "came this thick, thick letter from this woman, and I said to myself, 'This is going to be good. She's going to grovel for ten pages.' I opened it. No letter at all, but out fell a tract, 'Steps to Christ, Army and Navy Edition.'"

A highlight for the Nimitzes in the spring of 1948 was the Texas Festival, which combined a pilgrimage to the Alamo, a fiesta celebrating the Battle of San Jacinto, and the presentation by the Navy of the old battleship *Texas* to be a state monument. At Admiral Nimitz's request, Secretary Sullivan sent a plane to take him and Mrs. Nimitz from San Diego to Texas and back. For several days, in San Antonio and Houston, the admiral was the center piece in parades, celebrations, and dinners. At the presentation of the *Texas*, his five-star flag was broken at the main. After the celebrations, the Nimitzes visited Fredericksburg and Kerrville, where they greeted all the admirals's friends and relatives, including half brother Otto and half sister Dora. Chester made a special point of calling on his old teacher, Miss Susan Moore.

When the Nimitzes arrived back in southern California, they helped Kate move with her babies to a rented house in Coronado, and then climbed into Chrissy, this time with Freckles aboard, and headed back toward Berkeley and the Claremont Hotel. It was a gloomy trip. Chester was glum, seeing nothing ahead but more idleness and a stuffy hotel existence. Catherine shared his distaste for hotel life, particularly for having their meals in the dining room continually interrupted by people who recognized the admiral and came over to chat. Most distressing were the visits of parents who wanted to talk about sons lost in the Pacific War.

Toward the end of May, the Nimitzes' search for a house came to a happy conclusion. Unable for a long time to find anything suitable, they had become discouraged. They had in fact resorted to looking at rental property when the real estate agent suggested to Mrs. Nimitz that she ought to inspect a house that was for sale on Santa Barbara Road in North Berkeley. "I did," wrote Catherine in the diary, "I saw, I wanted!! Called Chester to come home and look and he saw and wanted. We drove directly to the office and deposited $1000 and made an offer. The rest of the day we hoped and hoped and prayed."

What they had found at 728 Santa Barbara Road was a large Spanish-style residence, one of a number of attractive houses set back from the sidewalk and fairly close together. At the rear of the lots, the ground dropped away sharply in a series of terraces, providing the view that Admiral Nimitz demanded. Across the back of 728, picture windows—in the living room, in the dining room, and in the breakfast room—afforded to westward a breathtaking panorama of San Francisco Bay. In the middle distance were the Golden Gate and Golden Gate Bridge, and beyond them a stretch of the broad Pacific was visible.

The asking price was $42,000, which was more than the Nimitzes could afford to pay, but at the agent's suggestion they offered $27,000. The owner, who had been called to Chicago to take an executive position with Sears, Roebuck and Company, made a counterproposal of $32,500 for house, drapes, carpets, and stove, and the Nimitzes accepted it, paying $20,500 cash and taking out a mortgage for the rest. The cash payment was from their wartime savings. The admiral, with only light personal expenses in Pearl Harbor and Guam, had allotted much of his pay to Mrs. Nimitz, who had squirreled away most of it for just such an opportunity as this.

Admiral Nimitz could hardly wait for the former owners of 728 Santa Barbara Road to get out. As they were leaving by the front door, the Nimitzes were moving in the back door. They were in their own home at last! Chester and Catherine at once began buying furniture, installing bookcases, painting patio chairs, and working on the back terraces. They called their new house Longview.

Though the Nimitzes acquired a part-time maid and a part-time gardener, they did most of the housework and yard work themselves. "The admiral was a mad gardener," said Mrs. Nimitz. "He gardened and he built compost heaps, and the soil that he finally got for the place was the most beautiful soil I've ever seen. You could crumble it so beautifully. And he took such pride in the things he planted."

Mary, having won the only "general excellence" award in her high school, came to spend the summer with her parents. In mid-summer Chet arrived in Berkeley to be executive officer of the University of California NROTC unit, which his father had founded in 1926. With him were Joan and the girls, Frannie, aged 8, and Betsy, 2. Joan was again pregnant. The Chester Nimitz

Juniors moved into the Santa Barbara Road house, and the Chester Nimitz Seniors happily baby-sat for them while they hunted for a house of their own. Nancy wrote from Washington that she was planning to come out to the West Coast to join this gathering of the Nimitz clan and look for a job.

Chet and Joan soon found a house and moved in. With the beginning of the fall semester, Chet was delighted, as his father had been, with the interesting new friends he met at the university. Like his parents, Chet loved music, and he was a skilled violinist. It is not surprising that he soon encountered the internationally famed Griller Quartet, then in residence at Berkeley. The next day, calling on his parents, he exclaimed, "God, what a wonderful time I've had! Yesterday I went up to listen to the Griller Quartet practice at the University of California in their music room. I've never heard such music."

Chet wrote a note of appreciation to Sydney Griller, first violinist and head of the group, and Griller invited him to come to their rehearsals whenever he pleased. This was the beginning of a long, friendly association between the Griller and Nimitz families. The quartet sometimes came and rehearsed in the Nimitzes' big living room, and Sydney and his wife, Honor, bought a house only a block from the Nimitzes. The admiral, always fond of children, became a sort of surrogate grandfather to their little daughter Catherine.

The elder Nimitzes combined hard work with an active social life. Besides gardening, furniture-painting, and general repair work, the admiral laid a floor in his unfinished attic. Mrs. Nimitz cooked, did the laundry, cleaned house, and, to save money, made most of her own clothes. The admiral was in constant demand for speeches and public ceremonies. He was made an honorary member of the famous Bohemian Club.

The Nimitzes had a steady stream of callers. They entertained at home most evenings when they were not themselves being entertained elsewhere. They went to most of the concerts of the San Francisco Symphony Orchestra, occasionally attended a play, opera, or movie, and were present at the major university athletic events. They nevertheless found time to baby-sit for the younger Nimitzes.

In the afternoon of November 6, 1948, Joan was rushed to the hospital. Her mother-in-law recorded in the Nimitz diary the big event of the evening: "Today proved to be *the* day! Sarah Catherine arrived at 7:40 p.m. safe and sound. At first I think her young father was disappointed but his great relief over Joan's safety and the fact that the baby was all right more than made up for any regrets. I am so pleased my little granddaughter shares my name! It's an honor for me." The admiral recorded that the baby weighed 6 pounds, 13 ounces.

At 11:30 a.m. on Thanksgiving Day, November 25, Nancy arrived at Santa Barbara Road, having driven alone across country and, en route to Berkeley, visited the Lay family at Coronado. A couple of days later, Grandmother Nimitz, exhausted from looking after children, grandchildren, and guests, and helping her husband to unwind, gave up. Leaving Nancy to look after her father, she retreated to the Oak Knoll hospital for a checkup and a week's rest.

To Nancy, newly arrived on the scene, it was more obvious than to the others that Admiral Nimitz was an unhappy man. For all his activity, he was quite simply bored. After years of heavy responsibility, of meeting great challenges, of making momentous decisions, he could now scarcely endure the futility of his daily pursuits. To lend them apparent weight, he scheduled everything strictly. Shortly after Nancy arrived at Berkeley, for example, he proposed a pleasure expedition to Drake's Bay, where Sir Francis Drake is supposed to have repaired his ships in 1579. Everybody agreed to the proposal, whereupon the admiral announced, "We will leave at 11:05."

At 11:05 Nimitz was seated in the front-hall chair wearing his battered felt hat and with his cane across his knees, extremely irritated that not everybody was ready. The party was under way in a quarter of an hour, but for Nimitz, accustomed to punctual obedience to his orders, that was a quarter of an hour too late. His day was ruined. With unrelenting sullenness he very nearly ruined everybody else's day.

Nancy regarded her father's intense dissatisfaction with the life he led as a kind of flaw in his character. This she defined as a "restless need to have an enterprise worthy of him to do, an inability to generate it within himself, and a kind of cold rage at not having something which demanded his effort."

The irony of the situation was that Admiral Nimitz had everything he once thought he needed to make him happy. He and Catherine were in good health. They had a home they loved. For the first time in 15 years they had all their children nearby. More grandchildren were arriving to comfort their old age. Some of the admiral's closest former associates in the Navy had retired and settled in the neighborhood: Charles Lockwood at Los Gatos, Kelly Turner at Monterey, Raymond Spruance at Pebble Beach.

There were other causes for satisfaction. His son-in-law, Commander Lay, was promoted to captain. Sergeant Cozard, whom the Nimitzes thought of as almost a member of the family, arrived in California to drive the admiral's official car. He retained the punctual habits of the Washington days. When practical, he made a dry run of any expedition ordered by Nimitz so as to fix exactly the times of departure and arrival.

In January 1949, Secretary Sullivan sent his personal plane to Moffett Field, California, to bring Admiral Nimitz to participate with him in President Truman's inaugural ceremonies. In Washington, Nimitz was made comfortable in the Secretary's yacht *Sequoia*. On Inauguration Day, the 20th, he sat on the President's platform to observe Mr. Truman take the oath of office and deliver his address. In the subsequent parade, Nimitz sat in the car with Sullivan, who was marshal of the 6th parade division. Also in the car were Bill Halsey, now a fleet admiral, and Archer Vandegrift, who had retired, the first marine officer to attain the rank of four-star general.

That evening Admiral Nimitz attended the President's reception, held at the National Art Gallery. He wrote in the diary: "Pres. Truman was very cordial when he saw me and took both my hands in his. He seemed bright and alert and completely impervious to the fatigue which was evident in Mrs. T's face." After a brief appearance at the inaugural ball and a drink at the Carroll Arms with the Texas Cavaliers, who had come from San Antonio to march in the parade, Nimitz got to the airport and enplaned at midnight. When he reached Moffett Field at noon the next day, Paige and Cozard were there to meet him.*

Thursday, March 10, 1949, was for Admiral Nimitz a busy and, in at least one respect, a momentous day. He recorded it in the diary:

> Mostly cloudy and rain all day. Spent all forenoon and first half of afternoon in S. F. at my office and in attending meeting of World Affairs Council of Northern California. Called on by Mr. Buckley and one other (a vice president of Anglo American Bank) official of American President Line and invited to become a director. Was called on Long Distance by Ad. Denfeld—CNO and asked if I were interested in being the Supervisor of Elections in Kashmir to determine whether that state should join Pakistan or India. Said I was interested if I could take Mother along. State Dept will call me at office about noon tomorrow. Admiral S. S. Robison arrived in midafternoon to spend several days with us. CWJr. & Joan came up to have a drink with us.

Mrs. Nimitz later recalled how she received the news about Kashmir:

> Admiral Robison had just arrived in this rain and I had just given him a highball, when I saw my husband coming up the walk. I went to open the door for him. As he came through the door, he thrust a paper in my hand and said, "Don't say anything to Admiral Robison." As he went to talk to the admiral, I opened the paper and here was this suggestion. You can imagine what it did to me. We'd just bought the house. We hadn't even got it fully settled. We had all our children around us for the first time in years, and here he was thinking of going. Well, I didn't say a word, but my mind was working a mile a minute. I don't know what I gave them for supper, but I did it.

Nimitz spent all the next day in San Francisco, mostly entertaining his old friend and patron, Robison, now a widower. They made calls, lunched at the Bohemian Club, and attended a stag cocktail party at the Presidio Officers' Club. Nimitz managed however to get a call through to the Navy Department and learned that his proposed title was Plebiscite Administrator under the United Nations Commission on Kashmir. He was at his office at noon to receive the expected call from the State Department. The caller was Assistant Secretary of State Dean Rusk. Rusk asked Nimitz to let the Department know by noon Monday whether he would accept the appointment.

Late Saturday morning Admiral Robison left the Nimitzes and went on to

---

* Characteristically, the Nimitzes loaded their diary with names—of families they called on or who came to call on them, of interesting persons they met at parties, of tradesmen they dealt with, of navy doctors and dentists who treated them, and of pilots and other crew members of planes they flew in.

visit elsewhere. Chester and Catherine worked in their garden all afternoon, talking, resolving the question concerning their future. "I really don't think there was much resolving," said Catherine. "I knew what the answer was going to be. It's so much nicer to take it pleasantly." In fact, Catherine was not utterly opposed to the appointment. She had her own streak of romance and adventure and had begun to be charmed at the notion of traveling to far-off and exotic lands.

That evening Chester wrote in the diary: "Mother and I have decided to make myself available for the U.N. job of plebiscite administrator for Kashmir and I will send the State Department a dispatch tomorrow."

On Monday, March 21, Admiral Nimitz received word that Pakistan and India had consented to his nomination, and U.N. Secretary-General Trygve Lie asked him to come to New York at the earliest moment for consultations. Nimitz telephoned Secretary Sullivan, requesting a plane for Wednesday night, March 23, and the Secretary agreed to send it.

All was now hustle and bustle as Chester and Catherine got out the suitcases and started packing, for how long only heaven knew. The Woos called and left farewell gifts. The Canagas came over Wednesday to see them off. The Nimitzes left Longview that day at 4:00 p.m. with two carloads of baggage. Nancy would be alone in the big house with only Freckles to keep her company. Chet and Joan promised to look in on her regularly.

The plane took off from Moffett Field at 5:30 p.m. with the Nimitzes, Lieutenant Paige, and Sergeant Cozard as passengers. They arrived at Washington's National Airport at nine o'clock the next morning. There followed a round of immunizations and applications for passports. Nimitz called on Secretary of the Navy Sullivan and Chief of Naval Operations Denfeld and was disappointed to learn that he could not have an all-navy team for the Kashmir operation because service people on active duty could not receive additional compensation, except in the form of a per diem allowance, a restriction that did not apply to himself. In the afternoon he made a call on the new Secretary of State, Dean Acheson, who turned him over to State Department officials for a briefing on the situation in Kashmir.

When Pakistan separated from India in 1947, the adherence of the state of Kashmir was in dispute, the Maharaja of Kashmir favoring union with India. To prevent such a union, Pakistani Moslems invaded Kashmir and threatened Srinagar, its capital. At that, the Maharaja formally joined his state to India and appealed for help from the Indian government, which flew in troops who defended the city. War raged in Kashmir until late 1948, when India brought the case before the U.N. Security Council. A U.N. Commission for India and Pakistan arranged a cease-fire and directed that the future of Kashmir should be decided by plebiscite. India and Pakistan had agreed to negotiate a truce and to withdraw their troops from Kashmir to facilitate the holding of the plebiscite, which it would be Admiral Nimitz's task to administer.

During the next two days, Nimitz conferred with Indian and Pakistani diplomats, who assured him that their governments would do everything possible to make his mission a success. At the State Department he received instruction from officials experienced in plebiscite administration. He visited the naval hospital at Bethesda to call on Admiral King but found that he was out, went to the White House to attend the awarding of a third Distinguished Service Medal to Admiral Leahy, and received a delegation that wanted him to add his signature to a scroll honoring General MacArthur.

On Monday, March 28, the Nimitzes went by train to New York, where they were conducted to quarters arranged for them at the River Club. Admiral Nimitz then called on the American representatives to the United Nations, Vice Admiral Bernhard H. Bieri and Senator Warren R. Austin, at the U.S. delegation headquarters on Park Avenue. He next reported to Trygve Lie and his executive assistant, Andrew W. Cordier. He ended his first day in New York conferring with the U.N. plebiscite experts.

Nimitz spent nearly all of Tuesday at the U.N. headquarters at Lake Success. Mrs. Nimitz came out and had a look at her husband's new office, which was quite the finest he had ever enjoyed. They were overwhelmed to learn that the admiral's salary from the United Nations was to be $26,000 a year, plus a $20 per diem allowance. This, added to his $15,000 annual salary from the Navy, was more money than they had ever expected to see. It was, in fact, for 1949, a very comfortable income.

With U.N. help, Admiral Nimitz began assembling a staff. Major General Harry J. Maloney, USA, Retired, consented to serve as deputy administrator. Nimitz's staff, which he intended to limit to a couple of dozen people, was comprised of citizens of the United States, Canada, France, China, and Great Britain, among them experts in every phase of the task with which he would be confronted. Because of the difficulty of paying Lieutenant Paige's salary, Nimitz sent him back to California and eventually sent Sergeant Cozard back also, intending to rely entirely on U.N. employees.

In his first enthusiasm, after he had mastered his basic problems, Nimitz dashed off an article, "The Task of the Plebiscite Mission," for the *United Nations Bulletin*. "I have already met some representatives of India and Pakistan," he wrote, "and I have been impressed by their ardent desire to secure a peaceful solution to this problem. I must say that with the good-will and support of all concerned, I am confident and optimistic about the outcome."

Until mid-April Admiral Nimitz was expecting to leave for Kashmir with Mrs. Nimitz and staff members by the end of the month. Then he was advised not to reach India before the truce agreements had been signed. By late April the signing date appeared receding into the future, as both interested nations raised objections to the truce provisions offered by the United Nations Commission on Pakistan and India. Nimitz kept setting later target dates for the departure of the Nimitzes and his staff for the subcontinent.

Despite the frustration caused by the delayed truce, Admiral Nimitz was happy in his service with the United Nations. He felt that he was again doing something really worthwhile. He attended many conferences and labored hard at planning, but enjoyed the work. He relished his discussions with the delegates and with the U.N. officers. When he had a little spare time, he would sit in on sessions of the Security Council or of various committees. Mrs. Nimitz spent much of her time at home painting or studying Hindustani, but she frequently visited the United Nations and sat with her husband as a spectator at meetings that were open to the public. For both of them a favorite was Eleanor Roosevelt's Human Rights Commission.

Admiral Nimitz abandoned his dieting so that he could enjoy the conversations at lunch in the U.N. dining rooms. There, he joined fellow U.N. personnel, or invited friends who lived in or were passing through the New York area to lunch with him and Catherine and then be given a quick tour of the U.N. headquarters. One day, for some reason, a bumpkin was seated at the Nimitz table. Looking about disapprovingly at the various skin colors in the room, he asked, "Do they allow foreigners to eat in here?" Catherine replied quietly, "There are no foreigners in the United Nations."

The Nimitzes were frequently invited to formal dinners given by delegates and others associated with the U.N. One dinner Catherine would never forget was given on the evening of April 26, 1949, by Secretary-General Trygve Lie to honor the outgoing president of the General Assembly, Herbert Vere Evatt, of Australia. Among the guests were Mrs. Ogden Reid, Hector McNeil, the Andrew Cordiers, Dean Rusk, Chinese ambassador Wellington Koo, and Andrei Gromyko, deputy Soviet foreign minister and chief Russian delegate at the United Nations. This was a time of international tension because of the blockade imposed on Berlin by the Soviet Union. Gromyko, known among the English-speaking delegates as "Old Stone Face" or "The Abominable 'No' Man," was believed to be one of the authors of the blockade.

As Catherine Nimitz, feeling elegant in her new white nylon evening gown, came out of the ladies' cloakroom, Chester stepped up to her and said, "Do you know who your dinner partner's going to be?"

"Is it going to be Gromyko?"

"Yes, it is."

"Well, I think I can get on with Gromyko very well."

When they went in to dinner, Gromyko was waiting to pull Catherine's chair out for her. As he sat down, she turned to him and said, "Let's drink a toast to peace."

"Let's," he responded, and they did.

Catherine asked him if Mrs. Gromyko was coming to the United States. He replied in a rather pained and tired voice, which made Catherine realize that he had been asked the same question many times by people who apparently supposed that Mrs. Gromyko stayed away out of disdain or mistrust. Gromyko explained that their son was getting ready to enter the University of Moscow and that only a Russian prep school taught the preparatory courses required for a Russian university. Mrs. Gromyko felt that she ought to stay to provide a home for the boy and to help him with his studies.

Catherine replied that she understood perfectly. Many a time she had had to give up being with Chester because their children were in school or getting ready for college.

Trygve Lie, who was sitting on Catherine's left, began talking business to Gromyko, who fell silent and looked annoyed. Finally, Gromyko said, "Let us not talk business at dinner."

"No," said Catherine, "let's not talk business at dinner. Let's talk about music and flowers."

Gromyko let out a sigh and said, "Yes, let's."

Mr. Lie, laughing a little sheepishly, turned away and began talking to the person on his left. Catherine asked Mr. Gromyko which he knew most about, music or flowers.

"Neither," replied Gromyko.

"Well, then," said Catherine, "I will proceed to tell you some good navy stories," and she launched into one of Chester's favorites. Presently the diners were startled and all heads turned as Old Stone Face broke into a hearty laugh. Catherine afterward remarked that she considered that quite an achievement on her part.

After dinner, the ladies retired to the drawing room, and the gentlemen disappeared to the upper part of the house. Hours passed. The ladies were worn out and ready to go to bed when the gentlemen finally came back down at 12:30.

During the drive home, the Nimitzes were talking about their experiences. Cozard, their driver, came up with an experience of his own. A gregarious fellow, he had spent the evening chatting with U.N. chauffeurs from all over the world. Suddenly he noticed the Russian chauffeurs off by themselves. He went over and asked them to come and join the group. They replied very quietly that they were not allowed to.

A few days later, when Catherine and Chester were lunching at the United Nations, Cordier joined them. "Oh, Andy," said Catherine, "I didn't have any difficulty with Gromyko. We got on beautifully."

Cordier looked at her quizzically. "You think we weren't watching you?" he said. "You were put there for that purpose. We were watching you very closely. It might interest you to know that on that night we took Gromyko upstairs after dinner and we broke the Berlin blockade."

While waiting to depart for India, the Nimitzes lived briefly at the River Club and at Hotel Chatham in New York City and stayed at the homes of friends. As the wait stretched on indefinitely, they sought more permanent quarters, and succeeded in having assigned to them two large, comfortable rooms in The Chimneys, a fine old English home that had been brought over from England, piece by piece, and rebuilt by a wealthy widow at Port Washington, Long Island. It had been rented by the Office of Naval Research for the Special Training Devices Center, which used it as a commissioned officers' mess and bachelor officers' quarters. Among the bachelors were several Waves and women scientists.

Of The Chimneys, Catherine wrote in the diary: "What a beautiful spot this is! Somehow it seems sacrilege to move this lovely old house from England where it belongs. The beautiful carving on windows and doors, the leaded windows and last but not least the magnificent chimneys! Never have I seen anything so utilitarian so beautiful."

As always, Chester managed to do a good deal of walking, especially on weekends. In late afternoons he and Catherine usually swam, in indoor pools in cold weather and in Long Island Sound when it was warm. Chester was rarely without access to a horseshoe pit. Most of the Nimitzes' weekends were devoted to social activities. They had many friends in the New York-Long Island area, and through their U.N. and naval connections they made many more. Several times they were invited to join yachting parties on the Sound.

Among the friends of whom the Nimitzes saw a great deal were the Gilbert Darlingtons. Dr. Darlington was an unusual combination of devout clergyman and highly successful financier. He had stopped preaching in churches because of deafness, but he remained a chaplain in the inactive Naval Reserve, and he was chaplain general of both the Military Order of the World Wars and the Naval Order of the United States. Since 1920 he had been treasurer of the American Bible Society.

In June 1949 the Bible Society promoted a national radio broadcast, with President Truman as the principal speaker. Dr. Darlington asked Admiral Nimitz to make a five-minute talk preceding the President's address. Nimitz protested that he was not very familiar with the Bible and had scarcely entered a church, except for weddings and funerals, since leaving the Naval Academy. "In fact," said the admiral, "I don't know whether I've ever been baptized."

Darlington drew from Nimitz an acknowledgment that reading the Bible, with its teachings of morality, devotion, and brotherhood, could improve society, and asked him to put that thought into a brief speech. Nimitz continued to protest that he was not the man for the assignment, but Darlington kept on insisting until Nimitz, ever reluctant to disappoint a friend, finally gave in. He worked on his speech, anxious not to give a false impression of his own beliefs and convictions. "I'm sure I had plenty of listeners who were waiting to hear Truman," he afterward wrote. "I tried to frame my talk in such a way that I could not be accused of being a hypocrite."

As it turned out, Nimitz's fatal admission, as far as Dr. Darlington was concerned, was that he did not know whether he had ever been baptized. Darlington was sure that if Nimitz had been baptized he would know about it. Therefore, he evidently had not, and he absolutely must be baptized without delay. Nimitz at first thought he could brush off the suggestion with a smile, but he underestimated the good doctor. Darlington at every opportunity renewed his campaign to have the admiral baptized. Nimitz at last began to lose patience. Not willing to go through a ceremony that implied doctrinal convictions he did not hold, he grimly told Catherine, "I won't be baptized." Then he added hopefully, "I think I probably *was* baptized."

"Why don't you write to Texas," said Catherine, "and ask whether you have been baptized?"

So Chester wrote to an uncle who was a judge, and asked him to look into the matter. "You needn't be too fussy about the sources," he wrote. "Just be sure you find the records."

The story got around the Nimitz family, and all recognized the parallel with the situation in Clarence Day's *Life with Father*. "O *Life with Father!*" they would say. "We're going to get Father baptized!"

"If I get baptized," said the admiral to Mrs. Nimitz, "you're going to be baptized too."

"I didn't shoot my mouth off in this situation," replied Catherine cheerfully. "I'm not going to have anything to do with this."

At last there came a reply from the Texas uncle. Chester had been baptized as an infant in the Lutheran Church. Dr. Darlington, appeased by this news, abandoned his campaign.

Admiral Nimitz had never ceased to keep himself informed concerning national defense policy, particularly as it affected the Navy. He was much interested in the *United States*, a 65,000-ton carrier whose keel was laid at Newport News, Virginia, on April 18, 1949. She was being built partly on his advice. Before his retirement as Chief of Naval Operations, he had advised Secretary Sullivan that the Navy needed carriers large enough to handle planes that could carry the 10,000-pound atomic bomb. An important reason for giving this advice was that the Air Force's new strategic bomber, the B-36, did not have the range to reach all parts of the Soviet Union from the United States.

When Sullivan requested funds to build the first oversized carrier, the *United States*, the Air Force hotly objected, because it regarded strategic bombing and delivery of the atomic bomb as its own monopoly. Secretary of Defense Forrestal, to head off an acrimonious interservice debate, met at Key West with the Joint Chiefs of Staff to make decisions regarding service roles and missions. Out of this meeting came an agreement that, while strategic bombing was primarily a function of the Air Force, the Navy and Marine Corps should be permitted to attack, with or without atomic weapons, any targets, as necessary, to accomplish their missions. The corollary of this agreement was that the Navy could build big carriers.

After funds for the new carrier had been allocated but before she was laid down, Forrestal, mentally and physically exhausted, resigned as Secretary of Defense. Naval officers in general looked upon his successor, Louis A. Johnson, with misgiving. Johnson had been an army officer in World War I and Assistant Secretary of War in the late 1930s. He had pushed the development of the B-17 and, since World War II, had been a director of the company that built the B-36. He was said to be in favor of taking naval aviation out of the Navy and putting it in the Air Force, and of transferring the marines from the Navy to the Army. A less complex and less sensitive man than Forrestal, he entered upon his office determined, as he said, to crack heads together, if necessary, to attain closer unification of the services and to build up the Air Force.

One of Johnson's first acts on becoming Secretary of Defense was to stop work on the *United States* and cancel plans for her completion. Secretary Sullivan resigned in protest. In his letter of resignation, dated April 26, 1949, which he released to the press, Sullivan told Johnson that scrapping the super-carrier "represents the first attempt ever made in this country to prevent the development of a powerful weapon. The conviction that this will result in a renewed effort to abolish the Marine Corps and to transfer all naval and marine aviation elsewhere adds to my anxiety."

In the morning of May 3, Nimitz at his U.N. office received a telephone call from Sullivan, who asked Nimitz to meet him at La Guardia Airport. The ex-Secretary arrived there just before noon and invited the admiral into his car. Leaving public life for good, he wanted to say goodby to his old friend with whom he had served in the Navy Department. Bitterly, he related to Nimitz the details of why the scrapping had been ordered and told him of other Johnson plans, which he deemed dangerous for the national defense.

Sullivan's successor was Francis P. Matthews, a banker and business man from Omaha, Nebraska. Appointed by President Truman on Secretary John-son's recommendation, Matthews knew next to nothing about the Navy. He confessed that his closest contact with sea power consisted of having once taken the oars of a rowboat. But Matthews was Johnson's man. He believed that Johnson could do no wrong and hence he was useful to the Defense Sec-retary.

Forrestal never recovered from the exhaustion with which he laid down the burdens of office. Beset with mental difficulties, he entered the naval hos-pital at Bethesda, Maryland. In the night of May 22, he went into a little kitchen to which he had access, opened the window, and jumped out. The next day Mrs. Nimitz wrote in the diary: "Word of Jim Forrestal's death reached us. Poor man, he had a heavier load than he could carry. He has done well by the Navy."

In August 1949 amendments to the National Security Act became law. These amendments, which Sullivan had opposed, replaced the National Mili-tary Establishment with a Department of Defense and brought Army, Navy, and Air Force into closer unity. The result was far from a complete merger of the services, but it increased Johnson's authority over the military departments and provided for the head of one of the services to act as chairman of the Joint Chiefs of Staff. That office was to rotate among the services, the first to serve being General Omar N. Bradley.

Though in August the Russians exploded an atomic bomb, Johnson per-sisted in economizing. He refused to spend all of the President's military budget, which was dangerously skimpy to begin with. Since most of his "sav-ings" were to be achieved by cutting expenditures for naval air, it was apparent that the Navy soon would be unable to support offensive air operations. Army spokesmen, including General Bradley, were recommending that the Army take over all amphibious operations. Some Air Force officers favored restricting the Navy to control of sea communications and antisubmarine warfare. These officers advocated limiting the Navy's air operations to hunting down submarines with small planes that would fly from a few escort carriers. Johnson seemed inclined toward these extremes, and Matthews was obediently following his lead.

Veteran aviator Captain John G. Crommelin was the first naval officer to sound the alarm publicly. On September 10, 1949, in defiance of regulations, he publicly charged the Air Force with attempting to dominate the defense budget and take over all air power, and he accused Johnson of trying to establish a dictatorship within the Defense Department. He pointed out that two of the Joint Chiefs of Staff with a "landlocked concept of national defense" could always outvote the Navy.

Matthews, supposing Crommelin to be a lone complainer, asked the senior naval commanders to comment on his allegations. Vice Admiral Gerald F. Bogan, another veteran naval aviator, then commanding a task force in the Pacific Fleet, seized the opportunity. To Matthews' surprise, Bogan wrote that he agreed completely with Crommelin. He added that in his opinion the "balderdash" that passed for unification in Washington was endangering the nation, and that morale in the Navy was lower than it had been at any time in his 33-year career.

Admiral Arthur Radford, then CinCPac, and, since the death of Mitscher and the retirement of Towers, considered the Navy's foremost aviator, endorsed Bogan's letter, adding that most naval officers agreed with Crommelin. Admiral Denfeld, not an aviator, attached a final endorsement, concurring with Radford. When Crommelin on October 4 leaked Bogan's letter with its endorsements to the press, Matthews angrily told Denfeld that his value as Chief of Naval Operations had probably been impaired.

Representative Carl Vinson's House Armed Services Committee, which had been investigating the B-36, expanded its inquiry to include the whole question of military unification. As first officer witness on this subject, it summoned Admiral Radford, who proved a most effective advocate for the naval point of view. He called the B-36 a "billion-dollar blunder," a popular "symbol of a theory of warfare, the atomic blitz, which promises...a cheap and easy victory if war should come."

To enable less articulate officers to make a good impression on the committee, Denfeld brought the brilliant Captain Arleigh Burke to the Pentagon to prepare their testimony. Admiral Radford remained in Washington to advise witnesses and otherwise help to strengthen the Navy's case. Representative Sterling Cole, of the Armed Services Committee, wrote to most of the top admirals asking for their views. Admiral Nimitz sent a reply setting forth what he believed to be the Navy's proper missions. He specified that his letter was not to be released to the press without the consent of the Secretary of the Navy.

Johnson and Matthews had assured newsmen that the officers appearing before the Vinson committee were free to express their own opinions, that there would be no reprisals if they expressed disagreement with the views the secretaries of Navy and Defense had advocated. Matthews took great pains, however, to make sure that Admiral Denfeld was "tamed," that when it came his time to testify he would not say anything in opposition to the secretaries' policies—policies which the President was inclined to favor.

In the morning of October 13, Admiral Nimitz, happening to be in Washington on U.N. business, drove over to the Pentagon to pay some courtesy calls. Denfeld was not in his office. His turn to testify before the Vinson committee had come. Nimitz did pay calls on Secretaries Matthews and Johnson. Giving Matthews the right of release on his letter and subsequently calling on him were acts of elementary courtesy which the admiral would not have thought of omitting. But Matthews, feeling isolated and shunned by senior naval officers, was touched by what seemed to him acts of sympathy on Nimitz's part.

So far as secretaries Matthews and Johnson, and even President Truman, were concerned, Admiral Denfeld's testimony was a bombshell. Since he had stated that he favored unification of the services, they had expected him at least partially to support their views, or in any case to remain silent on points in which he opposed them. Instead, Denfeld stated emphatically that he endorsed everything that Admiral Radford had said.

On the 14th, Nimitz, back at the United Nations, received a telephone call from Matthews. The Secretary said that he was in urgent need of advice. Nimitz offered to come back to Washington, but Matthews said no, he would come to New York. Would Nimitz join him the next day at the Hotel Barclay?

At the Barclay the following morning, Admiral Nimitz found Secretary Matthews in a state of agitation. He said he felt himself to be the victim of a conspiracy, with Denfeld the principal conspirator. "He tells me nothing," said Matthews. The Secretary added that he knew there was something going on down there in Arleigh Burke's and Admiral Radford's shop, something that had to do with unification and the B-36 controversy.

"The first time I was cut in on anything," said Matthews, "was when the congressional committee informed me of your letter. Admiral Nimitz, that was the first time I've been brought into this controversy. Denfeld never tells me anything. Is that right?"

Nimitz had no desire to participate in any disagreement between the Secretary of the Navy and the Chief of Naval Operations. He was particularly anxious not to appear critical of Denfeld, whom he liked. But, in all honesty, he had to admit that the Chief of Naval Operations had no business concealing facts about the Navy from the Secretary. "When I was CNO," said Nimitz, "I reported to Mr. Forrestal every morning, as soon as I had read the dispatches. I considered it my duty to keep him fully informed about all matters relating to the Navy."

While Nimitz could not possibly have been in agreement with all of

Matthews' views, he seems to have felt pity for this well-meaning but confused man who was caught between his duty to support the Navy and loyalty to his friend and patron, Secretary Johnson. The extent of Matthews' unfamiliarity with naval matters was revealed by his final question: "How can I get rid of Denfeld?"

It seemed impossible for a man to be Secretary of the Navy for six months and not know the answer to that elementary question. Nimitz patiently explained that the Commander in Chief of the Armed Services was the President and that it was the President's prerogative to remove any civilian or military official of the armed forces. He told Matthews that if he really believed he could not work with Admiral Denfeld, he should write to Mr. Truman, asking that Denfeld be transferred to some other duty, and stating the reasons for the request. He pointed out, however, that Matthews should not list among his reasons Denfeld's statements before the Vinson committee, since all officers had been guaranteed against reprisals for their testimony.

Secretary Matthews went back to Washington and wrote his letter, which he seems to have mulled over for several days. In it he asked President Truman that "for the good of the country" he be allowed to transfer Admiral Denfeld "to other important duties." He gave as his specific reason for the request, not Denfeld's testimony before the committee, but his endorsement of Bogan's letter. The President was only too glad to comply. In the afternoon of October 27, he opened his news conference with an announcement that he had received the request and had granted it. This news was broadcast by radio and television within the hour.

Late in the afternoon of Monday, October 31, Admiral Nimitz returned to The Chimneys from his U.N. office with a severe case of laryngitis and promptly went to bed. At suppertime there came a telephone call for him. Favoring his sore throat, the admiral asked Mrs. Nimitz to handle the call.

"I think you'll want to take this," said Catherine. "It's the President." Chester took the phone. He recorded the substance of the ensuing conversation in the diary:

> I was called to the phone by Pres. Truman who told me he was being pressured to return me to Washington to take up duties as CNO. He asked my reaction, and he got it as vigorously as my laryngitis would permit. I told him it would be a mistake in time of peace to return an older officer (beyond retirement age) to that job, when there were plenty of able young officers available. Also told him that my present job with UN, to which he had assented months back, had first claim on my services. . . . I said finally that only an order from him would bring me to Washington as CNO, and he said that he would never order me anywhere without consulting me first. He was most cordial and friendly.

Truman asked Nimitz to recommend some other officer to replace Denfeld. Nimitz replied that there were many good officers in the Navy suitable for the post. Truman asked him to name some. Nimitz offered the names of

Admiral Forrest Sherman, then commanding the Sixth Fleet, and Admiral Richard Conolly, Commander of U.S. Naval Forces in Europe.

"And of the two, which would you recommend?"

"Sherman is younger and even less involved in politics."

"Thank you," said Truman and asked Nimitz to repeat his recommendation, presumably so that it could be recorded.

Sherman was widely favored among naval officers as the admiral best fitted to bring peace to the troubled Navy Department. He was probably Truman's, and almost certainly Matthews', second choice—after Nimitz. In fact, Matthews had already ordered Sherman home from his headquarters in Lebanon. Sherman's plane landed at New York at 4:30 a.m. on November 1, and he went directly to Washington, where he was informed that he had been appointed Chief of Naval Operations. That evening he telephoned the good news to the Nimitzes, and Chester and Catherine congratulated him warmly. He never knew that Nimitz had recommended him.

Admiral Denfeld chose to retire rather than accept other duty. He wrote an article, "Reprisal: Why I Was Fired," which was published in *Colliers* the following March. Secretaries Matthews and Johnson lasted a little longer. Their policies were discredited when the Korean War broke out the following summer and revealed the weakness of American military power, trimmed to almost fatal inadequacy by misplaced pennypinching. Support from the carriers, which critics had called obsolete, saved the U.N. Eighth Army. The U.S. Seventh Fleet, by putting the 1st Marine Division ashore at Inchon, broke the stalemate at the Pusan perimeter. Said old soldier General MacArthur: "The Navy and the marines have never shone more brightly than this morning."

When Secretary Matthews in August 1950 indiscreetly called for a preventive war against the Soviet Union, President Truman shipped him off to Ireland as ambassador to get him out of the Pentagon and off the front pages. The following month Johnson's increasingly erratic behavior obliged the President to ask for his resignation. At Truman's request, General of the Army Marshall succeeded Johnson as Secretary of Defense.

During Admiral Nimitz's period with the United Nations, Mrs. Nimitz was obliged to commute between the east and west coasts. In May 1949 she flew west to be present when Mary graduated from high school "with the highest honors." Nancy needed looking after too, and so did the house. Hoping to escape from library work, Nancy was enrolled at the University of California, taking a crash course in Russian that consumed all her time, leaving none for house and grounds. Mrs. Nimitz repaired these omissions as best she could. Then, in mid-June, having entered Mary in summer school, she returned to Long Island.

At the end of July, Catherine was packing to go west again. When she had finished, she put her thoughts into the diary:

> Busy during the morning packing my clothes in those beautiful new suitcases! How really exciting to travel with "matched luggage." Almost too

much style for one who for thirty-five years has traveled with "any old kind." After all, the wardrobe I carried was more or less "any old kind" with the addition of dolls, toys, bottles and diapers. Now the wardrobe like the luggage is a bit more "matched"—no dolls, no toys, no diapers, no bot—oh well maybe *one*. I only hope that we will have happy times to equal those we had when the luggage was heterogeneous and the wardrobe slim.

Just before leaving to catch her train, she made one more entry, a quick parting message to Chester: "Good night my Darling. All my heart's love is yours entirely. I'll be with you in spirit always." As it turned out, that was Catherine's final entry, though Chester made daily entries for eight more months. Following Catherine's departure, he wrote: "I miss Mother greatly and console myself with the thought that our separation will not be too long— and also that she will be helping our children."

In September 1949 Nimitz recorded a happy result of his double salary: "Sent off final check to American Trust Co in Berkeley to complete payment . . . for our house at 728 Santa Barbara Road, Berkeley. It is a great relief to me to have this debt cleared. Too many people in my age bracket—the sixties have a habit of dropping off with heart attacks and I could not rule out the possibility in my case. Also the flying hazard, small as it is, might catch up with me. Now however my mind is easier and I do not have the constant fear that I might suddenly leave a huge debt if I had an accident."

Mrs. Nimitz meanwhile was busy looking after Longview, helping Nancy pack for a drive back across the continent, and seeing Mary entered as a freshman at Stanford University. Mary's entry into college was complicated by her right arm being in a cast, she having broken it while roller skating. Nancy, after a week's lonely driving, arrived at The Chimneys. She visited briefly with her father and with her Aunt Elizabeth Freeman at her home in Wellfleet. She then proceeded to Harvard University to begin work on a master's degree in the Russian regional studies program. Toward the end of September Mrs. Nimitz arrived back in New York. The admiral happily recorded the event: "Met Mother at La Guardia airport at 9 a.m. when her Constellation arrived from California. It was oh—so good to see her."

That fall Nimitz motored up to West Point to address the cadets, and told them, "I hope I don't live to see an H-bomb developed." From Chet came a letter announcing the sad end of Freckles, run over by a car. Professor Samuel Eliot Morison, who was writing his multi-volume *History of United States Naval Operations in World War II*, twice came down from Harvard to lunch with Nimitz at the United Nations and interview him. Admiral and Mrs. Nimitz and Nancy spent Thanksgiving with Elizabeth Freeman in Wellfleet. They were back at Wellfleet again for Christmas, this time joined by Mary, who had come by train from the West Coast for the holidays.

In January 1950, Admiral and Mrs. Nimitz went to Washington for Hap Arnold's funeral. Nimitz and Bill Halsey were honorary pallbearers. Although it was sleeting and snowing, the service was held in the outdoor amphitheater at Arlington National Cemetery. "It was a long and unnecessary ordeal for

Mrs. Arnold," wrote Nimitz. That evening the Nimitzes dined at Observatory House as guests of Admiral and Mrs. Forrest Sherman.

As early as June 1949, when both India and Pakistan rejected new truce proposals suggested by the U.N. Commission, Nimitz had begun to suspect that nothing would come of his plebiscite assignment. He suggested to Secretary-General Lie that his staff be dissolved in order to save the United Nations money. Lie agreed and in mid-June the staff met for the last time and then went on a month's leave preparatory to being disbanded. "Sorry to see them go," Nimitz wrote, "because they are a competent and hardworking group." In early July General Maloney applied for terminal leave.

In August 1949 Nimitz received from the U.N. Commission for India and Pakistan a dispatch asking if he would accept the task of arbitrating a truce in Kashmir. "Gladly," he replied. In his diary he noted: "It will probably be weeks before the commission reaches the stage of offering arbitration."

A couple of weeks later he wrote in the diary that he had received "a close-up description of Nehru [Jawaharlal Nehru, prime minister of India] in a rage over the Kashmir question—which makes me believe he will obstruct early settlement of truce and holding of plebiscite." The next day he learned that the U.N. Commission for India and Pakistan had canceled joint meetings scheduled to begin in New Delhi the following week. "Now it looks more doubtful than before that the truce can be arbitrated," he wrote, "so I believe the commission will now refer the matter back to UN. It now looks as if I will be kept here until sometime in Sept—by which time the matter should be back to the Security Council."

President Truman wrote to the prime ministers of both Pakistan and India urging them to accept Admiral Nimitz's arbitration. Prime Minister Nehru rejected Truman's plea and expressed annoyance at what he termed "American intervention." Nehru was scheduled to visit the United States in October. It was hoped that through personal contact with him the wrecked negotiations might be put back on the track.

Pandit Nehru arrived in Washington accompanied by his daughter, Mme. Indira Gandhi. In the evening of October 12, Secretary of State and Mrs. Acheson gave a dinner in their honor at Anderson House on Massachusetts Avenue. Admiral and Mrs. Nimitz went down from New York to attend.

After dinner Acheson made a complimentary speech, as expected, but he departed from the usual, tired practice of summarizing the history of "the close and fruitful relations between our two countries." Instead he chose to be original. In order to bring out the varied achievements of the visitor, he improvised a series of imaginary conversations between Nehru and great Americans of the past. He had George Washington talking to Nehru as one father of his country to another; Thomas Jefferson, as a fellow ideologist of democracy; Andrew Jackson, as to another tough political organizer and strategist; Abraham Lincoln, as to another leader who had suffered with his people through fratricidal strife.

It was a virtuoso performance, and it caught Nehru flat-footed. The Prime Minister was prepared only to return a routine reply to a routine speech. Displeased, he spoke so softly that Nimitz could not catch a word of what he said.

At the after-dinner reception, the guests were so numerous, about 90, that Admiral Nimitz barely met the Prime Minister, and Mrs. Nimitz did not meet him at all. At the earliest possible moment, Acheson spirited Nehru away to his own home. As the Secretary wrote afterward, "I had hoped that, uninhibited by a cloud of witnesses, we might establish a personal relationship. But he would not relax. He talked to me, as Queen Victoria said of Mr. Gladstone, as though I were a public meeting."

Admiral Nimitz afterward learned what took place. Acheson, after patiently listening to Nehru denounce the Dutch and the French, finally got the subject around to the question of Kashmir and the truce. The Prime Minister clothed his views in lofty language, but what it boiled down to was that he would not consent to a truce until all of Pakistan's troops, but none of India's, had been withdrawn from Kashmir. The inference was that Nehru would consent to a plebiscite in Kashmir only if he could be sure that it would favor union with India. Afterward, Acheson wrote wearily, "He was one of the most difficult men with whom I have ever had to deal."

Admiral Nimitz met Prime Minister Nehru twice again, at a reception at the Waldorf-Astoria Hotel given in his honor by the Indian delegation to the United Nations and at a luncheon at Trygve Lie's home in Forest Hills. At the luncheon, which chairmen of the General Assembly committees attended, Nehru unbent a little from his customary aloofness. Since he never brought up the matter of Kashmir, the situation remained unchanged.

In December the report of the U.N. Commission on India and Pakistan arrived and was taken up by the Security Council. Canada held the presidency for December and General Andrew G. L. McNaughton of that country presided. The Council voted in favor of a resolution, put forward by Norway, that McNaughton get representatives of India and Pakistan together with himself to seek a solution of the deadlock.

In February 1950 General McNaughton reported that his efforts to bring India and Pakistan to an understanding had failed. Sir Benegal Rau, of India, then made a long statement before the Council, expounding India's point of view. He was followed by Sir Lafrulla Khan, Pakistani foreign minister, who in the course of two days of oratory set forth Pakistan's side of the problem. Rau then came back with a long rebuttal. After that, the Security Council adjourned for a week in order, as Nimitz wrote, "to digest the torrent of words they had heard and devise a formula for further procedure. Their decisions will determine whether Mother and I go to India or return to California."

After long debate, the Security Council voted on a resolution to replace the U.N. Commission for India and Pakistan with a one-man U.N. representative. The vote was 8 to 0 in favor, with India and Yugoslavia abstaining and the Soviet Union boycotting the Council. Admiral Nimitz, having been informed that Pakistan would insist upon his being the representative, thought he might at last be going to India.

Anticipating that possibility, Mrs. Nimitz made another visit to the West Coast. "It was time for me to come back and look after the house," she said. "So many people had keys and were coming there to stay on weekends—friends of the children and the girls themselves."

Hardly had Catherine left when the Indian government, in another maneuver, firmly rejected the proposal that the U.N. representative and the plebiscite administrator should be the same man. That, of course, eliminated Admiral Nimitz, who concluded that his usefulness to the United Nations had come to an end. He could no longer conscientiously accept pay for results he saw no chance of producing. He therefore submitted his resignation.

Admiral Nimitz had received an emergency call from the president of the University of California, asking him to come to Berkeley and deliver the Charter Day address, substituting for Senator Austin, who was ill. Though the time was short, Nimitz consented, and at once set to work on his speech. He kept at it every spare moment until his plane left La Guardia on Saturday evening, March 18. On the plane he continued polishing the address, which was to be delivered the following Wednesday. On his arrival at the San Francisco airport, he was met by Paige and Cozard. He gave the speech to Paige for him to work over and have typed in a semi-final version. Cozard drove him across the bay bridge to Longview.

"Mother and Mary were waiting at home," wrote Nimitz in the diary, "and it was good to see them. The house and grounds are in perfect condition. After a bath I weighed 188 pounds, or 10 pounds more than when I left here last March. A regime of dieting is indicated and will be started at once."

By Charter Day, March 22, Admiral Nimitz believed that he and his speech were ready. Wearing cap and gown over his uniform, he mounted the rostrum with confidence and faced a large audience of students, faculty, and alumni. His address seemed to him to be well received. He got numerous compliments.

Afterward, while walking across the campus, Nimitz encountered a retired astronomy professor whom he had known in his NROTC days and who was now almost blind with age. "Good morning," said Chester, thrusting out his hand. The professor returned the greeting but obviously did not recognize the admiral. He asked Nimitz how he liked that speech. Before Chester could reply, the professor continued, "I've heard a hell of a lot better!"

Nimitz was at first taken aback. Then he began to laugh. It was a story he often told on himself.

That evening Admiral and Mrs. Nimitz attended the Charter Day dance. As they entered the ballroom, Chester received another surprise. The band struck up, "What Shall We Do with a Drunken Sailor?"

"It was a delightful Charter Day," said Catherine.

# CHAPTER 27

# LAST YEARS

T<small>RYGVE</small> L<small>IE</small> PERSUADED Admiral Nimitz to withdraw his resignation and remain in the employ of the United Nations—as a roving "good will ambassador." Nimitz consented because he recognized the need for such a post and, in doing so, he said that if India and Pakistan should come to terms, he would still be available as plebiscite administrator. In the course of the following two years, from speakers' platforms all over the United States, he explained the major issues before the United Nations and the solutions proposed. He thus helped to offset a growing disillusionment among Americans who had expected too much of the world organization.

Early in 1951, about a year after it began, Admiral Nimitz's roving commission was very nearly interrupted by orders from the American President. Following sensational charges made by Senator Joseph McCarthy, of Wisconsin, that there were Communists in the national government, President Truman appointed Nimitz to head a nine-man commission "to consider how best to protect the United States from subversion without endangering the freedom of American citizens." The President hoped thus to calm the national hysteria caused by McCarthy's repeated accusations. Nimitz accepted the appointment, but a Senate committee headed by Pat McCarran, of Nevada, set up standards that made confirmation of the Nimitz Commission members impossible. Sorrowfully, Truman wrote to Nimitz, "I had hoped that the Congress would be as anxious as I am to make sure that the Bill of Rights is not undermined in our eagerness to stamp out subversive activities."

In the summer of 1952, Admiral Nimitz, feeling that his new assignment with the United Nations had run its course, turned in his final, irreversible resignation. He recognized this time that he was in fact retiring, whatever regulations might state about five-star officers. To be sure, his government income was called salary rather than retirement pay, and he had a title, Special Assistant to the Secretary of the Navy in the Western Sea Frontier, but he correctly anticipated that he would hardly ever be asked for assistance.

There were, of course, alternatives to retirement. Colleges and universities, including the University of California at Los Angeles, offered Nimitz presidencies and chancellorships, and business and industry offered him high-salaried positions. He turned down all such offers. He felt that he was not equipped to head a university, and the prospect of entering business interested him not at all.

Chester Junior protested: "Dad, for God's sake, why don't you do it? ... You've performed your duty to your country. Now do something for yourself.... If you don't want the money, give it to your children."

Gradually the son came to appreciate the father's point of view. "He had this very strong feeling," said Chet years later, "that he represented the Navy to a lot of people who had lost relatives in the Pacific War, and that it would somehow undermine their feeling for the Navy...if the man who had been *the* naval commander, under whom their relative had served, acquired an image as other than that naval commander."

Mrs. Nimitz Senior agreed. "Chester felt that it was important that he, who had been asked to stay on as an elder adviser, should do it," she said, "and nothing was as important to him as to keep his place in history and not mix it with any business. He knew I didn't care about money. Therefore he could do it without depriving me of anything."

Joan Nimitz, Chet's wife, remembered something that her father-in-law said: "Well, now, Mother is the one. I've spent all my life doing things because the Navy wanted me to. Now I'm retired. She is the one who is going to decide where we live and what we do." Joan added, "I'm sure that Chester's mother hoped he would do something to occupy himself. Here he was, just full of energy and ability and good mind and everything else, and here he was just going to sit, because he wouldn't take a job of any sort. Totally disinterested in finances or money."

"He was maintaining an image until he died," said Chet.

Admiral Nimitz took very seriously his duties as regent of the University of California. He attended all the monthly meetings and immersed himself in the university's problems of finance, administration, and policy. He argued fruitlessly, as he had during his NROTC days, against the practice of setting up publishing as the main criterion for hiring, firing, and promoting faculty members. He felt that the university was missing or losing some excellent teachers through its continuing policy of "publish or perish."

More distressing to Nimitz was the university's decision to require all members of its faculty to take a loyalty oath. He saw that requirement as an ill-considered reaction to the national hysteria resulting from the McCarthy accusations, and he pointed out its futility. The loyal professors would be insulted, he said, and the disloyal would sign without a qualm and go on being disloyal.

The loyalty oath required at Berkeley was the main topic of discussion in the graduate student council at Harvard, and a young man from California was invited by the members to describe the situation to them. Nancy Nimitz, a member of the council, was filled with pride and also impressed with the fleetingness of fame when the young man said, "You know, there's a military man out there, a guy named Admiral Nimitz, who's one of the regents, and even *he* isn't for the oath."

In spite of his interest in the university's affairs, Nimitz still had time on his hands. As Nancy pointed out, "the amount of work he brought home in his briefcase from the regents' meetings would not keep a man of his ability busy more than two days. Of course at this time he was reading. This was the time when books on the war were coming out in great numbers. All these books were sent to him, so he had a lot of reading to do. He wrote his own letters, longhand, and he was an extremely punctilious correspondent. If you wrote a letter to him, you got a letter back within two days." When he liked a book, he would write a letter of appreciation to the author, then, usually, paste the author's answer inside the cover of the book.

Nimitz at last had a little time to think about himself. A friend sent him "A Prayer for Restraint," which he adopted for his own:

Lord, Thou knowest better than I know myself that I am growing older, and will some day be old.

Keep me from getting talkative, and particularly from the false habit of thinking I must say something on every subject and on every occasion.

Release me from craving to try to straighten out everybody's affairs.

Make me thoughtful, but not moody; helpful, but not bossy. With my vast store of wisdom, it seems a pity not to use it all—but Thou knowest, Lord, that I want a few friends at the end.

Keep my mind free from the recital of endless details; give me wings to get to the point.

Seal my lips on my many aches and pains. They are increasing, and my love of rehearsing them is becoming sweeter as the years go by.

I ask for grace enough to listen to the tales of others' pains. Help me to endure them with patience.

Teach me the glorious lesson that occasionally it is possible that I may be mistaken.

Keep me reasonably sweet; I do not want to be a saint—some of them are so hard to live with.

Help me to extract all possible fun out of life. There are so many funny things around us, and I don't want to miss any of them.

Although Admiral Nimitz never got over his habit of punctuality and of expecting promptness in others, he gradually mellowed and grew to accept a life without major responsibilities. More than ever before he took an interest in the activities of his family.

At Harvard, where she was working toward a master's degree, Nancy delved into Soviet politics, economics, and history. During her second year, expecting to work in Washington after receiving her degree, she talked with some government recruiters. When she visited Washington during Easter vacation in 1951, however, she was told that she could not receive a security clearance. Investigators, it seemed, had been looking into her past. Because the spirit of McCarthy was still pervading the land, they took a serious view of her radical activities as an undergraduate at George Washington University in the 1930s.

"I remember driving back to Cambridge in a glum frame of mind," Nancy wrote later, "not helped by having to change a tire at 2 a.m. on some main highway in New Jersey. I left Harvard for Wellfleet in June 1951, feeling not only unemployed but unemployable, and spent a delicious couple of weeks walking around the woods and beaches and listening to a Cimarosa oboe concerto on the phonograph. Then a telephone call came from someone at Rand, asking if I would be interested in a job there. (I had worked the summer before for a Harvard professor who was a Rand consultant, and he had evidently suggested that they rescue me.) I remember saying irritably that they wouldn't be able to clear me, and the voice at the other end said soothingly, 'Different places have different standards.' Rand employed me as a consultant in Cambridge until they succeeded in clearing me. (It took over a year.) I became a regular employee in Santa Monica on 7 December 1952."

At Stanford University, Mary Nimitz had majored in biology, a subject in which she had long been interested. Her interest seems first to have been stimulated by some little green turtles given her by Rear Admiral John F. Shafroth and by some sea shells sent her from the Pacific by Rear Admiral William L. Calhoun. During her school days at San Rafael, Mary became an avid collector of sea shells, some highly fragrant from the defunct inhabitants still inside. All during World War II, friends of her father sent or brought her unusual specimens. From turtles and shells, her interest gradually expanded to include living creatures of all sorts.

Mary's parents, as was their habit, fostered their daughter's interests in every way. Mrs. Nimitz even had the forbearance to raise no serious objections when Mary appropriated all 36 of her custard cups in which to observe the development of salamander larvae. But there were limits. When Mrs. Nimitz discovered that Mary had brought home cockroaches to observe, she made it plain that if any of them got loose in the house, Mary could expect to get out.

At the end of her freshman year at Stanford, Mary announced that she intended to become a communicant of the Roman Catholic Church. This was perfectly agreeable to her parents, who were not surprised and who, in any event, believed in letting their children make their own decisions, without interference and without unwanted advice.

Admiral and Mrs. Nimitz, though deeply religious in their own way, were unable to accept the doctrine of any established church, but they respected the religious beliefs of others. They did not have their children baptized because they thus would be making a decision for them, committing them to a set of beliefs and practices, before the children had reached an age at which they could make the choice for themselves. They did, however, send the children to Sunday School in order to give them some basis for deciding whether they wished to join a church.

Mary's interest in Catholicism grew out of her convent schooling. During World War II, when Mrs. Nimitz was busy at Oak Knoll Hospital, she had entered Mary as a boarder at Dominican Convent Lower School in nearby San Rafael. She made this choice both because of the school's high scholastic standing and because the girls there were strictly guarded.

"There was a danger," said Mrs. Nimitz, "and the Navy felt it, of Mary being kidnapped by somebody who wanted to upset the admiral, you see because she was young. So I decided that the only way she'd be safe was to put her in the convent. I'd known of this school for years, and I assure you nobody could have gotten near Mary. They took wonderful care of her."

When Admiral Nimitz approached the end of his tour as Chief of Naval Operations, he and Mrs. Nimitz sent Mary back to San Rafael, to Dominican Convent Upper School. Here Mary, thoroughly instructed in Catholic doctrine and accustomed to attending mass, concluded that she would be happy in the Catholic Church. She put off making the final decision several months, however, in order to test her feelings in secular surroundings.

Mary had in mind nothing less than following the example of the sisters who had taught her at the convent school. When she announced her desire to become a nun, both her parents appear to have been startled. The cloistered life she contemplated was far removed from anything the family was accustomed to. It seemed almost as if they were losing her. The admiral asked Mary to wait a year before making her final decision. Mrs. Nimitz continued to have periods of being upset, wondering if she had done the right thing in sending her daughter to the convent school.

"Look," said the admiral impatiently, "if Mary is happier doing that, I can't understand why anybody is moaning and groaning." Perhaps he saw in Mary's desire to serve and obey the Church a parallel to his own career in serving and obeying his country through the Navy.

At Stanford, in recognition of her high scholarly attainment, Mary was made a member of Phi Beta Kappa. In January 1953 she was graduated with distinction. She promptly started on a master's program in biology at Stanford but, having decided to begin her novitiate the following summer, she transferred almost at once to the University of California at Berkeley, in order to spend her last six months of secular life with her parents.

When it became known to the public that Admiral Nimitz's daughter was entering a convent, fanatics began annoying the family with crackpot telephone calls and mail. People even came to Longview at night and stuffed papers under the door. Admiral and Mrs. Nimitz during this period forbade Mary to answer phone calls, and they kept the rabid mail and circulars from her.

On August 1, 1953, the day Mary was to enter the convent, newspaper people began congregating there early in the morning, pencils and cameras at the alert. In some distress, Mother Margaret, the mother general, called Mrs. Nimitz. "They're over here waiting for Mary," she said, "and I've told them she isn't coming till after noon. Now they've just started over for your house."

"Fine," said Mrs. Nimitz, "we'll start over for the convent." En route they passed the newspaper crowd headed in the opposite direction. Nobody recognized Mary or her mother, who was driving.

Mary successfully passed through her six months as postulant and her year as a novice. She made her first profession in February 1955, having taken the rather formidable name of Sister M. Aquinas. While serving as a teaching sister, she completed her M.A. at the University of California and her Ph.D. at

Stanford. After teaching in Catholic girls' secondary schools for several years, she was assigned in January 1964 to teach at Dominican College of San Rafael in the Department of Biology, of which she became chairman in 1970.

When Mary was at the convent at San Rafael, Admiral and Mrs. Nimitz visited her often and made friends with the 345 other nuns. The latter loved the admiral's stories, of which he had a great number that were suitable for religious. He took an interest in the convent buildings and grounds and advised on tree-planting. When a fellow naval officer, distressed because his own daughter had chosen to enter a convent, asked Nimitz how he felt about his daughter becoming a nun, the admiral replied cheerfully that he never felt that he had lost a daughter but that he had in fact acquired 345.

Catherine and Chester had very strong beliefs about abiding by the Golden Rule and doing the best they could in this life, without expecting any reward in a life to come. "You don't know what's ahead of you," said Catherine, "but if there *is* anything, that's lovely. If there isn't, you will still have achieved what you set out to do, or come near it, if you do your very level best."

As if the Nimitzes had not had enough responsibility in rearing four children of their own, they in effect adopted four more: the Battha sisters, Maria, Magda, Margit, and Marta. The girls' parents had to remain in Hungary, but they sent their daughters out ahead of the advancing Russians, entrusting them to the care of the Catholic Church. The Church ultimately sent them to California, where they were placed under the guardianship of two harsh women in the southern part of the state and enrolled in Dominican School at San Rafael. Magda Battha and Mary Nimitz were classmates during their senior year in the upper school.

In the spring of 1949, when the elder Nimitzes were at the United Nations, Nancy, then living alone at Longview, went over to the school to bring Mary home for Easter vacation.

"Nancy," Mary said, "there are four Hungarian girls here on scholarships. They have no money to go anywhere and they haven't any friends around here. Couldn't we take them home with us?"

"Why, of course," said Nancy. "I'll ask Mother Margaret."

Mother Margaret was more than willing to let the Battha sisters go to Longview. "Oh, I'd be so grateful to have those girls have some place to go," she said.

So Nancy took Mary and the four Batthas home. Later she wrote her parents, "I've never known five such willing pairs of hands."

When Admiral and Mrs. Nimitz returned to Berkeley, and Mary was away at college, the Battha sisters were still welcome visitors at Longview for Thanksgiving, Christmas, Easter, and many weekends. With Mrs. Nimitz's permission, they often brought friends with them. "They all had keys to the house," said Catherine. "We never knew how many children we were going to have in, because they came from all over."

While Mary was a freshman at Stanford, she visited Dominican School and found Marta, youngest of the Batthas, ailing and listless. She called her mother, who came at once to San Rafael. To Mrs. Nimitz it appeared that Marta was more terrified than ill. With Mother Margaret's permission, she took the girl home with her and by gentle questioning at length drew from her an admission that she dreaded having to go back to southern California to spend the summer with the she-dragon who was her appointed guardian.

Admiral and Mrs. Nimitz swung into action. They decided that Maria, the eldest Battha, could provide a solution to the immediate problem of her sisters and their guardians. Maria had graduated from Dominican College and had a room and a job in San Francisco. Before the end of the semester, she would be 21 years old. The local authorities, under pressure from the admiral, who provided the necessary guarantees, arranged for Maria, immediately on becoming 21, to take over the guardianship of her sisters. The Nimitzes told Mother Margaret that if Dominican would take care of the girls' education, they would look after everything else. When Marta found that she did not have to go back to her former guardian, she promptly got well. "She was the happiest child I have ever known," said Mrs. Nimitz.

The next immediate problem was getting American citizenship for the Battha girls. The quota for new citizens was filled for that year, but Admiral Nimitz got in touch with his powerful friends in Washington and arranged to have a special bill put through Congress to make sure they got their citizenship.

Magda, Margit, and Marta all completed their work at Dominican College on scholarships. Magda wanted to do a year of postgraduate work at Mills College in Oakland and was prepared to go into debt to finance it. Instead, the Nimitzes paid for it out of their own slender means.

The Batthas came to think of Longview as their home and the Nimitzes as their family. When Magda, Margit, and Marta were married, Admiral Nimitz, as surrogate father, marched each of them up the aisle.

In 1954, Admiral and Mrs. Nimitz went to Europe, making their first visit there since 1913, when the Navy sent Chester to Germany to study diesel engines. The chief attraction this time was Chester Junior and his family. Chet was stationed in London, on duty with the North Atlantic Treaty Organization (NATO), and lived with his family outside the capital, at Wentworth, near Windsor Castle. Admiral Nimitz found the walking very fine at Wentworth.

From England the elder Nimitzes crossed to Holland and visited France, Italy, and the Island of Malta. For the first time since World War II they were enjoying a blessed anonymity; no strangers in Europe, it seemed, recognized Admiral Nimitz. The sole exception was in the train en route to Rome. Somebody spotted the admiral and passed the word. The Nimitzes were sitting quietly in their compartment reading when a noise outside attracted their attention and they looked up.

"My God, Chester," said Catherine. "What's all this?"

Outside in the corridor gazing into the compartment was a crowd of people standing packed, those in the rear on tiptoe craning their necks. All the Nimitzes could do was smile pleasantly and pretend to go on reading, but

Catherine muttered under her breath, "There's only one thing for us to do. If we want any peace, we're going to have to pull down our curtains."

At Malta the Nimitzes were guests of old family friend Vice Admiral James Fife, USN. Fife was deputy to Admiral Lord Louis Mountbatten, who at that time was serving NATO as Commander in Chief of all Allied forces in the Mediterranean, except the U.S. Sixth Fleet.

Admiral Fife wondered how he was going to entertain his guests. He need not have worried. When the Nimitzes arrived by plane, invitations from eminent Maltese were awaiting them. As word of the Nimitzes' graciousness spread, more invitations poured in than they could possibly accept. Lord and Lady Mountbatten gave a dinner for them and, with Fife, saw them off when they flew back to the mainland.

In the fall of 1955 Admiral and Mrs. Nimitz crossed the continent to visit the Lays at Arlington, Virginia, and attend the 50th anniversary homecoming of the admiral's Naval Academy class. Rear Admiral Walter F. Boone, superintendent of the Academy, invited Nimitz, as the ranking and most celebrated member of the class of 1905, to take the review of the midshipman regiment in the afternoon parade. Nimitz declined the honor and requested the superintendent to ask the president of the class, Captain A. B. Court, to take it.

To avoid problems of protocol and so as not to attract attention away from Court, Nimitz delayed his departure from Arlington late enough to miss the parade altogether. As he came downstairs at the Lays' house, resplendent in white uniform with gold, five-starred shoulder boards, the Lays' maid stared at him in awe. "Baby Doll," she exclaimed, "you sure do look sexy!"

The Nimitzes and Lays rode to Annapolis in an official car with a marine driver, both furnished by the Chief of Naval Operations. Their evening began at "the world's largest cocktail party" in Dahlgren Hall, where Nimitz stood under the "1905" painted in gold beneath the balcony and genially held court while nursing a drink in a paper cup.

As Nimitz and his classmates with their ladies arrived at the 1905 table in the huge mess hall, Nimitz said, "Now wait a minute. No man shall sit beside his wife." The couples accordingly separated and rearranged themselves. Nimitz soon realized that, so far as he was concerned, he had made a dreadful mistake, for he found himself seated between a pair of notorious chatterers who scarcely gave him a chance to eat. They spent most of the meal clamorously soliciting favors that Nimitz was in no position to grant. One of them wanted to get some sort of legislation through Congress.

After dinner the Lays and the Nimitzes met back at the car. The admiral turned to Mrs. Nimitz. "Mother," he said grimly, "we'll skip the 75th and I'll take you to the 100th. Oh, those women, those women!"

On the way back to Arlington, Nimitz entertained his fellow passengers by mimicking the chatter to which he had been subjected. He soon had the whole party, including the marine driver, shaking with laughter.

In August 1957 Chester Nimitz Junior retired from the Navy with the rank of rear admiral. In a public statement he gave as his reason his need to take a job that would earn him enough to educate his three daughters as he would like to see them educated. That consideration no doubt influenced him, but his main reason for retiring was that he was bored. After a childhood as a navy junior and nearly a quarter of a century as a naval officer, he wanted a change.

Fleet Admiral Nimitz told the press merely that he understood his son's decision, but to Chet he said, "I'm glad you did get out. I think it's high time."

"I'm not quite sure why he felt it was the right thing to do," said Chet, "but I think it was associated with what Eisenhower [referred] to as 'military-industrial complex.' . . . The Pentagon, he felt, had become greatly overmanned with civilians. The status of military people was unsatisfactory. Admirals were acting as messenger boys.

"He was distressed with the type of weaponry: impersonal rockets, air-to-air missiles, air-to-ground missiles, and intercontinental missiles.... This modern age of rockets and mass bombings...involved too many civilian casualties. It was no longer the exercise of military force to gain national ends against somebody else's military force, but a pretty cold-blooded business.

"I think he felt that the kind of person required by the armed forces was no longer the kind of person . . . he had tried to be."

Fleet Admiral Nimitz was staying in the service as a representative and symbol of the Old Navy that he loved, but he apparently did not expect his son to give the same sort of continuing loyalty to what the Navy had become.

The younger Nimitz had earned an excellent service reputation, particularly as a submarine skipper in World War II. He was entitled to wear a chestful of medals, including the Navy Cross, the highest decoration the Navy could award short of the Medal of Honor. For that reason and because of his name, he found a ready welcome in the world of business and industry. He worked for Texas Instruments, Incorporated, until 1961, when he transferred to another instrument-manufacturing concern, The Perkin-Elmer Corporation, in Connecticut. As a businessman, Chester Junior revealed a gift for administration comparable to his father's. Before he was 60, he had been both president and chairman of the board of Perkin-Elmer.

In 1958, at the Secretary of the Navy's request, Admiral Nimitz went to Washington to testify on behalf of the Navy before the Senate Armed Services Committee, of which Lyndon Johnson was chairman. Bill Leverton, then a captain, got himself assigned as Nimitz's aide and accompanied him to the Senate Office Building. There, from a front-row seat, he observed Admiral Nimitz and Senator Johnson matching wits. Leverton tells the story:

> Lyndon Johnson's technique was to give maybe a paragraph quote and say, "Do you agree with that?"
> The admiral said, "Can I see that in writing?"

"No."

"Well, read it one more time."

When Johnson had finished, the admiral said, "I agree with it if it doesn't mean so and so."

It was quite complicated and ambiguous language. Johnson would have to admit that it didn't mean that, so the admiral would agree with him.

In August of the following year, Admiral Nimitz went east again. He went alone, to attend Bill Halsey's funeral, and he stayed with Catherine Lay and her three boys in their Arlington home. Captain Junior Lay was away at sea. During this hasty visit, Nimitz could gladly have used an assistant with Bill Leverton's experience and know-how. Instead, the Navy Department sent him, along with an official car, a young officer who had had no experience at all as an aide and a driver who did not even know his way around Washington.

The day of the funeral turned out to be blazing hot, very rough on Admiral Nimitz, aged 74, fresh from the cooler weather of California. He intended that morning to make a quick trip to the Pentagon, but the driver got lost, and the aide was no help. They could see the Pentagon plainly in the distance, but it took them an hour to find the approaches to it and get on the road leading to the river entrance.

It was past noon when Nimitz and his hapless aide got back to the Lay residence. "We don't have any time for lunch," said the admiral. "I have to get dressed." And he hurried off to the guest room to get into his whites.

The aide, who was uncomfortably aware that he had been weighed and found wanting, timidly asked if he might change in the living room.

"Fine," said Kate.

At about that point the admiral, hot and bothered, came out and said to Kate, "Get me a pair of Junior's white uniform socks." He had unrolled those he had brought and found a big hole in one heel.

"Oh, gosh," said Kate, "Junior hasn't worn a white uniform in ages."

To hunt for the socks she had to climb a ladder into a tiny hotbox of an attic. "The temperature must have been 104," she said afterward. "I was dying and there was no time to waste. I finally managed to find a rather yellowed pair of Junior's white uniform socks and brought them down."

The aide now emerged from the living room and said piteously, "Look, have you got a safety pin?" A hook on the high collar of his uniform was missing.

Looking past the young man, Kate was shocked to see his discarded skivvies draped over a lamp atop the piano. Nevertheless she couldn't help feeling sorry for the poor fellow, who was in a state bordering on panic. She finally found a safety pin and tried to pin the collar. It was no use. The cloth was in two layers and starched. She might as well have tried to force a pin through a plank.

The admiral appeared in the doorway. "What are you doing?" he asked.

Kate and the aide spoke at the same time: "Trying to put a safety pin through...."

"There's no time for that," snapped the admiral. "Nobody's going to be looking at you anyway. Come on."

Off went Nimitz and his aide to the funeral, the young man's collar agape. Both were streaming with perspiration, and so was Kate.

The two officers returned in mid-afternoon, their uniforms limp and wrinkled. The admiral headed straight for the guest room, saying, "I'm going to take a shower."

The aide just stood, wearing a hangdog expression. Kate wondered what further boners he had pulled.

"How about a cold beer?"

"I'd love one," said the aide.

At that point the admiral came out of the guest room in his bathrobe and headed for the shower. Then he thought of his aide and turned back.

"Are you married?"

"Yes, sir."

"Your wife should have checked your uniform."

This was too much for Kate. She swung around to face her father. "*You're* married. Why didn't your wife check your socks?"

Later, speaking of the aide, Kate said: "Oh, poor man. I felt so sorry for him. I must admit when Dad got cooled off and had a beer, he was his usual affable self. I don't remember that man's name, but I guess he regarded this as one of the darkest days of his life."

When Admiral and Mrs. Nimitz returned to California from the United Nations, they resumed their habit of weekly attendance at the San Francisco Symphony Orchestra. They had seats up front because the admiral took particular pleasure in watching the musicians. Mrs. Nimitz was a member of the symphony board, and she and the admiral got to know the conductor and all the members of the orchestra. They became acquainted with people interested in the musical life of the San Francisco area, and they usually met and sometimes entertained visiting musicians.

As Admiral Nimitz grew older, his love for the classical composers seemed to deepen. His favorite was Brahms, notably his first, second, and fourth symphonies. He came more and more to loathe contemporary concert music, particularly works featuring dissonance.

One afternoon, after the Nimitzes had seated themselves in the concert hall, Chester glanced approvingly over his program and remarked to Catherine, "This is going to be just beautiful." He had read his program too hastily. He had assumed that the first work to be heard was by Robert Schumann, the classical composer, born in Germany in 1810. It was in fact by the modern American composer William Schuman, born exactly a hundred years later and at that time still very much alive. Catherine recognized her husband's mistake at once and said to herself, "Oh, boy, this is going to be wonderful!"

The musicians tuned their instruments, the conductor raised his baton, and the music started—one of William Schuman's most dissonant symphonies. A puzzled look came over the admiral's face. He knitted his brows. He looked accusingly at the musicians. Then he took his program and read it again—this time carefully. Thereafter he sat in grim silence. When the symphony was over, he expressed his feelings to Catherine in one disgusted word, "William!"

That evening the Nimitzes dined with the conductor and several members of the orchestra. Mrs. Nimitz told of the admiral's misreading and reaction, and the musicians roared with laughter. Thereafter, at concerts, when one of them spotted Admiral Nimitz in the audience and a modern work was coming up, he would whisper "William," to nearby musicians, and they would pass the word along to the rest of the orchestra.

In addition to musical and social events, the Nimitzes were faithful spectators of athletic contests, both professional and collegiate. As long as he was able, Chester continued to take long walks, but Catherine, crippled by arthritis, could not join him. She never gave up her daily swim, however, and in fact on her 73rd birthday swam her usual mile. Chester, on the contrary, did little swimming in his later years for fear that he might further impair his hearing, which seemed to be deteriorating.

Chester's favorite walks were in Tilden Park, in the hills behind Berkeley. He preferred walking with a human companion but sometimes he strolled only with his dog—Dina, a wire-haired dachshund, successor to the late Freckles, or Dina's successor, Gigi, a black poodle. He hiked the trails of hilly Tilden Park so often that he came to think of it almost as his own estate. A project of his was to plant in the park clumps of yellow lupine, a shrublike, flowering plant that flourishes along the Pacific coast. He had seeds brought over from Yerba Buena Island, where the plants grew abundantly. With a pocketful of the seeds he would stroll along, planting them in holes he made in the ground with his cane. At length his favorite trail blossomed with yellow flowers. The city of Berkeley marked the entrance of the trail with a small arch bearing the words: THE NIMITZ WAY.

At about the same time, state authorities gave the name "Nimitz Freeway" to a new high-speed road linking Oakland and San Jose. Such recognition gave the admiral great pleasure until he saw a headline in the newspaper: TWO KILLED ON NIMITZ.

Until his retirement from the Marine Corps in 1961, Cozard continued to drive Nimitz's official car. For unofficial transportation, Nimitz replaced his disintegrating Chrysler with a new Mercury. Sometimes he took the wheel himself, but his driving left something to be desired. "When he got behind the wheel, he went along okay," said Cozard, "but he sort of navigated the car, rather than driving it. If he went around one particular corner and swept a little wide, and maybe bounced off a pole just enough to scratch or bend a fender, later on he'd say, 'Let's not go that way. I think this street over here's a better street.'"

On one occasion when the admiral was driving down one of the steeply inclined streets of Berkeley, his footbrake failed, or he somehow lost control of it. As the car began wildly accelerating, it never occurred to him to use the emergency brake. The Mercury, rapidly gaining speed, crossed two heavily traveled streets without hitting anything. On the third street, Nimitz finally managed to turn the car and bring it to a stop. He attributed his escape from death ∩r injury to nothing less than divine intervention. He would say solemnly, "God was sitting on the seat beside me that day."

Though Admiral Nimitz's deafness grew worse in his old age, he never lost the ability to converse in small gatherings. In public meetings and especially at large cocktail parties, however, he was often at a loss. "People mutter," he would complain. Unable to follow conversations in such circumstances, he tended to carry on a monologue.

Longview was a mecca not only for the Lays and their three boys and for the Nimitz Juniors and their three girls but for navy men and friends of the Navy. The admiral had so many visitors, official and unofficial, that he was obliged to schedule his time. But he enjoyed the visits. Nothing gave him more pleasure than to "talk Navy" and reminisce about his career. He occasionally wrote an article or made a speech, but he generally avoided public utterances on the subject of World War II lest he inadvertently stir up a controversy. For the same reason he stubbornly refused to write or assist in the writing of his biography.

In late 1956, several civilian faculty members of the U.S. Naval Academy, including this writer, were planning to write a history of sea power through the ages, to be used as a textbook at the Academy and in the NROTC. They asked Admiral Nimitz to advise on their project and he consented to do so. He thus found a means of expressing some of his opinions about naval warfare and even about the conduct of World War II without specifically writing a memoir. For their part, the professors hoped to avoid the complaints that some officers had raised to their previous publications, arguing that civilians did not have a proper basis for assessing the military decisions of professionals.

The editor and chief author of the new book went to Berkeley for a conference with the admiral and was given a guiding principle: "Officers understandably resent having their operations publicly criticized by civilians. My suggestion to you is this: give all the facts, as accurately, objectively, and fairly as you can, but don't draw conclusions. Let the reader do that. Let the facts speak for themselves."

Of her father's work on the history of sea power, Nancy Nimitz said, "He construed his responsibilities to include stylistic revisions as well as digging deeper into problems of interpretation and facts. I remember coming into his office one morning and he was showing me the manuscript. I think this was one of the exercises that gave him more pleasure after he left Washington than almost anything else. Nothing gave him more pleasure than receiving the chapters of this voluminous book in typescript and going through them. I looked at his penciled notations, and there would be many places where he had crossed out a line or two—you know, ten words unnecessary—and it gave him pleasure to do so."

*Sea Power: A Naval History,* as the book was titled, appeared in the summer of 1960 in time for use in classes that fall. The section on World War II was subsequently published in the United States and England as *The Great Sea War.* Condensations of the parts dealing with operations in the Atlantic and Pacific were published in paperback as *Triumph in the Atlantic* and *Triumph in the Pacific,* respectively. *Sea Power,* as a whole or in part, was translated into seven languages.

Admiral Nimitz would not accept, or even discuss, remuneration for his share in *Sea Power* and its numerous offspring. He left the settlement entirely up to the editor and to his former aide, Eugene Fluckey, who in 1960 was a captain and head of the Science Department at the Naval Academy. The editor and Fluckey decided to contribute $1,000 in Nimitz's name toward the building of the Navy-Marine Corps Memorial Stadium, then under way in Annapolis, and to assign all royalties due Nimitz to the Naval Academy Athletic Association.

Though Nimitz deeply resented the mistreatment of prisoners of war by certain Japanese, he admired the Japanese people, and the latter, as they learned the true history of the war and Nimitz's attitude toward them, came to admire him. It became a regular practice for Japanese naval officers visiting the United States to call at Longview to pay their respects to the admiral.. They were always gladly received.

In the course of the disarmament of Japan by the occupation forces, the Russians contended that the memorial ship *Mikasa,* encased in concrete, was a fortress. They insisted that this reminder of their 1905 defeat by Admiral Togo be destroyed. The British and Americans refused to destroy the vessel, but they did remove her masts and her antique guns. With the ending of the occupation, the Japanese were free to put them back, but pacifist sentiment in Japan was then so strong that there was no move to do so. Instead, the famous old ship was roofed over and used for a dance hall.

When Nimitz learned from his Japanese callers of this debasement of the *Mikasa,* he wrote an article for the magazine *Bungei Shinju* reminding the people of Japan of the part Togo's victory had played in their naval heritage. He donated the 20,000 yen ($56) he received for the article to encourage the Japanese themselves to contribute money for restoring the *Mikasa.* In accepting Nimitz's contribution, Admiral Ko Nagasawa, chief of the Japanese Maritime staff, wrote:

> I should like to express my deep appreciation for your warm friendship you have shown us this time, and I do not know how much your beautiful deed has strengthened the ties between our countries and above all between the two navies.
>
> Your name will never be forgotten together with TOGO and MIKASA in the history of the Japanese Navy.

Admiral Nimitz's reminder and example stirred the Japanese into waging a campaign that soon produced enough money from government sources and public contributions to put the old vessel back in shape. The *Mikasa* was rededicated on May 27, 1961, Japanese Navy Day and the 56th anniversary of the Battle of Tsushima. Admiral Nimitz was invited to attend as a special guest of honor. He could not accept the invitation, but he sent his photograph, with the following message written across the bottom:

> To all those patriotic Japanese who helped to restore this famous ship *Mikasa*— flagship of Admiral Togo—your greatest naval officer—with best wishes from a great admirer and disciple.
>
> C. W. Nimitz, Fleet Admiral, U.S. Navy

Admiral Nimitz was also interested in seeing the Togo Shrine rebuilt. Erected in 1940 to honor the famous admiral, it was destroyed in the 1945 fire-bombing of Tokyo. A small, temporary shrine had been erected on the site, and a movement was under way to reproduce the original beautiful and imposing structure.

Admiral Nimitz found an opportunity to help with the restoration in 1962, when a Japanese publisher was preparing to bring out in Japanese the portion of *Sea Power* that deals with the Pacific phase of World War II. The publisher asked Nimitz to write a foreword for the book. Nimitz wrote the foreword, specifying that any pay due him for doing so be donated to the Togo Shrine restoration fund.

The publisher, who appreciated the power of publicity, decided to turn the presenting of the donation into a kind of pageant. At the American embassy in Tokyo, before newspaper reporters and photographers, he handed a check for 100,000 yen ($280) to Captain John G. Roenigk, U. S. naval attaché, who was representing Admiral Nimitz. Captain Roenigk then handed the check to Masayasu Kosaka, wartime governor of Tokyo, and retired Vice Admiral Shiegeo Uemura, former aide to Togo. Kosaka and Uemura represented the shrine.

The story of Nimitz's donation and a picture of the check transfer appeared in many Japanese newspapers, with the dual result that contributions for the restoration of the shrine poured in from Japanese citizens, and the book became a best seller in Japan. Published on December 7, Pearl Harbor day, as *Nimitz's History of the Pacific Ocean War*, it sold out in less than a month. A second printing was rushed through the presses to meet the demand.

*Nimitz's History* received highly favorable reviews, which tended mostly to be eulogies of Nimitz. One in *Asahi Shinbun* of January 7, 1963, contains this rather astonishing passage:

> It appears that Nimitz's excellent ability of command and leadership played an even more important role in the issue of the war than the ever-widening gap in the numerical and material strength between Japan and the United States. . . . The Japanese Navy had two major weak points from the

very beginning. One of them was lack of efficient command. . . . The other was the easy-to-decipher code used by the Japanese Navy. . . .

In April 1961, Lyndon Johnson, then Vice President, invited Admiral Nimitz to be his guest at the LBJ Ranch to help him entertain West German Chancellor Konrad Adenauer, who was in America on a state visit. At the urging of the Secretary of the Navy, the admiral accepted the invitation, and he and Mrs. Nimitz flew to Texas. On the 16th, Johnson, Adenauer, and Nimitz went by helicopter to nearby Fredericksburg, Nimitz's birthplace, where most of the citizens spoke German as well as English.

The helicopter landed at the fair ground. Here Nimitz and Johnson made speeches in English and Adenauer spoke in German. Vice President Johnson, a familiar neighbor, was somewhat neglected in the enthusiasm the Fredericksburg natives showed for Nimitz and for Adenauer, who reminded them of all that was best in their German heritage.

Following the speeches, the townspeople entertained their guests with a saengerfest featuring old German songs. The visitors then toured the city, each in a separate car, mainly so that Adenauer could see the old houses remaining from the original German settlement. Nimitz, to whom these were familiar, had his car pull out of the procession and went to visit two sick aunts, Tante Lise and Tante Minni, who were in separate hospitals. When the distraught Secret Service men who were responsible for Nimitz's safety finally caught up with him, Johnson and Adenauer had already left town in the helicopter, so they took the admiral back to the ranch by car.

During the 1950s Nimitz became, to the general public, mainly a name attached to an imposing title. General MacArthur and Admiral Halsey were far better known. Their colorful personalities and news-making statements attracted attention almost to the exclusion of other officers in the Pacific theater. But with the appearance of books on World War II, notably those of Samuel Eliot Morison, people began to appreciate the contributions made by the quiet but able man who had commanded military operations in the Pacific Ocean Areas. On his 75th birthday the Naval Academy midshipmen had a plaque presented to him:

Presented to
Fleet Admiral Chester W. Nimitz
with great respect and admiration
from the
Brigade of Midshipmen, U. S. Naval Academy
24 February 1960

The following year, the class of 1961, nearly 900 midshipmen, autographed a copy of *Sea Power* and sent it to Nimitz.

October 7, 1964, was declared Nimitz Day at Berkeley. The Naval Academy football team was there to play the University of California. From Annapolis came also a large contingent of faculty, staff, and officers, including midshipmen. The game was a sellout. The visitors' side of the stadium was packed with naval personnel from the San Francisco area and far beyond.

When it was suggested to Admiral Nimitz that he attend the game in uniform, he expressed doubt about the wisdom of wearing that symbol of military authority. The Vietnam War was hotting up. Students, particularly at the University of California, were beginning to react against all things military. Nevertheless Nimitz took a chance; he put on the blue and gold.

At half time, Clark Kerr, chancellor of the university, stepped up to a microphone placed at mid-field and introduced California's governor, Edmund Brown. There was an ominous amount of booing from the stands. Onto the field came an open car with two naval officers in the back seat. As the first stepped out, Kerr introduced him as Rear Admiral Charles S. Minter, superintendent of the Naval Academy. There followed a mild amount of applause.

Then the second officer stepped out and raised his cap, exposing a head of snowy hair. Almost before Kerr could introduce him as Fleet Admiral Nimitz, the many thousands in the stands leapt to their feet and let loose with applause, cheers, and whistles that soon became pandemonium. It was clearly a salute of affection. Though few of the people in the stands had seen Nimitz before and not many of them had served under him, he had obviously won their hearts. They knew him by reputation as an officer who had wielded enormous power without arrogance or ostentation, a forceful leader who had remained simple, friendly, and approachable while commanding millions of men.

By the early 1960s, keeping house at Longview had become something of a burden for Admiral and Mrs. Nimitz. For Catherine, increasingly afflicted with arthritis, climbing the stairs was painful. A solution to the problem was found in the summer of 1963 when Commander, Western Sea Frontier, was detached without relief and his duties were assumed by the commandant of the 12th Naval District. This move left Quarters One, Yerba Buena Island, without a tenant, and the Navy offered this spacious residence to the Nimitzes. They gladly accepted the offer and moved in. With the comfort of an elevator and of stewards to look after them and the house, they received their usual stream of visitors. The admiral went from time to time to his office in the Federal Building and continued to answer his heavy volume of mail. He had long since dispensed with the services of an aide, though as a fleet admiral he was authorized to have three.

In October 1963, while visiting his office, the admiral fell and shattered his right kneecap. After surgery and five weeks in the hospital, he was able to walk again, but subsequently developed severe pains in his right hip and lower back.

"He would come down to breakfast and be looking quite good," said Catherine. "We would go for a walk and throw sticks for Gigi to catch. By the time we walked back he was already beginning to look a little grim. It was just plain old pain and something you apparently can't do much for.... The pain was too deep for anything to touch it. I would say, 'Well, now, let me rub your back. Let me put something on it.' He'd say, 'Darling, it's where you can't reach it. There's nothing that you can do.'"

The admiral's ailment was diagnosed as osteoarthritis of the spine, perhaps the result of an injury he had suffered when a lieutenant and almost certainly aggravated by his recent fall. His spinal cord appeared to be compressed by calcium that filled the spine at the point of his early injury.

By the fall of 1965, Chester was in such pain that he decided to talk the matter over with Dr. Gale G. Clark, an eminent neurosurgeon at Oak Knoll. When he got back to Quarters One, he told Catherine, "I'm going to the hospital tomorrow and Dr. Clark is going to make some tests. He asked if you would come."

Catherine waited at the hospital while the tests were being made. When they were completed, Clark told her that an operation to free the spinal cord from pressure would be long and severe, and added that if he were to operate on a junior officer for a condition of this sort, he would not send him back to duty for at least three months. Admiral Nimitz, said Clark, was much too old for such an operation but insisted that he wanted it done, even though it might not bring relief.

"Go ahead and do it," said Catherine.

Clark scheduled the surgery for the next day, November 10, the birthday of the Marine Corps. It was an extremely delicate operation, lasting several hours. The surgeon had literally to whittle the bone from around the spinal cord. As Nimitz was regaining consciousness in the recovery room, he opened his eyes, recognized Dr. Clark, and grinned. "You know, doctor," he said, "tonight I was to have cut the marines' birthday cake. Instead, you've been cutting on me."

The operation was a complete success, but then Nimitz's old lung weakness manifested itself; he caught pneumonia. The doctors controlled the pneumonia with antibiotics and, by the end of November, the back pain had gone and the admiral could walk a little with two canes. Then he suffered a series of small strokes and showed evidence of congestive heart failure. Chester Junior, who had come from Connecticut to visit his parents, said to Catherine, "Mother, take him home. He's not going to live. Take him home."

At last, on Catherine's insistence, the doctors agreed to let Chester leave the hospital. On December 11 he went back to Quarters One in an ambulance and was made comfortable in a little sun room off the upstairs front porch. From there and sometimes from the porch itself, he could look across the bay to Oakland and Berkeley or watch the traffic on the bay bridge.

To help her look after Chester, Catherine appointed one of their staff, B. L. Estebal, a Filipino who had studied to be a hospital corpsman. "He was one of the loveliest characters you can imagine," said Catherine, "and he was just devotion itself to the admiral. Estebal could somehow get food into him when others couldn't. Estebal would say, 'Just one more mouthful, Admiral, just one more mouthful.' Estebal would have given him his bath before he had his breakfast, and then Chester would go back to bed. He spent most of his time there."

Occasionally visitors were permitted to see the admiral, only for a few minutes and rarely more than two at a time. The Navy arranged for Commander M. Scott Carpenter, the astronaut, to visit him. He and Nimitz had an enjoyable chat about the wonders of space travel. On Christmas Day, the Edward V. Brewers, the Nimitzes' Berkeley neighbors, paid a call.

"None of this two at a time," said Chester when he was told that the Brewers had arrived. "I know the Brewers as a family. I want to see them all." They found him seated in an armchair in bathrobe and slippers, with a blanket over his knees—"very well groomed."

On New Year's Day, 1966, Jack Redman and his wife called and found the admiral watching one of the bowl football games on television. "He looked rather thin and weak," said Redman, "but seemed genuinely pleased to see us. We had a glass of sherry with them. Although it was an effort for him to speak very much, he said, 'Jack, you can have something stronger if you like.'"

In January Admiral Nimitz was readmitted to Oak Knoll but, as he was manifestly unhappy there and the doctors could do little for him, they soon sent him home. Before long, he sank into a coma and was conscious only intermittently. Kate arrived from the East Coast accompanied by Dick, one of her twin sons, who was considering going to Cal Tech.

"Now I will say this to you," Mrs. Nimitz said to Kate. "If you insist on seeing your father, that's all right. But I really think you would be happier if you didn't."

Kate was only too glad to remember her father as she had last seen him, in robust health.

On Sunday, February 20, Catherine kept checking on the admiral because he was being tended that day by a hospital corpsman she did not know. At about five o'clock in the afternoon she found that the corpsman had put blankets on the admiral.

"You've got blankets on him."

"Yes," replied the corpsman, "he's shivering."

"He's not shivering, he's dying. You call and get the doctor right away." The corpsman dashed from the room.

Alone with Chester, Catherine put her hand on him and he stopped shaking. She leaned over and kissed him. He was dead when the doctor arrived.

Nancy, who had recently been visiting her parents, returned to Berkeley at once. Mary came over from San Rafael. Chester Junior flew in from the East Coast and took charge of the funeral arrangements. There was little arranging to do, for his father had planned everything.

Admiral Nimitz knew that he was entitled to a state funeral and burial in Arlington Cemetery, but he wanted neither. He wanted a simple graveside ceremony. For a burial place he had chosen a vacant strip along one of the roads in the Golden Gate National Cemetery at San Bruno, a few miles south of San Francisco. He had arranged with veteran Pacific Fleet admirals Raymond Spruance, Kelly Turner, and Charles Lockwood that they and their wives should be buried there with him and Catherine. Each admiral was to have a regulation headstone like the thousands of others in the cemetery. Virtually all the other headstones bear either a Christian cross or a Jewish star of David enclosed in a circle. Nimitz had specified that the circle on his headstone should show only his fleet admiral's five stars—not a religious symbol but evidence perhaps that he had done his best in this life.

For a man of Admiral Nimitz's eminence, it was, of course, impossible to have a really simple funeral. Though there was to be a memorial service for him at the National Cathedral in Washington, many friends and dignitaries went to California from all parts of the country. Naval Academy classmates of Chester came tottering on canes.

Half an hour after noon on February 24, 1966, Chester Nimitz's 81st birthday, his closed casket was placed in the Treasure Island Naval Station chapel. There it lay in state, and a ceremonial guard of all services was stationed. Viewers were permitted to file through the chapel until 1:45 p.m. Meanwhile, the family received friends in the adjacent officers' club annex.

At 2:00 p.m. the casket was removed to a hearse. A motorcade of about a hundred vehicles was formed and, with police escort, headed for the Golden Gate National Cemetery. The overpasses of the road to San Bruno were crowded with many hundreds of people, mostly service or ex-service men, who had been waiting for hours to catch a glimpse of the hearse.

At the cemetery gates, the casket was placed on a caisson, which was drawn by twelve navy enlisted men and followed by a caparisoned horse with trappings that included a navy sword. Along a route flanked by evenly spaced enlisted men from all the services, the procession moved slowly to the grave site.

"I remember a sailor who couldn't have been old enough to have served with Dad," said Kate. "He was standing there at attention so stiff that his back was arched, and he had tears streaming down his cheeks."

As the caisson reached the grave site, 70 navy jet planes flew over the cemetery, and a 19-gun salute was fired, followed by three volleys and the playing of Taps. The Protestant graveside committal service was read by Rear Admiral James W. Kelly, chief of chaplains. A prayer was offered by Nimitz's old friend Francis Cardinal Spellman, who had come from New York. Secretary of the Navy Paul Nitze then presented the national colors and the admiral's personal flag to Catherine.

Bruce Canaga died a few days later. "Wasn't it fine," said Catherine, "that these two went away so close together?"

To a friend who wrote offering condolences, Catherine replied, "I'm not feeling sad. To me, he has just gone to sea and, as I have done so many times in the past, some day I will follow him. In the meantime, he's always in my heart, and I can hear him laugh when I do something silly."

# ACKNOWLEDGMENTS

THIS BOOK OWES a great deal to my former colleagues and coauthors Henry H. Adams and J. Roger Fredland and to my wife Grace, all of whom read the typescript in its entirety and made numerous suggestions for improvements in style, accuracy, organization, and selection of materials. My wife also assisted in conducting interviews and in the research and did much of the final typing.

Rear Admiral Edwin T. Layton, USN (Ret.), Captain Joseph J. Rochefort, USN (Ret.), and Captain Laurance F. Safford, USN (Ret.) provided me with information concerning the contributions cryptanalysis and radio intelligence made to the winning of the war against Japan. Admiral Layton and Captain Rochefort read chapters 5, 6, and 7 in both their rough and semifinal forms, in an effort to clear them of inaccuracies.

At the U.S. Naval Institute, Thomas F. Epley, editorial director, gave me valuable advice in setting the tone of the book, Frank Uhlig, Jr., pointed out passages that needed clarification, and Mary Veronica Amoss skillfully edited the text, correcting inaccuracies and removing ambiguities. John T. Mason, Jr., head of the Institute's oral history project, not only conducted or directed most of the taped interviews on which this book is based in part, but was always ready with advice or assistance, and conducted additional interviews at my request.

Dean C. Allard, director of the Operational Archives Branch of the Naval Historical Center, and his assistants, Mae Seaton and Kathleen Lloyd, were helpful in solving research problems. Allard saved me considerable time by having some of the key materials I needed copied and sent to me.

Commander Thomas B. Buell sent me copies of materials related to Admiral Nimitz from the Naval War College. Helpful also were Philip Brower of the MacArthur Memorial Bureau of Archives, Norfolk, Virginia; Harry Schwartz of the National Archives; and the staff of the Nimitz Library at the U.S. Naval Academy.

C. M. Nelson placed at my disposal the fruits of his research for his unpublished biography of Admiral Nimitz. My colleague Paolo E. Coletta provided me with numerous items he encountered in the course of his researches, which were somewhat parallel to my own. Chief Warrant Officer W. A. Langenwalter, of the Naval Academy's Seamanship and Tactics Department, advised me on tactical formations. Charles A. Ware did a bit of research for me in Honolulu newspaper files. The Naval Academy encouraged my work and granted me a semester's leave to finish it.

The Nimitz family answered, usually by return mail, any questions I sent them, and none ever sought to have any control over, or to see in advance, what went into this book.

# SOURCES

## INTERVIEWS

The interviews conducted by the Naval Institute are indicated by an (N) following the name of the interviewee. These interviews were recorded on tape and transcribed, and the transcriptions were generally sent to the interviewees for correction. Where more than one person was interviewed on a single tape, the interview is usually identified in the Chapter Notes, below, by the name of the first person listed. In the following list, ranks (where applicable) are given before names, but USN and USN (Ret.) are omitted after names. The rank given is that held at the time of the interview.

E. Robert Anderson; Adm. Thomas C. Anderson, MC (N); Sister Aquinas (Mary Nimitz) (N); James W. Archer (N); Vice Adm. Bernard L. Austin (N); Capt. James Bassett, Jr. (N); Rear Adm. George W. Bauernschmidt (N); Mr. and Mrs. Edward V. Brewer, Jr. (N); Adm. H. Chester Bruton (N); Vice Adm. William M. Callaghan (N); H. Joseph Chase (N); Dr. Gale G. Clark; Capt. A. B. Court (N); George E. Cozard (N); Adm. Maurice E. Curts (N); Capt. Tracy D. Cuttle, MC (N); Rear Adm. Neil K. Dietrich (N); Rear Adm. William Waldo Drake (N); Mrs. Milton Durst and Mr. Guenther Henke (N); Vice Adm. George C. Dyer; Adm. James Fife (N); Rear Adm. Eugene B. Fluckey (N); Charles M. Fox, Jr. (N); Adm. Harry W. Hill; Mrs. Charles Kiene (Tante Lise) (N); H. Arthur Lamar (N); Rear Adm. Onnie P. Lattu (N); Catherine Nimitz Lay and Capt. James T. Lay (N); Rear Adm. Edwin T. Layton (N); Rear Adm. J. Wilson Leverton, Jr. (N); Rear Adm. Preston V. Mercer (N); Mrs. Preston V. Mercer; Rear Adm. Charles S. Minter, Jr.; Capt. Sam P. Moncure (N); Rear Adm. Stuart S. Murray (N); Vice Adm. Lloyd M. Mustin (N); Fleet Adm. Chester W. Nimitz (Columbia University oral history project); Mrs. Chester W. Nimitz, Sr. (N); Mrs. Chester W. Nimitz, Sr., and Nancy Nimitz (N); Rear Adm. Chester W. Nimitz, Jr., and Mrs. Nimitz, Jr. (Joan) (N); Nancy Nimitz (N); Capt. Ralph C. Parker; Capt. George S. Perkins (N); Rear Adm. Mell A. Peterson (N); Maj. Gen. Omar T. Pfeiffer, USMC (Ret.) (Marine Corps oral history project); Comdr. David W. Plank, CHC (N); Rear Adm. Allen G. Quynn (N); Adm. Arthur W. Radford; Dora Nimitz Reagan (N); Vice Adm. John R. Redman (N); Max O. Reinbach (N); Capt. Joseph J. Rochefort (N); Vice Adm. John F. Shafroth; Vice Adm. Paul D. Stroop (N); Rear Adm. Raymond D. Tarbuck (N); Herman Toepperwein (N); Rear Adm. Harold C. Train; Rear Adm. Odale D. Waters (N); Mr. and Mrs. Joe Wheeler, Jr. (N); Vice Adm. F. E. M. Whiting (N). Transcripts of most of these interviews are at the U.S. Naval Institute, Annapolis, Maryland.

## MATERIALS AT OPERATIONAL ARCHIVES, NAVAL HISTORICAL CENTER, WASHINGTON, D.C.

### Nimitz Papers

Note: The gathering of these papers was initiated by Fleet Adm. Nimitz and implemented by Rear Adm. Ernest M. Eller, former Director of Naval History. The papers were organized and are controlled by Dean C. Allard, director of the Operational Archives.

CinCPac Command Summary, or Gray Book. A kind of diary of the Pacific War as seen from CinCPac headquarters. The daily entries were initialed by Adm. Nimitz and staff officers. An important guide to dates. Summarizes important dispatches. Includes minutes of some meetings attended by Adm. Nimitz away from headquarters.

CinCPac-CinCPOA dispatch file (microfilm). Contains Confidential and Secret, but not Top Secret, dispatches, about a hundred a day.

CinCPac-CinCPOA letter file.

World War II letters from Adm. Nimitz, Sr., to Mrs. Nimitz, Sr. (As noted in the Preface, Mrs. Nimitz burned most of these daily wartime letters, but those that survive are useful.)

Letters from Fleet Adm. Nimitz to E. B. Potter from 1955 to 1965. About a hundred, mostly dealing with the book *Sea Power*, but containing answers to many questions concerning World War II decisions and operations. (Facsimile copies at Operational Archives.)

*Proceedings, Findings, and Sentence of the General Court-Martial in the Case of Ensign Chester W. Nimitz, U.S. Navy.*

Lamar, "Anecdotes." A collection of wartime experiences of Adm. Nimitz, as recalled by his personal aide, H. Arthur Lamar.

Miscellaneous letters, papers, and documents.

### Other materials

World War II CNO classified dispatch file (source for Top Secret and other dispatches not in CinCPac file).

ComSoPac War Diary, with dispatches.

Forrestal Diary. Secretary of the Navy James V. Forrestal's original diary, not a copy. Millis, *Forrestal Diaries*, listed in the bibliography, below, is made up of selections from this original.

## MATERIALS AT NAVAL WAR COLLEGE

Nimitz letters and lectures.

Interview with Adm. Raymond A. Spruance by Philippe de Bausset, *Paris-Match*, July 1965. Original transcript, before translation. (De Bausset, Washington representative of *Paris-Match*, asked Adm. Nimitz to write a sketch of his wartime experiences for an edition of his magazine commemorating the twentieth anniversary of the end of the war in the Pacific. Nimitz asked me to write the article, which he would revise and extend, and it would be published in *Paris-Match* under a joint by-line. Before I could get started, Nimitz's distaste for publishing his wartime memoirs reasserted itself, and he canceled the project. "Everything I have to say about World War II is in *Sea Power*," he said. De Bausset, facing a deadline, was aghast, but, enterprisingly, he went after Adm. Spruance. Spruance was not willing to write anything, but he agreed to submit to an interview.)

## MATERIALS AT NATIONAL ARCHIVES

Logs of the heavy cruiser *Augusta.*
Operational schedule of Battleship Division One.

## MATERIALS AT MACARTHUR MEMORIAL
## BUREAU OF ARCHIVES, NORFOLK, VIRGINIA

CinCSoWesPac file of classified radio dispatches. (Copies of dispatches used from this source have been placed in Operational Archives, Naval Historical Center, Washington, D.C.)

## THE NIMITZ DIARY

Fleet Adm. and Mrs. Nimitz jointly kept a diary in a series of notebooks from Dec. 15, 1947 to Mar. 20, 1950. Mrs. Nimitz kindly loaned the notebooks to me for use in preparing this biography.

## LETTERS

A number of letters, in addition to those cited in the Chapter Notes, below, provided useful background information. Most of these came in response to a notice in the *U.S. Naval Institute Proceedings*, April 1971, requesting readers who had stories or anecdotes about Adm. Nimitz to send them to me for use in this biography. The writers of these letters were:

Capt. Robert E. Bassler, Vice Adm. W. Gordon Beecher, Jr., Rear Adm. Richard B. Black, Rear Adm. P. N. Buckley, RN, Adm. Arleigh Burke, Paul R. Copeland, Jr., Capt. Paul C. Crisley, August Faltin, John T. Gotjen, Capt. J. L. Gracey, Capt. Andrew Hamilton, Eugene C. Johnston, Edward von der Porten, L. R. Raish, Cooper K. Ragan, J. R. Smith, Guenter Steuer, Capt. W. P. Willis, Jr.

## MATERIALS REFERRED TO ONLY IN CHAPTER NOTES

Newspaper and magazine articles (*U.S. Naval Institute Proceedings* is abbreviated *USNIP.*)
Official reports.
Letters not in the categories noted above.
Material that fits no other category is designated as "Record."

## BIOGRAPHIES, MEMOIRS, DIARIES, HISTORICAL STUDIES

References to the following works are identified in the Chapter Notes by the first word in the entry below, in most cases the last name of the author (or of one of the authors). Where necessary for further identification, a short title has been added.

Acheson, Dean. *Present at the Creation: My Years in the State Department.* New York: W. W. Norton & Company, 1969.

Adamson, Hans Christian, and George Francis Kosco. *Halsey's Typhoons.* New York: Crown Publishers, Inc., 1967.

Albion, Robert Greenhalgh, and Robert Howe Connery. *Forrestal and the Navy.* New York and London: Columbia University Press, 1962.

Appleman, Roy E., James M. Burns, Russell A. Gugeler, and John Stevens. *Okinawa: The Last Battle.* Washington, D.C.: Historical Division, Department of the Army, 1948.

Arnold, H. H., General of the Air Force. *Global Mission.* New York: Harper & Brothers, 1949.

Barbey, Vice Admiral Daniel E., USN (Ret.). *MacArthur's Amphibious Navy: Seventh Amphibious Force Operations, 1943–1945.* Annapolis, Md.: U.S. Naval Institute, 1969.

Barde, Robert Elmer. *The Battle of Midway: A Study in Command.* Ph.D. dissertation, University of Maryland, 1971.

Bartley, Lt. Col. Whitman S. *Iwo Jima: Amphibious Epic.* Washington, D.C.: Historical Branch, G-3 Division, Headquarters, U.S. Marine Corps, 1954.

Belote, James and William. *Typhoon of Steel: The Battle for Okinawa.* New York: Harper and Row, 1970.

Benjamin, Park. *The United States Naval Academy.* New York: G. P. Putnam's Sons, 1900.

Bishop, Jim. *FDR's Last Year: April 1944–April 1945.* New York: William Morrow & Company, Inc., 1974.

Blair, Clay, Jr. *Silent Victory: The U.S. Submarine War against Japan.* Philadelphia and New York: J. B. Lippincott Company, 1975.

Brownlow, Donald Grey. *The Accused: The Ordeal of Rear Admiral Husband Edward Kimmel, U.S.N.* New York: Vantage Press, 1968.

Buell, Thomas B. *The Quiet Warrior: A Biography of Admiral Raymond A. Spruance.* Boston: Little, Brown and Company, 1974.

Buhite, Russell D. *Nelson T. Johnson and American Policy toward China, 1925–1941.* East Lansing: Michigan State University Press, 1968.

Cannon, M. Hamlin. *Leyte: The Return to the Philippines.* Washington, D.C.: Office of the Chief of Military History, Department of the Army, 1954.

Caraley, Demetrios. *The Politics of Military Unification.* New York and London: Columbia University Press, 1966.

Casey, Robert J. *Torpedo Junction: With the Pacific Fleet from Pearl Harbor to Midway.* Indianapolis: The Bobbs-Merrill Company, 1942.

Churchill, Winston S. *History of the Second World War*, Vol. VI. Boston: Houghton Mifflin Co., 1953.

Clark, J. J., Admiral, USN (Ret.) with Clark G. Reynolds. *Carrier Admiral.* New York: David McKay Company, Inc., 1967.

Craig, William. *The Fall of Japan.* New York: The Dial Press, 1967.

Craven, Wesley F., and James S. Cate, eds. *The Army Air Forces in World II.* Chicago: University of Chicago Press, Vol. I, 1948; Vol. IV, 1950; Vol. V, 1953.

Crowl, Philip A. *Campaign in the Marianas.* Washington, D.C.: Office of the Chief of Military History, Department of the Army, 1960.

———, and Edmund G. Love. *Seizure of the Gilberts and Marshalls.* Washington, D.C.: Office of the Chief of Military History, Department of the Army, 1955.

Davis, Burke. *Get Yamamoto.* New York: Random House, 1969.

———. *Marine! The Life of Lt. Gen. Lewis B. (Chesty) Puller, USMC (Ret.).* Boston: Little, Brown and Company, 1962.

Doenitz, Admiral Karl. *Memoirs: Ten Years and Twenty Days.* Translated by R. H. Stevens. London: Weidenfeld and Nicolson, 1959.

Dyer, Vice Admiral George Carroll, USN (Ret.). *The Amphibians Came to Conquer: The Story of Admiral Richmond Kelly Turner.* 2 vols. Washington, D.C.: U.S. Government Printing Office, 1971.

Farago, Ladislas. *The Tenth Fleet.* New York: Ivan Obolensky, Inc., 1962.

Forrestel, Vice Admiral E. P. *Admiral Raymond A. Spruance, USN: A Study in Command.* Washington, D.C.: U.S. Government Printing Office, 1966.

Frank, Benis M. *Halsey.* New York: Ballantine Books, 1974.

Frank, Pat, and Joseph D. Harrington. *Rendezvous at Midway: U.S.S. Yorktown and the Japanese Carrier Fleet.* New York: The John Day Company, 1967.

Frost, Commander H. H., USN. *The Battle of Jutland.* Annapolis, Md.: U.S. Naval Institute, 1936.

Fuchida, Mitsuo, and Masatake Okumiya. *Midway: The Battle that Doomed Japan.* Annapolis, Md.: U.S. Naval Institute, 1955.

Furlong, Captain William R., USN, ed. *Class of 1905, United States Naval Academy.* Annapolis, Md., 1930.

Glines, Carroll. *Doolittle's Tokyo Raiders.* Princeton, N.J.: D. Van Nostrand Company, Inc., 1964.

Griffith, Samuel B., II, Brigadier General, USMC (Ret.). *The Battle for Guadalcanal.* Philadelphia: J. B. Lippincott Company, 1963.

Halsey, Fleet Admiral William F., and Lieutenant Commander Joseph Bryan III, USNR. *Admiral Halsey's Story.* New York: Whittlesey House, 1947.

Hart, Robert A. *The Great White Fleet: Its Voyage Around the World, 1907–1909.* Boston: Little, Brown and Company, 1965.

Heinl, Lieutenant Colonel Robert D., Jr., USMC. *Marines at Midway.* Washington, D.C.: U.S. Government Printing Office, 1948.

Hewlett, Richard G., and Francis Duncan. *Nuclear Navy, 1946–1962.* Chicago: University of Chicago Press, 1974.

Hezlet, Vice Admiral Sir Arthur. *Aircraft and Sea Power.* New York: Stein and Day, 1970.

Hopkins, Captain Harold, RN. *Nice to Have You Aboard.* London: George Allen & Unwin Ltd., 1964.

Hoyt, Edwin P. *How They Won the War in the Pacific: Nimitz and His Admirals.* New York: Weybright and Talley, 1970.

Hunt, Frazier. *The Untold Story of Douglas MacArthur.* New York: The Devin-Adair Company, 1954.

Isely, Jeter A., and Philip A. Crowl. *The U.S. Marines and Amphibious War: Its Theory and Its Practice in the Pacific.* Princeton, N.J.: Princeton University Press, 1951.

James, D. Clayton. *The Years of MacArthur*, Vol. II, 1941–1945. Boston: Houghton Mifflin Company, 1975.

Joan of Arc, Sister. *My Name is Nimitz*. San Antonio, Texas: Standard Printing Company, 1948.

Johnson, Ellis A., and Davis A. Katcher. *Mines against Japan*. White Oak, Silver Spring, Md.: Naval Ordnance Laboratory, 1973.

Kahn, David. *The Codebreakers: The Story of Secret Writing*. London: Weidenfeld and Nicolson, 1967.

Kenney, George C. *General Kenney Reports: A Personal History of the Pacific War*. New York: Duell, Sloan and Pearce, 1949.

King, Fleet Admiral Ernest J., USN, and Walter Muir Whitehill. *Fleet Admiral King: A Naval Record*. New York: W. W. Norton & Company, Inc., 1952.

Laurence, William L. *Dawn over Zero: The Story of the Atomic Bomb*. New York: Alfred A. Knopf, 1946.

Leahy, Fleet Admiral William D. *I Was There*. New York: Whittlesey House, 1950.

LeMay, General Curtis E., with MacKinlay Kantor. *Mission with LeMay*. Garden City, N.Y.: Doubleday & Company, Inc., 1965.

Lockwood, Charles A., Vice Admiral, USN (Ret.). *Sink 'Em All: Submarine Warfare in the Pacific*. New York: E. P. Dutton & Co., Inc., 1951.

———, and Hans Christian Adamson. *Battles of the Philippine Sea*. New York: Thomas Y. Crowell Company, 1967.

Lord, Walter. *Incredible Victory*. New York: Harper & Row, 1967.

MacArthur, General of the Army Douglas. *Reminiscences*. New York: McGraw-Hill Book Company, 1964.

Maclay, Edgar S. *The History of the United States Navy*. Vol. III. 1st ed. New York: D. Appleton and Company, 1904.

Mahan, Captain A. T., USN. *Naval Strategy: Compared and Contrasted with the Principles and Practice of Military Operations on Land*. Boston: Little, Brown and Company, 1911.

Matloff, Maurice. *Strategic Planning for Coalition Warfare, 1943–1944*. Washington, D.C.: Office of the Chief of Military History, Department of the Army, 1959.

———, and Edward M. Snell. *Strategic Planning for Coalition Warfare, 1941–1942*. Washington, D.C.: Office of the Chief of Military History, Department of the Army, 1953.

McHale, Francis. *President and Chief Justice: The Life and Public Services of William Howard Taft*. Philadelphia: Dorrance & Company, 1931.

Miller, John, Jr. *Guadalcanal: The First Offensive*. Washington, D.C.: Historical Division, Department of the Army, 1949.

Miller, Thomas G., Jr. *The Cactus Air Force*. New York, Evanston, and London: Harper and Row, 1969.

Millis, Walter, ed. *The Forrestal Diaries*. New York: The Viking Press, 1951.

Mitchell, Donald W. *History of the Modern American Navy: From 1883 through Pearl Harbor*. New York: Alfred A. Knopf, 1946.

Morison, E. E. *Admiral Sims and the Modern American Navy*. Boston: Houghton Mifflin Company, 1942.

Morison, Samuel Eliot. *History of United States Naval Operations in World War II*. 15 vols. Boston: Atlantic, Little, Brown and Company, 1947–1962.

Morton, Louis. *Strategy and Command: The First Two Years*. Washington, D.C.: Office of the Chief of Military History, Department of the Army, 1962.

Newcomb, Richard F. *Abandon Ship: Death of the U.S.S. Indianapolis.* New York: Henry Holt and Company, 1958.

————. *Iwo Jima.* New York: Holt, Rinehart and Winston, Inc., 1965.

————. *Savo: The Incredible Naval Debacle off Guadalcanal.* New York: Holt, Rinehart and Winston, Inc., 1961.

*Nimitz: The Story of Pearl Harbor as Seen from the Japanese Perspective with the Relationship between Admiral Togo and Admiral Nimitz.* (Booklet) Fredericksburg, Texas: Admiral Nimitz Center, 1975.

Phillips, Cabell. *The Truman Presidency.* New York: The Macmillan Company, 1966.

Pogue, Forrest. *George C. Marshall: Ordeal and Hope, 1939–1942.* New York: The Viking Press, 1966.

————. *George C. Marshall: Organizer of Victory, 1943–1945.* New York: The Viking Press, 1973.

Potter, E. B. *The Naval Academy Illustrated History of the United States Navy.* New York: Thomas Y. Crowell Company, 1971.

————, ed. *The United States and World Sea Power.* Englewood Cliffs, N.J.: Prentice-Hall, Inc., 1955.

————, and Fleet Admiral Chester W. Nimitz, USN, eds. *Sea Power: A Naval History.* Englewood Cliffs, N.J.: Prentice-Hall, Inc., 1960.

————, and Fleet Admiral Chester W. Nimitz, USN. *Triumph in the Pacific: The Navy's Struggle against Japan.* Englewood Cliffs, N.J.: Prentice-Hall, Inc., 1963.

Reynolds, Clark G. *The Fast Carriers: The Forging of an Air Navy.* New York: McGraw-Hill Book Company, 1968.

Richardson, James O., Admiral, USN (Ret.), and George C. Dyer, Vice Admiral, USN (Ret.). *On the Treadmill to Pearl Harbor: The Memoirs of Admiral James O. Richardson, USN (Retired).* Washington, D.C.: Naval History Division, Department of the Navy, 1973.

Richardson, Norval. *Texas: The Lone Star State.* New York: Prentice-Hall, Inc., 1943.

Robison, Samuel S., and Mary L. Robison. *A History of Naval Tactics from 1530 to 1930.* Annapolis, Md.: U.S. Naval Institute, 1942.

Rogow, Arnold A. *James Forrestal.* New York: The Macmillan Company, 1963.

Roosevelt, Eleanor. *This I Remember.* New York: Harper & Brothers, 1949.

Roscoe, Theodore. *United States Submarines in World War II.* Annapolis, Md.: U.S. Naval Institute, 1949.

Rosenman, Samuel I. *Working with Roosevelt.* New York: Harper & Brothers, 1952.

Sherman, Frederick C., Admiral, USN (Ret.). *Combat Command: The American Aircraft Carriers in the Pacific War.* New York: E. P. Dutton & Company, 1950.

Sherwood, Robert E. *Roosevelt and Hopkins: An Intimate History,* Rev. ed. New York: Harper & Brothers, 1950.

Smith, General Holland M., USMC (Ret.) and Percy Finch. *Coral and Brass.* New York: Charles Scribner's Sons, 1949.

Smith, Vice Admiral William Ward, USN (Ret.). *Midway: Turning Point of the Pacific.* New York: Thomas Y. Crowell Co., 1966.

Steinberg, Alfred. *The Man from Missouri: The Life and Times of Harry S. Truman.* New York: G. P. Putnam's Sons, 1967.

Taylor, Theodore. *The Magnificent Mitscher*. New York: W. W. Norton & Company, 1954.

Toland, John. *But Not in Shame: The Six Months after Pearl Harbor*. New York: Random House, 1961.

————. *The Rising Sun: The Decline and Fall of the Japanese Empire, 1936–1945*. New York: Random House, 1970.

Truman, Harry S. *Memoirs by Harry S. Truman*. Vols. I and II. Garden City, N.Y.: Doubleday & Company, Inc., 1955, 1956.

Tugwell, Rexford G. *The Democratic Roosevelt*. Garden City, N.Y.: Doubleday & Company, Inc., 1957.

Tuleja, Thaddeus V. *Climax at Midway*. New York: W. W. Norton & Company, 1960.

Turnbull, Archibald D., and Clifford L. Lord. *History of United States Naval Aviation*. New Haven, Conn.: Yale University Press, 1949.

Vandegrift, A. A., and Robert B. Asprey. *Once a Marine: The Memoirs of General A. A. Vandegrift, United States Marine Corps*. New York: W. W. Norton & Company, 1964.

Wilson, Eugene E. *Slipstream*. New York: McGraw-Hill Book Company, Inc., 1950.

Woodward, C. Vann. *The Battle for Leyte Gulf*. New York: The Macmillan Company, 1947.

# CHAPTER NOTES

*General:* (1) Originals or copies of all radio dispatches and, so far as possible, all letters and records cited below are deposited at the Operational Archives, Naval Historical Center. (2) The CinCPac Command Summary, or Gray Book, was an important source for all World War II chapters.


## 1. THE APPOINTMENT

Interviews: Adm. Nimitz, Sr., Mrs. Nimitz, Sr., C. W. Nimitz, Jr., Lay, Sister Aquinas, Lamar, Whiting, Plank, Robert Anderson, Shafroth. Letters: Adm. Nimitz, Sr., to Mrs. Nimitz, Sr., Dec. 20, 21, and 24, 1941. Record: Comdr. John L. Pillsbury, USNR (Ret.), reconstructed statement of Adm. Nimitz, Sr., on his appointment as CinCPac. Newspaper: *New York Times*, Dec. 7–24, 1941. Article: Fletcher Pratt, "Nimitz and His Admirals," *Harper's Magazine*, Feb. 1945. Books: Toland, *Shame* and *Rising Sun*; Hoyt; King; Morison, *Operations*, III; Potter, *Triumph*. Conversations of the author with Mrs. Nimitz, Sr.


## 2. CINCPAC FROM TEXAS

PEARL HARBOR     Interviews: Adm. Nimitz, Sr., Train, Drake, Layton, Parker. Letters: Adm. Nimitz, Sr., to Mrs. Nimitz, Sr., Dec. 26, 28, and 31, 1941, and Jan. 4, 9, 12, and 18, 1942. Record: Rough notes made by Rear Adm. William F. Fitzgerald, Jr., USN (Ret.) from interview with Fleet Adm. Nimitz, Oct. 15, 1964. Articles: Fleet Adm. Nimitz, "Our *Good* Luck at Pearl Harbor," *The American Weekly*, Dec. 7, 1957; E. B. Potter, "Chester William Nimitz, 1885–1966," *USNIP*, July 1966. Books: Brownlow; Toland, *Shame*; Smith, *Midway*; Barde.

ANCESTRY     Letter: Charles Henry Nimitz to Midshipman Chester W. Nimitz, Feb. 19, 1902 (a slightly inaccurate version is in Fleet Adm. Nimitz taped interview). Book: Joan of Arc.

TEXAS AND ANNAPOLIS     Interviews: Adm. Nimitz, Sr., Mrs. Nimitz, Sr., C. W. Nimitz, Jr., Reagan, Durst. Articles, books, newspapers: Fleet Adm. Nimitz, "My Way of Life," *Boys' Life*, Jan. 1966, and ms. of "Career by Chance," *San Francisco Examiner*, Mar. 17, 1957; Walter F. Edwards, ed., *The Story of Fredericksburg*, Fredericksburg, Tex., Chamber of Commerce, 1969; Julie Estill, *Admiral Chester W. Nimitz: His Heritage and Training*, Fredericksburg, Tex., 1942; E. B. Potter, "Chester William Nimitz, 1885–1966," *USNIP*, July 1966; Fredericksburg *Standard*, Fredericksburg, Tex., Oct. 13, 1945. Guenther Henke manuscript. Conversations of author with Nimitz relatives and associates in Fredericksburg and Kerrville.

## 3. HOLDING THE LINE

Interview: Parker. Letters: Adm. Nimitz, Sr., to Mrs. Nimitz, Sr., Feb. 28, Mar. 19 and 22, 1942. Record: Fitzgerald notes noted for preceding chapter. Books: Farago; Halsey; Casey; Hoyt; Toland, *Shame*; Fuchida; Morison, *Operations*, III and IV; King; MacArthur; Potter, *Triumph*; Barde. Radio dispatches: SecNav (Jan. 1942) 060230; ComInCh (Dec. 1941) 302740, (Jan. 1942) 021718, 202150, (Feb. 1942), 051555, 061513, 062352, 092245, 151830, (Mar. 1942) 091630; CinCPac (Jan. 1942) 220055, 280311, (Feb. 1942) 010736; CTF 16, (Mar. 1942) 050701; CTF 17, (Feb. 1942) 010040, 010623. Author's conversations with Fleet Admiral Nimitz.

## 4. BACKGROUND OF A STRATEGIST

Interviews: Adm. Nimitz, Sr., Mrs. Nimitz, Sr., Lamar, Parker. Letters: Adm. Nimitz, Sr., to Midn. W. S. Williamson, Jan. 23, 1962 (the beer party); to Potter, Jan. 18, 1963. Articles: Adm. Nimitz, Sr., "My Way of Life," *Boys' Life*, Jan. 1966, and "First Ship was Memorable," The Time of My Life series, Richmond *Times-Dispatch*, Sept. 1, 1961; *Washington Post*, Sept., Oct., 1901 (Sampson-Schley controversy). Nimitz Papers: *Proceedings, Findings, and Sentence of the General Court-Martial in the Case of Ensign Chester W. Nimitz, U.S. Navy*; U.S. Naval Academy, Registrar's files, "Nimitz, C. W."; Capt. George V. Stewart, undated memorandum to the superintendent, U.S. Naval Academy, in Naval Academy archives. Books: Benjamin; Mitchell; Halsey; Potter, *Sea Power*; Maclay; *Register of Alumni* (U.S. Naval Academy), 1956; *Lucky Bag* (Naval Academy yearbook), 1905; Morison, *Operations*, I; Roscoe; King; Mahan, pp. 166, 255; McHale; Hart; Furlong. Author's conversations with Fleet Admiral Nimitz.

## 5. CONFRONTATION IN THE CORAL SEA

Interviews: Layton, Rochefort. Letters: Layton to Potter, Apr. 8, 1970; David E. London, former manager of the St. Francis Hotel, to William Belote, Nov. 15, 1967 (details of Pope suite); Captain Laurance F. Safford, USN (Ret.) to Potter, Aug. 19, 1970. Books: Fuchida; Glines; Halsey; Kahn; Lord; Morison, *Operations*, IV; Toland, *Shame* and *Rising Sun*. Radio dispatches: ComInCh (May 1942) 111245; CinCPac (May 1942) 050321, 050329, 050345, 060239, 070245, 080703, 090031, 092219; CinCSoWesPac (May 1942) 080215; Com 14, Station Hypo, (May 1942) 082212; CTF 17 (May 1942) 042226, 072356, 080137, 080252, 080346, 080402. Admiral Layton and Captain Rochefort read and corrected this chapter.

## 6. PREPARING TO DEFEND MIDWAY

Interviews: Layton, Rochefort, Bassett. Letters: Adm. Nimitz, Sr., to King, May 29, 1942; to Mrs. Nimitz, Sr., May 31 and June 2, 1942; Rear Adm. Edwin T. Layton, USN (Ret.) to Potter, Apr. 27, 1975; Capt. Joseph J. Rochefort, USN (Ret.) to Potter, Dec. 14, 1971 and Apr. 30, 1975; Vice Adm. George C. Dyer, USN (Ret.) to Potter, Sept. 16, 1975. Article: Gordon W. Prange, "Miracle at Midway," *Reader's*

*Digest*, Nov. 1972. Books: Lord; Forrestel; Frank, *Midway*; Fuchida; Halsey; Heinl; Kahn; Morison, *Operations*, IV; Matloff, *1941–42*; Morton; Smith, *Midway*; Tuleja; Barde. Corrections to rough and next-to-final copies of this chapter by Layton and Rochefort.

## 7. THE BATTLE OF MIDWAY

Interviews: Layton, Rochefort, Curts, Adm. Mercer. Letters: Adm. Nimitz, Sr., to Potter, Apr. 24, 1965; MacArthur to Adm. Nimitz, Sr., May 29, 1942. Article: Gordon W. Prange, "Miracle at Midway," *Reader's Digest*, Nov. 1972. Radio dispatches: Mac-Arthur, incoming (May 1942) 280351; (June 1942) 010100, 020455. CinCPac: outgoing (May 1942) 160307, 160325, 180357, 180403, 210137, (June 1942) 040014, 040245, 040715, 040801, 040811, 040959, 041847, 042331, 042340, 050052, 050129, 050335, 050611, 050915, 051134, 051203, 051225, 060315, 060831, incoming, 041445, 041804, 041835, 042020, 042135, 042145, 042153, 042158, 042255, 05001?, unknown (apparently from CTF 17), 050204, 050414, 050415, 050430, 050510, 050645, 050730, 050742, 050850, 050912, 051341, 051345, 052000, 052020, 052036, 052355, 060235, 061115, 062123, 070735, 070740, 071330, 071915, Comdr. Flight O, 040415, Officer Controlling Flight 92 to Comdr. Flight 92, 041649 (evidently in error, should be 042204), Dutch Harbor, 041759, Com. 14, 042136, CTF 17, 050140, Midway, 050204. Corrections to rough and next-to-final copies of this chapter by Layton and Rochefort. The oft-repeated story of Commander, Torpedo Squadron 8 (from the *Hornet*), requesting and being denied permission to withdraw and refuel before attacking the Japanese carriers (Forrestel, p. 46; Casey, p. 379; Hoyt, p. 100) seems now disproved (*see* Barde, p. 172*n*.).

## 8. CHESTER AND CATHERINE

Interviews: Adm. Nimitz, Sr., Mrs. Nimitz, Sr., Adm. Mercer, Mrs. Mercer. Letters to Potter: John M. Thompson (who was in one of the crash boats that came to the rescue of Adm. Nimitz's plane), Apr. 6, 1971; H. C. "Pat" Daly (who gave the admiral his diathermy treatment), May 12, 1971; Sister Aquinas, Dec. 31, 1971; Comdr. Marshall L. Smith, USN (Ret.) (who drove Mrs. Nimitz's car and brought the admiral fresh underwear), Feb. 7, 1972; Nancy Nimitz, Oct. 23, 1972. Lieut. Nimitz's letter to his mother is in the Adm. Nimitz, Sr., interview. Articles: Stanley High, "Nimitz Fires When He Is Ready," *Reader's Digest*, Apr. 1953; Lieut. C. W. Nimitz, "Military Value and Tactics of Modern Submarines," *USNIP*, Dec. 1912. Lecture: Lieut. C. W. Nimitz, "Defensive and Offensive Tactics of Submarines," U.S. Naval War College, Newport, R.I., June 20, 1912. Books: Morton; Hoyt; Morison, *Operations*, VI; Dyer.

## 9. RISING STAR

Interviews: Adm. Nimitz, Sr. (including his letters quoted in this chapter), Mrs. Nimitz, Sr., C. W. Nimitz, Jr., Fife. Articles: Vice Adm. W. S. Anderson in "Comment and Discussion," *USNIP*, Oct. 1966; Nimitz, "The Navy's Secret Weapon,"

*Petroleum Today*, spring 1961; *The Times*, London, June 16 and 20 and July 2, 1913; *New York Times*, July 2, 1913; *Naval and Military Record and Royal Dockyard Gazette*, Vol. 31, 1913. Letter to Potter: August A. Busch, Jr., Jan. 12, 1972. Books: Furlong; Potter, *Illustrated History*, p. 141.

## 10. TACTICIAN AND TEACHER

Interviews: Adm. Nimitz, Sr., C. W. Nimitz, Jr., Mrs. Nimitz, Sr., Mrs. Nimitz, Sr., and Nancy Nimitz, Nancy Nimitz, Lay, Archer, Brewer, Chase, Cuttle, Lattu, Perkins. Letters: Nimitz to Adm. Charles L. Melson, Sept. 24, 1965, in Naval War College files; Nimitz to Capt. Samuel S. Robison, July 9, 1928 and May 30, 1929, in U.S. Naval Academy archives; Mrs. Nimitz, Sr., to John T. Mason, Jr., Jan. 16, 1970. Reports: SecNav Reports, 1923–26; BuNav Reports, 1923–26. Speeches: Fleet Adm. Nimitz, at Naval War College, Oct. 10, 1960, and Oct. 12, 1961, in Naval War College library. Books: Frost; Morison, *Sims*; Wilson; Robison; Mitchell.

## 11. THE *RIGEL* AND THE *AUGUSTA*

Interviews: Adm. Nimitz, Sr., C. W. Nimitz, Jr., Mrs. Nimitz, Sr., Lay, Leverton, Nancy Nimitz, Mustin, Lattu, Waters, Moncure. Letter: C. W. Nimitz, Jr., to Potter, Nov. 20, 1973. Records: BuNav Reports, 1931–1935; Log of the *Augusta*, 1933–35, at National Archives. Typed narrative: Rear Admiral E. M. Thompson. Books: Buhite; Furlong; Davis, *Marine!*.

## 12. FLAG RANK

Interviews: Adm. Nimitz, Sr., C. W. Nimitz, Jr., Mrs. Nimitz, Sr., Lay, Nancy Nimitz, Adm. Mercer, Bauernschmidt. Letters: Mrs. Nimitz, Sr., to John T. Mason, Jr., Jan. 16, 1970; Mrs. James T. Lay to Potter, Oct. 17, 1973. Article: Nimitz, "The Navy's Secret Weapon," *Petroleum Today*, spring 1961. Records: BatDivOne, 1938–39, at National Archives; CNO Reports, 1938, 1939. BuNav Reports, 1935–41. Book: Isely.

## 13. GUADALCANAL INVADED

Interviews: Bassett, Lamar, Drake, Layton, Redman, Peterson. Letters: Spruance to Potter, Dec. 1, 1964; Knox to Nimitz, Aug. 11, 1942; Nimitz to King, Sept. 2, 1942; Adm. Nimitz, Sr., to Mrs. Nimitz, Sr., Sept. 15 and Oct. 17, 1942. Nimitz Papers: Lamar, "Anecdotes." Record: ComSoPac War Diary, 1942. Books: Buell; Morison, *Operations*, IV and V; Potter, *Sea Power*; Newcomb, *Savo*; Reynolds; Albion; Halsey; Arnold; Hoyt; Vandegrift; Griffith; Miller, *Guadalcanal*; Toland, *Rising Sun*; Frank, *Halsey*; Miller, *Cactus*; Morton. Radio dispatches: CinCPac (Aug. 1942) 062045, 070231, 090341, 092033, 122025, (Oct. 1942) 162359; ComSoPac (Aug. 1942) 082140, 090310, 090544, 090640, 131400; CTF 61 (Fletcher), (Aug. 1942) 090620, 131400; CTF 62 (Turner), (Aug. 1942) 090815, 090725, 101220; CominCh (Aug. 1942) 121250.

## 14. GUADALCANAL RECAPTURED

Interviews: Drake, Layton, Adm. Mercer. Letters: Adm. Nimitz, Sr., to Mrs. Nimitz, Sr., Oct. 19, 21, 24, and 25, 1942; Knox to Nimitz, Oct. 24, 1942. Nimitz Papers: Lamar, "Anecdotes." Books: Halsey; Vandegrift; Hoyt; Morison, *Operations*, V; Griffith; Morton; Toland, *Rising Sun*. Radio dispatches: CinCPac, (Jan. 1943) 110221; CinCSoWesPac, (Jan. 1943) 131131.

## 15. CINCPAC AND CINCPAC STAFF

Interviews: Adm. Mercer, Layton, Lamar, Peterson, Drake, Callaghan, Redman, Tarbuck, C. W. Nimitz, Jr. Letters: Adm. Nimitz, Sr. to Mrs. Nimitz, Sr., Oct. 31, 1942; Capt. Bernard A. Lienhard, USN (Ret.) to Potter, Mar. 25, 1973. Nimitz Papers: Lamar, "Anecdotes." Speech: Adm. Isaac C. Kidd, Jr., Sept. 7, 1973, at dedication of Nimitz Library, U.S. Naval Academy (Nimitz's check-off list). Articles: Fletcher Pratt, "Nimitz and His Admirals," *Harper's Magazine*, Feb. 1945; Potter, "Chester William Nimitz, 1885–1966," *USNIP*, July 1966; Capt. Lienhard (above), "Have You Seen Chester?", *USNIP*, July 1974. Books: Davis, *Yamamoto*; Buell; Hoyt; Morison, *Operations*, VI and VII; Morton; Toland, *Rising Sun*; Lockwood, *Sink 'Em*; Blair; Kahn; Roscoe. Conversations of author with Fleet Admiral Nimitz.

## 16. LAUNCHING THE CENTRAL PACIFIC DRIVE

Interviews: Thomas Anderson, Lamar, Leverton, Spruance interview for *Paris-Match*. Letters: Nimitz to King, Apr. 8 and July 22, 1943. The quotation from President Roosevelt's letter to Adm. Nimitz is as Lamar recalled it in his interview and may not be exact. Nimitz Papers: Lamar, "Anecdotes." Articles: Fletcher Pratt, "Nimitz and His Admirals," *Harper's Magazine*, Feb. 1945; S. L. A. Marshall in "Comment and Discussion," *USNIP*, July 1966. Books: Morison, *Operations*, V, VI, VII; Halsey; Reynolds; Hoyt; Isely; Potter, *Sea Power*; Smith, *Coral and Brass*; Crowl, *Gilberts and Marshalls*; Matloff, *1943–1944*; Morton; Dyer; Buell; Forrestel.

## 17. GALVANIC AND FLINTLOCK

Interviews: Thomas Anderson, Hill, Lay, Lamar, Layton, Redman, Quynn, Spruance interview for *Paris-Match*. Letter: Adm. Nimitz, Sr., to Mrs. Nimitz, Sr., Nov. 29, 1943. Nimitz Papers: Lamar, "Anecdotes." Articles: Potter, "Nimitz"; Marshall; both *USNIP*, July 1966. Books: Reynolds; Morison, *Operations*, VII; Hoyt; Buell; Forrestel; Smith, *Coral and Brass*; Dyer; Isley; Clark; King; Halsey; Potter, *Sea Power*; Crowl, *Gilberts and Marshalls*. The Nimitz quotation "This is it. . . ." is based on Dyer. A slightly different version, previously published by me, was related by Fleet Admiral Nimitz in casual conversation. When he spoke to Dyer, Nimitz knew it was for publication, and Dyer read it back to Nimitz from his notes for possible correction. Radio dispatches: CinCPac (Nov. 1943) 212225; ComCenPac (Nov. 1943) 202334, 241807; CTF 17, Lockwood (Feb. 1944) 180653; CTF 52, Turner (Nov. 1943) 202201, 210710, (Feb. 1944) 010158, 020120; CTF 53, Hill (Nov. 1943) 210105, 210131, 210957; CTG 58.2, Montgomery (Feb. 1944) 180653; CominCh (Feb. 1944) 031517, 121451.

## 18. LEAP TO THE MARIANAS

Interviews: Thomas Anderson, Lamar, Layton, Adm. Mercer. Letters: King to Nimitz, Feb. 8 and 17, 1944; Nimitz to King, Feb. 18, 1944. Nimitz Papers: Lamar, "Anecdotes." Articles: Noel Busch, "Admiral Chester Nimitz," *Life*, July 10, 1944; Fletcher Pratt, "Nimitz and His Admirals," *Harper's Magazine*, Feb. 1945; Potter, "Chester William Nimitz," *USNIP*, July 1966. Books: Reynolds; Crowl, *Marianas*; Kenney; Matloff, *1943–1944*; Toland, *Rising Sun*; Halsey; Morison, *Operations*, VI, VII, VIII; Potter, *Sea Power*; Pogue, *Organizer of Victory*; Hoyt; Buell; Forrestel; Leahy; James; Bishop; Smith, *Coral and Brass*; Albion. The quotation beginning, "I'll tell you something you may not know . . ." is from Halsey, p. 186. Halsey places this conversation in Dec. 1943. Since MacArthur would have no basis for making such a statement at that time, I have assumed that Halsey's memory was at fault and that the conversation actually took place in Feb. 1944. Kenney, p. 349, gives a slightly different version of MacArthur's reaction. Radio dispatches: CinCSoWesPac (Mar. 1944) 150115; CinCPac (Mar. 1944) 151036.

## 19. OF GENERALS, ADMIRALS, AND A PRESIDENT

Interview: Lamar. Letters and memoranda: Adm. Nimitz, Sr., to King, Sept. 8, 1944; Marshall to King, Nov. 22, 1944; King to Marshall, Nov. 23, 1944. Document: CinCPac Op Plan No. 3–44, Apr. 23, 1944. Nimitz Papers: Lamar, "Anecdotes." Books: Lockwood, *Philippine Sea*; Roscoe; Morison, *Operations*, VIII; Reynolds; Buell; Potter, *Sea Power*; King; Matloff, *1943–1944*; Taylor; Smith, *Coral and Brass*; Hoyt; Dyer; Crowl, *Marianas*; Pogue, *Organizer of Victory*; Bishop; Halsey; Rosenman; Leahy; James; Hunt; Vandegrift. Radio dispatches: Com5thFleet, Spruance (June 1944) 190825, 211147; CTF 17, Lockwood (June 1944) 180016. I include Gen. MacArthur's final quotation on page 318 with some hesitation because I am not certain of the reliability of my source. It is an opinion, however, that MacArthur frequently expressed, though possibly not at this time and place.

## 20. RETURN TO THE PHILIPPINES

Interviews: Austin, Parker, Spruance interview for *Paris-Match*. Letters: Nimitz to King, Oct. 28, 1944; Adm. Nimitz, Sr., to Potter, Oct. 18, 1959, and May 1, 1965; C. W. Nimitz, Jr., to Potter, Feb. 16, 1970, and Aug. 8, 1974. Document: CinCPOA Op Plan No. 8–44, Sept. 27. Books: Lockwood, *Philippine Sea*; Morison, *Operations*, XII; Reynolds; Buell; Potter, *Sea Power*; King; Hoyt; Churchill; Pogue, *Organizer of Victory*; Potter, *U.S. and World Sea Power*; Woodward; Clark; MacArthur; Halsey; Cannon; Leahy. Admiral Nimitz's thoughts on Oct. 25, 1944, are based on conversations with the author. Nimitz said, "I knew perfectly well where Task Force 34 was." Radio dispatches (all Oct. 1944): Com3rdFlt, Halsey, 240130, 240252, 240400, 240434, 240612, 240838, 241104, 241124, 241800, 242204, 242348, 242355, 250027, 250215, 250217, 251226, 251317; Com7thFlt, Kinkaid, 240315, 241742, 241912, 242123, 242203, 242225, 242227, 242239, 242329, 250146, 250231, 250316, 252403, 251007; CTF 38, Mitscher, 240817, 240930, 240942, 242335; CTU 77.4.3, C. Sprague, 242207; CinCPac, Nimitz, 250044.

## 21. THE PHILIPPINES CAMPAIGN AND THE MOVE TO GUAM

Interviews: Bauernschmidt, Dyer, Fox, Lamar, Mrs. Nimitz, Sr., Nancy Nimitz, Whiting. Letter: Nimitz to King, Dec. 13, 1944. Articles: Robert S. Schwab, "A Narrow Escape," *USNIP*, July 1966, and E. B. Potter, "The Command Personality," *USNIP*, Jan. 1969. Books: Morison, *Operations*, XII and XIII; Potter, *Sea Power*; Hoyt; Reynolds; King; Leahy; Hopkins; Clark; Arnold; Adamson; Halsey; Craven. Conversations of the author with Fleet Admiral Nimitz.

## 22. IWO JIMA AND OKINAWA

Interviews: Sister Aquinas, Lay, Lamar, Nancy Nimitz, Mrs. Nimitz, Sr. Letters: Adm. Nimitz, Sr., to Mrs. Nimitz, Sr., Mar. 17 and 25, Apr. 8, 13, 16, and 24, 1945; Catherine Lay to Potter, Sept. 5, 1974; Sister Aquinas to Potter, Dec. 12, 1974. Newspaper: *New York Times*, Feb. 11, 1945. Document: Forrestal Diary (original). Article: Potter, "Chester William Nimitz," *USNIP*, July 1966. Books: Morison, *Operations*, XIV; Reynolds; Smith, *Coral and Brass*; Buell; Dyer; Newcomb, *Iwo Jima*; Bartley; King; Halsey; Hoyt; Johnson; LeMay; Craven, V; Toland, *Rising Sun*; Belote; Adamson; Potter, *Sea Power*; Vandegrift; Appleman; Bishop. Radio dispatches: CTF 52, Blandy (Feb. 1945) 181220; Com5thFleet, Spruance (Feb. 1945) 182115; CTF 51, Turner (Feb. 1945) 190150, (Apr. 1945) 010255.

## 23. VICTORY

Interviews: Lamar, Drake, Layton, Lay (includes letter: Adm. Nimitz, Sr., to Catherine Lay, Sept. 1, 1945), Mrs. Nimitz, Sr. (includes letter: Nimitz to Mrs. Nimitz, Sept. 2, 1945). Letters: Adm. Nimitz, Sr., to Mrs. Nimitz, Sr., Apr. 3, 5, and 26 and May 6 and 7, 1945; Adm. Frederick L. Ashworth to Potter, Jan. 2, 1975; King to Nimitz, May 11 and 12, 1945; Layton to Potter, Apr. 27, 1975. CinCPac/POA serial 0005057, May 19, 1945. Document: Forrestal Diary (original). Newspaper: *New York Times*, Aug. 14, 20, 29, and 31 and Sept. 2, 1945. Books: Hoyt; Laurence; Arnold; Halsey; King; Buell; Johnson; Newcomb, *Abandon Ship*; Toland, *Rising Sun*; Morison, *Operations*, XIV; Reynolds, Craig. Radio dispatches: CinCPac (Apr. 1945) 132346, 142242, 151406, 160250. Conversations of the author with Fleet Admiral Nimitz.

## 24. FROM CINCPAC TO CNO

Interviews: Lamar, Drake, Mrs. Nimitz, Sr., and Nancy Nimitz. Letter: Truman to Potter, Feb. 13, 1970. Document: Forrestal Diary (original). Record: "Fredericksburg's Tribute to Admiral Chester W. Nimitz," compiled by the Fredericksburg Chamber of Commerce. Newspapers and newsmagazines: *New York Times*, Oct. 2, 10, 11, and 13, Nov. 1, 10, 18, 20, and 21 and Dec. 16, 1945; Fredericksburg *Standard*, Oct. 13, 1945; *Time*, Oct. 22 and 29, 1945; *Newsweek*, Oct. 15, 1945. Books: Craig, Hewlett, Rogow, King, Taylor, Buell, Forrestel, Hoyt. Conversations of the author with Fleet Admiral Nimitz.

## 25. CHIEF OF NAVAL OPERATIONS

Interviews: Adm. Nimitz, Sr., C. W. Nimitz, Jr., Mrs. Nimitz, Sr., Nancy Nimitz, Lay, Fluckey, Bruton, Dietrich, Redman. Letters: Adm. Nimitz, Sr., to Potter, Mar. 9, 1965 (gun instructor story enclosed, "To give you a laugh!"); Public Information Office, University of Richmond to Potter, Jan. 6, 1975. Record: Nimitz Diary, Dec. 15, 1947–Mar. 5, 1948; CNO Reports, FY 1946, 1947, 1948. Newspapers and news-magazines: *New York Times*, Feb. 24, 1946, and Nov. 13, 1947; *Time*, Mar. 4, 1946; *Newsweek*, Mar. 4, 1946, and Oct. 27, 1947. Articles: Adm. Nimitz, Sr., in the following—"My Way of Life," *Boys' Life*, Jan. 1966; "The Navy: Investment in Peace," *Nation's Business*, May 1946; "Your Navy as Peace Insurance," *National Geographic*, June 1946; "Labor We *Thank* You," *American Federalist*, Oct. 1946; "Is the Navy Obsolete?" *Sea Power*, Nov. 1946; "Seapower Still Indispensable," Washington *News Digest*, Feb. 1947; Fleet Admiral William F. Halsey and Lt. Comdr. J. Bryan III, "Admiral Halsey Tells His Story," Part I, *Saturday Evening Post*, June 14, 1947. Books: Newcomb, *Abandon Ship*; Albion; Millis; Caraley; Doenitz; Potter, *Sea Power*; Hewlett. Conversations of the author with Fleet Admiral Nimitz.

## 26. FROM THE NAVY DEPARTMENT TO
## THE UNITED NATIONS

Interviews: Sister Aquinas, Lay, Mrs. Nimitz, Sr., Nancy Nimitz, Mrs. Nimitz, Sr., and Nancy, Fife, Cozard. Letters: Truman to Potter, Feb. 13, 1970; Nancy Nimitz to Potter, May 13 and 22, 1975. Record: Nimitz Diary. Newspaper: *New York Times*, Apr. 24 and 27, Oct. 28, and Nov. 1, 1949. Articles: Fleet Admiral William F. Halsey and Lt. Comdr. J. Bryan III, "Admiral Halsey Tells His Story," Part I, *Saturday Evening Post*, June 14, 1947; Nimitz, "The Task of the Plebiscite Mission," *United Nations Bulletin*, May 15, 1949, and "My 150 Days at the UN," *United Nations World Magazine*, Sept. 1949; Paolo E. Coletta, "The Defense Unification Battle, 1947–50: The Navy," *Prologue*, spring 1975; Adm. Louis E. Denfeld, "Reprisal: Why I Was Fired," *Collier's*, Mar. 18, 1950. Books: Rogow, Acheson, Steinberg. Conversations of the author with Fleet Admiral Nimitz and with Mrs. Nimitz.

## 27. LAST YEARS

Interviews: C. W. Nimitz, Jr., Nancy Nimitz, Mrs. Nimitz, Sr., and Nancy, Mrs. Nimitz, Sr., Lay, Plank, Fife, Court, Leverton, Cozard, Clark, Durst, Brewer, Redman. Letters: Adm. Nimitz, Sr., to Potter, May 31, 1963, Aug. 26, 1963, and May 4, 1965; Capt. John G. Roenigk to Adm. Nimitz, Sr., Jan. 10, 1963; Sister Aquinas to Potter, Apr. 5, 1970, and June 27, 1975; Nancy Nimitz to Potter, May 13 and 22, 1975; C. W. Nimitz, Jr., to Potter, June 9, 1975. Documents and records: Nimitz to Potter, "A Prayer for Restraint"; Dr. Gale G. Clark, Medical Report on Chester William Nimitz, U.S. Naval Hospital, Oakland, Calif., Jan. 6, 1966; Memorandum, Capt. D. H. Pugh to Comdr. Trotter, Aide to Fleet Admiral C. W. Nimitz, USN: Sequence of Events—Funeral of Fleet Admiral Chester Nimitz, USN. Newspaper: "Book Review Column," *Asahi Shinbun*, Tokyo, Jan. 7, 1963. Articles: E. B. Potter, "Chester William Nimitz, 1885–1966," *USNIP*, July 1966; E. M. Eller, "Mikasa Restored," *Shipmate*, Feb. 1962. Books: Truman, II; Phillips; Steinberg; *Nimitz*. Conversations of author with Fleet Admiral Nimitz and with Mrs. Nimitz, Sr.

# INDEX

Chester W. Nimitz, Sr., is abbreviated CWN